University of California, Berkeley

THE WELLNESS ENCYCLOPEDIA

University of California, Berkeley

THE WELLNESS

ENCYCLOPEDIA

The Comprehensive Family Resource for Safeguarding Health and Preventing Illness

From the Editors
of the University of California, Berkeley
WELLNESS LETTER

Houghton Mifflin Company
Boston 1991

For information about permission to reproduce selections
from this book, write to Permissions, Houghton Mifflin
Company, 2 Park Street, Boston, Massachusetts 02108

Library of Congress Cataloging-in-Publication Data

The Wellness encyclopedia : the comprehensive
family resource for safeguarding health and preventing
illness / from the editors of the University of California,
Berkeley wellness letter.

p.   cm.
At head of title: University of California, Berkeley.
Includes index.
ISBN 0-395-53363-5

1. Health—Handbooks, manuals, etc. 2. Medicine,
Preventive—Handbooks, manuals, etc.   I. University of
California, Berkeley, wellness letter.

RA776.W436 1991
613—dc20   90-5228
                                       CIP

Printed in the United States of America

RMV/10 9 8 7 6 5 4 3 2 1

This book is not intended as a substitute for
the advice of a physician. Readers who
suspect they may have specific medical
problems should consult a physician about
any suggestions made in this book.

Preface

It is becoming increasingly clear that the promotion of health and the prevention of disease is an interactive process involving the development of public policy and governmental actions and the empowerment of individuals to take control of their own well-being. Self-empowerment leads to changes in public policy: for example, many states have declared public places no smoking areas; food labeling regulations are being revised with consumer input; and citizens are calling attention to a host of environmental issues. These policy changes, in turn, facilitate changes in individual behavior. Helping people to bring about this type of change has always been a goal of the Berkeley School of Public Health. To that end, we began in 1984 to publish the *University of California, Berkeley Wellness Letter*—a newsletter designed as an authoritative source of health information for the lay person. Our intention was to create a publication that would clarify the often conflicting and superficial health information presented by the popular media. We chose the word "wellness" because it conveys what we consider to be a primary goal: leading a full and productive life. And one of the crucial tenets of wellness is that preventing illness is just as important as treating it—perhaps *more* important because many chronic diseases are incurable. Preventive health is something that can and should be practiced every day by every person.

In the spirit of the *Wellness Letter*, we have developed this encyclopedia. It is a comprehensive resource that differs from other medical reference books in that it focuses on tomorrow's health, rather than today's illness. Although there is a growing awareness about guidelines for preventive health, the average person has difficulty putting his or her knowledge into practice. Take one example: most Americans are aware of the connection between a high-fat diet and the incidence of heart disease and cancer, and 60 percent say they have made changes in their diet to reduce chronic disease risk. Yet the average daily fat intake remains at 37 percent of total daily calories—significantly higher than the amount recommended for good health—and fully half of the population gets an even greater percentage of their calories from fat.

This is not a reference book that should sit on your shelf until something goes wrong. The information here, like that in the *Wellness Letter*, contains positive, practical guidelines you can take advantage of right away. While the book draws on articles that have appeared in the *Wellness Letter*, all of the material has been expanded and updated. In these pages, you'll find recommendations on how to reduce your risk for developing chronic diseases, create a healthy diet, design an exercise program, prevent and treat minor illnesses at home, make the best use of the health care system when you need it, and banish environmental and safety hazards from your home and workplace.

SHELDON MARGEN, M.D.
Professor Emeritus, School of Public Health
University of California, Berkeley

Contents

Introduction

The concept of what it means to be healthy is changing. Most of us believe that if we are not sick, we are healthy. Even many doctors think of good health as simply the absence of illness, and of "health care" as efforts by medical personnel to cure people when they are sick. But it has become increasingly apparent that the best medical care, while certainly beneficial, is not sufficient to preserve and enhance health. To accomplish that, we need to take a more active approach. Wellness embodies such an approach in two ways. First, it is a way of living that stresses taking steps to prevent illness and prolong our lives. In addition, wellness represents something to strive toward—the optimum state of health and well-being that each individual is capable of achieving, given his or her own set of circumstances.

While the past twenty years have seen tremendous advances in medicine—in the development of new drugs and new diagnostic and surgical techniques— these discoveries have a downside: drugs are prescribed too readily; an excessive number of X-rays and other diagnostic tests are often ordered; hospitals have grown overcrowded and impersonal; and the cost of health care has soared.

Even when applied effectively, the medical approach to sustaining life is incomplete. Consider this: a major study showing that the mortality rate from heart disease has been dropping since 1963 also found that life-style changes in diet and smoking habits—rather than new medical treatments—accounted for over half of the decline. Another large-scale study at the Carter Center at Emory University showed that fourteen primary causes of illness and premature death— causes ranging from drug abuse to cancer and heart disease—were dramatically influenced by risk factors for which preventive action can be taken. (The six factors most frequently cited were tobacco, alcohol, injuries, unintended pregnancy, lack of preventive services, and improper nutrition.) Indeed, the researchers concluded that about two-thirds of the deaths under age sixty-five are potentially preventable.

The clear conclusion of these and other studies cited throughout this book is that we are not dependent on medical breakthroughs to achieve an enormous improvement in our health. Rather, good health depends to a large extent on certain life-style choices we make that include what we eat, how active we are, whether or not we smoke, the precautions we take to avoid injuries and accidents, how we deal with tension and anxiety, even how we manage the environments in which we live and work. This book is intended to inform you about these choices and to help you integrate them into your life. By doing so, you will not only greatly increase your chance of avoiding many illnesses and disorders, but will also very likely experience benefits that range from looking better and having more energy to learning how to work with your family, friends, and members of your community to solve health-related problems. As it improves your health, wellness also improves the quality of your life.

Bear in mind that wellness is not "alternative" medicine—it doesn't promote special diets, regimens that rely on vitamin supplements, herbal medications, or other treatments based on fads or anecdotal evidence. Nor is wellness a substitute for medical care when you are ill. Physicians, nurses, and other well-trained medical providers can diagnose, alleviate, and cure many types of health problems. Your doctor can also perform routine tests and examinations that can greatly increase your chances of avoiding or recovering from an illness. Nevertheless, the medical community by and large is devoted to helping people get well after they have become ill. The premise of wellness is that there are many ways to prevent problems that affect your health, and correct information is essential for you to make the proper choices.

The recommendations in this book

As the idea of taking charge of your own health has gained acceptance, claims about how to achieve wellness have proliferated. The mass media virtually overflows with experts and so-called authorities promoting various regimens for a healthy life style. Newspapers and magazines bombard us with advice on how to eat right, what to do about heart disease, when and how to exercise, and a hundred other health-related matters. Some of this information is straightforward, but a great deal of it is confused, contradictory, or misleading.

The information in the following pages is backed by the consensus of researchers and clinicians at the School of Public Health at the University of California, Berkeley, one of the nation's leading research and teaching institutions in this field. In drawing upon their expertise, the book provides recommendations that have emerged from reviews of hundreds of scientific studies. The intent is to sort out claims and misconceptions, and to supply explanations and guidelines that are clear, practical, and as up-to-date as possible.

Of course, knowledge in preventive health care is expanding rapidly, and new research is always being considered. However, we have made an effort to arrive at guidelines that will hold up over time—that are based not on one or two small studies, but on a more substantial base of research. For example, researchers may argue over exactly how much exercise is the optimal amount to lower the risk for heart disease. But several large-scale studies have shown unequivocally that even moderate amounts of physical activity offer a dramatic benefit compared to being sedentary. Clarifying such distinctions is one of the ways that this book serves as a truly authoritative reference source.

How to use this book

The Wellness Encyclopedia is divided into five major parts that correspond to key areas of wellness: Longevity, Nutrition, Exercise, Self-Care, and—one of the most recent areas of concern—Environment and Safety. Each of these parts contains chapters dealing with major topics; each chapter is organized around subtopics, with guidelines or special topics highlighted in charts, tables, and boxes. Many of the guidelines offer manageable steps on how to change old habits for healthier ones. You will also find tips and interesting facts concisely presented in the margin of almost every page of the book.

The index, which is detailed and extensively cross-referenced, simplifies access to information on any topic. The text also contains cross references to related topics.

In addition, the book has several special features. In the Nutrition section, you will find a sixty-two page guide that offers advice on a wide variety of foods, including shopping and preparation tips. Another feature—in the Self-Care section—is an eight-page illustrated guide to the body's major muscles and joints, useful for an understanding of how to prevent aches and pains. And a glossary at the back of the book provides brief definitions of key terms.

LONGEVITY

The first and foremost goal of wellness is preventing illness, especially illness that can shorten your life. Today, in Western societies, the health problems that most significantly affect longevity are chronic diseases such as heart disease, stroke, and cancer—the current leading causes of mortality. Researchers have determined that the factors promoting these illnesses are strongly linked to life style and behavior patterns, ranging from what we eat to unhealthy habits like smoking or a lack of exercise. This part of the book provides practical information on how you can lower your risk of chronic disease. In the following pages, you'll find that many of the recommendations for longevity overlap and work together; for example, a diet that reduces blood cholesterol levels also helps you lose weight and reduces your risk of developing certain kinds of cancer. The opening chapter clarifies the concept of health risk and includes a questionnaire to help you pinpoint areas of your life that may need attention. Subsequent chapters provide a detailed look at the most important risk factors that affect your health and explain what you can do to reduce them.

Health Risks: A Perspective

Efforts to identify health risks—and reduce them, if possible—are as old as medicine itself. Hippocrates advised his fellow physicians to "consider the seasons of the year and what effects each of them produces" and to take note of what people drank and ate and how they lived. Scientists today are still looking for the determinants of health, albeit with a little more sophistication and scientific knowledge. Epidemiology (literally, the study of epidemics) is the attempt to identify the factors that cause diseases and injuries in order to determine what the probabilities are that they will cause them, and to determine how to decrease or eliminate the identified risks. This is often referred to as risk hazard appraisal, which is of growing importance in medical science, especially in the effort to prevent disease and promote health. Once the risk factors are known, the next job is to make changes in the environment (for example, to persuade car manufacturers to install seat belts of a certain design) and to persuade people to change their behavior (for example, convince them to fasten the belts).

When reports in newspapers or magazines talk about risk, they are basically quoting odds. No one can honestly assure you that doing one thing will kill you, while refraining from doing it will keep you safe. For example, on the average, one out of ten smokers gets lung cancer, but a rare nonsmoker gets it. If you are an average smoker, your chances of getting lung cancer at any time of life are twenty-four times higher than those for a nonsmoker, and the risk increases as the amount of smoking increases.

In the science of risk assessment, there is no such thing as absolute safety; however, you can choose to widen or narrow your safety margins. And though scientists may assess the risks, it's often hard to evaluate what the experts say. The press seldom makes your task simpler. The headline "Alcohol shown to cause breast cancer" will attract more readers than "Study suggests alcohol intake slightly increases breast cancer risk for some women." It is always easier to oversimplify than to tell people how complicated things really are.

Examples of risk assessment

How do experts figure your odds against different risks? Here are two examples:

•You are about to plan a thousand-mile journey, and you aren't pressed for time. Rank the following means of transportation from the safest to the riskiest: bus, train, plane, and passenger car.

The answer is fairly straightforward. You are safest in a bus, and in greatest danger in an automobile. (More than ten people die per billion automobile and taxi miles; but it takes more than two billion bus miles to produce a fatality. Trains and planes are ten times safer than cars, but only about half as safe as buses.)

•You're a healthy forty-five-year-old man, slightly overweight. Your father and his brother both died in their fifties of heart disease. Your mother, now sixty-five, has had noninsulin-dependent diabetes (NIDDM, adult-onset or type II diabetes) for several years. Are you likely to get one of these ailments?

If your father died young of a heart attack, you have a good chance of following in his footsteps. Knowing your inherited liabilities, though, gives you an excellent opportunity to alter them. The genetic odds may be lowered significantly if you are not overweight, keep your blood pressure under control, and maintain a low blood cholesterol level. If your mother has diabetes, that's an indication that weight control and exercise are crucially important for you.

For many of us, familial tendencies constitute an emotional trap. People whose parents or grandparents died at comparatively young ages of heart disease or cancer, or some other disease with a genetic component, usually realize that this heritage works against them and may falsely conclude that taking care of their own health is irrelevant. On the other hand, if all your relatives were as indestructible as Winston Churchill—who drank brandy, smoked habitually, was overweight, yet lived into his eighties and died peacefully in his sleep—you may have an equally false sense of invulnerability.

Researchers may one day unravel the genetic code and come closer to accurately predicting your chances of getting a disorder such as heart disease or hypertension. But of the hundreds of diseases that have been genetically defined, most are fairly rare—the few that are more common include hemophilia, in which a blood-clotting factor is absent; sickle cell anemia, a blood disorder that occurs most commonly among people of African descent; cystic fibrosis; and certain forms of kidney disease. In many ailments that show signs of running in families, such as cancer, heart disease, or diabetes, heredity is only one factor in the mix. Your biological and cultural heritage and your environment interact, and it's the interaction that counts. Your diet or exercise habits or your environment may foster, or foil, the tendencies with which you were born.

Making sense of "increased risk"

Reports that warn about doubling or tripling your risk of heart disease, or any other specific illness, need to be viewed cautiously. You have to know how likely you are to get the disease in the first place. For example, if your chances of developing a certain illness are 1 in 100,000, a doubled risk brings you up to 2 in 100,000 (or 1 in 50,000). Those are still pretty low odds. However, if 1 out of 10 people develops this illness and you do something that doubles your risk, your chances are now 1 in 5. That's a very significant increase.

Let's say, for example, that you're a forty-three-year-old woman, a good cook, and you like a glass or two of wine with fine food. You've heard about a report stating that even moderate alcohol consumption may double a woman's risk of getting breast cancer—and that quitting now might not reduce the risk. Nevertheless, you stop drinking wine. Your sister is a teetotaler. Are you twice as likely to get breast cancer as she is?

In 1987, studies by two prestigious research groups independently demonstrated a link between alcohol intake and breast cancer. A woman who drank even as few as three beers or glasses of wine weekly was found to have a 50 percent greater lifetime risk of developing breast cancer than a nondrinking woman. Publicized along with that figure was another statistic: that one American woman out of eleven develops breast cancer at some time in her life. That's a risk of 9 percent. It seems logical to conclude, as many reporters did, that women drinkers run a risk closer to 14 percent, a terrifying narrowing of the safety margin.

But here's what very few of the reports made clear: the one-in-eleven figure applies to all American women indiscriminately, from age one to eighty-five. That is, it's a lifetime average and does not describe the odds for an individual over shorter intervals. The incidence of breast cancer in the population rises with age. A forty-year-old woman has about a 3.3 percent chance of developing breast cancer by age sixty. If she's a moderate drinker, her chances would increase by half—to about 4.8 percent—if the reported studies are correct. That's a little less horrifying than 14 percent.

Being realistic

Many people, of course, choose to focus on news that is reassuring rather than alarming. For example, say that you're fifty, female, and a smoker. Your last checkup showed that both your blood pressure and blood cholesterol level were somewhat higher than they should be. You know this means you risk a heart attack or stroke, but you read an article that said that even fifty-year-old male smokers with high blood pressure and elevated cholesterol levels have only a 13 percent chance of getting sick within six years. So you're looking on the bright side: you've got an 87 percent chance of staying healthy for the next six years. Is this a constructive attitude?

A fifty-year-old smoker, male or female, with elevated blood cholesterol and blood pressure is seriously courting cardiovascular disease. You may have only a 13 percent chance of developing it (though neither you nor your doctor has any way of predicting whether you'll fall into the lucky 87 percent who do not develop heart disease or the unlucky 13 percent who do). If these sound like favorable odds, you may decide not to make any changes in your habits. However, a more realistic way for you to consider the odds is as follows: if your risk factors are low (that is, you don't smoke and your blood pressure and blood cholesterol levels are low), your chance of having a heart attack between age forty and sixty-four is only 6 percent. But, if you continue to smoke and do nothing about your other risk factors, your chance of having a heart attack during these years is 40 percent. This is a very big difference. Giving up cigarettes, controlling your blood pressure, and lowering your blood cholesterol level would significantly widen your safety margin. Obviously, that's the constructive action to take.

Another example of this kind of reasoning can be seen in the relationship between oral contraceptives and heart attacks. High-dose oral contra-

When Risk Factors Synergize

If you smoke and drink, you are worse off than if you only smoke or only drink. Alcohol seems to multiply the cancer-causing effects of smoking—a phenomenon called synergism. A person who has one drink per day but doesn't smoke has a 60 percent higher risk of oral cancer than a nonsmoking teetotaler. A person who smokes up to pack of cigarettes a day and doesn't drink has a 52 percent higher risk than a nonsmoking teetotaler.

But the risk for a moderate smoker and drinker (a pack or less a day and one drink a day) is four times greater (400 percent) than that for a total abstainer. For a heavy smoker (two packs) and drinker (more than two small drinks a day), the risk is fifteen times greater. No one knows exactly why these risks synergize in this instance. However, if you both smoke and drink and decide you'll give up one of these habits, quit smoking. Overall, it's the more harmful of the two.

ceptives increase the risk of heart attack by a factor of 4.7. This sounds like a very large increase. However, if you're a twenty- to twenty-four-year-old woman, your heart attack risk is estimated to be less than 1 in 500,000. Thus a fivefold increase represents only about 5 in 500,000 (or 1 in 100,000). This means that if all the 8.5 million American women in this age group were to take oral contraceptives, eighty of them (instead of the expected seventeen) would die of heart attacks. This is many fewer deaths than might result from unwanted pregnancies in the same age group. Even this small risk has been markedly reduced by the introduction of low-dose estrogen contraceptives.

Interpreting health news

Nowadays almost anything can be called a study or be so designated by the press. Major journals in the medical field attempt to limit unproven or overstated claims by carefully reviewing what is submitted to them. However, a phenomenal amount of research is published each year: an average of 240,000 biomedical articles in English alone are indexed each year by the National Library of Medicine. If every study "proved" something, there would be no questions left unanswered. A dose of skepticism is always in order, even when the study comes from an important institution and appears in a respected journal.

Some years ago, for example, *The New England Journal of Medicine* published a study from Johns Hopkins Medical Institutions showing that heavy coffee drinkers had two to three times the risk of heart disease—a study conducted over many years and using many subjects. From reports in the media, it sounded like proof positive, unless you actually had a copy of the study and read it all the way to the end. The authors didn't ask participants about important risk factors such as their diet (did they habitually eat a lot of fat and cholesterol?), smoking habits, and exercise levels. It wasn't clear, therefore, whether coffee was at fault, or diet, or other factors altogether. "A need for further investigation" was the final word—though this didn't keep writers and reporters from citing this study as proof of the dangers of caffeine intake.

Or consider the two studies cited on page 8 that showed a link between alcohol consumption and breast cancer. Although the studies didn't ignore other risk factors, they illustrate several other problems. For example, the estimation of what the women actually ate and drank was based on poor data obtained only at the beginning of the studies, which lasted from four to ten

---

Health news isn't always good news.

Just because a study is reported on television or on the front page doesn't mean that it contains information that is useful for you. Here are some reasons why:

• Many studies are too small and too short to mean much—such as a study indicating that eating seventeen times a day lowers blood cholesterol levels which involved only seven subjects.

• Organizations such as the American Heart Association or the American Cancer Society routinely issue press releases, as do medical schools, drug companies, and food manufacturers. Some accurately represent scientific work, while others simplify or manipulate the facts. But press releases, even the most helpful ones, seldom present enough detail for the critical analysis necessary for careful reporting.

• Enterprising scientists, institutions, and corporations have been known to hire public relations experts to promote their work and help them land on the front page.

Words to Watch

The following words are commonly used in reporting scientific studies—and both reporters and lay readers often misinterpret their meaning.

Breakthrough: is so overworked as to be meaningless.

Contributes to, is linked to, is associated with: none of these terms means "causes."

Doubles the risk, triples the risk: may or may not be meaningful. Does the reporter tell you what your risk was in the first place? If your risk is 1 in a million, and you double it, that's still only 1 in 500,000. If your risk is 1 in 100, and increases by 25 percent, that is 1 in 80, which may be cause for concern.

Dramatic proof: probably neither.

Indicates, suggests: do not mean "proves."

In some people: does not mean "in all people."

May: does not mean "will."

Proves: scientific studies gather evidence in a systematic way, but they seldom prove anything. A dubious word.

years. The investigators did not determine the women's previous eating and drinking habits, or whether these habits changed while the studies were going on. In addition, they did not rule out the chance that something besides alcohol was increasing the cancer risk in the lives of moderate drinkers. What is more, a year later a researcher at the Centers for Disease Control in Atlanta reported that a new study of seven thousand women (based on a different approach) found no association at all between alcohol consumption and breast cancer.

When you read or listen to health news, keep the following points in mind:

Don't jump to conclusions. Changing your daily habits on the basis of a single study is almost never a good idea. Scientific findings should be duplicated by others for validity, and even then there's an element of uncertainty.

Try to distinguish between promising advances, reported as scientific news, and public health recommendations. If doctors at some medical center have just done the first successful liver transplant, that's interesting. But it doesn't mean there's now a cure for liver disease. On the other hand, if the Surgeon General or the American Cancer Society says "eat less fat" or "don't smoke," you can assume that many studies point in this direction.

Keep your skepticism in working order. Science is an uncertain undertaking. Progress is measured less often by dramatic insights than by the slow accumulation of knowledge. "Astounding" medical advances are rare. "Medical milestone" in a press report is like the word "natural" on a food package: something to arouse rather than allay your suspicions. No matter how enthusiastically a finding is hailed in the press, see what the experts are saying next week and next month.

Notice where the information is coming from. Does the author of the article cite any authorities, appear to rely on scientific evidence—or simply tell a lot of anecdotes? "Thousands of people say..." "It's well known that..." Is any source given for astounding statistics? Even fully sourced statistics can be wrong, of course, but if the author is willing to give sources, that may be a good sign.

Use your own logic and common sense. If the article says that the Japanese are healthier than Americans and claims it's because they eat more fish, stop and think. The Japanese also eat a lot of rice. They also sleep on mats instead of mattresses. How does the writer know it's the fish? The heart attack rate tends to be higher in countries where most households have telephones, but that doesn't mean the telephones are causing heart attacks.

Be wary when studies are cited to sell you a product. Manufacturers and industry groups have been known to stretch the truth.

Self-Assessment Quiz

The following questionnaire is designed to increase your knowledge and awareness of your overall health, and to highlight potential areas of concern. It doesn't pinpoint how you compare to the rest of the population, but the scoring chart at the end will show you areas where you are making healthy choices and where there is room for improvement. Keep in mind that although health risks associated with age, gender, and heredity are beyond your control, you can modify a range of other factors such as blood pressure, smoking, blood cholesterol levels, exercise, diet, stress, and excess body weight.

Circle "Yes" or "No"

Section A: PHYSICAL FITNESS

1. Do you exercise or play a sport for at least thirty minutes three or more times a week?	Y	N
2. Do you warm up and cool down by stretching before and after exercising?	Y	N
3. Do you fall into the appropriate weight category for someone your height and gender?	Y	N
4. In general, are you pleased with the condition of your body?	Y	N
5. Are you satisfied with your current level of energy?	Y	N
6. Do you use stairs rather than escalators or elevators whenever possible?	Y	N

NUMBER OF ANSWERS IN EACH COLUMN ⬤ ⬤

Section B: FAMILY HISTORY

Do you have a grandparent, parent, aunt, uncle, brother, or sister who:

1. Had a heart attack before age forty?	N	Y
2. Had high blood pressure requiring treatment?	N	Y
3. Developed diabetes?	N	Y
4. Developed glaucoma?	N	Y
5. Developed gout?	N	Y
6. Developed breast cancer?	N	Y

NUMBER OF ANSWERS IN EACH COLUMN ⬤ ⬤

Section C: SELF-CARE AND MEDICAL CARE

1. Do you floss your teeth daily?	Y	N
2. Do you have a dental checkup at least once a year?	Y	N
3. Do you use sunscreen regularly and avoid extensive exposure to the sun?	Y	N
4. For women: do you examine your breasts for unusual changes or lumps at least once a month?	Y	N
5. For men: do you examine your testicles for unusual changes or lumps at least once every three months?	Y	N
6. Do you usually know what to do in case of illness or injury?	Y	N
7. Do you avoid unnecessary X-rays?	Y	N
8. Do you normally get an adequate amount of sleep?	Y	N
9. Have you had your blood pressure checked in the past year?	Y	N
10. For women: have you had a Pap smear within the last two years?	Y	N
11. If you are over forty: have you had a test for glaucoma within the last four years?	Y	N
12. If you are over forty: have you had a test for hidden blood in your stool within the last two years? If you are over fifty: within the last year?	Y	N
13. If you are over fifty: have you had at least one endoscopic exam of the lower bowel?	Y	N

NUMBER OF ANSWERS IN EACH COLUMN ⬤ ⬤

Section D: EATING HABITS

	Y	N
1. Do you drink enough fluids so that your urine is a pale yellow color?	Y	N
2. Do you try special or fad diets?	N	Y
3. Do you add salt to foods during cooking and at the table?	N	Y
4. Do you minimize your intake of sweets, especially candy and soft drinks, and avoid adding sugar to foods?	Y	N
5. Is your diet well balanced (including vegetables, fruits, breads, cereals, dairy products, and adequate sources of protein)?	Y	N
6. Do you limit your intake of saturated fats (butter, cheese, cream, fatty meats)?	Y	N
7. Do you limit your intake of cholesterol (eggs, liver, meats)?	Y	N
8. Do you eat fish and poultry more often than red meats?	Y	N
9. Do you eat high-fiber foods (vegetables, fruits, whole grains) several times a day?	Y	N

NUMBER OF ANSWERS IN EACH COLUMN ◯ ◯

Section E: ALCOHOL, NICOTINE, AND OTHER DRUG USE

	Y	N
1. Do you smoke cigarettes, cigars, or a pipe, chew tobacco, or use other drugs?	N	Y
2. Do you limit yourself to no more than two drinks a day?	Y	N
3. Have family members or friends ever commented on or complained about your drinking or your use of other drugs?	N	Y
4. Have you been unable to recall things you did when you were drinking or using other drugs?	N	Y
5. Do you use alcohol or other drugs as a way of handling stressful situations or problems in your life?	N	Y
6. Do you read and follow the label directions when using prescribed and over-the-counter drugs?	Y	N

NUMBER OF ANSWERS IN EACH COLUMN ◯ ◯

Section F: ACCIDENTS

	Y	N
1. Do you drive after drinking alcohol or using other drugs, or ride with drivers who have been drinking or using other drugs?	N	Y
2. Do you obey traffic rules and stay within the speed limit when you drive?	Y	N
3. As a driver and passenger, do you wear a seat belt at all times?	Y	N
4. Are the vehicles you drive well maintained?	Y	N
5. Do you smoke in bed?	N	Y
6. Are you informed and careful when using potentially harmful products or substances, such as household cleaners, poisons, flammables, solvents, and electrical devices?	Y	N
7. Do you own a gun?	N	Y

NUMBER OF ANSWERS IN EACH COLUMN ◯ ◯

Section G: INTELLECTUAL LIFE, VALUES, AND SPIRITUALITY

	Y	N
1. Are you interested in, and do you keep up to date on, social and political issues?	Y	N
2. Are you satisfied with what you do for entertainment?	Y	N
3. Do you engage in creative and stimulating activities as often as you would like?	Y	N
4. Are you satisfied with the degree to which your work is consistent with your values?	Y	N
5. Are you satisfied with the degree to which your leisure activities are consistent with your values?	Y	N
6. Is it difficult for you to accept the values and life styles of others when they are different from your own?	N	Y
7. Are you satisfied with your spiritual life?	Y	N

NUMBER OF ANSWERS IN EACH COLUMN ◯ ◯

Section H: STRESS AND SOCIAL SUPPORT

1. Are you satisfied with the amount of excitement in your life?	Y	N
2. Do you find it easy to laugh?	Y	N
3. Do you hold in your angry feelings without expressing them?	N	Y
4. Do you make decisions with minimum stress and worry?	Y	N
5. Do you include relaxation time as part of your daily routine?	Y	N
6. Do you anticipate and prepare for events or situations likely to be stressful?	Y	N
7. Have you had to make difficult readjustments at home or work in the past year?	N	Y
8. Has a family member or close friend died, been seriously ill, or been injured within the past year?	N	Y
9. Are you a chronic worrier, subject to guilt feelings or self-punishment?	N	Y
10. Have your health, eating, or sleeping habits changed as a result of a stressful incident or situation during the past year?	N	Y
11. Are you able to fall asleep when you are ready and to sleep through the night uninterrupted?	Y	N
12. Do you wake up feeling rested?	Y	N
13. Do you have one or more persons with whom you can discuss personal concerns, worries, or problems?	Y	N
14. Do they make you feel respected and/or admired?	Y	N
15. Is there someone you can turn to if you need help, such as to lend you money?	Y	N
16. Are you satisfied with the support you provide to others?	Y	N

NUMBER OF ANSWERS IN EACH COLUMN ⬤ ⬤

Section I: ENVIRONMENT

1. Are you often in an environment that has significant air and/or noise pollution?	N	Y
2. Are you often exposed to asbestos, vinyl chloride, formaldehyde, or other toxins?	N	Y
3. Do you miss many days at work due to illness or just not feeling up to it? ("Work" refers to daily activities, including school or work in the home.)	N	Y
4. Do you often sit for periods of an hour or more at a time?	N	Y
5. Are you satisfied with your ability to plan your workload?	Y	N
6. Do you receive adequate feedback to judge your performance?	Y	N
7. Are you satisfied with your balance between work and leisure time?	Y	N

NUMBER OF ANSWERS IN EACH COLUMN ⬤ ⬤

Section J: SEXUALITY

1. Are you satisfied with your level of sexual activity?	Y	N
2. Are you satisfied with your sexual relationships?	Y	N
3. Are you satisfied with your use (or nonuse) of contraceptives?	Y	N
4. Are you satisfied with your use (or nonuse) of "safer sex" practices?	Y	N

NUMBER OF ANSWERS IN EACH COLUMN ⬤ ⬤

Scoring the Quiz

For each section of the quiz, write the number of answers you marked in the *lefthand* column in the blanks below.

Sections: **A**____ **B**____ **C**____ **D**____ **E**____ **F**____ **G**____ **H**____ **I**____ **J**____

In the circle graph below, shade in the number of subsections to correspond with the numbers you wrote above. Start with the innermost section. For example, if there are four answers marked in the lefthand answer column of section D, that portion of the circle graph will look like this:

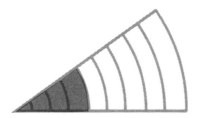

Sections that are *completely shaded:* you are making healthy behavior and life-style choices in these areas. Keep up the good work.

Sections that are *partially shaded:* with a little more awareness and effort in these areas, you could improve the quality of your life—and live longer.

Sections that are *barely shaded or not shaded at all:* there is significant room for increasing your health and satisfaction in these areas. Work first on those areas where you are most likely to be successful, then tackle the tougher sections.

Note: This grading system doesn't apply to section B, since you have no control over your family history. If you answered "yes" to several questions about family history, try to compensate by concentrating on the other areas over which you do have control.

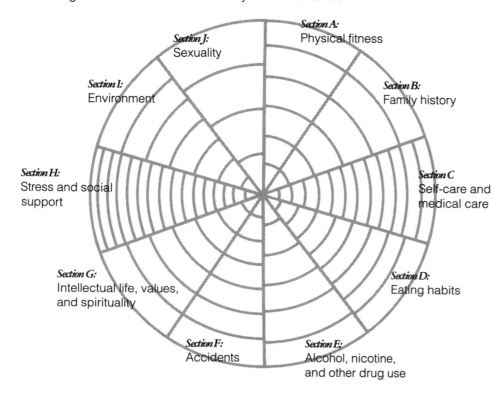

The Role of Diet and Exercise

The relevance of diet and physical activity to wellness cannot be overstated. The foods you eat and your level of physical activity affect a number of risk factors implicated in longevity, particularly blood cholesterol levels, hypertension, and obesity. Moreover, diet and exercise are the elements of your health care over which you have the most control.

Drawing on hundreds of studies, researchers have compiled considerable evidence showing the extent to which diet and exercise influence the risk of disease. This chapter summarizes the key findings concerning this connection; other benefits that you can derive from changes in diet and exercise, as well as specific recommendations, are covered in the nutrition and exercise parts of this book.

Diet and Longevity

The evidence that a proper diet can help prevent the leading chronic diseases comes from a wide range of sources: large-scale studies of what certain populations eat and the prevalence of various diseases in these groups; studies of humans and animals under experimental conditions showing how specific diets change their chronic disease risk; and laboratory experiments showing how chemicals alter the structure and function of cells and tissues in the test tube.

Based on these studies, scientists now estimate, for example, that 40 percent of all cancer incidence in men and nearly 60 percent in women are related to diet. Diet has also been clearly implicated in two of the three major factors in the development of heart disease—high blood cholesterol levels and hypertension. Furthermore, there is now a consensus among experts as to which dietary elements play a role in the development of disease. The American Cancer Society, the American Heart Association, the National Research Council, the National Cancer Institute, and many other scientific organizations all basically agree on the dietary changes individuals must make to reduce their risks of chronic disease. In addition, a comprehensive review of the available evidence on diet and health, conducted by the Surgeon General and released in 1989, confirmed the findings and recommendations of other organizations, and has been compared in importance to the 1964 Surgeon General's report on the relationship between tobacco use and disease.

What are the foods that play a role in disease prevention or promotion? Actually, it is not foods per se that contribute, but substances contained in foods. These range from fats—which in excessive amounts can contribute to heart disease—to antioxidant compounds, which can protect against cancer and other diseases, and enhance immune system functioning.

Fat. Of all the changes you can make in your diet, cutting back on fat will have the greatest effect on reducing disease risk. A diet high in fat has been strongly linked to an increased risk of heart disease and certain forms of cancer, such as breast, colon, rectum, endometrium, and prostate. A low-fat diet is also helpful to those with diabetes, since diabetes accelerates the development of heart disease. In particular, a diet high in saturated fat (the type found in animal products, such as meats and whole-milk dairy products, and in tropical vegetable oils—coconut, palm, and palm kernel) contributes to heart disease by raising levels of total blood cholesterol and low-density lipoprotein (LDL) cholesterol—the type referred to as "bad" cholesterol.

A high-fat diet also contributes to obesity, which is an independent risk factor for heart disease and cancer, and the primary risk factor for developing noninsulin-dependent diabetes mellitus (NIDDM, also called adult-onset or type II diabetes).

Dietary cholesterol. Cholesterol from foods (cholesterol is found only in animal products) contributes to the development of heart disease because it can raise blood cholesterol levels, but not to as great an extent as saturated fat. Elevations in total blood cholesterol levels from dietary cholesterol are predominantly in the form of LDL.

Sodium. In populations with a high-sodium intake, there is an increased incidence of hypertension. While not everyone is sodium sensitive—responding to a high-sodium intake with a rise in blood pressure—there is no way to tell who is and who is not. In addition, there is some evidence that high-sodium intake over a lifetime may cause some people to become sodium sensitive.

Alcohol. Alcohol consumed to excess increases the risk of cancer of the mouth, pharynx, esophagus, and larynx. These risks increase dramatically when alcohol is used in conjunction with tobacco. In addition, there is some association between alcohol intake and cancers of the pancreas, rectum, and breast. There is no evidence that alcohol causes these cancers, but once they have developed, alcohol may help promote their spread. Except when combined with smoking, the risk of cancer from alcohol appears to be most commonly linked with heavy alcohol consumption. And while a moderate intake of alcohol has been shown to slightly increase the levels of HDL ("good") cholesterol, heavy drinking can lead to decreased HDL levels, high blood pressure, and heart damage. In addition, drinking alcohol to excess can contribute to a decrease in bone mass, increasing the risk for developing osteoporosis.

Nitrites and nitrates. These chemicals, which are used to preserve cured meats—such as bacon, hot dogs, sausages, and ham—have been found to promote cancers of the stomach and esophagus in laboratory animals, most probably because the chemicals can be converted by stomach acid to nitrosamines, which are carcinogenic. Foods high in vitamin C may block the conversion of nitrites and nitrates to cancer-causing nitrosamines.

Char-broiled foods. Grilling or barbecuing foods can create cancer-causing agents. This is most dangerous when fatty meats are cooked over a heat source because when the fat drips on the coals or hot coils, it forms carcinogenic substances that are then deposited on the food by the rising smoke.

Fiber. Both soluble and insoluble fiber help prevent disease. In combination with a low-fat, low-cholesterol diet, soluble fiber—found in oat and rice bran, legumes, and many fruits and vegetables—has been shown to help control cholesterol in individuals with elevated levels. In those with diabetes, soluble fiber appears to lower blood glucose levels when it makes a substantial contribution to the diet. Insoluble fiber—the type found in wheat bran—has been associated with a lower risk of colon cancer. Researchers theorize that fiber does this by helping to speed the

Food Sources of Vitamin C
Asparagus
Blackberries
Broccoli
Cantaloupe
Cauliflower
Chinese cabbage
Grapefruit
Grapefruit juice
Kale
Kiwifruit
Kohlrabi
Mangoes
Mustard greens
Oranges
Orange juice
Peas, edible pod
Peppers
Raspberries
Red cabbage
Strawberries
Tangerines
Tomatoes
Tomato juice

elimination of waste matter and/or possibly by binding carcinogenic matter in the intestine in some way.

Antioxidants. Beta carotene (which the body converts to vitamin A), vitamins C and E, and the mineral selenium are antioxidant compounds that appear to protect against cancer and possibly other diseases because they neutralize free radicals—unstable molecules created by various normal chemical processes in the body, or by solar or cosmic radiation, cigarette smoke, and other environmental influences. In the human body, the most damaging free radicals are derived from the complex chemical process by which oxygen is utilized inside the cells. Chemically incomplete, free radicals may "steal" particles from other molecules, creating abnormal compounds and thus setting off a chain reaction that can damage cells by causing fundamental changes in their genetic material and other important parts of the cell. In simplest terms, the manner in which free radicals damage the body's cells is similar to the process by which oxygen causes paper to turn yellow or butter to turn rancid. Antioxidant nutrients render free radicals harmless by neutralizing them without becoming free radicals themselves. These antioxidant nutrients are abundant in fruits, vegetables, and grains: supplements are not necessary, and in the case of selenium, may be toxic.

Potassium. An adequate potassium intake may lessen the blood-pressure-raising effect of sodium, and independently contribute to a reduced risk of death from stroke. Potassium is abundant in fruits and vegetables. One study found that if you add even one piece of fruit or serving of vegetables or other food high in potassium to your regular diet, you may reduce your risk of fatal stroke by 40 percent.

Calcium. Calcium is the most important dietary factor associated with the risk of developing osteoporosis, a disease characterized by a decrease in bone mass. An adequate intake of calcium throughout life—and especially from birth to the age of twenty-five—can help build bone density and therefore ward off osteoporosis. Calcium obtained from foods is better absorbed by the body than calcium obtained from supplements.

Vitamin D. Vitamin D helps the body to absorb calcium. A number of studies have shown that elderly people are at increased risk for vitamin D deficiency. Milk—an excellent source of calcium—is usually fortified with vitamin D (choose low-fat or skim varieties). In addition, the body produces vitamin D in response to sunlight.

Cruciferous vegetables. These members of the cabbage family—such as broccoli, kale, brussels sprouts, and cauliflower—have been shown in studies with laboratory animals to be protective against certain forms of cancer. They contain substances called indoles, which may act as antioxidants.

Can diet cure disease?

Much of the research on diet and health focuses on the prevention—not the treatment—of chronic diseases. But the distinction between "reducing disease risk" and "delaying the onset of further symptoms" is sometimes blurred. Certainly, diet can help control many chronic diseases. For example, if you have diabetes, eating a diet high in complex carbohydrates and maintaining an appropriate weight can help keep the disease in check. Hypertensives may lower their blood pressure by losing weight and eating less sodium. And one study of people with severe heart disease, conducted by Dr. Dean Ornish and his colleagues

---

Food Sources of Beta Carotene

Apricots
Asparagus
Broccoli
Cantaloupe
Carrots
Cherries
Cress
Dandelion greens
Kale
Mangoes
Peaches
Peas
Romaine lettuce
Sweet potatoes
Spinach
Tomatoes
Winter squash

at the University of San Francisco, found that a vegetarian diet extremely low in fat (10 percent calories from fat) and cholesterol (five milligrams daily) can not only help keep more plaque from building up in the coronary arteries, but also help reduce the plaque already there and thus actually unclog arteries. In addition to changing their diet, the men and women in the study participated in a moderate exercise program, practiced stress management techniques, and quit smoking. After one year, the participants experienced a significant regression of the plaque that had built up in their arteries plus a reduction in chest pain. On average, total blood cholesterol levels dropped 24 percent, and levels of LDL ("bad" cholesterol) dropped a dramatic 37 percent. However, the study did not determine which, if any, of the life-style changes had the greatest effect; thus, diet alone may not be enough to reverse atherosclerosis.

In none of these instances, though, does diet cure chronic disease the way an antibiotic can wipe out an infection. Yet the myths proliferate, especially when it comes to fighting cancer. Claims have been made for a wide variety of dietary cures—everything from aloe vera to carrot and celery juice to vitamin B$_{15}$ (pangamic acid) supplements. One persistent belief is that macrobiotic diets have the ability to cure cancer. These diets consist chiefly of whole grains plus selected vegetables, a few fruits, seaweed, and occasionally some fish. The diet is progressive—that is, you are eventually supposed to cut out all foods except brown rice. This is just one example of how nutrition quackery can be especially harmful. Not only is there no evidence that any kind of macrobiotic diet can cure cancer, but it can actually interfere with the treatment of the disease by contributing to malnutrition and weight loss. Even worse, people might decide to substitute the diet for effective treatment.

Nevertheless, a proper diet—one that is low in fat, high in complex carbohydrates, and supplies an adequate amount of nutrients—can serve as an adjunct to medical intervention and treatment in the management of many diseases.

Exercise and Longevity

Perhaps the most comprehensive research on exercise and health is the series of studies conducted by Dr. Ralph S. Paffenbarger, Jr. and his associates at Stanford University. Underway for more than twenty-five years, the study has produced strong evidence that regular exercise is an important health-promoting factor. The study has examined the life styles of 16,936 Harvard alumni who entered college between 1916 and 1950 and ranged in age from thirty-five to seventy-four at the start of the study. Their exercise habits (self-reported) and mortality rates were followed from the mid-1960s until 1978. The exercises included walking, stair-climbing, and various sports.

The study found that, for the most part, the more a person exercised, the better his chances to outlive his peers. For example, during the twelve to sixteen years of observation, men who walked nine or more miles a week had a 21 percent lower mortality rate than those who walked three miles or less. In terms of calories burned per week, life expectancy improved steadily, starting at an expenditure of 500 calories per week on exercise (a 150-pound man burns off about 500 calories walking six miles) and continuing upward to 3,500 calories per week (the

Heart Disease and Exercise: Vital Statistics
After a two-year analysis of studies on the subject, researchers at the Centers for Disease Control in Atlanta found that the least active people were almost twice as likely to have heart disease as those who were most active. Furthermore, while smoking, high blood pressure, or high blood cholesterol may put an individual at higher risk for heart disease, the researchers point out that lack of exercise is so widespread it actually poses a greater threat to the cardiovascular health of the nation. Nearly 60 percent of Americans don't get any regular exercise, and 80 to 90 percent don't engage in a regular aerobic exercise program, which is the best way to keep the heart healthy. In contrast, 18 percent smoke a pack of cigarettes a day, 10 percent have a systolic blood pressure level above 150, and 10 percent have a blood cholesterol level over 268 mg/dl.

equivalent of walking six miles daily for a week). No additional benefit occurred above 3,500 calories a week, however. The beneficial effects of exercise were evident in all of the men studied, and the benefits tended to intensify with age.

The benefits of moderate activity

As Dr. Paffenbarger has pointed out, the Harvard alumni in his study were not necessarily typical of the general population. Their mortality rates from every major cause were generally half that of most white males—except for suicides, where their rate was 50 percent higher. Since those studied clearly enjoy a special status (white, male, and well-off economically), Dr. Paffenbarger cautioned against drawing sweeping conclusions for all of society. However, subsequent studies show that other groups in the population have benefited from being active—and that the greatest surge in life expectancy is derived by incorporating a relatively modest amount of activity into what was previously a sedentary life style.

For example, one study looked at three thousand railroad workers—all white, male, and middle-aged—over a period of seventeen to twenty years. The subjects who passed their leisure time being sedentary—defined as expending less than 250 calories a week in moderate- or low-intensity exercises like strolling, bowling, gardening, or cycling at an easy pace—had a 30 to 40 percent greater risk of dying from coronary heart disease as well as from all causes than those who expended between 1,000 and 2,000 calories a week in these activities. This was true even after adjusting for age, blood pressure, smoking, and blood cholesterol levels. The researchers estimated that it takes about thirty minutes of moderate activity every day to expend 1,000 calories in a week. As other studies have found, this one indicated that going beyond an average of about an hour's worth of moderate leisure activity a day (more than 2,000 calories a week) did not add to the health benefits.

A more well-rounded and systematic study, conducted by researchers at the Institute for Aerobics Research in Dallas, surveyed more than thirteen thousand healthy men and women for an average of eight years and related their exercise and activity habits to overall mortality. Subjects were evaluated according to objective standards of fitness—the results of treadmill tests. (In contrast, most earlier research relied only on how much people said they exercised; such self-reports, without any evaluative testing, are not as reliable.)

The results are impressive. Of five groups of people, divided according to fitness levels, the least-fit group (who were also the most sedentary) had the highest mortality rates by far. The big surprise was that the death rate dropped most sharply in the second-least-fit group, by 60 percent for men and 48 percent for women. To be in this group, the researchers estimated, all a person would have to do is walk briskly for thirty to sixty minutes every day. The three fittest groups—including people who jogged up to forty miles a week—derived relatively minor additional benefits.

In addition, the women (more than 3,100 of them) were found to benefit as much from being fit as the men. The few earlier studies of fitness in women were small and had ambiguous results. In this study, being physically fit lowered the risk not only of heart disease among both men and women, but also cancer (for which there is less evidence) as well as all causes of death. The researchers couldn't adjust for the fact that nearly all the participants were white and well-to-do. But they did adjust their data statistically to be sure that the higher mortality rate was

---

The Cancer Risk

While it has not been shown that a given level of physical activity per se can reduce your overall cancer risk, research suggests that exercise often modifies some of the risk factors associated with certain kinds of cancer. Obesity, for example, has been linked to cancer of the breast and the female reproductive system—and regular exercise helps promote weight loss. Several studies have also found that men who worked at sedentary jobs for most of their lives had a greater incidence of colon cancer (but not rectal cancer) than those in more active jobs.

Exercise will not counteract the effects of a high-fat diet or smoking. Still, it can contribute, even indirectly, to a reduced risk, and is recommended by the American Cancer Society as part of its cancer prevention program.

due to lack of fitness and not other important risk factors, such as age, smoking, high cholesterol or blood pressure levels, and family history of heart disease.

Fitness and aging

Our bodies change as we age. For example, aerobic capacity (the ability of the cardiovascular system to deliver oxygen to working muscles) declines slightly every year after age thirty. Heart muscle contractibility slowly declines, as does general muscle strength. Percentage of body fat, as opposed to lean muscle tissue, tends to increase with age.

Yet some people stay vigorous and active much longer than others. Most gerontologists now believe age-associated declines can be explained in terms of life style, habits, diet, and other factors not directly part of the aging process. Thus exercise may certainly be a factor in slowing the hands of time. Consider the following evidence:

• As reported in the *Journal of Gerontology,* a study of walkers in three age groups (19 to 29, 39 to 49, and 55 to 60 years old) showed that aerobic capacity is not necessarily correlated with age. That is, some fast walkers in the older group were as fit as those in the younger groups.

• A study at Western New Mexico University showed that postmenopausal women who engaged in high-intensity exercise programs significantly increased their cardiovascular endurance.

• Burning extra calories through exercise protects against the slow but steady weight gain that is a common pattern among Americans as they grow older.

• Exercise increases bone density in women over forty, many of whom are at high risk for menopausal bone loss.

• Comparisons of the mental agility of younger people and healthy older individuals who exercise at about the same level show that the elders react about as fast as their juniors and significantly faster than their sedentary peers. Regular aerobic exercise seems not only to help preserve neurological functioning into old age, but also potentially to enhance it in older people who have been sedentary.

If maintaining a healthy heart, strong muscles, and flexible joints is part of staying young, then exercise is part of the answer. Americans spend millions on potions that "guarantee" the glow of youth but accomplish nothing. Exercise, which can truly maintain your body's youthful functions, usually costs nothing.

Controlling Your Weight

For most people, "overweight" and "obese" are not scientific terms, but loaded words that trigger anxiety and frustration. Like gender and ethnicity, weight is an essential part of every person's self-image, and when pounds go haywire, the result is distress. Our culture is, to put it mildly, preoccupied with weight. Weight gain is always noticed and generally perceived as an important change—in an adult, usually for the worse. Bathroom scales are almost as common as bathrooms; millions of people weigh themselves daily as part of their morning routine.

In our culture, the ideal human body is lean and trim with an abdomen taut as an army cot—an image depicted everywhere and a model to which few conform. Some surveys show that as many as 90 percent of Americans believe they weigh too much—indeed, two-fifths of Americans are following some weight-loss program at any given moment—and even small children worry about diets. Lurking in the back of our minds is the notion that fat is the visible evidence of self-indulgence and a weak will. And according to the National Institutes of Health, of all the health risks of being overweight or obese, probably none has a more adverse effect than the psychological suffering. Fortunately, medical discoveries of the past few years have begun to offer new ways of thinking about overweight and obesity.

What is obesity?

Although often used interchangeably, "overweight" and "obese" do not mean the same thing. Obesity is a medical term meaning the storage of excess fat in the body. Often referred to as a "disease," obesity is actually a sign of what may well be a spectrum of different kinds of disorders—genetic or environmental. In fact, there is no single definition of obesity. It may be simply an extreme degree of overweight, but a person can be overweight without being obese: a 250-pound six-foot linebacker, for example, may be overweight according to ordinary standards, but may actually have a below-average amount of body fat. In contrast, a person in a normal-weight range but with very sedentary habits could have a small muscle mass and be storing excess fat and thus be classifiable as obese. About one-third of all Americans are above their ideal weight as determined by standard tables, and for the majority of them, the excess weight is in the form of body fat, not muscle mass. Of this group, about half exceed their ideal weight by 20 percent or more and hence are classified as obese.

Risks of too much poundage

Doctors have observed for many years that overweight and obesity are associated with greater risk for some diseases, and the evidence continues to accumulate. (The risks are greatest for the very overweight and the obese; if you're only a few pounds—less than 10 percent—over your desirable weight, your increased risks are small.)

Hypertension is 5.6 times higher in overweight people aged twenty to forty-four and twice as high for those forty-five to seventy-four. An Australian study of young overweight hypertensives, published in *The New England Journal of Medicine,* showed them all to be prone to the kind of heart enlargement usually associated with high blood pressure. One group was placed on a weight-reduction regimen, and although they lost an average of only eighteen pounds, their systolic and diastolic blood pressure dropped significantly. Moreover, their heart size decreased somewhat, providing additional evidence of the connection between being overweight and cardiovascular disease.

Numerous other studies have shown the relationship between being overweight and high blood cholesterol levels as well as heart attacks. Although diabetes is probably an inherited disease, noninsulin-dependent diabetes mellitus (NIDDM, also called adult-onset or type II diabetes), can be delayed or averted by weight control. Diabetes is three times as frequent in overweight people as in those who are not overweight. Studies conducted by the American Cancer Society have shown that certain cancers (of the colon and prostate in men, of the uterus in women, and of the breast in post-menopausal women) are more prevalent in the obese than in the nonobese.

In addition, obesity puts women in particular at increased risk of heart disease. A study conducted at Harvard Medical School of 115,000 women aged thirty to fifty-five found that of all the women in the study who developed heart disease during an eight-year period, 40 percent of them had no other risk factors (diabetes, family history, smoking, or high cholesterol, for example) except being 20 percent

Men who are 30 percent overweight have a 70 percent higher risk of developing coronary heart disease than those at their recommended weight level.

How Much Should You Weigh?

Those who exceed their ideal weight by 20 percent or more (for example, a 180-pound person whose ideal weight is 150) are seriously endangering their health. But how to determine your "desirable" weight is still a matter of controversy. The fastest, though not the most accurate, way to determine what you should weigh is to consult a standard height/weight table. By far the most widely known are the Metropolitan Life Insurance tables, based on the mortality figures of policy holders. According to an analysis in the *Annals of Internal Medicine,* one trouble with these tables is that they take no account of many factors that affect weight—family history, race, or age, for instance. At age fifty, even the trim and muscular weigh more than they did at twenty-five, and there is some evidence that modest weight gain between age twenty-five and sixty-five is healthy.

A better way to define overweight is to measure the proportion of fat in the body, but this is a difficult task to do accurately, even with professional training. Therefore, the preferred way to figure out your healthy weight is to calculate your body mass index—the figure you get by dividing your weight in kilograms by the square of your height in meters. This is the most useful figure because it minimizes the effect of height and provides reasonable guidelines for defining overweight. You can calculate your body mass index by following the steps below. (A calculator, while not a necessity, will help.)

1. To convert your weight to kilograms, divide the pounds (without clothes) by 2.2: _____.

2. To convert to meters, divide your height in inches (without shoes) by 39.4 (_____), then square it: _____.

3. Divide (**1**) by (**2**): _____. This is your body mass figure.

For men, desirable body mass is 22 to 24. Above about 28.5 is overweight. Body mass above 33 is seriously overweight.

For women, desirable body mass is 21 to 23, overweight begins at about 27.5, and seriously overweight is above 31.5.

or more over their ideal weight. And of this group, 70 percent were women in the very obese category (they were at least 30 percent over their ideal weight). Women who had been slim at age eighteen and gained weight in adulthood seemed to be at increased risk.

Clearly, then, weight has a serious and direct effect on longevity and seems to take its greatest toll in those under fifty. Leading health professionals have already stated that younger overweight people stand to gain even more by reducing than do the middle-aged and elderly.

Does body shape matter?

People with "apple" shapes (fattest in the abdomen area) have a greater risk of coronary artery disease, stroke, hypertension, and diabetes than those with "pear" shapes (fattest in the hips, buttocks, and thighs). In addition, researchers have found that fat distribution may also affect the risk of breast cancer in postmenopausal women. It's long been known that increased body weight is a risk factor for various cancers, but several studies have indicated that women who tend to store fat in the midsection and upper body are at even greater risk.

Men are more likely than women to store excess fat in the midsection and develop a "beer belly" whether they drink alcohol or not. Women typically store fat lower on the body. Because of these gender differences, researchers suggest that sex hormones determine where fat is deposited. Still, women can be "apple-shaped," too, with all the risks that that entails. Heredity and physical activity level are other major factors affecting your "shape."

While fat in the hip and thigh region is mainly stored just under the skin, fat in the midsection is stored deeper inside the body. Scientists theorize that abdominal fat also releases more fatty acids, leading to a rise in triglycerides and some forms of cholesterol in the bloodstream, and interfering with the action of insulin in the body (thus increasing the risk of diabetes). The elevated risk of breast cancer, the researchers theorize, may be due to increases in the availability and activity of estrogen associated with abdominal obesity.

The role of fat

Fat cells are not mere storage tanks for excess calories, they cushion organs and insulate against the cold. More important, the ability to store excess energy for future use is one of the miracles of evolution. With fat in reserve, animals and, later, early humans could range through wide and inhospitable areas where food might be scarce.

Smoking appears to cause a dangerous redistribution of fat to the abdomen, even though smokers tend to weigh less than nonsmokers. On the other hand, when smokers quit and then gain weight, it tends to accumulate around the hips.

Calculating Waist-to-Hip Ratio

To evaluate your risk of developing disease based on your fat distribution, determine your waist-to-hip ratio as follows:

1. Measure your waist at the navel, then your hips at the greatest circumference around the buttocks.

2. Divide the waist measurement by the hip size. This is your waist-to-hip ratio.

A waist-to-hip ratio greater than 1.0 for men and 0.8 for women indicates an increased cardiac risk. This means that, ideally, the circumference of a man's waist shouldn't exceed that of his hips; a woman's waist should measure no more than 80 percent of her hips.

For example, a woman who has a waist measurement of 28 inches and a hip measurement of 38 inches has a waist-to-hip ratio of 28 divided by 38 or 0.74. Since this is less than 0.8, it is a healthy waist-to-hip ratio.

Holiday Planning

Holidays can be hard for people trying to lose weight—but they don't have to be. Many traditional holiday meals can be modified to be more healthful. Consider the sample menus below:

Holiday Feasting Breakfast to Midnight

PLAN 1	Calories	PLAN 2	Calories
Breakfast		**Breakfast**	
1 cup orange juice	110	1 cup orange juice	110
2 slices toast	135	2 slices toast	135
1 tbsp butter	100	1 tbsp jam	55
1 tbsp jam	55	1 cup coffee with	
2 eggs, scrambled in butter	220	low-fat milk	15
1 cup coffee with cream	35		
Total	**655**	**Total**	**315**
Appetizers		**Appetizers**	
10 potato chips	105	5 pretzels	120
with creamy dip	120	with low-fat yogurt dip	35
5 crackers with cheese	175	Raw vegetables with salsa	40
1 cup egg nog	340	½ cup egg nog	170
Total	**740**	**Total**	**365**
Dinner		**Dinner**	
8 oz champagne	170	4 oz champagne	85
6 oz turkey, white and dark		6 oz turkey, white meat,	
meat, with skin	345	no skin	230
¼ cup gravy	30	¼ cup low-fat gravy	20
1 cup stuffing	500	1 cup low-fat stuffing	125
2 candied sweet potatoes	285	1 cup acorn squash	115
1 cup buttered steamed green beans	70	1 cup steamed green beans	35
2 rolls, buttered	240	2 rolls	170
¼ cup canned cranberry sauce	105	¼ cup low-sugar cranberry sauce	85
1 slice pecan pie, with whipped cream	520	1 slice pumpkin pie	145
Total	**2,265**	**Total**	**1,010**
Supper		**Supper**	
Turkey sandwich, with mayonnaise,		Turkey sandwich, with low-fat stuff-	
cranberry sauce, stuffing	450	ing, cranberry sauce, gravy	210
1 slice pecan pie	495	1 slice melon	45
1 cup whole milk	150	1 cup skim milk	85
Total	**1,095**	**Total**	**340**
DAY'S TOTAL	**4,755**	**DAY'S TOTAL**	**2,030**
Percent calories from fat	***45%***	***Percent calories from fat***	***11%***

One veterinarian reports that overweight dogs have 75 percent more cardio-vascular problems and 50 percent more cancers and locomotion problems than thinner dogs. The message: slim dogs, like slim people, live longer, healthier lives.

The development of fat cells in the body is very precisely orchestrated, and their number (thirty to forty billion in the average adult) is carefully regulated. In the last trimester before birth, the fetus prepares for the uncertainties of life outside the womb by beginning to accumulate fat cells. For the first six months of infancy, the number of fat cells continues to increase. This rate slows through childhood, and the total number of accumulated cells depends on genetic and environmental factors, especially nutritional ones. (Although some data indicate that obesity in childhood predisposes a person to obesity for life, not all fat babies grow into fat adults.) At puberty, the body again significantly increases the number of its fat cells, with females taking on more than males, since the *(Text continued on page 28.)*

Myths About Weight Control

Myth: Eating grapefruit burns away fat.

Fact: No food can cause fat to be burned away. Dozens of diets based on eating vast quantities of grapefruit claim that grapefruit, or grapefruit concentrate in the form of a pill, contains enzymes that digest fats and so burn them away. There are no known ingested enzymes that will increase the rate at which the body burns fat.

Adding fruit to your diet can be good for you. But there is nothing in grapefruit that will digest calories or cut appetite. In addition, a crash diet of grapefruit and eggs, or grapefruit and bacon and eggs, or some of the other high-fat, high-protein foods that are often recommended along with grapefruit, can raise your cholesterol level.

Myth: Taking diet pills is a good way to lose weight.

Fact: Weight lost with artificial reducing "aids" usually comes right back. Only reformed eating habits can take weight off and keep it off. The major ingredient of many reducing pills is a drug called phenylpropanolamine (PPA), which is a stimulant. When PPA is taken in large doses, its effects resemble those of amphetamines, or "speed." Even in low doses, the immediate effect of PPA is to constrict the blood vessels and speed up the heart, resulting in acute elevation of blood pressure. It can produce such side effects as anxiety, sleeplessness, headaches, irregular heart rhythm, and even lead to strokes or seizures.

Although many health authorities feel uneasy about recommending PPA, the Food and Drug Administration (FDA) has approved it as an over-the-counter reducing aid. It does tend to suppress appetite, and some studies have shown that over the short term, its use can result in slightly greater weight loss than if a placebo is taken. But results are minimal at best—and there's no evidence that it helps to promote long-term weight loss.

Myth: Your stomach shrinks when you eat less.

Fact: Your stomach cannot shrink, no matter how little you consume. If you eat enormous amounts of food, it can expand, but once empty it returns to normal size. If you diet for several days, your appetite level does indeed drop for reasons that medical science does not yet understand. However, this has nothing to do with the size of your stomach.

Myth: Fasting can lead to permanent weight loss.

Fact: As part of a fad diet, fasting is usually ineffectual. Total fasting as a medical treatment for severe obesity was first introduced about thirty years ago. A drastic method that is both risky and usually uncomfortable for the patient, fasting indeed results in a rapid initial weight loss, but most of the loss is fluid and minerals, rather than fat. As the fast continues, the person does lose body fat, but also considerable lean body mass (especially muscle) and more minerals. However, after a certain point in the fast, the body's energy production slows and the rate of loss of both fat and lean body mass decreases.

Depending on the duration of the fast, the amount of muscle and electrolyte (mineral) loss can become critical and usually represents a significant portion (30 percent or more) of the weight loss. Because of the dangers of a prolonged fast, this technique is rarely recommended any longer, even for the morbidly obese. Few people who actually lose weight by this means maintain their loss, and some may sustain permanent injury.

Myth: Toast is less fattening than bread.

Fact: Toast retains all of the calories of the bread it is made from. Many diet plans call for a slice of dry toast with a meal, as though toast were a special diet food. It may look more austere, but a slice of toast has the same 60 to 70 calories that a slice of bread has. Toasting removes only moisture.

Myth: Celery has "negative calories" because it takes so much work to chew it.

Fact: Celery is very low in calories, but not so low that chewing it burns more calories than it contains. An eight-inch stalk has only 6 calories, but chewing celery or anything else burns about the same amount of calories per minute as just sitting. Basically, celery, as well as iceberg lettuce and cucumbers, are nearly calorie-free—not because of the energy required to chew them, but because of their high water content.

Myth: Potatoes are very fattening.

Fact: A five-ounce potato baked in its skin has about 130 calories—no more calories than a serving of cottage cheese or tuna (water-packed) of the same weight, and 20 percent fewer calories than a serving of brown rice. Moreover, potatoes have no fat and no cholesterol, are low in sodium and high in fiber, vitamin C, niacin, and potassium. They are also a good source of complex carbohydrates. Potatoes become a problem food only when you fry them in oil or slather them with butter, gravy, sour cream, or melted cheese. Like other high-carbohydrate foods, such as pasta and bread, it's not the potato that's fattening, it's what you top it with.

Myth: Removing cellulite requires special treatment.

Fact: The whole idea of cellulite is nonsense. Cellulite is simply plain old fat asserting itself. Much of the body's fat is stored directly beneath the skin, where strands of connective fiber separate fat cells into compartments. When the cells increase in size, they bulge out of these compartments, giving the skin a crosshatched appearance in some individuals. Whether you develop this condition depends mainly on the amount of fat in your body, the strength of the connective fibers, and the thickness of the skin. In women, the fibers are taut, the skin is thin, and the fat between fibers tends to bulge. In men, the fibers are more flexible and the skin thicker, so the fat is more evenly contained.

Special creams, brushes, lotions, rub-downs, or rubber pants won't get rid of cellulite. It will, however, yield to the same regimen that gets rid of any fat—proper diet and regular aerobic exercise.

Myth: Electric muscle stimulators can make you trim.

Fact: The ads for electric muscle stimulators—claiming that you can lose weight and firm up without moving a muscle—sound too good to be true, and they are. Electric stimulators, devices that claim to provide "passive exer-cise" ("3,000 sit-ups without moving an inch," as one ad says) are only "the latest in vanity-type quackery," according to the Food and Drug Administration.

Electric muscle stimulators contract muscles by passing a current (from batteries or line current) through electrodes applied to the skin. Study after study has shown that regular use of electric stimulation produces no significant change in body weight or body fat. Researchers at Northeastern University in Boston found that this treatment burned only six calories in thirty-five minutes when applied to the buttocks, thighs, and abdomen.

Even if electric muscle stimulators burned a lot more calories, they wouldn't trim the treated areas, since spot reduction is a myth. The body draws energy from fat stores located throughout the body, not selectively from the parts that are being exercised or electrically stimulated at that time.

Myth: In order to lose weight, you need to give up all sweets.

Fact: Including a reasonable amount of sweets in a weight-loss plan may help to ensure that a diet will succeed.

The key to losing weight and keeping it off is to adopt healthy eating and exercise habits that you can stick to for a lifetime. It is unrealistic to expect that you will never again for the rest of your life eat a piece of chocolate or a slice of cake. In fact, there is some evidence that a craving for sweet foods is not a matter of flabby willpower, but has a chemical basis in some individuals. Nutritionists at the Massachusetts Institute of Technology have suggested that the hunger for sweets may be regulated in part by serotonin, one of several brain chemicals that appear to control many physiological functions. When we eat sweets, our brains normally respond by releasing increased amounts of serotonin. This causes us to feel satisfied.

Researchers speculate that some obese people crave carbohydrates because they "need" extra serotonin. Whether this theory is borne out by further research or not, you can include small amounts of dessert-type foods in your diet and still lose weight, provided that you don't do it too often and that you control your portion sizes.

female body must be prepared for the possibility of pregnancy and the further demands of lactation.

By early adulthood the body has accumulated most of the fat cells it will ever have. Although people may subsequently gain a great deal of weight, their fat cells generally do not increase in number but only in size (in cases of extreme obesity, however, there is an increase in the number of fat cells). And while fat cells can shrink, they never disappear. In an experiment conducted at Rockefeller University in New York City, rats were put on a starvation diet. They lost some fat, but not their fat cells. As the diet continued, they lost muscle, organ, and connective tissue, but even at the point of death, their fat cells decreased in size but not in number and their brain cells remained intact. Clearly, fat cells are programmed to guard themselves zealously.

It is also speculated that the body has a "set point," or precise amount of fat it "decides" to maintain. Even if you cut down your caloric intake, this set point may be hard to change. This is one theory as to why it may be so difficult to diet and why people may be prone to put weight back on when dieting stops. There is also some evidence that people prone to obesity expend calories at a lower rate than others, even at the same level of activity.

The genetic factor

Why some people are fat and others are thin is a question that medical science is not yet able to answer. The old platitude that blames overweight on overeating is true, but doesn't tell the whole story about obesity. Food in the United States is plentiful, cheap, and available twenty-four hours a day, and many people not only overeat, but eat a lot of high-fat, high-calorie foods that contribute to weight gain. However, there are some people who eat anything they want and never gain weight, and studies show that obese people do not eat an inordinate amount of calories. In fact, they often eat less than nonobese people do. Perhaps more important than overeating, far too many Americans spend their leisure time inactively—shopping, driving around, or watching television, for instance. From an environmental standpoint alone, then, it is no wonder that obesity and overweight are as prevalent as they are in this country.

Yet there are other factors at work, including race, gender, economic status, and possibly genetics. Black men between the ages of thirty-five and fifty-five are more likely to be overweight than white men in the same age group, and black women thirty-five to fifty-five are almost twice as likely to be overweight as their white counterparts. For reasons not well understood, those who live below the poverty line, particularly women, are more likely to be fat than people at the top of the economic heap.

Although the tendency to be overweight appears to run in families, until recently no one was sure whether this is a matter of eating habits or heredity. But a study reported in *The New England Journal of Medicine* by Dr. Albert Stunkard and his colleagues concluded, "Genetic influences have an important role in determining human fatness in adults, whereas the family environment alone has no important effect." Dr. Stunkard studied 540 middle-aged adults who had been adopted as children. Their body mass index bore little relation to their adoptive parents' index; instead, the daughters tended strongly to follow the pattern of their biological parents, particularly of their mothers, although the sons showed no such

Does TV lead to weight gain?

Men who watch television for at least three hours a day are twice as likely to be obese as those who watch less than an hour. And an article in Pediatrics *stated that the prevalence of obesity in teenagers increased by about 2 percent for every additional hour of daily television viewing. Many researchers suggest that the relationship between excessive television watching and obesity is reciprocal—one reinforces the other. In addition, television viewers may be encouraged to eat more food, thanks in part to exposure to thousands of ads on television for high-calorie snacks.*

relationship to either set of parents. This again emphasizes the complex relationship of genetics and environment to obesity.

Still, a genetic tendency toward being overweight does not doom a person to be fat—any more than a familial tendency in the other direction guarantees thinness. Studies have shown that rats bred for thinness can still get fat on a diet of snack foods; animals genetically prone to be fat will get fatter on the same diet. But both groups lose weight if returned to a normal maintenance diet. Furthermore, even fat-prone rats can be saved from obesity if their physical activity is increased.

If you know that overweight runs in your family, you can use the knowledge preventively. Because Americans, as a whole, live a relatively sedentary life style and have plenty of food available to them, individuals looking to lose weight have to make an effort to keep active and eat a low-fat, high-carbohydrate diet that is moderate in calories.

Why crash diets don't work

Still, the advice "eat less and exercise more" is often too simplistic to be of much help. Furthermore, you already know that if through some feat of self-denial you manage to lose a few pounds, you'll almost certainly gain them back within six months. Or you may suffer through two weeks of deprivation only to find that you haven't lost a pound. What advice do the experts have for such problems?

No matter how much weight you want to lose, the reducing process has two phases: first, the time it takes to drop the desired number of pounds, which most people want to do as quickly as possible; and second, the development of a life style that will keep the weight off. The second is the hard part because it has to continue for the rest of your life. That's why most diets emphasize the first phase only—the easy part. But the truth is that diets meant to lose weight fast won't keep you thin and may be harmful.

Three factors work against the dieter. One is that the body rather quickly adapts to a lower food intake by lowering its metabolic rate and thus resists burning off fat. When you restrict your diet and lose ten pounds, the body "becomes used to" that restricted diet. Then, if you increase your food intake, even though you still eat less than before your diet, the body treats the increase as an excess, and you gain weight.

The second element working against the dieter is the fact that the weight lost in the early part of a strict diet program is not fat, for the most part, but water.

Third, if the dieter consumes less than 1,200 calories a day, he may lose muscle tissue as well as fat. So even though the dieter loses weight, he is actually fatter than he was before the diet because the percentage of body fat goes up. This is not the goal of a good diet, which is to reduce weight without losing much muscle tissue.

The consequences of crash dieting

People who try one crash diet after another, losing weight only to regain it, are doing themselves more harm than good. Some research suggests that people who get caught up in the "yo-yo" cycle take progressively longer each time to shed pounds, and gain them back progressively faster. Studies of groups as diverse as obese patients, high-school wrestlers, and laboratory rats all suggest that repeated loss-and-gain cycles trigger metabolic changes that make it a little harder to lose weight each time you start over. It took the eighty obese patients in the first study

Very-Low-Calorie Diets: Do They Work?

The very-low-calorie diet—400 to 800 calories a day in the form of powdered egg or milk-derived protein supplements mixed with liquid—is, in effect, a modified fast designed for the very overweight. These new "liquid diets" are administered by hospitals and physicians who keep close tabs on their patients' health—a far cry from the over-the-counter liquid protein supplements of the 1970s, withdrawn when the Centers for Disease Control reported sixty deaths attributable to their use. Unlike today's diets, the protein in these early supplements was collagen-based; its inadequate amino-acid composition (plus possibly a lack of carbohydrates) led to a dangerous loss of lean muscle mass, including heart muscle. Also, these early diets didn't provide for adequate potassium intake, which may have resulted in serious disturbances of heart rhythm.

A new formula

In addition to protein, today's supplements contain varying amounts of carbohydrates and the Recommended Daily Allowance for most nutrients. Mixed with liquid, these supplements are taken three to five times a day at meal and snack times. Other than eight glasses of water or more a day, that's all you get. (Some programs do allow you to munch on raw vegetables to satisfy the need to chew.) Very-low-calorie diet programs usually last three months. After one to three months on a maintenance diet of 1,250 to 1,500 calories, the patient may repeat the program. Reportedly, hunger pangs are rarely a problem, possibly because low intakes of calories lead to the manufacture of substances called ketones that are thought to suppress hunger. More importantly, the programs include regular electrocardiograms (ECGs), blood and urine tests, and visits to the doctor, as well as exercise regimens, nutrition education, and support groups.

Medical supervision is key

Medical supervision is extremely important when you're on such a diet program. One complication that can occur is an increased incidence of gallstones probably due to the sluggish flow of bile on a very low-fat, low-calorie diet. This problem and others can be watched for and prevented when you're under a doctor's care.

The very-low-calorie diet, extreme though it is, has earned medical recognition as sound therapy for people whose obesity puts them at risk for such problems as diabetes, hypertension, and heart disease. On the other hand, such drastic dieting is generally regarded as overkill for people who simply want to lose a few pounds from their hips or thighs; most programs won't admit you unless you are 20 to 30 percent above your ideal weight. And no one should undertake a program that provides fewer than 1,200 calories a day without a doctor's advice. Not all researchers or physicians, though, agree that even seriously obese patients benefit from such austere diets.

Studies made by researchers conducting these diet programs indicate high rates of short-term success. Two- to five-pound losses per week are common, and over three months most patients lose forty to sixty pounds. As yet, there are few long-term studies to indicate how many people manage to keep the weight off permanently—and it is weight-loss maintenance that ultimately validates any weight-reduction program. One study at San Diego State University found that while people who actually completed a very-low-calorie program (45 percent) lost an average of 84 percent of their excess weight, they regained 59 to 82 percent of their initial excess within thirty months. "This is disappointing, but may be exactly what should be expected," commented the researchers, since overweight individuals "have learned to overeat and underexercise."

Learning to eat less

The best very-low-calorie-diet programs include a maintenance phase of up to eighteen months devoted to re-educating patients in long-term weight-management techniques—in short, to improving their eating patterns and changing their life styles. For everyone, these patterns, which include cutting back on calories and engaging in regular physical activity, are the only ways to control weight in the long run; you can't safely shed pounds overnight again and again. And for the obese, since their condition can be life-threatening, a carefully monitored very-low-calorie diet may well prove of real help.

more than a third longer to lose weight the second time around, even though they were fed the same diet. Among a group of twenty-seven teenage wrestlers, those who crash-dieted repeatedly to "make weight" for matches had significantly lower resting metabolic rates than those who didn't. As for the rats, a group put on a yo-yo cycle took twice as long to lose the same amount of weight the second time around, but gained it back three times as fast.

What appears to happen is this: when you go on a stringent crash diet, you burn both fat and lean muscle mass; when you regain those lost pounds, you get back more fat than lean. Why? Possibly because the body interprets drastic dieting as a mortal threat and in an effort to maintain essential life processes, slows the rate at which it burns the calories involved in these processes (the basal metabolic rate). Yo-yo dieting thus affords the body repeated opportunities to build up its efficiency at storing energy—a function of fat cells. Muscle cells, on the other hand, burn calories, so that along with lost muscle mass, some of your body's calorie-burning potential disappears. Another ominous outcome is that the weight that is regained is more likely to be in the upper body than the lower, and that type of weight distribution—the "apple-shaped" body—has been linked to an increased risk of heart disease.

The average American gains seven pounds between the ages of twenty-five and thirty-four, with women gaining slightly more weight than men.

Evaluating a weight-control plan

Having established that fad diets don't work, what does? For most people, nutritionists and doctors usually recommend a diet of no fewer than 1,200 calories a day, composed of nutritious, low-calorie, low-fat foods such as fruits, vegetables, whole grains, lean meats, fish, and low-fat dairy products. Although people get discouraged with these sensible diets because they work slowly, sticking to a sensible plan ensures that the weight will stay off.

Some of the popular diet plans from best-sellers, magazines, and organizations can help those individuals who feel they need a regimen to get started. Here's how to distinguish a good plan from ineffective or harmful ones:

Pass up any diet plan that:

•Emphasizes a particular food (for instance, grapefruit, wheat germ, or yogurt) above all others.

•Guarantees that you'll lose a certain number of pounds, especially a large number of pounds—for example, "Lose up to ten pounds a week."

•Is described as "first," "new," "innovative," "easy," or "fast"—there's nothing new or quick about losing weight.

•Uses fanciful theories to explain how a combination of certain foods (such as fruits and grains only) can improve your health and lead to weight loss. Food-combining theories have been around for a long time and have never been shown to promote weight loss—unless the menus they suggest happen to be low in calories.

•Omits one food group or major nutrient, such as carbohydrates. To stay healthy, you need to choose foods that supply all nutrients. The once-fashionable high-protein, low-carbohydrate diets are high in fat. Furthermore, although they may lead to rapid weight loss initially, it comes mostly from water loss, followed by loss of muscle tissue rather than fat.

•Recommends a total daily intake of fewer than 1,200 calories, unless you're under medical supervision. Besides being hard to follow, minimalist diets don't ensure you of proper nutrition. (For the truly obese, liquid diets—400 to 800

Tactics and Strategies for Weight Control

- Eat slowly.
- Clear your refrigerator and pantry of high-calorie foods and snacks; stock only what you intend to eat on your new diet.
- Eat less fat and more complex carbohydrates (grains, fruits, and vegetables).
- Limit your intake of butter, ice cream, cheese, salad dressings, and oils.
- Avoid packaged snacks, cookies, and high-fat baked goods.
- Use nonstick cooking utensils.
- Bake, broil, or poach meats and steam vegetables (instead of frying or sautéing them in fat).
- Switch to using skim milk and low-fat dairy products.
- Exercise regularly.
- Take up enjoyable activities that don't involve food (such as gardening, adult education, or sports).
- Get counseling or join a support group on a long-term basis.

The Truth about Food Combining

While some beliefs about food combining—eating specific foods in the right combinations—are religious or cultural in origin, most are pure faddism. There is no scientific evidence that any one food should not be combined with another. Many fad diet plans will tell you, for example, that starches shouldn't be eaten in the same meal as proteins, and that improperly combined foods "putrefy" the body. But what the advocates of food combining don't tell you is that all foods, even when eaten individually, are combinations of fat, protein, and carbohydrates to begin with.

calories—may be useful for immediate weight loss; these require strict medical supervision and can be quite expensive. See page 30.)

- Tells you to take megadoses of vitamin and mineral supplements to make up for losses in foods. Be especially suspicious if "special formula" supplements are sold along with the diet plan.

Look for a diet program that:

- Relies on low-calorie foods that are high in nutrients, particularly fruits, vegetables, and whole grains, and is low in fat.
- Offers variety so you don't get bored with the diet.
- Fits the way you live. Allowance should be made—and advice given—for people on the go or those who are not expert cooks.
- Emphasizes slow weight loss and long-term change of eating habits. It shouldn't promise weight loss exceeding two pounds weekly.
- Offers instruction in the principles of nutrition, in addition to daily menus and charts. If the diet is successful, the day will come when you won't need the plan anymore.
- Includes exercise as part of the weight loss regimen.
- Has been designed, or at least carefully reviewed, by someone with good credentials in nutrition—for instance, someone with a degree in nutrition, dietetics, or a related academic discipline from an accredited college or university.
- Offers strict medical care by a trained nutritionist or physician, if you opt for a rigorous formula or special diet. Make sure the person who developed the program is well qualified.

The diet key: eating low-fat

Recent studies now support the theory that it's not just the number of calories you eat that cause weight gain or loss, but also which type of foods those calories come from. A study from Harvard Medical School looked at 141 women (age thirty-four to fifty-nine) and found that after adjusting for age, physical activity, alcohol, and smoking, there was virtually no correlation between calorie intake and body weight. The degree of excess weight was linked to fat consumption (notably saturated fat), however, independent of calorie intake. Another study, from Stanford University School of Medicine, followed the eating habits of 155 sedentary, obese men (age thirty to fifty-nine) and came to similar conclusions: the proportion of daily calories that came from fat, not the number of calories per se, was directly related to the degree of obesity (total body weight and percentage of body fat).

Is fat more fattening?

A gram of fat yields more than twice as many calories as a gram of carbohydrates (about 9 to 4). Scientists have assumed that one calorie is pretty much like another, and that if you eat more calories than you expend, those calories will be stored as fat, whether they came from fat, protein, or carbohydrates. That fact is not likely to change. But it is now complicated by the question of "efficiency:" are some types of calories, depending on their source and the metabolic state of the individual consuming them, used more efficiently in chemical reactions in the body and stored more easily as fat?

In recent years investigators have found evidence that the body may be able to convert dietary fat into body fat with greater ease than it can convert carbohydrates (starches and sugars) into body fat. Experiments at the University of Massachusetts Medical School, for example, suggest that if you consume 100 excess carbohydrate calories, 23 of those calories will be used simply to process those foods, and thus only 77 of them will end up being stored as reserve energy (body fat). But, the studies suggest, only 3 calories are burned in the processing and storing of 100 fat calories—20 less than it takes to process 100 carbohydrate calories. Still, this small difference can't completely explain the substantial loss of weight that occurs on a high-carbohydrate diet, compared to a high-fat diet, as some studies have reported. For example, if you consume 2,000 calories a day and cut your fat intake from 40 percent of calories to 20 percent (exchanging 400 fat calories for 400 carbohydrate calories), your metabolic savings would be only about 80 calories per day. That could account for a loss of only about two pounds in three months.

No one knows precisely why one person gains more weight than someone else who eats similarly and is as active. Certainly, what goes in (caloric intake) must be

Studies suggest that increasing the amount of gratification and fun in daily life that is unrelated to eating can help ensure that a weight-loss plan will succeed. Researchers have found that most of the pleasurable activities in an overweight person's life are related to eating. Normal-weight people, in contrast, have a wider spectrum of enjoyable activities, such as hobbies or work.

Calorie-Saving Substitutions

Instead of:	Have:	Calories Saved
¼ cup sour cream (125 calories)	¼ cup plain low-fat yogurt (70 calories)	55
3 oz beef, prime rib, untrimmed (360)	3 oz beef, lean round, trimmed (160)	200
3 oz French fries (270)	3 oz baked potato (80)	190
1 cup whole milk (150)	1 cup skim milk (85)	65
¹⁄₁₂ frosted chocolate cake (205)	¹⁄₁₂ unfrosted angel food cake (125)	80
1 cup canned plums, in light syrup (160)	3 fresh plums (110)	50
3 oz chicken, dark meat, with skin, coated, fried (260)	3 oz chicken, light meat, skinless, baked (150)	110
½ cup premium ice cream (175)	½ cup fruit sorbet (110)	65
2 eggs scrambled in butter (190)	1 whole egg and 1 white scrambled in nonstick pan (95)	95
1 bagel, 1 oz cream cheese (300)	1 bagel, with 1 oz cottage cheese, 1% fat (220)	80
2 cups fettuccine Alfredo (800)	2 cups spaghetti, with tomato sauce (450)	350
2 oz potato chips (320)	4 cups popcorn, no oil or butter (100)	220

used (caloric expenditure) or be stored. But though we can measure caloric intake, it's trickier to measure how many calories the body burns. Energy output depends on many variables, including your basal metabolic rate (the bare-necessity energy required for vital functions at rest), energy expenditure from activities, and the energy required for processing food. Caloric efficiency is another factor complicating the picture, and further studies are being conducted to determine its exact effects on body weight.

Does this prove you'll lose weight, as some people claim, on a diet high in carbohydrates and low in fat? There's no guarantee. Inevitably, to shed pounds, you must burn more calories than you consume. But the most efficient way to lose weight is to cut down on high-fat, high-calorie foods (such as whole milk, butter, ice cream, oils, salad dressings, fatty meats, and most cookies and cakes) and eat a greater proportion of foods with high bulk and low-caloric density (fruits, vegetables, grains, and even such starchy items as potatoes).

How exercise helps

Restricting calories and fat is only part of the weight-loss story. For most people, a regular exercise or sports program is essential for losing weight and maintaining the loss. Not only are you likely to enjoy exercise once you get into the habit, but it will also dispose of a certain number of calories.

The only exercise that burns fat, and thus helps you to lose weight, is aerobic exercise—activities such as running, cycling, walking, and cross-country skiing, which use large muscle groups and can be maintained for an extended period, thus burning more calories than anaerobic activities such as weight lifting and sprinting. Moreover, aerobic exercise requires oxygen to fuel the muscles. Without oxygen, your body cannot burn fat for energy.

As well as expending calories, exercise helps in weight loss and weight maintenance by building muscle tissue. Ultimately, if you're trying to lose weight, what counts isn't just how many pounds you take off but what kind of body tissue is lost. The goal should be to shed fat while sparing important "lean body mass," such as muscle, organ tissue, and bone. The problem of losing tissue other than fat is especially serious in very-low-calorie diets. In one study conducted at the University of Minnesota, caloric intake of participants was cut by 45 percent, and changes in the dieters' weight and body composition were observed for a period of twenty-four weeks. During the first twelve weeks, 54 percent of the weight lost was lean body mass; in the second twelve-week period, a third of what was lost was lean tissue.

But research has shown that a proper low-calorie diet combined with exercise can help dieters maintain lean body mass while increasing the burning of fat. To maintain that increased body tone, your body uses more calories—even at rest—eventually drawing on fat. As a result, your percentage of body fat decreases and you improve your fat- to lean-ratio. Deposits of fat gradually decline, revealing contours of muscle that were there all along.

Exercise and appetite

Many people fear that exercise will increase their appetite and that the calories they burn while exercising will be more than made up for by the extra food they'll eat. But evidence shows that most people who work out moderately eat about the same

Eating soup at the start of a meal can curtail appetite by giving the body time to notify the brain that the stomach is filling up.

as they would if they didn't exercise—or slightly more. Although competitive athletes in strenuous training eat more than they would otherwise, the extra calories seldom overtake their increased energy expenditure.

How your appetite will respond to exercise depends on many variables, such as frequency, duration, and intensity of exercise; initial accumulation of body fat; metabolic rate; as well as the amount and type of food available after exercise. Among the recent studies, one looked at a group of college men, none of them overweight. It found that the harder they exercised, the less hungry they were during the first few hours after their workouts; however, their hunger increased slightly during the next several hours. Another study found that lean women who exercised moderately compensated by eating slightly more—but only enough to maintain their caloric intake/expenditure equilibrium. Yet when the same researchers conducted two studies of obese women, they found that the women did not compensate for exercise by eating more, despite free access to meals and snacks. Remember, however, that the results of such short-term experiments cannot explain the body's regulation and adaptation processes during a long-term exercise regimen.

There is, in short, no definitive evidence that exercise always increases or always reduces appetite to any degree. But it is probable that, over the long haul, the calories burned during regular exercise will more than make up for any slight increase in appetite that you may experience.

Keeping weight off

Most people who lose weight regain it—and more. But some people succeed in keeping it off. What's the secret of their success? No one knows, but recently the experts have tended to downplay the "willpower" aspect. Overeating is similar to other forms of addiction. To understand it, you must ask why the addiction exists. Keep in mind that losing weight is not a moral issue. You may hear foods described as "sinfully rich" or "wickedly delicious," but food is not sinful. Nor are you morally deficient if you fall off the wagon. Most people do fall off occasionally, or get pushed off by circumstances. Remember that people trying to change other lifelong habits—smoking, for example—usually have two or three relapses (returns to the old habits) before they succeed. *(Text continued page 38.)*

Keeping Track of How Much You Eat

If you want to shed pounds while eating a balanced diet, the key is watching your portion sizes. But study after study has shown that people are very poor estimators of portion sizes, and most of us have trouble accurately describing or even remembering what we've eaten the day before. Indeed, during the first week or so of your new eating program, it may be wise to keep a diary of what you eat as well as how much—measured as precisely as possible. Don't forget to include estimated amounts of toppings, gravies, and garnishes. If your eating plan allows only three ounces of skinless chicken breast, do you know what a three-ounce portion looks like on the plate? It's not much bigger than a pack of playing cards or the palm of your hand.

In order to stick to an eating plan, a kitchen scale is as wise an investment as a bathroom scale. Use it when you cook, especially for such calorie-dense foods as meat, fish, or cheese. The scale will help you to train your eye to remember what a reasonable portion looks like so that eventually you won't have to rely on scales or calorie counters. Be sure your kitchen is equipped with measuring cups and spoons, and follow all of your recipes to the letter.

Calorie Burning: An Activity Guide

The following chart gives you the approximate number of calories burned per minute for a variety of activities. Exactly how many calories are expended by an individual depends on many factors. For example, the more you weigh, the more calories you'll burn because of additional effort during physical activity. Other factors that influence calorie burning are: your level of fitness, your proportion of body fat to muscle, air temperature and humidity, and how efficiently you perform a particular activity. Still, this chart gives you a rough estimate. The first column of numbers represents the calories burned per minute per one pound of body weight; multiply this number by your weight to get an estimate that is correct for you. Calculations are provided for 110, 150, and 190 pounds. To determine how many calories you burn during an extended period of activity, simply multiply the per-minute calculation for your weight by the number of minutes you perform the activity.

| | | CALORIES BURNED PER MINUTE | | |
| | Per Pound | Per Body Weight | | |
Activity		110 lb	150 lb	190 lb
Ax chopping, fast	0.135	14.8	20.2	25.6
Skin diving, considerable motion	0.125	13.8	18.8	23.8
Skiing, cross-country, uphill	0.125	13.7	18.7	23.7
Running, 6-min mile	0.115	12.6	17.2	21.8
Boxing	0.101	11.1	15.1	19.2
Squash	0.096	10.6	14.5	18.3
Running, 8-min mile	0.095	10.4	14.2	18.0
Jumping rope, 145 jumps per min	0.089	9.8	13.4	16.9
Judo	0.088	9.7	13.2	16.8
Running, 9-min mile	0.087	9.6	13.1	16.6
Racquetball	0.081	8.9	12.1	15.4
Jumping rope, 125 jumps per min	0.080	8.8	12.0	15.2
Treading water, fast	0.077	8.5	11.6	14.7
Cycling, racing	0.076	8.4	11.5	14.5
Swimming, backstroke	0.076	8.4	11.5	14.5
Snowshoeing, soft snow	0.075	8.3	11.3	14.3
Jumping rope, 70 jumps per min	0.074	8.1	11.0	14.0
Swimming, breaststroke, fast	0.074	8.1	11.0	14.0
Swimming, crawl, fast	0.071	7.8	10.6	13.5
Climbing hills, with 44-lb load	0.066	7.3	10.0	12.6
Digging trenches	0.065	7.2	9.8	12.4
Marching, rapid	0.065	7.1	9.7	12.3
Skiing, cross-country, walking	0.065	7.1	9.7	12.3
Climbing hills, with 22-lb load	0.064	7.0	9.5	12.1
Basketball	0.063	6.9	9.4	11.9
Forking straw bales	0.063	6.9	9.4	11.9
Horseback riding, galloping	0.062	6.8	9.3	11.7
Aerobic dance, intense	0.061	6.7	9.1	11.6
Field hockey	0.061	6.7	9.1	11.6
Running, 11.5-min mile	0.061	6.7	9.1	11.6
Chopping down trees	0.060	6.6	9.0	11.4
Football	0.060	6.6	9.0	11.4
Climbing hills, with 9-lb load	0.058	6.4	8.7	11.1
Swimming, crawl, slow	0.058	6.4	8.7	11.1
Sawing by hand	0.055	6.1	8.3	10.5
Climbing hills, with no load	0.055	6.0	8.2	10.4
Skiing, cross-country, moderate speed	0.054	5.9	8.0	10.2
Lawn mowing	0.051	5.6	7.6	9.7
Horseback riding, trotting	0.050	5.5	7.5	9.5

Activity	CALORIES BURNED PER MINUTE			
	Per Pound	Per Body Weight		
		110 lb	150 lb	190 lb
Scrubbing floors	0.049	5.4	7.4	9.3
Shoveling coal	0.049	5.4	7.4	9.3
Tennis	0.049	5.4	7.4	9.3
Aerobic dance, medium	0.046	5.1	7.0	8.8
Cycling, 9.5 mph	0.045	5.0	6.8	8.6
Badminton	0.044	4.8	6.5	8.3
Weight training, circuit training	0.042	4.6	6.3	7.9
Hoeing	0.041	4.5	6.1	7.8
Stacking firewood	0.040	4.4	6.0	7.6
Weight lifting, free weights	0.039	4.3	5.9	7.4
Golf	0.038	4.2	5.7	7.3
Shoveling grain	0.038	4.2	5.7	7.3
Walking, normal pace, fields and hills	0.037	4.1	5.6	7.1
Walking, normal pace, asphalt road	0.036	4.0	5.5	6.9
Plastering	0.035	3.9	5.3	6.7
House painting, exteriors	0.035	3.8	5.2	6.6
Walking, normal pace, plowed field	0.035	3.8	5.2	6.6
Sawing, power	0.034	3.7	5.0	6.4
Weeding	0.033	3.6	4.9	6.2
Table tennis	0.031	3.4	4.6	5.9
Gymnastics	0.030	3.3	4.5	5.7
Playing drums, sitting	0.030	3.3	4.5	5.7
Archery	0.029	3.2	4.4	5.5
Cycling, 5.5 mph	0.029	3.2	4.4	5.5
Fishing	0.028	3.1	4.2	5.4
Food shopping	0.028	3.1	4.2	5.4
Mopping floors	0.028	3.1	4.2	5.4
Scraping paint	0.028	3.1	4.2	5.4
Treading water, normal	0.028	3.1	4.2	5.4
Croquet	0.026	2.9	4.0	5.0
Window cleaning	0.026	2.9	4.0	5.0
Raking	0.025	2.7	3.7	4.7
Carpentry	0.024	2.6	3.5	4.5
Dancing, ballroom	0.023	2.5	3.4	4.3
Volleyball	0.023	2.5	3.4	4.3
Cooking	0.022	2.4	3.3	4.1
Wallpapering	0.022	2.4	3.3	4.1
Canoeing	0.020	2.2	3.0	3.8
Sewing, by machine	0.020	2.2	3.0	3.8
Billiards	0.019	2.1	2.9	3.6
Horseback riding, walking	0.018	2.0	2.7	3.5
Piano playing, sitting	0.018	2.0	2.7	3.5
Conducting music	0.017	1.9	2.6	3.3
Drawing, standing	0.016	1.8	2.5	3.1
Driving tractor	0.016	1.8	2.5	3.1
Sewing, by hand	0.015	1.6	2.2	2.8
Typing, manual	0.014	1.5	2.0	2.6
Writing, sitting	0.013	1.4	1.9	2.4
Standing still	0.012	1.3	1.8	2.2
Typing, electric	0.012	1.3	1.8	2.2
Card playing	0.011	1.2	1.6	2.1
Eating, sitting	0.010	1.1	1.5	1.9
Knitting	0.010	1.1	1.5	1.9
Lying still	0.010	1.1	1.5	1.9
Sitting still	0.009	1.0	1.4	1.7

Boosting Self-Efficacy

Self-efficacy—your perception of your own ability to do a specific task—can be affected by past performance. If you've tried to break a bad habit and succeeded, breaking other bad habits will be all the more easier for you. If you've tried and failed, however, you may find it more difficult. Here are some suggestions for boosting self-efficacy:

1. Think about a similar thing you have succeeded in doing. Maybe you haven't been able to give up potato chips or stick to an exercise program, but you did quit smoking. Or perhaps you have overcome your fear of public speaking or mastered some other difficult task.

2. Recruit your family and/or friends as a support group. Tell them what helps you and what does not.

3. Find a role model. If necessary, join a support group.

4. Don't undertake too much at one time. Start with the easiest tasks first, or parts of tasks. Use a one-day-at-a-time philosophy. Instead of saying, "I'm going to lose weight," say, "I'm going to lose one pound this week," and outline a plan for doing it.

Such relapses usually occur within the first three months. The same is true about eating lapses. But lapses and relapses simply mean that it's time to start over. In fact, according to many studies, analysis of what triggers your relapses can stiffen your resolve.

Researchers believe that emphasis should be placed on techniques to maintain change, rather than on the initial commitment to change. Sometimes, breaking a hard-to-keep vow can lead to feelings of inadequacy and guilt that in turn lead to further relapses. Slips may signal an emergency, but they aren't the end of the world. A slip should be viewed as an opportunity from which you can learn a lesson and then try to do better the next time.

It isn't enough just to say no: you have to plan ahead so you can see temptation coming. This is easier to do in light of an increased awareness of why some situations are particularly dangerous for you. As soon as you realize that, in defiance of all resolutions to the contrary, you've gone overboard on your eating, take a hard look at what you've done and why. Ignore the feelings of guilt and inadequacy and concentrate on the reasons why you decided to control your eating in the first place.

Then review the conditions that led to your slip so you can recognize the warning signs next time and stiffen your resolve. Studies by psychologist G. Alan Marlatt of the University of Washington have identified three primary high-risk situations that account for 75 percent of all relapses:

Negative emotional states. Watch out if you are bored, tense, angry, or frustrated. That's when you are most likely to return to old habits.

Interpersonal conflicts. If you've had an argument at home or at work, you may return to old eating habits in compensation or in revenge.

Social pressures. It may not be easy to stick to your newly developed eating patterns at a business lunch or a party.

Plan strategies to cope with the type of situations that are the most dangerous. The details will differ from person to person, but there are three basic strategies for structuring your resistance:

1. Develop a positive addiction. Rather than rewarding yourself with ice cream or potato chips, become "addicted" to a healthful habit. Take up anything from gardening to jogging that will leave you feeling deprived if you don't get your daily fix.

2. Stay away from temptation. If you always have cake and coffee when you play bridge, don't play bridge for a while. Don't wander "aimlessly" through the baked goods section of the supermarket.

3. Learn to wait out the urge. Ride it like a surfer rides a wave: you know that all waves subside. And see through your own stratagems. Don't keep goodies around in case friends drop in when you know your own cravings will be hard to suppress.

Finally, be prepared to rehearse all or parts of these strategies several times: only practice will make perfect. And have confidence in your ability to change. Studies show that if you believe in your ability to reach a particular goal—a concept defined as self-efficacy—you are more likely to reach it. When beset with difficulties, people who entertain serious doubts about their capabilities slacken their efforts or give up altogether, whereas those who have a strong sense of self-efficacy exert great effort to master the challenges. Nonetheless, allow plenty of leeway for mistakes, and regard each of them as a fork in the road. One path leads to total relapse, the other to continued change for the better.

Cholesterol

Americans are conscious of cholesterol as never before, but not necessarily clearer about its relationship to health. Although some experts question whether high blood cholesterol levels cause heart disease in everybody, there is substantial evidence that, in most cases, the connection between high blood cholesterol levels and heart disease is as incontrovertible as the link between smoking and lung cancer. This connection is strongest in men under fifty. For young women and for everybody over fifty, the link is weaker, but still signficant. This section covers factors that affect your cholesterol level and gives you techniques for controlling it.

What is cholesterol?

Cholesterol is a white, waxy, fat-like substance. Although we usually think of it as found only in the bloodstream, it is actually present in all of the body's tissues. Cholesterol is essential to life: among other things, it is used in the outer membrane of cells; as a fatty insulation sheath around nerve fibers; and as a building block for certain hormones.

Despite its importance to life, cholesterol isn't an essential nutrient—you don't have to consume any to stay healthy. Most of the cholesterol in your bloodstream is manufactured in your body—primarily by the liver—from the fats, proteins, and carbohydrates you eat. The body produces varying amounts, usually about 1,000 milligrams a day. In addition, the average American consumes 400 to 500 milligrams of cholesterol in food every day. In foods, cholesterol is found only in animal products, such as meats, eggs, and dairy products. So, in a sense, there are two different "types" of cholesterol, though chemically they're the same—the type that comes from food (called dietary, or preformed, cholesterol), and that made by the body, both of which end up in the blood.

Just how cholesterol is distributed throughout the body is not entirely clear, but researchers now hypothesize that the mechanism works like this: the liver puts together packages called lipoproteins, made of proteins, cholesterol, and triglycerides (fats either made by the body or derived directly from foods). The largest of these are called very-low-density lipoprotein, or VLDL. As it circulates through the bloodstream, VLDL drops off the triglycerides to the muscle and fat cells to be used for energy or stored for later use. When VLDL drops off its triglycerides, it breaks up into smaller low-density lipoprotein, or LDL. LDL carries cholesterol throughout the system, dropping it off where it can be used for cell metabolism. Cholesterol carried by LDL that is not used, broken down by the liver, or excreted, is left to circulate in the bloodstream where it accumulates in the arterial walls. Nodules, called plaque, are eventually formed, decreasing the flow of blood over time—a condition known as atherosclerosis—and favoring the formation of blood clots. This may ultimately cut off the flow of blood: in the coronary arteries, this leads to a heart attack, and in the cerebral arteries, a stroke.

The liver makes another type of molecular package known as high-density lipoprotein, or HDL. Like the other lipoproteins, HDL is composed of proteins, fats, and cholesterol, but HDL carries less cholesterol than LDL. As it circulates through the bloodstream, HDL seems to have the beneficial capacity to pick up cholesterol and bring it back to the liver for reprocessing or excretion. In simple terms then, LDL brings cholesterol into the system, so it's often called "bad" cholesterol, and because HDL clears cholesterol out of the system, it has been dubbed "good" cholesterol. (If you have trouble remembering which is which, think "lousy" for LDL and "helpful" for HDL.) *HDL (as well as LDL) is formed only in the body. You can't eat "good" cholesterol; no type of cholesterol you eat is good for you.*

Cholesterol and diet

A diet rich in cholesterol and—even more significantly—in saturated fat can increase your blood cholesterol level. There are many other factors that affect your blood cholesterol level, and some people, no matter how little fat and cholesterol they eat, may continue to have high blood cholesterol levels because of genetic disorders, diabetes, or other metabolic diseases. For most people, though, diet remains the first defense against elevated blood cholesterol.

The connection between diet and cholesterol levels was shown as early as 1913, when the Russian pathologist Nikolai Anitschkow demonstrated that rabbits would develop atherosclerosis if they were fed a diet rich in cholesterol. And in the following years, other studies showed clear links between elevated blood cholesterol levels and atherosclerosis in humans.

Other evidence has indicated that high blood cholesterol levels are related to high intakes of saturated fat. The Finns, for instance, who have the highest levels of saturated fat in their diets of any national group, have the highest cholesterol levels, and the highest rate of heart disease, too. Americans, with a slightly less rich diet, have the second highest level of heart disease. And the Japanese, who eat a diet very low in saturated fat, have the lowest levels of blood cholesterol and cardiovascular disease of any developed nation.

In addition, studies have demonstrated that blood cholesterol can be lowered by diet. In one study, a group of physicians in Holland put thirty-nine subjects on a strict diet that contained only 100 milligrams of cholesterol a day. The diet also

Cholesterol

Foods that Affect Blood Cholesterol Levels

Increases Cholesterol

Meats
Shrimp
Egg yolks
Butter
Tropical oils
Hydrogenated fats
Shortening
Coconut
Chocolate
Cocoa butter
Ice cream

Decreases Cholesterol

Vegetables
Vegetable oils
Dried peas and beans
Fruits
Barley
Oats

Nine Factors That Influence Blood Cholesterol

Lowers cholesterol:

Soluble fiber. Beans, oats, fruits, and vegetables are good sources.

Polyunsaturated fat. This lowers LDL, or "bad," cholesterol. Safflower, sesame, and soybean oil are good sources.

Monounsaturated fat. Studies have shown that this also lowers cholesterol. Olive oil is a good source.

Fatty fish. These contain special polyunsaturated fatty acids called omega-3s, which may lower cholesterol.

Aerobic exercise. Although overall cholesterol remains the same, regular exercise helps increase HDL ("good") cholesterol.

Raises cholesterol:

Excess weight. If you're overweight, each two pounds of excess weight adds, on average, one mg/dl to your total blood cholesterol.

Foods high in saturated fat. More than any other factor, a diet high in saturated fat raises blood cholesterol levels. Sources of saturated fat include beef, butter, whole-milk dairy products, dark meat poultry, poultry skin, and coconut, palm, and palm kernel oils.

Foods high in cholesterol. Only animal products contain cholesterol. Eggs and organ meats are the richest sources.

Smoking. Increases LDL ("bad") cholesterol and decreases HDL ("good") cholesterol.

called for two parts polyunsaturated fat for every one part saturated fat. By the end of two years, the subjects had lowered their cholesterol levels by an average of 27 milligrams. Diet alone, it was demonstrated, could lower cholesterol levels and keep them low for at least two years.

The cholesterol/heart disease link

Several studies have provided more exact information about the relationship between cholesterol and heart disease. In a ten-year study conducted by the National Heart, Lung, and Blood Institute, almost four thousand men between the ages of thirty-five and fifty-nine were divided into two groups. One group was given the cholesterol-lowering drug, cholestyramine; the other group was given a placebo. By the end of the study, the drug-taking group lowered their blood cholesterol levels 8.5 percent below that of the control group—and those who reduced their cholesterol levels also reduced their incidence of heart attack by an astonishing factor: they had 19 percent fewer heart attacks than the control group. The study's conclusion: for every 1 percent drop in cholesterol levels, there is a 2 percent reduction in heart disease risk.

Your cholesterol level: "normal" vs. "safe"

Blood cholesterol levels are measured by withdrawing a small amount of blood—usually from your arm—to be analyzed in a lab. The result, a number that is usually between 150 and 300, is the number of milligrams of cholesterol per deciliter of blood (that's about a tenth of a quart, or a little less than half a cup). The average American has a cholesterol level of 210 milligrams per deciliter (mg/dl). Until recently, this average was considered "normal"—that is, an acceptable level. Lately, though, doctors have begun to question this assumption: Americans as a whole, with their rich diet of meat and dairy products, have blood cholesterol levels that are far too high to be healthy, which may partially explain why they have such a high incidence of heart attack and stroke. The so-called "normal" American levels of cholesterol help to produce "normal" levels of one-and-one-half million heart attacks a year.

Experts now believe that to be at low risk for heart disease, people under age thirty should reduce their blood cholesterol levels to 180 mg/dl or less, and those over age thirty to less than 200 mg/dl (see box on page 43). While there is no magic number—a point at which your blood cholesterol level automatically passes from safe to dangerous—the risk of heart disease rises continually with increasing levels of blood cholesterol, though it doesn't rise markedly until levels exceed 200 mg/dl. And the rate of coronary heart disease begins to accelerate rapidly above the 220 level. *Thus, many researchers believe that cholesterol levels should be as low as possible; well below 200 mg/dl is excellent.*

HDL and LDL

If the results of your cholesterol test show that you are in a risk category for developing heart disease, it is likely that your doctor will order another blood test—one that measures the amount of HDL and LDL cholesterol in your bloodstream. If your HDL levels are low, you are more prone to developing arterial deposits. At least four studies have found that people with "safe" total cholesterol levels—below 200 mg/dl—may still be at risk for coronary artery disease if their

It's not true that low cholesterol levels increase your risk for developing cancer. People suffering from cancer often do have low cholesterol levels, but it's generally thought to be the cancer that produces the low levels, not the other way around.

Who's at Risk?

It is estimated that about 25 percent of all Americans have high cholesterol, and another 25 percent borderline high. According to the experts, a complete lipid profile (usually including LDL, HDL, and triglycerides) should be ordered only if you have high total cholesterol or if you have a borderline-high level along with either prior coronary artery disease or at least two of the following risk factors: being male (heart disease rates are three to four times higher in men than in women in middle age, and about twice as high in the elderly); a family history of premature coronary artery disease; cigarette smoking; high blood pressure; obesity; diabetes; and an HDL reading below 35 mg/dl.

	Total Cholesterol (mg/dl)	LDL Cholesterol (mg/dl)
Desirable	under 200	under 130
Borderline high	200 to 239	130 to 159
High	240 or more	160 or more

HDL CHOLESTEROL AND RISK OF CORONARY HEART DISEASE

	HDL Cholesterol Men	Women	Ratio of Total Cholesterol to HDL Men	Women
Very low (½ average)	over 65	over 75	under 3.4	under 3.3
Low risk	55	65	4.0	3.8
Average risk	45	55	5.0	4.5
Moderate risk (2 times average)	25	40	9.5	7.0
High risk (3 times average)	less than 25	less than 40	more than 23	more than 11

Only one out of every three Americans knows that cholesterol is found solely in animal products, such as meat and dairy products, according to a recent Food and Drug Administration survey. Many think that vegetable oils also contain cholesterol.

HDL levels are low; and, conversely, that some people with elevated total cholesterol levels (in this case, usually women) may not be at high risk if their HDL levels are high. Average HDL levels in adult Americans are about 45 to 65 mg/dl, with women averaging higher than men. Studies suggest that levels above 70 of HDL cholesterol may protect against heart disease, while those below 35 signal coronary risk. Female sex hormones tend to raise levels of HDL; this may help explain why women are usually protected against atherosclerosis during their childbearing years, when estrogen production is high.

Despite these current findings, the way doctors understand or treat high cholesterol hasn't changed. It's just that the emphasis has switched. Until now, physicians have focused on elevated total cholesterol and LDL because the evidence linking them to heart disease is substantial. But when they look at LDL, doctors now normally also look at HDL as well. Some researchers prefer to go by the ratio of total cholesterol to HDL in order to get the whole picture. It's important to remember that no clinical study has demonstrated that people with low HDL levels can actually decrease their risk of heart disease solely by raising these levels. Complicating matters is the fact that there are different types, or subclasses of HDL and LDL, which interact in complex ways and appear to have different effects on coronary risk.

Controlling cholesterol

If you are trying to control your blood cholesterol level, you must limit not only the amount of cholesterol you consume, but also the amount of saturated fat, which appears to stimulate the body's production of cholesterol. Experts now recommend that you reduce dietary cholesterol to no more than 300 milligrams per day and keep your total fat intake at 30 percent or less of your total daily calories, with no more than 10 percent of those calories coming from saturated fat.

Although they're often mentioned together, cholesterol and fat are not the same thing. Cholesterol is found only in animal products—meats, poultry, dairy products, and eggs. Plant foods—vegetables, fruit, nuts, grains, and vegetable oils—contain no cholesterol at all. Both plant and animal products can contain fat, however. Saturated fat is found primarily in animal products—beef, pork, whole milk products, and poultry skin—and in three vegetable oils, coconut, palm, and palm kernel. Although foods high in saturated fat tend also to be rich in cholesterol, some foods are high in one but not the other. Organ meats (liver and kidney, for example) and eggs have lots of cholesterol but only moderate amounts of fat. Sour cream, butter, and lard, on the other hand, are rich sources of fat but not particularly high in cholesterol.

In addition to reducing the amount of saturated fat and cholesterol in your diet, there are other steps you can take to keep your cholesterol level down:

Substitute unsaturated fats for saturated fats. Studies have shown that polyunsaturated fats (such as safflower and corn oil) and monounsaturated fats (such as olive oil) help to lower blood cholesterol levels. Monounsaturated fats may help maintain or increase the level of HDL cholesterol as well. But this doesn't mean you should add any of these fats to your diet—you should still keep your total fat intake at or below 30 percent of your daily calories. Less than one-third of these calories should come from saturated fat, and less than one-third should come from polyunsaturated fat; monounsaturated fat should make up the rest. To achieve this, for example, replace butter in cooking with olive or corn oil. Or substitute fish for some of the red meat and poultry in your diet. Some types of fish are high in a polyunsaturated fat known as omega-3 fatty acids, which have been shown to have cholesterol-lowering benefits.

Lose weight, if necessary. Not only does excess body fat raise your total blood cholesterol and LDL levels, but it is also an independent risk factor for heart disease. On average, each two pounds of excess body fat contributes one mg/dl of total cholesterol. And one study has found that weight loss—whether by cutting calories or increasing exercise—resulted in a 10 percent increase in HDL, and more than a 40 percent increase in the subcomponent (HDL2) that is supposed to be protective against heart disease, while total cholesterol and LDL levels remained the same.

Exercise. A program of regular aerobic exercise may help lower total cholesterol and raise HDL. To get this benefit, as well as the other benefits exercise offers, you should exercise at least three times per week for thirty minutes a session.

Increase your consumption of foods high in soluble fiber. Oat bran is certainly the most familiar of these foods, since highly publicized studies have reported that it can lower cholesterol levels by up to 19 percent if consumed in the context of a low-fat, low-cholesterol diet. Oat bran is not the only source of soluble fiber; it is also found in legumes and other vegetables, such as black-eyed peas, kidney beans, carrots, split peas, corn, and prunes. Sweet potatoes, zucchini, and broccoli have some soluble fiber, as do bananas, apples, pears, and oranges, as well as many other fruits and vegetables. No one can say just how much soluble fiber you need to eat each

Fatty meat has about the same amount of cholesterol as lean cuts, since cholesterol is found primarily in the lean tissue, not the fat. Untrimmed fatty beef has about 82 milligrams of cholesterol in three ounces, while well-trimmed lean beef has about 79 milligrams. Untrimmed, high-fat cuts of beef, however, can still contribute to high cholesterol levels, since they are high in saturated fat.

day to lower your blood cholesterol (in the studies with oat bran, the participants ate a bowl of oatmeal and five oat bran muffins daily), but if you regularly eat a high fiber, low-fat diet that includes a variety of the vegetables and fruits listed above and some oatmeal or oat bran daily, you may see results next time you have a cholesterol check—particularly if the level was previously elevated. Studies indicate that soluble fiber has a greater cholesterol-lowering effect on individuals with elevated cholesterol levels than on those with levels within the "safe" range.

Don't smoke. Smoking increases total cholesterol and reduces HDL, and is an independent risk factor for heart disease as well.

Cholesterol-lowering drugs

The primary candidates for cholesterol-lowering drugs are those individuals who do not respond to changes in diet. Drugs should be used only when diet (along with exercise) is not effective; they are usually prescribed only if six months of careful dieting fails to reduce blood cholesterol levels below 200 mg/dl. And even when drugs are prescribed, *individuals still need to follow a diet low in fat and cholesterol for the drugs to be most effective.*

Your doctor can prescribe several cholesterol-lowering drugs that can produce significant results in some individuals; however, none of these drugs are without some side effects. Cholestyramine and colestipol, for example, have an unpleasant taste and can cause nausea, gas, and bloating. Lovastatin appears less likely to cause unpleasant or serious side effects than other cholesterol-lowering drugs, but its long term safety and ultimate effectiveness against heart disease remains in question. According to one study, megadoses of niacin—taken under a doctor's supervision—can produce a 10 percent drop in cholesterol and a 21 percent reduction in nonfatal heart attacks, but can cause flushing, stomach irritation, irregular heartbeat, impaired regulation of blood sugar levels, and liver dysfunction.

Psyllium-containing over-the-counter laxatives—which are rich in soluble fiber—also appear to lower total cholesterol and improve the ratio of LDL to HDL. But these laxatives can cause bloating, gas, diarrhea, and abdominal cramping, and may result in a dependency on the laxative for normal bowel function. In addition, an excessive fiber intake may interfere with the absorption of certain minerals. (This is less likely to be a problem with high-fiber foods, since they tend to be rich in minerals and more than make up for any losses.) For these reasons, it is unwise to use this type of laxative to lower cholesterol without a doctor's recommendation and advice.

No one should elect to take any type of prescription or over-the-counter drug to lower cholesterol without first consulting his or her doctor. Individuals taking these drugs need to be monitored by a physician to check for side effects, regulate dosages, and judge the effects of the drugs on cholesterol levels.

What you need to know about cholesterol testing

Having your blood cholesterol measured is a relatively simple and inexpensive process. The problem is in getting accurate results and then a sound interpretation of the figures.

This blood test is complicated to run in a laboratory. Different labs use a variety of methods that yield differing results. Analyses done in doctor's offices—especially by someone not trained in laboratory techniques and on machines that are poorly standardized—may be particularly unreliable. And not all clinical lab methods for determining blood cholesterol levels end up with values that are comparable to those used by the Lipid Research Clinics (LRC). This nationwide research group, working with experts at the National Institutes of Health (NIH), has developed a standardized method for determining blood cholesterol concentrations and has used it on a large group of patients. Based on these numbers, national estimates of the risks of elevated cholesterol have been made. Research has found that two commonly used clinical lab instruments indicated significantly higher cholesterol levels than those obtained when the same sample was analyzed by the LRC method. Ask your doctor if the values his lab gives are comparable with those obtained by the LRC and if the lab participates in any recognized quality-control program to ensure the accuracy of their cholesterol determinations. Even under the best circumstances, different labs and different equipment can yield different results from the same blood sample.

Other factors that affect your test

In addition, various factors unrelated to the lab can affect blood cholesterol levels. If it's winter, your reading will probably be higher. The cause of this seasonal shift is unknown, but it may be because people tend to eat fattier foods and to exercise less in winter. Even your body position at the time of blood withdrawal can influence the measurable concentration of blood lipids. When you are prone, you blood becomes diluted. Still, there are measures you can take to ensure you are getting the best possible result from your cholesterol test:

•Don't exercise before your test. Exercise can cause a temporary rise in cholesterol levels—as much as 10 to 15 percent—for up to an hour after you've stopped exercising.

•Cholesterol levels can be affected by illness, some medications, pregnancy, and recent heart attack or surgery. If any of these conditions apply to you, discuss them with your doctor.

•Sit down for at least five minutes before your blood is taken. Having blood taken while you are standing or lying down can skew the results.

•Don't eat anything for twelve hours prior to your blood test, if you are having your HDL/LDL levels measured.

•Have at least two tests performed and schedule them a month or two apart. Since cholesterol levels fluctuate, the average of two tests will give a more accurate picture, provided both results are within thirty points of each other.

Assessing the results of cholesterol tests

When the results from your cholesterol test come back from the lab, ask your doctor for the exact number. Be cautious about accepting statements such as "you're perfectly normal" or "everything is okay." You may find that you must take charge of your health in this important area: in 1985 the American Health Foundation in New York gave finger-stick cholesterol tests (a machine that measures cholesterol levels from a pinprick with results available in two minutes, useful for screening purposes only) to twelve thousand people. Those with high cholesterol were advised to see their doctors. Of three hundred such people interviewed by phone later, more than 70 percent said their doctors simply told them "to do nothing" or "not to worry." A 1986 survey of doctors showed that one doctor in three remained unconvinced that high cholesterol levels increase the risk of heart disease, and one out of two doubted that a low-fat diet had a large impact on the prevention of coronary heart disease.

A cholesterol reading above 200 mg/dl should concern both you and your doctor. If this is what your test shows, here's what may ensue:

•Your physician may ask for a confirmatory test. If the results are the same but still not high enough to put you in a high-risk category, the doctor should advise you to make life-style changes, if necessary (exercise, stop smoking, lose weight) as well as to go on a cholesterol-lowering diet. He should give you solid information on how to go about this, or send you to a nutritionist who can advise you.

•If your cholesterol level is high for your age, the doctor will need further information about your blood. This may include a measure of your triglyceride level and of HDL and LDL levels. Together these measurements make up your "lipid profile."

•If your cholesterol is moderately elevated, another important number to know is the ratio between your total cholesterol and your HDL. A higher HDL level may be protective against heart disease. (See box on page 43.)

•Depending on your lipid profile, your doctor may prescribe a drug as well as ask you to modify your diet. Although there are now some effective but very expensive drugs for the treatment of hypercholesteremia (high cholesterol levels), alterations in diet and personal habits often account for the most dramatic changes.

Hypertension

The typical image of a person with hypertension (high blood pressure) is an overweight, overworked male executive with a very short fuse. The truth is, high blood pressure affects people of all ages, races, social classes, sizes and shapes, women as well as men, and even children—a total of more than 60 million Americans. Moreover, at least 20 million of them are currently on antihypertensive drugs, spending more on such medications (approximately 2.5 billion dollars a year) than on drugs for any other diagnosis. Although great strides have been made in recent years to control this condition, often it still goes untreated or uncontrolled.

What is blood pressure?

Every cell in the body needs a constant supply of blood to bring in oxygen and nutrients and to remove waste products. The force that keeps blood moving comes from the heart, but a complex system of nerve signals, hormones, and other elements regulates the blood flow to each organ by widening or constricting small muscular blood vessels called arterioles, much like a faucet controls the flow of water. Blood pressure thus depends on a number of factors, including how much blood is flowing through the arteries, the rate of blood flow, and the resiliency of the arteries' walls.

Blood pressure fluctuates from moment to moment. Among the factors influencing it are the time of day (it is lowest in early morning) and your degree of physical exertion or anxiety. Although blood pressure tends to go up with age in industrial societies, population studies have found that in nonindustrialized countries, there is actually little increase in blood pressure with age.

Measuring blood pressure

Blood pressure is commonly measured by wrapping an inflatable cuff around the upper arm. Air is pumped into the cuff until circulation is cut off; when a stethoscope is placed over the cuff, there is silence. Then as the air is slowly let out of the cuff, blood begins to flow again and can be heard through the stethoscope. This is the point of greatest pressure (called systolic), and is usually expressed as how high it forces a column of mercury to rise in a tube. At its highest normal pressure, the heart would send a column of mercury to a height of about 120 millimeters. At some point, as more and more air is let out of the cuff, the pressure exerted by the cuff is so little that the sound of the blood pulsing against the artery walls subsides and there is silence again. This is the point of lowest pressure (called diastolic), which normally raises the mercury to about 80 millimeters.

Normal blood pressure is thus usually said to be 120/80 (systolic/diastolic) or less, measured in millimeters of mercury (abbreviated as mm Hg).

Both systolic and diastolic readings are important, but diastolic pressure has traditionally been emphasized because it is less subject to fluctuations. However, recent studies, including the ongoing Framingham heart study, have revealed that systolic pressure may be as significant a heart attack predictor as diastolic pressure.

Monitoring Your Own Blood Pressure

For some people, monitoring blood pressure at home can be a good idea. For example, if you're trying to lower your blood pressure by dieting or medication, you may be encouraged by frequent evidence that you're succeeding. Some medications require monitoring to minimize side effects. Equally important, a few people are "office" hypertensives—their pressure goes up just from being in a medical setting. The only way they get an accurate reading is by measuring at home.

Guidelines for measurement

You will need a health professional to teach you how to measure your blood pressure accurately. Remember, blood pressure varies from minute to minute. Body position and other factors, especially smoking, can cause pressure to rise. Prior to taking your blood pressure, you should avoid smoking for thirty minutes (or better still, do not smoke at all), and you should relax for about ten minutes beforehand in a quiet room. Take your pressure at the same time each day and under the same conditions so you can compare readings. One high reading should not alarm you, but consult your doctor if high readings persist. (Try to take your pressure occasionally when you are emotionally upset.)

Choosing the right equipment

Selecting accurate equipment may not be easy. You can buy a sphygmomanometer (a blood pressure measuring device) for as little as eighteen dollars, but many are wholly unreliable. Unfortunately, price is no guide to quality. Equipment comes in three types:

1. The old-fashioned mercury-filled glass column with cuff and bulb attached. This is very accurate but heavy and inconvenient for home use, and mercury will escape if the tube breaks. A stethoscope is required.

2. Mechanical-aneroid equipment with a cuff, bulb, and a clocklike gauge. This is also dependable and less awkward than the mercury column. You need a stethoscope for this one, too.

3. Electronic-digital equipment with cuff and bulb and with the gauge and stethoscope contained in one unit. This is easy to use and pleasingly high-tech in look; it is also the most costly and the least likely to give you an accurate reading.

Both the mechanical-aneroid and the electronic-digital equipment must be checked for accuracy against a mercury unit at least once a year, and possibly more often. Thus, it makes sense to buy from a medical supply house or other supplier who will perform this service for customers.

A reputable supplier should also be able to advise which kind of equipment will be accurate enough for your purposes. Make sure the cuff is the right size. If it's too tight or too loose, you won't get accurate readings. And you'll need a wider cuff if your arm is large.

Myth: Low blood pressure can be just as bad as high blood pressure.

Fact: *Low blood pressure, also known as hypotension, can, in rare cases, be a sign of underlying disease, but most of the time it is something to be grateful for.*

However, one form of temporary low blood pressure can cause lightheadedness. Known as orthostatic hypotension, it occurs when you stand up suddenly. Your cardiovascular reflexes work quickly to prevent blood from pooling in your ankles and legs, but a too rapid change in position may tax these reflexes, especially in older people.

If you get dizzy frequently, ask your physician to help you discover the cause. If it's orthostatic hypotension, pace yourself when rising from a prone position, especially when getting out of bed. Sit for a moment before you stand, and stand a moment before walking. Walking in place briefly and pulling in your abdominal muscles several times before taking a step will aid in the return of blood from the legs.

What causes hypertension?

In some people, the system that regulates blood pressure goes awry: arterioles throughout the body stay constricted, driving up the pressure in the larger blood vessels. Sustained high blood pressure—above 140/90 mm Hg, according to most experts—is called hypertension. About 90 percent of all people with high blood pressure have "essential" hypertension—meaning that it has no identifiable cause. In the remaining 10 percent of cases, the elevated blood pressure is due to kidney disease, diabetes, or another underlying disorder.

About 70 percent of people with high blood pressure have relatively "mild" hypertension—systolic pressure between 140 and 159, diastolic pressure between 90 and 104. This is usually only the first stage, since many cases worsen over time if untreated. And many researchers believe that even slightly elevated blood pressure (85 to 89 diastolic), called borderline hypertension, can be a health hazard if it persists for years.

Hypertension is known as the "silent killer" because it doesn't produce any symptoms—at least none that most people are aware of—until considerable damage has already been done. Untreated high blood pressure is the leading cause of strokes, which occur at a rate of half a million a year in the United States. As a result of hypertension, the heart, because it has to work harder, may become enlarged and less efficient. The added pressure also damages the artery walls, increasing the likelihood of fatty plaque being deposited, leading to scarring and hardening of these vessels (atherosclerosis). This in turn can reduce the flow of oxygen to the kidneys, heart, and eyes, or allow a blood clot to form in a narrowed artery. Life insurance studies show that untreated mild to moderate high blood pressure cuts life expectancy by three to six years on average; severe hypertension, by eight years or more. However, once detected, high blood pressure is usually controllable.

Risk factors you can't change

Certain unalterable conditions put you at greater risk for developing hypertension. If you fall into one of the following categories, you can avoid compounding your risk by making life-style changes.

Heredity. Those with a family history of hypertension are twice as likely to develop it as others. Many children of hypertensive parents have slightly elevated blood pressure even as infants.

Race. Hypertension is more common and generally more severe among blacks than among whites. For reasons not completely understood, blacks—especially males—tend to develop high blood pressure earlier in life, and much more often with fatal results.

Pregnancy. Hypertension is not related to a person's sex. However, during pregnancy, some women—even those who have never had high blood pressure—develop it.

Risk factors you can change

Although heredity and race are unalterable, you can do something about other risk factors for high blood pressure. For some people, dietary and life-style changes may help prevent hypertension, or at least postpone it or reduce its severity. Such changes (under a doctor's supervision) are also the first step in treating people with mild hypertension, who may thus be able to avoid or postpone the need for antihypertensive drugs. If these steps fail to lower elevated blood pressure after three to six months, antihypertensive drugs will probably be necessary. And if you are put on such drugs, you should continue to modify your behavior, since this may help you get by on a lower dose and thus reduce any adverse side effects the drugs may cause.

There's no guarantee that the dietary and life-style changes described below will prevent hypertension or lower elevated blood pressure. Still, even if they don't, they offer other potential health benefits, most importantly a reduction in risk factors for cardiovascular disease. Some factors, such as caffeine and emotional state, cause transitory rises in blood pressure, which you need not worry about unless you are hypertensive.

The following factors lower blood pressure:

Exercise. There is growing evidence that regular physical exercise can reduce mildly elevated blood pressure over the long term. One study looked at fifty-two men with mild hypertension. The subjects were divided into three groups: two groups took hypertension medication and the third group took a placebo. The men, all of whom were previously sedentary, then started a ten-week exercise program, combining twenty minutes of aerobics (stationary cycling or walking/jogging) and thirty minutes of weight training (in the form of circuit training) three times a week.

The nondrug group experienced a lowering of blood pressure as substantial as that of the two drug groups, dropping from 145/97 to 131/84 mm Hg on average in seven weeks. "There was no added benefit to the use of either drug in these patients," according to the researchers. However, the participants' exercise regimen was supervised by the researchers and the study lasted just ten weeks. The big "if" with exercise is commitment; treatment for high blood pressure is a lifelong endeavor. Under normal circumstances, the men may not have exercised as conscientiously. In addition, if the drug dose had been individualized rather than a standard amount, the drug therapy may well have had added results.

Nevertheless, other research has shown that even when exercise alone doesn't control hypertension, exercise may help some people get by on a lower dose of medication and thus reduce any adverse effects the drug may have.

Aside from its blood pressure-lowering potential, exercise is often accompanied by other healthful life-style changes, such as weight reduction and decreased sodium and alcohol consumption. Exercise strengthens the cardiovascular system and reduces the risk of heart disease. It can also help control diabetes, which is another heart disease risk factor. Most experts recommend aerobic exercise for twenty to thirty minutes at least three times a week. Hypertensives should avoid lifting heavy weights, since this can temporarily raise blood pressure to dangerous levels. (See marginal on page 50.)

Calcium. Some studies suggest that eating too little calcium may result in high blood pressure readings. This link is a weak one, however, and no long-term effect has been proven as yet. Therefore, you should not increase your calcium intake above the recommended dietary allowance (1,200 milligrams per day between the ages of eleven and twenty-four; 800 milligrams per day after that. Post-menopausal women should consume 1,200 to 1,500 per day, according to the National Institutes of Health). Low-fat dairy products and some leafy green vegetables—such as broccoli and spinach—not pills are the best sources of calcium, since these are also high in potassium and other possible antihypertensive nutrients, such as magnesium.

Magnesium. Studies suggest that a magnesium deficiency may be linked to hypertension. Get your magnesium from foods—such as low-fat dairy products and grains—not from supplements.

Potassium. An adequate potassium intake may help prevent or lower high blood pressure. A diet that contains grains, fruits, and vegetables will supply plenty of potassium since it is abundant in these foods. In addition, by cutting down on high-sodium foods and substituting unprocessed foods, you'll probably consume more potassium. Avoid taking potassium supplements unless you are under a doctor's supervision.

Polyunsaturated fats. When they replace saturated fats in the diet, polyunsaturated fats may cause a reduction in blood pressure. However, you should keep your total fat intake to no more than 30 percent of your total daily calories, with no more than 10 percent of those calories coming from polyunsaturated fats.

Relaxation techniques. Biofeedback, hypnosis, meditation, and other relaxation techniques may produce a modest, temporary reduction in blood pressure in some

High blood pressure, smoking, and elevated cholesterol increase the risk of heart attack more in middle-aged women than in men of the same age. While the average fifty-five-year-old woman who has none of these risk factors is slightly less likely to have a heart attack than a man of that description, her risk rises disproportionately as each risk factor is added.

people. But these reductions usually aren't reliable or predictable. They are not useful as a first line treatment for hypertension, but may be useful as an adjunct to treatment in some circumstances.

The following factors raise blood pressure:

Sodium. Study after study has found that population groups consuming a lot of sodium (usually in the form of table salt) have a high incidence of hypertension. People who cut down on sodium are likely to make other dietary changes that may lower blood pressure. However, about 10 percent of the population are genetically "sodium sensitive"—that is, their blood pressure responds to the amount of sodium they consume. This group accounts for about one-quarter to one-third of the cases of hypertension in the United States. Still, it is advisable for everyone to cut down on their sodium intake since there is no practical way to determine in advance who is sodium sensitive and who is not. Furthermore, genetic resistance to sodium may be weakened by high sodium intake over many years. Limit your sodium consumption to 2,400 milligrams per day.

Overweight. This is a factor in about 60 percent of all cases of hypertension. The obese (20 percent or more over ideal weight) are twice as likely to have high blood pressure as the nonobese. Even small weight losses can lower blood pressure significantly in overweight hypertensives.

Alcohol. One of the most common remediable causes of hypertension in the United States is alcohol consumption. Alcohol's effect on blood pressure appears to be completely reversible. Limit your intake to two drinks a day (a drink equals one and a half ounces of eighty-proof spirits, five ounces of wine, or twelve ounces of beer) or less.

Smoking. Smoking briefly raises blood pressure but its long-term effect on hypertension is not clear. Nevertheless, smoking is a risk factor for heart disease—as is hypertension. Therefore, smoking compounds the risk.

Caffeine. Like smoking, caffeine causes a transitory rise, but the long-term effects on hypertension appear to be minimal. Habitual consumers may develop some tolerance to its effect on blood pressure. Hypertensives can try doing without caffeine to see if their blood pressure comes down.

One survey of major U.S. insurance companies found that a thirty-five-year-old man who had uncontrolled high blood pressure of 170/95 mm Hg would pay more than twice as much for life insurance as a man with normal blood pressure.

Smoking

None of the habits that can damage the health of human beings has been as clearly documented—or as widely publicized—as smoking. There is simply no room for debate: smoking promotes heart disease and cancer, and is the major cause of premature, preventable deaths in the United States. Smoking can make you sick if you're healthy, and make it harder to recover if you do get sick.

By virtue of the massive evidence concerning the dangers of smoking, millions of Americans have given up the habit. Nearly half of all Americans who have ever smoked have quit. About 1.3 million Americans become former smokers each year, and more and more Americans now view smoking as socially unacceptable. At the same time, however, most heavy smokers continue to smoke. In fact, even after having a heart attack, many smokers refuse to give up the habit. And each year about one million young persons start—that is, about three thousand each day. So there is a need to be reminded of smoking's risks, and to learn the most effective ways to break the life-threatening habit.

The harmful elements in smoke

There are three constituents in tobacco smoke that, in concert, cause most of the premature deaths in smokers. Smoke contains a number of gases, the most dangerous of which is carbon monoxide; when inhaled, it passes into the bloodstream, where it interferes with the ability of red blood cells to transport oxygen. Carbon monoxide may account for the breathlessness of some smokers, and also affects vision, hearing, and judgment.

Smokers also inhale tars—microscopic particles that form sticky, resin-like substances in the lungs. Not only do tars impair the function of the respiratory system, but some of the chemicals in them are carcinogenic—that is, they can produce cancer in tissues with which they come in contact.

The most insidious element in tobacco is nicotine, a powerful, central nervous system stimulant that is highly addictive. In the view of many experts, an addiction to nicotine is the leading reason (though not the only one) why smoking is so difficult to foreswear. In addition, nicotine directly affects blood pressure, heart rate, skin temperature, hormone production, muscle tension, and pain sensitivity.

The damage to your health

More than 350,000 premature deaths a year are attributable to smoking. Up to age sixty-five, people who smoke a pack a day (twenty cigarettes) or more die at almost twice the rate of nonsmokers in the same age group. Smokers suffer from nonfatal ill effects as well, particularly respiratory problems. If you smoke, you risk the adverse effects cited on page 54. (Although smoking is clearly most harmful to smokers, evidence is mounting that the secondhand smoke generated by smokers can pose health risks for nonsmokers who are frequently exposed to it. The environmental considerations concerning "passive smoking" are explained on page 488.)

Cancer. The deadliest risks from smoking are cancer of the lungs, throat, and mouth. Pack-a-day smokers are fourteen times more likely to die from these cancers than nonsmokers. Lung cancer is largely a disease of smokers, and because it is difficult to detect until it reaches an advanced stage, over 90 percent of the cases are fatal. Most smokers also tend to swallow small amounts of smoke, which puts them at higher-than-average risk for cancer of the esophagus. And carcinogenic chemicals that are absorbed into the bloodstream increase a smoker's risk of bladder cancer.

Heart disease. Smoking is a major risk factor in heart attacks, to the extent that more than 200,000 deaths from cardiovascular disease (out of a total of 750,000) are related to smoking—many more than the total number of smoking-related deaths from cancer and pulmonary disease.

Smoking contributes greatly to atherosclerosis in coronary arteries, which impedes blood flow to the heart. Smoking damages the lining of the arteries (which is thought to encourage the formation of arterial plaque); it raises total blood cholesterol and lowers HDL (the "good," protective cholesterol); and it increases the stickiness of blood platelets, making a clot in the narrowed arteries more likely. In addition, nicotine makes the heart beat faster, which requires more oxygen; yet the carbon monoxide in smoke cuts down on the amount of oxygen the blood can carry. Smoking also raises blood pressure temporarily, and it may constrict coronary arteries as well, which makes them less able to supply oxygen to the heart when increased physical effort demands it.

Together, these are perfect conditions for a heart attack, and people who smoke at least a pack a day are more than twice as likely to suffer a heart attack as nonsmokers; even more sobering, they are as much as four times more likely to die from it within an hour.

Respiratory problems. The tars in tobacco smoke gradually impair the cilia, the tiny hairs in lungs and airways that sweep mucus and foreign particles toward the throat for clearing. At the very least, damaged cilia cause extra mucus to accumulate, producing a "smoker's cough." Heavy smoking will eventually destroy the cilia, making the smoker more susceptible to colds, chronic bronchitis, and

Is smoking a few cigarettes a day harmful?

Obviously it's worse to smoke a lot, but no amount of smoking is free of risk. The exact amount of damage depends on a host of variables: what type of cigarette you smoke, how long you've smoked, how much you inhale, as well as genetic factors. How much you smoke each day is also important, for there is a dose-response relationship between smoking and lung cancer, heart disease, and chronic respiratory disease. In other words, the more you smoke, the greater your risk. One study found that men who smoked from one to nine cigarettes daily had a nearly five times greater risk of dying from lung cancer than nonsmokers; for those smoking ten to nineteen cigarettes, it was nine times greater.

Why Do You Smoke?

This test, based on one by the U.S. Department of Health and Human Services, will help you determine why you smoke. Jot down your answers as you go.

True or False: I smoke. . .
1. because I light up automatically and don't know I'm doing it.
2. because it's relaxing.
3. because I like handling cigarettes, matches, and lighters.
4. to help deal with anger.
5. to keep from slowing down.
6. because it's unbearable not to.
7. because I enjoy watching the smoke as I exhale it.

8. to take my mind off my troubles.
9. because I really enjoy it.
10. because I feel uncomfortable without a cigarette in my hand.
11. to give myself a lift.
12. without planning to—it's just part of my routine.

Results: "True" answers to 5 and 11 indicate that you smoke for stimulation; to 3 and 7, that pleasure of handling is important; to 2 and 9, that you seek relaxation; to 4 and 8, that you need a tension-reducing crutch; to 6 and 10, that you have a physiological addiction; to 1 and 12, that you smoke from habit. No doubt you smoke for a combination of these reasons.

No Safe Way to Smoke

In an effort to continue their habit, yet mitigate the risks, some smokers take up cigar and pipe smoking in the belief that these are less harmful. Studies are revealing, however, that cigars and pipes can be fully as risky as cigarettes, particularly for those who used to smoke cigarettes.

Smokers who have smoked only a cigar or pipe rarely inhale the smoke, which generally puts them at low risk of lung cancer (though they are at high risk for cancers of the mouth and lips). But former cigarette smokers who switch to cigars or pipes are at increased risk for lung cancer because they tend to inhale the smoke and to smoke a lot. Both habits are carryovers from cigarette smoking.

Studies of carbon monoxide levels in the blood indicate that virtually all former cigarette smokers inhale smoke from pipes and cigars—though many are unaware of it. By inhaling the smoke, they are able to maintain nearly the same level of nicotine in their blood as they had when they smoked cigarettes. And since pipe and cigar smoke is much higher in tar than cigarette smoke, these may actually pose a higher risk of lung cancer than cigarettes. In addition, studies indicate that the increased risk of heart attack associated with cigarette smoking may continue unabated in men who switch to cigar smoking.

Remember, too, that even if you don't inhale on your cigars or pipe and have never smoked cigarettes, the smoky environment that you are creating ("side-stream exposure") may increase your risk of both lung cancer and heart disease.

other respiratory infections. Smoking is also the leading cause of emphysema, a condition that damages air sacs in the lungs and gradually destroys the lungs' elasticity, causing labored breathing and chronic shortness of breath.

The benefits of quitting

Smoking is an instance where your body—even after decades of smoking—will forgive you if you stop. The cardiac benefits start to accrue almost immediately such that, in two years, much of your risk of heart disease will have disappeared. Within five to ten years, your risk will be no greater than if you had never smoked. The risk of lung cancer and other malignancies begins to decrease steadily after you quit, and after ten years your risk is almost as low as that of nonsmokers—even if you had smoked for years. If you suffer from bronchitis or emphysema, you can expect an improvement in breathing almost at once. As an added benefit, nonsmokers have stronger bones and less chance of getting osteoporosis.

Indeed, nothing you do for your health—not even dieting and exercise—pays as many dividends so quickly as giving up smoking.

Why it's hard to quit

Psychology and physiology play complex roles in the smoking habit. Nicotine is a psychoactive, addictive drug that causes marked alterations in body chemistry. It acts through specialized cell formations in the brain and muscles, but unlike alcohol or other psychoactive drugs, it does not produce dramatic evidence of intoxication, and thus people underestimate its power.

Inhaled nicotine goes almost immediately to the brain, rapidly producing a sense of euphoria, particularly if you are smoking the first cigarette (or pipe or cigar) of the day. By taking more or fewer puffs, inhaling more or less deeply, and pacing your cigarettes, you unconsciously try to recreate this feeling again and again. What appears to be casual and random behavior is instead highly controlled. Nicotine not only affects blood pressure, heart rate, and other bodily

Heavy Smokers and Quitting

There's been some argument about whether the failure rate was higher among heavy smokers (more than a pack a day) who tried to quit than light smokers (less than a pack a day). Investigators monitoring data on over five thousand smokers found that light smokers were twice as likely to quit and stay cigarette-free as heavy smokers. But if you're in the multiple-pack-a-day category, don't despair. A study from the University of Kentucky Medical Center followed 108 heavy smokers enrolled in a hospital-based program that provided group sessions and nicotine gum. At the end of one year, 45 percent of them were verified as nonsmokers (the others had relapsed or dropped out). Three years later, 80 percent of those who had managed to stay off cigarettes for a year were still not smoking.

functions, it also alters mood. You are not merely imagining that smoking a cigarette enhances your powers of concentration or soothes your anxiety. Yet the tense, uptight feeling that a cigarette supposedly relieves can itself be caused by nicotine. It's a vicious cycle.

Smoking is not just a matter of nicotine, however. Typically, an adolescent starts smoking to gain peer approval, to express his rebelliousness, or simply out of curiosity. What psychologists call "modeling" is a strong factor. If the people you admire smoke, you may emulate them.

As you begin to smoke, you learn that just handling cigarettes can be a pleasurable activity. You learn to associate them with such pleasures as mealtime, or the end of classes or work, or with the relief of tension. Smoking has cosmetic uses, too. A pipe makes a man look wise, a cigar is the mark of a connoisseur, a cigarette makes a woman look worldly—at least according to prevailing social stereotypes, which are largely created by advertising.

According to cigarette advertising, the brand you choose confirms your masculinity or your femininity, identifies you as avant-garde or as a risk-taker, and can lend you the appearance of being rugged or sophisticated. The charming, healthy, intelligent-looking young men and women in ads (who mostly aren't shown smoking) are swimming, playing tennis, sailing, or engaging in some other appealing activity.

All of this makes the smoking habit undeniably powerful: most people who smoke would like to break the habit, yet nine out of ten American smokers have tried to quit and failed on at least one occasion. On the other hand, an estimated 43 million people have succeeded—a sure sign that you can choose not to smoke.

Keys to quitting

Nearly every method—no matter how odd—has worked for somebody. If you know former smokers, interview them. Chances are you'll find some go-it-aloners, others who joined a group, and even one or two who swear by hypnosis or acupuncture. The important thing is to find a method that suits your needs. A previous failure is nothing to be ashamed of. If you've tried and failed, and are now trying again, that simply indicates the strength of your motivation. Giving up tobacco is a learning process. Like learning to ride a bike, it may take more than one try.

Going it alone or joining a group. In the past, 95 percent of the millions of people who quit were thought to have quit on their own. Abstinence rates for formal programs were alleged to be quite low, and a study published in 1982 claimed that self-quitters were two or three times more successful than people who sought professional help of some kind. But new data shows that self-quitters and program-seekers are basically similar in their motivations; in their ability (or lack of it) to break the habit; and in their success rates at long-term abstinence. Go it alone if you wish, but don't ever forget that professional help and support groups do help some people—and you may be one of them.

If you want a group program, the local chapter of the American Cancer Society can supply information, and so can most public libraries. The yellow pages (look under "Smoker's Information and Treatment Centers") will also tell you what's available nearby. There are live-in programs and five-day plans. You will probably find a list of counselors, clinics, hypnotists, acupuncturists, and other self-proclaimed experts in behavior modification. Remember that there is no scientific

It's never too late to quit.
Even for older, long-term smokers who already show signs of heart disease, the health risks from smoking are partly reversible by quitting. In the well-known Coronary Artery Surgery Study, researchers examined nearly two thousand male and female smokers over age fifty-four, most of whom had coronary artery disease. They found that 807 people who quit smoking the year before the study and abstained for six years had substantially lower death rates than those who continued to smoke—largely as a result of fewer heart attacks. And the improved survival rate was seen even in the oldest abstainers.

evidence that hypnosis, acupuncture, or "total immersion" are effective. Whichever method you choose, ask in advance what the costs will be, what the dropout rate is, what percentage of people in the program succeed in quitting for an entire year, and whether there is any follow-up.

Drugs to cope with withdrawal. Clonidine, an antihypertensive drug, has been used to control alcohol and drug withdrawal symptoms, and although the Food and Drug Administration (FDA) has never approved it for such use, some doctors have prescribed it to cut down cigarette cravings. But a recent study failed to show that clonidine offered any benefits to people trying to quit. And a recent, exhaustive scientific review of the experimental use of various drugs to combat nicotine withdrawal concluded that the only effective treatment currently available is nicotine itself, in the form of nicotine chewing gum. Nicotine gum requires a prescription, and eventually you have to kick the gum habit. But nicotine gum combined with a stop-smoking program can be highly effective (close to a 50 percent success rate, according to some reports).

Finding a substitute. The best way to quit smoking varies according to which kind of smoker you are, what you think you get out of smoking, and what it seems to do for you. See the box on page 54 to get a better understanding of what keeps you smoking; knowing why you smoke will help you find substitutes that enable you to quit. For example:

•If you smoke for stimulation or a lift, find a healthy substitute, such as a brisk walk or moderate exercise.

•If you smoke for pleasurable relaxation or to relieve tension (sometimes it's hard to tell which is which), physical exertion, social activity, a new hobby, deep breathing, or even eating and drinking can serve as a partial substitute.

•If the physiological addiction factor is high, you may need to go "cold turkey." Actually, doing without nicotine may be the only way to teach yourself to do without it. To work up to quitting, set a final date, then smoke too much for a day or two, which should increase your distaste for cigarettes. Next, try cutting back by switching to a brand you dislike. This will decrease your nicotine intake and alleviate later withdrawal symptoms. Some people have quit by switching to low-tar, low-nicotine cigarettes for a week or two, then quitting completely. Others have found help in nicotine chewing gum, the only catch being that the gum is also addictive, so eventually you have to take the final step and quit the gum.

•If the habitual factor is strongest, work to alter your daily patterns. Cut down gradually—eliminate a certain number of cigarettes each day. Form the habit of asking yourself if you really want the cigarette you are about to light. You may be surprised at how often you say no.

•If handling the cigarettes is important, try doodling, or playing with some small object in your fingers. Take up a craft such as embroidery that supplies tactile sensations.

A plan for quitting on your own

If you decide to quit on your own, choose a weekend (but not a holiday) or some time when you are under the least possible outside stress and have some time to devote to yourself. Throw out all cigarettes, matches, lighters, and ashtrays. Visit the dentist and have the tobacco stains removed from your teeth. Steer clear of friends and family members who smoke. Plan lots of activity for the day you quit.

Some people, especially young ones, actually take up smoking as a way to stay slim. Researchers at Memphis State University recently found that among students who smoke, 39 percent of the women and 25 percent of the men do so as a dieting technique. As a means of staying svelte, this is a markedly poor bargain. The health risks from smoking just aren't worth it.

Go places where smoking is not permitted—museums, department stores, theaters. Take public transportation. Swim, jog, ride a bike, or play tennis. Try to avoid any activity that you associate strongly with smoking.

It is realistic to expect unpleasant or even severe withdrawal symptoms, which may include headaches, constipation, productive coughing, drowsiness, a sore mouth, impaired concentration, irritability, mood swings, an increased desire to snack, and depression. However intense your symptoms may be, they are temporary and in no way threatening to your health and well-being. The worst symptoms should subside after a week or two. Intense cigarette cravings usually last only three to five minutes. When you feel the craving, take a break or a walk. Have something to eat or drink. Brush your teeth often, and use a tasty mouthwash. Breathe deeply or do stretching exercises.

Count the dividends. All the experts suggest plenty of self-congratulation in the first few days. As part of treating yourself well, add up the costs of smoking—just the short-term costs of tobacco and paraphernalia, throwing in a calculation for accidental damage to clothing and furniture. After a week or two, buy yourself a present with the money saved. Or calculate your savings for a month or a year (plus interest) and see what reward you will be able to give yourself or your family.

As your withdrawal pangs subside, the rewards will begin to accumulate. After only a week, your body will be free of nicotine. You will notice that your senses of smell and taste are a keen source of pleasure. Your food, breath, body, and clothing will smell better. Your cough will go away. Breathing will be easier. You will no longer have to go to the trouble of buying tobacco. Newly created nonsmokers are also pleased with the sense of mastery and accomplishment that accrues. Most important, you will add healthy years to your life.

Smoking and weight gain

Researchers have known for some time that smokers generally weigh less than nonsmokers and that many people who quit smoking gain weight—an average of five to ten pounds. This weight increase may be caused by a difference in the number of calories smokers consume or by physiological differences between smokers and nonsmokers. The popular explanation for these weight swings is that smokers are jittery types who eat less than others and when they quit compensate by devouring every candy bar and cookie in sight. New evidence, however, suggests that people who stop smoking tend to gain weight not only because they turn to food as a substitute for the nervous habit or for the oral gratification once provided by cigarettes, but also because of metabolic changes that occur when they kick the habit.

Over the years studies have shown that nicotine slightly accelerates basal metabolic rate (the basic rate at which energy is expended to maintain essential body functions). That is, smokers burn more calories when they are at rest than nonsmokers. One of the most recent studies, at the University of Pittsburgh, found that nicotine causes your metabolic rate to increase to an even greater extent during light activity—by about 12 percent (compared to 5 percent during rest). Thus, when you quit smoking, your rate of energy expenditure—at rest and during everyday activities—slows back down, enough to promote weight gain.

The researchers themselves admitted, however, that this metabolic change would probably account only for a difference of 31 to 69 calories during an eight-hour day—which would show up as only about an extra pound over the course of a month. That's within the normal weight range of most people and doesn't account for the five or ten pounds that the average smoker rapidly gains after quitting. So while these findings are interesting, they don't actually explain what happens in real life. We still don't know how much of the weight gain can be attributed to a change in eating habits, to activity levels, or to physiological changes.

If you smoke, don't put off quitting because you know it will probably cause you to gain weight. You can compensate for any shift to a lower metabolic rate that may occur when you quit by either consuming fewer calories or exercising more. In fact, by doing just that, a large portion of smokers maintain or eventually lose weight when they give up cigarettes.

•During the first week after quitting, which is likely to feature compulsive munching, eat raw vegetables and fruit instead of high-calorie snacks. In the next weeks, slightly reduce portion sizes and lower the proportion of fatty foods you eat.

•Aerobic exercise is a great calorie burner, and it helps keep your mind off cigarettes. At a slower pace, walking as little as an additional mile a day can completely make up for your slowed metabolism.

How to stay an ex-smoker

One of the myths about smoking is that quitting is mainly a matter of willpower. True grit is essential, but not sufficient in itself. According to a report in the *American Psychologist,* quitting is "a dynamic process, not a discrete event." That is, if smoking is central to your life (and for most smokers it is), you have to do more than just quit. After you've won the battle with acute withdrawal symptoms, you'll have to plan new activities and new ways to relax that don't depend on nicotine. Here are some tips for avoiding a relapse:

•The thought of never smoking again can sometimes feel overwhelming. When you have that thought, tell yourself that you are quitting just for today.

•The first three months are dangerous. Avoid smokers and smoking situations such as cocktail parties.

•When you feel the urge for a cigarette, try any of the relaxation techniques outlined on page 409.

•Be prepared for tough times. You'll find yourself making excuses to have "just one"—but having "just one" is never worth the risk. If you're tempted, remind yourself how hard it was to quit, and rehearse the benefits you've enjoyed as a nonsmoker: "I've saved money, I don't cough all the time, I'm proud of myself," and so on. Having a friend to confide in, especially a reformed smoker, can help.

•Don't be fooled into thinking you can become an "occasional" smoker, even after a year of not smoking. It's true that a few former smokers can smoke a cigarette on Saturday night and not get hooked again. But it's also true that some people, according to a study of five thousand smokers and quitters, "cycle from smoking to nonsmoking and back again" most of their lives.

•Don't be alarmed or ashamed at falling off the wagon. If you do, quit again.

Alcohol

Millions of people enjoy an occasional alcoholic beverage, and for most adults, moderate drinking—whether of beer, wine, or spirits—is not associated with any health risk. When consumed in excess, however, alcohol acts as a toxic drug, with pronounced short-term and long-term consequences. After tobacco, alcohol abuse is the leading cause of premature death in America—and the drinker is by no means the only victim. Alcohol is associated with the loss of more than 100,000 lives annually. These include deaths not only from alcohol-related diseases (such as cirrhosis of the liver) but also from traffic accidents. Alcohol is associated with about half of the 50,000 or so fatalities that occur each year on the nation's highways; among those killed are pedestrians, motorcyclists, and bicyclists who had been drinking. Another half a million people are injured each year in traffic accidents involving alcohol.

Alcohol also contributes to serious hazards in the home, especially falls and house fires, and to drownings. People who drink habitually are more likely to smoke and hence to doze off and start fires with unextinguished cigarettes. Nor are the highways and the home the only places where trouble occurs. Reduced productivity and lost employment due to drinking cost an estimated 71 billion dollars annually. In addition to such statistics are the immeasurable emotional and psychological costs: the damage done to family life, for example, by a parent's drinking habits.

Amid all the bad news about alcohol, there is definitely some good. For one thing, Americans have been drinking less alcohol—and lighter forms of it—since the mid-1970s, reversing the trend of heavier drinking in the post-World War II era. As a direct consequence of the campaign against drinking and driving, the number of intoxicated-driver fatalities decreased steadily throughout the 1980s. And everywhere, even among people who regularly drink and serve alcohol, new attitudes prevail. Food writers in national newspapers and magazines urge party-givers to keep the cocktail hour short, not to serve alcohol before dinner, and even to deprive intoxicated guests of their car keys, if necessary, to keep them off the road.

Equally important, the abuse of alcohol is now being recognized as a complex biological and psychological disorder, and such recognition may help more heavy drinkers come to terms with their habit.

Alcohol in your bloodstream

A natural product of fermentation, alcohol is the most widely used of all drugs. Its effect on the mind and body depends on how much of it is consumed over what period of time. The amounts of different alcoholic beverages usually designated as one drink—five or six ounces of wine, twelve ounces of beer, and an ounce and a half of eighty-proof spirits—all put the same amount of pure alcohol into the bloodstream, about two-thirds of an ounce.

How fast alcohol passes into the bloodstream depends on many variables. Unlike most other substances, alcohol can be absorbed through the stomach as well as the small intestine, allowing it to reach the bloodstream more quickly. Because the alcohol in beer and wine is less concentrated than in spirits, it is absorbed more slowly than the alcohol in, say, straight whiskey. On the other hand, the carbon dioxide in champagne and in drinks mixed with soda seems to increase the absorption of alcohol (see the box at right for average blood alcohol levels per drink). Eating while or before drinking, particularly if you eat high-fat foods, slows down absorption. There is thus some rationale for eating rich hors d'oeuvres with drinks.

When the alcohol in one drink is absorbed into the bloodstream, it takes the body up to two hours to metabolize it. Because alcohol is removed this slowly from the blood, even one drink per hour produces a steady increase in blood alcohol levels. Once the alcohol is in the bloodstream, nothing can be done to hurry the process of metabolizing it. You cannot run or swim alcohol away or get rid of it by eating a meal, taking a cold shower, or drinking coffee.

Blood alcohol concentration can be estimated from intake and body size and accurately measured in body fluids and breath. The concentration is related not only to weight but also to the ratio of muscle to fat. Leaner individuals have more water in their bodies into which the alcohol is distributed. Since males usually have proportionately less body fat than females, they will have lower blood alcohol concentration after consuming the same amount of alcohol for the same body weight over the same period of time. The general response to various concentration levels is shown in the box above. However, responses to a given blood concentration level vary from one person to the next and even in the same person under different circumstances.

Effects of Alcohol in Your Blood

How drinking affects your physical and psychological state depends upon the concentration of alcohol in your blood—which, in turn, is related to the amount you drink in a given period of time and your body weight, as indicated below.

Percentage of Blood Alcohol Concentration

Body Weight (lb)	Number of Drinks in Two Hours*				
	2	4	6	8	10
120	0.06	0.12	0.19	0.25	0.31
140	0.05	0.11	0.16	0.21	0.27
160	0.05	0.09	0.14	0.19	0.23
180	0.04	0.08	0.13	0.17	0.21
200	0.04	0.08	0.11	0.15	0.19

Resulting Condition

Blood Alcohol Concentration	Effect
0.05%	Relaxed state; judgement not as sharp
0.08%	Everyday stress lessened
0.10%**	Movements and speech become clumsy
0.20%	Very drunk; loud and difficult to understand; emotions unstable
0.40%	Difficult to wake up; incapable of voluntary action
0.50%	Coma and/or death

*1 drink equals 1½ ounces 80-proof alcohol, 12 ounces beer, or 5 ounces wine.

** Most states use 0.10 as the lowest indicator of driving while intoxicated. A few states use 0.08, while some go as high as 0.12.

More than two-thirds of all American teen-agers have used alcohol, and one-third drink enough to hurt their school performance or get in trouble with the law. The majority of these youthful drinkers start early, before they have even turned thirteen.

Short-term effects of alcohol

Because all cells in the body can absorb alcohol, even its immediate effects (only partially described here) can be wide-ranging. Of all the changes it causes, none is more dramatic than the effect of alcohol on the central nervous system. Some experts have suggested that the effects of alcohol on human behavior are caused by "disorders" of cell molecules. Judgment, memory, and sensory perception are all progressively impaired as blood alcohol concentration level rises. Alcohol depresses the parts of the brain that integrate behavior. Thoughts begin to get jumbled; concentration and insight are dulled. The exhilaration of the first drink or two may turn into profound depression. Alcohol causes sleepiness, but at the same time disrupts normal patterns of sleeping and dreaming.

Alcohol also acts as a diuretic: it stimulates the kidneys to pass more water than is being consumed. The dehydration that results contributes to what is perhaps the most unpleasant short-term physical effect of too much alcohol—the hangover. No remedy has ever been found for this debilitating combination of dry mouth, sour stomach, headache, and exhaustion. The remedies for curing a hangover have ranged from eating cabbage—a palliative proposed by the ancient Greeks—to a stiff morning drink. In fact, passage of time is the only effective remedy; more alcohol will simply make matters worse.

The effects of moderate drinking

Regularly consuming moderate amounts of alcohol—which is defined as averaging one or two drinks per day by the National Institute on Alcohol Abuse and Alcoholism—has not been linked to any significant health problems. In fact a number of studies support the idea that coronary heart disease is more likely to develop in nondrinkers than in those who have one or two drinks a day. In addition, X-ray studies show that moderate drinkers are less likely to have clogged coronary arteries than nondrinkers.Why this is so remains uncertain. Some research has shown that an increase in HDL cholesterol is associated with moderate alcohol intake, but it's questionable whether this actually has a protective effect.

Higher levels of alcohol intake than one or two drinks per day, though, are associated with a decrease in HDL cholesterol, and have considerable adverse effects on other cardiovascular functions. Because of the other potential health risks associated with alcohol, most doctors don't prescribe moderate drinking as a preventive for coronary heart disease. However, moderate drinkers who have recovered from a heart attack may be advised that they can continue to have one or two drinks a day. And healthy people who drink small amounts need not worry that they are increasing their risk of a heart attack.

Breast cancer risk. Some studies have indicated that drinking alcohol increases a woman's risk of developing breast cancer, while other studies have not demonstrated any relationship between this disease and drinking (see page 8). If you're a woman wondering whether an occasional drink will do you harm, the answer is still up in the air: no cause-and-effect relationship between alcohol and breast cancer has yet been demonstrated. Certainly, more medical research needs to be done. In the meantime, if you are a woman who drinks occasionally, you needn't be overly concerned that you are exposing yourself to risk.

Pregnancy. Pregnant women who drink heavily risk giving birth to children who suffer from fetal alcohol syndrome, characterized by mental retardation, poor coordination, hyperactivity, heart defects, and structural abnormalities of the face or limbs. Because no safe level of alcohol consumption during pregnancy has been determined, pregnant women (and those likely to become pregnant) are advised not to drink at all.

According to a report from the Centers for Disease Control in Atlanta, drunken driving accounts for a far greater loss of years of potential life than any single alcohol-related disease. Of the more than forty-seven thousand Americans killed in automobile crashes in 1988, 39 percent were legally drunk. (For most people, this is the equivalent of having about four drinks in two hours; if drunken driving was defined more conservatively, the percentage would be much higher.)

Nine Ways to Drink Less (or Not at All)

1. Let your waistline be your incentive. For the same 215 calories in two seven-ounce gin and tonics, you can have three ounces of broiled, trimmed sirloin and get the meat's additional nutrients.

2. If you do drink, measure your consumption: five ounces of wine, twelve ounces of beer, or one-and-a-half ounces of spirits is the maximum that a 160-pound man should consume within an hour and a half to two hours. A lighter person should drink less. If the drink vanishes before the time is up, switch to a juice or soft drink.

3. At a restaurant, order food first, not a cocktail. That way you'll probably have time for only one drink before the meal is served.

4. Schedule your business meetings at breakfast time.

5. Avoid drinks made with carbonated mixers, especially if you're thirsty. You'll gulp them down.

6. If there is a convenient place to set a drink down, do that in preference to holding the glass constantly in your hand.

7. If you are drinking a glass of good wine, sip some water on the side. Make the wine last. Savor it.

8. Try a spicy Bloody Mary without the vodka.

9. Remember that the pressure to have a drink may be in your imagination. It is becoming more and more acceptable to say "no thanks" to alcohol.

Risks of heavy drinking

According to the National Institute on Alcohol Abuse and Alcoholism, a person who averages more than two drinks a day can be considered a heavy drinker. As consumption increases beyond two drinks, so do the risks to health; indeed, chronic, excessive use of alcohol can seriously damage nearly every function and organ of the body. These physical consequences of drinking cannot be reversed, but many of them can at least be halted once drinking is discontinued.

The brain. One of the organs most damaged by alcohol is the brain. CAT (computerized axial tomography) scans of the head show that heavy, prolonged alcohol consumption can actually cause the brain to shrink and the ventricles, or cavities, within the brain to enlarge.

The gastrointestinal tract. Alcohol is a stomach irritant, and it also adversely affects the way the small intestine transports and absorbs nutrients, especially vitamins and minerals. Added to the usually poor diet of heavy drinkers, this often results in severe malnutrition. And though alcohol is not a food, it does have calories and can contribute to obesity. Heavy drinking also produces a whole spectrum of pancreatic disorders and can inflame the large and small intestines.

The liver. Alcohol is metabolized in the liver, and so excessive alcohol consumption directly interferes with the liver's cell function. Initially, alcohol causes fatty deposits to accumulate, resulting in an enlarged liver. Ultimately, damage to the liver can cause cirrhosis, which is estimated to affect one in five chronic heavy drinkers. In cirrhosis, healthy cells are destroyed and there is an overgrowth of scar tissue. The various functions of the liver, including the elimination of normal products of metabolism from the bloodstream and blood flow through the liver, gradually deteriorate. Though incurable and often fatal, the disease can be slowed if it is detected at an early stage and if the patient stops drinking.

The cardiovascular system. For many years doctors have observed that high blood pressure and alcohol abuse go together; moreover, according to a number of recent studies, heavy drinkers are indeed more likely to have high blood pressure than teetotalers. Heavy alcohol consumption also damages healthy heart muscle or adds

Are nonalcoholic beers and wines a healthy substitute for alcoholic beverages? That depends. "Nonalcoholic" on a label does not mean alcohol-free, but simply that a beverage contains less than 0.5 percent alcohol per volume. (Only a product labeled "alcohol-free" must contain none at all.) For most people, 0.5 percent is an undetectable trace. But for a recovering alcoholic, some experts fear that these beverages may be the first step back to drinking. If strict abstinence is your goal, fruit juices, seltzer, and similar beverages may be the wisest choice.

Another possible hazard of nonalcoholic beverages is sulfites, which are present in ordinary wine and beer and can cause severe allergic reactions in a small percentage of the population. However, nonalcoholic beverages usually carry an ingredients list, so you can check for sulfites if you are sensitive to them.

extra strain if the heart muscle is already damaged, and increases the risk of heart attacks and heart disease.

Other effects. The direct effects of alcohol abuse are only part of the story. In the words of one study, "the alcoholic abusing only alcohol is very rare." Heavy drinkers also tend to be heavy smokers and are also more likely to take and misuse other drugs, such as tranquilizers. Alcohol itself is not a carcinogen, but excessive use of it, particularly in combination with tobacco, increases the chance of cancers of the mouth, larynx, and throat. Alcohol abuse appears to play a role in stomach and colorectal cancers and possibly in liver cancer as well. It can complicate and interfere with the treatment of cancer and other diseases.

Women drinkers and health risks. Though men have long outnumbered women as problem drinkers, studies have shown that drinking and drinking-related problems among women are on the rise. Today, 60 percent of women drink alcoholic beverages, the highest percentage ever. Perhaps as many as 25 percent of those women are heavy drinkers, and certainly they are susceptible to the consequences. In fact, women who drink the same amount as men—or even less—appear to be more vulnerable than men to medical problems, and to develop them more quickly than men. One study showed that women who had been drinking for a shorter period of time than men (fourteen versus twenty years) had nearly the same rates of alcohol-related diseases as the men. Women apparently develop liver disease at lower levels of alcohol intake and with shorter drinking histories than men, even correcting for their lighter body weight and smaller lean body mass.

Heavy drinking in women also puts them at risk for osteoporosis, the shrinking and weakening of bone tissue.

Alcohol and alcoholism

An estimated 15 million adults have more than two drinks a day. About 18 percent of that group have more than four drinks a day, and this group is at risk for becoming seriously addicted to alcohol. At which point someone becomes alcoholic

---

Alcohol: Do You Have a Problem?

Alcohol problems occur at all educational and social levels, and in every age group. Although no objective definition exists for "problem drinking," there are general guidelines to indicate whether someone is having trouble controlling his or her alcohol intake. Ask yourself the following questions. If the answer to any of them is yes, you need to re-examine how alcohol is affecting your health, safety, and relationships with others.

1. When under pressure at your job, do you calm down with a drink at lunch?

2. Do you ever have hangovers?

3. Do family quarrels most often occur after you have had a drink or two?

4. Does your family think you drink too much?

5. Have you ever injured yourself or another person after drinking?

6. Are you often on—and off—the wagon?

7. If you drink regularly, do you know how much you spend at the liquor store or in restaurants, or do you avoid the calculation?

8. Do you avoid situations where you think it would be impossible for you to get a drink if you wanted one?

9. When pouring yourself a second or third glass of wine or beer, or mixing the additional highball, do you reassure yourself that you deserve it?

10. If you know that you have to drive home in an hour, do you go ahead and have a second drink anyway?

is widely debated, as is what causes alcoholism or to what extent it is an disease. Alcohol itself is not the cause of alcoholism. Paradoxically enough, most people can drink occasionally and sparingly throughout their lives and never succumb to alcohol abuse. Medical science cannot yet explain why one person has little or no interest in alcohol, while another habitually drinks to excess.

One factor that seems to predispose individuals to alcoholism is heredity. Studies have shown that a significant number of children of alcoholic parents, even when raised in a nonalcoholic household, become alcoholics. This suggests that their ability to handle alcohol may be genetically determined. Also, recent studies conducted in Japan have shown that 50 percent of all Asians do not produce the liver enzyme that metabolizes alcohol, so they cannot drink at all without becoming ill. Perhaps the chemistry of the body will prove to be the key to whether a person can drink moderately or not. Still, this does not mean that everyone with the hereditary tendency must become an alcoholic.

Treating alcohol abuse

One problem in treating alcohol abuse is that, for health professionals as well as for the drinker, it is often hard to define when a person has crossed the line from moderate to heavy drinking. A person who is chronically drunk in public is no doubt an alcoholic. But not all heavy drinkers advertise their problem by falling down in the street, losing their jobs, causing traffic accidents, or getting arrested. Many people drink secretly, or only on weekends, only in the evening, or even only once a month. They may successfully hold down a job or practice a profession. Yet at some point, whatever their drinking patterns may be, they have lost their ability to control alcohol intake.

There are several signals that a person is in danger from alcohol:

•drinking for relief of pain and stress;

•pattern drinking (drinking every day or every week at a certain time, particularly in the morning);

•making alcohol the center of life or of all pleasurable, relaxing activities.

Increasingly, alcohol abuse has become treatable. Therapists have devised many different approaches to alcoholism, and a number of organizations—particularly Alcoholics Anonymous and Al-Anon—can help you or a family member deal with a drinking problem. Whatever the approach, though, the critical factor is probably the drinker's desire to stop.

Hosting Parties Without Alcohol

•Have plenty of non-alcoholic beverages on hand and make sure they are as accessible and as attractive as the alcoholic drinks. Serve these beverages in glasses, not in paper or plastic cups.

•If it's a dinner party, try to serve dinner promptly, before there's time for a second drink.

•Experiment with various juices and beverages until you come up with an alcohol-free concoction all your own. Or stick to traditional punches and blends, but leave out the alcohol.

NUTRITION

Good nutrition is the cornerstone of good health. Not only is eating right crucial for the proper growth and functioning of your body, but there is strong evidence that it can offer protection from many chronic diseases as well.

Eating healthfully isn't as difficult as some people think. You don't necessarily have to make radical changes in the way you eat or give up your favorite foods. This part of the book outlines the steps you can take to achieve an optimal diet—one that supplies you with the nutrients you need and promotes longevity by emphasizing foods low in fat and high in complex carbohydrates. Guidelines and suggestions are provided for incorporating these steps into your daily meals.

The following chapters cover the various components of diet individually, sorting out the benefits and misconceptions and indicating which foods you should try to eat on a daily basis and which ones to limit. There is also a section that shows you how to decipher food labels and an extensive guide to help you select and prepare the healthiest versions of different foods.

The Healthy Diet

Over the last decade, Americans have been bombarded with a plethora of dietary advice. Every month, it seems, a new dietary recommendation is issued by one authoritative source or another, not to mention the "fad" diets that appear regularly on the best-seller list. As a result, many Americans are aware that making some changes in their diet would benefit their health, particularly with regard to lowering their risk of heart disease and cancer. Yet it isn't always clear to them which dietary guidelines are important or how to apply them on a day-to-day basis.

Actually, developing healthy eating habits isn't as confusing or as restrictive as many people imagine. The first principle of a healthy diet is to eat a wide variety of foods, rather than emphasize any one category. This is important because different foods make different nutritional contributions.

Another basic rule for an optimal diet is that fruits, vegetables, grains, and legumes—the foods high in complex carbohydrates and fiber, low in fat, and free of cholesterol—should make up more than half of the calories you consume; the rest should come from low-fat dairy products, lean meats and poultry, and fish. These foods will help keep your fat and cholesterol intake relatively low and ensure that you get the proper amounts of vitamins and minerals.

You should also try to maintain a balance between calorie intake and calorie expenditure—that is, don't eat more food than your body can utilize. Otherwise, you will gain weight. The more active you are, therefore, the more you can eat and still maintain this balance.

Following these basic rules doesn't mean that you have to give up your favorite foods. As long as your overall diet is low in fat and high in complex carbohydrates, there is nothing wrong with an occasional cheeseburger or ice cream cone. Just limit how frequently you eat such foods and eat small portions. You can also view healthy eating as an opportunity to expand your repertoire by trying foods—especially vegetables, grains, or fruits—that you don't normally eat. There's no reason that eating right has to mean eating foods that are bland or unappealing.

Twelve steps to a healthy diet

1. Keep your total fat intake at or below 30 percent of your total daily calories. Limit your intake of fat by choosing lean meats, poultry without the skin, fish, and low-fat dairy products. In addition, cut back on vegetable oils and butter—or foods made with these—as well as on mayonnaise, salad dressings, and fried foods.

2. Limit your intake of saturated fat to less than 10 percent of your fat calories. A diet high in saturated fat contributes to high blood cholesterol levels. The richest sources of saturated fat are animal products and tropical vegetable oils, such as coconut or palm oil.

3. Keep your cholesterol intake at 300 milligrams per day or less. Cholesterol is found only in animal products, such as meats, poultry, dairy products, and egg yolks.

4. Eat a diet high in complex carbohydrates. Carbohydrates should contribute at least 55 percent of your total daily calories. To help meet this requirement, eat five or more servings of a combination of vegetables and fruits, and six or more servings of whole grains or legumes daily. This will help you obtain the twenty to thirty grams of dietary fiber you need each day, as well as provide important vitamins and minerals. Make sure to include green, orange, and yellow fruits and vegetables, such as broccoli, carrots, and cantaloupe, and citrus fruits. These foods are thought to help protect against developing certain types of cancer.

5. Maintain a moderate protein intake. Protein should make up about 12 percent of your total daily calories. Choose low-fat sources of protein.

6. Eat a variety of foods. Don't try to fill your nutrient requirements by eating the same foods day in, day out. It is possible that not every essential nutrient is known and eating a wide assortment of foods ensures that you will get all nutrients. In addition, this will limit your exposure to any pesticides or toxic substances that may be present in one particular food.

Calculating Fat Calories

To determine the percentage of calories from fat in a food, follow these steps:

Example:
325 calories, 11 grams of fat

1. Multiply the number of grams of fat in a serving by 9 (the number of calories in a gram of fat).

11 x 9 = 99

2. Divide the result by the number of calories in a serving.

99 ÷ 325 = 0.3046

3. Multiply your answer by 100, then round to the nearest whole number.

0.3046 x 100 = 30.46 or 31

This food would get 31 percent of its calories from fat.

7. Avoid too much sugar. Besides contributing to tooth decay, sugar is a source of "empty" calories, and many foods that are high in sugar are also high in fat.

8. Limit your sodium intake to no more than 2,400 milligrams per day. This is equivalent to the amount of sodium in a little more than a teaspoon of salt. Cut back on your use of salt in cooking and on the table; avoid salty foods; check food labels for the inclusion of ingredients containing sodium.

9. Maintain an adequate calcium intake. Calcium is essential for strong bones and teeth. Get your calcium from low-fat sources, such as skim milk and low-fat yogurt.

10. Get your vitamins and minerals from foods, not from supplements. Especially avoid supplements that provide more than the Recommended Dietary Allowance (RDA) for any one nutrient.

11. Maintain a desirable weight. Balance energy (calorie) intake with energy (calorie) output. Eating a low-fat diet will help you maintain—or lower—your weight, as will regular exercise.

12. If you drink alcohol, do so in moderation. Drink no more than the equivalent of one ounce of pure alcohol per day. This is the amount in two twelve-ounce beers, two small glasses of wine, or one and a half fluid ounces of spirits. Excess alcohol consumption can lead to a variety of health problems. And alcoholic beverages can add many calories to your diet without supplying any nutrients. (Pregnant women should avoid all alcoholic beverages because of the damage alcohol can cause to the developing fetus.)

Do you need to worry about meeting the RDAs?

The Recommended Dietary Allowances (RDAs) were developed by the Food and Nutrition Board of the National Research Council, a committee funded in part by the federal government. This group, made up of scientists from a variety of specialities, evaluates the current research on nutrition to establish estimates of nutrient requirements for protein, calories, eleven vitamins, and six minerals. In addition, the committee has established a range of safe and adequate intakes for two more vitamins and five more minerals for which insufficient scientific evidence exists to establish an RDA, but which are known to be toxic at levels only several times the upper limit of the committee's recommended range. The RDAs are designed to apply to healthy individuals and are adjusted for men, women, and children, and for different age groups, as well as for pregnant women. They are revised about every five years to include any new information about human nutrient needs.

How the Body Uses Food

Food—or more accurately, the nutrients it contains—is essential to life. These nutrients are broken down into three types: *macronutrients*—carbohydrates, protein, and fats—present in foods in large amounts; *micronutrients*, the vitamins and minerals, present in much smaller amounts; and *water*, a basic component of all foods.

Each type of nutrient has primary functions, but they all interact to carry those functions out. The macronutrients provide energy and help maintain and repair the body. Vitamins regulate the chemical processes that take place in the body. Minerals assist with this, and play a role in body maintenance as well, notably in the formation of new tissue, including bones, teeth, and blood. Water—perhaps the most essential nutrient—is present in all cells. Among other things, it provides a fluid medium for all chemical reactions in the body, and for the circulation of blood and removal of waste; serves as a lubricant in joints; and plays a critical role in regulating body temperature.

ATP: the body's fuel

The ability of the body to perform all its various functions—from nerve transmission to digesting food to strenuous exercise—depends on the presence of a substance called adenosine triphosphate, or ATP. The body produces ATP from the nutrients supplied in foods. As nutrients are broken down, the chemical bonds holding them together are split apart, releasing energy. About 60 percent of that energy is disseminated as heat; the rest is stored in the form of ATP and is released gradually in reactions regulated by special enzymes. If the body were not able to store energy in the form of ATP, all of the energy provided by foods would be released at once and we would have to consume food constantly in order to survive. The body's supply of ATP, in turn, must be continually renewed either from foods or from stores of carbohydrates or body fat.

Getting energy from foods

Your body is always burning a mixture of the macronutrients for energy. At rest and low levels of activity, carbohydrates provide 40 to 50 percent of the body's energy needs. Carbo-hydrates are the most efficient fuel for the body because they can be broken down to produce energy almost instantly. The body breaks down the carbohydrates you eat into their simpler form, glucose, which must be present in order for the cells to produce ATP. Excess glucose is converted to a substance called glycogen and stored in the muscles and the liver; glycogen in the liver can readily be transformed back to glucose as needed by the body. When the muscles and liver contain as much glycogen as they can hold, any excess is converted to body fat.

Fat—either from foods or from body fat stores—also provides energy, but not as readily as carbohydrates. During digestion, fats are broken down into glycerol and fatty acids. Glycerol can quickly be converted to glucose, and the fatty acids, in the presence of sufficient amounts of oxygen, can be metabolized to produce ATP. During continual activities of moderate intensity—such as long-distance cycling or brisk walking—your body begins to rely more on fats and less on carbohydrates for energy. After twenty to thirty minutes of activity, fats begin to contribute more to the energy supply. The longer the activity, the more your body uses fat for fuel. Any dietary fat that is not burned is converted to body fat.

Protein is metabolized into amino acids, which are used to build and repair the body's tissues. Some protein can be, however, used for energy, especially during intense endurance or strength training regimens. Excess protein, like excess carbohydrate or dietary fat, is converted to body fat.

Measuring energy

The energy that food provides is measured in kilocalories, which are more commonly referred to as calories. Scientists determine the number of kilocalories in a food by burning it in a laboratory device called a calorimeter and measuring the amount of heat produced. A kilocalorie represents the amount of heat necessary to raise the temperature of one liter of water one degree Celsius. Carbohydrates and proteins contain four kilocalories per gram. Fat contains nine kilocalories per gram and alcohol contains seven per gram.

Nutritional Needs Through the Years

Calorie and nutrient requirements vary according to age and growth rate, as the chart below indicates. For women, they also change during pregnancy and lactation. To satisfy an increased need for calories at different stages of life, it is important to choose foods that are nutrient-dense—that is, foods that provide a good amount of vitamins and minerals for the number of calories they contain. The RDAs for specific nutrients by age, weight, and sex are summarized in the chart on page 74.

Age Group	Special Concerns	Recommendations
Infants to age 2	High metabolism and rapid growth rate make it especially important to meet proper calorie and nutrient requirements of this age. Enough water is essential, since a greater percentage of an infant's body weight consists of water.	Breast milk or formula generally provide enough nutrients, calories, and water to sustain an infant during the first four to six months. Vitamin D, fluoride, or iron supplements may be prescribed by a pediatrician. Supplemental water should be given to a baby who has been ill (vomiting, diarrhea, or fever), or who has been exposed to hot weather. Check with a pediatrician as to when solid foods can be added. Don't restrict fat intake since fat is essential for energy and proper growth.
Children age 2 to adolescence	These children need to consume enough calories to sustain periods of rapid growth. Pay special attention to ensuring proper intake of calcium and iron.	Teach children healthy eating behavior at this stage. Start children on a low-fat, high-complex-carbohydrate diet. Switch to low-fat dairy products and lean meats and offer plenty of fruits, vegetables, and whole grains. Limit intake of sugary snacks. Patterns of growth affect appetite. Teach children to eat only when hungry and to stop eating when they are full. Ensure proper nutritional intake by offering a few choices among healthy foods, not by encouraging a child to eat everything on his or her plate.
Adolescents	There is variation in the rate of growth of adolescents and therefore in their caloric needs. Maintain the proper intake of calcium and iron. Dieting—common in this age group—can shortchange teens on nutrition.	Adults can help ensure that teens get adequate nutrition by stocking healthful foods—low in fat, cholesterol, and sodium, and high in nutrients. On average, about 25 percent of a teen's calories come from snacks, so keep healthy snack foods on hand, such as low-fat yogurt, rice cakes, bread sticks, sliced raw vegetables, low-fat cottage cheese, and part-skim mozzarella. Encourage increased physical activity over dieting to help control weight.
Adults	Growth stops, so energy needs decrease. Maintain adequate intakes of nutrients, especially calcium and iron and eat foods low in fat, cholesterol, and sodium, and high in carbohydrates and fiber.	Balance calorie intake with energy expenditure. Choose foods that are high in complex carbohydrates and low in fat. Get vitamins and minerals from foods, not from supplements. Consume alcohol and caffeine only in moderation.
Older individuals	With age, caloric needs may decrease, depending on level of activity. Constipation may be a problem. Some prescription drugs can hamper the absorption or modify effects of certain nutrients, so check with your doctor or pharmacist.	As individuals grow older, nutrient needs remain virtually the same as for younger adults. However, some individuals over the age of 65 do not get enough vitamin D. Be sure to consume low-fat dairy products fortified with vitamin D or spend some time outside each day so that sunlight can stimulate the body's production of this vitamin. Inadequate zinc intake is also common; good sources of zinc include lean meats, whole grains, and legumes.
Pregnant women	More calories are needed to support the mother and fetus. Increased need for protein, vitamins B_6 and B_{12}, folacin, calcium, iron, zinc, and fluoride.	A weight gain of 25 to 30 pounds is recommended during pregnancy; 2 to 4 pounds per month during the first trimester and about a pound per week after that. (A large majority of this weight gain is from the baby, the placenta, and the increased volume of fluid in the woman's body.) Avoid alcohol and smoking completely. Drugs—prescription or over the counter—should be taken only on the advice of a physician.
Lactating women	About 500 extra calories per day are needed to maintain the production of milk. There is an increased need for calcium, protein, magnesium, zinc, and fluids.	Lactating women should eat nutrient-dense foods and consume approximately two quarts of liquid daily. Avoid alcohol and decrease caffeine. Drugs should be taken only after consulting a physician.

Nutrition and Exercise

The dietary needs of athletes and other active individuals are, with a few small adjustments, not very different from those recommended for all healthy people. Active individuals expend more energy than sedentary people, so they do need to consume more calories; the exact number depends on age, body size and composition, activity, and level of training. The chart below tells what percentage of daily calories should come from carbohydrates, protein, and fat.

A diet deficient in essential nutrients can make you feel weak, slow you down, and make you perform below par. But there's no evidence that exceeding the RDAs by taking supplements will improve performance under normal circumstances. In some cases large doses of supplements can prove detrimental.

Nutrient	Importance for Exercise	Recommendations	Comments
Carbohydrates	The most efficient fuel for the body.	Should supply 55 to 60% of daily calories for all people, 60 to 70% for endurance athletes. No more than 15% of total calories should come from simple carbohydrates (sugars), the rest from complex carbohydrates.	Can't be stored in large amounts. By eating more complex carbohydrates, you may increase energy reserves (glycogen) in muscles and liver, thus prolonging time before exhaustion.
Protein	Needed to build, maintain, and repair tissue.	Protein needs of sedentary and most active people are about the same. The adult RDA is easily met when 12% of calories come from protein. Protein supplements are unnecessary and expensive.	The average American gets more than enough protein. Excess protein won't build muscles— only exercise does. Extra protein is stored as fat.
Fats	The most concentrated and abundant form of energy in the body, fat stores serve as the primary fuel during prolonged aerobic exercise.	For all people, less than 30% of daily calories should come from fat, and less than 10% from saturated fat. Besides being a health risk, a high-fat diet may impair performance. Avoid fatty foods before exercise, since they can take three to four hours to digest.	Don't confuse body fat and excess dietary fat; body fat is the stored form of dietary protein, carbohydrates, and fats. Even lean people have more than enough fat stores for energy production.
Vitamins	Needed for the metabolism of carbohydrates, protein, and fats.	Active people generally don't require supplementary vitamins. If their increased caloric intake comes from a varied, balanced diet that is high in complex carbohydrates, it should provide all the vitamins they need.	Contrary to popular opinion, vitamins don't build muscles or provide energy. There's no evidence that large doses of any vitamin will improve performance.
Minerals	Needed for the metabolism of carbohydrates, protein, and fats. Iron is vital for oxygen transport. Sodium and potassium help maintain the body's water balance.	A varied diet generally provides enough minerals for active people, with the possible exception of iron. All adult women should consume at least 1,000 milligrams of calcium daily, preferably from foods rather than supplements.	Losses of sodium through perspiration are actually quite small and can usually be replenished by a normal diet. Salt tablets are rarely necessary.

Recommended Dietary Allowances[a]

Category	Age	Weight[b] (lb)	Height[b] (in)	Protein (g)	Vitamin A (μgRE)[c]	Vitamin D (μg)[d]	Vitamin E (mgα)[e]	Vitamin K (μg)	Vitamin C (mg)	Thiamine (mg)
Infants	0-6 months	13	24	13	375	7.5	3	5	30	0.3
	6-12 months	20	28	14	375	10	4	10	35	0.4
Children	1-3	29	35	16	400	10	6	15	40	0.7
	4-6	44	44	24	500	10	7	20	45	0.9
	7-10	62	52	28	700	10	7	30	45	1.0
Males	11-14	99	62	45	1,000	10	10	45	50	1.3
	15-18	145	69	59	1,000	10	10	65	60	1.5
	19-24	160	70	58	1,000	10	10	70	60	1.5
	25-50	174	70	63	1,000	5	10	80	60	1.5
	51 plus	170	68	63	1,000	5	10	80	60	1.2
Females	11-14	101	62	46	800	10	8	45	50	1.1
	15-18	120	64	44	800	10	8	55	60	1.1
	19-24	128	65	46	800	10	8	60	60	1.1
	25-50	138	64	50	800	5	8	65	60	1.1
	51 plus	143	63	50	800	5	8	65	60	1.0
Pregnant women				60	800	10	10	65	70	1.5
Lactating women	1st 6 months			65	1,300	10	12	65	95	1.6
	2nd 6 months			62	1,200	10	11	65	90	1.6

[a]The allowances, expressed as average daily intakes over time, are intended to provide for individual variations among most normal persons as they live in the United States under usual enviromental stresses. Diets should be based on a variety of common foods in order to provide other nutrients for which human requirements have been less well defined.

[b]Weights and heights of Reference Adults are actual medians for the U.S. population of the designated age. The use of these figures does not imply that the height-to-weight ratios are ideal.

[c]Retinol equivalents. 1 retinol equivalent= 1 μg retinol or 6 μg beta carotene. To calculate IU value: for fruits and vegetables, multiply the RE value by ten; for animal-source foods, multiply the RE value by 3.3.

It is important to note that the RDAs are *recommendations*, not *requirements*. Individual dietary needs vary greatly, and the RDAs are set at a level that is assumed to cover the nutrient needs of most people, plus a generous margin of safety. Therefore, the RDAs should not be viewed as the minimum amount of a nutrient required, but as an estimate of a safe and adequate intake; over a period of time, an intake below the RDA may leave some people deficient in a particular nutrient and in some cases, and for some nutrients, a regular intake far in excess of the RDA may have unpleasant side effects, or even be toxic.

The Recommended Dietary Allowances should serve as a rule of thumb; most people should aim at getting 100 percent of the RDA for each nutrient daily, but not worry too much if on any particular day they fall slightly below or above it. Without even trying, most Americans meet the RDAs from their regular diets. The only exceptions may be getting enough calcium and iron. You should pay special attention to meeting the daily recommendation for these nutrients since they can be difficult to get and are not always absorbed readily by the body. Calcium is found in low-fat dairy products, canned salmon and sardines eaten with bones, and some leafy green vegetables. Good sources of iron include lean beef, poultry, clams, beans, and peas. (For information on the RDAs for the various vitamins and minerals, according to age groups, see the chart above; the U.S. RDA, the standard used on food labels, is explained in detail on page 111.)

Riboflavin (mg)	Niacin (mg NE)[f]	Vitamin B6 (mg)	Folate (µg)	Vitamin B12 (µg)	Calcium (mg)	Phosphorus (mg)	Magnesium (mg)	Iron (mg)	Zinc (mg)	Iodine (µg)	Selenium (µg)
0.4	5	0.3	25	0.3	400	300	40	6	5	40	10
0.5	6	0.6	35	0.5	600	500	60	10	5	50	15
0.8	9	1.0	50	0.7	800	800	80	10	10	70	20
1.1	12	1.1	75	1.0	800	800	120	10	10	90	20
1.2	13	1.4	100	1.4	800	800	170	10	10	120	30
1.5	17	1.7	150	2.0	1,200	1,200	270	12	15	150	40
1.8	20	2.0	200	2.0	1,200	1,200	400	12	15	150	50
1.7	19	2.0	200	2.0	1,200	1,200	350	10	15	150	70
1.7	19	2.0	200	2.0	800	800	350	10	15	150	70
1.4	15	2.0	200	2.0	800	800	350	10	15	150	70
1.3	15	1.4	150	2.0	1,200	1,200	280	15	12	150	45
1.3	15	1.5	180	2.0	1,200	1,200	300	15	12	150	50
1.3	15	1.6	180	2.0	1,200	1,200	280	15	12	150	55
1.3	15	1.6	180	2.0	800	800	280	15	12	150	55
1.2	13	1.6	180	2.0	800	800	280	10	12	150	55
1.6	17	2.2	400	2.2	1,200	1,200	320	30	15	175	65
1.8	20	2.1	280	2.6	1,200	1,200	355	15	19	200	75
1.7	20	2.1	260	2.6	1,200	1,200	340	15	16	200	75

[d] As cholecalciferol. 10 µg cholecalciferol = 400 IU of vitamin D.

[e] α -Tocopherol equivalents. 1 mg d-α tocopherol = 1 α -TE.

[f] 1 NE (niacin equivalent) is equal to 1 mg of niacin or 60 mg of dietary tryptophan.

Estimated Safe and Adequate Daily Dietary Intakes of Selected Vitamins and Minerals[a]

Category	Age	VITAMINS		TRACE MINERALS[b]				
		Biotin (µg)	Panthothenic acid (mg)	Copper (mg)	Manganese (mg)	Fluoride (mg)	Chromium (µg)	Molybdenum (µg)
Infants	0-6 months	10	2	0.4-0.6	0.3-0.6	0.1-0.5	10-40	15-30
	6-12 months	15	3	0.6-0.7	0.6-1.0	0.2-1.0	20-60	20-40
Children and adolescents	1-3	20	3	0.7-1.0	1.0-1.5	0.5-1.5	20-80	25-50
	4-6	25	3-4	1.0-1.5	1.5-2.0	1.0-2.5	30-120	30-75
	7-10	30	4-5	1.0-2.0	2.0-3.0	1.5-2.5	50-200	50-150
	11 plus	30-100	4-7	1.5-2.5	2.0-5.0	1.5-2.5	50-200	75-250
Adults		30-100	4-7	1.5-3.0	2.0-5.0	1.5-4.0	50-200	75-250

[a] Because there is less information on which to base allowances, these figures are not given in the main table of RDAs and are provided here in the form of ranges of recommended intakes.

[b] Since the toxic levels for many trace elements may be only several times usual intakes, the upper levels for the trace elements given in this table should not be habitually exceeded.

Breakfast

Most of us were brought up to believe that breakfast is an important meal—perhaps the most important. Yet about one out of every four adults usually or always skips it. Is this a cause for worry? What do nutritionists know about breakfast?

Some of the best and worst foods in the American diet are served at breakfast. Such foods as bacon, sausage, butter, and cream cheese add considerable amounts of saturated fat to traditional breakfasts, while doughnuts, Danish pastries, syrupy pancakes, and store-bought muffins add sugar, fat, and calories. Many breakfast cereals also supply hefty doses of sugar and sodium, especially for children. And eggs, a staple of the American breakfast, provide one-third of all the cholesterol consumed in the United States. If your breakfast supplies all the cholesterol or most of the sodium you should eat for the entire day, you may not be able to compensate for these excesses later on in the day, since it would be difficult to consume only foods that contain none of these substances.

On the other hand, it is probably easier to incorporate wholesome foods into your diet at breakfast than at other meal. Many low-fat, low-cholesterol foods are ideal morning fare, supplying nutrients that may be hard to get in later meals. Breakfast is also an important source of fiber.

Does breakfast affect performance?

Researchers have never proven that skipping breakfast is harmful to the health of adults. It may be possible that suddenly starting to skip breakfast has negative effects on those who normally eat in the morning, but that routinely omitting breakfast may have little or no effect on adults. Although there are no adequate studies on whether physical or mental performance is altered by skipping breakfast, there's considerable anecdotal material reporting that children who skip breakfast have a decreased attention span.

The argument for eating a good breakfast revolves around the idea that the body needs refueling after the twelve or so hours of overnight fasting. Foods do affect blood sugar (glucose) levels, but the links between blood sugar and performance, mood, and feelings of hunger and tiredness are not fully understood. In any case, the effect on glucose levels will depend on the specific food and the individual. So there's no reason to believe that you should eat anything for breakfast just to get something in your stomach in the morning. Eating a nutritious breakfast of food that maintains you through the morning does make sense, however, particularly for children and adolescents.

Weight control

Some people skip breakfast because they are trying to lose weight and this is an easy place to cut calories. Others skip it because they think eating breakfast increases their appetite later in the day. But, in fact, studies suggest that eliminating breakfast does not help in weight control. Many people who skip meals "starve and stuff" themselves, and are more likely to eat snacks—usually high in calories and low in nutrients—and be obese than those who eat three balanced meals. In any case, a healthful, high-fiber breakfast will of course be much more conducive to weight control than one loaded with fat, sugar, and thus calories.

A fast-food cheese Danish can contain more calories and twice as much fat as a fast-food hamburger.

The foods that provide a good breakfast—and suit most Americans' eating patterns—are some form of complex carbohydrates (such as breads or cereals containing fiber, protein, vitamins, and minerals), which will help provide a steady supply of blood sugar. Also recommended is fruit or fruit juice high in vitamin C, and low-fat or skim milk or other dairy product. A small amount of fat helps provide a sense of satiety. Most adults enjoy coffee or tea, which is harmless in reasonable quantities.

If you prefer chicken and vegetables, there's no harm in that. What people eat for breakfast is largely a cultural matter. In Japan, for instance, it often includes salad and soup, and in Norway, smoked fish and bread. But you should try to get fruit juice, whole grains, and milk products at lunch or dinner if you leave them out at breakfast. Try to avoid foods high in sugar, which tend to be low in nutrients. Also, limit traditional breakfast foods that are high in fat, cholesterol, and sodium because of the damage they do to your heart, arteries, and waistline.

About 12 percent of all soft drinks are consumed in the morning.

A Better Breakfast

Eggs
Egg yolks are high in cholesterol, so most people should eat no more than four per week. For a cheese omelet, use one whole egg with one to three whites, low-fat cottage cheese, and chopped, cooked vegetables. Season with thyme, basil, dill, or a combination of herbs.

Butter
This spread is high in fat and cholesterol, so you should limit your intake. For cooking, use a nonstick pan or a pan lightly coated with vegetable oil. On bread, substitute apple butter or all-fruit spreads that have little or no added sugar.

Margarine
It has the same fat and calorie content as butter, but it is rich in polyunsaturates and free of cholesterol. However, those listing a hydrogenated oil first are usually higher in saturated fat. Diet margarine contains more water, so it has half the calories and fat.

Cream cheese
Not a good choice, since it is very high in fat and cholesterol, and low in calcium and protein for a cheese. Substitute low-fat cottage cheese, pot cheese, or farmer cheese; you can blend these with low-fat yogurt, dry mustard or dill, and pepper.

Whole milk
Substitute low-fat or skim milk; blend in strawberries, bananas, or low-fat yogurt if desired. You can also thicken skim milk, and boost its nutrients, by adding dry nonfat milk.

Bread
Almost all bread has 70 to 80 calories per slice (about an ounce). Bread made from 100 percent whole wheat flour is the most nutritious. Commercial pumpernickel and rye usually contain mostly white flour; look for whole-grain varieties.

Bagels
These are made from high-protein flour and little fat.

Croissants
These rolls contain butter and sugar, which add saturated fat, cholesterol, and calories. They are also low in fiber.

Bran muffins
Rich in fiber, niacin, and iron. Store-bought muffins are usually high in fat and sugar (honey is just as high in calories). If you make muffins, use whole-grain flour, bran, one egg plus one white, dried fruit or fruit juice (instead of sugar), skim milk or low-fat yogurt. Add bananas, carrots, or cranberries, if desired.

Pancakes
Use whole wheat flour instead of white. Or, try buckwheat pancakes. Use skim milk and low-fat yogurt instead of whole milk, and substitute an egg white for at least one egg.

Pancake syrup
Substitute fresh or puréed fruit, applesauce, or juice concentrate blended with tapioca.

French toast
Use whole wheat bread and egg whites with skim milk and vanilla (or grated orange rind).

You don't have to give up all your favorite breakfast foods to eat healthfully. See the box on page 77 for suggestions on how to salvage your current menus.

Lunch

For most people, lunch is a meal eaten hurriedly in the middle of a busy workday. As a result, people tend to choose foods that are quickly prepared and convenient to eat: a sandwich and a bag of chips from the local deli or coffee shop, a slice of pizza, or a fast-food burger and fries. Many of these foods, however, are high in fat and sodium and low in fiber. Fortunately, you don't have to give up convenience for health; most traditional lunch fare can be modified to be more healthful.

Sandwiches

At home, in brown bags, and at restaurants, sandwiches are a standard lunch. But some of the old favorites—ham and Swiss, egg salad, pastrami—may be dealing out more calories, cholesterol, and fat than most of us want to consume at one sitting—particularly if the ham and Swiss are on a croissant and the roast beef comes with plenty of mayonnaise. Any one of the classic sandwiches in the first half of the chart (page 80) could put you over the limit of no more than 30 percent of your total daily calories from fat. The sandwiches in the second half are healthier alternatives. To create sandwiches that are more nutritious and lower in fat, follow these suggestions:

•Whole-grain breads give you more minerals and fiber than white breads or buns. Most bagels and pita breads (check labels) are low in sodium as well as fat. Open-faced sandwiches are a good way to economize on calories.

•Processed sandwich meats like bologna, liverwurst, and salami are usually high in saturated fat and cholesterol, and all have large amounts of sodium. Roasting your own chicken or turkey breast (and removing the skin) for sandwiches is worth the effort: you'll cut down on calories, fat, and sodium. Discard all the visible fat on roast beef, ham, or pork, and limit the amount of meat you use on a sandwich.

•Instead of cheese or mayonnaise, add slices of vegetables or fruit to make a sandwich moister and tastier.

•A tasty, low-fat sandwich dressing can be made with plain, low-fat yogurt, or by blending equal parts of low-fat cottage cheese and buttermilk, flavored with herbs and spices, or with mustard powder, horseradish powder, lemon juice, minced garlic, or ground ginger. A tablespoon of such a mixture has only 9 calories and a trace of fat.

•Ketchup and prepared mustard are low-calorie, low-fat flavor boosters—10 to 24 calories per tablespoon. But they are high in sodium, with 150 to 180 milligrams per tablespoon. You can make sodium-free mustard by mixing mustard powder with water. Prepared horseradish has half the calories and one-tenth the sodium of mustard or ketchup.

Salad bars

Offering much more than just lettuce and tomatoes, the salad bars found in many delis and restaurants can make a quick and nutritious lunch. Still, you must choose wisely; a study conducted at Mississippi State University found that students who ate a salad-bar lunch generally consumed more fat and calories than those who ate a hot meal. This isn't surprising when you consider that in addition to fresh vegetables and fruit, and legumes, salad bars are stocked with such high-fat items as coleslaw, cheese, potato salad, and bacon bits. And most people top their choices off with a few ladles full of salad dressing, which is also high in fat.

Still, the salad bar offers many options for the health-conscious diner. Just keep the following guidelines in mind:

•Choose your selections carefully. Stick to vegetables, fruits, and legumes for the most part. Cottage cheese can also be a good choice, provided it is the low-fat variety—but that can be hard to determine.

•Sodium is another problem at salad bars. Ask if salt or MSG (monosodium glutamate), a source of sodium, is used in preparing the selections.

•Be aware that such widely varied foods as avocadoes, olives, sunflower seeds, bacon bits, cheese, and diced ham are high in fat and sometimes sodium. If you want to include items such as these, use them sparingly—think of them as condiments rather than the main focus of your salad.

•Avoid salad dressings or limit the amount you use. A typical small ladle at a salad bar holds about two tablespoons of dressing, so two ladles full of Italian, French, or blue cheese dressing contain about 300 calories, almost all of them from fat. Try using mustard, soy sauce, salsa, lemon juice, or vinegar mixed with a small amount of oil instead.

•Pre-dressed selections such as pasta or three-bean salad, marinated vegetables, and tuna fish are often doused with oil or mayonnaise. These items are also more likely to contain added sodium.

•Some salad bars offer hot foods as well. Many, such as macaroni and cheese, fried chicken, and meatballs are high in fat and sodium. However, roast chicken or turkey would make a healthful addition to your salad. Soup can be another low-fat option if it is vegetable based, though it is likely to be high in sodium. Cream soups and those made with beef are often high in fat as well.

Fast food

One-fifth of all Americans (forty-five million) eat in a fast-food restaurant on a typical day and many people rely on these establishments to provide them with a quick, hot lunch. But they may be shortchanging themselves nutritionally. Between 40 and 55 percent of the calories in most fast-food meals come from fat, mostly in the form of saturated fat, the kind that raises blood cholesterol levels. Sandwiches are very high in sodium—usually between 700 and 900 milligrams. Specialty items such as cheeseburgers with bacon may pack 1,300 to 1,950 milligrams. Add in salty french fries and other fixings and you easily consume the entire maximum recommended daily allowance of sodium (2,400 milligrams) in one sitting. In addition, fast food is low in fiber and calcium and high in calories. While fast food provides protein, this isn't a reason to eat it since most Americans get more than enough protein already. American children tend to eat enough protein to meet the RDA twice over.

Still, there are healthy choices to be made at a fast-food restaurant. A few chains provide nutritional information upon request, so you can get the specifics about the foods you choose, but in general, here are some fast-food guidelines:

A Safe Salad Bar
A salad bar should offer more than just nutritious foods. Items that require refrigeration should be sitting in enough ice to keep them cool. The bar should have an overhanging cover that keeps dust and other contaminants from settling on the food. And an employee should be on hand to make sure that customers do not touch food with their hands or with serving utensils that have dropped on the floor; otherwise, foods, especially high-protein foods like eggs and meat, can become contaminated.

Comparing Sandwiches

	CLASSIC SANDWICHES				
	Ingredients	Calories	Cholesterol (mg)	Fat (g)	Fat Calories
Roast beef and Swiss	3 oz roast beef (rib), 2 oz Swiss cheese, 1 tbsp Russian dressing, 2 slices rye bread	580	128	33	51%
Tuna, oil-pack	3 oz oil-pack tuna, 1 slice tomato, lettuce, 1 tbsp mayo, 2 slices white bread	400	53	23	52%
Turkey and ham club	2 oz turkey roll, 3 oz ham, 1 tbsp mayo, 2 oz Swiss cheese, 3 slices white toast	745	140	46	56%
Egg salad	1 egg, 1 tbsp mayo, 1 slice tomato, lettuce, 2 slices white bread	315	281	19	55%
Bacon, lettuce, and tomato	3 slices bacon, lettuce, 1 slice tomato, 1 tbsp mayo, 2 slices white toast	325	24	22	61%
Reuben	3 oz corned beef, 1 oz Swiss cheese, 1/4 cup sauerkraut, 1 tsp mustard, 2 slices white bread	455	107	25	50%
Ham and cheese on croissant	3 oz ham, 2 oz Swiss cheese, lettuce, 1 tbsp mayo, 1 croissant	730	122	51	63%
Peanut butter and jelly	3 tbsp peanut butter, 1 tbsp jelly, 2 slices white bread	465	0	26	50%
	HEALTHY SANDWICHES				
Turkey	3 oz turkey breast, 1 slice tomato, lettuce, 1 tbsp dressing*, 2 slices whole wheat bread	290	60	5	16%
Tuna, water-pack	3 oz water-pack tuna, 1 tbsp dressing*, 1/4 apple, lettuce, 2 slices whole wheat bread	305	49	3	9%
Chopped ham and vegetable pita	1 oz extra-lean ham, chopped bell pepper, 1/4 cup sprouts, 1 tsp mustard, 1 pita pocket	220	13	3	12%
Hard-boiled egg-white salad	2 egg whites, 1 tbsp dressing*, 2 tbsp diced celery, 2 tbsp chopped watercress, 1 bagel	245	1	2	7%
Chicken salad	3 oz chicken breast, 1 tbsp dressing*, lettuce, 2 tbsp alfalfa sprouts, 2 slices whole wheat bread	315	74	4	11%
Roast beef	3 oz roast beef (round rump), 1/4 cup shredded fresh cabbage, 1 tsp mustard, 2 slices rye bread	310	76	10	29%

* Dressing made from plain low-fat yogurt with added spices (curry, mustard, garlic, dill, etc.) to taste.

•Look for a restaurant with healthy options. Some chains offer salad bars, low-fat salad dressings, fruit juices, low-fat or skim milk, and whole-grain buns. Salad bars and whole-grain buns can help compensate for the lack of fiber, and salad bars add vitamins A and C, which are scarce in typical fast-food fare.

•Choose roast beef—it's almost always leaner than burgers.

•Choose single plain burgers. Skipping the "special sauce" or mayonnaise can save 100 to 150 calories (nearly all from fat). Skipping the bacon and cheese can cut more than 200 calories plus a good amount of saturated fat and cholesterol.

•Avoid the chicken and fish in fast-food restaurants; they are almost always breaded and fried—in vegetable oil or even in beef tallow. Chicken nuggets and sandwiches often contain ground chicken skin (very high in fat). Six of these nuggets have as much fat as one and a half cups of standard ice cream.

•Watch out for "extra crispy" fried chicken—its texture comes from extra fat.

•If baked potatoes are available, order one instead of french fries; just skip the sour cream, melted cheese, and butter.

The healthiest lunch

Packing your own lunch is the easiest way to retain control over what you eat—it can be as simple as a healthful sandwich and sliced raw vegetables or yogurt and a few pieces of fruit. If you choose, you can invest in a thermos, an insulated lunch bag (both of which will allow you to keep hot foods hot and cold foods cold) and various sized plastic containers. This way, foods such as soups, salads, pasta, stews, and chili, along with leftovers, can regularly be on your lunchtime menu. If you have access to a refrigerator or microwave oven, you have even more choices. For example, you can prepare a number of individual meals and freeze them at the beginning of the week so you have a selection to bring to work.

Dinner

For many people, dinner is the most important meal of the day. It is usually the largest; according to food consumption surveys by the United States Department of Agriculture (USDA), Americans consume 42 to 45 percent of their total daily calories at dinner. The foods eaten at dinner contribute a significant amount of nutrients to the diet, but also a large proportion of the day's fat, cholesterol, and sodium.

It can be difficult to change eating habits at dinner; it is the meal most likely to be shared with other members of the household, and therefore must accommodate everyone's tastes. One easy way to start is to make dinner a lighter meal; most nutritionists recommend that individuals spread their caloric intake more evenly throughout the day. Beyond that, however, creating a more healthful dinner doesn't mean you have to make drastic changes in the foods that you normally would eat.

A steady diet of dinners centering around red meat can contribute more fat, cholesterol, and protein than is healthy. Fortunately, there are many alternatives to traditional "meat and potatoes" fare:

•Try skinless, light-meat poultry or fish instead.

•Use meat as an adjunct to a meal rather than as the centerpiece. Add a small amount of beef or pork to flavor an oriental-style vegetable dish; make a beef stew using lots of vegetables and a small amount of beef; for a light dinner, sliver steak or roast beef and add to a salad.

•Go completely meatless—for example, serve pasta, rice and beans, or a vegetable stir-fry with tofu as a main course.

Healthy accompaniments

Choosing more healthful appetizers and side dishes can improve the nutritional quality of your meals as well:

•Good starter choices include: vegetable crudités—raw carrots, celery, and peppers, and steamed cauliflower and broccoli—with a dip made from low-fat yogurt, a green salad with low-fat dressing, a vegetable- or chicken-based soup (heartier

Vegetarian Diets

The term vegetarian sometimes conjures up visions of people living on a steady diet of nuts and berries, but the vegetarian way of eating—high in fiber and usually low in saturated fat and cholesterol—has lost its bohemian image and entered the health mainstream. Studies show that vegetarians are less at risk for heart disease, diabetes, and various cancers (notably of the colon) than the average American. They tend to have lower blood pressure and cholesterol levels, and are closer to the optimal weights in the insurance companies' acceptable-weight tables. They are also less often afflicted with digestive-system disorders such as constipation.

It's true, of course, that some of the benefits attributed to what vegetarians eat may accrue from how they live: many abstain from tobacco, drugs, and alcohol, as they do from flesh and fowl. And they tend to exercise more. But whether vegetarian health gains arise from diet or life style, they are reassuring enough to have spurred the American Dietetic Association to issue a position statement approving vegetarian diets as "healthful and nutritionally adequate when appropriately planned."

Vegetarian is a catchall term that includes the following:

Vegans (total vegetarians), a small minority, abstain from all foods of animal origin.

Lactovegetarians include dairy products as protein sources. Such a diet isn't necessarily low in fat and cholesterol unless skim or low-fat milk products are used.

Lacto-ovovegetarians eat eggs as well as dairy foods. Most American vegetarians fall into this category.

Semivegetarians occasionally supplement a diet of vegetables, cereals, fruit, and dairy products with a little meat, fish, or chicken. Eating lean meat from time to time doesn't undo the beneficial effects of a vegetarian diet. Most low-fat, "heart-healthy" meal plans—which suggest eating meat as side dishes or condiments in small amounts, rather than as main courses, and increased consumption of grains and beans as protein sources—are essentially semi-vegetarian diets. So are many ethnic cuisines.

Planning a diet

If vegetarians plan their diets with some care, they are no more prone to deficiencies than meat eaters. While lacto-ovo- or semivegetarians choose from most or all of the basic food groups, strict vegans may be shortchanged on certain essential nutrients.

The potential deficiencies in strict vegetarian diets are:

Vitamins. Vitamins B_{12} and D are found only in animal products. A lack of B_{12} can bring on anemia as well as degenerative changes in the central nervous system. But these conditions are rare, even in strict vegetarians. If you're not eating meat, dairy products, or eggs, you'll have to get your B_{12} from fortified products or a supplement.

Vitamin D is necessary for calcium absorption, and a deficiency can cause rickets in children. But you need very little of this vitamin and, given adequate exposure to the sun, the body is able to synthesize it. Riboflavin, one of the B-complex vitamins, is found primarily in meat, eggs, and dairy products, though broccoli and almonds are good sources.

Minerals. Calcium is found mostly in animal products, and the iron and zinc found in plant foods are not as well absorbed as those in meat and dairy products. Women, in particular, need to make sure they are consuming enough iron and calcium, which can be a problem if they are vegans.

Peas, lentils, and wheat germ are good sources of zinc; broccoli, kale, collard and mustard greens, and fortified tofu contain calcium (though it may not be as well absorbed as the calcium in animal products); beans, potatoes, dried fruit, and fortified cereals and breads supply iron; and you can enhance your body's absorption of iron by eating foods rich in vitamin C (berries, citrus fruits, tomatoes, red bell peppers, and broccoli) with your nonmeat iron sources.

Protein. Many grains and legumes are surprisingly good sources of protein, but unlike the protein in meat, fish, or eggs, that in plant foods is incomplete—that is, it has insufficient amounts of one or more essential amino acids. The trick is to combine proteins that complement one another so that together they form a complete set of amino acids—for instance, legumes (peas, peanut butter, lentils, beans) with whole-grain bread, rice, or other cereals.

Contrary to common belief, you don't have to combine complementary foods at the same meal to get the effects of a complete protein. If you eat a wide variety of foods (especially if you eat even a small amount of meat or dairy products), you will absorb a full complement of all the amino acids you need as long as complementary proteins are eaten within a few hours of each other.

Variety is the key

It takes only a little planning to keep a vegetarian diet healthful and nutritionally adequate. If you decide to follow a strict vegetarian regimen, the word to remember is variety. Eat a wide range of foods: fruits, vegetables, whole-grain breads and cereals, legumes (such as soybeans, chick-peas, lima beans, lentils), nuts, seeds, and soy products. Dairy products made from low-fat or skim milk, and an egg now and then, make it easier to get the full range of nutrients.

Some studies have found that children who were brought up as vegetarians or were breast-fed by vegetarian mothers are smaller than other kids. And vitamin and mineral deficiencies can be particularly harmful for children. It's a good idea to have a qualified nutritionist evaluate the diet of any infant or child brought up on a strict vegetarian diet.

Ingredient Substitutes

Many recipes call for inordinate amounts of sugar, salt, and fat. But these are not always essential components of delicious food; many dishes taste fine without them, or with less of them. Try the suggestions below. (Remember that baking recipes are more exact that other types of recipes, so you may have to experiment more.)

In place of:	Substitute:
Whole egg	2 egg whites
Whole milk	Low-fat or skim milk
Sour cream	Low-fat yogurt; low-fat cottage cheese puréed in a blender with a little lemon juice
Sugar	Half the amount in most recipes; for baking, reduce to 1/4 cup of sugar for every cup of flour
Cream	Evaporated skim milk or nonfat dry milk with a little water added
Salt	Omit and/or substitute mixed herbs and spices, or lemon or lime juice
Ground beef	In casseroles: kidney beans; in lasagna or sauces: ground turkey breast
Bacon	Canadian bacon or boiled ham
Cream cheese, on bagels or toast	Neufchâtel cheese, part-skim ricotta, or low-fat cottage cheese
Mayonnaise	Imitation mayonnaise or plain low-fat yogurt flavored with a little mustard
Butter or oil (for sautéing)	Use nonstick cookware and/or sauté in broth or wine
White flour	Substitute whole wheat flour for half the flour in the recipe

Turkey is one of the leanest types of poultry, except for the self-basting variety, which is injected with butter or vegetable oil (corn, soybean, or coconut oil). To keep your turkey low in fat, baste it with chicken stock.

soups, such as lentil, can often serve as a main course.)

•Serve brown rice instead of white with your meal to add potassium, phosphorus, and fiber.

•Other healthful side dishes include: steamed vegetables; grains such as wheat pilaf; baked potatoes topped with salsa or low-fat yogurt rather than sour cream or butter; and legumes flavored with herbs and spices.

Healthy cooking

One of the easiest ways to begin to make your dinner more healthful is to alter your preparation techniques. If, for example, you plan to have chicken for dinner, you can keep it relatively low in fat by choosing light meat over dark, removing the skin before cooking, and baking, broiling, or poaching it instead of frying. Four ounces of chicken prepared in this manner has just 175 calories and five grams of fat compared with the 195 calories and eleven grams of fat in the two and a half ounces of meat on a fried drumstick.

Other easy preparation techniques can improve the health benefits of foods. Use a nonstick skillet, for example, or cook with wine or stock instead of

Healthy Dining Out

BREAKFAST	
Choose	**Avoid**
Whole-grain cereals—such as shredded wheat, oatmeal or bran cereals—with skim milk; bran muffins, whole wheat toast, bagels, or English muffins with jam or low-fat cottage cheese; pancakes or waffles with fresh-fruit toppings and low-fat yogurt.	Eggs, bacon, sausage, ham, butter, cream cheese, fast-food biscuits or muffins, doughnuts, croissants, Danish pastries, hash browns, cereals high in fat or sugar (including granola).

LUNCH AND DINNER		
	Choose	**Avoid**
Salads	Salads containing fresh vegetables or fruit, protein-rich chick-peas or kidney beans; for dressing, oil and vinegar, lemon juice, or low-calorie bottled dressing; ask for dressing on the side and use sparingly.	Marinated vegetables, bacon bits, eggs, cheese, butter-fried croutons, avocado, meats, pre-dressed pasta salads; creamy salad dressings, mayonnaise, or sour cream; coleslaw and potato, macaroni, chicken, or tuna salads made with mayonnaise.
Soups	Minestrone, chicken noodle, and vegetable soups in a non-cream base; split pea, lentil, or other bean soups; potato-leek soup.	Soups made with cream such as New England clam chowder or cream of tomato; most soups have a high sodium content and so should be avoided if you are sensitive to sodium.
Appetizers	Raw vegetables, steamed or broiled seafood.	Cheese, pâtés, nuts, corn or potato chips, pretzels, cream dips.
Main courses	Pasta or rice with vegetables or legumes and no cream sauce or butter; seafood that is steamed or broiled; white meat poultry and lean red meat (ask that fat be removed from meat and skin from poultry before cooking); food that is baked, steamed, roasted, or dry-broiled in lemon juice or wine; lean cold cuts such as turkey or chicken breast; pita and whole-grain breads and muffins.	Liver, duck, goose, poultry with skin, and processed meats; food that is fried, sautéed, creamed, escalloped, marinated in oil, or basted; food in a cheese, butter, gravy, hollandaise, mayonnaise, or cream sauce; casseroles and quiches; fatty cold cuts such as bologna and salami; cheese, creamy dressings, or mayonnaise; "diet plates" consisting of a beef patty or high-fat (4 percent milk fat) cottage cheese; sodium-restricted dieters should avoid foods that are smoked, pickled, or in a broth.
Side dishes	Steamed, boiled, baked, or raw vegetables; low-fat yogurt topping for baked potatoes.	Vegetables or starches cooked or prepared with fats (oil, butter, mayonnaise, or sour cream) or cheese; coleslaw, potato and macaroni salad.
Desserts	Fresh fruit, sherbet, sorbet, skim or low-fat milk in coffee.	Cakes, pies, cookies, pastries, canned fruit in heavy syrup, ice cream, custards, and cheese made from whole milk.

butter—this eliminates the need for added fat. Steam or microwave vegetables instead of boiling them in order to preserve nutrients, and use lemon juice or herbs and spices in place of butter or salt to flavor them—this saves on fat, calories, cholesterol, and sodium. (Other healthy food preparation techniques for specific foods are outlined in the Wellness Food Guide on pages 148-209.) Modifying your recipes to substitute for ingredients high in fat, cholesterol, sugar, and sodium is another way to make your meals more healthful. (See chart on page 83.)

Dining out

Dining in a restaurant can pose some difficulties for those interested in eating healthfully. While many people make nutritious choices when eating at home, they often ignore healthy eating habits when eating out. It's no wonder; many dishes offered in restaurants are high in fat and calories and commonly used preparation methods can further increase the fat and calorie count. Still, it is possible to make nutritionally sound choices in almost all types of restaurants by following a few simple guidelines:

•Choose items that are poached, steamed, broiled, or roasted. Avoid creamed, pan-fried, and sautéed dishes, as well as buttery, cheesy, and crispy ones.

•Ask how foods are prepared. Many restaurants are willing to accommodate special requests in preparing foods. For example, ask that the meal be prepared without salt or MSG; broiled or baked instead of fried; cooked in margarine or vegetable oil instead of butter; served with dressings or sauces on the side. You can also request that the fat be trimmed from meats and the skin removed from poultry before cooking.

•See if substitutions are possible. For example, can you get a baked potato instead of french fries? A green salad instead of coleslaw?

•Start your meal with a low-fat appetizer such as a green salad, a tomato- or broth-based soup, shrimp cocktail, a raw vegetable platter, or an artichoke (minus the butter sauce). Appetizers can help fill you up so that you don't feel the need to order a rich entree. A slice of bread or a couple of breadsticks (minus the butter) are also good low-fat appetizers.

•If your table is provided with a bowl of chips, fried noodles, or nuts, ask the waiter to take them away.

•Consider ordering a few appetizers for dinner instead of a main course.

•Stick to entrees that center on foods such as chicken breast, fish, pasta, shellfish, or other low-fat foods. If you want to order a richer entree, such as a T-bone steak, order an appetizer and share the entree with a dining companion.

•Many ethnic restaurants—such as Chinese or Italian—offer cuisines that tend to be healthier than ours.

Approximately 40 percent of restaurant owners now offer healthful menu selections lower in fat, cholesterol, sodium, and calories.

Carbohydrates

A decade or so ago, bread and potatoes had a bad name among weight-conscious people. Popular diet books were likely to warn you off these foods and guide you firmly toward broiled steak and salad. Today, however, carbohydrates, especially "complex" carbohydrates, are back in favor. Pasta is on the menu even in the most expensive restaurants; large helpings of meat on the dinner table are more likely to be blamed for their "fattening" properties than are baskets of bread.

Instead of just another dietary fad, the new attitudes may reflect a better understanding of what's good for us. For although carbohydrates (or any other single nutrient) are not a magic road to health, they are the body's largest source of energy. Moreover, carbohydrates are in bountiful supply on the American table, as in most parts of the world, and—unless purchased in highly processed forms such as breakfast cereals—are the most economical of foods.

What are carbohydrates?

The term covers an immense variety of edibles. Refined sugar, pears, strawberries, whole wheat bread, apple pie, popcorn, white flour biscuits, green peas, cole slaw, a hot dog bun, and sweet potatoes are all sources of carbohydrates. In fact, all sugars and starches that we eat and most types of fiber, too, are carbohydrates. However, many types of fiber cannot be broken down by the body and used as energy. Varied though these foods may be in color, taste, texture, and nutritional content, the carbohydrates contained in almost all of them are transformed by the body into one essential substance—glucose, the main sugar in the blood and the body's basic fuel. For animals as well as humans, glucose serves as the primary source of energy.

Complex is best

There are two general types of carbohydrates:

Simple carbohydrates are the sugars, which include glucose and fructose from fruit and vegetables, lactose from milk, and sucrose from cane or beet sugar.

Complex carbohydrates, which are actually large chains of glucose molecules, consist primarily of starches as well as cellulose or fiber that occurs in all plant foods. Starch takes other forms, too, including dextrin, which helps form the appetizing crust on bread when it is toasted or baked. Moreover, starches can be modified or refined, as in cornstarch, which is used for thickening sauces and other culinary purposes. Starch is the storage form of carbohydrates in plants; the storage form in humans and animals is glycogen.

In both humans and animals, unlike plants, the ability to store carbohydrates is limited, but small amounts of glycogen can be stored in the liver and in muscle. The body can quickly transform the glycogen in the liver into glucose for release into the bloodstream when needed for energy. Amounts of carbohydrates that are in excess of what can be stored as glycogen become fat.

Since the majority of carbohydrates are broken down into glucose, why does it matter which carbohydrates you consume? Complex carbohydrates are better for us than simple carbohydrates because foods high in sugars are more likely to come in "empty packages." That is, they are what commercials are fond of calling "pure food energy," which means calories without added nutritional value.

By contrast, the calories in foods high in complex carbohydrates usually bring a lot of nutritional extras with them. Two slices of whole wheat bread, for example, may contain 130 calories—as compared with 150 in a soft drink. But in addition to carbohydrates, the bread also contains five grams of protein, one gram of fat, as well as small amounts of riboflavin, thiamine, niacin, calcium, iron, and, of course, dietary fiber. None of these nutritional benefits are available in the soft drink.

Fiber is a crucial item in the carbohydrate package, and comes from such plant foods as whole grains, fruits, and vegetables. Insoluble fiber provides bulk in the intestine and hence helps to regulate bowel movements. It may also protect against colon cancer. Soluble fiber also helps lower blood cholesterol levels and thus may reduce the likelihood of cardiovascular disease. Because of our high consumption of refined flours—which have less fiber than whole-grain flour—and our preference for high-protein and sugary foods over whole grains, fruit, and vegetables, fiber has tended to decrease in the average American diet. (For more information on fiber, see pages 89-93.)

Will carbohydrates make you fat?

If you are trying to control your weight or lose several pounds, you have probably heard contradictory things about carbohydrates. Dieters often shun starchy foods—beans, potatoes, pasta—in favor of foods high in protein such as lean meat, and stay away from soft drinks, candies, and rich desserts believing that sugar is fattening.

It may come as a surprise that—gram for gram—both simple and complex carbohydrates contain exactly the same number of calories as protein, 4 calories per gram. Fat, on the other hand, has 9 calories per gram. Thus, if you have your choice of a five-ounce baked potato and three ounces of broiled lean hamburger, remember that the potato has fewer calories than the meat. This is because in addition to protein, the meat inevitably contains a fair amount of fat. And rich desserts aren't fattening because of sugar, but because they are loaded with fat. Foods high in complex carbohydrates tend to be low in fat and are usually not fattening. They are likely to be high in

A high-carbohydrate, low-fat diet can reduce the risk for five of the ten leading causes of death in the United States: coronary heart disease, stroke, atherosclerosis, diabetes, and certain forms of cancer. These chronic diseases are responsible for more than two-thirds of all deaths.

High-Carbohydrate Dishes

You should get 55 to 60 percent of the calories you eat each day from carbohydrates. No more than 15 percent of your total calories should come from simple carbohydrates; the rest should come from complex carbohydrates. The dishes below more than fulfill these requirements.

	Calories	Carbohydrates (g)	Carbohydrate Calories
Bean and rice salad, 6 oz	225	36	64%
Pasta with vegetables, 10 oz	310	49	63%
Pasta salad, 5 oz	160	25	62%
Potato-leek soup, 8 oz	100	17	68%
Cornmeal, pancakes, 6 oz	365	70	76%
Baked potato with ratatouille topping, 6 oz	95	16	67%
Apricot-banana-bran bread, 4 oz	290	47	64%

Foods High in Complex Carbohydrates

	Total Carbohy-drates (g)	Sugars (g)	Complex Carbohy-drates (g)
Bread, 1 slice	13	1	12
Corn flakes, 1 oz (low sugar)	24	2	22
Pasta or rice, ½ cup, cooked	20	0	20
Beans, 1 cup, cooked	40	0	40
Potatoes, corn, or peas, 1 cup	30	6	24
Carrots or beets, 1 cup	12	6	6
Broccoli, 1 cup, cut up	7	0	7

Potatoes are an excellent source of complex carbohydrates, but potato chips are not. Eating eight ounces of potato chips is like adding twelve to twenty teaspoons of vegetable oil (usually hydrogenated) to an eight-ounce potato.

nutritional quality as well; a diet that omits them will leave you seriously short of vitamins, minerals, and fiber.

...Or help you lose weight?

As for the claims that complex carbohydrates can actually help the dieter, the answer is a hopeful maybe. Because fruits and vegetables, which are usually rich in complex carbohydrates, have a high water content and relatively few calories, they are obviously useful in any weight-control program. For one thing, they allow you to vary your food intake in a satisfying way. They also satisfy your appetite. Foods high in fiber are particularly useful in this respect because fiber fills you up, but is not digestible and supplies no calories.

Furthermore, some studies suggest that carbohydrates are less effectively transformed into body fat than dietary fat is. Nevertheless, it is probably too much to claim that complex carbohydrates actually "help you lose weight."

Carbohydrates and the athlete

Since carbohydrates in the form of glycogen are stored in the liver and muscles and provide energy for muscle contraction, it is a commonly held belief among athletes that loading up on carbohydrates before a competition can postpone the time to exhaustion and improve their performance. The classic "carbo-loading" regimen took a week and called for depleting the body's stores of glycogen through exercise and a low-carbohydrate diet, followed by rest and a very high carbohydrate intake. Most sports nutritionists now advise against this dietary manipulation because it is hard to follow, may produce undesirable side effects (such as lethargy, weight gain, and cardiac rhythm abnormalities), and is unnecessary. Sports physiologists have devised a simpler version of carbohydrate loading; during the two to three days before an endurance event, simply increase your complex carbohydrate intake and slightly decrease your level of exercise.

However, studies have shown that, at best, any form of carbohydrate loading is of limited value, even in long-distance events, since muscles can store only so much glycogen. Anybody who eats a balanced, high-carbohydrate diet and is in reasonably good physical condition has enough glycogen stores in the muscles and liver to meet the demands of *short*-duration exercise of approximately one hour or so. Moreover, during *long*-duration, moderately intense exercise—such as cycling for two hours—the muscles are able to use more fat than carbohydrates as their main source of energy. The improvement in performance that comes from carbohydrate loading, if there is one, is usually small. So the best advice is to stick to the balanced, high-complex-carbohydrate diet that should be eaten on a daily basis.

Fiber

Fiber is not a single substance. It is an enormous group of widely different chemical substances with varied physical properties. Fiber is divided into two basic types—soluble and insoluble—and five major forms: cellulose, hemicellulose, lignin, pectin, and gums. Moreover, foods differ in the type and amount of fiber they contain. But all types of fiber have two things in common: they are found only in plant foods and they are resistant to human digestive enzymes (that is, they pass through the digestive tract without being completely broken down). While other basic foods are nearly all digested and absorbed as they pass through the small intestine, fiber enters the large intestine more or less intact. Being indigestible, fiber also contributes no nutrients to the body, and so for many years, no one thought removing it from food was bad (hence, the popularity of "softer" white bread over whole wheat). But nutritionists have discovered that fiber performs valuable functions precisely because it is not digested.

Insoluble vs. soluble

Insoluble fiber— which includes cellulose, some hemicellulose, and lignin—is like a sponge: it absorbs many times its weight in water, swelling up within the intestine. Insoluble fiber is found mainly in whole grains and, in the form of cellulose and lignin, on the outside of seeds, fruits, legumes, and other foods. For example, wheat bran, which contains cellulose, is the outer protective layer of a grain of wheat. This outer material is often the chewiest part of foods, and for that reason it is often removed when food is processed by milling, peeling, boiling, or extracting. But it is best to eat unrefined foods since insoluble fiber is key in promoting more efficient elimination by increasing stool bulk and may alleviate some digestive disorders. It is also thought to play a role in colon cancer prevention.

Soluble fiber— which includes pectin, gums, and some hemicellulose—is found in fruits, vegetables, seeds, brown rice, barley, oats, and oat bran. It can help produce a softer stool, but does less to help the passage of food; rather, it works chemically to prevent or reduce the absorption of certain substances into the bloodstream. Soluble fiber appears to lower blood cholesterol levels and retard the entry of glucose into the bloodstream, an especially important factor for diabetics.

Crude vs. dietary

Because fiber is such a complex group of substances, it is difficult to measure. Older methods employed strong chemicals that "digested" the food (and in the process destroyed some of the insoluble and much of the soluble fiber); what was left was called crude fiber. New methods use milder chemicals and enzymes to analyze dietary fiber.

Dietary fiber is the more accurate and complete measure, but it has not yet been determined for all foods. Nutrition information provided by the United States Department of Agriculture (USDA) usually lists crude fiber content. Thus, you'll still see crude fiber listed on many food labels, even though it is considered

Fiber Content of Foods

Getting the recommended 20 to 30 grams of fiber per day need not be difficult. Newer methods of analyzing fiber are more accurate, so many of the foods you don't think of as high in fiber in fact are. The measures below, provided by Dr. James W. Anderson of the University of Kentucky College of Medicine, are for dietary fiber and are more accurate. To maximize fiber intake, choose unrefined versions of foods (such as brown rice over white rice) whenever possible.

		Serving Size	Dietary Fiber (g)
Grains	Bread, white	1 slice	0.6
	Bread, whole wheat	1 slice	1.5
	Oat bran, dry	1/3 cup	4.0
	Oatmeal, dry	1/3 cup	2.7
	Rice, brown, cooked	1/2 cup	2.4
	Rice, white, cooked	1/2 cup	0.8
Fruits	Apple, with skin	1 small	2.8
	Apricots, with skin	4 fruit	3.5
	Banana	1 small	2.2
	Blueberries	3/4 cup	1.4
	Figs, dried	3 fruit	4.6
	Grapefruit	1/2 fruit	1.6
	Pear, with skin	1 large	5.8
	Prunes, dried	3 medium	1.7
Vegetables	Asparagus, cooked	1/2 cup	1.8
	Broccoli, cooked	1/2 cup	2.4
	Carrots, cooked, sliced	1/2 cup	2.0
	Peas, green, frozen, cooked	1/2 cup	4.3
	Potato, with skin, raw	1/2 cup	1.5
	Tomatoes, raw	1 medium	1.0
Legumes	Kidney beans, cooked	1/2 cup	6.9
	Lima beans, canned	1/2 cup	4.3
	Pinto beans, cooked	1/2 cup	5.9
	Beans, white, cooked	1/2 cup	5.0
	Lentils, cooked	1/2 cup	5.2
	Peas, blackeye, canned	1/2 cup	4.7

Fiber values from Plant Fiber in Foods, *Second Edition, James W. Anderson, MD. HCF Nutrition Research Foundation, Inc., P.O. Box 22124, Lexington, KY 40522*

outdated. While no existing methods for extracting fiber can measure all of its types precisely, the newer methods do measure more substances, so the amount of dietary fiber in a food is usually two to five times larger than its crude fiber.

The benefits of fiber

In the early 1970s, researchers linked a high-fiber intake among rural Africans with a low incidence of diseases all too common in industrialized Western countries. Although not all of the findings have been confirmed, a number of studies have indicated that the various types of fiber may help prevent or improve the following conditions and diseases:

Constipation. By promoting more efficient elimination, whole-grain fiber almost inevitably halts common constipation when taken with adequate amounts of fluid. The fiber and the water it retains produce a larger, softer stool that the digestive system can pass quickly and easily. Without an adequate intake of fiber, a small hard stool forms that takes far more time and effort to expel. Moreover, when fiber enters the large intestine, about half of it is broken down by bacteria. This yields many more complex chemicals, which in turn help initiate bowel movements. African villagers consuming fiber-rich diets typically hold food in their large intestine for much less time than Americans. In clinical studies, subjects who increased their fiber intake increased the frequency, bulk, and ease of bowel movements. Most doctors now recognize fiber (along with adequate fluid intake) as the safest, most effective way to prevent and treat constipation.

Intestinal disorders. About 30 to 40 percent of adults fifty years old and over suffer from diverticulosis, a condition in which intestinal pressure causes tiny pouches to form in the wall of the large intestine. When the pouches trap feces, they can become painfully inflamed, a condition called diverticulitis. Fiber, which was once thought to cause the inflammation, may actually keep it from occurring by reducing the pressure and allowing the feces to be swept out of the pouches. Moreover, several studies suggest that it may actually help prevent, though not cure, diverticulosis. Similarly, a high-fiber diet has been successfully used to treat the constipation often seen in irritable bowel syndrome—spasmodic contractions of the large intestine that can cause gas, nausea, and abdominal pain. (People with either of these disorders should consult their physicians before starting a high-fiber diet.)

Cancer. Colon cancer, the second most common form of cancer in the United States, is rare among people with a diet low in meat and rich in high-fiber foods. The evidence is not yet conclusive that fiber is protective, but a 1989 study showed that insoluble fiber—in the form of wheat bran—has a direct effect on people who have precancerous polyps of the colon. This four-year study followed fifty-eight men and women at very high risk of colon cancer because of an inherited condition characterized by the continuing development of numerous polyps in the colon and rectum starting early in life. Over time such polyps gradually enlarge and become malignant. Half the subjects had their regular diet supplemented by a wheat-bran cereal high in insoluble fiber (they ate a total of 22.4 grams of fiber a day); the others were given a low-fiber look-alike cereal (they ate an average of 12.2 grams of fiber a day, about as much as the average American). Over the course of the study, polyps were more likely to have shrunk both in size and number in the people on the high-fiber cereal. Though this study looked at a select group at very high risk for cancer, the researchers believe that the findings apply to everyone.

No one knows exactly how fiber may protect against this cancer, but there are several likely mechanisms. It may move intestinal contents faster through the bowel, thus decreasing the length of time the bowel wall is exposed to potential carcinogens. And fiber may dilute carcinogens as well or possibly bind or inactivate them in some way.

Heart disease. An elevated cholesterol level is known to be one of the chief risk factors in heart disease, and a number of studies have linked high-fiber intake with low levels of cholesterol. However, wheat bran, the most popular fiber source, has little if any effect on cholesterol. Only soluble fiber produces a significant reduction. Although the mechanism of this action has not been fully explained, it's proposed that fiber may alter fat or cholesterol absorption in the large bowel. Some studies suggest that soluble fiber produces a reduction in LDL ("bad") cholesterol levels without decreasing HDL ("good") cholesterol levels.

Fig bars contain twice as much fiber and less than half the fat calories of most cookies. Still, they are high in sugar and calories, so save them for occasional treats.

Gallstones. While the evidence is not conclusive, fiber is thought to prevent gallstones from forming in two ways: by stimulating bile flow from the liver and by preventing bile reabsorption.

Diabetes. Elevated blood sugar levels are a major problem in diabetes. Researchers have shown that fiber may have a potent effect on blood sugar levels. In studies conducted by Dr. James W. Anderson of the University of Kentucky College of Medicine, V.A. Medical Center at Lexington, diabetics placed on high-carbohydrate, high-fiber diets were able to dramatically reduce their insulin requirements. Other studies have also shown that a high-carbohydrate, high-fiber diet improves glucose tolerance. Exactly why isn't clear, but one theory is that the gums in soluble fiber may delay the emptying of the stomach or even the absorption of glucose. Still, some investigators propose that it may be factors other than fiber, including total carbohydrate intake or a low-fat, low-calorie diet. Nevertheless, it appears that individuals suffering from both noninsulin-dependent diabetes (NIDDM, also called adult-onset or type II) and insulin-dependent diabetes (IDDM, also called juvenile or type I) would benefit from increasing their fiber intake, under the supervision of their physicians.

Obesity. People who eat high-fiber diets are seldom obese, and for good reason: high-fiber diets are usually low in fat, and fiber fills you up without adding calories. Indeed, several studies have shown that high-fiber foods enhance the feeling of satiety. But fiber itself doesn't lower the number of calories your body absorbs. The weight control benefits from fiber come from the fiber in foods, not in supplement form (see box on page 93).

Increasing your fiber intake

Suddenly increasing the amount of fiber you eat can cause problems. One common consequence is intestinal gas due to fermentation in the colon. Usually this isn't serious and subsides once the bacteria in your system adjust to the fiber increase. You can reduce the chances of gas or diarrhea by adding fiber-rich foods to your diet gradually.

One of the potential adverse effects of a high-fiber diet is the tendency of fiber to bind some minerals—such as magnesium, calcium, and in particular trace minerals, such as zinc and iron—and to lessen their absorption. There is some evidence that because of this mechanism an extremely high intake of fiber could create mineral deficiencies in people whose diet is nutritionally poor. This should not be a problem for most Americans who consume a wide variety of foods. Moreover, high-fiber foods are usually rich in minerals which compensates for any losses.

The daily intake of fiber for Americans averages about twelve grams. Most authorities agree that we should be consuming at least twice that amount. The National Cancer Institute recommends eating foods that provide twenty to thirty grams of fiber a day. While it helps to be aware of the amount of fiber in various foods, you can ensure an adequate fiber intake by gradually adopting these steps:

•Eat a variety of foods—the less processed the better. Bran, for example, is a superb source of fiber. However, consuming it in the form of whole-grain cereal is more nutritionally sound than merely adding bran flakes as a supplement to your food because in addition to the fiber, you get the vitamins, minerals, and flavor. There is no evidence that bran or other fiber supplement can compensate for an otherwise unhealthy diet.

Ounce for ounce, kidney beans have three times more dietary fiber than green beans, and raspberries have four times as much cherries.

Fiber Supplements

Can fiber in a bottle play the same role in weight reduction that a diet high in fiber can? Manufacturers of fiber supplements would like you to think so. And they may be right; there have been few studies so far, but there is some suggestion that fiber pills might be helpful in producing the same feeling of satiety produced by high-fiber foods. Still, much more research is needed to determine the safety of the use of fiber supplements over the long term. Moreover, getting fiber from supplements rather than from food is a little like getting vitamins from pills instead of from food. Here are four reasons not to use fiber supplements:

•Fiber pills alone won't make you slim. First of all, there's no conclusive evidence that fiber by itself decreases appetite. Second, the diets described in the fiber supplement packages— which you must follow if you expect to lose weight while taking the supplements—usually add up to about 1,200 calories a day, and on that allowance you would lose weight without fiber supplements. Even with them, you'll still need willpower.

•Fiber pills actually have little fiber in them. Five pills, at the recommended premeal dose, usually supply 2.5 grams of fiber—about as much as an apple or three rye wafers, but at a greater expense. So even if you swallowed the recommended fifteen pills daily, you're not getting that much fiber.

•Fiber is a large group of widely different substances, and no one knows precisely their optimal combinations. The fiber in the supplements may be unbalanced or incomplete. In contrast, if you eat a wide variety of foods, you're likely to get all kinds of fiber.

•Fiber binds some minerals in the foods you eat. Foods high in fiber contain minerals, so you more than make up for any losses; fiber supplements contain no minerals.

The fiber values of cooked vegetables and fruits are frequently higher than their raw counterparts. That's because water may be lost in cooking, causing fiber to make up a greater proportion of the total.

•Eat more fruits and vegetables. They are excellent low-calorie sources of fiber and provide essential vitamins and minerals as well. Eat them unpeeled, such as baked potatoes or apples with their skin, whenever possible.

•Drink plenty of liquids. Otherwise fiber can slow down or even block proper intestinal digestion.

•Spread out your fiber intake. Getting all of your fiber at one sitting may cut the benefits and increase the chance of unpleasant side effects. As a rule of thumb, try to eat foods high in insoluble and soluble fiber at every meal.

This approach will not only increase your fiber consumption, but should also help you reduce the sugars and fatty meats that most of us eat too freely. That is another way in which fiber, though not a nutritional panacea, is an excellent form of health insurance.

Fat

As most people see it, fat is the villain in the nutritional scenario, clogging the arteries and settling around the waist. They forget that we need to consume some fat to remain healthy. As with many other nutrients and foods, the question about fat is: how much and which kinds should we eat?

Americans have one of the fattiest diets in the world; about 37 percent of all calories consumed today come from fats. Most of this fat intake occurs at the expense of carbohydrates. The chief sources of fat in the diet include meats, poultry, and dairy products, as well as vegetable oils and shortenings. Most nutritionists recommend that only 30 percent of our total daily calories come from fat, and that we should try to get more of these calories from plant sources or fish, rather than animal sources.

What are fats?

Technically called lipids, fats come in solid or liquid (oil) form. All are insoluble in water. Although carbohydrates are the body's main source of food energy, fats are the most concentrated source, supplying 9 calories per gram; carbohydrates and proteins have 4 calories per gram. High-fat foods are thus always high-calorie foods. The important functions of fats in the body include:

•Store energy. Fats serve as the storage substance for the body's excess calories, filling the balloonlike adipose cells that insulate the body. Extra calories from carbohydrates and proteins as well as from fats are stored as body fat.

•Maintain healthy skin and hair.

•Carry fat-soluble vitamins (A, D, E, and K).

•Supply "essential" fatty acids, so named because the body can't make them and must get them from foods. Linoleic acid is the most important of these, especially for the proper growth and development of infants. Essential fatty acids are the raw materials for several hormonelike compounds, including prostaglandins, which help control blood pressure and other vital bodily functions.

•Regulate levels of cholesterol in the blood.

•Promote satiety, because they slow the emptying of food from the stomach.

Fatty acids: saturated vs. unsaturated

Most fats in foods are triglycerides, which consist of three fatty acids attached to a glycerol molecule. These fatty acids vary in length and in degree of saturation by hydrogen atoms—and it is these variations that determine the properties of different fats. All fats are combinations of saturated and unsaturated fatty acids. Fats containing mainly saturated fatty acids are described as "highly saturated," while fats that are primarily polyunsaturated or monounsaturated are described as "highly unsaturated."

Saturated fatty acids are loaded with all the hydrogen atoms they can carry. Fats that are largely saturated come chiefly from animal sources and include butter, milk fat, and the fat in meats; two vegetable oils—coconut and palm oils—are also highly saturated. Highly saturated fats are usually solid at room temperature and keep well.

Unsaturated fatty acids do not have all the hydrogen atoms they can carry. Depending on the number of missing hydrogen atoms, these fatty acids are called either *monounsaturated* (olive, peanut, canola, and avocado oils are largely monounsaturated) or *polyunsaturated* (corn, safflower, and sesame oils are primarily polyunsaturated). The important dietary unsaturated fats come from plants and fish. They generally are liquid at room temperature and may become rancid quickly since the absence of hydrogen makes the carbon atoms very reactive with oxygen.

A manufacturing process called *hydrogenation* adds hydrogen atoms to unsaturated fats, thus making them more saturated. The fats in margarines and shortenings are often hydrogenated because this makes them harder and more stable. Depending on the degree of hydrogenation, these artificially saturated vegetable fats are no better for you than comparably saturated animal fats.

Fats and heart disease

Many factors affect blood cholesterol levels and thus the risk of developing cardiovascular disease. Surprisingly, there does not appear to be a simple direct relationship between *dietary* intake of cholesterol and *blood* cholesterol levels in all people.

Researchers estimate that only about 20 percent of the population is genetically hypersensitive to dietary cholesterol—that is, their blood cholesterol levels jump when they eat high-cholesterol foods. There's no simple test for cholesterol hypersensitivity. (For more information on cholesterol, see pages 40-41.)

Nevertheless, dietary changes, especially involving fats, *can* have a significant effect on blood cholesterol levels. In fact, the type of fat you eat influences blood cholesterol levels more than dietary cholesterol does. Saturated fats usually elevate the levels of LDL ("bad") cholesterol and raise overall cholesterol levels. That's why limiting your cholesterol intake but not your consumption of saturated fats can result in high blood cholesterol.

In contrast, polyunsaturated fats tend to lower the amount of LDL ("bad") cholesterol, thus reducing the amount of artery-clogging cholesterol in the bloodstream. Moreover, the unique polyunsaturated fats in fish oil offer an additional benefit: they make the blood less likely to clot, thus reduc-

Like the oil that comes from it, coconut is one of the richest sources of saturated fat. Three-quarters of the 100 calories in an ounce of raw coconut come from saturated fat. But like all plant foods, coconut is cholesterol-free.

Hidden Fats

Potatoes, rice, bagels—low-fat foods, right? Not if you're talking about some supermarket varieties. When buying processed foods, look at ingredients lists for hidden saturated fats in the form of tropical oils (coconut, palm, and palm kernel), hydrogenated or partially hydrogenated vegetable oils (hydrogenation makes an oil more saturated), as well as cheese and butterfat. The following is a sampling of unlikely places where saturated fats often lurk:

Side dishes
Packaged potato mixes
Packaged rice dishes
Stuffing/breading mixes
Frozen vegetables in sauce
Gravies (canned or bottled)
Refried beans

Snacks
Crackers
Bagel/pita bits
Microwave popcorn

Breakfast foods
Granola cereals
Nondairy creamers
Flavored instant coffee mixes
Toaster pastries

ing the chances of artery blockage and heart attack. However, some animal studies using large quantities of polyunsaturated fat have suggested that in addition to lowering LDL cholesterol, polyunsaturated fats also lower the beneficial HDL cholesterol. (This may not increase heart disease risk if the levels of both types of cholesterol drop proportionately.) In contrast, some studies have shown that monounsaturated fats, such as olive oil, may be able to reduce total cholesterol by decreasing the amount of damaging LDL cholesterol in the blood without producing a reduction in HDL cholesterol. Whether nut oils, such as peanut oil, which are high in monounsaturated fat also help to reduce heart disease risk is not clear at this time.

Eating large amounts of any kind of fat increases your chance of becoming overweight or obese, which is another risk factor in cardiovascular disease. Reducing overall fat intake and raising the *ratio* of unsaturated to saturated fats is no guarantee of protection against heart disease, but it does increase the odds in your favor because it has the potential to lower blood cholesterol levels. Such a diet is recommended to everyone, especially if you have elevated blood cholesterol levels, or if you smoke, have high blood pressure, have a family history of heart disease, or are in another high-risk group for heart disease.

The special role of fish oil

Fish oil contains a unique kind of polyunsaturated fatty acid called omega-3, which the fish get by eating certain plants, particularly those growing in cold water. Omega-3s significantly reduce blood clotting. They make platelets less likely to stick together and to blood vessels, lessening the chance of a heart attack due to a coronary artery clot. Fish oil may also prevent hardening of the arteries, since it appears to be even more effective than polyunsaturated vegetable oils in lowering triglyceride levels in the blood, while slightly raising HDL cholesterol.

The best way to get omega-3s is to include at least two servings of fatty fish, such as salmon or mackerel, per week in your diet. Fish oil pills, a highly advertised alternative, can actually be dangerous (see box on page 97). Vegetable oils are also being touted as alternative sources of omega-3s, but they contain only linolenic acid and not the longer-chain eicosapentaenoic acid (EPA) and docosahexaenoic acid (DHA) found in fish oils. While fish are able to convert the linolenic acid in algae and other sea plants into EPA and DHA, the human body cannot do this to any significant degree. Nor has it been shown that the fatty acids in these oils can reduce blood clotting as much as marine omega-3s.

Fats and cancer

The relationship between fat intake and certain types of cancer is more controversial than the link to heart disease. Many scientists have noted that, with a few exceptions, countries with a high national fat intake also have the highest cancer rates. American women, for instance, have a six-times higher rate of breast cancer than Japanese women, who eat much less fat. Some studies have suggested that a diet high in fat—saturated or unsaturated—increases the risk of cancer of the colon and breast, and possibly of the ovary, uterus, and prostate.

The mechanism for the link between a high-fat diet and cancer has not been determined, but there are theories. A diet high in fat affects the secretion of some sex hormones, which might cause cancer in the reproductive organs. Moreover,

You can defat homemade sauces, soups, gravies, and broths by straining out the solids and chilling the liquid separately. As it cools, the fat rises to the top of the liquid, where it congeals for easy removal.

Fish Oil Supplements

Fish oil has a protective effect on heart disease because it lowers trigylceride levels and reduces the tendency of the blood to clot. Researchers speculate that this is why Eskimos and the Japanese, whose diets include vast amounts of fatty fish, have such a low incidence of cardiovascular disease.

In light of this, a wide array of fish oil supplements have come on the market appealing to those who want the advertised benefits, but not the fish. But these supplements are not the great nutritional breakthrough they are advertised to be. Here are a few reasons why you should get your fish oil from fish, not from pills:

• Many questions remain about the effectiveness, safety, and optimal dose of fish oil in its various forms. Not much is known about potential long-term side effects either. In other words, we have no idea what is an optimal and safe dose of fish oil.

• Those same Eskimos who have a low incidence of heart disease have a high risk of hemorrhagic stroke, perhaps because of the decreased clotting ability of their blood. Fish oil's anti-clotting effect can be dangerous in an accident or during surgery.

• Fish oil in liquid (such as in cod liver oil) or in capsule form may contain pesticides or other contaminants, especially if it is made from fish livers, where these compounds tend to concentrate. Furthermore, cod liver oil is overly rich in vitamins A and D, which can be toxic in high doses (no more than a tablespoon or two a day should be taken).

• Prolonged consumption of fish oil may result in a vitamin E deficiency. Some manufacturers have therefore added this vitamin to their supplements.

• It is unclear whether fish oil by itself provides all the health benefits of fish. These fatty acids may work with other elements in the fish not found in the supplements. On the other hand, some supplements contain ingredients of questionable value, such as lecithin.

• Besides its oil, fish is rich in protein, iron, B vitamins, and other nutrients. Also, it can take the place of meats that are high in saturated fat. Pills cannot cancel out the effects of a high-fat, high-cholesterol diet. You don't have to eat huge amounts of fish to improve your cardiovascular health. Studies suggest that two to three servings a week are enough.

Skinless dark chicken and turkey meat contains more than twice as much fat as skinless light meat. It also has about 20 percent more calories and 10 percent less protein than light meat.

high-fat diets increase the amount of cholesterol and bile acids that are in the colon, which may then be converted by bacteria that are present there into carcinogenic by-products.

Some animal studies have implicated *large* intakes of the type of polyunsaturated fat found in plants and therefore in vegetable oils is implicated in the development of certain types of cancer. For this reason, in addition to their high calorie content, you should not go overboard on polyunsaturated fats even though they are known to help lower blood cholesterol levels.

How much fat should you eat?

Virtually all health organizations and government agencies recommend that Americans reduce their fat intake and blood cholesterol levels. The American Heart Association and American Cancer Society say that only 30 percent of all calories consumed each day should come from fats. While most Americans consume about twice as much saturated as polyunsaturated fats, the American Heart Association recommends approximately equal amounts: less than 10 percent of all caloric intake should come from saturated fat, up to 10 percent from polyunsaturated fats, and the remainder from monounsaturated fats.

Some health professionals advocate that total fat consumption should drop to 20 percent, and a few recommend that only 10 percent of calories come from fats. Eliminating that much dietary fat is very difficult, and unnecessary for most people. (*Text continued on page 103.*)

Fat and Cholesterol Content of Foods

Fat. The amount of fat in a serving of each food is listed in grams (there are about 28 grams in an ounce). Foods high in fat are printed in BLUE; this indicates that more than 30 percent of their calories come from fat. While you should limit your intake of the foods in blue, you don't have to avoid them entirely. The key to a healthy diet is to balance high- and low-fat foods so that no more than 30 percent of your daily calories come from fat.

Saturated fat. This is the type of fat that can raise blood cholesterol levels. Foods high in saturated fat (more than 10 percent of the total calories) have an "S" printed next to their fat content. The major sources of saturated fat are meat (notably beef, pork, lamb, and cold cuts), poultry skin, whole-milk dairy products (such as cheese and butter), and three vegetable oils—coconut, palm, and palm kernel.

Cholesterol. The second most important dietary factor in controlling your blood cholesterol level is limiting your intake of cholesterol from foods. You should consume no more than 300 milligrams of cholesterol a day. Cholesterol is found only in animal products, such as meats, fish, poultry, eggs, milk, and cheese. Plant foods—such as grains, fruits, vegetables, and vegetable oils—contain no cholesterol.

DAIRY AND EGGS

	Calories	Fat (g)	Saturated Fat (g)	Cholesterol (mg)
Cheese				
American, 1 oz	105	9 S	4	27
American spread, 1 oz	82	6 S	4	16
Blue, 1 oz	100	8 S	5	21
Cheddar, 1 oz	115	9 S	6	30
Cottage, creamed, ½ cup	108	5 S	3	15
Cottage, low fat, ½ cup	104	2 S	1	10
Cream, 1 oz	100	10 S	6	31
Feta, 1 oz	75	6 S	4	25
Gouda, 1 oz	101	8 S	5	32
Mozzarella, part skim, 1 oz	72	5 S	3	16
Mozzarella, regular, 1 oz	80	6 S	4	22
Muenster, 1 oz	105	9 S	5	27
Parmesan, 2 tbsp	50	4 S	2	8
Provolone, 1 oz	100	8 S	5	20
Ricotta, part skim, ½ cup	170	10 S	6	38
Ricotta, whole milk, ½ cup	216	16 S	10	63
Swiss, 1 oz	105	8 S	5	26
Milk and Cream				
Buttermilk, 1 cup	100	2 S	1	9
Chocolate milk, whole, 1 cup	208	8 S	5	30

	Calories	Fat (g)	Saturated Fat (g)	Cholesterol (mg)
Eggnog, 1 cup	342	19 S	11	149
Heavy cream, whipped, ¼ cup	103	11 S	7	41
Evaporated milk, skim, 1 cup	200	1	0	9
Half and half, 1 tbsp	20	2 S	1	6
Milk, 2% fat, 1 cup	120	5 S	3	18
Milk, 1% fat, 1 cup	100	3 S	2	10
Milk, skim, 1 cup	85	0	0	4
Milk, whole, 1 cup	150	8 S	5	33
Sour cream, ¼ cup	123	12 S	8	26
Yogurt				
Low fat, fruit, 1 cup	230	2	2	10
Low fat, plain, 1 cup	145	4 S	2	14
Nonfat, plain, 1 cup	125	0	0	4
Whole milk, plain, 1 cup	140	7 S	5	29
Eggs				
Egg, whole	80	6 S	2	274
Egg, yolk	65	6 S	2	274
Egg, white	15	0	0	0

FATS AND OILS

	Calories	Fat (g)	Saturated Fat (g)	Cholesterol (mg)
Butter, 1 tbsp	100	11 S	7	31
Cocoa butter, 1 tbsp	120	14 S	8	0
Coconut oil, 1 tbsp	120	14 S	12	0
Lard, 1 tbsp	115	13 S	5	12
Palm oil, 1 tbsp	120	14 S	7	0
Palm kernel oil, 1 tbsp	120	14 S	11	0
Vegetable oil, other, 1 tbsp	120	14 S	2	0
Margarine, liquid, 1 tbsp	102	11 S	2	0
Margarine, soft tub, 1 tbsp	100	11 S	2	0
Margarine, stick, 1 tbsp	100	11 S	2	0
Mayonnaise, imitation, 2 tbsp	70	6 S	1	8
Mayonnaise, regular, 2 tbsp	200	22 S	3	16
Tartar sauce, 1 tbsp	75	8 S	1	4

	Calories	Fat (g)	Saturated Fat (g)	Cholesterol (mg)
Salad dressings				
Blue cheese, 2 tbsp	154	16 S	3	0
French, low calorie, 2 tbsp	44	2	0	0
French, regular, 2 tbsp	134	13 S	3	0
Italian, low calorie, 2 tbsp	32	3	0	0
Italian, regular, 2 tbsp	137	14 S	2	0
Russian, low calorie, 2 tbsp	46	1	0	0
Russian, regular, 2 tbsp	151	16 S	2	0
Thousand island, low calorie, 2 tbsp	50	4	0	4
Thousand island, regular, 2 tbsp	120	12 S	2	8

BREADS AND GRAINS

Breads and pastries	Calories	Fat (g)	Saturated Fat (g)	Cholesterol (mg)
Bagel, plain	200	2	0	0
Bread, French, 1 slice	100	1	0	0
Bread, Italian, 1 slice	85	0	0	0
Breadcrumbs, dry, grated, 1 cup	390	5	2	5
Bread, (oatmeal, white, wheat, whole wheat, rye), 1 slice	65	1	0	0
Croissant, 1	235	12	4	13
Danish, fruit, 2½ oz	235	13 S	4	56
Doughnut, glazed, 2½ oz	235	13 S	5	21
English muffin, 1	140	1	0	0
Pancake, from mix, 1 (4")	60	2	1	16
Pita bread, 1	165	1	0	0
Tortillas, corn	65	1	0	0
Waffle, from mix, 3 oz	205	8 S	3	59

Cereals, hot, cooked	Calories	Fat (g)	Saturated Fat (g)	Cholesterol (mg)
Corn grits, 1 cup	145	0	0	0
Cream of Wheat, 1 cup	86	0	0	0
Oatmeal, 1 cup	145	2	0	0
Wheatena, 1 cup	168	1	0	0

Cereals, ready to eat	Calories	Fat (g)	Saturated Fat (g)	Cholesterol (mg)
All Bran, 1 cup	204	2	0	0
Cheerios, 1 cup	88	2	0	0
Corn flakes, 1 cup	88	0	0	0
Granola, ⅓ cup	125	5 S	3	0
Raisin Bran, 1 cup	180	1	0	0
Rice Krispies, 1 cup	110	0	0	0
Shredded Wheat, 1 cup	151	2	0	0
Wheaties, 1 cup	100	0	0	0

Crackers	Calories	Fat (g)	Saturated Fat (g)	Cholesterol (mg)
Graham crackers, plain, 2	60	1	0	0
Melba toast, plain, 4	80	0	0	0
Rye wafers, 4	110	2	1	0
Saltines, 4	50	1	1	4
Snack type, round, 4	60	4 S	1	0
Wheat, thin type, 4	35	1	1	0
Whole wheat, 4	70	4 S	1	0

Grains and pasta	Calories	Fat (g)	Saturated Fat (g)	Cholesterol (mg)
Barley, cooked, 1 cup	200	2	0	0
Couscous, cooked, 1 cup	201	0	0	0
Egg noodles, cooked, 1 cup	200	2	1	50
Noodles, chow mein, canned, 1 cup	220	11	2	5
Pasta, cooked, 1 cup	190	1	0	0
Rice, brown, cooked, 1 cup	230	1	0	0
Rice, white, cooked, 1 cup	225	0	0	0
Rice, wild, cooked, 1 cup	166	1	0	0

LEGUMES

	Calories	Fat (g)	Saturated Fat (g)	Cholesterol (mg)
Black beans, cooked, 1 cup	225	1	0	0
Great northern beans, cooked, 1 cup	210	1	0	0
Kidney beans, canned, 1 cup	230	1	0	0
Lentils, cooked, 1 cup	215	1	0	0
Lima beans, cooked, 1 cup	260	1	0	0
Navy beans, cooked, 1 cup	225	1	0	0
Pinto beans, cooked, 1 cup	265	1	0	0
Soybeans, cooked, 1 cup	235	10	1	0
Split peas, cooked, 1 cup	231	1	0	0
Tempeh, ½ cup	165	6	1	0
Tofu, 4 oz	81	5	1	0

FISH AND SHELLFISH

(4 oz except caviar)	Calories	Fat (g)	Saturated Fat (g)	Cholesterol (mg)
Carp, cooked	185	8	2	96
Caviar, 2 tbsp	80	6	0	188
Cod, cooked	120	1	0	63
Clams, breaded, fried	231	13 S	3	70
Clams, cooked	169	2	0	77
Crab, Alaskan king, cooked	111	2	0	61
Crayfish, cooked	130	1	0	203
Haddock, cooked	128	1	0	86
Halibut, cooked	160	3	0	47
Lobster, cooked	112	1	0	82
Mackerel, cooked	299	21	5	83
Mussels, cooked	197	5	1	64
Oysters, cooked	157	6	1	125
Perch, cooked	134	1	0	131
Pike, cooked	129	1	0	57
Salmon, pink, canned	159	7	2	45

(4 oz)	Calories	Fat (g)	Saturated Fat (g)	Cholesterol (mg)
Salmon, sockeye, fresh, cooked	247	13	99	2
Sardines, canned in oil, with bones	238	13	3	162
Scallops, breaded and fried	245	13	3	70
Scallops, cooked	128	1	0	61
Shrimp, breaded and fried	277	14	2	202
Shrimp, cooked	113	1	0	223
Snapper, cooked	146	2	0	54
Squid, fried	200	8	2	297
Swordfish, cooked	177	6	2	57
Trout, rainbow, cooked	173	5	1	83
Tuna light, canned in oil	226	9	2	21
Tuna light, canned in water	150	2	0	21
Tuna, blue fin, fresh, cooked	210	7	2	56

POULTRY

(4 oz)	Calories	Fat (g)	Saturated Fat (g)	Cholesterol (mg)
Chicken				
Dark meat, with skin, roasted	289	18 S	1	104
Dark meat, without skin, roasted	203	10 S	1	106
Light meat, with skin, roasted	253	13 S	1	96
Light meat, without skin, roasted	175	5	0	97
Light meat, with skin, batter dipped, fried	317	17 S	1	96
Capons, with skin, roasted	262	13 S	4	98
Goose				
With skin, roasted	349	25 S	8	104
Without skin. roasted	272	14 S	6	110

(4 oz)	Calories	Fat (g)	Saturated Fat (g)	Cholesterol (mg)
Turkey				
Breast meat, without skin, roasted	154	1	0	95
Dark meat, with skin, roasted	253	14 S	1	102
Dark meat, without skin, roasted	214	8 S	1	97
Light meat, with skin, roasted	225	9	1	87
Light meat, without skin, roasted	179	3	0	79
Turkey roll, light meat	168	8 S	2	0
Duck				
With skin, roasted	385	32 S	4	96
Without skin, roasted	228	13 S	1	101

BEEF

(4 oz)	Calories	Fat (g)	Saturated Fat (g)	Cholesterol (mg)
Beef frankfurter (cured)	360	32 S	14	70
Bottom round, trimmed, select cut, braised	245	10 S	4	110
Bottom round, untrimmed, prime cut, braised	285	14 S	5	110
Brisket, trimmed, braised	275	14 S	7	106
Brisket, untrimmed, braised	447	37 S	15	106
Chuck, blade roast, trimmed, select cut, braised	293	16 S	6	121
Chuck, blade roast, untrimmed, choice cut, braised	443	35 S	15	118
Corned beef, cooked	287	22 S	7	112
Eye of round, trimmed, roasted	209	8 S	3	79
Ground beef, lean, baked (medium)	306	20 S	8	89
Ground beef, extra lean, broiled	291	18 S	7	113
Ground beef, regular, broiled	333	21 S	9	115
Liver, pan fried	248	9 S	3	551
Pastrami	399	33 S	12	106
Prime rib, trimmed, broiled	320	22 S	9	94
Rib eye, trimmed, choice cut, broiled	257	14 S	6	91

(4 oz)	Calories	Fat (g)	Saturated Fat (g)	Cholesterol (mg)
Rib eye, untrimmed, choice cut, broiled	337	24 S	10	95
Round, trimmed, select cut, broiled	210	8 S	3	94
Salami	299	24 S	10	74
Sirloin, trimmed, broiled	238	10 S	4	102
Sirloin, untrimmed, (all grades), broiled	320	20 S	9	58
T-bone steak, choice cut, trimmed, broiled	245	12 S	5	91
T-bone steak, untrimmed, choice cut, broiled	370	28 S	12	96
Tenderloin, trimmed, roasted	240	13 S	4	98
Tenderloin, untrimmed, prime cut, broiled	363	26 S	11	98
Top loin, trimmed, select cut, broiled	217	9 S	3	87
Top loin, untrimmed, prime cut	387	29 S	12	91
Top round, trimmed, broiled	218	7	3	96
Top round, untrimmed, prime cut, braised	271	13 S	5	97

PORK

	Calories	Fat (g)	Saturated Fat (g)	Cholesterol (mg)
Bacon, 3 strips	109	9 S	3	16
Bologna, 1-oz slice	70	6 S	2	14
Canadian bacon, grilled, 4 oz	211	9 S	3	66
Ham, fresh, trimmed, roasted, 4 oz	251	13 S	4	107

	Calories	Fat (g)	Saturated Fat (g)	Cholesterol (mg)
Ham, fresh, untrimmed, roasted, 4 oz	336	22 S	9	106
Pork loin, trimmed, roasted, 4 oz	274	16 S	5	102
Sausage, Italian, cooked, 4 oz	369	31 S	10	89

VEGETABLES AND JUICES

	Calories	Fat (g)	Saturated Fat (g)	Cholesterol (mg)		Calories	Fat (g)	Saturated Fat (g)	Cholesterol (mg)
Artichoke, cooked, 1 cup	55	0	0	0	Peppers, sweet, raw, 1	20	0	0	0
Asparagus, cooked,					Potatoes, baked with skin,				
4 spears	15	0	0	0	1 large	220	0	0	0
Beans, snap, cooked, 1 cup	45	0	0	0	Potatoes, french fried,				
Bean sprouts, raw, 1 cup,	30	0	0	0	in vegetable oil, 2 oz	160	8S	3	0
Beets, cooked, 1 cup	55	0	0	0	Potatoes, mashed, with milk,				
Broccoli, cooked, 1 cup	45	0	0	0	and margarine, 1 cup	225	9	2	4
Brussels sprouts, cooked,					Potato salad, with				
1 cup	60	1	0	0	mayonnaise, 1 cup	360	21	170	4
Cabbage, raw, 1 cup,	15	0	0	0	Pumpkin, canned, 1 cup	85	1	0	0
Carrot, raw, 1 medium,	30	0	0	0	Sauerkraut, 1 cup	45	2	0	0
Cauliflower, cooked, 1 cup	30	0	0	0	Spinach, raw, 1 cup	10	0	0	0
Celery, 1 stalk	5	0	0	0	Squash, summer, cooked,				
Corn, cooked, 1 cup,	135	0	0	0	1 cup	35	1	0	0
Cucumber, 6 large slices	5	0	0	0	Sweet potatoes, baked,				
Eggplant, cooked, 1 cup	25	0	0	0	1 medium	115	0	0	0
Jerusalem artichoke,					Tomatoes, canned, 1 cup	50	1	0	0
raw, 1 cup,	115	0	0	0	Tomatoes, raw 1 medium	25	0	0	0
Kale, cooked, 1 cup	40	1	0	0	Tomato juice, 1 cup	40	0	0	0
Lettuce, 1 cup	10	0	0	0	Tomato paste, ¼ cup	55	1	0	0
Mushrooms, raw, 1 cup	20	0	0	0	Tomato sauce, 1 cup	75	0	0	0
Okra, 8 pods	25	0	0	0	Turnips, cooked, 1 cup	30	0	0	0
Onions, chopped, ¼ cup	14	0	0	0	Vegetable juice cocktail,				
Parsnips, cooked, 1 cup	125	0	0	0	1 cup	45	0	0	0
Peas, cooked, 1 cup	125	0	0	0	Water chestnuts, 1 cup	70	0	0	0

FRUITS AND JUICES

	Calories	Fat (g)	Saturated Fat (g)	Cholesterol (mg)		Calories	Fat (g)	Saturated Fat (g)	Cholesterol (mg)
Apple, 1 medium	80	0	0	0	Grapes, 10	35	0	0	0
Apple juice, 1 cup	115	0	0	0	Grape juice, 1 cup	155	0	0	0
Applesauce, unsweetened,					Honeydew melon,				
1 cup	105	0	0	0	4-oz slice	45	0	0	0
Apricots, 3	50	0	0	0	Kiwi, 1	45	0	0	0
Apricots, canned in juice,					Nectarines, 1 medium	65	1	0	0
1 cup	120	0	0	0	Orange, 1 medium	60	0	0	0
Apricots, dried, 5 medium					Orange juice, 1 cup	110	0	0	0
halves	42	0	0	0	Peaches, 1 medium	35	0	0	0
Avocado, 1 medium	305	30 S	5	0	Peaches, canned in juice,				
Banana, 1 medium	105	1	0	0	1 cup	110	0	0	0
Blackberries, 1 cup	75	1	0	0	Pear, 1 medium	120	1	0	0
Blueberries, 1 cup	80	1	0	0	Pineapple, fresh, 1 cup	75	1	0	0
Cantaloupe, ½	95	1	0	0	Pineapple, canned in juice,				
Cherries, 10	50	1	0	0	2 slices	70	0	0	0
Cranberry juice cocktail,					Pineapple juice, 1 cup	140	0	0	0
1 cup	145	0	0	0	Plums, 1 medium	35	0	0	0
Cranberry sauce, canned,					Prunes, 5	115	0	0	0
1 cup	420	0	0	0	Prune juice, 1 cup	180	0	0	0
Dates, 5	115	0	0	0	Raisins, 1 oz	80	0	0	0
Figs, 5	238	1	0	0	Raspberries, 1 cup	60	1	0	0
Grapefruit, ½ medium	40	0	0	0	Strawberries, whole, 1 cup	45	1	0	0
Grapefruit juice,					Tangerines, 1 medium	35	0	0	0
unsweetened, 1 cup	95	0	0	0	Watermelon, diced, 1 cup	50	1	0	0

NUTS AND SEEDS

	Calories	Fat (g)	Saturated Fat (g)	Cholesterol (mg)		Calories	Fat (g)	Saturated Fat (g)	Cholesterol (mg)
Almonds, 1 oz	165	15	1	0	Peanuts, roasted in oil, 1 oz	165	14 S	2	0
Cashews, dry roasted, 1 oz	165	13 S	3	0	Peanut butter, 2 tbsp	190	16 S	3	0
Chestnuts, roasted, 1 oz	69	1	0	0	Pecans, 1 oz	190	19	2	0
Coconut, dried, shredded,					Pistachios, 1 oz	165	14	2	0
sweetened, 1 oz	143	10 S	8	0	Sesame seeds, 1 tbsp	45	4 S	1	0
Hazelnuts, 1 oz	180	18	1	0	Sunflower seeds, 1 oz	160	14	2	0
Macadamia, roasted in oil,					Walnuts, 1 oz	170	16	2	0
1 oz	205	22 S	3	0					

SWEETS AND SNACKS

	Calories	Fat (g)	Saturated Fat (g)	Cholesterol (mg)		Calories	Fat (g)	Saturated Fat (g)	Cholesterol (mg)
Cakes (2-oz slice)					**Frozen desserts**				
Angel food	125	0	0	0	Ice cream, ½ cup	135	7 S	4	30
Coffee cake	180	5	1	28	Ice cream, premium, ½ cup	175	12 S	7	44
Devil's food, with chocolate					Ice milk, ½ cup	92	3 S	2	9
frosting	191	6 S	3	28	Sherbet, ½ cup	135	2	1	7
Gingerbread	156	4	1	0	Sorbet, ½ cup	100	0	0	0
Carrot, with cream cheese					Fruit and juice bars	70	0	0	0
frosting	225	12	2	43					
Cheesecake	170	11 S	6	103	**Pies** (2-oz slice)				
					Apple	146	6 S	2	0
Candy (1 oz)					Blueberry	137	6	1	0
Caramels	115	3 S	2	1	Custard	119	6 S	2	61
Chocolate, milk, with					Lemon meringue	142	6 S	2	57
almonds	150	10 S	5	5	Pecan	230	13	2	38
Fudge	115	3 S	2	1	Pumpkin	115	6 S	2	39
Jelly beans	105	0	0	0					
Marshmallows	90	0	0	0	**Puddings**				
					Chocolate, ½ cup	150	4 S	2	15
Condiments					Custard, baked, 1 cup	305	15 S	7	278
Chocolate topping, fudge					Rice, ½ cup	155	4 S	2	15
type, 2 tbsp	125	5 S	3	0	Tapioca, ½ cup	145	4 S	2	14
Jam or jelly, 1 tbsp	55	0	0	0					
Honey, 1 tbsp	65	0	0	0	**Snack foods**				
Maple syrup, 2 tbsp	122	0	0	0	Cheese puffs, 1 oz	160	10	4	TK
					Popcorn, 1 cup, air popped	30	0	0	0
Cookies					Popcorn, popped in oil,				
Chocolate chip, 4 small	185	11 S	4	18	with 1 tbsp butter, 1 cup	155	15 S	8	31
Fig bars, 4	210	4	1	27	Potato chips, 1 oz	150	10	3	0
Oatmeal raisin, 4	245	10	3	2	Pretzels, 1 oz	110	1	0	0
Peanut butter, 4	245	14 S	4	22	Tortilla chips, 1 oz	150	8	1	0
Shortbread, 4	155	8 S	3	27					
Vanilla wafers, 4	74	3	1	10					

FAST FOOD

	Calories	Fat (g)	Saturated Fat (g)	Cholesterol (mg)		Calories	Fat (g)	Saturated Fat (g)	Cholesterol (mg)
Cheeseburger, single,					French fries, fried in veg-				
plain, on bun	320	15 S	6	50	etable oil, regular order	235	12 S	4	0
Cheeseburger, 2 patties,					Hamburger, single, plain,				
with condiments, on					on bun	275	12 S	4	36
double-decker bun	649	35 S	103	13	Pancakes, with butter				
Chicken, fried, dark meat,					and syrup	519	14	6	57
2 pieces	430	27 S	7	165	Pizza, cheese, one slice	109	3	1	7
English muffin, with egg,					Potato, baked, with cheese				
cheese, Canadian bacon	383	20 S	9	234	sauce and broccoli	402	21 S	9	20
Fish sandwich, with tartar					Roast beef sandwich, plain	346	14	4	52
sauce	431	23	5	55	Salad, tossed, with chicken	105	4	1	72

Should children follow a low-fat diet?

Cardiologists generally agree that limiting a child's fat intake *from age two onward* will help reduce the odds against eventually developing coronary heart disease. Since the average American is estimated to have one chance in three of a significant cardiovascular event (such as a heart attack or stroke) before age sixty, prevention is important.

The major symptoms of clogged coronary arteries seldom become manifest until adulthood. However, the fatty streaks and fibrous plaques that are probable precursors of atherosclerosis can appear in early childhood. Autopsies of young soldiers killed in battle during World War II and the Korean and Vietnam conflicts often revealed a significant accumulation of coronary plaque. It is estimated that 5

Lower-Fat Substitutes

Instead of eating:	Substitute:	To save:
1 croissant	1 plain bagel	35 calories, 10 grams fat
1 whole egg	1 egg white	65 calories, 6 grams fat
1 oz cheddar cheese	1 oz part-skim mozzarella	43 calories, 4 grams fat
1 oz cream cheese	1 oz cottage cheese (1% fat)	74 calories, 9 grams fat
1 tbsp whipping cream	1 tbsp evaporated skim milk, whipped	32 calories, 5 grams fat
4 oz skinless roast duck	4 oz skinless roast chicken	53 calories, 8 grams fat
4 oz beef tenderloin, choice, untrimmed, broiled	4 oz beef tenderloin, select, trimmed, broiled	86 calories, 11 grams fat
4 oz lamb chop, untrimmed, broiled	4 oz lean leg of lamb, trimmed, broiled	250 calories, 32 grams fat
4 oz pork spareribs, cooked	4 oz lean pork loin, trimmed, broiled	180 calories, 18 grams fat
1 oz regular bacon, cooked	1 oz Canadian bacon, cooked	111 calories, 12 grams fat
1 oz hard salami	1 oz extra-lean roasted ham	75 calories, 8 grams fat
1 beef frankfurter	1 chicken frankfurter	67 calories, 8 grams fat
4 oz oil-pack tuna, light	4 oz water-pack tuna, light	76 calories, 7 grams fat
1 regular-size serving fast-food french fries	1 medium-size baked potato	125 calories, 11 grams fat
1 oz oil-roasted peanuts	1 oz roasted chestnuts	96 calories, 13 grams fat
1 oz potato chips	1 oz thin pretzels	40 calories, 9 grams fat
1 oz corn chips	1 oz plain air-popped popcorn	125 calories, 9 grams fat
1 tbsp sour cream dip	1 tbsp bottled salsa	20 calories, 3 grams fat
1 glazed doughnut	2-oz slice angel food cake	110 calories, 13 grams fat
3 chocolate sandwich cookies	3 fig bar cookies*	4 grams fat
1 oz unsweetened chocolate	3 tbsp cocoa powder	73 calories, 13 grams fat
1 cup ice cream (premium)	1 cup sorbet	150 calories, 24 grams fat

Fig bar cookies have 15 more calories.

Most packaged microwave popcorn contains as much fat (partially hydrogenated soybean, cottonseed, or coconut oil) per ounce as most cookies, along with more than twice as many calories as conventional popcorn. It's also high in sodium. Make your own at home using a hot-air or microwave popper, which requires no oil, and use the salt-shaker sparingly.

percent of all five- to fourteen-year-olds in the United States have blood cholesterol levels above 200 mg/dl.

All high-risk children—those with a parent who develops any form of cardiovascular disease before age fifty-five or a parent who has high blood cholesterol that is not controllable by diet—should have a cholesterol test. The American Health Foundation and some pediatricians recommend routine testing of all children between the ages of two and five to get a baseline cholesterol reading.

You should limit fat intake to 30 percent of the total calories in a child's diet (over age two), with less than 10 percent of daily calories coming from saturated fat. Cholesterol intake should be no more than a hundred milligrams for each 1,000 calories consumed, not to exceed three hundred milligrams a day.

The overall diet must, of course, be nutritionally balanced, and its total calorie count adjusted to your child's growth rate so as to maintain a desirable body weight. Restricting the fat will help overweight children lose unwanted pounds, but that is not the diet's primary purpose.

More important, the diet is likely to produce a small, but noticeable, decrease (10 percent on average) in your child's cholesterol level. Best of all, the diet can start your child on a long life of healthful eating habits.

How to cut down on fat

These tips will help you reduce your intake of fat—especially saturated fat:

•Read labels carefully to determine both the amount and type of fats in packaged foods you buy. To determine the number of calories that come from fat, multiply the grams of fat in a serving by nine. Then divide this number by the total calories in the serving to get the percentage of calories coming from fats.

•Substitute fish or chicken (preferably light meat, skinless) for some red meat.

•Eat more meatless meals. Use vegetables or grains as the main dish.

•Select lean meats and eat smaller portions (three to five ounces). Trim off all visible fat.

•Use skim or low-fat milk and milk products.

•Limit your intake of fats and oils, particularly those high in saturated fat, such as butter, cream, lard, heavily hydrogenated fats (some margarines), shortenings, and foods containing coconut or palm oil. Choose a margarine that has at least twice as much polyunsaturated fat as saturated.

•Broil, bake, or boil foods instead of frying them in fat.

•Moderate your use of fat-laden snack foods, such as potato chips and corn chips as well as cookies, cakes, and pastries.

Red meat, poultry, and fish provide about 34 percent of the fat in the American diet. Dairy products and eggs contribute about 15 percent. The bulk of fat—44 percent—comes from vegetable oils, shortening, butter, and margarine.

Protein

Much has been said about protein in our diets—that we need it (as of course we do), that athletes should load up on it, that not all proteins are created equal, that we eat too much protein and should therefore cut down our consumption of meat and dairy products and fall back on fruits and vegetables to maintain ourselves. How much protein do we need to be healthy?

The basic component: amino acids

Aptly enough, the word "protein" is derived from a Greek root meaning "of first importance," and protein—which constitutes about one-fifth of an adult's body weight—is the basic material of life. Muscles, organs, bones, cartilage, skin, antibodies, some hormones, and all enzymes (the compounds that direct chemical reactions in cells) are made of protein.

Yet protein is not a single, simple substance, but a multitude of chemical combinations. The basic structure of protein is actually a chain of amino acids that can form many different configurations and can combine with other substances. Twenty-two amino acids have been identified in the proteins of the human body. The possible arrangements can be almost infinite, and tens of thousands of different proteins have been identified.

Proteins are constantly being broken down in our bodies. Most of the amino acids are reused, but we must continually replace some of those that are lost. This process is known as protein turnover. Our need to keep this process going begins at conception and lasts throughout life. Without dietary protein, growth and all bodily functions would not take place.

While plants and some bacteria can manufacture all the amino acids they need, the human body can manufacture only thirteen. The amino acids we can make are known, somewhat confusingly, as the "nonessential" amino acids. They are in fact essential, but not as part of our diet. The nine "essential" amino acids are those we have to eat. They are histidine, isoleucine, leucine, lysine, methionine, phenylalanine, threonine, tryptophan, and valine. We can either get them from plant protein directly or by eating animals that consume plants and animals.

When we eat foods containing protein, the digestive system breaks it down to the constituent amino acids, which enter the body "pool" of amino acids. Each cell then assembles the proteins it needs using the building blocks available. If, however, one or more of the needed amino acids is in short supply or not available at all, others that may be on hand cannot be utilized to form a protein. This is why it is important to eat a diet that contains all of the essential amino acids plus enough additional amino acids to allow for synthesis of the "nonessential" amino acids.

Getting complete protein

Nutritionists use the phrases "complete protein" and "incomplete protein" to describe the proteins provided by various foods. If a food supplies a sufficient amount of the nine essential amino acids, it is called a complete protein. Virtually all proteins from animal foods are complete. Foods that lack or are short on one or more of the essential amino acids—such as some fruits, grains, and vegetables—are called incomplete proteins. Such plant-derived foods can nonetheless be excellent sources of protein if eaten in combinations that supply all of the essential amino acids. For example, the amino acids missing in a vegetable can be provided by eating a grain product, another vegetable, or an animal-derived protein at the same meal. (If you are eating adequate amounts of protein generally, the complementary foods can be eaten within a few hours of each other and still supply complete protein.)

Bread, a staple of the human diet for thousands of years, is rich in the amino acid methionine, but low in lysine. Legumes are rich in lysine, but poor in methionine; when legumes and bread are eaten together, however, you get a complete protein. That lunch box favorite the peanut butter sandwich is an example of this complementarity. The peanuts provide the amino acids that the grain lacks, and vice versa. Without understanding the chemical reasons for what they were doing, cooks the world over have come up with complementary combinations of proteins: beans or peas or lentils and rice; beans and brown bread or cornbread; corn and lima beans. Most of the diets in the world contribute adequate amino acids and protein; an exception is a diet based mostly on tubers (such as sweet potato or manioc), common in some parts of Africa.

Animal vs. vegetable

That meat and other animal products are the most readily available sources of complete protein is perhaps the reason why humans have been such ardent hunters and fishers, as well as domesticators of animals. The protein content, by weight, of cooked meat, fish, poultry, and milk solids is between 15 and 40 percent. The protein content of cooked cereals, beans, lentils, and peas ranges from 3 to 10 percent. Potatoes, fruits, and leafy green vegetables come in at 3 percent or lower. Soybeans and nuts have a protein content comparable to meat, but, depending upon how they are prepared, their proteins may not be as easily digested. However, recent

Beans provide nearly as much protein as meat, and are much lower in fat and calories. One cup of cooked beans contains 12 to 25 grams of protein, which is 25 to 50 percent of the RDA.

Protein Requirements

The body cannot store protein, so it needs a fresh supply every day. The Food and Nutrition Board of the National Academy of Sciences has established a daily Recommended Dietary Allowance (RDA) for protein based on a person's age and weight. According to the Academy, because most people in the United States eat meat and dairy products regularly, the average protein intake is higher than what most people need. So you should easily meet the following RDAs:

•The RDA for adults is 0.8 grams of protein for each kilogram (2.2 pounds) of body weight. This works out to 44 grams for a 120-pound person, 55 grams of protein for a weight of 150-pounds, and 66 grams for 180 pounds. These allowances assume that you eat a mixed diet of proteins—some high-quality (complete), some low-quality (incomplete).

•If, like most Americans, you consume mostly high-quality protein, your total requirement will therefore be *slightly* less. If you get almost all your protein from plant sources, it will be *slightly* greater. The variation due to the type of diet is no more than approximately 15 percent.

•Children under eighteen need some additional protein to allow for growth, and the younger they are, the more protein they need per pound of body weight.

•Pregnant women are allocated an additional 10 grams of protein per day by the RDA, lactating mothers an extra 12 to 15 grams during the first six months.

research suggests that in a mixed or even totally vegetarian diet, the issue of digestibility is not too important. For someone eating a whole grain and vegetable diet, no more than 15 percent of the protein consumed would be unavailable because of problems with digestibility.

The fact that we are omnivorous, that is, we can eat both meats and plants, has contributed to the survival of the human species. But as anthropologists have pointed out, human beings have overwhelmingly preferred meat to other foods, when they could get it. And a number of experts attribute the general good health, increased height, and longevity of people of developed countries today to their high-protein diets (this theory, however, ignores other important environmental factors that have led to improved health).

Other authorities regard American's meat eating as excessive, since it is a source of saturated fat, which may contribute to coronary heart disease, cancer, and stroke. Moreover, a diet high in animal protein—the typical diet for adult Americans—increases the loss of calcium in the body (though no long-term studies have been done to indicate whether a habitual high-protein intake increases the risk of osteoporosis.) Another potential problem with such a high-protein diet is the strain it puts on the kidneys in having to excrete extra waste products from the protein breakdown.

Fortunately, nutritionists have found that adding even small amounts of animal protein to plant foods can boost their protein quality—for example, using a light meat sauce on spaghetti, sprinkling cheese on macaroni, or adding half a cup of milk to breakfast cereal.

Can extra protein make you stronger?

The cells of muscles, tendons, and ligaments have to be maintained with protein. Hemoglobin, which carries oxygen through the bloodstream, is a protein. Given these physiological facts, many people try to eat more protein in their quest for a stronger body or to improve athletic performance. Others actually want to add poundage, preferably in the form of muscle. In the old days, in their quest for added protein, athletes were likely to wolf down T-bone steaks or drink raw eggs. Today they often turn to high-tech, high-protein powders, liquids, tablets, wafers, capsules, and bars.

Don't swallow such claims: they have not been supported by studies on athletes. A basic understanding of how protein works in the body helps explain why. Protein is indeed needed to build and maintain not only muscles but all cells in the body. But consuming more protein won't by itself stimulate muscle growth. Excess protein simply breaks down in the body and is burned for energy (though carbohydrates and fats are the main energy sources) or, if not used, is most likely converted to fat. Thus, though many people believe the more protein they eat the better, this is simply not true.

Besides protein, the supplements usually contain isolated amino acids, vitamins and minerals, and sometimes more exotic ingredients such as ginseng and bee pollen. These products' protein sources include whey, soy, egg white, gelatin, yeast, and nonfat dry milk. Most contain thirteen to twenty-three grams of protein per dose, as much as two or three ounces of chicken or other meat, though some tablets and wafers have only a few grams of protein. While some of the supplements claim that their isolated amino acids are better absorbed by the body than

Supplements for athletes often tout hydrolyzed protein—a type of pre-digested protein that has been broken apart into small fragments called peptides and amino acids. While hydrolyzed protein can simplify digestion for people with certain digestive diseases or metabolic disorders, healthy individuals do not need hydrolyzed protein; it does not enhance the protein quality of foods, nor does it help build strength or endurance.

Sources of Protein

The foods below are all good sources of protein. The listed protein amounts are averages. Many foods that are relatively high in protein are also high in fat, so the chart indicates the percentage of fat accompanying each food. Try to limit your intake of protein sources that derive more than 30 percent of their calories from fat.

	Protein (g)	Fat Calories
Dairy and eggs		
Cheddar cheese, 1 oz	7	70%
Cottage cheese		
(2% milk fat), ½ cup	16	17%
Egg, 1 medium	6	68%
Ice cream, hard, vanilla,		
½ cup	2	48%
Milk, skim, 1 cup*	8	5%
Mozzarella, part skim,1 oz*	8	56%
Ricotta, part skim, ½ cup*	10	53%
Yogurt, low-fat, plain		
1 cup*	12	25%
Meat and fish (4 oz)		
Chicken, light meat,		
roasted, no skin	31	26%
Ground beef,		
extra lean, broiled	33	56%
Sirloin steak, choice cut,		
trimmed, broiled	35	37%
Tuna, canned, in water	33	12%
Turkey breast,		
roasted, no skin	24	6%
Grains		
Oatmeal, 1 cup cooked	6	12%
Rice, brown,		
1 cup cooked	5	4%
Spaghetti, 1 cup cooked	6	5%
Whole wheat bread,		
2 slices	6	13%
Legumes and nuts		
Almonds, 1 oz	6	82%
Cashews, dry roasted,1 oz	4	71%
Lentils, ½ cup cooked	8	4%
Lima beans,		
½ cup cooked	8	3%
Peanut butter, 2 tbsp	10	76%
Red kidney beans,		
½ cup canned	8	4%
Soybeans, ½ cup cooked	10	38%
Tofu, 4 oz	9	55%

Low-fat dairy products often contain added milk solids, which increase the protein content slightly.

whole protein, healthy individuals have no problem digesting and absorbing the amino acids from whole protein. Furthermore, consuming large quantities of isolated amino acids is not advised, since the body needs a balanced mixture of amino acids in order to synthesize protein. The excessive intake of a single amino acid may interfere with the absorption of other amino acids and as a result inhibit protein synthesis.

The one promise the supplements *are* likely to deliver on is weight gain, since they are meant to be consumed in addition to your regular food, and many of them are calorie-dense. Consumed as directed in two glasses of whole milk, some powders can add more than 1,000 calories a day to your diet. The weight you gain will probably be mostly fat, however, unless you start to exercise more. *Only strength-building exercise, not supplements, builds muscles.* Excessive amounts of protein offer no benefits whatsoever, but can produce serious negative effects, chiefly dehydration, diarrhea, and calcium loss, and may aggravate liver or kidney disease as well.

Other claims

Numerous claims have been made for the curative powers of various amino acids, and some are sold over-the-counter in drugstores and health food stores. One amino acid, lysine, has been touted as a treatment for herpes. Another, argenine, has been featured as a "growth hormone releaser" that makes you lose weight as you sleep. Probably the most widely used amino acid supplement is L-tryptophan, which has been taken by millions of Americans in recent years. Some researchers have suggested that this amino acid relieves insomnia, but scientific studies are still inconclusive in that regard. In fact, there is absolutely no scientific evidence to back up any of the claims for amino acid supplements. Moreover, unlike most vitamin supplements, for instance, amino acid pills are not on the Food and Drug Administration's Generally Recognized as Safe (GRAS) list. In fact, in December, 1989 the FDA halted all sales of L-tryptophan—and products in which it's listed as a major ingredient—because of the development of a blood disease in some people taking as little as one gram a day. Called eosinophilia-myalgia, the disease causes muscle pain and an abnormally high count of one type of white blood cell. It can result in high fever, weakness, joint pain, swelling of the arms or legs, rashes, shortness of breath, and death. As a general rule, taking amino acid supplements is unnecessary and potentially unhealthy, unless there is a deficiency in the digestive system. Studies with animals have shown that abnormally large intakes of amino acids can create imbalances of those substances in the body.

A normal diet: more than enough protein

You need adequate protein intake to build muscles, but if you eat a normal, balanced diet, it is hard not to get enough protein. Even strict vegetarians get enough of it if they eat grains and vegetables in proper quantities and combinations. Government surveys show that the typical American consumes about one hundred grams of protein per day, nearly twice as much as the Recommended Dietary Allowance (see box on page 106). For most people, five ounces of fish or meat supplies more than half the RDA, for instance, and two cups of milk would take care of the rest. In general, the RDA is easily met when 12 to 15 percent of your total caloric intake comes from protein.

Regardless of how much they exercise, even professional athletes do not need to go out of their way to consume extra protein. Recent studies suggest that some endurance athletes or heavy-duty weight lifters may need more protein than the RDA, but since they are usually consuming more calories, they get the extra protein with little trouble. Say, for instance, a body builder or wrestler consumes 4,000 calories a day; if 12 percent of these come from protein, he's consuming a whopping 120 grams of protein, much more than enough for any exercise regimen.

Since the only way to build muscle is to exercise, you should therefore eat the same healthful diet recommended for everybody—one high in complex carbohydrates (bread, cereal, pasta, fruits, and vegetables) and low in fat (poultry, fish, lean meat, and low-fat dairy products). If you're trying to gain weight, just eat larger meals plus additional healthful snacks.

Four ounces of dry pasta provides about 20 percent of the RDA for protein, as much as two large eggs. And some high-protein pastas have twice that much.

Vitamins

A vitamin is an organic substance that your body requires to help regulate metabolic functions within cells. Only very tiny amounts of vitamins are needed to carry out these functions—and, as a general rule, your body cannot manufacture vitamins, so nearly all come from food.

Myths abound concerning the health benefits of vitamins. Indeed, vitamin supplements may be the most misunderstood, and misused, substances in the realm of health. Between 35 and 40 percent of American adults take vitamin supplements, but the simple truth is that a healthy person who eats a well-balanced diet has no need for vitamin supplements: regular meals that include fresh vegetables, fruit, whole-grain cereals, fish, lean meats, and low-fat dairy products provide all of the vitamins a normal person needs for good health.

Taking extra vitamins in the form of supplements will not make a person live longer, give you a better sex life, or make you a better athlete, despite all the claims. The continuing hoopla over vitamins has inspired thousands of careful scientific studies, and in almost every case researchers have found that vitamins simply cannot perform the miracles that some people say they will.

What vitamins do

Vitamins are absolutely essential to life. Among the myriad tasks they perform are: promoting good vision, forming normal blood cells, creating strong bones and teeth, and ensuring the proper functioning of the heart and nervous system. While vitamins themselves do not supply energy, some do aid in the efficient conversion of foods into energy. The consensus among scientists is that there are thirteen vitamins needed by humans: A, C, D, E, K, and eight vitamins often referred to as the B-complex—thiamine, riboflavin, niacin, B_6, pantothenic acid, biotin, folacin, and B_{12}. These can be categorized as either fat-soluble (A, D, E, K) or water-soluble (the B vitamins and vitamin C). The distinction is important because the body stores fat-soluble vitamins for relatively long periods (usually in the liver and in fat tissue), whereas water-soluble vitamins, which are stored in various tissues, remain in the body for only a short time; symptoms associated with a deficiency of water-soluble vitamins can occur within weeks to several months if the vitamins are not replenished.

Each vitamin carries out specific functions, and if a certain vitamin is lacking or is improperly used by the body, a particular deficiency disease usually results. In such cases vitamins *have* worked miracles. Vitamin C has cured scurvy; vitamin A has cured night blindness; B vitamins have restored stamina and alleviated mental disturbances—but *only* when the lack of these vitamins in the diet was the cause in the first place.

Recommended intakes

There are two sets of guidelines for daily vitamin consumption. The Recommended Dietary Allowances (RDAs), published by the Food and Nutrition Board of the National Research Council and revised periodically, are generally used by most nutritionists. The U.S. Recommended Daily Allowances (U.S. RDAs), an older and simplified version of the RDA, are the official standards used on food labels, which usually cite vitamin content by listing the percentages of the U.S. RDA that a food provides. The differences between the RDA and the U.S. RDA are minimal: whereas the RDA gives specific guidelines for men, women, different age groups, and pregnant or lactating women, the U.S. RDA gives one set of guidelines for all people over age four (except pregnant or lactating women).

Both sets of guidelines have been the cause of some confusion since surveys have shown that many Americans do not consume enough vitamins to meet these guidelines—a fact that vitamin manufacturers and advertisers have seized upon. Actually both these sets of guidelines were deliberately set high so that there would be a comfortable margin of nutritional safety: the majority of Americans probably do not need the amounts of vitamins specified in these guidelines. If the amounts actually needed are not met, the risk of deficiency does increase. But if Americans really were seriously deficient in vitamins, there would be rampant deficiency diseases, such as pellagra, beriberi, scurvy, and night blindness.

Who needs vitamin supplements?

People rarely *need* vitamin supplements. Even so, supplements have been viewed as the lazy man's path to good nutrition: busy people who skip breakfast and grab a fast-food lunch think they can take a nutritional shortcut—a couple of vitamin pills. In fact, though, vitamins work with other nutrients in food; they cannot replace food or necessarily turn a junk-food diet into a healthy one.

Certain groups may be prone to vitamin deficiencies, but in many cases these needs can be met through a normal diet. You should seek nutritional advice if you fall within one of these groups:

Pregnant women. These women need more vitamins than other adults, but not megadoses. According to the RDAs, pregnant women should get 15 to 50 percent more vitamins each day (but 100 percent more vitamin D and folacin). Some physicians recommend supplements during pregnancy, though a woman can generally meet her increased vitamin needs through a good diet. Vitamin megadoses have been linked to severe birth defects. If a pregnant woman takes megadoses of vitamin C, her baby could be born with a dependence on large amounts of C and develop scurvy when he gets only the normal amount in his food. Recent research indicates that vitamin supplements containing folic acid can decrease the incidence of neurological tube defects (for example, spinal bifida). This is probably due to a low intake of folic acid in the American diet.

The elderly. Some elderly people may need supplements because they reduce their consumption of foods that are good sources of vitamins.

Frequent aspirin takers. Aspirin interferes with the metabolism of vitamin C and folacin, so people who take aspirin regularly—arthritis sufferers, for example—should ask their physicians about supplements.

Heavy drinkers. Heavy alcohol consumption often depletes B vitamins and vitamin C in the body.

Smokers. People who smoke appear to use up vitamin C at a faster rate than nonsmokers. A committee of the National Academy of Sciences recommends that the RDA for smokers be 100 milligrams (as compared to 60 milligrams for non-

Myth: Vitamin B_{12} shots give energy.

Fact: Doctors who administer B_{12} shots to make their patients "feel better" are either misinformed or practicing bad medicine. B_{12} is vital for life and health—among other key functions, it controls essential processes in all tissue cells and acts to maintain bone marrow. But you need it only in minute amounts.

A deficiency of B_{12} is usually caused by an inability to absorb the vitamin from food because the stomach can't secrete a substance essential to the absorption. People suffering from this disorder, known as pernicious anemia, must receive B_{12} in regular injections. Since one sign of B_{12} deficiency is a feeling of weakness, the notion somehow arose that B_{12} injections, popularly called "liver shots," could buck up weary people and make them feel vigorous.

B_{12} will not alleviate ordinary fatigue, cure an iron deficiency, or make a person feel "up to par."

Vitamins: Facts and Myths

Vitamin/Food Sources	What It Does	Myths
Vitamin A. Liver, eggs, fortified milk, carrots, tomatoes, apricots, cantaloupe, fish.	Promotes good vision; helps form and maintain healthy skin and mucous membranes; may protect against some cancers.	Cures cancer; enhances normal vision; promotes smooth, youthful skin.
Vitamin C. Citrus fruits, strawberries, tomatoes.	Promotes healthy gums, capillaries, and teeth; aids iron absorption; may block production of nitrosamines; maintains normal connective tissue; aids in healing wounds.	Prevents or cures cancer; reduces cholesterol and protects against heart disease; prevents allergies; cures a wide range of infections; cures arthritis.
Vitamin D. Fortified milk; fish; also produced by the body in response to sunlight.	Promotes strong bones and teeth; necessary for absorption of calcium.	Cures arthritis.
Vitamin E. Nuts, vegetable oils, whole grains, olives, asparagus, spinach.	Protects tissue against oxidation; important in formation of red blood cells; helps body use vitamin K.	Prevents or alleviates coronary heart disease; enhances sexual performance; improves muscle strength and stamina; heals burns and wounds; slows aging.
Vitamin K. Body produces about half of daily needs; cauliflower, broccoli, cabbage, spinach, cereals, soybeans, beef liver.	Aids in clotting of blood.	None.
Vitamin B$_1$ (thiamine). Whole grains, dried beans, lean meats (especially pork), fish.	Helps release energy from carbohydrates; necessary for healthy brain and nerve cells and for functioning of heart.	Prevents fatigue; cures depression.
Vitamin B$_2$ (riboflavin). Nuts, dairy products, liver.	Aids in release of energy from foods; interacts with other B vitamins.	Cures baldness; improves vision.
Vitamin B$_3$ (niacin). Nuts, dairy products, liver.	Aids in release of energy from foods; involved in synthesis of DNA; maintains normal functioning of skin, nerves, and digestive system.	Fights heart disease; alleviates schizophrenia; cures depression.
Vitamin B$_5$ (pantothenic acid). Whole grains, dried beans, eggs, nuts.	Aids in the release of energy from foods; essential for synthesis of numerous body materials.	Cures allergies; helps you cope with stress; restores gray hair to normal color.
Vitamin B$_6$ (pyridoxine). Whole grains, dried beans, eggs, nuts.	Important in chemical reactions of proteins and amino acids; involved in normal functioning of brain and formation of red blood cells.	Helps arthritis; cures migraines; relieves nausea; acts as a tranquilizer; relieves nervous and muscle disorders; prevents tooth decay; lowers blood cholesterol.
Vitamin B$_{12}$. Liver, beef, eggs, milk, shellfish.	Necessary for development of red blood cells; maintains normal functioning of nervous system.	Helps nervous disorders.
Folacin. Liver, wheat bran, leafy green vegetables, beans, grains.	Important in the synthesis of DNA; acts together with B$_{12}$ in the production of hemoglobin.	Alleviates mental illness; cures anemia.
Biotin. Yeast, eggs, liver, milk.	Important in formation of fatty acids; helps metabolize amino acids and carbohydrates.	Cures baldness; alleviates muscle pain; cures dermatitis.

smoking adults). A balanced diet—indeed, even an eight-ounce glass of orange juice—easily satisfies this higher RDA.

Megadoses: do they work?

In the belief that "if a little is good, a lot is better," many people take megadoses of vitamins, particularly A, C, and E. In fact, the body requires just tiny amounts of vitamins. This is because most vitamins are coenzymes (or integral parts of coenzymes) that assist enzyme function in your body. To do this, some of them need to link up with certain proteins, called apoenzymes, to form complete enzymes. But the body produces only limited amounts of apoenzymes, so the need for vitamins is limited. If you consume such a vitamin in amounts greater than its available apoenzyme, the excess has no nutritional value and is just excreted. Taking megadoses thus does not enhance normal bodily functions.

Many people with cancer have taken extremely large doses of vitamin C in the belief that it can cure the disease. But studies, including one undertaken at the Mayo Clinic, have conclusively shown that vitamin C does not cure cancer or prolong the life of cancer victims.

There may be some truth to the belief that vitamin A—not as the preformed vitamin, but in the form of its precursor, beta carotene—and vitamin C protect against cancer: people who regularly eat foods rich in these vitamins have been found to have lower incidence of cancers of the lung, larynx, bladder, and esophagus than people who eat lesser amounts of them. In addition, Vitamin E has also been shown to have cancer-protecting properties. But no one knows if this protective effect is due to the vitamins themselves or due to other substances in these foods, although extensive studies are underway to investigate this problem. Studies have shown that it is helpful to eat nutritious foods—not to gobble large amounts of vitamin supplements.

Perhaps the most famous apostle of vitamin megadoses is Dr. Linus Pauling, whose 1970 book *Vitamin C and the Common Cold* convinced millions that megadoses of C would prevent colds, shorten their duration, or ameliorate their symptoms. Since the publication of that book, more than thirty studies have measured the effects of vitamin C and found that large doses have no capability of preventing colds and only a minimal effect on making a cold sufferer feel better faster.

Megadoses of vitamins are not only wasteful, they are potentially hazardous. For every popular report on the benefits of megadoses, the medical literature can respond with documented cases of bodily harm from large doses of vitamins. Recent studies have shown that most vitamins are toxic when taken in large doses, although the differences between the RDAs and toxic levels may vary greatly. Relying on supplements makes it all too easy to far exceed recommended levels of vitamins, whereas it's almost impossible to reach megadose levels if you get your vitamins through the foods you eat.

There is no difference between "natural" and man-made vitamins. Their chemical formulas and usability by the body are the same.

Minerals

Minerals, especially in pill form, have come in for their share of attention and miracle claims in recent years. Minerals are unquestionably essential to a host of vital processes in the body, from basic bone formation and enzyme synthesis to the regulation of the heart muscle and the normal functioning of digestion. The latest research, while not conclusive, suggests that deficiencies of certain minerals—and excess levels of others—may play a role in causing such ailments as cardiovascular disease, diabetes, high blood pressure, and cancer. Minerals taken in amounts significantly larger than the Recommended Dietary Allowances (RDAs) may in some cases do serious harm. As is true of vitamins, the best way to ensure an adequate supply of minerals is to eat a varied and balanced diet.

The essential twenty-two

Unlike the organic compounds we call vitamins, minerals are inorganic substances—that is, they do not contain carbon—that are basic constituents of the earth's crust. Carried into the soil, groundwater, and sea by erosion, they are taken up by plants and consumed by animals and humans.

While there are more than sixty different minerals in the body, those currently identified as essential number some twenty-two. Seven of these—calcium, chloride, magnesium, phosphorus, potassium, sodium, and sulfur—are generally designated as "macrominerals," or major minerals; those that are present in the healthy body in quantities exceeding 0.005 percent of body weight. The other fifteen are termed "microminerals," or trace minerals, and include chromium, copper, fluorine (fluoride), iodine, iron, manganese, molybdenum, selenium, and zinc—to name those best understood at present. Very possibly the list of recognized microminerals will grow as researchers succeed in mapping in greater detail the complex chemistry of life.

As components of the body, minerals are present in small amounts. All together, they add up to perhaps 4 percent of the body weight. But this amount is in no way indicative of the relative importance of minerals to the functioning body. The 0.00004 percent of your body that is iodine is no less critical to survival than the approximately 1.5 to 2 percent that is calcium. The key to good health lies in maintaining the proper percentages.

Recommended intakes

Precisely how much of any mineral the body needs to maintain good health is still hotly debated by experts. Consequently, there are RDAs for just seven minerals; for five others, the National Academy of Sciences makes what are more cautiously termed "estimated safe and adequate daily dietary intakes."

Because of the complex interactions between minerals and the dangers of overdosing, no one should self-prescribe mineral supplements in amounts greater than the RDAs or estimated intakes. (Too much calcium in supplement form, for exam-

Minerals: Facts and Myths

Mineral/Food Sources	What It Does	Myths
Calcium. Milk and milk products, sardines and salmon eaten with bones, dark green leafy vegetables, shellfish, hard water.	Builds bones and teeth, maintains bone density and strength; helps prevent osteoporosis; helps regulate heartbeat, blood clotting, muscle contraction, and nerve conduction.	Helps prevent insomnia and anxiety.
Chloride. Table salt, fish.	Maintains normal fluid shifts; balances blood pH; forms hydrochloric acid to aid digestion.	None.
Magnesium. Wheat bran, whole grains, raw leafy green vegetables, nuts (especially almonds and cashews), soybeans, bananas, apricots, spices.	Aids in bone growth; aids function of nerves and muscle, including regulation of normal heart rhythm.	Cures alcoholism, prostate problems, kidney stones, and heart disease.
Phosphorus. Meats, poultry, fish, cheese, egg yolks, dried peas and beans, milk and milk products, soft drinks, nuts; present in almost all foods.	Aids in bone growth and strengthening of teeth; important in energy metabolism.	Reduces stress; accelerates growth in children; helps reduce arthritis.
Potassium. Oranges and orange juice, bananas, dried fruits, peanut butter, dried peas and beans, potatoes, coffee, tea, cocoa, yogurt, molasses, meat.	Promotes regular heartbeat; active in muscle contraction; regulates transfer of nutrients to cells; controls water balance in body tissues and cells; helps regulate blood pressure.	Cures acne, alcoholism, allergies, burns, and heart disease.
Sodium. Table salt, salt added to prepared foods, baking soda.	Helps regulate water balance in body; plays a role in maintaining blood pressure.	Lowers fevers; prevents stroke.
Chromium. Meat, cheese, whole grains, dried peas and beans, peanuts.	Important for glucose metabolism; may be a cofactor for insulin.	Cures diabetes and hypoglycemia.
Copper. Shellfish, nuts, beef and pork liver, cocoa powder, chocolate, kidneys, dried beans, raisins, corn oil margarine.	Formation of red blood cells; cofactor in absorbing iron into blood cells; helps produce several respiratory enzymes.	Stimulates hair growth in bald men; relieves anemia.
Fluorine (fluoride). Fluoridated water and foods grown or cooked in it; fish, tea, gelatin.	Contributes to solid bone and tooth formation; may help prevent osteoporosis.	Causes cancer.
Iodine. Primarily from iodized salt, but also seafood, seaweed food products, vegetables grown in iodine-rich areas, vegetable oil.	Necessary for normal function of the thyroid gland and for normal cell function; keeps skin, hair, and nails healthy; prevents goiter.	Causes anemia.
Iron. Liver, kidneys, red meats, egg yolks, peas, beans, nuts, dried fruits, green leafy vegetables, enriched grain products.	Essential to formation of hemoglobin, the oxygen-carrying factor in the blood; part of several enzymes and proteins in the body.	Controls alcoholism and menstrual discomfort.
Manganese. Nuts, whole grains, vegetables, fruits, instant coffee, tea, cocoa powder, beets, egg yolks.	Required for normal bone growth and development, normal reproduction, and cell function.	Helps asthma, diabetes, sterility, and fatigue.
Molybdenum. Peas, beans, cereal grains, organ meats, some dark green vegetables.	Important for normal cell function.	None.
Selenium. Fish, shellfish, red meat, egg yolks, chicken, garlic, tuna, tomatoes.	Complements vitamin E to fight cell damage by oxygen-derived compounds.	Cures cancer and arthritis.
Zinc. Oysters, crabmeat, beef, liver, eggs, poultry, brewer's yeast, whole wheat bread.	Maintains taste and smell acuity; normal growth and sexual development; important for fetal growth and wound healing.	Relieves angina and cirrhosis.

Chelated Minerals

The term "chelation" (pronounced "key-lay-shon") comes from the Greek for "claw" because this process binds a metallic element to another substance. The chelated minerals found on more and more drugstore shelves—most often iron, zinc, magnesium, potassium, or calcium—are generally bonded to amino acids, the chemicals which are the building blocks of protein.

The manufacturers claim that by being linked to amino acids, chelated minerals are absorbed more quickly by the body. Non-chelated minerals, they say, must wait in the intestine until they are combined with amino acids, which slows their absorption. In fact, when the chelated supplement reaches the intestine, the mineral is quickly separated from the amino acids and absorbed like nonchelated minerals. There is no evidence that chelated minerals are absorbed any quicker or better than other minerals.

Take away the amino acids from chelated minerals and you have ordinary mineral supplements, which most people don't need anyway, since a varied and balanced diet provides all the minerals they need. Unless prescribed by a doctor, no one should take doses of mineral supplements greater than the RDAs or estimated safe intakes because of the complex interactions between minerals and the dangers of overdosing.

Don't confuse chelated minerals with oral chelation products. These combinations of vitamins, minerals, and amino acids have been banned by the Food and Drug Administration (FDA) as unapproved drugs.

Bananas are often mentioned as a food high in potassium, but potatoes contain nearly twice as much. One large banana has 450 milligrams of potassium, while a large baked potato with its skin contains about 850 milligrams (the skin alone has about 235 milligrams).

ple, can interfere with the absorption of iron and other minerals.) If you believe you ought to increase your mineral intake, make changes in your diet according to the chart on page 115 or get professional advice.

Some minerals—such as phosphorus, potassium and sodium—are so plentiful in the average diet that deficiencies are virtually unknown. If anything, the problem is that we consume too much of some of these minerals. Excess phosphorus, which impairs the absorption of iron, may be a problem for people who habitually consume soft drinks. Americans also tend to eat sodium excessively, contributing to high blood pressure, kidney disease, and heart disease.

Iodine deficiency, which causes goiter and other thyroid disturbances, was once a major health problem in certain inland parts of the United States where iodine was absent from the soil and thus from food crops. But the widespread use of iodized table salt and the nationwide marketing of food products from areas that do have high iodine content make iodine deficiency a rare condition in developed countries today.

Of all minerals, Americans are most likely to consume too little calcium, iron, and zinc. A lack of zinc can delay puberty, impair the healing of wounds, and decrease sensations of taste and smell. And low levels of zinc in pregnant women may lead to fetal abnormalities.

Calcium and especially iron deficiencies are more commonly found in women than in men and are frequently related to the physiological demands of childbearing and menstruation. The RDA for women for iron is higher than that for men. Moreover, the problem of maintaining adequate iron intake during pregnancy has led the National Research Council to recommend that pregnant women take iron supplements.

Sodium, Calcium, and Iron

Sodium, calcium, and iron are three minerals of particular concern in the American diet. On average, we consume too much of one (sodium), and too little of the others. This chapter explains the functions of each of these minerals and provides you with suggestions on how to alter your intake of them.

Sodium

Many people do not realize that there is some sodium in nearly everything we eat. Chemically, sodium is a metallic element, and it is usable in the human system only when it occurs in combination with another element. Its most common form is table salt (NaCl, or sodium chloride), which is actually only about 40 percent sodium. A number of unprocessed foods contain salt, but usually not in significant amounts; much of the salt that we consume we add deliberately, usually to enhance flavor. Salt is also an effective preservative, and for thousands of years salted fish and meats and brine-treated vegetables have been staples of the human diet.

How much is too much?

For a number of years many doctors and public health officials have been warning people about the dangers of consuming excessive amounts of sodium, and the public has reacted to a remarkable degree. In the last several years our intake of salty foods has fallen off by 30 percent, and the food industry—alert to this trend—is introducing an increasing number of processed foods that are lower in sodium. Yet our per capita sodium intake is still very high, between two and three times the recommended maximum daily intake of 2,400 milligrams.

The convenience foods and fast foods and snacks that Americans love are often storehouses of salt. But fast foods are not necessarily the worst culprits. A meal in the most expensive restaurant—or dinner on the airplane—may be loaded with salt. Many recipe books tell us to add salt to anything we cook. (See chart on page 121 for the sodium content of commonly eaten foods.) In addition, there is sodium in baking powder, in the flavor-enhancer MSG (monosodium glutamate), and in such widely used preservatives as sodium benzoate and sodium propionate. The milligram count goes up more if you drink beverages containing sodium saccharin or take any of dozens of over-the-counter medicines such as antacids and cough syrups. When you add up the sodium in a day's ration of liberally salted home-cooked foods and then factor in the snack foods Americans eat so casually, the sum can be staggering. What will this do to people in the long run?

In light of the broad antisodium trend that has recently emerged, it may come as a surprise to hear that there is still a debate within the scientific community about what sodium intake to recommend. Sodium intake appears to be linked with hypertension, an ailment that leads to heart attacks, strokes, and kidney failure. Yet, of the 18 percent of the population with hypertension (and another 12 percent with borderline hypertension), only about half are sufficiently sensitive to sodium that they can be adversely affected by a high salt intake. A number of experts therefore believe that the majority of people do not need to reduce their sodium intake. So, they ask, why badger them about it?

On the other side of the question are arrayed equally respected experts who maintain that sodium is used to dangerous excess in our modern diet. They add that even though some people may never be made ill by a high salt intake, all of us must be cautious.

Need vs. craving

Sodium is not merely a flavor enhancer; it is a mineral essential to health. Sodium permeates the body. All cells in the body are bathed in a fluid that maintains cell function; this fluid contains particles that are mostly (90 to 95 percent) sodium salts. The ratio of particles to fluid determines the fluid balance of the entire body. If the body is retaining more sodium, it must also retain more water to maintain a proper particle/fluid ratio.

The body's daily requirement for sodium varies with each individual, but in any case the amount is quite small. The minimum sodium requirement is about 115 milligrams per day—roughly the amount of sodium in one-twentieth of a teaspoon of salt. The National Academy of Sciences recommends a minimum daily sodium intake of about 500 milligrams to maintain good health (though if you are sweating profusely, your intake may need to be higher).

In a healthy body many organs interact to regulate the amount of sodium in the system. The chief monitors are the kidneys, adrenal glands, heart, and brain. They do their job with amazing efficiency and accuracy. Although your sodium intake may vary from day to day, the amount of sodium in your body generally does not vary by more than 2 percent. Your regulatory system will conserve sodium if you need it and excrete it if you have an excess. However, the total amount of sodium in the body can be influenced significantly by substantial changes in diet, climate, or level of physical activity.

Saltwater fish are generally no higher in sodium than freshwater fish. Fish have an internal regulatory system that prevents their flesh from taking up sodium from the water.

Iodized Salt

Iodized table salt has been part of the American diet since the 1920s, when it was introduced to counteract a type of goiter (an enlargement of the thyroid) caused by the iodine deficiency then widespread in some parts of the country. With the advent of adding iodine to salt, goiter has nearly disappeared.

If you cut down on your salt intake, is there any reason to worry about getting enough iodine? Not really. We get our iodine from a variety of sources; in fact, only about 55 percent of the salt consumed in the United States is iodized. Iodine is widely dispersed in the food supply. It occurs in seafood and in crops grown near the seacoast, but its chief source is dairy products (cattle take it in from iodized salt licks and iodine-supplemented feed). Iodine is also used in some preparations to condition bread dough.

As a result, iodine deficiency is rare. The daily RDA is 150 micrograms, and the Food and Drug Administration's Total Diet Study shows that the average 2,900 calorie-a-day diet contains more than two-and-a-half times the RDA, excluding the use of iodized table salt. Only in the northernmost states are there truly low levels of iodine in the soil. In these areas, you may want to add a daily pinch of iodized table salt to your food—though remember that all you need is half a teaspoon of iodized salt *from all sources*, including processed foods, to meet your needs.

Flavor without Salt

People who are placed on a low-sodium diet or those who choose to cut down on salt as a sensible health precaution often complain that foods aren't as tasty as they used to be, and that salt substitutes taste bitter. But retraining your taste buds is not so difficult. Your gustatory system has resources that you may have overlooked up to now.

Combining tastes

We can distinguish only four main taste sensations—sweet, sour, salty, and bitter— which may seem like a small repertoire until you consider the possible combinations. Not only can these four basic tastes be combined, but the other senses can be brought into play as well. For example, taste and smell are two entirely different sensory systems, but they greatly influence one another. Indeed, expert cooks have known for centuries that taste, aroma, texture, visual appeal, and temperature are all important parts of the sensation we call flavor. By selecting interesting foods, serving them attractively, and using alternate methods of adding tang to your foods, you can often compensate for the lack of salt.

Boosting flavor

A few drops of lemon juice, for example, not only perk up flavor but also seem to give even small amounts of salt more bounce. Just why a sour taste should work as an enhancer of or substitute for a salty taste when they are so different has never been explained. (Kosher cooks discovered the salt-sour crossover generations ago when they began using "sour salt," a preparation of powdered citric acid or tartaric acid, in place of sodium chloride in some dishes.) And don't forget herbs and spices, particularly the various forms of pepper. Many cuisines use vinegar and pepper in combination to stimulate taste buds.

Some packaged vegetable and herb mixtures contain salt, so be sure to check the ingredients listed on product labels.

If the sodium level in the body falls acutely, it can trigger an appetite for salty foods—for example, after severe vomiting or diarrhea, or as a result of the profuse sweating that accompanies sustained and strenuous exercise on a very hot day. In such circumstances the body can release a hormone called angiotensin, which acts on the brain and can stimulate an intense appetite for salt (as demonstrated so far only in laboratory experiments with rats).

But the salt craving that people experience daily is not based on a physiological need for more sodium. It is instead a self-perpetuating cycle caused by salt itself. People who eat a lot of salty foods experience frequent cravings for sodium because their systems are used to it. The cycle can be broken with relative ease. People who are cutting down on salt generally report that it is not hard, certainly easier than giving up cigarettes, and that after several weeks they no longer crave foods that are highly salted.

Sodium and hypertension

Despite advances in our knowledge of how sodium functions in the body, the mechanism of hypertension and how sodium affects it is still not clearly understood. About 5 to 10 percent of the people who have high blood pressure develop it as a result of having diabetes or kidney disease. Such cases, called "secondary" hypertension, can be alleviated by treating the underlying disease. The remaining 90 to 95 percent of hypertension cases have what is known as "essential" hypertension and it is this condition that continues to puzzle researchers. The cause is unknown. But researchers have identified factors that, either alone or working in combination with one another, increase the risk of developing high blood pressure:

Sodium Labeling

Beginning in 1986, the FDA required food manufacturers to list the milligrams of sodium per serving on all nutrition labels. Words such as "low sodium" on a label have not always meant a great deal, but now labels must carry the standard terminology listed below. Note that "unsalted" does not mean sodium free.

Claim on Label	FDA Requirement
Low sodium	Less than 140 mg per serving
Very low sodium	Less than 35 mg per serving
Sodium free	Less than 5 mg per serving
Reduced sodium	75% or greater reduction
Unsalted	No salt added

Are salt substitutes better than regular salt?

If you have high blood pressure and your doctor has told you that salt may endanger your health, then the answer is yes. Instead of sodium, the substitutes contain potassium, which may make your food taste bitter. People with kidney disease or certain endocrine diseases should avoid these substitutes.

"Lite" salts are combinations of sodium and potassium that contain about 40 percent of the sodium in common table salt, but taste almost as salty; however, they are not really sodium substitutes, since they still contain some.

Actually, if you do without salt or salt substitutes for a few weeks, you'll be surprised how quickly your taste buds adjust. See the box on page 119 for alternative ways to season foods.

cigarette smoking, habitual alcohol intake, obesity, psychological stress, certain dietary factors, and genetics. Age is also a factor: in industrialized societies, blood pressure tends to go up with age.

Studies have found that population groups that consume a lot of sodium tend to have a high incidence of hypertension, and groups that consume little sodium have a relatively low incidence. In northern Japan, for example, salt consumption is enormous—about 20 to 25 grams per day, which is three to four times higher than average consumption in the United States—and the prevalence of hypertension is also very high. Among the studies now being conducted to test the salt/hypertension link has been one in Kenya, among the Luo tribe. The preliminary findings indicate that the Luo who live in the countryside, where the diet is low in sodium, tend to have a low incidence of hypertension. But when members of this tribe migrate to urban areas, where the diet is higher in sodium, the incidence of hypertension goes up.

Many experts are reluctant to draw conclusions from studies such as these because other factors aside from salt intake may have influenced the levels of hypertension in these groups. For example, some rural diets include large amounts of fresh vegetables that are rich in potassium, a mineral that may protect against hypertension. And in the Kenya study, the rise in blood pressure was also associated with weight gain and psychological stress. More recently, though, a large international cooperative project called the Intersalt Study has offered convincing evidence of the relationship between sodium intake and blood pressure. Among ten thousand participants from thirty-two countries, researchers found that, with few exceptions, a low sodium intake was significantly correlated with a low incidence of high blood pressure. While acknowledging that the results of the study are subject to various interpretations, the committee that directed Intersalt concluded that the evidence strongly supports the contention that sodium intake is an important factor in the occurrence of hypertension.

Are you sodium sensitive?

Heredity also plays a key role in determining a person's susceptibility to hypertension. For reasons that are not at all clear, some people seem to be "sodium sensitive"; that is, their blood pressure responds to the level of sodium intake. Others are "sodium resistant" and do not show a significant rise in blood pressure even if they consume a lot of sodium. Current estimates indicate that up to 90 to 95 percent of the population is sodium resistant. Only 5 to 10 percent of the U.S. population—roughly twelve to twenty-five million people—are sodium sensitive. This group encompasses about half of the cases of hypertension in the United States.

Two recent studies have revealed that salt sensitivity increases with age. Researchers at the Indiana University School of Medicine measured the blood pressure response of groups of hypertensives and healthy people (aged seventeen to seventy-two) to injections of a saline solution. Among the hypertensives the reaction to the increased salt intake varied directly with age—the older the subject, the more pronounced the reaction. Among those who were not hypertensive the salt solution raised blood pressure only among those older than fifty. With aging, kidney function tends to slow down, and the body generates less of the substances that promote sodium excretion.

A complementary study at Wayne State University suggested that as people grow older they experience a decline in their ability to excrete sodium. Thus their sodium intake may have a greater effect on their blood pressure, since the body can no longer get rid of the mineral as efficiently.

The fact that so many of us seem to be genetically sodium resistant is the crux of the public health debate over the usefulness of discouraging excessive salt intake. If the majority of us are not sodium sensitive, why do we have to restrict our salt? There are good reasons to do so. In the first place, before hypertension develops it is impossible to determine who is sodium sensitive. In the second place, even though you may not be salt sensitive at forty, your sensitivity may increase with the years. There is also the possibility that the genetic resistance to sodium can be weakened by very high sodium intake over a lifetime and by other life-style factors such as stress.

Recommended intake

The real worry is that we are getting far more sodium than we need—5,000 to

Salt and sodium are not interchangeable terms. By weight, table salt is only 40 percent sodium, the rest chloride.

Sodium Content of Foods

LOW SODIUM	Sodium (mg)
Coffee, 1 cup	1
Fruit juice, 1 cup	2-10
Fruit, 1	2-5
Tea, 1 cup	5
Broccoli, ½ cup	8
Tomato, 1	14
Soft drinks, 1 cup	10-60
Eggs, 1	69
Beef, pork, lamb, poultry, fish (fresh), 3 oz	60-100

MEDIUM SODIUM	
Clams, steamed, 3 oz	95
Butter, salted, 1 tsp	115
Margarine, 1 tsp	115
Milk, 1 cup	120
Cake, 2 oz	150-400
Ketchup, 1 tsp	180
Bread, 2 slices	200-600

HIGH SODIUM	
Yellow mustard, 1 tsp	188
Potato chips, 1 oz	250
Cheese, cheddar, 1½ oz	300
Tuna, canned, 3 oz	250-500
Lobster, steamed, 3 oz	326
Olives, black, 2 oz	385
Ham, cured, 2 oz	400-800
Cheese, cottage, ½ cup	425
Pancakes, 3 prepared	400-800
Soy sauce, 1 tsp	420
Parmesan, 1 oz	528
Frankfurter, 1	450
Roll, crescent, 2 oz	500
Tomato juice, 6 oz canned	500
Pizza, 1 slice	500-1,000
Cheese, American, 1½ oz	600
Pickle, dill, 2 oz	700
Hamburger, 1 prepared (Big Mac, Whopper)	1,000
Spaghetti and meatballs, canned, 7½ oz	1,000
Soup, canned, 10 oz	1,000-1,500
TV dinner, 11 oz	1,000-2,000

7,000 milligrams is still the average daily intake. The Food and Drug Administration and various professional groups have been carefully reviewing the evidence for and against sodium and have decided that a sodium intake of 2,400 milligrams per day is the maximum amount for healthy individuals. People under a doctor's care for hypertension may be advised to consume less. And there are other medical conditions, such as heart or kidney disease, that may require an adjustment in sodium intake.

Although the case against salt is not ironclad, it is only prudent to heed the evidence that does exist. Hypertension is a life-threatening ailment—that much is perfectly clear. Unless you are under a doctor's orders to do so, you need not take drastic measures. But avoid reaching for the saltshaker automatically, and avoid the snacks and processed foods that are loaded with sodium. The health risks are too great to justify an overload of salt.

The average American is eating about three times as much cheese now as in 1950. Cheese is a good source of calcium, but unfortunately an even richer source of fat.

Calcium

Bones are active tissues, constantly taking up and releasing calcium to maintain skeletal strength and density. All individuals, therefore, need to consume calcium regularly. An adult's bones still need two-thirds of the calcium required when he or she was growing and presumably drinking a quart of calcium-rich milk each day. Yet it appears that, starting in adolescence, many individuals consume too little calcium, mainly because they decrease their intake of dairy products. Over the long-term, a decreased calcium intake contributes to the development of osteoporosis, a condition of bone thinness and fragility that primarily afflicts postmenopausal women. (The condition also appears—rarely—in elderly men.)

The reasons why women are particularly vulnerable to calcium deficiencies are complex. During pregnancy the fetus makes increased calcium demands on a woman's system, and the high demands continue during lactation. During and after menopause the decline in estrogen may impair the bones' ability to retain calcium, or actually lead to rapid loss.

The role of calcium
Calcium is the essential factor in building bones and teeth; indeed, about 99 percent of the calcium in the body is found in the bones and teeth. The remaining 1 percent or so is found in the cells and in the fluid that surrounds them. This minute amount plays an important role. Adequate calcium intake is needed for proper clotting of the blood, for proper muscle contraction (and therefore helping to regulate heartbeat), and for proper nerve transmission. In addition, calcium helps to maintain normal blood pressure, and according to some studies, may play a role in preventing and alleviating hypertension.

Building strong bones
In order to perform these functions, the cells must have calcium available on demand. Bones serve as a bank for calcium, storing the mineral and then supplying the cells with it when they need it.

The body begins to build bone mass in infancy and continues to do so throughout childhood and young adulthood. In order to achieve maximum bone density, the body must have a calcium intake high enough to maintain the structural integrity of the bones and to compensate for calcium losses through excretion. The exact age at which the body stops forming new bone is unclear, but it appears that peak bone mass is not reached until the age of twenty-five, and may extend into the third decade of life. During these formative years, therefore, it is important to get the proper amount of calcium to ensure maximal bone formation and to continue to meet recommended allowances thereafter.

The body continually reprocesses bone in a cycle of formation and resorption. During the early years, the primary activity is formation; in the latter years, resorption predominates, and bone mass begins to slowly decline in most individuals after fifty. This decline is not debilitating in individuals whose bone stores are adequate. However, an inadequate calcium intake throughout the first two or three decades of life can leave an individual at risk for osteoporosis.

We also lose the ability to absorb calcium efficiently as we age. During childhood, a period of rapid bone growth, the body may absorb up to 75 percent of the calcium ingested. As growth slows, so does the absorption rate. Adolescents absorb 20 to 40 percent of ingested calcium and adults, on average, only 15 percent. This is another reason why it is important to consume adequate calcium during the early years of life when the body can make the most efficient use of it.

While calcium is the primary factor in building strong bones, it is not the only one. Other minerals such as manganese, magnesium, fluoride, copper, zinc, and boron also contribute to bone formation. Vitamin D, lactose, and protein (at the recommended level) help the body absorb calcium. In addition, regular weight-bearing exercise, such as walking, and not smoking help the body build and maintain bone density.

Recommended intakes

The daily Recommended Dietary Allowance (RDA) for calcium is 800 milligrams a day for adults, and 1,200 milligrams a day for children and young adults from ages eleven to twenty-four as well as for pregnant or lactating women. However, a National Institutes of Health consensus panel has recommended that postmenopausal women consume 1,200 to 1,500 milligrams of calcium. Yet the typical American woman consumes less than 600 milligrams of calcium a day.

Getting enough calcium

The best calcium sources are dairy products, particularly milk, yogurt, and cheeses. Whole milk dairy products, however, are also concentrated sources of fat, and should be consumed in moderation. The solution is to consume adequate amounts of low-fat dairy products such as 1 percent or nonfat milk, low-fat or nonfat yogurt, and lower-fat cheeses such as part-skim mozzarella and ricotta—all are just as high, if not higher, in calcium than high-fat versions. For example, one cup of whole milk has 291 milligrams of calcium; nonfat milk has 316.

If you do not like milk, try yogurt or kefir. If you have trouble digesting dairy products (a condition known as lactose intolerance), try yogurt, which is easier to digest, or milk treated with the enzyme lactase. There are also good nondairy sources of calcium: leafy green vegetables, such as turnip greens and broccoli, and canned salmon or sardines eaten with the bones. Other foods, while by no means

Myth: Cottage cheese is a good source of calcium.

Fact: *Compared to milk, yogurt, and other cheeses, cottage cheese is a meager source of calcium. Low-fat varieties of cottage cheese are a good source of protein. But all types of cottage cheese retain only 25 to 50 percent of the calcium in the milk they were made from, since the special curdling procedure used to make cottage cheese encourages the loss of calcium into the whey, which is then drained.*

As a result, a four-ounce serving of cottage cheese has only 70 to 80 milligrams of calcium (dry curd has only 23). Just one ounce of most hard cheeses has two to four times as much—for example, cheddar has 205 milligrams. Hard cheeses, though, are too high in fat to serve as a daily supplier of calcium. Low-fat or skim milk and low-fat yogurt make excellent calcium staples. Yogurt retains all the calcium in the milk it was made from—about 300 milligrams per cup.

Sources of Calcium

The most plentiful sources of calcium are dairy products, which, unfortunately, can also be high in fat. However, low-fat dairy products often contain slightly more calcium than their higher fat counterparts; low-fat, nondairy sources of calcium are also available. This chart compares the calcium content of selected foods with their percentage of calories from fat.

DAIRY PRODUCTS			
	Serving Size	Calcium (mg)	Fat Calories
Milk, skim	1 cup	316	5%
Milk, 1%	1 cup	313	26%
Milk, 2%	1 cup	313	36%
Milk, whole	1 cup	291	48%
Yogurt, plain, low-fat	1 cup	415	25%
Yogurt, plain, nonfat	1 cup	452	3%
Yogurt, fruit, low-fat	1 cup	314-383	18%
Blue cheese	1 oz	150	72%
Brie	1 oz	52	70%
Cheddar	1 oz	204	74%
Feta	1 oz	140	72%
Mozzarella, part skim	1 oz	207	56%
Provolone	1 oz	214	72%
Ricotta, part skim	¼ cup	167	53%
Swiss	1 oz	272	72%
American	1 oz	174	74%
VEGETABLES			
Beet greens, cooked	1 cup	164	0%
Broccoli, cooked	1 cup	178	0%
Swiss chard, cooked	1 cup	102	0%
Collards, cooked	1 cup	148	0%
Dandelion greens, cooked	1 cup	147	26%
Kale, cooked	1 cup	94	22%
Mustard greens, cooked	1 cup	103	0%
Turnip greens, cooked	1 cup	249	0%
Spinach, cooked	1 cup	244	0%
CANNED FISH			
Salmon, sockeye, canned, with bones	3½ oz	237	38%
Sardines, canned, in water, with bones	3½ oz	240	72%
MISCELLANEOUS			
Almonds	1 oz	75	79%
Figs	3	81	0%
Rhubarb, cooked, with sugar	½ cup	174	0%
Soybeans, cooked	½ cup	66	38%
Tofu	3½ oz	90	56%

considered good sources, do contribute some calcium in the diet. For example, one cup of cooked carrots contains 48 milligrams of calcium, and one orange has 52 milligrams.

Calcium supplements

The Surgeon General, the National Research Council, and many nutritionists recommend that, first and foremost, calcium should come from food sources. Getting calcium through food ensures that you are also getting the other nutrients that work together to develop bone mass and help the body absorb calcium. In addition, calcium-containing foods are excellent sources of other vitamins and minerals.

If you absolutely cannot get enough calcium through your diet, taking a supplement is better than ignoring calcium altogether. But remember that calcium supplements are not a magic bullet. Supplements are usually taken by women who are approaching, or have reached, menopause, and there is no evidence that calcium supplementation at this stage of life can compensate for a lifelong inadequate calcium intake. Nor is there any evidence that calcium in supplement form by itself will help ward off osteoporosis. In fact, estrogen replacement therapy in postmenopausal women has been shown to be much more effective than calcium supplementation in decreasing loss of bone mass.

If you decide to take calcium supplements or if your doctor recommends them, treat them as something you add to an already balanced diet, not something you consume instead of a mineral rich food. Generally, the least expensive form of supplement is calcium carbonate; there is really no evidence that other, usually more expensive, supplements are better absorbed. Take it with meals to enhance absorbability.

Keep in mind that you should not take supplements in excess of the RDA or, if you are a postmenopausal woman, the National Institutes of Health recommendations. An excess of calcium can lead to the formation of kidney stones in susceptible individuals. Furthermore, while large amounts of calcium may not be toxic for healthy individuals, no one really knows what constitutes an overdose. Little research has been done on long-term intakes over 2,500 milligrams a day, since getting that much calcium from food has been nearly impossible. We do know, however, that large doses of calcium can interfere with the absorption of other nutrients, such as iron and zinc.

Calcium-fortified foods

In recent years, dozens of calcium-fortified foods have become available or are in test markets—foods such as calcium-fortified orange juice, bread, and soda as well as supermilks and yogurts containing enough calcium to meet your daily needs in a single serving. Will these products allow you to get your calcium through foods?

Eating a calcium-fortified product is like taking a calcium tablet along with the food. Proponents of calcium fortification compare it to other forms of fortification, such as the iodine now added to most table salt, which virtually eliminated goiter in the United States. But, as discussed above, the link between calcium and osteoporosis is not clear-cut. Many researchers now doubt whether calcium *by itself* can slow the rate of bone loss, especially in postmenopausal women.

Since different foods have different amounts of added calcium, which are absorbed at different rates, it can be difficult to calculate how much calcium you're getting and whether you are consuming too much. In contrast, it's easy to remember that three to five glasses of milk or servings of other calcium-rich foods will supply the 1,000 to 1,500 milligrams of calcium you need each day. It is also easy to keep track of calcium in pill form.

Finally, it hasn't been determined how much of the calcium added to these foods is really absorbed and retained by the body. Not only can the type of calcium compound affect how well the mineral is absorbed, but so can other substances in the food. For instance, fiber can bind calcium and make it less available to the body, so calcium-fortified breakfast cereals or breads may be poor sources of calcium. On the other hand, one of the reasons that milk and dairy products are reliable sources of well-utilized calcium is that they contain lactose and vitamin D, which enhance calcium's absorption. In any case, very few of the fortified foods have been tested for calcium absorbability or retention.

The average American today is drinking 61 fewer quarts of whole milk a year than in 1955, and 38 quarts more of low-fat or nonfat milk. That leaves a net decline of 24 quarts of milk per person per year—and a likely shortfall in calcium of about 80 milligrams a day (10 percent of the RDA).

Iron

Iron deficiency is one of the most common nutritional shortfalls in the United States today. Up to 15 percent of women of childbearing age have some form of iron deficiency. In some developing countries, where people eat less meat and where fewer foods are iron-enriched, half the population may be iron deficient.

All cells in the body contain iron, which plays a vital role in many biochemical reactions. Most iron is incorporated in hemoglobin, the oxygen-carrying protein that gives blood its red color, and in myoglobin in muscle. Iron is stored in the liver, spleen, bone marrow, and other tissues. Low iron intake over a long period can gradually lead to a depletion of these stores, especially if the body is losing blood, as in menstruation.

Why you need iron

The initial stage of iron deficiency usually has no symptoms. It occurs when the body's iron stores are depleted or exhausted, a condition reflected by a drop in the blood's iron levels and an increase in transferrin—a protein that transports iron through the bloodstream. As the iron supply to the bone marrow dwindles, so does the marrow's ability to produce healthy red blood cells, which require iron. If the iron balance worsens, full-blown iron-deficiency anemia—characterized by low hemoglobin levels—can gradually develop. Since iron is an essential component of hemoglobin, a shortage of iron can impair the transport of oxygen from the lungs to the body's cells; as a result, work performance will be impaired. It can take months or even years for symptoms of iron deficiency—such as weakness, shortness of breath, paleness, poor appetite, and increased susceptibility to infection—to become evident. These usually disappear when iron stores are rebuilt.

Groups with higher iron needs

An iron deficit isn't necessarily due to poor eating habits. An otherwise balanced diet may not supply adequate iron if you are in one of the following groups:

Menstruating women. Because monthly blood losses increase iron needs, women aged eighteen to fifty have a higher RDA (see box on page 127). Women who bleed heavily should pay special attention to their iron intake.

Dieters, especially women. The average balanced American diet offers about six milligrams of iron per 1,000 calories. Thus the less you eat, the less likely you are to get enough iron. In particular, women consuming less than 1,500 calories a day will find it hard to get their RDA.

Pregnant women. Iron needs increase due to higher blood volume and the demands of the fetus and placenta.

Endurance athletes. Long-distance runners tend to have a higher incidence of iron depletion, manifested by below-normal iron stores. The physiological mechanism of these changes is uncertain, and researchers haven't determined whether they impair performance in the absence of anemia.

Vegetarians and people who don't eat red meat. Beef, pork, and lamb are among the richest sources of iron. The iron in vegetables, grains, and beans is not nearly as well absorbed by the body. Dairy products have negligible amounts.

Infants, children, and teenagers. Youngsters need a high iron intake because of their rapid growth. Some studies have found that iron deficiencies even without anemia can adversely affect the learning and problem-solving capacity of children. Pediatricians often recommend supplements for infants and preschoolers; most infant formulas are fortified with iron. Menstruating adolescents who are still growing are at high risk, especially if they eat poorly or go on crash diets.

Factors that affect iron absorption

Only a small amount of the iron you eat is absorbed by your body, so you must consume substantially more iron than your body actually needs. The absorption process is affected by dietary as well as physiological variables:

•The amount of iron you consume.

Prune juice is very high in iron (3 milligrams per cup versus 0.5 milligrams in most other fruit juices). But because it naturally has so much sugar, it is also high in calories (200 calories per cup). Its laxative effect is the same as that of whole prunes.

•The form of iron in your foods. Not all iron is the same: heme iron, which makes up about 40 percent of the iron in animal tissues, is much better absorbed than nonheme iron, which makes up the rest of the iron in animal tissues, and all of the iron in dairy products and eggs; in vegetables, fruits, and grains; and in the supplements used to enrich flour and cereals.

•Composition of your meals. Dietary factors such as vitamin C enhance the availability of iron in a meal. Others, such as oxalic acid in spinach, inhibit absorption of this mineral.

•Your body's needs. If your iron stores are low or you have a greater need because of rapid growth or pregnancy, you absorb more iron through the intestinal tract. When your stores are plentiful, the body reduces its iron absorption rate.

The RDA for iron is based on the rough estimate that 10 percent of all iron is absorbed. Thus the RDA for men is set at 10 milligrams to provide the estimated 1 milligram of *absorbed* iron they need each day. The recommendation for women varies by age (see below). Until recently, it was set at 18 milligrams for menstruating women—the recommendation specifies ages eleven to fifty—to provide the 1.5 to 2 milligrams they need. But in 1989, a committee of the National Academy of Sciences recommended that iron intake be reduced to 15 milligrams since it has been difficult for women to get 18 milligrams and the lower amount was found to be sufficient.

The iron content of a half cup of spaghetti sauce increases from 3 to 50 milligrams or more when simmered in a cast-iron pot for a few hours.

Increasing your iron intake

As iron absorption is a complex process—it varies according to the foods you eat, how you combine them, and your body's need—here are some steps that will help you get the most iron from your diet:

•Eat red meats (lean, of course), since these are rich in heme iron, the most readily absorbed form. Liver is one of the best sources, but should be eaten no more than once a week because of its high cholesterol content. Chicken and fish usually contain one-third to one-half the iron in red meat.

•Peas, beans and corn are relatively good plant sources of iron. You can also choose breads, cereals, and pasta labeled "enriched" or "fortified." Unrefined whole grains, such as whole wheat bread, supply a fair amount of iron, but this is removed during the refining process. Enrichment makes such foods comparable to their unrefined counterparts in nutrient value. Fortification adds more iron than was originally in the grain.

•Try to eat foods high in vitamin C at most meals, since it helps the body absorb iron, especially from a meatless meal. For instance, if you drink a glass of orange juice with iron-enriched breakfast cereal, you may double or triple your iron absorption. Besides citrus fruits and juices, other good sources of vitamin C include tomatoes, sweet peppers, broccoli, cauliflower, leafy greens, strawberries, and even potatoes (with skin). Try to distribute your vitamin C intake so that you consume

Daily RDAs for Iron

Age	Iron (mg)
less than 6 months	10
6 months–3 years	15
4–10 years	10
11–18 years	15
19–50 years (men)	10
(women)	15*
over 51	10

*During pregnancy, the National Academy of Sciences recommends 30 to 60 milligrams of supplemental iron, as prescribed by a physician, continuing after childbirth for two to three months.

Sources of Iron

Any table listing the iron content of foods presents only part of the picture, since this mineral is absorbed better from some sources than others. About 15 to 30 percent of the iron in meat, fish, and poultry is absorbed, compared to an average of 5 percent from vegetables, fruit, grains, and eggs. In addition, some foods contain substances that hinder absorption.

The figures below are for the total iron content and don't take into consideration how well it is absorbed.

Sources of Heme Iron	Amount	Iron (mg)
Beef liver, sautéed	3 oz	7.5
Clams	3 oz	5.2
Oysters, raw	3 oz	4.8
Pork chop, broiled	3 oz	3.3
Steak, lean, broiled	3 oz	3.0
Sardines, canned	3 oz	2.5
Chicken, dark meat, cooked	3 oz	2.0
Lamb, broiled	3 oz	1.7
Tuna, canned	3 oz	1.6
Ham	3 oz	1.2
Chicken, white meat, cooked	3 oz	1.0
Salmon or white fish, broiled	3 oz	1.0

Sources of Nonheme Iron	Amount	Iron (mg)
Dried apricots	3 oz	4.0
Molasses, blackstrap	1 tbsp	3.2
Baked beans	½ cup	3.0
Potato, baked, with skin	1 medium	2.8
Almonds	2 oz	2.7
Lima beans, dried, cooked	½ cup	2.1
Raisins	3 oz	1.9
Spaghetti, enriched, cooked	1 cup	1.4
Brewer's yeast	1 tbsp	1.4
Peas, cooked	½ cup	1.2
Breakfast cereal, enriched or fortified	1 oz	1-10
Egg	1	1.0
Broccoli, cooked, chopped	½ cup	0.9
Peanut butter	3 tbsp	0.9
Bread, enriched or whole-grain	1 slice	0.7

some at each meal. Consider the effect of vitamin C, for instance, on a vegetarian meal of navy beans, rice, cornbread, and an apple. By adding seventy-five milligrams of vitamin C—as in a cup of steamed broccoli or five ounces of fresh orange juice—you could get three to seven times more *absorbable* iron from this meal.

•Another way to improve the absorption of the nonheme iron in vegetables, fruits, and grains is to eat them with meat and fish, which are rich in heme iron. Try chili beans with lean ground beef, for instance, or peppers and chicken. The body's absorption of nonheme iron can vary by up to tenfold, depending on the presence of heme iron and other inhibiting and enhancing substances in the meal.

•Cook in cast-iron pots to increase the iron content of foods. The more acidic the food (such as spaghetti sauce) and the longer it cooks, the higher the increase in iron content.

Iron supplements

If you eat meat and combine foods wisely, you probably don't need an iron supplement, especially if you are a man or a postmenopausal woman. However, some doctors will suggest supplements for vegetarians, infants, and young children. (The RDA now includes a recommendation for pregnant women.) Despite the claims made in some advertisements, don't expect iron pills or elixirs to "perk" you up or improve your athletic performance unless your body is chronically lacking in iron.

In any case, self-treatment with iron supplements is not recommended, even if you think you have an iron deficiency or anemia. If something is amiss with your blood, you should consult a doctor to find out why. Self-diagnosis is foolhardy for several reasons. First of all, weakness and fatigue can be symptoms of many other conditions besides anemia. Secondly, not all anemias are due to inadequate iron intake. Some result from other nutritional shortages (such as a lack of folacin) and won't respond to iron supplementation. Many cases of anemia are not due to diet at all. For instance, one of the most common causes of iron-deficiency anemia in older people is internal bleeding, which requires prompt medical care, particularly if it is due to a cancer of the gastrointestinal tract.

Finally, if you really are suffering from iron-deficiency anemia, this should be corrected under a doctor's supervision. If your doctor prescribes iron supplements, take them on an empty stomach—one hour before or two hours after meals—for best absorption. However, if you are extremely sensitive to iron, you may need to take supplements with meals to prevent stomach upset.

Self-prescribed supplements are also hazardous to a small number of individuals who are susceptible to iron toxicity because their bodies don't properly regulate iron absorption. While it's nearly impossible to get too much iron from diet alone, these people—about 0.35 percent of the population—may get an overdose from potent pills and elixirs, possibly damaging the liver, pancreas, heart, or immune system. Excessive iron intake can also impair the absorption of other trace minerals, particularly zinc and copper. As is true of other nutrients, you are always better off getting your iron from foods in a well-balanced diet than from pills.

Over a lifetime, the average woman will need almost twice as much iron as a man.

Sugar

For many years sugar has had a bad reputation. At the very least, it has been considered a junk food and an indulgence. More seriously, it has also been said to cause heart disease, obesity, cavities, hyperactivity in children, and diabetes. While it's true that sugar per se is a source of "empty" calories—that is, it provides no nutritional value aside from energy—it certainly isn't the dietary villain it has been portrayed as. At the same time many of us consume more sugar than we realize because of its prevalence in many of the foods we eat, particularly processed foods and soft drinks.

Types of sugar

To most people, sugar means white table sugar (sucrose) made from cane or beets. However, there are actually dozens of sugars: in their pure form they have such names as fructose, glucose (also called dextrose), maltose, lactose, and sugar alcohols like sorbitol and xylitol. In addition, sugars are often identified by their sources, such as maple syrup, honey, corn syrup, and molasses.

All sugars are essentially the same and none offers significant nutritional advantages over another (except blackstrap molasses, which is rich in iron). Therefore, there is no difference between honey or brown sugar and table sugar. And the sugar in fruit is no better than the sugar in a candy bar. Fruit actually contains a combination of fructose, sucrose, and glucose. In fact, sucrose is the main sugar in some fruit, such as oranges, melons, and peaches. The health bonus that comes from eating fruit lies in their vitamin, mineral, and fiber content, not in the type of sugar they contain.

Some differences do lie in the degree of sweetness, however. Fructose, for example, is much sweeter than other sugars, so far less of it is needed to make foods taste sweet. On the other hand, xylitol and sorbitol are much less sweet than other types, so more of them has to be used to produce a sweet taste.

Glucose: an essential element

The body needs sugar. Glucose, the main sugar in the blood and a basic fuel for the body, is essential to the functioning of all cells, particularly brain cells. But you don't need to eat any sugar to supply your body with glucose. All you need is complex carbohydrates, also known as starches, which are found in foods derived from plants—grains, vegetables, and fruits. In some circumstances glucose can be derived from the breakdown of protein or fat.

When you eat something sugary, it is broken down to the simplest sugars (unless the food's sugars are already in their simplest forms). For instance, during digestion sucrose is broken down into glucose and fructose, which enter the bloodstream through the walls of the small intestine and travel to the body's cells and the liver. With the aid of the hormone insulin, the cells absorb glucose and use it as energy. Some glucose is stored in the liver and muscle in the form of glycogen. Glycogen in the liver can be readily reconverted to glucose when energy is needed.

Most of the fructose is also converted to glucose by the liver. The liver can also convert sugar into some of the building blocks of protein—amino acids. Any excess sugar, like any extra calories, is converted into fat and stored.

Myths about sugar

Obesity. Sugar alone is not to blame for obesity. Eating more calories than you burn up adds pounds to the body—and for most people the lion's share of excess calories comes from eating too much fat, not sugar. In fact, some studies have found, surprisingly, that lean people tend to eat more sugar (and less fat) than obese people. People often blame sugary foods for weight gain, forgetting that cakes, ice cream, chocolate, and cookies derive most of their calories from fat, not sugar, and that fat has more than twice the calories of sugar. Many a "sweet tooth" may actually be a "fat tooth." This doesn't mean you won't gain weight if you add sugary snacks to your diet. But it's calories, not sugar, that cause weight gain, and fat provides far more of the calories in the American diet than sugar does.

Pour eight ounces of water in a glass and add six teaspoons of sugar—that is the concentration of sugar in some soft drinks.

> ## Other Names for Sugar
>
> Sucrose—or table sugar—isn't the only form of sugar that can be added to a product. Even when a label claims "sugar free," it still can contain some type of caloric sweetener, and one form is no more nutritious than another.
>
> | | |
> |---|---|
> | Barley malt | Honey |
> | Brown sugar | Invert sugar |
> | Cane sugar | Lactose |
> | Corn sweetener | Maltose |
> | Corn syrup | Mannitol |
> | Dextrose | Maple syrup |
> | Fructose | Sorghum |
> | Glucose | Sorbitol |
> | Grape sugar | Sucrose |
> | Grape sweetener | Sugar |
> | High fructose corn syrup | |

Heart disease. A few studies had indicated that sugar could raise blood cholesterol levels in most individuals, but a task force of scientists convened by the Food and Drug Administration (FDA) concluded in 1986 that there was no conclusive evidence that a high sugar intake is a risk factor for heart disease, whether by raising blood cholesterol, triglycerides (a fat in the blood), or blood pressure, "in the general population." However, some researchers suggest that a small number of "carbohydrate-sensitive" individuals with insulin or triglyceride levels that are high to start with may be particularly sensitive to sugar (especially fructose) and respond by increasing cholesterol and triglyceride levels.

Diabetes. Eating too much sugar is not the cause of diabetes. This misconception arises because diabetes is characterized by high levels of blood sugar (glucose). Excessive sugar consumption is indeed very dangerous for diabetics, who must curtail their sugar intake. But sugar doesn't cause this disorder. Obesity is probably the leading risk factor for noninsulin-dependent diabetes—and as stated above, sugar is not the major culprit behind most cases of obesity. Family history of the disease and advancing age are other important factors.

Hypoglycemia. Many people claim to suffer from low blood sugar, or hypoglycemia—and blame it for their fatigue, drowsiness, light-headedness, or anxiety, for instance—but true hypoglycemia is rare. Long-term severe hypoglycemia can be life threatening; it isn't a disease, but may be a warning sign of a serious disorder that can disrupt the body's ability to regulate sugar.

When low blood sugar occurs in response to food, it's called reactive hypoglycemia. Normally, however, the liver maintains a relatively constant level of blood sugar. After a meal, blood sugar rises and then returns to normal within two to three hours, as insulin allows the body's cells to utilize it. Some foods—sugary ones as well as some starchy ones—tend to cause a greater rise in insulin, which may result in a rather precipitous drop in blood sugar.

Studies have found that few people with chronic fatigue or restlessness actually have a concurrent drop in blood sugar. Conversely, most people have no adverse symptoms when their blood sugar temporarily dips.

Quick energy. A drop in blood sugar can, however, cause problems when you are exercising. Sugar eaten right before exercise or an athletic event is likely to be counterproductive and may inhibit performance. Many people believe that eating a candy bar or some other sugary snack before an athletic event will give them quick energy. But you'd actually be better off offering a candy bar to your opponent rather than eating it yourself. Sugar indeed raises glucose levels and thus provides some energy for a short while. In response, however, the insulin released temporarily drops the glucose level even lower than it was to start. Thus if you eat candy right before a long workout, it can cause you to become exhausted faster, since your body has to call on its energy reserves (glycogen) earlier than it normally would. In contrast, many complex carbohydrates, found in foods such as beans or whole wheat pasta, cause less of a glucose response in the body.

An exception: consuming a sugar snack or beverage during a workout lasting longer than two hours (such as a marathon) may help maintain your blood sugar level, stave off fatigue, and enhance your performance by supplying you with supplementary energy.

Behavior. It's a common belief that individuals can become addicted to sugar and that a high sugar intake can lead to all sorts of behavioral changes from hyperactivity in children to aggressiveness in adults. There is no evidence that sugar is addictive; people don't become physically dependent on sugar—that is, when they stop eating it they don't experience physical withdrawal symptoms associated with truly addictive substances. There is a popular belief that refined sugar, like drugs, causes a "high" or "rush"—in this case by boosting blood sugar. Other foods, however, such as bananas or dried fruit, may raise blood sugar just as much and no one claims they're addictive.

It is true that humans have an inborn preference for sweets. This may have evolved as a protective mechanism to ensure that our early ancestors ate enough high-calorie foods or tended to choose nontoxic foods such as fruit. And people do crave pleasurable foods, but this does not qualify as an addiction.

Despite the fact that many parents blame a high sugar intake for their children's uncontrollable behavior, several reviews of existing studies have found no strong evidence that sugar causes hyperactivity in children. A 1988 University of Washington study came to the same conclusion.

The jury is still out as to whether there's any consistent cause-and-effect relationship between sugar and behavior. Early investigators reported that eating excessive sweets may lead to aggressive and even criminal behavior in adults. However, some experiments during the last decade have found that a meal high in carbohydrates (whether sugars or starches) and low in protein may lead to a relaxed feeling, sleepiness, and decreased alertness by boosting the level of a brain neurotransmitter called serotonin.

Although the average American has cut consumption of table sugar (sucrose) to about 60 pounds a year, per capita intake of all types of caloric sweeteners, including corn syrup and all other forms of sugar, is up to about 150 pounds per year.

Sugar Substitutes

The ideal sugar substitute would have to be a chemical miracle: sweeter than sugar, with no bad aftertaste, calorie-free, colorless, odorless, water soluble, heat tolerant, nontoxic, noncarcinogenic, cheap, and safe for the teeth. So far, no sugar substitute meets all these demands. The most widely used sugar substitutes are the artificial sweeteners, saccharin and aspartame (brand names: NutraSweet and Equal). (Cyclamate, another artificial sweetener, is widely used in other countries, but has been banned in the United States.) The effectiveness and safety of both of these products have been widely debated.

The two main groups of people who use sugar substitutes are diabetics and those trying to lose weight. And that would include almost everybody, since nearly everyone diets from time to time. Yet, according to the Food and Drug Administration (FDA), there is no evidence that drinking diet soft drinks or eating artificially sweetened foods will help a person lose weight. The consumption of diet sodas and other artificially sweetened products has dramatically increased and yet Americans are heavier than ever. Even for diabetics the need to avoid all sugar is open to question, since diabetic diets have been liberalized to allow a controlled amount of sugar.

Still, if you want to use sugar substitutes in cooking or at the table, or buy products that contain them, neither saccharin or aspartame are harmful when kept to a modest level. But one problem with these products is that you have no way to gauge the amount of artificial sweeteners they contain, since manufacturers are not required to list the amount of saccharin or aspartame used in foods on the label. For example, the FDA says it is safe for a healthy, 150-pound adult to consume up to 3.5 grams of aspartame a day. A child weighing 50 pounds who downed a two-liter bottle of diet soda (containing 1.2 grams of aspartame) would have exceeded that. Since the aspartame content is not listed on the label, however, you would have no way of knowing.

Aspartame vs. Saccharin

	Safety	Who Should Not Use	Advantages	Disadvantages
Aspartame	Allergic reactions, such as swelling of the larynx, have been reported. Can have a toxic effect on the fetal brain.	Pregnant and lactating women, children, and those with phenylketonuria (PKU).	180-200 times sweeter than sucrose. No aftertaste. Minimal calories. Doesn't promote tooth decay.	Loses sweetness when heated so not good for hot drinks or cooking.
Saccharin	Found to cause bladder cancer in laboratory animals, but not proven to be a carcinogen for humans. Still, foods containing saccharin must carry warning labels.	Pregnant and lactating women, and children.	300 times sweeter than sucrose. No calories. Doesn't promote tooth decay. Can be used in cooking.	Tastes bitter.

Sugar and tooth decay

The connection between sugar and cavities is the only well-substantiated argument against sugar. Still, just eating sugar isn't enough to cause cavities. Half of all children in the United States today have no cavities at all, though they're eating as much or more sugar than ever. Many factors play a role in tooth decay—including the strength of tooth enamel, which has been greatly improved by long-term fluoridation of most of America's water supply. In any case, while refined sugar remains the leading dietary cause of tooth decay, it is not the only food that promotes cavities. Sugars such as fructose in fruit and lactose in milk may promote decay, as may some foods high in fermentable carbohydrates, such as bread and rice. Other variables also affect tooth decay: the consistency of the food, how long the food remains on the teeth, and of course, how well and how often you clean your teeth.

Recommendations

There is no reason to severely restrict your consumption of sugar, unless you are a diabetic or carbohydrate sensitive (and even most diabetics are allowed occasional sweets). The best advice is the United States Department of Agriculture's vague admonition to "avoid too much sugar." This, however, may not be easy to do since sugar is a popular addition to many of the processed foods that are so common-place in the American diet. While the amount of refined sugar (sucrose) we eat has dropped since 1975, the total amount of sugars in the typical American diet has remained the same. That's because there has been a large increase in the use of corn syrup, especially the very sweet and inexpensive high-fructose corn sweetener now used in most sodas and many processed foods. Sugar is, in a sense, the number-one food additive; it turns up in some unlikely places such as soups, spaghetti sauces, fruit drinks, frozen dinners, cereals, and yogurts as well as in breads, condiments, canned goods, and of course, soft drinks and what we call "sweets." Added to this are the sugars that are found naturally in fruits, vegetables, and dairy products. This amounts to each American consuming, on average, 133 pounds of sugar a year, which accounts for about 20 to 25 percent of all calories and 500 to 600 calories per day per person. Provided that an individual's overall diet provides the proper balance of nutrients, this isn't necessarily harmful. Ideally, however, sugar should contribute no more than 15 percent of your total daily calories.

Keep in mind, however, that most "sweets" are high in fat and calories and relatively low in nutrients. If the cola you're drinking is taking the place of skim milk, it's a bad trade-off. But if you're eating a balanced diet that is low in fat and high in complex carbohydrates, there is no reason to go out of your way to avoid sugar. Indeed, by eating such a diet, you will automatically be restricting your sugar intake.

Brown sugar is simply white sugar (sucrose) with small amounts of molasses or burnt sugar added for coloring; it offers no nutritional advantages.

Caffeine

Caffeine is a mind-altering drug, possibly the most popular drug there is, as well as one of the most ancient. It occurs naturally in more than sixty plants and trees that have been cultivated by humans since the beginning of recorded history. Whether they get their caffeine in coffee, tea, cocoa, headache remedies, or soft drinks, nearly everyone ingests at least some caffeine daily. Most adult Americans begin their day with coffee or tea; others, including many children, get their morning start with a cola. The average American coffee drinker consumes three cups a day. Yet many people worry about caffeine's side effects. In sufficient amounts it can bring on the jitters, and at one time or another caffeine has also been accused of causing pancreatic cancer, heart disease, breast disease, high blood pressure, high blood cholesterol levels, and birth defects. But does it indeed play a part in all of these health problems?

The effects of caffeine

Caffeine is one of a group of compounds called methylxanthines, which act directly to stimulate certain neurotransmitters in the central nervous system, with effects throughout the body. Depending on how much you consume, it can temporarily step up your heartbeat and your metabolism, increase stomach-acid secretion and urine production, dilate some blood vessels, and constrict others. It wards off drowsiness and increases alertness. One of the documented effects of caffeine is that it shortens reaction time. Precisely how it affects intellectual activity is hard to define, but German researchers have found that caffeine improves reading speed without increasing errors. Another study stated broadly that "caffeine produces an increased capacity for sustained intellectual effort." Other studies, however, have shown that caffeine does not affect verbal fluency, numerical reasoning, or short-term memory. As for athletes, some researchers have claimed that caffeine may enhance performance at endurance events for a variety of reasons, but the evidence is inconclusive.

Aside from shortening simple reaction time, caffeine does not appear to help in the performance of more complex motor tasks, and it may even be slightly disruptive. Depending on your body weight and physical condition, your habituation and sensitivity to caffeine, as well as the amount you consume, caffeine can produce trembling, nervousness, chronic muscle tension, irritability, throbbing headaches, disorientation, sluggishness, depression, and insomnia—otherwise known as coffee nerves. Some people can drink two or three cups of coffee in an hour without experiencing much of an aftereffect. Others, if unaccustomed to caffeine, can get jittery after one cup.

How much is too much?

Such adverse reactions are rare among healthy adults when coffee or tea is drunk moderately; that is, in quantities of about 200 to 250 milligrams daily (about two cups of brewed coffee—see chart on page 137). The effects of caffeine tend to be more severe among people who don't ingest it regularly; regular consumers seem to take caffeine's effects in stride. Children run a risk of their own version of coffee nerves, since one cola for a small child may have the same effect as four cups of coffee for an adult. The authors of one study found behavioral changes in children who drank the equivalent of six cans of cola, not an unusual amount on a warm day, which adds up to more than 270 milligrams of caffeine. But the same researchers later found that children who regularly consume caffeine are less affected than children who do not. It appears unlikely that caffeine causes hyperactivity.

Many, perhaps all, such discrepancies in studies of the effects of differing amounts of caffeine can be explained by the fact that researchers have not consistently distinguished between habitual coffee consumers and the occasional laboratory volunteer who ingests large doses of caffeine over the course of an experiment. A dose of 250 milligrams given to a regular coffee drinker has no significant effect on blood pressure, heart rate, respiration, metabolic rate, blood glucose concentration, or cholesterol level. But caffeine administered to subjects who haven't been consuming caffeine for a week or two can raise all these rates and levels.

Myths about caffeine

Heart disease. Research into caffeine and heart disease is dogged by inconclusive and contradictory findings. Researchers at the University of Maryland School of Medicine reviewed ten studies investigating the link between coffee consumption and coronary heart disease. Two studies found a link, one found the evidence inconclusive, and seven discovered no link at all. Of the two studies in the first group, the Boston Collaborative Drug Surveillance Program study showed a 60 percent higher risk of heart attack among hospital patients who drank one to five cups of coffee a day, and a 120 percent higher risk among drinkers of six or more cups, compared to nondrinkers. The second study, of male medical students at the Johns Hopkins Medical Institutions, showed a two- to threefold greater risk of coronary heart disease among coffee drinkers.

But both studies proved to be flawed. In the Boston study, the coffee-drinking subjects who had had heart attacks were compared to a non-coffee-drinking control group with other diseases. The Johns Hopkins study did not look at other factors that may increase the risk of heart disease, such as a high-fat diet, lack of exercise, job stress, and personality.

A study of 14,500 men and women in Tromsö, Norway, showed that blood cholesterol and triglyceride levels were higher among coffee drinkers (as much as 14 percent higher in people who drank nine or more cups of coffee a day). But further analysis of these findings suggested that the coffee drinkers also tended to smoke, consume more fats, and lead sedentary lives. Coffee drinking, the researchers concluded, may therefore indicate an unhealthy life style. At this time it is still inconclusive as to whether caffeine alone raises cholesterol levels.

The sole heart problem definitely pegged to caffeine is irregular heartbeats, or arrhythmias, and people subject to such irregularity should stay away from caffeine, particularly if they are recovering from a heart attack.

Benign breast disease. The fibrocystic tissue that forms in the breasts of some women can be lumpy and painful. Some doctors advise women with fibrocystic breasts to limit their intake of caffeine. But several recent studies—including a report on more than 3,300 women issued by the National Institutes of Health—

have found no relationship between caffeine consumption and fibrocystic disease. Nor is there any evidence that giving up caffeine by itself eases the discomfort some women experience.

Cancer. Despite reports of links between coffee drinking and cancer of the bladder and pancreas, studies have failed to confirm them. The authors of a 1981 study suggesting a link between pancreatic cancer and coffee reversed their findings in a second study carried out five years later. And an evaluation of more than 16,000 men and women who were observed between 1967 and 1979 found no correlation between coffee drinking and cancer at any body site, including the breast, bladder, and pancreas.

Other ills. It's hard to evaluate caffeine's impact on health because so many other risk factors may be involved. As the Tromsö and other studies indicate, many people who drink a lot of coffee are also heavy cigarette smokers, and high coffee consumption often goes hand-in-hand with lack of exercise, high-fat diets, and other factors that do put people at risk for a variety of ailments. But no one has shown that caffeine alone is responsible for any of the ills mentioned here, or for others, such as human birth defects. Nor is there any evidence that caffeine poses a hazard to infants nursed by mothers who drink moderate quantities of coffee.

Nevertheless, many doctors counsel prudence, advising pregnant women, nursing mothers, children, and people with heart disease to abstain from caffeine altogether or restrict their intake to two hundred milligrams a day. Caffeine in moderate amounts is not known to be bad for children. Still, a growing child is better off drinking milk or fruit juices than picking up the cola or coffee habit.

Coffee or tea?

A cup of brewed tea has about forty milligrams of caffeine on average, less than half of what you get in a cup of coffee. The exact amount depends on the type of tea and how long it is brewed. Green teas generally have less caffeine than black. And loose teas contain less caffeine than the same brands when brewed from tea bags.

Many people believe that tea contains tannins, which are known to interfere with the body's absorption of iron, protein, and other nutrients. It is true that tea contains a variety of substances called polyphenols, which give tea its astringent taste. Some of these polyphenols are chemically similar to tannins,

Percolated or drip coffee typically contains twice as much caffeine as instant.

Caffeine Content

This chart will help you calculate your daily caffeine intake. But remember, caffeine content varies widely, depending on the product you use and how it's prepared.

BEVERAGES		
	Serving Size	Caffeine (mg)
Coffee, drip	5 oz	110-150
Coffee, perk	5 oz	60-125
Coffee, instant	5 oz	40-105
Coffee, decaffeinated	5 oz	2-5
Tea, 5-minute steep	5 oz	40-100
Tea, 3-minute steep	5 oz	20-50
Hot cocoa	5 oz	2-10
Cola	12 oz	45

FOODS		
	Serving Size	Caffeine (mg)
Milk chocolate	1 oz	1-15
Bittersweet chocolate	1 oz	5-35
Chocolate cake	1 slice	20-30

OVER-THE-COUNTER DRUGS		
	Dose	Caffeine (mg)
Anacin, Empirin, Midol	2	64
Excedrin	2	130
NoDoz	2	200
Aqua-Ban (diuretic)	2	200
Dexatrim (weight control aid)	1	200

but they don't have the nutrient-binding effect of true tannins. For many years tea polyphenols were marketed as bioflavonoids or vitamin P, with numerous medicinal claims made for them. The Food and Drug Administration (FDA) considers them ineffective, so they are no longer available for purchase in the United States.

Should you give it up?

If you're a healthy adult who enjoys coffee or tea, there's no evidence that caffeine will do you any harm. If it gives you a lift or a reason to relax in the midafternoon, there's no reason to deprive yourself of caffeine's benefits. If you think caffeine may be robbing you of a sound night's sleep, by all means try cutting out caffeine in the evening. If you get jittery and nervous from it at any time of day, it makes sense to cut back.

Many people who occasionally suffer from nothing worse than coffee nerves may want to cut down on coffee drinking or stop entirely. Since caffeine is a mildly habit-forming drug, some heavy coffee and tea drinkers may experience withdrawal symptoms twelve to sixteen hours after their final dose: drowsiness, headache, lethargy, irritability, the blues, nausea. Even passing up the regular after-dinner cup can cause morning-after headache. Such symptoms can be avoided simply by cutting back gradually. You can switch to drinking decaffeinated coffee or other caffeine-free beverages, which, however, may also have unwanted side effects.

Decaffeinated coffee

Many people, unwilling to give up the pleasures of coffee, choose decaffeinated coffee: it has much of the taste and aroma of "real" coffee, but almost no caffeine.

One worry, which turned out to be of little significance, was the use of the solvent methylene chloride to extract the caffeine in some brands. This chemical was shown to cause cancer when inhaled by laboratory animals, which is why its use was banned in hair sprays. But scientists found no carcinogenic effect when the animals drank the chemical. In any case, the residue in decaf is virtually nil, and the FDA has approved it for use in decaffeination. There are also plenty of water-processed decaffeinated coffees now available, though they usually cost more and offer no particular health advantages.

Another inflated concern about decaf grew out of a study conducted at Stanford University that suggested that decaf raises levels of LDL, the "bad" cholesterol in blood. At the end of the two-month study, which compared coffee drinkers with decaf drinkers and subjects who gave up coffee altogether, the decaf drinkers purportedly showed an average increase of five milligrams per deciliter in LDL, while the regular-coffee drinkers and abstainers showed no significant change in LDL. Researchers had no idea why any of this had happened, but they doubted that it was the absence or presence of caffeine that caused the difference. One possibility they hazarded was that the type of bean may have caused the rise since the regular coffee used in the experiment is made from a different type of bean than the decaf. In a well-designed study, though, both groups would have drunk coffee made from the same kind of beans. Moreover, this study was small (only 181 men) and brief, and the reported difference of five milligrams in blood cholesterol between the two groups is of no significance.

A cup of coffee ice cream contains an average of 19 milligrams of caffeine. That's more than twice the amount found in chocolate ice cream, but far less than the caffeine in brewed coffee.

Food Labeling

Manufacturers of packaged foods are required to provide certain information on their food labels. This information must state: the common or generic name of the product; the name and address of the manufacturer and/or distributor; the net contents; and a list of ingredients, unless the product is standardized. When an ingredients list appears on a food label, the Food and Drug Administration (FDA) requires that all ingredients be listed and that they are listed in descending order by weight. (Flavorings, spices, and colors—with the exception of yellow dye no.5, however, need not be listed by their specific name, and can be referred to as "artificial" or "natural" flavoring or coloring.)

In addition, manufacturers are required to provide full nutritional information if: protein or vitamins or minerals are added; a claim is made about any nutrient or the nutritional quality of the food; or it is intended for special dietary uses. (Some examples of claims are: "high in iron"; "dietetic"; and "provides you with 100 percent of the U.S. RDA for ten vitamins and minerals.")

About half of all packaged foods today display nutritional information. Some food manufacturers provide nutritional information on products when not required to do so, but many don't. The sample label on page 141 shows you the minimum amount of nutritional information that must be listed when such information is given.

Reading the fine print

Why do some foods not list any ingredients at all? Ketchup, cheddar cheese, peanut butter, and margarine are among some three-hundred-odd staples that don't have to list ingredients or nutrients because they are made according to a "standard of identity"—a recipe specifying concentrations of various ingredients—regulated by the FDA. For example, if the jar says "mayonnaise," it must contain vegetable oil, vinegar and/or lemon juice, and egg yolk; these ingredients don't have to be spelled out. Certain optional ingredients, however, such as salt, sweetener, and preservatives, must be listed. Some manufacturers voluntarily list the ingredients on standardized foods; others provide ingredients lists at the consumer's request.

Most foods are not standardized, so they must list their ingredients. Even so, an ingredients list can be deceptive when it comes to sugar and sodium, and less than clear about flavoring and colorings (see the sample label on page 141).

Fat and cholesterol

Food labels tell little about the two problem nutrients that may be most important to you—fat and cholesterol. A nutrition label must list how many grams of fat there are in a serving, but seldom anything beyond that, and very few foods indicate what percentage of their calories come from fat. A breakdown of the fats into unsaturated and saturated fatty acids is optional. Cholesterol content is also optional, unless a claim is made about it.

A Labeling Glossary

Enriched. A process whereby nutrients lost during processing are replaced, approximately, by the manufacturers. For instance, when wheat is turned into white flour, it loses at least 50 to 80 percent of many nutrients. Of these, iron, niacin, thiamine, and riboflavin are replaced; but other nutrients lost in the milling process, such as fiber, zinc, and copper, are not restored.

Fortified. These foods contain added vitamins and minerals that were not originally in the food or were present in smaller amounts. Breakfast cereals are commonly fortified.

Imitation. A food that has had its formula altered so that it has less nutritional value than the product it resembles. Imitations are not necessarily bad. Imitation margarine, for example, is so called because it has less fat than required by the government standard for margarine—but that's good for you.

Light or "lite." A virtually meaningless term. If it refers to reduced calories, full nutritional information must be provided. But light can also refer to pale color, low sodium, taste, reduced alcohol, or fluffy texture. When applied to processed meats and poultry, "light" means that products have at least 25 percent less fat than usual.

Low-calorie. Food labeled in this manner must contain less than 40 calories per serving and less than 0.4 calories per gram. A salad dressing with 35 calories per tablespoon may seem to be "low-calorie" because of its small serving size, but it would not qualify since it contains more than 0.4 calories per gram.

Natural. When applied to meat or poultry, it means the food is minimally processed and free of artificial ingredients. But for other foods "natural" has no legal meaning. Many foods labeled as such are highly processed, and loaded with fat, sugar, and preservatives. A "natural" flavor must come from a juice, oil, leaf, herb, or spice, but something containing "all natural flavor" may still have artificial colors and preservatives. Perhaps "natural," like the term "health food," should be a warning rather than a reassurance.

Organic. A term that has no legal meaning. The USDA, however, does not allow it to be used on meat or poultry. Some states use this term if no pesticides are used where crops are grown or if no chemicals are in the feed or water given to animals.

Reduced calorie. These foods must have at least one-third fewer calories than the regular preparation. The nutritional comparison must be shown on the label.

RDA. Recommended Dietary Allowance. This is the estimated amount of various nutrients needed each day to maintain good health. Most RDAs vary slightly according to age and gender; pregnant or lactating women have special RDAs. These are ballpark figures, so consuming somewhat more or less than the RDAs won't hurt. Food labels utilize a condensed version of the allowances called the U.S. RDA, which is the level of the RDAs for all people over age four. These are expressed in percentages on food labels.

Sugarless and sugar-free. While products labeled in this manner must not contain sucrose (table sugar), they still can contain honey, glucose, fructose, or sugar alcohols such as xylitol or sorbitol.

Spotting saturated fat

If you are trying to reduce your intake of saturated fat, food labels don't make your job easy. Look for foods made with highly polyunsaturated vegetable oils, such as corn, safflower, sunflower, sesame, or soybean oil, or highly monounsaturated oils such as olive or peanut oil. Limit your intake of foods containing coconut, palm, or palm kernel oil—like animal fats such as butter or lard, these are highly saturated and thus raise blood cholesterol levels. Also cut down on foods containing hydrogenated oils, since hydrogenation makes fats more saturated. (The phrase "partially hydrogenated" tells you little—since it can mean anything from 5 to about 60 percent saturated.)

How to Read a Food Label

No legal meaning. Product can still contain preservatives, artificial flavoring, and other additives.

When comparing brands, make sure serving sizes are the same.

This number must be within 20 percent of the actual calorie count. Thus a serving of this granola can contain anywhere from 104 to 156 calories.

Amount of saturated and unsaturated fatty acids as well as cholesterol must be listed if health claims are made about them on the package.

These eight nutrients must be listed. Listing of other nutrients is optional, unless they have been added or a claim is made for them. Listed amounts don't account for any losses that may occur during cooking or preparation.

Ingredients are listed in descending order according to weight. This gives you no idea how much of any ingredient is actually used. Standardized foods don't have to list ingredients.

Specific flavors, colors (except yellow no. 5), and spices don't have to be listed by name; general terms like this are allowed. If you are allergic to some of these, write to food manufacturers to find out which ones they use.

BHT stands for butylated hydroxytoluene, a common preservative in cereals and other foods. Preservatives, thickening agents, emulsifiers, and other additives must be listed on labels. Most of those used today are safe, but a few, such as sulfites, pose health risks for some people. Others, including BHT, are under continuing review.

Granola Cereal

ALL NATURAL

NUTRITION INFORMATION

SERVING SIZE	1 ounce
SERVINGS PER PACKAGE	16
Calories	130
Protein	3 g
Carbohydrates	16 g
Fat	6 g
Sodium	95 mg

PERCENTAGE OF U.S. RDA

Protein	4
Vitamin A	*
Vitamin C	*
Thiamine	6
Riboflavin	2
Niacin	2
Calcium	2
Iron	4

*Contains less than 2% of the U.S. RDA of this nutrient.

INGREDIENTS: Rolled oats, brown sugar, corn syrup, sugar, raisins, peanuts, honey, nonfat dry milk, salt, vegetable oil (one or more of the following: soybean, hydrogenated palm, and/or coconut oil), artificial and natural flavors, preservative BHT, MSG.

Sugars, fiber, and complex carbohydrates are lumped together under carbohydrates. A separate fiber listing is optional; it must be listed if a claim is made about it. There are no regulations concerning fiber labeling. Consumer groups have asked the FDA to make dietary fiber a mandatory part of standard labeling.

Remember, no more than 30 percent of your total daily calories should come from fat. To figure out what percentage of calories in a food comes from fat, multiply the grams of fat by 9 (calories in a gram of fat) and divide by the total number of calories. A serving of this granola gets 42 percent of its calories from fat: 6 times 9 equals 54 fat calories, divided by 130 total calories equals 0.42, or 42 percent. That's a lot, since most cereals are low in fat.

The U.S. RDA for calcium is 1,000 mg per day, so 2 percent is only 20 mg.

"Sugar" means sucrose (table sugar) on a label. But sugar comes in many forms, and these are listed separately, like the brown sugar, corn syrup, and honey seen here. When these are added up, sugar may actually be the predominant ingredient.

Soybean is the only unsaturated oil here. Since palm and coconut oils, which are highly saturated, usually cost less, they are used in many foods.

Monosodium glutamate is a flavor enhancer and a source of sodium. Sodium is found in at least 70 compounds used in foods besides salt, including baking soda (sodium bicarbonate). You should not consume any more than 2,400 milligrams of sodium a day.

The Future of Food Labeling

Spurred on by the confusion in food labeling terminology, in 1990 the Food and Drug Administration (FDA)—along with Congress and many consumer groups—began to develop regulations that would make it simpler for Americans to follow the dietary guidelines—such as eating more fiber and less fat, calories and cholesterol—that health officials and nutritionists keep emphasizing. These proposals are still evolving as the FDA gathers comments from industry and the public. Some consumer groups and public health organizations are advocating broader changes and stricter regulations. If any changes occur they are not likely to take place until at least 1992. However, here are the key FDA proposals:

	Current Status	FDA Proposal
Nutritional labeling	Required on packaged foods only when a claim is made about nutrient content, or when the product is fortified with vitamins, minerals, or protein. This covers 30% of FDA-regulated foods. Another 30% of foods display nutrition data voluntarily. That leaves 40% of packaged foods with no nutrition data.	Would be required on nearly all foods regulated by the FDA (exceptions include spices, foods prepared in retail stores, and restaurant food). Foods regulated by the USDA, including meat and poultry, would not be covered. Nutritional data for fresh fruits and vegetables would be described on shelves or booklets.
Ingredients lists	Most foods must list ingredients. Ingredients are listed in descending order by weight, without quantities. Exceptions are about 300 standardized foods (such as mayonnaise and ketchup) that don't have to list ingredients included in their federal "standard of identity."	Nearly all FDA-regulated products, including standardized foods, would list ingredients.
Nutritional values	When a nutrition label is used, it must include calories, protein, carbohydrates, fat, sodium, iron, vitamins A and C, calcium, thiamine, riboflavin, and niacin.	New labels would add saturated fat, fiber, and cholesterol, plus calories from fat. (The percentage of calories derived from fat would not be listed.) Thiamine, riboflavin, and niacin would be optional, as few Americans are deficient in them.
Serving size	Up to the manufacturer. Small sizes are often chosen to make foods seem lower in calories, fat, sodium, etc.	Would require uniformity of serving size based on a commonly consumed portion as determined by the FDA.
Labeling terms	Terms such as "low-fat," "high fiber," "light," and "natural" are undefined or poorly defined.	Formal definitions for such labeling terms would be required.
Health claims	Since the mid-1980s, these have proliferated in a legal limbo. About 40% of new products bear health claims. Proposed regulations have stalled. For the most part, the FDA has not fought even the most questionable claims, leaving this to the states.	These must be supported by "significant agreement" about scientific evidence (may be difficult to judge). Claims would be permitted in these well-established areas: cutting back on fat may reduce risk of heart disease and cancer; limiting salt may reduce risk of hypertension; calcium may help prevent osteoporosis. Model claim messages will be developed by the U.S. Public Health Service.

It's hard today to find processed foods that don't contain a cholesterol-raising fat. The problem is, many labels don't specify which oil is used, listing just "vegetable oil" instead. Many others list an array of oils—for instance, "contains one or more of the following: soybean, hydrogenated cottonseed, and/or palm kernel oil." This gives manufacturers a choice when prices fluctuate. When presented with such a list, assume the worst, since the saturated oils tend to be cheaper and have a longer shelf life. Even if a product label makes the claim that it "contains no tropical oils," you still should read the ingredients list to see which, if any, type of fat it does contain.

Some labels confuse the issue further by hailing the foods as containing "100 percent vegetable oil" or being "cholesterol free." Only animal products contain cholesterol. But even if they contain no cholesterol, foods high in saturated fat can raise levels of cholesterol in the blood.

Can you believe the health claims?

Some food companies have started making health claims on the labels of their products—for instance, suggesting that the vitamin A in butter will keep your skin smooth, or that vegetable oils reduce your risk of heart disease. Since 1906, such claims have been prohibited by the FDA, but in recent years the agency has relaxed its standards (though not officially). As a result, there are only very vague guidelines as to what a food manufacturer can and cannot say. While it is unlikely that the claims on labels will ever resemble the absurd, pre-1906 claims (Grape Nuts, for example, was advertised as a cure for tuberculosis, malaria, and appendicitis), some consumer groups are worried that the routine use of health claims might open the door to deceptive claims that most shoppers—at least those without graduate degrees in nutrition—will be unable to evaluate.

The basic rule of thumb for judging health claims is not to put much stock in them. No one food can provide health benefits by itself, and while a food may have some positive attributes, it may have negative health effects as well. A food rich in calories, fat, cholesterol, and/or sodium may be promoted on the basis of some nutrient that you could easily get elsewhere: the vitamin A in butter, for example. Or an emphasized nutrient in a product may actually be poorly absorbed by the body because of other substances in the food. The best course of action is to read the ingredients list and nutritional information and use them to help you decide whether the food can contribute to a well-rounded diet

Food Additives

Food additives are hardly new: they have been with us for thousands of years, probably starting with the discovery that salted meat lasted longer. And they are not likely to go away, since Americans depend on an ever-wider variety of convenience foods that require additives. Some of these substances offer indisputable health benefits, but most additives are used solely to make foods more attractive and palatable to consumers. Surveys show that few things worry consumers more than additives, particularly "chemicals" or "artificial ingredients" in foods. Are these fears well founded?

Our food supply is more closely scrutinized and additives more strictly regulated than ever before. In the "good old days" a century ago, eating was really risky, since foods weren't well preserved or carefully handled. Adulteration of foods was common—for instance, toxic metals were used in food coloring, and copper sulfate in bread. No one claims that such acutely toxic compounds are being added to our foods today. Instead, consumers worry about long-term safety. Their fears have been heightened in recent years by the banning of the artificial sweetener cyclamate and other substances approved by the Food and Drug Administration (FDA) that were subsequently shown to cause cancer in animals. In addition, food scientists as well as consumers are concerned about the health implications of "indirect" additives—that is, substances that find their way into foods during packaging and storage.

The most commonly used additives are sugar, salt, and corn syrup, which together with baking soda, pepper, and a dozen other substances, make up about 98 percent (by weight) of all additives in the United States. Notice that these are all "natural." Yet natural substances can be health hazards—just look at sassafras bark extract (known as safrole and formerly used to flavor root beer) or aflatoxin (found in a mold that grows on peanuts), both known carcinogens. On the other hand, there's no reason to worry about the great majority of artificial ingredients. Laboratory-made vitamins and some flavors, for instance, are exact replicas of natural substances, and since they have identical chemical structures, the body can't tell them apart. Other chemicals have no natural counterparts, and while this isn't necessarily bad, they arouse the most fear in consumers.

Who is protecting you?

Food additives are extensively studied and regulated, primarily by the FDA. Legislation in 1958 and 1960 required manufacturers to prove the safety of any new additive; before that, the burden was on the government to prove the health danger of a substance.

Margin of safety. If manufacturer-sponsored tests prove an additive is safe, the FDA sets guidelines for its use. Generally, food manufacturers can use only one-hundredth of the least amount of an additive shown to be toxic in lab animals.

The Delaney clause. This is the most restrictive provision of the 1958 law, stating that a substance shown to cause cancer in animals or man may not be added to food in any amount. Food manufacturers argue against this rule on the grounds that in some cases the cancer risk is minuscule, or that any risk is outweighed by the benefits the additive may provide—as with nitrites and saccharin, weak carcinogens that are still on the market.

Testing for safety. Even under the best circumstances, absolute safety of an additive can never be proven. Any substance may be harmful when consumed in excess. Animal studies, which are our primary mode of testing, have limitations. They may not be effective in assessing the degree of cancer risk from long-term use because of the animals' short life spans. Moreover, it is hard to make precise comparisons between animals and humans. Other questions concern possible interactions of the hundreds of additives we consume.

GRAS. The 1958 law exempted about seven hundred "generally recognized as safe" (GRAS) substances from testing because of their long history of use without any harmful effect. This grandfather clause has turned out to be somewhat problematic. Many of the most widely used—and controversial—additives are on the GRAS list. The FDA has been re-evaluating all GRAS substances and has banned some or restricted their use. The controversies surrounding artificial colors and some preservatives are discussed in the box below.

Smart choices

•Eat fresh or minimally processed foods as much as possible, since they usually have few additives. Avoid junk foods (such as cookies, candy, and soda), which are not only chock-full of artificial colors and other additives, but are also of little nu-

---

Controversial Additives

Artificial colors

The most controversial food colors are the so-called coal-tar dyes, which were originally derived from coal tar but now come from other sources. Many have been banned by the FDA, including red no. 2 in 1976, then the most widely used food coloring in the United States. To ensure that it contains no harmful contaminants, each batch of food coloring has to be certified by the FDA. (Other dyes don't have to be certified; they are derived from natural products, such as caramel and annatto, or are pure chemicals.)

Only a handful of certified artificial dyes remain on the FDA's approved list, yet they account for most food coloring used today. All are under fire as suspected carcinogens, especially red no. 3, found in maraschino cherries, pistachio nuts, gelatin desserts, and other foods. In addition, yellow no. 5 can cause allergic reactions in a small segment of the population. Hence, it is the only dye that must be listed by name on food labels; others can be listed as "artificial coloring." Manufacturers seem to be aware of consumer concern,

and a few have ceased adding artificial dyes to some of their products.

BHT and BHA

Like many forbidding-sounding chemicals, butylated hydroxytoluene and butylated hydroxyanisole are allowed to go by their initials: BHT and BHA. These preservatives are used to retard rancidity in vegetable oils, potato chips, candy, cereals, and many convenience foods. Though on the GRAS ("generally recognized as safe") list, they have been plagued by controversy for years. Some studies have shown that BHT causes cancer in rats, while a few have actually found that it may prevent cancer in certain circumstances. The FDA is still reviewing BHT and BHA. Meanwhile, some companies have stopped using these chemicals, substituting natural preservatives such as ascorbic acid, citric acid, or vitamin E. Going against this trend, the United States Department of Agriculture allows meat processors to add BHT and BHA to raw and cooked meat-based toppings for pizza and to meatballs.

A Food Additive Primer

Additives do many jobs—the Food and Drug Administration lists thirty reasons why they may be added. Most of the estimated three thousand compounds deliberately added to foods fall into the following categories. The great majority of them are safe; safety questions are discussed under "comments."

Type	Functions	Common Uses	Comments
Preservatives Nitrates, nitrites, BHT, BHA, benzoic acid, ascorbic acid, sulfites, calcium propionate	Retard spoilage from bacteria, molds, and fungi; keep fats/oils from turning rancid; delay browning, as in cut fruit.	Most processed or prepared foods.	Nitrates and nitrites promote cancer in lab animals, so limit your intake of cured meats. Sulfites may cause allergic reactions, especially in asthmatics. BHT and BHA are under continuing review.
Nutrients Vitamins and minerals	Replace nutrients lost in processing, or add those lacking in the diet.	Processed flour, rice, cereals, salt, margarine, milk.	Most vitamins are artificially synthesized but are chemically identical to the natural substances.
Flavor enhancers MSG, hydrolyzed vegetable protein, maltol	Modify taste or aroma of food.	Gravies, oriental foods, canned vegetables, soup mixes.	Some people are allergic to MSG. Hydrolyzed vegetable protein can produce MSG when heated and combined with salt.
Flavors Vanilla, spices, seasonings, artificial flavorings	Improve flavor; restore flavor lost in processing.	Baked goods, soft drinks, and many other products.	Largest category of additives. Can be listed on labels in general terms, such as "artificial flavors" or "spices."
Colors Annatto, carotene, caramel, fruit juice, synthetic colors	Make food appealing by giving an appetizing, characteristic color.	Used in virtually all kinds of processed foods.	Synthetic dyes are most widely used; their safety is under continuing review. Only yellow no. 5 must be listed by name on labels, because of allergic reactions.
Sweeteners Natural sugars (e.g. fructose, corn syrup); artificial sweeteners (saccharin, aspartame)	Give food a more agreeable flavor.	Candies, baked goods, soft drinks, and many processed foods.	Many consumers are concerned about artificial sweeteners because of questions about saccharin and the banning of cyclamates in 1970.
Emulsifiers (mixers) Lecithin, mono/diglycerides, polysorbate	Keep liquid particles evenly mixed and homogenous.	Baked goods, frozen desserts, puddings, gelatins, dressings.	Help disperse oils and flavors. Most come from natural sources.
Stabilizers, thickeners, texturizers Gums, carrageenan, gelatin, flour, pectin, cellulose, starch	Improve consistency and provide desired texture.	Most prepared desserts, sauces, baked goods, fruit products, soups.	Many are natural carbohydrates that absorb water in foods. Affect "mouth feel" of foods—i.e., prevent ice crystals from forming in ice cream.
pH control agents Citric acid, acetic acid, other acids, alkalis, buffers	Control acidity or alkalinity, thus affecting texture and taste.	Soft drinks, confections, baked goods, fruit products.	Also used to prevent botulism in low-acid canned goods such as beets. Some acids help in the rising of dough.

tritional value—high in calories, sugar, fats, and/or sodium. This is especially good advice for children, who are the main consumers of junk foods and are at increased risk if there are any health problems with additives.

•Read food labels. But remember, additives aren't always listed: more than three hundred standardized foods don't have to list their ingredients. Ice cream, for example, can contain some twenty-five specified additives without having to list any of them.

•Limit your intake of foods listing "artificial colors." Substitute products colored by real fruit juice. Still, an occasional maraschino cherry won't harm you.

•Eat a variety of foods. This will limit your exposure to any one additive, should it turn out to have long-term risks.

Wellness Food Guide

Which fruits and vegetables are the best sources of vitamin C? What's the difference between beef graded choice and beef graded select? Is goat's milk more nutritious than cow's milk? Is margarine better for you than butter? Answering these questions and many others, this chapter serves as a complete guide that covers a wide variety of foods in the following categories: Produce, Dairy and Eggs, Grains and Legumes, Meat and Poultry, Seafood, Fats and Oils, Snacks and Desserts, and Convenience Foods. Each entry provides you with nutritional information, shopping tips, and guidelines for preparing and storing foods.

PRODUCE

Fruit

Apples

Although there are seven thousand varieties of apples, only twenty are widely available in this country, and a mere eight varieties account for 75 percent of sales—Delicious, McIntosh, Golden Delicious, Rome Beauty, Jonathan, Wine-sap, York, and Stayman. They vary in taste and texture, but nutritionally are pretty much the same. A medium-sized apple has roughly 65 to 85 calories, depending on how sweet it is—the sweeter the apple, the more fructose (fruit sugar) it contains. Unpeeled apples are a good source of fiber but aside from that, this fruit provides very little nutritional value. An apple in its skin will give you only about 10 percent of your daily requirement for vitamin C (storage decreases the vitamin C content) and some potassium. Still, their high soluble fiber and low-calorie content and variety of sweet-tart tastes make them very good snack and dessert choices.

Choose apples that are firm and free of wrinkles, soft spots, and bruised areas. Store apples in the refrigerator; apples stored at room temperature will deteriorate quickly and become mealy. Kept in the refrigerator, apples will stay fresh for two weeks or more depending on the variety.

Apricots

Apricots are rich in beta carotene, the substance that the body transforms into vitamin A. Three medium-sized apricots provide about half of the daily requirement for vitamin A and only 50 calories. Apricots are also rich in potassium and they are a good source of fiber.

Choose fruits that are golden, plump, and juicy-looking. Ripe fruit gives slightly when pressed. Avoid apricots that are very soft (overripe), hard (underripe), or greenish-yellow in color. Ripe apricots should be stored in the coldest part of the refrigerator and eaten promptly.

Bananas

Bananas are the most popular fruit in the United States; pound for pound, more bananas are sold than any other fruit. It's no wonder: bananas are inexpensive and available year round. What's more, they are easy to chew and digest, making them ideal foods for babies and the elderly. Bananas are always picked green and allowed to ripen en route to the market, so it is not unusual to find very green fruit in the supermarket. In fact, allowing bananas to ripen on the tree would result in mushy, overripe, and damaged fruit by the time it arrived at the store. Bananas are a good source of potassium and fiber. A medium-sized banana has about 100 calories.

Choose bananas that are yellow, but green at the tips and free of dark spots, bruises, or gashes. These bananas will not be quite ripe, so store at room temperature for a few days. Bananas are at their sweetest when they are solid yellow and flecked with brown spots. When they reach that stage, they can be put in the refrigerator to prevent further ripening. Refrigeration will darken the skin, but this does not affect the fruit inside. Overripe bananas can be mashed and used in breads, cakes, and muffins.

Blueberries

Blueberries are a perfect summer food. Light and flavorful, they can be eaten by the handful, in cereal, added to fruit salads, stirred into muffin mix, or used to top pancakes or yogurt. A cup of fresh blueberries has just 87 calories and supplies about one-third of your daily vitamin C requirement and provides small amounts of potassium, iron, and vitamin A. Blueberries are also an excellent source of fiber.

Choose berries that are dark blue, dry, plump, and uniform in size. Avoid those that are shriveled or moldy and those in boxes stained with juice. Before storing, pick over the fruit and discard stems, leaves, and any berries that are shriveled, squashed, moldy, or green. Do not wash the berries until just before eating. Blueberries will keep for about a week in the refrigerator, but are best used within a few days of purchase.

Cranberries

Cranberries are high in fiber and potassium. A half cup of chopped fruit contains just 27 calories and supplies 13 percent of the daily requirement for vitamin C. You enjoy all these benefits if you eat dishes prepared with raw berries and not much sugar, such as homemade cranberry-orange relish. But if you like cooked cranberry sauce, finding a low-calorie commercial product is virtually impossible (unless it contains artificial sweetener). The added sugar in store-bought cranberry sauce increases the calories to 209 per half cup and cooking significantly reduces the vitamin C content. Fresh cranberries are a wonderful addition to muffins, cookies, and pies, and are delicious in stuffing for baked apples, squash, and chicken.

Choose plump, well-formed berries with a deep red luster. Cranberries are almost always sold in clear plastic bags, which makes it easy to check the quality. It's rare to find bad cranberries, though, since inferior ones are sorted out during the packing process. Cranberries will keep for about a week in the refrigerator; about six months in the freezer. Do not wash them until ready to use. Frozen cranberries do not need to be thawed before using them in dishes or recipes.

Fruits and vegetables provide virtually all the vitamin C (92 percent) and half the vitamin A (49 percent) in the nation's food supply, but only 9 percent of the calories.

Dried fruit

Drying is a time-honored method for preserving food; fruit is dried either in the sun or by forced hot air. This process reduces the fruit's water content, usually from about 80 percent to between 15 and 35 percent. As a result, the nutrients are concentrated, leaving the fruit high in minerals—especially iron, copper, and potassium—and sometimes beta carotene, a precursor of vitamin A. Dried fruit is also a compact source of fiber.

The catch is that drying also concentrates the fruit's sugar—and calories. Dried fruit may contain as much as 70 percent sugar by weight, a higher percentage than that of many cookies and approaching that of some candies. In return for the high mineral content,

---

NUTRITIONAL CONTENT OF
Dried Fruit

Fruit (3½ oz)	Calories	Dietary Fiber (g)	Iron (mg)	Vitamin A (IU)
Apples, 10 rings	240	10.6	1.4	0
Apricots, 12 halves	240	8.1	4.7	7,240
Dates, 12	275	8.7	1.2	50
Figs, 6	255	18.5	2.2	130
Peaches, 8 halves	240	N/A	4.0	2,160
Pears, 6 halves	260	11.0	2.1	3
Prunes, 12	240	16.1	2.5	1,990
Raisins, ⅔ cup	300	6.8	2.1	10

---

you are getting a relatively calorie-dense snack food, and, since dried fruit tends to stick to your teeth, an increased risk of tooth decay. (Try to brush and floss your teeth, or at least rinse your mouth with water, after eating dried fruit.) Fruit also loses most of its vitamin C when dried.

Choose dried fruit that has not been "glazed" or had sugar added. Sulfite preservatives are often added to light-colored fruit such as apples, peaches, pears, apricots, and golden raisins to keep them from turning brown. These preservatives can produce allergic reactions in some people—especially asthmatics—and many experience severe, sometimes even fatal reactions to them. Manufacturers are required to list these preservatives—usually sulfur dioxide—clearly on packages, shipping containers, and bulk bins. Sulfite-sensitive people should be sure to check labels and ask whether or not the fruit has been treated when buying from an unlabeled bin. Fortunately, there are some sulfite-free, light-colored fruits; these are usually labeled as such.

Fruit and vegetable juice

Most people drink juice to get vitamin C. In fact, orange juice is the major source of this vitamin in the American diet. But orange juice isn't the only juice high in vitamin C, and vitamin C isn't the only reason to drink juice. The range of juices is wider than ever—from tart to sweet, prosaic to exotic, in old-fashioned bottles to unrefrigerated mini-boxes. How can you tell the good juices from the bad?

The next best thing to whole fruits and vegetables is their juice. Most of their nutrients are retained, but nearly all fiber is lost. Here are some of the nutritional bright spots:

• All citrus juices are high in vitamin C, containing up to twice the daily Recommended Dietary Allowance (RDA) in an eight-ounce glass.

• Most red or orange-colored juices are rich in beta carotene. Thus red or pink grapefruit juice has forty-four times more beta carotene than white grapefruit. The champion is carrot juice: an eight-ounce glass supplies twelve times the amount of beta carotene needed to meet the RDA for vitamin A. (Fortunately, beta carotene isn't toxic, even at high levels, because the body converts it to vitamin A only according to its needs.)

•Potassium is abundant in nearly all fruit and vegetable juices, with carrot, prune, tomato, and orange juice at the top of the list.

•One juice is high in iron: a cup of prune juice provides 30 percent of the RDA for men, 20 percent for women.

Fresh vs. frozen vs. reconstituted. Do you sometimes wonder if the vitamin C is really there when you pick up a carton of orange juice? The amount of vitamin C in eight ounces of juice can range from about 80 to 160 milligrams. It depends on many factors over which you have no control: the variety of oranges (most brands are made from several varieties), their ripeness, the climate in which they grew, and how they were handled, processed, packaged, and stored. Many studies have compared various types of packaging and brands for nutritional content. It has been found, for example, that since vitamin C deteriorates when in contact with oxygen, there's increased risk of vitamin C loss in plastic jugs and some wax-coated cardboard cartons, which are permeable to air. Fortunately, because citrus fruit is so rich in vitamin C, you can generally assume that, despite the variations, a glass of nearly any type of orange juice you buy will provide at least 100 percent of the RDA.

Freshly squeezed juice usually has the highest vitamin C content, followed by frozen or canned (which retain their vitamin C for months), then chilled cartons and unrefrigerated mini-boxes. Chilled cartons, especially if they have been reconstituted, usually contain less vitamin C and have a shorter shelf life. One study found that an unopened carton of orange juice lost only 2 percent of its vitamin C a day when kept at forty degrees Fahrenheit. That's not much, but it can be a problem if juice is kept for long periods. So when buying a chilled carton of juice, check the date on it, which should indicate the last day it can be sold (an average of twenty-seven days after packaging). If the date is close or has passed, there may be significant loss of vitamin C—and of taste.

Vitamin A and C in Juices

Juice (8 oz)	Calories	Vitamin A* (IU)	Vitamin C (mg)
Apple, canned/bottled	115	2	2**
Apricot, canned	140	3,300	1**
Carrot, canned	95	63,000	22
Cranberry cocktail, bottled	144	9	90
Grape, canned/bottled	155	20	trace**
Grapefruit, pink, fresh	95	1,100	94
Grapefruit, white, fresh	95	25	94
Lemon, fresh	60	49	112
Orange, fresh	110	496	124
Papaya, canned	140	277	8
Peach nectar, canned	135	643	13**
Pineapple, canned	140	12	27
Prune, canned	180	9	11
Tangerine, fresh	105	1,037	77
Tomato, canned	40	1,350	45
V-8 vegetable, canned	47	3,000	36

*The values given for vitamin A are based on the estimated conversion of the beta carotene present in the juice.
**Vitamin C may be added. If so, it will be listed on the label.

Once you get the juice home, store it properly. A refrigerated carton can last two to four weeks (depending on its date) before there's a serious loss of vitamin C and taste. The same is true of frozen juice once it is reconstituted, and of canned juice once it is opened. To protect the vitamin C from air, store juice in a tightly closed glass container and keep it at forty degrees Fahrenheit or below.

Since nutrition isn't a major issue when choosing among orange juices, that leaves taste and price. Taste tests have found that nothing compares to fresh-squeezed; it is also most expensive. Frozen orange juice rates second in taste, and is usually least expensive. Don't think that all orange juice in cartons is fresh-squeezed; most are made from frozen concentrate shipped to regional packagers.

Read the labels. When buying fruit juice, watch the wording on labels. If something is simply called "juice," it must be 100 percent juice. "Drinks," "beverages," "punches," "juice blends," "-ades," and "juice cocktails" usually contain little fruit juice—the rest being water and sugar, such as corn syrup. The juice content is seldom disclosed on labels, since the Food and Drug Administration (FDA), bowing to pressure from packagers, doesn't require it. So you would be hard put to know some brands of fruit punch are only 10 percent juice, for instance, or some types of cranberry juice cocktail are just 27 percent juice. (Pure cranberry juice is not available commercially; sugar, water, and/or other juices are added, as well as vitamin C.) As long as you know what you're getting,

---

Exotic Fruits

It used to be that fruit was just apples, pears, oranges, a few other delicious but pedestrian varieties, and maybe an occasional pineapple. But thanks to improved horticultural methods and shipping, dozens of tropical or otherwise exotic fruits are now sold in specialty shops and well-stocked supermarkets around the country, sometimes year-round. Some types are now grown commercially in California, Hawaii, or Florida. All are expensive, however, so don't expect to replace your daily apple with a guava or persimmon.

Exotic fruits can be added to fruit salads, green salads, or cereal, made into jellies or preserves, or used in toppings or sauces for ice cream or for other fruits. Still, the best way to eat these fruits is by themselves—as low-calorie snacks and healthful desserts.

Fruit (3½ oz edible portion)	Calories	Vitamin A (IU)	Vitamin C (mg)	Comments
Guava	51	790	184	Sweet and aromatic. Use in pies or tarts, or for preserves.
Kiwifruit	61	175	98	Sweet-tart flavor. Good in fruit salads and tarts. High in potassium.
Kumquat	63	300	37	Small orangelike fruit. Good in fruit salads and pies.
Lychee	66	0	72	Grapelike flesh. Use in salads.
Mango	65	4,000	28	Peachlike flavor and spicy aroma. Must be fully ripe before eating. Good source of niacin.
Papaya	39	2,000	62	Mellow flavor. Use over ice cream or in fruit salads.
Passion fruit	97	700	30	Intense sweet flavor. Good when scooped out as a topping for fruit or ice cream. High in iron and potassium.
Persimmon, Japanese	70	2,170	8	Sweet and spicy. Must be ripe. Good in puddings and cakes. American variety is higher in vitamin C.
Quince	57	40	15	Aromatic. Tart when raw, sweet when cooked. Use in preserves, pies, stews, or as a cooked dessert.

there's nothing wrong with some of these beverages. But in some cases these products cost more than real juices, so you're paying a lot for water. If you want diluted fruit juice, you're better off mixing real juice with water or seltzer yourself. You'll cut calories, and you'll know what you're drinking.

Grapefruit

Grapefruit comes in white, pink, and red varieties. All are good sources of vitamin C, and because pink and red grapefruits contain beta carotene, they are a fair source of vitamin A. Grapefruit is low in calories—40 per half—and virtually fat free, but those are the only characteristics that qualify it as a diet food. It has no special properties that can help burn fat or otherwise cause you to lose weight. Grapefriut is, however, a good source of fiber and potassium.

Choose grapefruit that feels heavy for its size and with a thin skin; this indicates that it is juicy. Minor blemishes on the skin do not affect the fruit inside, but avoid grapefruit with any soft spots. Grapefruit can be stored at room temperature if you plan to eat it within a few days, though you may find it tastier when it's been chilled. Stored in the refrigerator it will keep for several weeks.

Lemons and limes

These citrus fruits don't offer much nutritionally simply because unlike oranges or grapefruits, they are rarely eaten out of hand. Still, they are fairly high in vitamin C and they can make a significant nutritional contribution when used to replace salt or butter as a seasoning or used as a low-fat salad dressing. The juice of a lemon or lime will also serve nicely as a low-fat marinade. And, of course, you can use fresh lemons to make your own lemonade;

that way you'll be able to control the amount of sugar added. Lemons can also be squeezed over cut fruits to prevent browning. Keep a few lemons and limes on hand; fresh-squeezed juice is more flavorful than bottled.

Choose lemons and limes that are heavy for their size and feel firm to the touch. The skin should be glossy and rich-colored. Avoid spongy fruit or those with thick skins. Stored in the fruit bin of the refrigerator, they will keep for about two weeks.

Melons

Two of the most widely available melons are cantaloupe and honeydew. Orange-fleshed cantaloupe is one of the best nutritional buys in the fruit world. Just half a melon provides you with more of vitamins A (in the form of beta carotene) and C than you need daily. It is also a good source of potassium and contains only 95 calories. Honeydew melon is large and creamy- or yellowish-white on the outside and light green on the inside. One four-ounce slice of honeydew contains just 45 calories.

Choose cantaloupes with rinds covered with thick, close netting; avoid those with any smooth areas. The ends should slightly yield to pressure, be free of any stem, and have a full, fruity fragrance. Honeydews should have a smooth velvety surface and give a little when pressed at the blossom end (opposite the stem end). Ripen melons at room temperature; once ripe, store in the refrigerator.

Nectarines

Nectarines are a member of the peach family but are not, as some people believe, a cross between a peach and a plum, or simply a fuzzless peach. One large nectarine has only 65 calories and contributes one-fifth of your total daily

You can get more juice from a fresh lemon or lime by rolling it with light pressure between your hands—preferably under warm or hot water—before squeezing.

requirement for vitamin A as well as some potassium.

Choose well-colored fruits—deep yellow with a red blush. In order to ripen properly, nectarines must come to maturity on the tree—once picked, they will get softer, but not sweeter—so avoid those that are hard and green or dull colored. Mature fruit will soften at room temperature. Nectarines are ready to eat when there is a slight softening along the seam. Store ripe fruit in the refrigerator, but for maximum flavor, serve at room temperature.

Oranges

Oranges are of two types: eating and juice. Popular eating oranges include: the navel, a large seedless orange that is meaty and flavorful; the temple, a juicy, sweet-tart cross between an orange and a tangerine; and the Valencia, a medium-sized, thin-skinned orange. Temples and Valencias also make good juice oranges. Relatives of the orange—tangerines, clementines, tangelos, and mandarins—are also good for eating. Varieties of oranges that are used primarily for juice include Hamlin, Pineapple, and Parson Brown.

Oranges, as most people know, are an excellent source of vitamin C—one orange more than fulfills your daily requirement. They are also a fair source of vitamin A. Tangerines have less vitamin C than oranges, but are a better source of vitamin A. Both are good sources of potassium. Oranges provide a small amount of calcium as well. A medium-sized orange has about 60 calories, a medium-sized tangerine, about 35 calories.

Choose oranges that are firm and feel heavy for their size. Lightweight oranges will be dry. A very rough surface often indicates a thick skin, and therefore little fruit inside. Color is not an indication of quality: many perfectly ripe oranges have green streaks through their skin. Tangerines and tangelos also should feel heavy for their size. Their skin is naturally loose, so the fruit will not feel firm. As with oranges, a slight greening does not mean the fruit is not ripe. Carefully check oranges and tangerines sold in plastic bags for mold before buying. Mold spreads very quickly—especially in tangerines—and can spoil the whole bag. Store oranges in a cool place or in the refrigerator. Store tangerines in the fruit bin of the refrigerator.

Peaches

Peaches are a fair source of potassium, vitamin A (in the form of beta carotene), and fiber. A medium-sized peach has 35 calories.

Choose peaches that are just beginning to soften. A ripe peach will have a creamy yellow and red color and a peachy smell. Do not buy fruit that is rock hard or has a greenish tinge—it will not ripen. Ripe peaches are very susceptible to bruises and should be handled with care. Ripen peaches at room temperature and store ripe fruit in the refrigerator.

Pears

There are many varieties of pears sold. Bartlett and Comice pears are soft, juicy, and sweet. They are also very fragile. Bosc and D'Anjou are firmer, but still very sweet and juicy. Depending on size and variety, pears contain between 85 and 120 calories. They are excellent sources of fiber and also contain small amounts of vitamins and minerals.

Choose pears that are firm, but not rock hard, and ripen them at home. (Pears are never left to ripen on the tree.) To ripen, place the fruit in a perforated paper bag and leave at room

Ripe oranges sometimes undergo a process known as regreening. This occurs when a ripe orange pulls some green chlorophyll from its stems and leaves back into its peel. Such greenish oranges are extra ripe and thus often sweeter than other oranges.

temperature for a few days. Pears are at their best when perfectly ripe; they are ready to eat when the flesh around the stem gives to gentle pressure. Avoid those pears with gashes or bruises and those that have gone soft at the blossom end. Ripe pears should be stored in the refrigerator.

Pineapples
Pineapples contain small amounts of vitamins and minerals and are a good source of fiber. Fresh pineapple is much more flavorful than canned. A cup of diced fresh pineapple has about 75 calories.

Choose fresh pineapples that are golden-yellow in color and heavy for their size. Pineapples do not ripen after they are picked, so they do not need any time to ripen at home. Contrary to popular folklore, you cannot tell if a pineapple is ripe by the ease with which a leaf is removed. A good indication of ripeness is a strong, pleasant pineapple fragrance. Avoid any pineapple that has soft spots. Buy the largest one you can use, since the amount of waste is the same regardless of the size of the fruit. Pineapples should be eaten as soon as possible, but will keep for a short time if stored in the refrigerator.

Plums
There are many types of plums that offer a variety of colors, tastes, and textures. Some popular varieties include: Santa Rosa, a deep red plum with yellow flesh; El Dorado, a large plum with reddish-blue skin and pink-tinged flesh; the mirabelle, a small aromatic, golden-yellow plum; and Italian prune, a small purple plum (this variety is dried to make prunes). The nutritional content of plums depends on the variety, but generally they are good sources of potassium and fiber and contain some vitamin A and iron.

One medium-sized plum contains about 35 calories.

Choose plums with good color for the variety you are choosing. Plums should be slightly soft. Avoid any plums that are very hard (as well as those that have gone too soft), bruised, or those that are shriveled. Store plums in the refrigerator.

Raspberries
Raspberries, and their cousins, blackberries, are good sources of fiber, potassium, and vitamin C. They also contain small amounts of vitamin A and iron, and blackberries contain a small amount of calcium as well. A cup of raspberries has just 60 calories; a cup of blackberries has 75 calories.

Choose berries that are plump with good color. Avoid containers that are stained, or contain berries that are moldy or mushy. Raspberries and blackberries are very perishable, and are best eaten on the day purchased. Do not wash the berries until you are ready to eat them.

Strawberries
Strawberries are delicious, beautiful, and nutritious. Strawberries have just 100 calories per pint or 37 calories for a standard half-cup serving, which also provides 100 percent of the recommended daily allowance of vitamin C and more fiber than a slice of whole wheat bread. They are also a good source of potassium.

Strawberries retain most of their vitamin C only if the green stem caps are still attached. Don't remove the caps until just before you are going to eat the strawberries.

Choose strawberries that have a lustrous red color and are firm to the touch. Avoid boxes of berries that show signs of leakage, or contain moldy-looking berries (check the bottom of

Some fresh fruits, such as pineapple and papaya, contain protein-digesting enzymes that may cause lip and mouth irritation. Cooking (which takes place prior to canning) inactivates the enzymes.

the box); mold will rapidly spread to the rest of the berries. Opt for small or medium-sized berries rather than large ones; though they may look pretty, large berries are often not as sweet and flavorful as smaller ones. Stored in the refrigerator, strawberries will keep for a day or two. Do not wash them until you are ready to eat them.

Watermelon

Watermelon has a very high water content, making it a good, flavorful, low-calorie thirst quencher. One cup of cubed watermelon has just 50 calories. It is a good source of vitamin A and potassium and contains some vitamin C as well.

Choose whole melons with a smooth, dull, exterior and a creamy yellow underside. You can more accurately judge the quality of a watermelon if you choose precut sections. The flesh should be deep red, moist, and fresh-looking. Avoid pale-fleshed watermelons or those that look dehydrated. Store whole melons in a cool room; wrap cut watermelon in plastic and store it in the refrigerator. Use watermelon within a few days.

Vegetables

Artichokes

Globe artichokes are usually served as an appetizer rather than as a side dish since they take a lot of concentration to eat. To remove the edible flesh, each leaf must be pulled off and scraped along the front teeth. But the effort is well worth it, both for flavor and nutrition. One medium-sized artichoke contains, on average, 55 calories and provides some protein, calcium, iron, and potassium. Artichokes are also very high in fiber. To make the most of the low-calorie count, stay away from traditional high-fat dipping sauces and serve artichokes with fresh lemon juice or a light vinaigrette.

Choose artichokes with tightly closed, fresh-looking leaves. A few dark spots on the leaves do not indicate spoilage as long as the vegetable looks healthy overall, but avoid any with extensive spotting or discoloration. Artichokes are best used as soon as possible. They will, however, keep in the refrigerator for four or five days.

Asparagus

Asparagus is very low in calories: eight spears have just 30. Asparagus also provides some potassium, vitamin A, and iron, and is a good source of fiber.

Choose bright green asparagus with compact, pointed tips. The stalks should be round: flat stalks can be tough and stringy. Thick stalks are more tender than thin ones. Once you get them home, trim the stem ends of the asparagus and wrap the bases in a damp paper towel. Store asparagus in the refrigerator crisper. Asparagus loses its flavor if kept too long, so use it within a few days of purchase.

Avocados

Avocados are the exception to the rule that fruits and vegetables are low in fat and calories. One-half of an avocado has 150 calories, 89 percent of which come from fat. Still, the majority of that fat is monounsaturated, and therefore may lower cholesterol levels. Furthermore, avocados are rich in potassium, niacin, and vitamin A and contain a fair amount of iron.

Choose avocados that have no bruises or sunken spots. Avocados are ripe when they yield to light pressure. Those that are not quite ready to eat can be ripened at room temperature. Store avocados that are already ripe in the refrigerator.

Fresh, Frozen, or Canned

Because it tastes better, many people prefer fresh produce. Nutritionally, too, fresh is better—in theory, that is, but not invariably. For maximum nutrition, fruits and vegetables should be harvested and eaten the same day. Still, even produce transported a thousand miles or more and left in the bin for a day or two can be full of nutrients.

Fresh produce. To get the most from fresh produce, shop frequently and use fruits and vegetables as quickly as you can. Don't peel, slice, or chop anything until just before you are ready to cook and/or serve it. If you don't have to cut, don't. String beans, for example, retain more flavor and vitamins if cooked whole. Avoid buying precut produce such as cantaloupe. At least ask the manager how long cut fruits have been sitting around. Never soak fruits and vegetables, and wash them as little as is consistent with cleanliness. Choose a quick-cooking method (microwaving, for example, or steaming) over the long, slow boil that leaches out minerals and partially destroys vitamins. Always cook vegetables with a cover. No matter how careful you are, processing of any kind always destroys some nutrients.

If produce looks or feels wilted and pallid, or if you have inadvertently allowed the broccoli to sit in the crisper for a week, you'll be better off with a frozen or even a canned vegetable for dinner.

Frozen produce. Frozen food that has been scrupulously handled can be more nutritious than fresh that has sat in the grocery for days. Frozen fruits, in particular, may retain more vitamin C than fresh fruit that has been abused in transport or storage. Don't buy packages with ice crystals on the outside; this indicates that the food has thawed and refrozen. Pack frozen fruits and vegetables in a double bag and get them home fast. Your home freezer should stay at zero degrees Fahrenheit. If something begins to thaw, you can salvage it by cooking it as soon as possible.

Canned produce. The extended heating process of commercial canning destroys some vitamin C and B vitamins, as well as A and E—90 percent in some cases. Minerals survive heating, but significant quantities—up to 50 percent—of manganese and zinc, for example, can be lost if the canned liquid is not used. Storing canned vegetables for more than a year can increase nutrient loss unless room temperature is kept below sixty-five degrees. Though most canned produce lacks the flavor and texture of fresh or even frozen, it still has enough nutrients to be worth eating.

Is garlic beneficial?
Studies have shown that garlic oil (specially extracted to retain its active ingredients) inhibits the coagulation of blood, reduces LDL cholesterol, and increases HDL cholesterol.

Only garlic oils extracted in this way have these benefits; the garlic pills, oils, and extracts sold in health food stores are processed in such a way that the healthful ingredients have been removed.

Unfortunately, the subjects in these studies downed the equivalent of ten cloves of garlic a day, an amount that may produce unpleasant side effects, such as diarrhea, nausea, vomiting, body odor, and bad breath.

Beans

Snap beans, which are also called green beans or string beans, are either green or yellow, and are a good source of iron, potassium, and vitamin A (yellow beans are much lower in this vitamin than green, however) and contain a small amount of calcium as well. They are also a good source of fiber. One cup cooked has 45 calories. Lima beans, fresh or frozen, are higher in protein, calories (one cup cooked has 170), and fiber, and lower in vitamin A than green beans. They, too, are a good source of iron.

Choose snap beans that are brightly colored green or yellow depending on their variety. The beans should look young and tender and feel velvety. Avoid those that are bulging with seeds since these will be old and tough. Snap beans will keep for a few days wrapped in plastic in the refrigerator. Fresh lima beans are sold in their pods. Choose pods that are bright green and well filled. Avoid those that have brown spots or look old. Baby lima beans are usually more tender. Lima beans should be refrigerated and stored in their pods uncovered. They will keep three to five days.

Beets

While canned beets are most popular, fresh beets are crisper and more flavorful; they can be steamed, boiled, or baked. Never peel beets until after cooking and leave some of the stem on

Exotic Vegetables

Interest in vegetables has risen in the past few years, and many supermarkets and produce stands have begun stocking varieties that you wouldn't have found, or perhaps even heard of, ten years ago. They're no more nutritious than your old favorites, but they can add variety and interest to your diet. There are squashes of all descriptions, as well as uncommon newcomers such as daikon (Japanese radish) and jicama (the so-called Mexican potato), and salsify (used by American cooks of the last century and now undergoing a revival). The following guide sorts out some of the newer vegetables you are likely to see, most of which are not really new at all—just less familiar than broccoli or carrots in American markets.

For variety as well as nutrition and good taste, these vegetables are well worth trying. Many can be eaten raw; all are easy to cook. Some of the larger vegetables (spaghetti squash, for example) may come with a small label affixed that offers tips on cooking and handling. Like all vegetables, these are relatively low in calories and relatively high in vitamins, minerals, and fiber.

Bok choy (Chinese mustard cabbage). Large white stem, dark green leaves, mild flavor, shaped like a head of celery. Can be stir-fried, added to soups, or eaten raw in coleslaw or salads, like any cabbage. A half-cup serving (cooked) has 10 calories, some calcium, one-third of your daily requirement of vitamin C, and half your daily requirement of beta carotene, which the body converts to vitamin A.

Celeriac (celery root). Bulbous white root, rough brown skin, celerylike flavor. Peel, then slice or julienne. Good raw if marinated in lemon juice or a flavorful dressing; also good in soups. A half-cup serving has 20 calories and also contains small amounts of beta carotene, iron, and calcium.

Chayote squash (mango squash or mirliton). Dark green. May be avocado-shaped or round. Zucchini-like flavor. Peel, then boil, bake, or stir-fry like any summer squash. The large seed is edible, too. Unpeeled halves can be stuffed with shrimp, ground meats, or rice and diced-vegetable combinations and then baked. A half-cup serving has 19 calories, plus small amounts of beta carotene, vitamin C, and potassium.

Daikon (Japanese radish). White carrot-shaped root. Crisp and spicy. Good raw in salads or sliced as a dipping vegetable. Can be added to soups, stews, or stir-fries. A half-cup serving has about 10 calories, with some vitamin C and potassium.

Fennel (finocchio, anise). Large bulb-shaped base (the edible part) with pale green, feathery tops. Common in Italian cooking. Mild licorice flavor. Trim, slice, and serve raw in salads or as a dipping vegetable. Add to soups and stir-fries. A half-cup serving has about 15 calories, some beta carotene, and calcium.

Jerusalem artichoke (sunchoke, girasole). Small brown bulb with crisp white flesh. Nutty flavor. Not related to artichokes. Peel, slice, and serve raw in salads, or steam and substitute for potatoes as a side dish. A half-cup serving has 57 calories, plus some calcium, iron, and phosphorus.

Jicama (Mexican potato). Light brown skin; round but slightly flat; crisp, sweet, white flesh. Needs peeling. Good raw, served sliced and cold, in salads or with dips. Or steam or stir-fry quickly. Can be dressed with lemon juice and chili powder for an hors d'oeuvre. A half-cup serving has 25 calories and almost one-quarter of your daily vitamin C requirement.

Salsify (oyster plant). A carrot-shaped root with black or white skin. Mild flavor, somewhat like asparagus. Steam whole, then peel and slice. Like potatoes, raw salsify darkens quickly when peeled. A good side dish or addition to soup. A half-cup serving has 35 calories, plus some calcium and iron.

Spaghetti squash. Yellow, football-shaped, with stringy but tender and flavorful yellow flesh. Halve and steam until tender, then use a fork to shred the pulp into "spaghetti." Serve plain, with pasta sauces, or with a small amount of olive oil and grated cheese. Cooked and cooled, it can be added to salads. A half-cup serving has 23 calories, some beta carotene, B vitamins, and potassium.

top for boiling. Beets contain more sugar than any other vegetable, but one cup (sliced) has only 60 calories. Beets are a good source of potassium, iron, and fiber.

Choose beets that are firm and smooth with a deep red color. The greens, if attached, should be fresh-looking. Remove green tops before storing. They keep about two weeks in the refrigerator.

Broccoli

Broccoli is the nutritional leader of the cruciferous family of vegetables, the type that studies suggest may protect against colorectal, stomach, and respiratory cancers. One cup chopped and cooked contains 45 calories and provides you with 90 percent of your daily requirement of vitamin A, 200 percent of vitamin C, 6 percent of niacin, 10 percent of calcium, 10 percent of thiamine, 10 percent of phosphorus, and 8 percent of iron. It is also rich in potassium and fiber.

Choose crisp stalks and flowerets that do not show any yellow. The stalks should look young and tender, not woody. Fresh broccoli will keep for a few days if wrapped in plastic and stored in the refrigerator.

Brussels sprouts

This vegetable looks like a miniature cabbage; indeed, it is a member of the cabbage family and like other cruciferous vegetables has cancer-protecting properties. Brussels sprouts are an excellent source of fiber and vitamin C. They are a good source of protein, vitamin A, potassium, and iron, and brussels sprouts also contain a small amount of calcium.

Choose tightly compact, firm heads with good color. Avoid those that are puffy and soft or those with a strong odor. Brussels sprouts kept in a plastic

bag in the refrigerator will stay crisp and green. Use within a few days.

Cabbage

Cabbage can be eaten cooked or raw, although some people have trouble digesting it raw. Cabbage is a good source of fiber and vitamin C, and, like its relatives, broccoli and cauliflower, has cancer-protecting potential. One cup raw has 15 calories; one cup cooked has 30.

Choose heads that are tightly closed without signs of worm holes or bruises. The heads should be firm, not puffy, and feel heavy for their size. Unwashed cabbage will keep for a week to ten days—sometimes longer—if placed in a plastic bag and refrigerated.

Carrots

Long been rumored to have properties that can improve vision, carrots are, in fact, good for your eyes: they are rich in beta carotene, which the body converts to vitamin A—a crucial nutrient for the functioning of the retina. But vitamin A won't cure nearsightedness or farsightedness and can improve vision only if vision problems result from a vitamin A deficiency, which is a rare condition in this country. Still, beta carotene is believed to be a protector against cancer and carrots may also help lower blood cholesterol levels.

One seven-inch carrot has about 30 calories and contains enough beta carotene to supply your body with more than four times the Recommended Dietary Allowance (RDA) for vitamin A (the deeper orange the color of the carrot, the more beta carotene it will contain). This root vegetable is also rich in potassium and a good source of soluble fiber.

To retain maximum nutrients, scrub carrots but leave them unpeeled, unless the skin is very tough or blem-

Vegetables with high fiber are green peas, lima beans, parsnips, sweet peppers, broccoli, carrots, green beans, brussels sprouts, and sweet potatoes.

ished. Carrots contain more natural sugar than any other vegetable, except for beets, and thus they make a healthful addition to items such as quick breads, cakes, and muffins.

Choose carrots that are firm and well-shaped with good color. Avoid those that are cracked, shriveled, or rubbery. When buying carrots with their green tops still attached, make sure the greens are fresh-looking. Carrots keep well in the refrigerator. Green tops should be removed from carrots before storing.

Cauliflower

One of the cruciferous vegetables that may offer protection against some forms of cancer, cauliflower can be eaten cooked or raw, although some people have trouble digesting it uncooked. One cup of cauliflower diced and cooked is high in vitamin C, fiber, and potassium, and contains 30 calories. Frozen cauliflower is not as flavorful as fresh; it often tastes soggy and bland.

Choose white, firm, clean flowerets with no discoloration. The leaves should be green and fresh-looking. Store cauliflower wrapped in plastic in the vegetable bin of the refrigerator.

Celery

Because of its high water content, celery is nearly calorie free; one eight-inch stalk has just 6 calories. It is, however, low in nutrients, supplying just a small amount of potassium. Still, celery does contain some fiber and makes a flavorful addition to soups and stews (celery leaves can also be used in making broth), or a healthful snack.

Choose bunches of celery that are tightly closed at the bottom. The stalks should be fresh-looking and free of bruises and growth cracks. The leaves should also look fresh. Avoid

celery that is limp. Store celery in the refrigerator; wrapped in plastic, it will keep for about two weeks.

Corn

Corn on the cob is best in season (May through September), for that is when its flavor is at its peak. An ear of corn has just 85 calories and is a good source of fiber. Corn provides a small amount of protein, phosphorus, and potassium. Yellow corn also contains a small amount of vitamin A.

Choose corn that has been picked that day and has been kept cold, or at least shaded from the sun. Do not buy corn that has already been husked. The husks should have a good green color and be free from decay where the silk ends. If possible, pull back the husk and look for well-formed, plump kernels. Eat the corn as soon as possible; the sugar in corn begins to turn to starch the moment it is picked. If you cannot eat the corn right away, store it in the coldest part of your refrigerator; cold temperatures retard the change from sugar to starch.

Cucumbers

Cucumbers are low in calories—six large slices have just 5 calories—but otherwise have little nutritional value. Their high water content, however, makes them particularly refreshing on a hot summer day. Full-sized cucumbers are usually waxed and should be peeled before eating; smaller-sized kirbys are usually not waxed and therefore do not need peeling.

Choose cucumbers that are slender and firm to the touch. Cucumbers should have a good green color and not be dull green or yellow. Avoid any overly large cucumbers and those with shriveled ends. Cucumbers will keep for about a week if they are stored in the refrigerator.

Creamed corn contains no cream or dairy products, but it does have cornstarch and sugar, which add calories. Canned whole-kernel corn may also contain sugar.

160

Eggplant

Eggplant comes in many colors—white, purple, purple-black, yellowish-white, red, and striped—but the most common is the the dark purple, pear-shaped variety. Eggplant is a good source of fiber and potassium. To get the most from its fiber content, do not peel eggplant before eating. One cup cooked has just 50 calories.

Choose eggplant that feels firm to the touch and is heavy for its size.

Dark purple eggplant should have a clear, satiny color. Avoid any with soft spots or bruises. Small eggplants are often more tender. Eggplant will keep for about a week if refrigerated and wrapped in a plastic bag to prevent moisture loss.

Greens

If iceberg lettuce is the only type of greens you eat, you are selecting the one weakling in a family of nutritional

NUTRITIONAL CONTENT OF
Raw Greens

Greens (3½ oz)	Calories	Vitamin A (IU)	Vitamin C (mg)	Dietary Fiber (g)	Calcium (mg)	Iron (mg)	Comments
Iceberg, or crisphead lettuce	13	33	4	.9	19	0.5	The most popular kind of lettuce, but the least nutritious.
Butterhead, bibb, or Boston lettuce	13	970	8	1.5	35	0.2	Sweet and delicate taste.
Romaine, or Cos lettuce	16	2,600	24	2.1	68	1.4	Strong taste. Used in Caesar salads.
Loose-leaf lettuce	18	1,900	18	2.1	68	1.4	Sweet and delicate taste.
Arugula, or roquette	23	7,400	91	N/A	309	1.2	Strong and peppery. Spices up a salad.
Chicory, or curly endive	23	4,000	24	1.6	100	0.9	Slightly bitter. Mix with milder greens. Radicchio is a red variety.
Escarole	17	2,050	7	N/A	52	0.8	An endive with broad leaves.
Spinach	22	6,700	28	2.4	100	2.7	Eat raw or cooked. High in folacin and potassium. Its iron is poorly absorbed by the body.
Watercress	11	4,700	43	3.3	120	0.2	Pungent. In cabbage family. Add to salads or sandwiches.
Beet greens	40	7,340	36	N/A	164	2.7	Eat cooked. High in potassium. Moderately high in sodium.
Dandelion greens	45	14,000	35	3.3	187	3.1	Pungent. Very nutritious. Use young leaves in salads; sauté tough leaves.
Turnip greens	27	7,600	60	3.9	190	1.1	Strong flavor. More nutritious than the root vegetable. Eat raw or cooked.
Swiss chard	19	3,300	30	N/A	51	1.8	Mild flavor. Steam or sauté.
Kale	50	8,900	120	6.6	135	1.7	Mild, cabbage-like taste. Cook or use in salad. Highly nutritious
Collards	19	3,300	23	3.2	117	0.6	Strong flavor. In cabbage family; related to kale. Steam or sauté.

champions. Any other lettuce or leafy green vegetable would be a better choice. Most other greens are excellent sources of vitamin C and beta carotene (a precursor of vitamin A), and good sources of iron, fiber, folacin (a B vitamin), and calcium. As a general rule, the darker green a leaf vegetable is, the more nutritious. Romaine and loose-leaf lettuce thus have up to five times as much vitamin C and six times as much beta carotene as iceberg lettuce. What's more, greens—especially kale, collards, and others in the cabbage family—may help lower the risk of cancer. The iron in greens is not as easily assimilated by the body as iron from animal sources, but iron absorption is enhanced by vitamin C—by eating tomatoes or red peppers in your salad, for example.

Choose greens with good color for their variety. Leaves should be fresh-looking, not wilted. Avoid any greens with brown, rusty spots or obvious damage (torn, bruised leaves, or insect damage). Check the cut end of lettuce; it should be cream-colored, not brown. Wash and dry greens and store them in a plastic bag in the refrigerator. Do not store lettuce with apples, pears, or tomatoes because these fruits emit ethlene gas which can cause brown spotting on the leaves. Greens will keep a few days to a week in the refrigerator, depending on the variety.

Mushrooms

If you thought that mushrooms were just a tasty decoration, it should come as good news that they offer a significant amount of some vitamins and minerals. One cup of *Agaricus bisporus*, the common cultivated mushroom sold in supermarkets, has just 40 calories cooked and drained and provides you with 15 percent of the RDA for iron, 28 percent of the RDA for riboflavin,

35 percent of the RDA for niacin, and is high in potassium. Drained, canned mushrooms are less nutritious. The vitamins and minerals may be lost during processing or may seep out into the cooking liquids. Try to use the liquid in some part of your meal. But check the label on the can to make sure that salt and high-fat ingredients such as butter have not been added.

Shiitake mushrooms are another commonly found type. These mushrooms, which are available fresh or dried, are intensely flavorful and usually high priced. They have more calories, but fewer minerals than *Agaricus bisporus*. Dried shiitake mushrooms have highly concentrated calories and minerals by weight, but because of their strong flavor they are used in much smaller quantities. They must be soaked before cooking.

Choose mushrooms with tightly closed caps. Even if the gills show, the mushrooms may still taste good, but avoid any that are pitted or spongy-looking. Store mushrooms in a paper bag in the refrigerator and use them as soon as possible.

Onions

Raw or cooked, onions can be used in a wide variety of dishes. They enhance the flavor of foods by irritating the membranes of the nose and mouth, and therefore are a good addition to low-sodium diets.

There are many varieties of onions. The most common is the yellow globe onion, which has a strong flavor and is used mostly for cooking. Spanish or Bermuda onions are milder and can be eaten raw or cooked. Sweet red Italian onions have a mellow flavor and are often eaten raw in sandwiches and salads. Shallots—a cross between garlic and onion—have a sweet flavor. Chives and scallions are immature onion plants; only the leaves of chives are used and scallions (which are sold with their green tops attached) are picked before the bulb has a chance to form. Chives are sprinkled on food just before serving and scallions are sliced and used raw.

Onions are a good source of fiber and provide a fair amount of potassium. Scallions provide a good amount of vitamin A if their green tops are eaten. A half cup of chopped onions has about 75 calories; a half cup of chopped scallions has 13.

Choose onions that are firm and well-shaped with no soft or soggy spots. Their dry, paper-thin protective skin should be intact. Avoid onions that have sprouted. Scallions and chives should be green and fresh looking. Store onions in a cool dry place, or in the refrigerator. They will keep in either place for several weeks. Do not store onions with potatoes as they will draw moisture from the potatoes and rot very quickly. Both scallions and chives should be stored in the refrigerator vegetable bin and used within a few days.

Parsnips

This relative of the carrot has served as a good source of starch for four thousand years but was largely replaced by the potato in the nineteenth century. Unjustly neglected today, it has a sweet, nutty flavor, particularly in the winter, when it is most abundant. Parsnips are a good source of vitamin C and folacin, and an excellent source of fiber; one cup of cooked slices has about 120 calories.

Choose small to medium, well-shaped parsnips; large ones can be tough and taste woody. Avoid those that are limp and shriveled. Wrapped in plastic, parsnips will stay fresh for several weeks in the refrigerator.

Peas

Most of the peas in this country are sold frozen, but finding fresh peas is well worth the search because the flavor is so much better. Fresh peas are tender and sweet. Some varieties, such as sugar snap and snow peas (or Chinese peas), can be eaten pods and all. Peas are very high in protein for a vegetable and provide a good amount of iron, potassium, vitamin A, phosphorus, and niacin. They contain about 125 calories per cup, cooked. Snow peas are high in protein, iron, vitamin C, and potassium, and provide a small amount of calcium as well. One cup of cooked snow peas has 65 calories.

Choose uniformly green young pods that are well filled, and velvety to the touch. Pods that look as though they are about to explode or those that are yellow are overly mature and will taste tough and mealy. Snow peas should be bright green and look crisp and fresh. To prevent the conversion from sugar to starch, store peas uncovered in their pods in the refrigerator. Eat them as soon as possible.

Peppers

The most popular variety of peppers is the bell, aptly named for its shape. This type can be either green, red, or yellow. While green peppers are a good source of vitamins A and C, red peppers are an even better source of these vitamins; one red pepper provides 84 percent of the RDA for vitamin A and nearly two and a half times the vitamin C needed daily. Both shades are good sources of potassium and fiber and have just 20 calories per pepper. Varieties of hot peppers, such as cayenne, jalapeño, chili, and hot cherry, are also high in nutrients and low in calories, but are usually not eaten in quantities large enough to make any significant nutritional impact.

Are hot peppers harmful?

Hot peppers—such as jalapeño and chili—contain a natural substance called capsaicin that produces a burning sensation in the mouth, causes the eyes to water and the nose to run, and even induces perspiration. Many people enjoy the sensation, but wonder if hot peppers cause any harm. Fortunately, they don't. In countries where hot peppers are used heavily in cooking, there is no higher incidence of stomach ulcers. Nor will hot peppers cause or aggravate hemorrhoids, since capsaicin is broken down before it reaches the lower intestine. Of course, if hot peppers give you heartburn, you should limit your consumption of them.

Choose peppers that are firm and well shaped with good bright red or green color. They should be thick fleshed and free of soft spots and wrinkled skin. Store peppers in a plastic bag in the refrigerator. They will keep for about a week.

Potatoes

Potatoes have a reputation for being fattening, but this is not the case. One medium-sized baked potato with its skin has just 220 calories and is virtually fat free. Potatoes are bad for those watching their weight only when they are fried or served with high-calorie, high-fat toppings such as sour cream and butter. Potatoes are a good source of fiber, iron, phosphorus, potassium, vitamin B_6, and niacin, and a fair source of vitamin C. New potatoes are not a different variety, but the young, small, thin-skinned potatoes of any variety that are harvested early. They are similarly nutritious.

To get the most nutrients from potatoes, you should eat the skin, since many nutrients are concentrated in or just below it. The only reason to avoid the skin is if the potato has a greenish tinge. That's chlorophyll, a sign that the potato has been exposed to too much light after harvest. It's also an indication that solanine (a naturally occurring toxin) may be present in increased amounts, especially in the skin. Eating such damaged potatoes may occasionally cause cramps, diarrhea, and fatigue. Potato sprouts contain lots of solanine, too. Although undamaged potatoes also contain some solanine, the concentration is very low in most American-grown varieties. You would have to eat about twelve pounds of them at a single sitting to be affected adversely.

If you don't like the taste of potato skin, even if it's undamaged, remember to peel it carefully. Cutting away too much will remove the nutrients just below the skin.

Choose potatoes that have not sprouted and are virtually unblemished. Avoid those that have shriveled skin or are soft, wilted, or green. If a potato you have at home has seen better days, pare away all the green areas, including the skin, and gouge out all sprouts. But if it has become excessively soft or sprouted, discard it. Store potatoes in a cool, dry, dark area. If stored properly, potatoes will keep for several months—new potatoes, several weeks—but it is best to buy potatoes in small amounts unless you plan to use them within a week or two.

Rutabagas

Often called yellow turnips, rutabagas are actually a different plant. One cup, cubed and cooked, provides more than half of your daily requirement for vitamin C and small amounts of calcium, iron, and potassium as well. Rutabagas are a good source of fiber.

Choose rutabagas that are firm and feel heavy for their size. Do not refrigerate. Stored in a cool place, rutabagas will keep for several months.

Squash

Squash is broadly divided into two varieties: summer, which includes zucchini and pattypan; and winter, which includes acorn, butternut, buttercup, Hubbard, and pumpkin. One cup of summer squash sliced has just 35 calories and provides a small amount of potassium. At 80 calories, one cup of winter squash, baked and cubed, provides nearly one and a half times the vitamin A (in the form of beta carotene) you need daily and a good amount of potassium. Pumpkin is even more nutritious: a cup of canned pumpkin has 85 calories (one cup fresh, cooked, has 50) and is high in iron, potassium, and vitamin A. All squashes are good sources of fiber.

Choose summer squashes that have a rind soft enough to puncture with your fingernail. They should be free of bruises and soft spots. Small- to medium-sized summer squashes are best in flavor and texture. Winter squashes should have a smooth, hard rind and be free of soft spots. They should feel heavy for their size. Summer squashes are very perishable. Store them in the refrigerator and use them as soon as possible. Winter squashes are more hardy; they will keep for several months if stored in a cool, dry area.

Sweet potatoes

Sweet potatoes either have a dry, light yellow flesh or a moist, deep yellow or orange flesh. The latter are sometimes called yams, but they are not true yams, which are grown in the tropics. One four-ounce sweet potato, baked and peeled, has 115 calories and provides nearly five times the RDA of vitamin A. Sweet potatoes also contain some potassium and fiber and small amounts of iron and calcium.

Choose small- to medium-sized sweet potatoes with tapered ends. They should be firm and smooth-skinned. Avoid those with shriveled or discolored ends. Sweet potatoes will keep in a cool room for about two weeks.

Tomatoes

The best tasting fresh tomatoes are found during the summer months. But though out-of-season tomatoes are not as tasty, they aren't necessarily less nutritious. Instead of being left to ripen on the vine, out-of-season tomatoes are picked at the stage called "mature green," still firm enough to ship, but only just at the point of turning red. To complete the ripening at their destina-tion, they are "gassed" with ethylene, a plant hormone that is part of the natu-ral maturing process. Ripened either with ethylene or on the vine, however, tomatoes are a good source of vitamins A and C and potassium. One five-ounce tomato has just 25 calories.

Choose vine-ripened tomatoes when possible. These should be firm and plump and have a strong tomato fra-grance. Avoid soft overripe tomatoes with blemishes, bruises, soft spots, or growth cracks. Store tomatoes in a warm location away from direct sun-light until ripe. Once ripe, store in the refrigerator. Ripe tomatoes will keep for about a week.

Turnips

Sold in bunches with their greens, early white turnips are marketed immediately after harvesting, so they are small and tender. Older ones are left in the field to mature until their skin toughens, making them easy to ship and store. One cup of boiled, cubed white turnips has 30 percent of the RDA of vitamin C and just 30 calories. Turnips are also a good source of fiber.

Choose turnips that are small, firm, and fairly smooth. If the greens are attached, they should be fresh looking and not wilted. Avoid those with obvi-ous fibrous roots. Store turnips in the refrigerator crisper and use them with-in a week.

DAIRY AND EGGS

Milk

Milk is a highly nutritious food that provides nearly all the substances essential for good health in people of all ages. It is particularly rich in high-

Water chestnuts, commonly used in Chinese cuisine, are not nuts, but tubers. Unlike nuts, they are low in calories (about 14 calories per ounce, approximately four water chestnuts) and almost fat-free.

quality protein, calcium, vitamin D, riboflavin, and other vitamins and minerals. One cup of milk on average supplies about 15 to 20 percent of an adult's daily protein needs, 25 percent of the vitamin D needed, as well as between 25 and 38 percent of the calcium needed.

Milk and milk products are primary dietary sources of calcium, which is essential for the growth and maintenance of bones and teeth. One cup of milk has about 300 milligrams of calcium. The daily RDA of calcium for children under age eleven is 800 milligrams, for teenagers and young adults, the daily RDA is 1,200 milligrams, and for most older adults, it is 800 milligrams.

For postmenopausal women, different rules apply: since, after menopause, women are particularly subject to osteoporosis (a gradual weakening of the bone structure, which puts them at greater risk for fractures), they must be sure to get extra calcium. A report of the National Institutes of Health recommends that postmenopausal women maintain a daily intake of 1,000 to 1,500 milligrams of calcium—an amout that is equivalent to three to four cups of milk (or three or four servings of yogurt or cheese).

Milk does have some drawbacks: whole milk contains a considerable amount of saturated fat and cholesterol, which can be harmful to the cardiovascular system. After the age of two years, it is advisable to switch to low-fat or skim milk.

Skim and low-fat milk are as nutritious as whole milk except that they are deprived of fat-soluble vitamins—for example A and D. In the United States, they are therefore always fortified with vitamin A (usually in greater quantities than in whole milk) and almost always vitamin D.

Most nondairy powdered creamers have as many calories as light cream and contain coconut oil, which is even more saturated than butterfat.

Caution on raw milk

Almost all milk is pasteurized these days; less than one percent of the 280 million glasses of milk drunk every day by Americans is raw milk. Yet this small percentage that escapes pasteurization is the subject of much debate among health food proponents, public health officials, and consumer groups. Milk is an excellent vehicle for bacterial infection, and in the nineteenth century it led to widespread outbreaks of disease. That's why pasteurization—a mild heating process that kills dangerous microorganisms in milk—is considered one of the greatest advances in food sanitation of all time.

Raw milk is still legally sold in some states, but that doesn't mean that it is safe to drink. In 1987, sixty-two Californians died from listerial bacteria in cheese made from unpasteurized milk and sixteen thousand Midwesterners were struck by salmonella poisoning after drinking improperly pasteurized milk.

Despite this, some people still believe that unpasteurized milk is more nutritious, since the heat of pasteurization destroys some nutrients, and that raw milk enhances resistance to disease. However, researchers have detected no nutritional advantages to raw milk. Current techniques of pasteurization heat milk for such brief periods that there is little effect on nutrients, only a nutritionally insignificant decrease in thiamine, vitamin B_{12} and vitamin C. There's no evidence that raw milk enhances resistance to disease. It has been shown, however, that raw milk contains infectious bacteria and has been implicated in outbreaks of disease.

Combating lactose intolerance

Many people cannot digest more than a small amount of milk because of its

NUTRITIONAL CONTENT OF
Milk

Milk (8 fl oz)	Calories	Fat (g)	Fat Calories	Comments
Whole (3% fat)	150	8	48%	Usually fortified with vitamin D. High in saturated fat and cholesterol. Total fat content may vary from state to state. Best only for children under the age of two.
Low-fat (2% fat)	120	5	38%	Close in taste and texture to whole milk. Vitamins A and D almost always added. Too high in fat to be an acceptable choice for those on a low-fat diet.
Low-fat (1% fat)	100	3	27%	Low in fat; good choice for those on low-fat diets or those trying to restrict calories. Vitamins A and D almost always added.
Skim (nonfat)	80	trace	5%	Virtually fat free. Best choice for those on a low-fat diet. Should not be given to children under the age of two.
Buttermilk (1% fat)	100	2	18%	Tart and creamy. Low in fat and and cholesterol. Usually made from skim or low-fat milk. Easily digested; bacteria breaks down about 25 percent of lactose. Usually not fortified with vitamins A or D.
Dry (nonfat, reconstituted)	80	trace	5%	About as nutritious as fresh skim milk. Virtually fat- and cholesterol-free. Fortified with vitamins A and D. Thin consistency, flat taste; clumps in hot liquids.
Evaporated (canned, made from whole milk, undiluted)	340	20	53%	High in fat and cholesterol. Sterilized; long shelf life if can is turned over every few months. Can be used undiluted when specified in recipes, otherwise must be diluted. Slightly carmelized taste.
LactAid™ (lactase treated, 1% fat)	100	2	18%	Helps lactose intolerants digest milk. Contains lactase, which breaks down at least 70 percent of lactose in milk. Slightly sweet taste.
Goat's milk (whole)	168	10	54%	High in fat. Contains mostly the same proteins as cow's milk, so those allergic to cow's milk will probably be allergic to goat's milk, too.

Half-and-half has twice as many calories and three times as much fat as whole milk. Heavy cream contains seven times as many calories and eleven times as much fat as the same amount of milk.

lactose (milk sugar). The inability to digest milk occurs because the enzyme lactase, which breaks down the milk's lactose in the intestines, is produced in increasingly smaller quantities in most people after infancy. While lactose intolerance most often affects blacks, Asians, and other people who traditionally consume few milk products, a large portion of the general population may suffer from this enzyme deficiency as they grow older.

To avoid the discomfort of this malady—cramps, gas, diarrhea—sufferers can try consuming fermented milk products such as buttermilk, kefir, or yogurt, since some of the lactose is broken down by the bacterial cultures in these products. Those who are lactose intolerant can also try drinking milk treated with the enzyme lactase which is available in the dairy case of many supermarkets.

Is goat's milk better?

Goat's milk and the cheese made from it are no more nutritious than cow's milk. It contains most of the same nutrients. The calcium content of goat's milk is slightly, but not significantly, higher than that of cow's milk. Its vitamin A content is higher, too, but so is the fat content. Cow's milk comes in low-fat versions, but goat's milk, so far, is sold only as whole milk. A cup of it has 165 calories and ten grams of fat, and more than half the calories come from fat.

Goat's milk contains a higher percentage of smaller fat globules, which in theory are more easily broken down by digestive enzymes, so some people think it is more digestible than cow's milk. But when cow's milk is homogenized, so that the cream does not rise to the top, the large fat globules in it are broken down. No human studies have shown that either homogenized cow's milk or goat's milk is more quickly digested than other kinds of milk. And the lactose levels are comparable, so if you are lactose intolerant, goat's milk is not the answer.

If you like the tangy taste of goat's milk, just make sure it has been pasteurized. Raw goat's milk is subject to the same type of bacterial contamination as cow's milk.

Cheese

Cheese is a concentrated form of milk, minus its liquid or whey. That makes it a mixed blessing—high in protein but also in saturated fat; usually full of calcium but also sodium; rich and creamy but loaded with cholesterol.

About eight pounds of milk go into a pound of most types of cheese, with the result that just one ounce (an average slice) of cheese contains approximately as much fat and protein as a cup of milk. Some nutrients found in milk are lost when the whey is drained, in particular the B vitamins and some minerals. Also removed is most of the lactose (milk sugar); this makes cheese good for people who have difficulty digesting lactose. However, most of the calcium (except in cottage cheese and other soft cheeses), vitamin A, and phosphorus from the milk remain in the cheese.

Can cheese be low-fat?

Because almost all the fat from the milk is concentrated in it, cheese is one of the most potent sources of saturated fat and cholesterol—worse than most meats. Since the fat is so essential to the taste of cheese, it's hard to produce a cheese low in fat. Some cheesemakers are using nonfat or low-fat milk to make reduced-fat cheese. On average, this practice removes only two to four grams of fat per ounce: the five to seven grams of fat in an ounce of the low-fat type is better than the nine in regular cheddar, for example, but it's still a lot. The terms "low-fat," "lower-fat," "light," or "lite" are virtually meaningless when used by cheese manufacturers, since the Food and Drug Administration (FDA) has never defined them. When manufacturers use these terms, however, they are required to provide nutritional labels, so you can at least check if the products really are low in fat.

Still, some old standbys are low or moderate in fat. Low-fat or dry-curd cottage cheese and part-skim ricotta, for example, contain less than three grams of fat per ounce and are the best choices for people on a low-fat diet.

You can boost the calcium content of any dish by adding nonfat dry milk. Stir into soups, sauces, stews, and gravies, or add to casseroles, rice, and cereals.

NUTRITIONAL CONTENT OF
Cheese

	Calories	Fat (g)	Fat Calories	Calcium (mg)	Sodium (mg)
American, 1 oz	105	9	77%	190	400
Blue, 1 oz	100	8	72%	150	396
Camembert or brie, 1 oz	85	7	74%	60	200
Cheddar, 1 oz	115	9	70%	205	200
Cottage, creamed, ½ cup	108	5	42%	63	425
Cottage, dry curd, ½ cup	62	trace	7%	23	9
Cottage, low-fat, ½ cup	104	2	17%	78	459
Cream, 1 oz	100	10	90%	20	85
Feta, 1 oz	75	6	72%	140	315
Mozzarella, part skim, 1 oz	80	5	56%	207	150
Mozzarella, whole milk, 1 oz	80	6	68%	147	106
Muenster, 1 oz	105	9	77%	205	175
Neufchatel, 1 oz	74	7	85%	21	113
Parmesan, 1 oz	130	9	62%	390	528
Provolone, 1 oz	100	8	72%	214	248
Ricotta, part skim, ½ cup	170	10	53%	335	154
Ricotta, whole milk, ½ cup	216	16	66%	255	104
Swiss, 1 oz	105	8	67%	275	150

Although they are dairy products, butter, cream, and cream cheese contain virtually no calcium and are concentrated sources of fat.

Whole-milk and part-skim mozzarella, whole-milk ricotta, feta, and creamed cottage cheese are higher in fat—four to six grams of fat per ounce—and so should be eaten in moderation.

Large markets and gourmet shops are starting to stock more exotic or new varieties of low-fat cheeses. Some of the types to look for:

Gammelost. This semisoft blue cheese from Norway is made from sour skim milk and has a sharp, aromatic flavor. One ounce contains about 60 calories and 0.3 grams of fat. It's comparatively low in sodium, too—85 milligrams.

Sapsago. Made from slightly sour skim milk plus buttermilk, Sapsago takes a bit of getting used to. Very hard, light green, and with a pungent herb flavor, it is best used as a grating cheese like Parmesan. One ounce contains about 65 calories and two grams of fat. Like Parmesan, however, it is very high in sodium—520 milligrams per ounce. Sapsago comes from Switzerland, but this cheese is also made in Germany, where it is usually called Schabizger, Glarnerkäse, Grunerkäse, or Krauterkäse.

Hoop or baker's cheese. Previously used primarily by bakers and in special diets, this soft cheese is now available at many markets. The curd is separated from the whey and isn't cooked or washed, which gives it a distinctive acidic taste. One ounce has about 85 calories, less than a gram of fat, and, because it's unsalted, just ten milligrams of sodium. Hoop or baker's cheese is good in dips, spreads, and many cooked dishes. (For a creamy dip, mix it with some low-fat or nonfat yogurt.) If you can't find it at your market, you can approximate it by rinsing low-fat cottage cheese in cold water using a fine mesh strainer.

Another low-fat option: yogurt cheese

Yogurt cheese—yogurt drained so that the whey is removed—can be an excellent substitute for high-fat cheeses, sandwich spreads, and dips. (See marginal at left.) If it is made from low-fat or nonfat yogurt, this cheese contains only a gram of fat or less per ounce.

What makes yogurt cheese special is that it picks up the flavor of anything it's mixed with. For example, two parts yogurt cheese can be blended with one part mayonnaise (real, imitation, or light) to make a sandwich spread that tastes like the real thing, but has much less fat and fewer calories, while adding a little calcium to boot. You can also use yogurt cheese as a substitute for butter, margarine, cream cheese, or sour cream. For a vegetable dip or topping, add herbs or spices like garlic and chives. Yogurt cheese can also be used to make a truly low-fat cheesecake.

Making Nonfat Yogurt Cheese

Yogurt cheese is easy to make at home. Follow these simple instructions:

1. Line a medium-sized strainer with dampened cheesecloth—or use a yogurt cheese funnel— and place it over a bowl.
2. Place plain nonfat yogurt in the strainer or funnel and let it drain uncovered in the refrigerator overnight.
3. What remains in the funnel is yogurt cheese. Discard the whey that has drained into the bowl.
4. If you are not using the cheese immediately, place it in a tightly covered container and keep refrigerated.

Each ounce of yogurt yields 1/2 ounce of yogurt cheese.

Yogurt

Yogurt is merely milk—generally cow's milk in this country—curdled by the addition of bacteria. Like the milk it is made from, yogurt is a nutritious food. Eight ounces supply 20 to 25 percent of your daily protein needs and 300 to 400 milligrams of calcium—about as much as a glass of milk—and is a good source of riboflavin, phosphorus, and potassium.

Yet, despite claims to the contrary, yogurt isn't necessarily a "diet food." The number of calories and amount of fat in it depend on which type of milk it is made from (whole, low-fat, or skim milk, to which may be added cream and nonfat milk solids) as well as the type and amount of sweetener (sucrose, fructose, corn syrup, honey, molasses, or some combination) it may contain. A cup of yogurt can have 90 calories or nearly 400, no fat or eleven grams (supplying up to 45 percent of all calories). Plain yogurt has no sugar, but vanilla, coffee, and lemon varieties

NUTRITIONAL CONTENT OF Yogurt			
(8 oz)	Calories	Fat (g)	Calcium (mg)
Whole-milk			
plain	140-210	5-11	275-400
flavored	230-390	5-11	200-350
Low-fat			
plain	140-160	4	300-450
flavored	220-280	3	300-400
Nonfat			
plain	90-110	0	300-450
flavored	150	0	250-300
Low-fat yogurt drink			
flavored	180	2	250-400
Kefir, low-fat			
plain	110	3	300-550
fruit	150	3	250-530

contain the equivalent of three and a half teaspoons of sugar, and fruit flavors up to seven teaspoons. And whereas a cup of yogurt made from skim milk has merely four milligrams of cholesterol, whole-milk brands contain about thirty milligrams.

If you are watching your weight or fat intake, steer away from highly sweetened, flavored yogurts and those made from whole milk. The various "styles" don't make a difference nutritionally. Sundae-style yogurt has the fruit on the bottom; Swiss- and French-style have yogurt and fruit already mixed (the Swiss-style is thicker because it contains a solidifying agent such as gelatin).

As for drinkable yogurt and frozen yogurt, look for the same things you look for in regular yogurt: low fat and low sugar. If you do, they'll be much better for you than a fast-food shake or an ice-cream sundae. You can also make your own shakes using low-fat yogurt and skim milk. And you can use plain low-fat yogurt on baked potatoes, fruit, and salads and in dips as a healthful alternative to sour cream, mayonnaise, and commercial dressings; in cakes and spreads in place of cream cheese; in shakes instead of ice cream.

Yogurt is especially appealing to many people who have difficulty digesting milk sugar (lactose). During the fermentation process, the bacteria convert much of the lactose into lactic acid, which accounts for yogurt's tangy taste (the more sour the yogurt, the less lactose it contains). So if you are lactose intolerant, you may not have a problem digesting yogurt.

Other benefits of yogurt are far more theoretical. Earlier studies had suggested that the live bacteria in nearly all yogurts could lead to beneficial changes in the bacterial population of the intestines. However, present research offers little support for this.

You can also try kefir, which is not really yogurt but a different, related fermented-milk product popular in Europe for years. Supposedly made from a different strain of bacteria as well as kefir yeasts, kefir has the same nutritional assets as yogurt but with a less sour taste.

Eggs

Most dietary guidelines limit egg intake to two or three a week because eggs (more precisely yolks) are such a concentrated source of cholesterol—about 275 milligrams per large egg, according to the United States Department of Agriculture (USDA). But a re-examination of a large sample of eggs in a study by the Egg Nutrition Board suggests that the cholesterol content of eggs may be about 24 percent less than this, about 213 milligrams per large egg. This drop may be due to changes in the way the chickens are fed and bred and to changes in the way cholesterol is analyzed. In addition, some chicken farmers claim that special breeding and feeding (some birds are being fed cholesterol-lowering fish oil, for instance) have enabled them to reduce their eggs' cholesterol content even further, but these claims have been largely undocumented, or, in some cases, fraudulent.

Before you rush to the store for these "improved" eggs, keep in mind that 200, or even 175, milligrams of cholesterol still goes a long way toward the suggested daily allotment of 300 milligrams from all sources. Also, like any specialty item, "low-cholesterol" eggs have a premium price—as much as 30 percent higher than regular eggs.

In all other ways, an egg is an egg. There is no difference between brown

Is yogurt a cure-all?
It has been suggested that yogurt with active cultures may be useful in restoring bacterial balance in the intestine in individuals who have been taking antibiotics, which can kill good bacteria along with the bad. However, this has not been well demonstrated and there's nothing magical about yogurt. It won't make you live longer, improve digestion, or permanently implant good bacteria in your system.

eggs and white eggs in terms of nutrition or taste. The shell color depends on the breed of chicken that lays it and no one breed of chicken is known to lay better eggs than another. And a pale egg yolk is just as nutritious as a dark one. The color depends on the amount of xanthophyll—a natural yellow pigment found in chicken feed—present in the yolk, not beta carotene as is sometimes claimed.

Egg substitutes

Anyone serious about cutting down on cholesterol should consider egg substitutes. Either frozen or powdered, these products usually have no cholesterol at all. But there's a trade-off: though most of the substitutes use egg whites, many also contain sodium—sometimes in the form of MSG (monosodium glutamate) and artificial coloring, flavoring, and preservatives. Brands that contain no egg white (just starch and leavening agents) are good for people with egg allergies; they can be used in baking but not scrambling.

How do these "fake" eggs taste? Though they do resemble the real thing when cooked, taste varies from product to product. It also depends on

what they're used for: some will be better for omelets, some better in baking. It's largely a matter of personal choice. Cost is another factor. Most packages contain the equivalent of six to eight eggs at nearly double the price of a dozen eggs.

There's another, easier way to cut the cholesterol you get from eggs: substitute two whites for every whole egg. Omelets can be made using whites, nonfat dry milk, and skim milk, plus chopped vegetables and seasoning. Some recipes, such as soufflés and some cakes and muffins, call only for whites; chopped hard-cooked whites can also be used as a garnish for salads and vegetables. Cutting out all egg yolks may make some breads and other dishes dry and tasteless; in that case use two whites plus one whole egg instead of two eggs.

GRAINS AND LEGUMES

Whole Grains

Whole grains—except in the form of flour—are something of a mystery to many American cooks. While most people are familiar with rice as a side dish, or oatmeal as a breakfast cereal, other whole grains, such as cracked wheat and barley, are too often overlooked as potential main or side dishes. Such foods as kasha or bulgur may sound a little too mysterious. And often only health food stores stock special grains.

Yet whole grains are high in complex carbohydrates, low in fat, and rich in protein and fiber, as well as some B vitamins. Many are also fairly good sources of calcium and iron. The average cup of cooked whole grains con-

NUTRITIONAL CONTENT OF
Eggs and Egg Substitutes

	Calories	Fat (g)	Cholesterol (mg)	Sodium (mg)	Fat Calories
Whole egg	80	66	213	69	68%
Egg white	15	0	0	50	0%
Egg substitute, frozen (2 oz)	25-60	0-3	0	80-130	0-45%
Egg substitute, powdered (half packet)	60	4	7	124	60%
Egg substitute, powdered, no egg white (1½ tsp)	15	0	0	0	0%

tains only about 200 calories and is as easy to prepare as rice or dried pasta.

Types and uses

Kasha is simply a term for roasted buckwheat kernels that are cooked like rice; bulgur is precooked wheat berries, which can also be handled much like rice. Mediterranean and Middle Eastern cuisines feature many famous whole-grain dishes: couscous, a delicious combination of cracked wheat berries (millet can be used, but the packaged product is usually ground semolina) with meat, vegetables, or even fruits; tabbouleh, a cold salad made of cracked wheat or bulgur, chopped tomatoes, mint, and parsley; and pilafs, cooked combinations of grains with meats or vegetables. There are endless adapta-tions of these dishes using everyday ingredients. Other whole grains, such as rye and oats, while not ready substitutes for rice or pasta, can be incorporated in bread, meat loaf, and other baked dishes. And one grain can, of course, be mixed with another.

Three unusual names on the chart on page 174 are amaranth (Greek, meaning "immortal grain"), triticale (the term combines *triticum* and *secale*, Latin words for "wheat" and "rye"), and quinoa (pronounced KEEN-wa, a Quechuan word meaning "the mother grain"). Amaranth and quinoa are native to South America. Both are high in protein, minerals, and vitamins; supermarkets and health food stores carry them. Triticale, also high-protein, is a hybrid created about a century ago.

Wild Rice

One form of rice is not a grain but a grass seed (Zizania aquatica). It's native to North America and was once basic to the diet of the Chippewa and the Dakota tribes. Today, almost all wild rice is planted and grown in paddies. Nutty and rich in flavor, wild rice is more expensive than regular rice, but if you occasionally buy some as a treat, you're getting some nutritional extras. One cup cooked contains just 135 calories and is high in protein (6.3 grams per cup), low in fat, and a good source of B vitamins.

Wheat Germ vs. Wheat Bran

For years people have been buying wheat germ to sprinkle on breakfast cereals, yogurt, and salads or add to baked goods and casseroles. Now, with the spotlight on fiber, wheat germ has been joined on supermarket shelves by wheat bran. Together, wheat germ and bran account for most of wheat's nutritional value. What are the differences between the two?

Wheat germ. This is the wheat kernel's embryo; it's what develops into a new stalk of grain if planted. It is often removed in milling because it contains a fair amount of fat (polyunsaturated), which tends to go rancid, thus increasing the risk of spoilage in stored whole wheat flour, bread, and other products. One ounce contains 30 percent of the U.S. RDA for both thiamine and vitamin E, and 10 percent of that for iron and riboflavin. It also has 100 calories, nine grams of protein, three grams of dietary fiber, and three grams of fat. Defatted wheat germ is available, but it's lower in vitamin E; unlike regular wheat germ, it doesn't have to be stored in the refrigerator.

Wheat bran. This is the kernel's outer shell, usually sloughed off during milling. It contains a whopping twelve grams of dietary fiber per one-ounce serving (this is primarily insoluble fiber, the kind that may be protective against colon cancer). One ounce contains 40 percent of the U.S. RDA for both niacin and magnesium, plus 15 percent of that for iron. It also has 60 calories, five grams of protein, and one gram of fat.

Removing the germ and bran results in the familiar white flour used in most cooking and baking. This is made up chiefly of the third component of the kernel, the starchy endosperm, a source of energy and protein but with most other nutrients removed. While it's true that some of the nutrients (iron, niacin, thiamine, and riboflavin) lost in the milling process are replaced when white flour is enriched, the flour remains low in fiber as well as some trace nutrients (such as zinc and copper).

If you eat whole wheat cereals and baked goods, you're already getting the germ and bran. Other whole-grain cereals and baked goods, including rye and oats, offer comparable nutritional riches. But even if you eat these, bottled wheat germ and bran are concentrated sources of these nutrients that are convenient to add to baked goods. You can sprinkle them on nearly everything, adding not only nutrients, but also flavor and texture.

NUTRITIONAL CONTENT OF
Grains

Grain (1 cup cooked)	Protein (g)	Fat (g)	Dietary Fiber (g)	Iron (mg)	Comments
Amaranth	15	7	4.5	11.8	High in protein, iron, and calcium. Native to South America; available in health food stores. Whole kernels sold pearled (polished). Good as side dish or cereal. Flour used in bread, tortillas, cookies, and cereal.
Barley	8	1	8.2	2.1	Available as "pot" or "Scotch" barley (whole kernels) or pearl barley (polished). Both good in soups and stews and for side dishes, puddings, and cereal. May lower blood cholesterol.
Buckwheat	12	2	11.4	3.8	Not a true grain but a seed. Roasted kernels can be cooked like rice as a side dish (kasha). Flour can be mixed with wheat for bread and pancakes. Distinctive, nutty flavor.
Millet	12	4	3.0	3.0	High in phosphorus and B vitamins. Used chiefly as animal feed in the United States but available in health food stores. Good as side dish or as a substitute for bread stuffings in poultry. Swells enormously in water.
Oats	16	6	2.7	4.2	Whole kernels (groats) take an hour to cook. Flattened rolled oats require less time. Oat flour (oatmeal processed in a blender) can be used in bread, pastry, meatloaf, and casseroles. May lower blood cholesterol.
Quinoa	16	7	4.6	6.6	High in protein, calcium, and iron. Good in puddings, soups, and stir-fries. Whole-grain version must be washed and strained. Flour can be used in combination or alone for baking. Native South American grain.
Rice, brown	5	1	4.8	1	Unpolished rice; retains the bran and germ that contain the majority of nutrients and fiber. Nutty flavor. Requires forty-five to fifty minutes of cooking time.
Rice, white	4	trace	trace	1.8	Less nutritious than brown rice because the bran and germ have been removed. Usually enriched with iron and other nutrients.
Rye	12	2	11.4	4.6	Low-gluten content produces heavy bread. Cracked rye makes good cereal. Rolled rye from health food stores can be added to meat loaf and casseroles. Good in soups. Flour mixes well with wheat and/or oats.
Triticale	11	2	9.9	2.6	Wheat/rye hybrid; early man-made grain. Comes whole, cracked, and as flour. Flour low in gluten, best combined with wheat for bread making. Commercial brands of triticale bread available in supermarkets.
Whole wheat	10	2	9.6	3.5	Comes as whole berries or cracked. Whole berries need two to three hours of cooking, cracked about fifteen minutes. Both good for cereals, casseroles, and soups. Bulgur (hulled, parboiled wheat) is good for tabbouleh salad and other cold side dishes. Sweet, nutty flavor.

Remember that many whole grains, especially wheat, keep best in the refrigerator. The natural oils in the bran and the germ (the outer parts, which are removed in refining) tend to spoil quickly, especially in warm environments. This is why whole grains tend to be more costly, and one reason why most grains are refined in the first place—to increase their shelf life.

Cereals

With more Americans concerned about fiber than ever, hot and cold cereals have become increasingly popular. While cereal grains are naturally high in fiber and low in fat, sodium, and sugar, this is not always true of the final products on supermarket shelves. Some brands have only a trace of fiber left, while others are as salty as potato chips or, if they are targeted toward children, as sugary as a candy bar.

Ready-to-eat cereals are grains (rice, wheat, corn, oats) that have been exploded into puffs, pressured into flakes, shredded and spun into little biscuits, or perhaps extruded into some fanciful shape. Then the product is toasted. Next, in many cases, vitamins are sprayed on. Some cereals have many added ingredients: sugar, both brown and white, honey, molasses, corn syrup, and other sweeteners, as well as nuts, raisins, salt, and preservatives. Since the vitamins are added to the cereal, they are often also listed among the ingredients.

Nevertheless, if you keep your own concerns in mind—which probably include more fiber and less salt, sugar, and fat—you can find what you want in a cereal. Here are some guidelines for sorting out the nutritional information on the box, which can approach a legal document in complexity.

Check the ingredients list. A grain or grains should be listed first. The shorter the list, usually the less highly processed the cereal.

Determine how much sugar is in it. If sugar—or any of its many forms such as corn syrup, honey, maltose, or dextrose—appears high on the ingredients list, or if there is more than one sweetener listed, you can be pretty sure that the cereal is high in added sugars. Another way to check, however, is to calculate the ratio of carbohydrates to protein; it should be about eight to one, or in others words, for every one gram of protein, there should be no more than eight grams of carbohydrates. If it is thirty grams of carbohydrates for every two grams of protein, you are probably getting lots of sugar.

Look for brands with a high fiber content. Some have seven to thirteen grams of fiber per serving (enough to supply one-third to one-half of your recommended intake), while many high-sugar cereals contain less than a gram.

Scrutinize the label for the fat content. Most cereals are low in fat, but check the ingredients list for the addition of oils, such as coconut or palm kernel. Granola cereals are almost always high in fat because they usually contain nuts, coconut, and coconut oil. You can keep the fat content low by using one percent or skim milk.

Ignore vitamin claims. Nearly all brands today are fortified with vitamins and minerals. If your diet is reasonably balanced, there's no need to eat a cereal fortified with 100 percent of the U.S. RDAs for vitamins and minerals. This is like taking a multivitamin pill with your cereal—a pill you pay a premium for.

Watch out for sodium. If you are trying to reduce your salt intake, look for a cereal containing little or no sodium, such as shredded or puffed wheat, or

More breakfast cereal is consumed in the United States than anywhere else in the world.

Adding Oat Bran to Your Diet

Cookies, breads, cakes, crackers, and cold cereals; these are just a few of the types of products that are now being touted as being made with oat bran. And consumers, eager to incorporate this cholesterol-lowering grain into their diets, are gobbling these products up. But just because a product contains oat bran doesn't mean that it's good for you. When choosing oat bran products, keep the following in mind:

•Plain oatmeal or oat bran is a better source of soluble fiber than processed foods.

•Be sure to check the ingredients list of any oat-bran-containing food. Some oat bran products actually contain very little oat bran. Oats should be the first ingredient listed, or at least be very high among the ingredients.

•Read the label for fat content, too. Some oat bran products contain saturated or hydrogenated oils that actually raise blood cholesterol and thus may cancel out any benefits the oats offer.

A better way to add oat bran to your diet is to use it in your own recipes:
•Make your own oat flour by putting oatmeal through the blender. Use it for breading, baking, and thickening sauces, as you would any other flour.

•Toast oatmeal on a baking sheet in the oven at a moderate temperature. Use it as a snack or as a topping for salads or desserts.

•Add oat bran to pancakes, baked goods, and meat loaf.

•Get into the muffin-making habit, using oat flour and oat bran as part of the mix. Most muffin recipes take only five minutes to stir up and twenty minutes to bake. In recipes that call for eggs, use egg whites only. Reduce or omit sugar and honey; instead add applesauce, raisins, dates, mashed banana, or frozen orange juice concentrate for sweetening. Substitute corn or safflower oil for butter. Reduce or omit salt.

About 8 percent of the food commercials aired during Saturday morning children's programming are for products of "low nutritional value," according to a study at the University of Delaware. Ads for high-sugar products, such as candy and cereals, prevail.

puffed rice. Most cold cereals have two to three hundred milligrams or more of added sodium per serving.

Hot cereals

Hot cereals are usually made from unrefined grains—most notably oats and wheat—which are high in fiber and vitamins and minerals, and low in fat. While most hot cereals lack the sugar and salt that is often added to cold cereals, some are made from refined grains and therefore lacking in fiber and some vitamins. Even with hot cereals, you would be wise to peruse the ingredients list.

Oats and oat bran. Oats come in two forms: oatmeal and oat bran. Four varieties of oatmeal are available—steel-cut, rolled or old-fashioned, quick, and instant. The difference is in the cook-ing time (finer cuts cook more quickly) and texture, not in the nutritional value. The exception is instant oat-meal, which can be loaded with salt, sugar, and sometimes even fat.

Oat bran— simply the outer coat-ing of the oat grain—has become pop-ular because of its cholesterol-lowering abilities. The effective ingredient is the water-soluble fiber, which can be found not only in oat bran but in legumes and many vegetables and fruits. (Oatmeal contains the bran of the oat, and therefore soluble fiber, but not as much per serving as oat bran.)

Oat bran cannot, however, undo the effects of eating a three-egg omelet. Oats, like any cholesterol-lowering agent, are effective only in the context of a low-fat, low-cholesterol, high-fiber diet. And no one can say how much soluble fiber you need to eat each day to lower your blood cholesterol. In studies where cholesterol level reductions were dramatic, subjects ate a bowl of oatmeal and five oat bran muffins daily—not a diet most can stick to forever. Nevertheless, if you begin to incorporate some oat bran into your heart-healthy diet and regularly eat fruits and vegetables high in soluble fiber, you should see results at your next cholesterol check—particularly if your cholesterol level was previously elevated.

Wheat. Wheat berries and cracked wheat (bulgur) are sold in supermarkets and health food stores and make a nutritious, high-fiber breakfast cereal. Most of the fiber in wheat is insoluble, the type that can be helpful in preventing constipation and may protect against colon cancer. A few brand-name hot wheat cereals are sold nationally. Wheatena, which is made from toasted whole wheat, is made from the whole grain and therefore is high in nutrients and fiber. Cream of Wheat and Farina, on the other hand, are cereals that have been processed and have had the bran—and therefore the fiber and most of the nutrients—removed from them.

Rice. Most rice cereals are sold as baby cereals. These products are ordinarily made from white rice. There are brown rice cereals available—usually in health food stores—and these are higher in fiber.

Corn. The most familiar type of hot corn cereal—at least in the south—is hominy or grits. Unfortunately, turning corn into hominy involves removing the bran and germ of the corn, and therefore most of the nutrients and fiber. Cornmeal made into porridge or polenta, is a better choice; although most brands of cornmeal have been degermed to prevent them from deteri-

orating, some types of cornmeal retain the fiber-rich bran.

Other grains. Hot cereals also come in the form of barley, buckwheat, millet, and rye. These uncommon whole-grain varieties are usually available in health food stores.

Bread

The beauty of bread is in its simplicity, at least in theory. The basic ingredients are flour, water, yeast, and salt. Though not essential, fat and sweeteners are usually added. In addition, however, most supermarket breads also include additives that improve their baking quality and extend their shelf life. Since formulas vary according to type of bread and brand, it is important to read labels and compare ingredients. Unfortunately, many "optional" ingredients in breads are not required by law to be on the label.

Bread is a good source of complex carbohydrates, protein, and—if whole grain—of fiber, vitamins, and minerals. It is not particularly fattening—about 70 calories per slice. Most importantly, three-quarters of these calories come from carbohydrates, and almost none from fat.

White versus whole wheat

Many people believe that enriched white bread is as nutritious as whole wheat bread, but this simply is not the case. Enriched white bread is made from bleached white flour. While four nutrients markedly decreased in the milling process—iron, thiamine, niacin, and riboflavin—are replaced, enriched white flour is woefully low in fiber as well as a host of trace nutrients such as zinc and copper, which are largely removed during milling.

Enriched white bread is better than

NUTRITIONAL CONTENT OF
Breads

Bread	Calories	Protein (g)	Fat (g)	Comments
Whole wheat, 1-oz slice	70	3	1	Must be made from 100 percent whole wheat flour. Good source of vitamins, minerals, and fiber. May contain sugar, honey, and molasses, which add calories. Bread labeled "wheat bread," "cracked wheat," or "sprouted wheat" usually contains white flour.
White, enriched, 1-oz slice	75	3	1	Made from white flour, which lacks the bran and germ of the wheat grain. Most of the lost nutrients are not replaced, even in "enriched" flour, which has only niacin, thiamine, riboflavin, and iron added. Fiber is reduced. Avoid bleached flour.
Rye, 1-oz slice	70	3	trace	Most rye breads contain mostly white flour. Look for rye flour, especially whole-rye flour, as a primary ingredient.
Pumpernickel, 1-oz slice	70	3	trace	Most American loaves are made from white and rye flour colored with caramel, so they have no advantage over white or rye bread.
Italian/French, 1-oz slice	80	3	trace	Loaves made at local bakeries are usually free of preservatives and they may contain little or no sugar or fat. Look for whole-grain varieties.
Bagel, plain	200	7	2	Usually made of high-protein flour and little or no fat, making it dense. Egg bagels contain added fat and cholesterol.
Pita	165	6	1	Often made just of flour, salt, and water. May have sweeteners and additives.
Croissant	235	5	12	Contains butter and sugar. High in saturated fat, cholesterol, and calories.
English muffin	140	5	1	Has no nutritional advantage over white bread.

the plain variety (which has lost up to 70 percent of the nutrients of whole grain), but it is a very poor second choice to high-quality whole wheat bread, meaning bread made of 100 percent whole wheat flour or a mixture of whole-grain flours, such as barley, brown rice, millet, and oats. Consumers must read the label: just because a bread is brown in color does not mean it is truly whole wheat. Some commercial whole wheat breads use primarily white flour with small amounts of whole wheat flour added to satisfy labeling requirements, and larger amounts of burned sugar syrup to give them a dark brown color. Other whole wheat breads, while still made of nutrient-rich flour, are also heavily laced with honey and brown sugar or molasses. One of the best breads is Italian or French bread from small local bakeries or baked at home. These loaves are often made without fat and may come in nutritious, whole-grain varieties.

Pasta

Pasta has come into its own. For years it had been dismissed in America as fattening and non-nutritious, and only recently have Americans learned that pasta—a staple around much of the world for centuries—is actually a nutritious food.

Pasta, meaning "paste" in Italian, is rich in complex carbohydrates, high in protein, and low in fat, cholesterol, and sodium (unless you pour on cheese, cream, butter, and salt). And despite its reputation, pasta is not especially fattening. In fact, a main-course plateful of spaghetti with simple tomato, vegetable, or fish sauce usually contains fewer calories than a steak or a tuna salad sandwich.

Types of pasta

Pasta is a simple product made essentially of flour and water. The flour is usually semolina, a high-protein variety milled from hard, golden durum wheat, which produces a truly fine pasta with a mellow flavor and sturdy texture. If the pasta will be shaped as noodles, eggs are mixed in, adding small amounts of protein, fat, and cholesterol. Whole wheat pasta is formed from unprocessed whole wheat flour containing bran and germ; it has a brownish color, a nutty taste, and additional protein and fiber. Other high-protein varieties substitute soy flour for some of the semolina. Varieties touted as "light" or "high protein" have fewer carbohydrates and more protein because they contain wheat germ, yeast, or other protein rich ingredients. Vegetable powder or juice, such as that made from spinach, tomatoes, or artichokes, may also be added to basic pasta; while this enhances the taste, it improves the nutritional content only slightly. Properly speaking, most Oriental noodles are not pasta, since they are made from rice flour or vegetable starches rather than whole wheat flour.

Despite the growing popularity of

Some people rinse pasta to wash away starch. Don't do it. Rinsing pasta only increases the loss of nutrients—and cools off the pasta.

NUTRITIONAL CONTENT OF
Pasta

Average main-course servings of pasta are about four ounces dry, which cooks up to two cups cooked; side-dish or appetizer servings are about two to three ounces dry. Because of absorption of water, four ounces of dry spaghetti weighs ten ounces when cooked al dente and thirteen ounces when cooked to a softer consistency.

Pasta (4 oz dry)	Calories	Protein (g)	Fat (g)	Comments
Regular spaghetti, shell, or other types of pasta	380	14	2	Domestic and imported brands and vegetable-enriched varieties (such as spinach) have approximately the same nutritional value.
Egg noodles	400	14	4	Slightly higher in fat and cholesterol due to eggs.
Whole wheat	400	15-20	2	Higher amounts of fiber and trace minerals.
Soy wheat	400	25	3	High in protein; available at many health food stores.
High-protein (or "light")	420	20-30	2	Almost 50 percent more protein (from wheat germ or yeast) than regular pasta.

fresh pasta in supermarkets and specialty stores, pasta is one food for which fresh doesn't necessarily mean best. A good commercial dried pasta made from durum wheat can be just as tasty as fresh store-bought pasta or pasta made at home from all-purpose flour—and it's often more nutritious.

Toppings for pasta

The most popular topping for pasta by far is tomato sauce, or meat and tomato sauce, usually from a jar or a can when one is pressed for time. Yet many canned or bottled sauces are fairly high in sodium and fat. Some brands can contain up to eight hundred milligrams of sodium per half-cup serving—a large portion of your daily allowance—and get up to 47 percent of their calories from fat. They may also contain significant amounts of sugar or corn syrup. As with all prepared foods, it is important to check the labels.

Homemade sauce: easy and better

A good tomato sauce need not simmer all afternoon to be flavorful. You can make your own in very little more time than it takes to boil the pasta. Buy canned tomato purée, tomato paste, and/or crushed tomatoes with no salt added; all are virtually fat-free. (If good fresh tomatoes are available, simply chop them up and cook to taste.) Cook some minced onion in a small amount of beef or chicken stock, then add the canned tomato product, and—if you wish—a small amount of very lean ground beef. Season with black pepper, plenty of garlic, and such characteristically Italian herbs as basil, oregano, and rosemary. If you're cooking without salt, you can add flavor with other combinations, too: experiment with a touch of curry, cumin, or chili powder.

Other low-fat sauces

There's no law that says spaghetti has to be topped with a tomato sauce. You can make delicious sauces with fresh vegetables simmered in stock until crisp-tender. Herbs and spices will improve the flavor. For a meat sauce, add chunks of skinless white-meat turkey or chicken, then toss with the pasta. A tablespoon of grated Parmesan cheese per serving adds a lot of flavor, with only about 25 calories and two grams of fat.

Dried Beans and Peas

Virtually any bean—or its culinary cousin, the pea—is chock-full of protein, complex carbohydrates, fiber, B vitamins, iron, potassium, and magnesium. At the same time, these legumes (vegetables borne in pods) are usually very low in fat and sodium, free of cholesterol—and inexpensive. With all these nutritional advantages, the wonder is that, except for regional cooking such as Tex-Mex or Southern, beans have fallen out of favor in the American diet.

Many people keep away from beans because they think they are very fattening. In fact, one cup of cooked beans (about two servings as a side dish) has only 200 to 300 calories. Beans are much lower in calories than meat, and provide nearly as much protein. (One cup of cooked beans will provide you with twelve to twenty-five grams of protein, which is 25 to 50 percent of the RDA). While the vegetable protein contained in beans is incomplete—that is, low in at least one essential amino acid—it is easy to complete by also eating grains, dairy products, or a small amount of meat. In fact, it's actually hard *not* to complete the protein in beans.

Versatility and variety are other advantages of beans. There are hundreds of varieties, many available in different colors and under various names. When purchased dried, as they usually are, they have a long shelf life, but need to be rinsed and soaked before cooking. Dried peas and beans may contain small pebbles, bits of soil, or other debris, so its always a good idea to wash them under running water and to look at them by the handful so that you can easily find any foreign material and remove it.

Soaking the beans for at least a couple of hours is usually necessary before cooking, but most packages have suggested shortcuts, such as letting them stand in hot water for an hour.

Like little sponges, beans absorb whatever flavors are added to the soaking or cooking liquid. Many beans are available frozen or canned, with little loss of nutrients. (Beware of the high sodium level in canned beans, though; rinse canned beans before cooking whenever possible.)

Research has turned up more good news about these legumes. Not only are beans free of cholesterol and almost free of saturated fat, but they contain soluble fiber—the type that may actually lower cholesterol levels. In addition, beans are a boon to diabetics. Because beans are digested slowly, they cause a gentle rise in blood sugar, thus requiring less insulin than most carbohydrate-rich foods.

A common problem with beans is flatulence, due mainly to the presence of certain complex sugars that cannot be digested and that cause gas and bloating. To reduce gas significantly, discard the water after soaking, then boil the beans in a large quantity of water, and then discard the water again

---

Meatless Meats

Many meat substitutes, or analogues, as they've come to be called, are made with traditional soy products like tofu, a soybean curd; tempeh, cooked and fermented soybeans; or miso, a fermented soy paste. Others are based on modern laboratory-produced soy derivatives. You can buy meatless beef, meatless turkey, and meatless chicken—some meatless meats even have a smoked taste.

Ounce for ounce, these products contain as much protein as meat. Most of the oil (largely polyunsaturated) is removed from soy protein concentrates and isolated soy protein, so they are virtually fat-free. Another advantage of isolated soy protein is that it contains much less of the carbohydrates that may cause flatulence.

Unfortunately, in most meatless meats, soy protein is not all you're getting. Processors generally add oils and fats (some partially hydrogenated) to soy protein concentrates and isolated soy protein to fake the look and taste of beef, bacon, ham, tuna, or even luncheon meats. Some soy-based products have as much fat as lean ground beef, but less saturated fat and no cholesterol. They may also contain artificial colorings and flavorings—even a jolt of sodium in the form of MSG (monosodium glutamate), soy sauce, or salt. Vitamins and minerals may be added, too, but compared to meat, many of these products remain notably deficient in iron, zinc, and other trace minerals.

You can concoct your own meat analogue at home, using cooked soybeans or other high-protein legumes (chick-peas, lentils, pinto beans) and adding chopped onion, celery, herbs, perhaps cooked barley or rice, and salt to taste. These can be shaped into patties and browned in a nonstick pan.

If you would rather try a commercial product, remember that no meat substitute will completely mimic the taste and texture of meat. And as with all prepared foods, it's worthwhile reading the labels. Some meatless products are as high in fat as real hot dogs; many are also high in sodium. In some cases, you'll be at least as well off nutritionally with lean meat—except for its cholesterol content.

Tofu Tips

Often used in Asian cooking, tofu—a high-protein soybean curd used in everything from soup and salad to dessert—has become a popular staple in this country. That's good news: tofu is low in fat, cholesterol, and sodium, and is inexpensive. But unfortunately, tofu is often sold in open markets or the vegetable section of a store, sitting out in a tray of water, unrefrigerated—inviting coliform bacteria to grow. High levels of bacteria can cause gastrointestinal tract ailments including nausea, vomiting, and diarrhea.

To lower your risk, choose dated fresh-looking products sold in sealed, refrigerated packages. Even properly packaged products, though, may not be microbe free. To be completely safe, heat the tofu for two minutes in boiling water before using it.

NUTRITIONAL CONTENT OF
Dried Beans and Peas

Bean (1 cup cooked)	Calories	Protein (g)	Fat (g)	Comments
Black beans	225	18	1	Highly nutritious, especially rich in iron and protein.
Black-eyed peas	190	16	1	More accurately called black-eyed beans. High in fiber.
Garbanzo beans (or chick-peas)	270	18	5	High in calories, fat, and protein.
Great Northern beans	210	14	1	High in fiber.
Kidney beans	230	16	1	High in fiber.
Lentils	215	16	trace	Good source of iron. Need no pre-soaking.
Lima beans	260	16	1	Good source of iron.
Mung beans, sprouted	26	6	trace	Often used for sprouting.
Navy beans	225	15	1	Good source of iron.
Peas, split	230	16	1	Need no presoaking. More protein but much less vitamin A and C than fresh green peas.
Pinto, pink, and red beans	265	15	1	Similar to kidney beans. High in fiber.
Soybeans	235	20	10	Highest in protein but also in fat; protein is most complete of all beans. Good source of iron.

Sprouted alfalfa, mung beans, lentils, peas, soybeans, and wheat are more nutritious than their unsprouted counterparts. Beta carotene, vitamin C, and most B vitamins are all synthesized as the sprouts grow.

(don't use the water as a soup base). This method can eliminate more than half of the gas-producing complex sugars in the beans.

MEAT AND POULTRY

Beef

We eat about 17 percent less beef today than we did a decade ago, a decline best explained in two words: fat and cholesterol, both linked to an increased risk of heart disease. Noting the preference for low-fat protein, the beef industry is now aggressively marketing leaner products. Ranchers are crossbreeding leaner, larger cattle with traditional breeds. In addition, cattle are being fed more grass and less corn and being sent to market younger so they will develop less fat. And meatpackers and retailers are trimming more external fat, often leaving only one-eighth to one-quarter inch. As a result, beef is now significantly leaner than it was twenty years ago.

But beef's fat content is widely variable, and only the leanest pieces are as low in fat as broiled fish or skinless chicken. Despite the industry's efforts to promote lean beef, it's often hard to recognize a low-fat piece of beef.

One way to tell fatty beef from lean is to look at it. If the beef is marblized—that is, there are interior streaks or specks of fat—it is fatty. A better way is to consider grade and cut. The best grade, "prime," is the fattiest, followed by "choice" and "select." "Select" is the new name for the "good" grade of meat that was often sold under a store's brand name. The United States Department of Agriculture (USDA) changed the name of this grade to make it sound more appealing as part of an effort to encourage people to eat leaner meat. "Select" has, on average, 20 percent less fat than "choice," and 40 percent less fat than "prime." Even if they have to sacrifice a little taste, many people would opt for the leanness of "select" meat. And "select" meat is also cheaper than other grades.

Still, "choice" beef can be low in fat, if you select the right cuts. Top round, eye round, London broil, and sirloin tip are leaner cuts, while brisket, rib roast, and short ribs are among the fattiest cuts. And as the chart at lower right shows, the best way to cut the fat content of meat is still with a knife—trim all external fat before cooking.

In addition to this government-regulated terminology, there is a voluntary rating system you can use to gauge the fat content of your meat:

Nutri-Facts labels. These were developed by the meat industry for beef, pork, and lamb, and are in use in many large supermarket chains. The labels are affixed to meat counters, not to individual packages of meat. They list the amount of fat, cholesterol, calories, and seven other nutrients in three ounces of well-trimmed cooked meat (the equivalent of about four ounces raw). These figures, based on the latest USDA testing, are averages for all grades of meat of that cut, so they are

most accurate for "choice" meat. When shopping for low-fat beef, look for a Nutri-Facts label listing less than eight grams of fat.

How about hamburgers?

Evaluating the fat content of packaged hamburger meat can be even more difficult than judging full cuts. The packages may carry seemingly helpful labels such as "75 percent lean," "lean," or "extra lean," but this terminology can be misleading. Beef labeled "75 percent lean" is 25 percent fat *by weight*, which is a lot of fat. Thus a patty made from this meat would derive more than 70 percent of its calories from fat, since, ounce for ounce, fat has more than twice as many calories as lean meat. And while a steak or other cut of beef labeled "lean" must have no more than 10 percent fat by weight, and "extra lean" no more than 5 percent, these standards don't apply when the meat is ground. "Lean" or even "extra lean" ground beef can have as much as 22 percent fat by weight, with this fat supplying about 70 percent of total calories.

Still, there is a way to get a burger you can trust. While hamburgers have acquired a bad name among health-conscious people, they are a good source of protein, and even a fast-food

The Wellness Burger
You can still enjoy hamburgers on a low-fat diet if you follow these steps:

1. Go to a store that has a butcher, choose a very lean cut of round, then ask him to trim all the fat and grind the meat for you. This will result in a burger with only 20 percent of its calories coming from fat.
2. Use three ounces of meat for each patty.
3. To make the lean beef less dry, mix it with tomato juice, chopped onion, or Worcestershire sauce before cooking.
4. Broil or panbroil your burger instead of frying it.
5. If you like cooked onions and mushrooms for a garnish, simmer them in stock (or water and wine) instead of sautéing them in butter.
6. Place the burger on a whole wheat bun (or whole wheat bread). Add a slice of tomato and some lettuce.

This hamburger will have 315 calories, 7 grams of fat, 34 grams of protein, 72 milligrams of cholesterol, and 415 milligrams of sodium.

Choice vs. Select Beef

Beef (3½ oz, broiled)	Calories	Fat (g)	Fat Calories
Tenderloin			
choice, untrimmed	271	18	59%
choice, trimmed	207	10	42%
select, untrimmed	254	15	55%
select, trimmed	196	8	38%
Top round			
choice, untrimmed	213	9	38%
choice, trimmed	194	7	30%
select, untrimmed	207	8	36%
select, trimmed	184	5	26%

Beef: Cooking Tips

Though conventional wisdom says that fatty beef tastes better and is more tender than lean, taste tests suggest that lean beef can be just as flavorful and tender, if it is prepared correctly.

• Trim all external fat before cooking.
• Reduce normal cooking times by 20 percent when using lean beef, since it cooks faster and becomes tough when overcooked. Don't be deceived by the redness of the meat: lean pieces cooked to a medium degree may look rare. Use a meat thermometer to measure doneness. Or, use the finger test: the meat is done when it gives a little when pressed.
• Broil meat so that the fat can drip off. Drain fat well when sautéing ground beef for chili or spaghetti sauce.
• To seal in the juices, sear meat in a skillet or roasting pan before cooking it.

burger has a fair amount of B vitamins, iron, and zinc. The trick is to create your own home-cooked burger made from carefully selected ground beef. (See the marginal on page 183.)

Hormones: should you worry?

Every so often, concern is expressed in the media about the hormones—natural sex steroids estradiol (estrogen), progesterone, and testosterone, and two synthetic ones—that are used in the raising of 70 to 90 percent of American cattle to make the animals gain weight faster. Numerous studies have shown that this concern has not been warranted.

The Food and Drug Administration (FDA) says hormone-treated beef is safe to eat. At the prescribed dosages used in feedlots, these hormones have been certified safe. There is virtually no evidence to the contrary. The residues left in meat are so minuscule that a pound of beef contains about fifteen thousand times less hormone than is produced each day by an average man—and several million times less than what's produced by a pregnant woman. And don't forget that many foods naturally contain estrogen: milk contains five times more estrogen by weight than hormone-treated beef, and wheat germ seventeen hundred times more.

The claim that hormones pose health risks may be based on an experience with a synthetic estrogen called diethylstilbestrol (DES). Banned as a carcinogen in Europe and the United States, black-market DES was injected into calves in Italy. The treated veal was used for baby food in 1981, and it was claimed—but never scientifically proven—that babies of both sexes who ate the veal grew breasts, and girls began to menstruate.

Hormones used in American beef today are chemically quite different from DES. And the way cattle today receive the hormones is far safer. Instead of injecting these substances into muscle tissue that may be eaten, feedlot operators implant time-release hormone pellets behind animals' ears, which are not used for human food.

American consumer groups have by and large supported the FDA's stand on hormones. However, some groups, including the Center for Science in the Public Interest, are concerned about the potential misuse of hormones in cattle. If the hormone pellet is placed not behind the ear but in a part of the animal that is used for ground beef— the neck or breast, for example—as a 1986 study by the USDA showed sometimes happens, a consumer might get more hormone that is proven safe.

You may wonder why the hormones are used at all, if questions of safety remain. Hormone implants save U.S. cattlemen about 650 million dollars per year, and part of these savings are passed on to consumers. A one-dollar hormone pellet behind the ear means the animal will consume about four fewer bushels of corn (a twenty-dollar savings) and reach market weight eighteen days sooner (15 percent faster than if untreated). It will be more docile and it will gain approximately fifty pounds more lean muscle tissue than an untreated animal. So not only do we save money and resources, but we also get leaner meat.

If you still feel concerned about hormone treatment, you don't have to give up beef. Some certified untreated beef is already on the market, and in light of the current debate, more is likely to become available—at a premium price. From the evidence now available, though, you don't need to switch to untreated beef.

Poultry

Chicken and other poultry provide high-quality protein for people who are turning away from beef, lamb, and pork, which can be high in saturated fat. In fact, a small portion (three to four ounces of cooked poultry without bones or skin) provides about half the daily adult protein requirement and has half to one-third the calories and fat of a similar portion of steak. Poultry is also a good source of B vitamins, but has less iron than red meat.

Chicken. Chicken is one of the nutritional success stories of the century. Since the 1940s, revolutionary changes in the way chicken is bred and raised have made it more abundant and affordable than ever before. When shopping for chicken, look for plump, firm meat with no off odor or slimy texture. The skin may be white or yellow, depending on what the bird was fed, but skin color has no relation to quality or nutrition. Choose white meat over dark; dark meat has far more fat and a little more cholesterol. Trim away all visible fat before cooking and discard the skin. This will reduce the fat content by as much as half. Roasted light meat without skin has the best nutritional value; roasting at a low temperature for a long period melts

---

A Better Barbecue

Whether you're using a gas or electric grill or charcoal, barbecuing—a low-temperature cooking method—does create compounds that experts deem carcinogenic (cancer-causing). This probably occurs much less during oven broiling, because the heating coil is above the food and the cooking process is faster. The principal danger lies in cooking fatty meat over a heat source. When the fat drips on the coals or hot coils, it forms carcinogenic substances that the smoke picks up and deposits on the food. Moreover, carcinogens are formed when flames hit the meat. Here are some tips for minimizing this effect:
- Pick low-fat meats for broiling.
- Cover the grill with foil and then punch holes to let the fat drip out.
- Avoid flare-ups. Burning meat juices and

fats produce harmful smoke.
- Keep a squirter bottle close by in case coals flame. If the smoke gets too heavy, use the water to reduce it.
- Wrap vegetables and fish in foil to preserve flavor and protect them from the smoke.
- Baste foods while cooking, but not with fat. Lemon juice, wine, barbecue sauces, or combinations thereof will add flavor.
- When cooking poultry or thick meat, try poaching or microwaving them until partially cooked, then finish them on the grill. This cuts cooking time and reduces exposure to smoke.
- After cooking, scrape off heavily charred material on the meat surface.
- Don't cook out every day. As with other good things, moderation is in order.

away the most fat. If you prefer fried chicken, don't bread it, since the coating will absorb fat.

Turkey. Skinless turkey breast is one of the leanest meats—a 3½-ounce portion has less than a gram of fat, which contributes only 5 percent of its 135 calories. Like chicken, turkey is now available in parts—breasts (with bones or without), drumsticks, and cutlets, for example—so you can have the benefits of turkey without having to wrestle with a sixteen-pound bird that takes hours to cook.

More and more supermarkets are offering ground turkey, too—which can serve as a substitute for high-fat ground beef in many recipes. Still, ground turkey generally contains dark meat and skin, so it's higher in calories and fat than light meat. To keep it low in fat, have a butcher grind light meat for you. (Remember, ground turkey usually needs lots of seasoning; tomato

A yellow chicken isn't necessarily more nutritious or healthier than a pale one. Yellow skin is due to the amount of yellow corn in feed. Some poultry suppliers add other substances containing yellow pigment, such as marigold petals, to give the birds a healthy-looking glow.

NUTRITIONAL CONTENT OF
Poultry

Poultry (3½ oz edible portion)	Calories	Fat (g)	Fat Calories	Cholesterol (mg)	Sodium (mg)
Broiler-fryer chicken					
light meat, with skin, roasted	222	11	45%	84	75
dark meat, with skin, roasted	253	16	57%	91	87
light meat, with skin, batter dipped, fried	277	15	49%	84	287
light meat, no skin, roasted	173	5	26%	85	77
dark meat, no skin, roasted	205	10	44%	93	93
Roasting chicken					
light meat, no skin, roasted	153	4	24%	75	51
dark meat, no skin, roasted	178	9	46%	75	95
Capon					
flesh and skin, roasted	229	12	47%	86	49
Turkey					
light meat, with skin, roasted	197	8	37%	76	63
dark meat, with skin, roasted	221	12	49%	89	76
light meat, no skin, roasted	157	3	17%	69	64
breast meat, no skin, roasted	135	1	5%	83	52
dark meat, no skin, roasted	187	7	34%	85	79
ground, dark and light meat, with skin	233	14	54%	65	111
Turkey cold cuts					
Pastrami	141	6	38%	53	1,045
Ham	128	5	35%	65	933
Barbecued breast slices	128	4	28%	65	1,050
Bologna	199	15	68%	99	878
Salami	196	14	64%	82	1,004
Smoked breast	123	4	29%	65	747
Duck					
flesh and skin, roasted	337	28	75%	84	59
flesh, no skin, roasted	201	11	49%	89	65
Goose					
flesh and skin, roasted	305	22	65%	91	70
flesh, no skin, roasted	238	13	50%	96	76

juice, egg white, and herbs can add moisture and flavor.)

If you opt for the traditional whole bird, avoid self-basting turkeys since the basting solutions contain, for the most part, fat—usually highly saturated coconut oil or partially hydrogenated soy or corn oil—water, and sodium. The water and the sodium help keep the bird juicy; the fat is used mostly for flavoring. Butter is an ingredient in some basting solutions. Baste the turkey yourself to keep it juicy. Instead of using turkey drippings—which are a concentrated source of fat—try basting with defatted chicken or turkey stock. Or skim the fat from the drippings before you baste. To make a low-fat gravy, you can use a gravy separator, which looks like a measuring cup with the spout at the bottom. This utensil makes it easy to separate the fat from the flavorful juices and discard it.

Turkey cold cuts. Turkey cold cuts are another poultry option. Unfortunately, these are often high in fat and always loaded with sodium, which serves as a preservative. Many are made from high-fat dark meat, and some brands contain high-cholesterol organ meats, such as the heart and gizzard. One brand of turkey bologna (advertised as "80 percent fat-free" by weight) gets 77 percent of its calories from fat and has 1,100 milligrams of sodium in just one three-ounce serving.

Look for cold cuts that have one gram or less of fat per ounce (at least 95 percent fat-free by weight). In many cases, turkey pastrami, ham, and breast slices fill this bill. Turkey bologna and salami tend to be nearly as rich in fat as their beef counterparts. Turkey "breast" cold cuts are low in fat, but don't think you're getting only sliced turkey; the meat has been processed and filled with additives such as

modified food starch. The fat content of turkey roll depends on whether it is made primarily from dark or light meat; it contains gelatin, sugar, and other fillers and flavorings. You're better off with sliced fresh turkey from the deli counter.

When buying turkey cold cuts, be sure to check ingredients lists carefully for sodium and sugar. Sodium comes in many forms besides salt. As a basic rule of thumb, any ingredient that has sodium as part of its name is going to be a source of sodium, including monosodium glutamate—MSG—a popular additive in turkey products. Kosher turkeys have been heavily salted and then rinsed, so sodium levels vary. Products that are barbecue-flavor and smoked are not only likely to be high in sodium, but may contain nitrites (a potential carcinogen) as well. Sugar also comes in many forms: dextrose, corn syrup, and honey are just a few of the types of sugar used in turkey cold cuts. There is no reason to choose sweetened turkey.

Duck and goose. These birds are bred today to have more meat and less fat and bones, but they are still high in saturated fat. Except for special occasions, avoid duck and goose. When you do choose to have them, be sure to roast them so that some of the fat melts away.

Proper storage

All fresh poultry is much more prone to contamination by salmonella than other meats. Store it in the coldest part of the refrigerator. If possible, buy poultry that has not been frozen—it is less likely to spoil and the flavor will be better—and cook it within two days. The safest way to thaw frozen poultry is overnight in the refrigerator, or in a microwave if you plan to cook it immediately. Do not refreeze poultry

A Safe Turkey Stuffing

When stuffing a whole turkey, it's important to guard against salmonella poisoning. Remember that the bacteria present in raw poultry can get into the stuffing and multiply. To prevent contamination, follow these steps:

•Stuff the bird loosely (tightly packed stuffing cooks more slowly.) Don't stuff the bird until you are ready to roast it.

•Consider cooking the stuffing separately—it's easier. Flavor the cavity with a little chopped onion, celery, and herbs.

•After cooking, check the stuffing temperature with a thermometer. You should get a reading of 165 degrees.

•Remove the cooked stuffing from the turkey and serve it separately. Don't allow a stuffed bird to sit around the kitchen for hours. Refrigerate leftovers as soon as you can. Remember that rice stuffings are high in starch and should be handled just like bread stuffings.

that has thawed. As another precaution, thoroughly wash your hands, knives, and cutting surfaces after handling raw poultry.

Pork

Because so many pork products—especially bacon, sausage, spareribs, and hot dogs—are high in fat, pork has a dubious reputation. But, in fact, many cuts of pork are 25 to 50 percent leaner than they were twenty-five years ago, thanks to changes in the breeding and feeding of hogs. Other advantages of pork include: the fat in pork is slightly less saturated than that in beef; and pork is an excellent source of B vitamins (especially thiamine), zinc, iron, and high-quality protein.

According to recent research at Iowa State University, pork may be even leaner than indicated by the figures in the chart at right from the U.S. Department of Agriculture (USDA). For instance, the Iowa researchers found that $3\frac{1}{2}$ ounces of broiled center loin has less than half the fat—four grams, contributing only 24 percent of the meat's 161 calories.

Getting the most from pork

To keep pork lean and flavorful, try the following:

•Choose lean cuts, such as tenderloin, center loin, fresh pork leg, or lean ham. Fattier cuts of pork (such as ribs, loin blade, and shoulder) and pork-based meats (sausage, bacon, ribs, etc.)—still the most popular fare—are hard to justify on a heart-healthy diet.

•If you're trying to minimize your salt intake, avoid all cured pork products such as bacon, ham, and other cold cuts.

•Trim all visible fat from pork before cooking.

What's a hot dog really made of?
Hot dogs are made of either beef, pork, or poultry, as well as the following: corn sweeteners, salt, spices, smoke flavoring, soy flour, soy protein or dried milk as fillers; and sodium nitrate or other preservatives such as sodium erythorbate, BHT, or BHA. Some people worry that hot dogs contain animal by-products (such as pork stomach, snout, heart, spleen, lips, and cartilage), but few brands actually do. The real problem with nearly all hot dogs—even those made from chicken or turkey, which generally contain ground skin—is that they get, on average, 70 percent of their total calories from fat and are high in sodium.

NUTRITIONAL CONTENT OF
Pork

Meat (3½ oz edible portion, fat trimmed)	Calories	Fat (g)	Fat Calories
Center loin, broiled	231	10	39%
Tenderloin, roasted	166	5	26%
Leg (ham), roasted	220	11	45%
Ham, cured, fresh	131	5	34%
Spareribs, braised	397	30	69%
Italian sausage	323	26	72%

•Limit portion sizes—say, three to five ounces at a meal—so that your cholesterol intake won't exceed three hundred milligrams a day from all sources. Pork, like all meats and poultry, contains twenty to twenty-five milligrams of cholesterol per ounce, whether it's lean or fatty. Meat can go a long way in dishes such as kabobs, sautés, and stir-fries.

•To keep lean meat moist and flavorful, marinate it in fruit juice, honey, or sherry. Experiment with seasonings such as thyme, ginger, rosemary, mint, garlic, fennel seed, or oregano.

Cooking pork

Because of the danger of trichinosis, be sure to cook pork to an internal temperature of at least 160 degrees Fahrenheit—"medium," no traces of pink—according to the Food Safety and Inspection Service, which formerly recommended a temperature of 170 degrees ("well done"). Freezing meat at 5 degrees for 20 days will also kill trichinae. The leaner the meat, the more quickly it will cook—so don't overcook it. When microwaving pork, cover the meat so that heating is even; and if the meat has bones, make sure that the meat near the bones is completely cooked.

Wild Game

Most people lack the opportunity—or the desire—to make venison, buffalo meat, and game birds a regular part of their diet. And thus, the nutritional values of game may seem beside the point. Yet "wild" meat, usually farm-raised, is appearing more and more often in restaurants and markets, especially in the West; and you can order venison, quail, and other game by mail. Many people still hunt and serve wild game in season.

In fact, game is better for you than most other meats. Wild animals usually don't get fat, and when they do the meat is only slightly marbled. Thus game is generally low in fat than beef or pork. A 3½-ounce serving of bison steak contains only about two grams of fat, compared with thirteen grams in a similar serving of chuck roast (prime

grade). The calorie count is less, too (135 for the buffalo, 205 for the beef). Since cholesterol is found in all animal tissue, lean or fat, beef and buffalo have about the same amount (sixty-two milligrams), which doesn't crowd the recommended daily limit of three hundred milligrams. Like all meats, wild game is rich in vitamins and minerals.

Cooking tips

•The low fat content is one reason why venison and other game steaks are chewy. If you're cooking a tender cut, you might braise it in a liquid so it doesn't dry out. Chops can be marinated and then broiled. Tough cuts need longer braising or stewing.

•Most chefs recommend low cooking temperatures for game, since high heat tends to toughen it. Simmered in a liquid for an hour or two, with vegetables and spices added, venison makes a good stew.

•When cooking game birds, as with any poultry, it's a good idea to remove the skin, since that's where much of the fat is.

NUTRITIONAL CONTENT OF
Wild Game

Game (3½ oz raw)	Calories	Protein (g)	Fat (g)	Cholesterol (mg)
Buffalo (bison)	135	25	2	62
Guinea hen	110	21	3	63
Pheasant	135	24	4	66
Quail	135	22	5	70
Rabbit	125	22	4	65
Squab	140	18	8	90
Venison	125	21	3	67

Note: game animal figures are for lean meat only; game bird figures are for flesh only (no skin). These numbers may vary, depending on the species and type of muscle analyzed.

S E A F O O D

Fish

Like meat and poultry, fish is an excellent source of protein. But unlike these other animal foods, most types of fish are relatively low in calories, fat, and cholesterol. While a four-ounce serving of trimmed, broiled sirloin has 241 calories, ten grams of fat, and 102 milligrams of cholesterol, the same size serving of broiled snapper has just 146 calories, two grams of fat, and 54 milligrams of cholesterol.

Fish also supply certain vitamins—particularly the B vitamins thiamine, riboflavin, and niacin—and are a good source of potassium. Higher-fat fish, such as salmon, tuna, sardines, and mackerel, are rich in vitamins A and D, and saltwater fish are the best natural source of iodine.

Fish and heart disease

Not only does fish tend to have less fat than meat, but the fat in fish is highly polyunsaturated and so preferable to the fat in meat, which is mostly saturated. (It is saturated fat that raises blood cholesterol levels.) Moreover, fish fat contains a special group of polyunsaturated fatty acids known as omega-3s. Research has shown that omega-3s can protect against heart disease by reducing the ability of the blood to clot, which lessens the chance of a heart attack caused by a blood clot in the coronary arteries. Omega-3s also lower levels of triglycerides, a type of fat in your blood that, when elevated, is associated with an increased risk of heart disease in some individuals.

Eating even small amounts of fish appears to significantly reduce the risk of fatal heart attack. In one of the most recent studies confirming this benefit, two thousand men in Wales, all of whom had previously suffered a heart attack, were divided into three groups, each of which was told to follow a different commonly recommended type of "heart-healthy" diet: one group was advised to eat more fish, one to eat more fiber, and one to eat less saturated fat. After two years, the fish group, which ate an average of about ten ounces of fish a week, had a 29 percent lower mortality rate (from all causes, but entirely attributable to a reduction in deaths from heart disease) compared to the other groups.

The study did not allow for a fair judgment about the benefits of either a high-fiber regimen or a low-fat diet, since the subjects in those two groups did not alter their fat and fiber intake substantially. What the study suggested, though, was that it may be easier for many people to add modest amounts of fish to their diet than to dramatically cut down on fat or substantially boost their fiber intake.

A guide to fat content

Researchers have found that the higher the fat content of fish, the greater the cardiovascular benefits. As a rule, darker fish contain more oil than light fish. The highest fat content is found in deepwater fish like tuna, which need the fat as insulation against cold water. Herring, mackerel, salmon, and sardines are also fatty, containing between 5 and 20 percent fat by weight. Moderately fatty fish that have between 2 and 5 percent fat include bass, bluefish, halibut, ocean perch, pollock, rockfish, and smelt. Lean fish—less than 2 percent fat—include flatfish like flounder and sole. Although lean fish have less fat, a greater percentage of the fat they do contain is in the form of omega-3 as compared to fatty fish.

Is fresh fish safe?

Many people worry about eating fish because of the potential hazards of chemical pollution. A few simple precautions, however, can allow you to eat fish with less worry. The key to safety is variety—don't eat the same fish every day, week after week. This protects you against repeated doses of pollutants, if any are present. Keep in mind these other safety guidelines:

• Saltwater fish caught in the open ocean are less likely to be polluted than lake fish.

• Farm-raised fish may or may not have been raised in pure water; it depends on the locality. Check the source with your fish merchant.

Fish High in Omega-3 Fatty Acids
Salmon
Mackerel
Herring
Sardines
Sablefish
Lake trout
Fresh tuna
Canned albacore tuna
Whitefish
Anchovies

Fish Moderately High In Omega-3s
Halibut
Bluefish
Rockfish
Rainbow and sea trout
Ocean perch
Bass
Hake
Pollock
Smelt
Mullet

•When you catch fish, be sure you are fishing in waters that are not polluted. When you buy your fishing license, you often will be given information on polluted waters in the area. If it is not provided, ask for this information or check with the local health department about it. And throw the bigs ones back. The younger and smaller the fish, the lower the level of toxic residues.

•Before cooking fish, trim off fatty areas — usually in the back and belly and in any dark meat just under the skin — since this is where toxic residues may accumulate. When possible, broil fish, since this cooking method tends to reduce residues.

Selecting fresh fish

To choose the best-quality fish:

•Buy fish from a reputable fish dealer. Not all stores sell seafood that is reliably fresh.

•In the market, fish should be stored on a bed of ice. Whole, dressed fish can be directly on the ice, but fish fillets and steaks should be placed on a metal tray or on plastic wrap so that they do not come into direct contact with the ice.

•Fresh fish smells mild, sweetish, and clean. Do not buy any fish that has a fishy, sour, or ammonia like odor.

•When purchasing whole fish, look for bright, clear, unsunken eyes; moist, shiny skin; and bright red or pink gills. The flesh should feel firm and spring back when you touch it. Look for fish fillets and steaks that are moist and firm.

•Frozen fish—which can be as fresh as fresh fish if it was flash-frozen soon after being caught—should be solidly frozen when purchased. Avoid any frozen fish that has ice crystals or that is discolored.

•Refrigerate fresh fish immediately

Fish: Cooking Tips

•Fish can be baked, poached, steamed, broiled, stir-fried with a small amount of vegetable oil, or microwaved. These cooking methods allow you to retain the moistness of the fish without having to add much fat.

•Fish ceases to become a low-fat food when it is cooked with butter or topped with a high-fat cream sauce. Try adding flavor without fat by marinating the fish in lemon or lime juice or wine; using herbs and spices (bay leaf, curry powder, dry mustard, fennel, green pepper, marjoram, paprika and tarragon all enhance the flavor of fish); or making a cream sauce from low-fat or nonfat yogurt.

•For maximum flavor, it is important not to overcook fish. The best way to judge cooking time is to cook fresh or thawed fish ten minutes for every inch of thickness. Cook frozen fish twenty minutes for every inch of thickness. (These guidelines do not apply when microwaving fish.) Fish is cooked when it has just turned opaque and the flesh barely flakes when it is separated with a fork.

Fish is a low-fat, low-sodium food, unless it's the deep-fried kind from the supermarket's freezer. Fat supplies half the calories in most frozen deep-fried fish, and a single serving contains 350 to 550 milligrams of sodium.

---

and use it as soon as possible; fish can spoil within a day or two.

Caution on raw fish

Fish are notorious carriers of a wide variety of parasites, some of which can infect humans. In the past, these parasites were not much of a problem in this country since Americans generally cook their fish, and adequate cooking (or freezing) destroys the organisms. However, the growing popularity of raw fish dishes such as sushi, sashimi, and ceviche has led to an increase in reports of fish tapeworm and roundworm infection, especially on the West Coast and in Alaska.

You should, therefore, minimize your intake of raw or undercooked fish. For those who still like the taste of raw seafood, the safest way to eat sushi is in

Fish (3½ oz)	Calories	Protein (g)	Fat (g)	Fat Calories	Cholesterol (mg)
Cod	105	23	1	7%	55
Haddock	112	24	1	7%	74
Halibut	140	27	3	19%	41
Herring	203	23	12	53%	77
Mackerel	262	24	18	62%	75
Mullet	150	25	5	30%	63
Ocean perch	121	24	2	15%	54
Perch	117	25	1	8%	115
Pike	113	25	1	6%	50
Pollock	113	24	1	8%	96
Rockfish	121	24	2	15%	44
Salmon, Coho	185	27	8	39%	49
Salmon, sockeye	216	27	11	46%	87
Sea bass	124	24	4	29%	53
Smelt	124	23	3	22%	90
Snapper	128	26	2	14%	47
Swordfish	155	25	5	29%	50
Trout, rainbow	151	26	4	24%	73
Tuna, fresh	184	30	6	29%	49

Nearly all shrimp (95 percent) sold in the United States has been frozen without significantly affecting its taste or nutritional content.

a reputable restaurant. Experienced sushi chefs know which species are likely to be infected and how to spot larvae and often times the fish is frozen first, which also reduces the risk of parasitic infection. The fish has to be handled carefully so that the flesh doesn't come in contact with the gut, which often harbors parasites. Also, the fish must be kept as cold as possible and served quickly to avoid bacterial contamination. Unless you have learned the specific steps for preparing raw fish, don't do it yourself.

If you should experience severe stomach discomfort or vomiting after eating raw fish, make an appointment with your doctor and tell him what you have eaten.

Shellfish

Shellfish is divided into two categories: mollusks and crustaceans. Mollusks are surrounded either wholly or partially by a hard shell. Common types include clams, oysters, scallops, and mussels. Crustaceans have segmented bodies and are covered with a thin shell. The most common type of crustaceans are lobster, shrimp, crab, and crayfish. Any of these shellfish is low in calories and is an excellent source of protein, iron, and the trace minerals zinc and copper. Most types also contribute a significant amount of B vitamins and iodine to the diet and are not particularly high in sodium.

Cholesterol and fat content

One of the popular misconceptions about shellfish is that it is high in cholesterol. This misunderstanding arose from traditional methods of food analysis that identified certain fats in shellfish that are similar to cholesterol as the true cholesterol. Newer analytical methods indicate that the cholesterol content of most shellfish is lower than that of canned tuna or broiled chicken breast. Even shellfish with the highest cholesterol levels are only slightly higher in cholesterol than lean beef, veal, or pork. (The exception here is shrimp, which has nearly twice the amount of cholesterol of a same size serving of beef.)

What's more, all types of shellfish are low in fat (unless, of course, they are breaded and fried or served in a butter sauce) and particularly low in saturated fat. Foods high in saturated fat are more responsible for raising blood cholesterol levels than foods high in dietary cholesterol.

Some types of shellfish also contain moderate amounts of omega-3 fatty acids. Those containing the most are oysters, mussels, and crab.

Shopping for and storing shellfish

The following tips will help you in selecting high-quality shellfish as well

A Shellfish Substitute

Surimi—you may never have heard of it, but if you like shellfish, you probably have eaten it. For centuries the Japanese have been making these "kneaded foods" from fish paste, which is flavored, textured, and then artfully shaped into over two thousand products—from fish balls to fish sausage and hot dogs. Surimi is becoming a booming industry in this country, too, as substitutes for expensive crabmeat, shrimp, lobster, and scallops. In supermarkets it may be labeled "sea legs" or "imitation crab meat," but on restaurant menus there's often no indication that the shellfish dishes are actually made from surimi.

What's surimi?

Most American surimi is made from Pacific pollack, a lean, white-fleshed fish. After the skin and bones are removed, the fish is ground up and then repeatedly washed and strained, which removes blood, pigment, the fishy odor, as well as some fat, niacin, and potassium. Sugar and/or sorbitol is added to this white, odorless, flavorless protein concentrate to decrease damage from freezing, and salt, starch, and sometimes MSG (monosodium glutamate) are added to enhance the flavor and texture. This pulp is flavored either naturally (with real shellfish or liquid from boiled shells) or artificially. Finally, coloring may be added, and then the pulp is shaped like crab legs or lobster tails, for instance.

Telling the difference

Surimi can be a fraud if you get it when you have ordered and paid for real crab salad or lobster Newburg. The Food and Drug Administration (FDA) insists that surimi products be labeled "imitation" if they resemble any actual type of seafood and are nutritionally inferior to it. The ingredients must always be listed—for instance, "crab-flavored minced pollack." That doesn't stop manufacturers from burying this information in tiny print and picturing real lobster or crab on packages. However, even a magnifying glass won't help you in restaurants and at sushi bars and deli counters, where the surimi is removed from its package, added to various dishes, and often served as real shellfish.

The bottom line is that, unless you are on a sodium-restricted diet, surimi is a good way to add low-cholesterol fish protein to your diet.

Surimi: pluses and minuses

Advantages:
- Low cholesterol (up to 75 percent less than shellfish).
- Rich in high-quality protein.
- Readily available.
- Good ratings for taste and texture when used in salads, casseroles, soups, and with sauces.

Disadvantages:
- High sodium (up to ten times more than real shellfish).
- About 25 percent more calories than comparable shellfish.
- Reduced niacin and potassium.
- Gelatin-like texture.
- Not good when eaten alone.

Discard the greenish tomalley, or liver, in lobsters or the "mustard" (hepatopancreas) in blue crabs. If the shellfish have lived in contaminated water, these body parts may have high concentrations of PCBs (polychlorinated biphenyls, a class of chemicals that are toxic) and cadmium (a toxic element).

as give you guidelines for safe storage of shellfish:

- Buy shellfish only from licensed stores and markets.
- Be sure the seller is storing the shellfish properly. Shellfish should be kept cold: surrounded by ice but not in direct contact with it.
- Clams, oysters, and mussels that are still in their shells must be sold alive. Buy only those with tightly closed shells, or those that snap shut when they are touched. Lobsters and crabs are also often sold alive. Buy the ones that are lively and feel heavy for their size.
- When buying shucked clams, oysters, and mussels, choose those that are plump, free of broken shell, and in a clear liquid.
- Make sure that all frozen shellfish has been kept solidly frozen. Avoid those that have begun to thaw, or those that contain ice crystals or show any sign of discoloration.
- Refrigerate shellfish immediately after purchase.
- Keep live shellfish alive until you

are ready to cook them. Clams, mussels, and oysters should be stored in a well-ventilated area of your refrigerator, not in tightly closed plastic bags or containers. Lobsters and crabs also need ventilation and should be stored covered with damp paper towels. Discard any shellfish that has died during storage.

•Fresh, uncooked shellfish spoils quickly. Keep refrigerated and use it within a day or two of purchase.

Caution on raw shellfish

Cherrystone clams and raw oysters are a favorite with many people. And while most Americans are aware that eating raw shellfish from contaminated waters could make them sick, many have assumed that if they heeded periodic health prohibitions regarding the eating of raw clams and oysters, they could enjoy them worry free the rest of the time. Unfortunately, this is no longer the case. Medical authorities warn that the eating of raw shellfish, even when it is certified clean, carries considerable risks. The problem, they say, lies in the inadequacy of current tests for shellfish contamination and in the policing of the shellfish industry.

The tests, conducted on a regular basis by state and conservation agencies under the supervision of the Food and Drug Administration (FDA), are designed to measure levels of coliform bacteria. These pathological microorganisms, harbored in the intestines of warm-blooded animals and in their feces, find their way into fresh and salt water from untreated sewage. Clams and oysters, which live by filtering fifteen to twenty gallons of water per day, become concentrated storehouses of such bacteria if they live in polluted waters. Because of this, harvesting has been limited to those areas that are certified clean, but waters that are clean of coliform bacteria are not necessarily free of other sewage-related microorganisms. Furthermore, the regulation of the shellfish industry is irregular at best. A handful of agents are charged with overseeing some ten million acres of approved shellfish beds along the Atlantic, Gulf, and Pacific coasts.

Therefore, anyone eating raw shellfish from any area runs a risk of gastrointestinal infection and the diarrhea, nausea, abdominal cramps, and vomiting that go along with it. Shellfish-borne viruses pose additional risks for persons not in good health, such as individuals with cancer, diabetes, or a disease that impairs immunity.

Inadequately cooked shellfish, too, can be a source of infection. Steamed clams, for example, are typically cooked just to the instant of opening, about one minute, so the clam never gets hot enough inside to inactivate any virus present. If it is health certainty you want, learn to like your steamed clams on the rubbery side; for safety, they should be cooked for at least six minutes.

Canned Fish

To most Americans, "fish" means canned tuna—we eat nearly three pounds of it per person each year. But tuna isn't the only type of canned fish available; salmon and sardines also come conveniently packaged. And like fresh fish, canned fish has many nutritional assets. It provides as much protein as meats and is rich is niacin, potassium, and, if bones are eaten, calcium. Canned salmon, sardines, and solid white albacore tuna are also good sources of omega-3 fatty acids.

Fresh from the sea, fish is low in calories. But when fish is canned, processors often add fat in the form of vegetable oil. This added oil usually doubles the calories in the fish and adds up to ten times more fat. Only 15 percent of the calories in water-pack tuna come from fat, compared to over 60 percent in oil-pack tuna. Another reason why water packed is preferred is that draining the oil can remove the valuable omega-3 fatty acids: one study found that while draining the water from water-pack tuna was found to remove only about 3 percent of the omega-3s, draining vegetable oil removed 15 to 25 percent because these fatty acids are oil-soluble. Still, if you prefer the taste of oil-pack tuna, you should be sure to drain the oil; this eliminates about a third of the total calories and half the fat.

Salt is more of a problem: processors usually add four to ten times the amount of sodium naturally in saltwater fish. Fortunately, "low-salt" and "no salt added" varieties are available. "Low-salt" tuna, for example, usually has about 50 percent less added sodium, leaving about two hundred milligrams in three ounces. Tuna marked "no salt added" contains 90 percent less sodium than regular cans, so it is good for people on sodium-restricted diets. To avoid paying a premium price for low- or no-salt tuna, rinse regular water-pack tuna, which removes most of the sodium.

FATS AND OILS

Vegetable Oils

A tablespoon of oil here and there may not seem like a big deal, but vegetable oils account in large part for a major shift in American eating habits in recent years. These oils are simply fat in liquid form. While we have cut back on animal fats, in 1987 we consumed about 50 percent more veg-

NUTRITIONAL CONTENT OF
Canned Fish

Fish (3 oz)	Calories	Protein (g)	Fat (g)	Cholesterol (mg)	Calcium (mg)	Sodium (mg)	Comments
Tuna							
in oil	200-250	19-21	15-19	40-60	10	300-500	High in B vitamins, especially
oil drained	140-200	22-24	8-12	40-60	10	250-450	niacin. Solid white tuna is slightly
in water	90-110	21	1	40-60	10	300-500	lower in fat and calories than chunk
low salt	90-110	21	1	40-60	10	200	white or chunk light.
no salt added	90-110	21	1	40-60	10	40	
Salmon (with bones)							
pink (humpback)	120	17	5	35	150-200	350-450	The redder the fish, the fattier and
red (sockeye)	160	17	8	35	150-200	350-450	moister. Rich in vitamin B$_{12}$, lots of added sodium. Lower in calcium if bones are not eaten.
Sardines (with skin and bones)							
in oil	250-350	16	20-30	85-100	250-350	400-600	Higher in cholesterol and fat than
oil drained	175-250	20	9-18	85-100	300-400	400-600	tuna or salmon. Rich in iron and
in water	200	16	16	85-100	250-350	400-600	vitamin D. Skinless and boneless
no salt added	200	16	16	85-100	250-350	100	sardines have no calcium and
in tomato sauce	200	15	15	75-90	250-350	700	reduced nutrients.

etable oil than we did in 1967—in our cooking oils, margarines, baked goods, fried foods, mayonnaise, and salad dressings. Our *total* fat consumption has, as a result, risen slightly.

Nutritionists agree that we should increase the ratio of polyunsaturated/saturated fats in our diet to help lower blood cholesterol levels and thus reduce the risk of heart disease. Moreover, some research suggests that *mono*unsaturated fats—abundant in olive oil and the new canola oil—are almost as good in lowering cholesterol.

However, no vegetable oil is 100 percent unsaturated. Corn, soybean, safflower, and other kinds of oil all contain some saturated fatty acids. In fact, coconut and palm kernel oil actually contain a higher percentage of saturated fatty acids than animal fats do.

Despite these substantial variations, many shoppers do not know which type of vegetable oil is in the cooking or salad oil they buy. According to a survey by the National Sunflower Association, price and brand loyalty were found to be key considerations,

There are no nutritional differences between extra-virgin, virgin, fine, and ungraded olive oil. These terms relate to differences in the way the oil is extracted from olives. Extra-virgin olive oil, the most expensive, comes from the first pressing and is minimally processed.

Vegetable Oils: A Fat Breakdown

FATTY ACID CONTENT

Oils, least to most saturated	Poly-unsaturated (%)	Mono-unsaturated (%)	Saturated (%)	Unsaturated/ Saturated Fat Ratio	Comments
Canola	32%	62%	6%	15.7:1	Best fatty acid ratio.
Safflower	75%	12%	9%	9.6:1	Highest in polyunsaturates.
Sunflower	66%	20%	10%	8.6:1	Sometimes used in place of olive oil, but blander.
Corn	59%	24%	13%	6.4:1	Heavy taste. Often used for deep frying.
Soybean	59%	23%	14%	5.9:1	Most commonly used oil—in baked goods, salad dressings, margarine, mayonnaise.
Olive	9%	72%	14%	5.8:1	Highest in monounsaturated fat. Expensive.
Peanut	32%	46%	17%	4.6:1	More pronounced flavor than safflower oil.
Sesame seed	40%	40%	18%	4.4:1	Used in Oriental and Middle Eastern cooking. Flavorful.
Cottonseed	52%	18%	26%	2.7:1	Higher in saturated fat. Used in processed foods and salad dressings.
Palm kernel	2%	10%	80%	0.2:1	Palm and coconut oils are the only vegetable oils
Coconut	2%	6%	87%	0.1:1	high in saturated fat. Used in baked goods and candies.

Note: These percentages do not add up to 100% because other fat-like substances make up the total composition.

rather than the type of oil. Shoppers also reported that they were attracted to their brand because of its "low cholesterol" content. They were apparently unaware that no vegetable product contains cholesterol, which is found only in animal products.

Consumers are even less aware of the type of "invisible" oil in processed foods such as crackers, cakes, frozen dinners, snack foods—even nondairy creamers. These often contain highly saturated coconut or palm kernel oil.

The chart on page 196 lists the breakdown of fatty acids in various oils. All oils contain about fourteen grams of fat and 120 calories per tablespoon, plus a fair amount of vitamin E. The higher the ratio of unsaturated/saturated fatty acids, the more healthful the oil. This doesn't mean that you should merely add unsaturated oils to your diet. The trick is to cut down on *all* fats. But when you do eat fat, try to make it as unsaturated as possible.

Choosing and using oils

•Read labels on store-bought foods and avoid those containing coconut or palm kernel oil, which have a long shelf life but are highly saturated. Also avoid foods with hydrogenated oils, since hydrogenation makes the fat more saturated.

•Heat cooking oil before adding food. The food will sit in the oil for a shorter time and absorb less of it.

•Stir-fry vegetables and meat (cut up in small pieces). Using this method, you can cook food faster and with very little oil.

•Use a spray-on vegetable oil, such as Pam, which can coat a pan with a mere quarter teaspoon of oil.

•Make your own salad dressing, using two parts safflower or sunflower oil to one part vinegar or lemon juice. Add fresh or dried herbs or mustard.

Butter and Margarine

A bewildering array of margarine products and substitute butters—semisoft spreads, squeezable liquids, even powders—has expanded what used to be a small corner of the dairy section in the supermarket. Three out of four Americans today use margarine regularly, often because they think it is better for them than butter. Are they making the right choice?

If you're trying to follow a "heart-healthy" diet, you should limit your use of butter, since most of its calories come from saturated fat, and it contains a fair amount of cholesterol. Of course, if your diet is sensibly low in fat and cholesterol, a daily pat of butter won't hurt you. But if you or members of your family eat a lot of butter, switching to a butter substitute or blend can make a big difference.

Here are some of your options:

Margarines. As in butter, 100 percent of margarine's calories come from fat, but the fat is largely polyunsaturated; good for spreading and cooking. None of the major brands have any cholesterol, since almost all are made from vegetable oils (though the Food and Drug Administration does allow lard—which is animal fat—to be used).

Vegetable-oil spreads. These contain less than the 80 percent fat by weight required in a margarine and are no better or worse than margarine.

Diet or reduced-calorie margarines. One way to cut fat is to use a "diet" margarine. Though all of its calories still come from fat (about 45 percent fat by weight), it is diluted with water, so it has half the fat and calories of regular margarine per tablespoon.

Butter-margarine blends. These are anywhere from 15 percent to 40 percent butter. Thus they contain some of butter's cholesterol and saturated fat, as well as its taste.

Sprinkle-on powders. Made from carbohydrates, these powders are virtually fat- and cholesterol-free. They melt well on hot, moist foods like baked potatoes. But they won't do for spreading on toast, in recipes, or for sautéing.

Choosing a margarine or spread

How much saturated fat a margarine or spread contains depends both on which vegetable oil it contains and how it was made. When shopping for a margarine or spread, let the label be your guide:

•Most margarine products tell how much saturated and polyunsaturated fats they contain. Look for one with at least twice as much polyunsaturated as saturated fat. If a brand doesn't give you a breakdown of fats, be suspicious.

•Although all the oils commonly used in margarines are high in polyunsaturated fat and low in saturated fat, they vary substantially. Those lowest in saturated fat are safflower, sunflower, and corn oil, in that order.

•If a hydrogenated or partially hydrogenated oil is listed first, the product is likely to be more saturated. To make oil solid and prolong its shelf life, manufacturers add hydrogen molecules—a process called hydrogenation. It transforms good unsaturated vegetable oil into a more saturated kind.

•The softer or more fluid a margarine is, the less saturated it is likely to be. For this reason, *liquid or tub margarines are almost always better than stick margarines.* One sign of a high polyunsaturate content is a liquid oil as the first ingredient, rather than a partially hydrogenated oil.

•Watch the sodium content, which tends to be relatively high. Salted margarine is just as undesirable as salted butter. Unsalted varieties are available.

Margarine with water listed as the first ingredient has one-third to one-half less fat than the average margarine.

Snack Foods

Salty, crunchy foods are second only to sweets as America's favorite snacks. Popcorn, pretzels, and even potato chips can all be healthful foods, provided you choose them carefully (or, in some cases, make your own) and eat them in reasonable amounts. After all, they are little more than corn, wheat, or potatoes—low-fat sources of complex carbohydrates and fiber plus some protein, vitamins, and minerals.

Yet these staples can become problem foods when, during processing, they are fried in oil and coated with salt or sometimes sugar. In addition, chips and prepopped popcorn frequently contain highly saturated palm or coconut oil, or a hydrogenated oil (hydrogenation makes vegetable oils more saturated, thus giving them a longer shelf life). Most of these snacks are, however, cholesterol-free.

Healthful chips, popcorn, and pretzels

•If you are trying to cut calories, stick to plain, unbuttered popcorn. By substituting one cup of plain popcorn for a one-ounce bag of potato chips, you save 135 calories and ten grams of fat. You would have to eat two quarts of plain popcorn to get the calories in twenty potato chips.

•Make your own popcorn. Prepopped corn and packaged kernels meant to be popped in microwave ovens are expensive and usually coated with oil and salt. You can eliminate all oil by heating plain kernels in a hot-air popper or in a special microwave popper. Otherwise, brush the pan with a small amount of highly unsaturated oil (such as safflower, sunflower, or canola oil). Use only a sprinkling of salt, or substitute herbs or spices.

•Buy unsalted pretzels—an excellent low-fat snack food.

•Make your own potato chips. See the recipe at right.

•Don't buy a large bag of chips if, like many people, you are likely to finish it in a sitting or two. As the chart below shows, an eight-ounce bag of chips has fifty to eighty grams of fat—as much as most people should eat in an entire day.

•Eating eight ounces of potato chips is like adding twelve to twenty teaspoons of vegetable oil (usually hydrogenated) and a teaspoon of salt to an eight-ounce potato.

•Avoid commercial dips, which are high in fat (from whole milk, cream cheese, coconut oil, and/or hydrogenated vegetable oil), calories, and sodium.

They have, on average, three times more calories and ten times more fat than homemade dips using low-fat yogurt or low-fat cottage cheese.

Nuts

Compact. That's the best word to describe nuts. Within their small walls, these kernels have a lot to offer—both good and bad. Ounce for ounce they are packed with protein (10 to 25 percent by weight), B vitamins, vitamin E, minerals (iron, calcium, copper, zinc, potassium, and magnesium), and fiber; however, they are also crammed with fat and calories, far too much and too many to serve as your primary source of protein.

Still, if you choose your nuts carefully and eat them in moderation, they make a nutritious occasional food. One

The Lightweight Chip
Here's a recipe that takes potato chips out of the junk-food category.

Ingredients:

One large baking potato (about 3/4 pound)

Vegetable oil cooking spray (or, if you prefer, a teaspoon of bottled oil)

Paprika

Preheat the oven to 400 degrees F. Scrub the potato well and slice it thinly. Lightly coat a large baking sheet with cooking spray (or oil the sheet with a small amount of oil on a paper towel). Arrange the slices in one layer, overlapping them slightly if necessary, then spray the slices lightly with cooking spray (or brush with remaining oil). Sprinkle with paprika. Bake 30 minutes, turning once, then reduce the heat to 300 degrees. Bake another 15 to 20 minutes, or until the chips are crisp and brown.

NUTRITIONAL CONTENT OF
Snack Foods

	Calories	Fat (g)	Sodium (mg)	Comments
Popcorn (1 cup)				Excellent snack food—low in calories, high in fiber and iron. Plain popcorn is nearly fat-free, but if you add oil and/or butter, about half the calories will come from fat. Limit the amount of salt you add.
plain, air-popped	30	trace	0	
popped in oil, with salt	40	2	100-300	
sugar-coated	140	1	0	
Potato chips (15 chips)	150-170	10	130-300	One ounce of chips has most of the nutrients in a small potato (high fiber, potassium, niacin, vitamin E). However, about 60 percent of calories come from oil (fat), which is usually hydrogenated. BBQ and bacon-flavored chips are especially high in sodium.
unsalted	150-170	10	20	
Pretzels (1 oz, 5 medium/2 large)	110	1	400-650	Good low-fat snack food, but usually highly salted. Made from wheat flour enriched with iron, niacin, thiamine, and riboflavin; whole wheat varieties are also available.
unsalted	110	1	30	
Tortilla and other corn chips (1 oz)	150-160	7-9	160-260	About 60 percent of calories come from fat. Taco-flavored chips are highest in sodium. Look for unsalted varieties.
Cheese puffs or twists (1 oz)	160	10	300-350	Made from corn meal, with a small amount of cheese. High in fat and sodium.

Nuts

	Serving Size	Calories	Protein (g)	Fat (g)	Comments
Almonds, raw	1 oz	165	6	15	Best ratio of nutrients to calories; good source of calcium, riboflavin, vitamin E. Primarily monounsaturated fat. Often blanched to remove dark skin.
Brazil nuts, raw	1 oz	185	4	19	High in fat, calories, and calcium.
Cashews, dry roasted	1 oz	165	4	13	Usually roasted, but raw cashews are less greasy and have slightly less fat and calories.
Chestnuts, fresh, roasted	1 oz	69	1	trace	Always cooked (roasted or boiled) or dried. More carbohydrates and less protein, fat, and calories than other nuts.
Coconut, dried, sweetened, shredded	¼ cup	118	1	8	Low in protein, high in sugar. Fresh coconut contains fewer calories. Fat is mostly saturated.
Hazelnuts (filberts), raw	1 oz	180	4	18	High in fat, though primarily unsaturated. Often ground and used in baked goods.
Macadamia nuts, roasted in oil	1 oz	205	2	22	High in fat and calories, low in protein.
Peanuts roasted	1 oz	180	7	15	Good nutritional value—highest in protein, high in calcium, niacin, and vitamin E. Primarily monounsaturated fat.
dry-roasted	1 oz	170	7	14	
partially defatted	1 oz	145	10	10	
raw	1 oz	160	7	14	
Peanut butter	2 tbsp	190	10	16	Fat is primarily monounsaturated, but some commercial brands contain hydrogenated oils, which can increase the amount of saturated fat. Some brands also contain sugar.
Pecans, raw	1 oz	190	2	19	High in fat and calories and low in protein.
Pistachios, dry roasted	1 oz	165	6	14	Avoid those dyed with red artificial coloring. High in iron. Fat is primarily monounsaturated.
Walnuts, English, raw	1 oz	170	7	16	High in fat and calories. Fat is primarily polyunsaturated.

mitigating factor is that although most nuts are at least half fat, it is primarily unsaturated. Also, like all plant foods, nuts contain no cholesterol.

Raw nuts. Nuts are sold with or without their shells, except cashews, which are always marketed shelled. Raw nuts should be kept in their shells until eaten, since the shells offer great natural protection for months. Shelled raw nuts become rancid quickly if they are not refrigerated; better still, they should be kept in an airtight container. To inhibit spoilage, almost all shelled nuts are sold, and should be stored, in airtight jars, cans, and plastic bags.

Roasted nuts. Unfortunately, many people like their nuts "roasted," which is actually a form of deep frying. Roasting nuts in oil (usually highly saturated coconut oil, and/or peanut oil) can destroy some vitamins and increase the amount of saturated fat. The cooking oil also adds a few calories—about 10 calories per ounce—besides giving them a greasy taste. And after their oil bath, the nuts are usually heavily salted. Peanuts, the most popular nut in America, are also the most frequent victim of the roasting and salting process. (Peanuts are actually legumes, like dry beans and lentils, but are commonly considered nuts.) One cup of salted peanuts has roughly one thousand milligrams of sodium—about half the suggested daily intake of this mineral.

Dry-roasted nuts. Dry-roasted nuts are one alternative to regular roasted ones. They contain the same nutrients, but since they are not cooked in oil, they are slightly less fatty. A much better alternative is partially defatted peanuts. About 60 percent of the fat—as well as almost half the weight and calories—is removed from these nuts when they are roasted under pressure, but their protein and nutrients remain intact. One ounce of defatted peanuts thus contains 60 percent more nuts and 40 percent more protein than regular nuts, but 30 percent less fat. In any case, choose unsalted nuts.

Caution on peanuts

Peanuts can be the source of another health hazard—aflatoxin, a common mold that grows on peanuts as well as on corn and other crops. If ingested in large amounts, it is known to be a factor in liver cancer. Although it is impossible to produce a peanut crop completely free of aflatoxin, this does not mean that peanuts and peanut butter on the market are likely to be unsafe. The Food and Drug Administration has set a maximum permissible level at twenty parts per billion, and the United States Department of Agriculture inspects peanut shipments for any sign of the mold and will ban any crop with detectable contamination. In addition, most American food processors have established rigorous programs to monitor the presence of aflatoxin, and most peanut products fall considerably below the allowable twenty parts per billion; in practice most are voluntarily keeping the level of aflatoxin down to less than two parts per billion.

Thus, commercial peanut butter and commercially packaged, roasted and dry-roasted peanuts are likely to be safe. Another protective factor: any added salt helps protect against mold. However, you should take the following precautions when buying and using peanuts and freshly ground peanut butter:

• Keep an eye on the peanuts you buy in the shell. Discard any peanuts that are discolored, shriveled, or moldy-looking.

• Peanut butter that is ground for you in a store may not be as safe as commercial brands. Peanuts that sit

You would have to eat about 32 cups of air-popped popcorn (unbuttered) to get the 840 calories in a cup of peanuts. Another plus for popcorn: less than 3 percent of its calories come from fat, compared to 76 percent of the peanuts' calories. And it's high in fiber.

around after they have passed inspection have a chance of picking up mold. Also, freshly ground peanut butter won't contain any added salt, so it needs refrigeration.

•If peanut butter from any source becomes moldy, don't just skim off the mold, as you might cut the mold off cheese to salvage the good part. Throw the whole jar out.

Crackers

Ounce for ounce, some popular crackers contain as much fat and sodium as the cheese you put on them. About 60 percent of the calories in some crackers come from fat, for instance. Others have virtually no fat or sodium and instead pack healthy amounts of fiber. Unfortunately, jazzy advertisements and ambiguous labels may make it hard to tell what is really in your favorite brand.

Most cracker packages contain no nutritional information beyond a list of ingredients. (Only those brands that make nutritional claims—such as being high fiber or low salt—have to list specifics about nutrients.) Ingredients are listed by weight in descending order. So if corn syrup, honey, brown sugar, and/or molasses appear toward the top of the list, you know that the crackers contain lots of sugar calories. As a general rule, the shorter the ingredients list—you can find crackers that are made with just flour, plus a little salt—the fewer the nutritional drawbacks.

Fat. One of the easiest ways for fat to sneak into your diet is in crackers and other baked goods. If you are trying to cut down on fat, try varieties that are virtually fat-free, such as matzo and some Scandinavian imports. If these are too dry for you, look for brands that list fat toward the bottom of the ingredients list. Crackers "made with 100 percent vegetable oil" are no better than those made with butter or lard if the oil is coconut, palm, or palm kernel oil. These tropical oils are at least as saturated as animal fats. Keep an eye out for hydrogenated or partially hydrogenated oils as well: these can be nearly as undesirable as tropical oils since hydrogenation makes them to some degree more saturated.

To add to your confusion, most cracker labels today list a group of oils, such as "soybean, hydrogenated cottonseed, palm kernel, and/or coconut oil," which gives the manufacturer a choice. However, since coconut, palm, and palm kernel oils

---

NUTRITIONAL CONTENT OF

Crackers

Crispbreads and matzo-type crackers are lowest in both calories and fats, but even a matzo-like cracker will hit the fat jackpot if spread with Camembert or topped with cheddar. The crackers below are listed in order of fat content—from lowest to highest.

	Crackers per Ounce	Calories	Fat (g)	Sodium (mg)
Rice Cakes	3	105	trace	105
Crispbread, rye, lite	3	120	trace	80
Matzo	1	110	trace	3
Crispbread, no salt	5	70	trace	3
Crispbread, fiber, with sesame	5	100	trace	335
Crispbread, rye	5	100	trace	325
Ry Krisp, original	4	80	trace	224
Melba Toast, wheat, unsalted	10	112	trace	7
Crispbread	3	140	1	125
Zwieback	4	125	2	72
Stoned Wheat Thins	4	130	2	110
Ry Krisp, sesame	4	120	3	296
Saltines	10	130	3	400
Graham	4	120	3	230
Crispbread, fiber plus	3	105	3	138
Table water crackers	9	112	5	68
Triscuits	7	125	5	180
Waverly Wafers	8	145	6	384
Round, snack type	9	160	9	291
Goldfish, original	60	150	10	250

are inexpensive and have a long shelf life, as do hydrogenated oils, it's likely that one of them will be used. The only benefit of these tropical oils is that they all are, like all vegetable products, free of cholesterol.

One way to test how much fat is in a cracker is to rub the cracker with a paper napkin—if it leaves a grease mark, there's lots of oil, even if it's an unsaturated vegetable oil.

Wheat vs. whole wheat. The words "wheat," "stone ground wheat," or even "a blend of hearty wheats" on a package sound promising but actually tell you little. As smart shoppers know, "wheat flour" and "white flour" are highly refined; this milling process removes most of the bran and germ from the whole grain, thus eliminating much of the fiber and many trace minerals originally in the grain. Most "wheat" crackers are actually the equivalent of 50 to 90 percent white flour. If you want 100 percent whole wheat, make sure "whole wheat" is the first and only type of flour listed among the ingredients, as in some crispbreads or whole wheat matzo. Other whole grains—such as rye or rice—are just as nutritious.

Fiber. Only those brands boasting a high-fiber content tell you how much dietary fiber they contain, and it's usually a hefty four to five grams or more per ounce. Some 100 percent whole-grain crackers contain nearly as much fiber. But most of the old favorites are made from refined wheat or white flour, so they contain only about one gram of fiber per ounce.

Sodium. For flavor's sake, most crackers contain a fair amount of salt. If you are on a low-sodium diet, you can take advantage of the growing number of low-salt or no-salt brands. Many crackers actually taste better with less salt.

Cookies

While it's true that no one has yet invented a cookie that is good for you, some cookie manufacturers are taking steps in the right direction. Some, for instance, have rewritten their recipes to exclude palm and coconut oils—two highly saturated fats. Cookies aren't much more than flour, sugar, and fat, but usually the overwhelming emphasis is on fat. While in the average cookie, about 40 percent of the calories come from fat, in some brands 60 percent are fat calories. The trick is to find a type of cookie with a less-than-average fat content (primarily unsaturated)—plus, if possible, reduced sugar and moderate-to-high fiber. Few cookie labels provide nutritional information, so, to know what you are getting, you have to learn to decipher the ingredients list.

Here's what to look for in cookies and what to avoid:

Fat. Vegetable oil, butter, and lard are the main fats in cookies. Butter and animal fats are the least desirable because they are highly saturated and contain cholesterol. Palm oil is as saturated as animal fats, and coconut oil even more saturated, but, like all vegetable products, they are both cholesterol-free. Hydrogenated or partially hydrogenated vegetable oils may also be very saturated. Your best bets are brands that contain plain, unhydrogenated vegetable oil, such as soybean or corn. However, such oils aren't any lower in calories than other fats, just less saturated.

Remember, in addition, that chocolate is packed with lots of fat, which is mostly saturated. All nuts and peanut butter are also concentrated sources of fat, though the fat they contain is mostly unsaturated.

All of the calories in cotton candy, hard candy, and jelly beans come from sugar.

The average American consumes about eleven pounds of cookies each year.

Beware of "Healthy Snacks"

A lot of food companies try to take the guilt out of snacking by offering products that appear to have a healthy image. Below is a sample of a few snacks that sound promising, but often don't deliver. This doesn't mean you should rule out all of the following products—just don't be lulled into a false sense of security by a healthy-sounding name. Always read labels.

Bran muffins. Bakery or deli bran muffins will contain fiber if they contain bran. The question is how much. Most store-bought muffins have far more hydrogenated oils, sugar, and eggs than oat or wheat bran. Check the ingredients list: if bran is close to the bottom, you're being rooked. Look for whole wheat flour as the main ingredient, not "wheat flour" (that is, refined white flour). If the muffin weighs heavily in your hand (some are 5 ounces or more) and has a sticky surface, it is likely to have as many calories and fat as any cupcake.

Carrot cakes. Carrots are healthful (rich in beta carotene and fiber), but carrot cakes are surprisingly rich in drawbacks. They are almost inevitably dense and moist, usually signs of a high-fat content. A typical cake may contain more than a cup of oil, which has nearly 2,000 calories by itself, or about 200 calories per slice—all fat calories—before adding the other ingredients. You'll find that nearly all store-bought carrot cakes also contain a variety of sugars, refined flour, eggs, and shortening, plus cream cheese and more sugar in the frosting. In the interest of health, you'll almost always be better off with apple pie, even though it may be loaded with sugar.

Banana cakes and breads. Most commercial banana cakes offer few, if any, advantages over chocolate cake. For instance, the list of ingredients in one widely sold banana cake begins with sugar, continues with partially hydrogenated vegetable shortening (partly saturated, in effect), and then flour. Only then comes the alibi for it all, bananas. Like carrot cakes, banana cakes usually get 40 to 50 percent of their calories from fat. You'll be better off making your own banana bread, which requires less fat and sugar. Store-bought banana breads, however, may be as full of fat as cakes. Look for flour first among the ingredients and shortening toward the bottom.

Granola bars. When granola bars first arrived on the market, they were a mixture of rolled oats, dried fruit, nuts, seeds, honey, some sugar, and a variety of oils but they contained both protein and carbohydrates in sufficient quantity to be better for you than most candy bars. Over the years, the ingredients of granola bars have changed so that now many granola bars commonly contain candy ingredients such as caramel, chocolate, and marshmallow afloat in increasing amounts of saturated oils and sweeteners. As a result, granola bars are practically nothing more than fat and sugar. The small amount of oats and nuts remaining give them a nutritional edge over candy bars, but it is slight.

Sugar. Whether it goes by the name brown sugar, molasses, fructose, corn syrup, dextrose, syrup, or sugar, it's sugar. And its calories are deficient in nutrients. Many brands of cookies include several sugars scattered throughout their ingredients lists; when these are added together sugar may constitute the cookies' main ingredient. Some cookies labeled "natural" are sweetened with dried fruits (which are a source of fiber) or fruit juice, which may contribute a few nutrients, but neither of these are lower in calories than refined sugar.

Calculating the fat

Unfortunately, most cookie manufacturers don't list the amount of fat on their packages; but three types of cookies tend to be lower in fat—ginger snaps, graham crackers, and fruit bars. Calories are a good clue to fat content: if the cookie has more than about 150 calories per ounce, it's probably packed with fat (cookies containing dried fruit are exceptions, since these types are high in calories but not necessarily in fat). Shortbread, butter cookies, and cookies that are made with nuts, nut butters, or chocolate tend to be the highest in both fat and calories.

If you enjoy cookies as an occasional treat, you needn't be too concerned about their nutritional benefits or shortcomings. But if you can't open a bag without eating at least six of them—which means consuming as much as thirty grams of fat and 480 calories or more in many popular brands—you might think twice about your choice of sweets: four ounces (two scoops) of premium ice cream have about eighteen grams fat and 265 calories—and regular ice cream, ice milk, and frozen yogurt far less. You could even have a serving of graham crackers with your ice cream and consume fewer calories and less fat than you would on a cookie binge. Eating more than two or three of most kinds of cookies adds up to is just that—a fat and calorie binge.

Frozen Desserts

It used to be that choosing a frozen dessert was a simple affair—the only decision was which flavor ice cream you wanted. The supremacy of ice cream is being challenged, however, by other frozen desserts, such as ice milks, sherbets, sorbets, frozen fruit and juice bars, frozen yogurts, frozen tofu, and products made with polydextrose, a derivative of cornstarch that helps provide a creamy consistency without the cream. This expanded variety of frozen treats should allow more people who are trying to cut back on fat, cholesterol and calories to satisfy their needs and tastes.

Fat. The major health drawback of ice cream is its fat content, which is largely saturated. By law, ice cream must contain at least 10 percent milk fat by weight; premium ice creams are

16 to 20 percent milk fat by weight. This means that standard ice cream gets about 48 percent of its calories from fat; premium ice cream 53 percent or more. Nuts and some other flavorings in ice cream can increase the fat content. Ice milk contains less fat by weight (2 to 7 percent milk fat) and usually gets less than 30 percent of its calories from fat. Frozen yogurt is basically ice milk with cultures and has a similar fat count, although there are nonfat varieties of frozen yogurt. When shopping for these products, it is important to compare nutritional information; for instance, the difference between a lower-fat ice cream and a higher-fat ice milk or frozen yogurt

Make sure your frozen yogurt is made from low-fat or nonfat milk. Brands made from whole milk (or those containing added fat) can contain as much fat as ice cream.

Frozen Desserts*

	Calories	Fat (g)	Fat Calories
Ice cream, ½ cup			
standard	135	7	47%
premium	175	12	62%
Ice milk, ½ cup	92	3	30%
Frozen yogurt, ½ cup	125	3	22%
Frozen tofu, ½ cup			
light	90	trace	0%
regular	230	14	55%
Sherbet, ½ cup	135	2	13%
Sorbet, ½ cup	100	0	0%
Polydextrose product, ½ cup	50	0	0%
Fruit and juice bar	70	0	0%

All values on this chart may vary widely from brand to brand depending on the amount of sugar, milk solids (including fat), and air in the products.

is not that great. Compare labels when choosing a frozen tofu product, too. Depending on the brand, frozen tofu can get any where from 0 to 55 percent of its calories from fat, although the fat is primarily unsaturated. Sorbets, sherbets, frozen fruit and juice bars, and frozen desserts made with polydextrose products are virtually fat-free.

Cholesterol. Most frozen desserts contain little cholesterol or, if they're nondairy, none at all. Ice cream contains the most: about thirty milligrams per half-cup—as much as in a glass of whole milk. Dense premium brands have about fifty milligrams of cholesterol per half cup.

Calories. If you are concerned only with calories, ice cream is hardly the worst culprit: a half-cup of standard ice cream contains anywhere from 125 to 175 calories, not much when compared to some other sweets, such as apple pie (350 calories per slice). However, premium ice creams contain extra fat and less air, and thus pack added calories (250 or more in a half-cup). Ice milk, frozen yogurt, low-fat frozen tofu, sherbet, and sorbet average about 100 calories per half-cup serving. Polydextrose products contain anywhere from 50 to 80 calories per half cup and frozen fruit and juice bars are even lower, containing between 40 and 70 calories per bar.

CONVENIENCE FOODS

Frozen Dinners

Most of us succumb now and again to the convenience of frozen dinners. Fortunately, there's been a shift in style in the supermarket freezer department from old standbys like Salisbury steak with french fries to frozen entrees aimed at health-conscious, weight-conscious shoppers.

Not all entrees labeled "lean" or "lite" are better than conventional TV dinners. Most have fewer calories (250 to 400 calories per serving) than the conventional frozen dishes (400 to 700 calories) but often less food. And they can still be loaded with fat, salt, sugar, flavor enhancers, and starchy fillers. Few packages list fiber, cholesterol, and the breakdown of saturated/polyunsaturated fat, and many don't list vitamin and mineral content. Skip brands that don't have any nutritional labeling beyond the ingredients, or else write to the company for some nutritional information.

Here's what to look for in a healthful frozen dinner or entree:

Less than 850 milligrams of sodium. That's about a third of the recommended daily maximum for most people. If you're on a sodium-restricted diet, even that amount will be too much. Like so many processed foods, most frozen meals—even those low in fat and calories—are sabotaged by an unacceptable amount of sodium (sometimes containing over 2,000 milligrams per serving) in an attempt to hype the flavor.

Less than ten grams of fat. In a 300-calorie serving, that means fat contributes less than 30 percent of the calories. (Since each gram of fat has 9 calories, to compute the percentage of calories that comes from fat, multiply the number of grams of fat by nine and divide this figure by the total number of calories.) Look for primarily unsaturated fat. Fish and poultry are usually low in fat, unless they are deep-fried: fat supplies half the calories in most deep-fried frozen fish. Similarly, pasta entrees are basically low-fat, provided you keep away from the cream and

Milk chocolate is lower in fat than semisweet chocolate: 30 percent of its calories are from fat compared to 45 percent in semisweet.

butter sauces. Even vegetarian dishes can be overwhelmed by oil and high-fat ingredients.

Little or no added sugar. Sugar in its variety of forms (sucrose, dextrose, high frutose, corn syrup, honey, molasses, etc.) shouldn't rank high in the ingredients list (ingredients are listed by weight). These sugars add unnecessary—and unwanted—calories to your chicken, pasta, vegetables or other frozen dishes.

Little or no cholesterol. Since few brands list cholesterol, just remember that three ounces of red meat or chicken have about 25 percent of the recommended daily maximum. Fish has less, and vegetarian dishes, including tofu, contain no cholesterol.

Few additives. Some brands don't use any additives. Check the ingredients list—the word "natural" doesn't tell you anything.

Even the best of these frozen dishes don't make completely balanced meals. Most are low in such vital nutrients as calcium, vitamins A and C, and fiber. So supplement them with a salad or vegetable side dish, whole-grain bread, low-fat dairy products, and fruit for dessert. These will also make the meal more filling. A small green salad, a slice of bread, a glass of skim milk, and a pear will add only about 300 calories to your low-calorie meal.

Of course, you can make your own frozen entrees for those days when you can't face cooking from scratch. Not only will they usually be less expensive but you will have full control over what goes into them.

Soups

We think of soup as comforting, nourishing, and sometimes downright medicinal. Canned or packaged varieties are easy to prepare, and dieters often resort to a cupful to stave off hunger. But even at their best, commercially available soups are seldom meals by themselves. Many are about 90 percent water, which helps account for their relatively low calorie count. Considering the average size of a serving, and then figuring only 10 percent of that as potentially nutritious, the outlook can be pretty dismal. A single serving usually provides less than 10 percent of the daily Recommended Dietary Allowance of vitamins, protein, and minerals.

The exceptions to this 90-percent-water rule are those nutritious soups made with beans, lentils, or peas (all excellent sources of fiber and protein), and chunky vegetable soups made with carrots, whole tomato pieces, and cauliflower, for instance.

Sodium. This is one nutrient that soups don't lack. Except for specially marked low-sodium varieties, almost all packaged soups contain 600 to more than 1,000 milligrams of sodium per eight-ounce serving. If you finish the whole canful of soup, like many people do, and eat it with other high-sodium foods, you can consume the entire recommended daily maximum of sodium (2000 to 3,000 milligrams) in one meal.

Fat. Most vegetable or noodle soups are low in fat. Creamy varieties, however, are generally rich (as much as 60 percent of their calories come from fat), as are the condensed types made with whole milk rather than water. Thus, milk-based New England clam chowders tend to be much higher in fat than tomato-based Manhattan chowders. When reading the labels, look out for palm, palm kernel, and coconut oils, chicken or beef fat, and butter—all highly saturated.

One way to defat soup is to chill it

Processed foods, such as frozen dinners and canned soups, contribute 75 percent of the sodium in the American diet.

in its can so that the fat congeals on top; then remove this layer. If you are preparing a milk-based soup, use low-fat or skim milk instead of whole milk. To add spice without adding extra salt, experiment with cayenne pepper, cloves, dill, basil, oregano, or garlic.

Many vegetable or bean soups contain meat stock, so if you're a vegetarian, read ingredients lists carefully.

Condiments

Sandwich ingredients—beef, ham, cheese, and bread—have all come under nutritional scrutiny. But what about mayonnaise, mustard, ketchup, and other condiments? The two danger points here are sodium and, in one important case, fat. You can buy low-sodium mustard and Worcestershire sauce and "lite" versions of mayonnaise and even ketchup. Less familiar condiments such as chutney, horseradish, and salsa are flavorful alternatives with few nutritional drawbacks, except that a few brands may contain large amounts of salt.

Mayonnaise. "Hold the mayo" is definitely the way to go: the only high-fat condiment, mayonnaise is an emulsion of oil, egg yolk, and vinegar; the regular version is almost 100 percent fat. However, since it is made with liquid vegetable oil (usually soybean), mayo is not particularly high in saturated fat. Despite its egg content, it contains only a small amount of cholesterol—about five milligrams per tablespoon. Thus a mayonnaise that is "cholesterol-free" is not an improvement.

Homemade mayonnaise is not nutritionally superior to store-bought. A standard recipe calls for two egg yolks and one cup of oil. And since it is made with raw eggs and without preservatives, homemade mayonnaise

may be a source of food poisoning due to salmonella.

Products labeled "salad dressing," as well as "light," "diet," or "imitation" mayonnaise—in which water and starch or another thickener replace some of the oil—may contain one-half to two-thirds the calories of real mayo, and less than half the fat. There's even a tofu-based product with only one gram of fat per serving.

If your palate demands real mayonnaise, use a teaspoonful rather than a tablespoonful on a sandwich, or blend the mayo with plain low-fat yogurt. Flavor yogurt with a little mustard, lemon juice, and pepper to add to the mayonnaise in chicken or tuna salad. Tartar sauce and the "secret sauce" used on fast-food hamburgers are both mayonnaise-based: substitute a light mayo or plain low-fat yogurt with a little chopped pickle mixed in. And although it's not usually suggested as a low-fat substitute, even sour cream is a better choice than mayonnaise when you're making a dip: a tablespoon of sour cream has only about 25 calories and 2.5 grams of fat—just one-quarter the calories and fat that are in mayonnaise. Using plain low-fat yogurt is even better.

Ketchup. Although it consists mainly of tomatoes, the average ketchup is 20 percent sweetener and contains up to 180 milligrams of sodium per tablespoon. Even the national-brand "lite" ketchup has a fairly high sodium level, although a dietetic brand labeled "low-sodium" contains practically no sodium at all. Other substitutes for the ketchup lover with a sodium problem include tomato paste or purée, or low-sodium or homemade spaghetti sauce (for use in recipes). Some brands of bottled Mexican *salsa ranchera* and taco sauce contain slightly less sodium than regular ketchup, as do Worcestershire, steak

The worst sodium offender among condiments is soy sauce, which may contain more than one thousand milligrams of sodium per tablespoon. Although "light" versions have 30 to 40 percent less sodium, one tablespoon can still contain approximately six hundred milligrams of sodium.

NUTRITIONAL CONTENT OF
Condiments

Product (1 tbsp)	Calories	Fat (g)	Sodium (mg)
Mayonnaise	100	11	80
reduced-calorie	50	5	85
Salad dressing	70	7	86
light dressing	45	4	95
Tofu-based mayo spread	20	1	100
Ketchup	16	trace	156
"lite"	8	0	110
low-sodium	6	0	5
Sweet pickle relish	21	0	107
Worcestershire sauce	12	0	147
low-sodium	12	trace	57
Steak sauce	12	trace	275
Salsa ranchera	5	0	81
Taco sauce	4	0	110
Yellow mustard	11	trace	188
Dijon-style	24	trace	465
low-sodium	15	trace	3
Apple chutney	41	0	34
Prepared horseradish	4	0	50

Tartar sauce has three-quarters of the calories in mayonnaise, plus two to three times the sodium.

Mustard. The natural pungency of mustard somewhat limits the amount you use, but even a tablespoonful can pack a major sodium wallop. If you need to watch your sodium intake, buy a no-salt-added mustard; dilute the mustard with some plain low-fat yogurt; or mix your own from dry mustard powder (you'll find basic directions on the package). Vary the strength, texture, and flavor by using water, vinegar, or milk as the liquid.

Chutney. Usually served with Indian food (but equally good with cheese, plain meats, and poultry), sweet-and-spicy chutneys are fruit- or vegetable-based relishes. All contain negligible fat; however, some are very high in sodium. Look for chutneys made from apples, tomatoes, cranberries, and other fruits at health food stores or specialty markets. If you can't find a salt-free chutney, choose one that has salt at the bottom—not the top—of the ingredients list. Or substitute apple, cranberry, or other fruit sauces, which are low in sodium and are virtually fat-free.

Horseradish. Though its pungency complements meat, poultry, and vegetables, prepared horseradish is not often used as a condiment. And while it is usually made with salt, its sodium content is fairly low. Combine it with low-sodium mustard for an eye-opening sandwich spread, blend it with plain low-fat yogurt to make a less biting sauce, or stir it into applesauce for a traditional Austrian accompaniment to beef. Powdered horseradish can be mixed with water or other condiments to make a tasty sauce.

sauce, and pickle relish; most chili sauces, barbecue sauces, and cocktail sauces have even *more* sodium than ketchup. Perhaps the best option is to make your own Mexican-style *salsa cruda* (raw sauce), a combination of chopped tomatoes, chilies, onions, lemon or lime juice, and spices, to satisfy your cravings for a topping with tomato flavor.

EXERCISE

Exercise can have a surprising number of benefits: it can improve your cardiovascular fitness and muscular endurance, which translates into an increase in energy; it can dramatically reduce the risk of coronary artery disease; it may also help lower blood pressure and cholesterol levels, and aid in weight control; and it appears to give self-esteem a measurable boost, and in general to improve your sense of well-being.

You can derive these benefits at any age, and, indeed, exercise—or at least staying physically active—appears to be increasingly important the older we get. Many of the problems commonly associated with aging—increased body fat, decreased muscular strength and flexibility, loss of bone mass, lower metabolism, and slower reaction times—are often signs of inactivity that can be minimized or even prevented by exercise. The following chapters explain the basic components of fitness, present guidelines for exercising safely, and contain entries covering a complete range of exercise activities.

The Elements of Fitness

Fitness is an elusive concept. According to the President's Council on Physical Fitness, it is "the ability to carry out daily tasks with vigor and alertness, without undue fatigue, and with ample energy to enjoy leisure-time pursuits and to meet unforeseen emergencies." Yet physical fitness means different things to a dancer, marathon runner, lumberjack, mailman, and weight lifter. And it's a relative term: you may be fitter than you were last year or than your neighbor, but there's no clear-cut point at which you are "fit." One fact is clear, though: if fitness is the goal, exercise is the way to get there.

There are four basic elements of physical fitness: cardiovascular endurance, muscular strength, muscular endurance, and flexibility. Each can be measurably improved with regular exercise. But keep in mind that exercising to build fitness is not the same thing as working out to improve athletic performance. For example, Olympic weight lifters have extraordinary muscular strength—they can heft tremendous weights, but they do it only in single efforts; football players typically have great muscular endurance but less cardiovascular endurance than runners or other long-distance athletes; yet while runners may build exceptional cardiovascular endurance, they commonly neglect their upper-body strength. To be truly fit, you should develop all four elements, not just one or two.

The most important element

While each element is a part of being fit, the most vital is cardiovascular endurance. Physiologically, cardiovascular endurance is the sustained ability of the heart, blood vessels, and blood to carry oxygen to the cells, the ability of the cells to process oxygen, and the ability of the blood, once again, to carry away waste products. Since every cell in the body requires oxygen to function, there is no more basic element of fitness than this—to see that the heart, lungs, and circulatory system do their job.

Cardiovascular endurance is built up through exercises that enhance the body's ability to deliver ever larger amounts of oxygen to working muscles. To achieve this, the exercise must utilize the large muscle groups (such as those in the legs) and, most importantly, it must be sustained. When you exert yourself physically, muscles first draw on quick sources of energy within their own cells, which can be obtained without any increase in the body's supply of oxygen; hence, short-term efforts—such as sprinting or lifting a heavy weight—scarcely need any oxygen. (Such activities are known as *anaerobic*, a word derived from two Greek words meaning "without air.") But when exercise lasts longer than a minute or two, the muscles get most of their energy from processes that require an increased supply of oxygen delivered to the muscles and tissues. Because of the role played by oxygen, such activities are called *aerobic* (meaning "with air"). Aerobic activities include running, brisk walking, swimming, cycling, rowing, cross-country skiing, rope skipping, and aerobic dance. (For a guide to these activities, see pages 231-257.)

With regular aerobic exercise, your heart will eventually be able to pump more blood and thus deliver more oxygen with greater efficiency. Moreover, your muscles will develop a greater capacity to use this oxygen. This is part of what is called the aerobic "training effect." Because your heart is stronger, it can pump more blood per beat, and as a result your heart rate, both at rest and during exertion, will decrease. Your heart will also acquire the ability to recover from the stress of exercise more quickly.

Your training heart rate

In order to achieve a training effect, the American College of Sports Medicine (ACSM) suggests performing aerobic-exercise sessions of *fifteen to sixty minutes a day, three to five days a week.* Furthermore, to get the most from aerobic exercise, you should exercise at a level of intensity called your *training heart rate.* The easiest way to compute this is to subtract your age from 220—that's your maximum heart rate (MHR)—then take 60 percent and 80 percent of that number (multiply the number by 0.6 and by 0.8). The results are the upper and lower end of your target heart rate zone: while you exercise, your heart rate per minute should fall somewhere between these two numbers.

Maximum and Training Heart Rates by Age

Age	Maximum Heart Rate (per minute)	TRAINING ZONE		
		60% Rate	80% Rate	90% Rate
20	200	120	160	180
25	195	117	156	175
30	190	114	152	171
35	185	111	148	166
40	180	108	144	162
45	175	105	140	157
50	170	102	136	153
55	165	99	132	149
60	160	96	128	144
65	155	93	124	140

Don't let pulse-taking and various computations make exercise frustrating. Once you've become an experienced exerciser, you may no longer need to take your pulse—you'll simply know how it "feels" to work out at your training heart rate. On the other hand, if you're a competitive athlete and are carefully monitoring your progress, or if you need to be extra cautious (for instance, if you have heart disease or high blood pressure), your heart rate will always be a crucial tool.

The benefits of aerobic exercise

Aerobic exercise, when regularly performed, helps keep elevated blood pressure at normal levels, reduces the risk of heart disease, and can help control weight gain. There is increasing evidence that it can raise the level of HDL ("good") cholesterol in the blood. And such exercise is important in the management of diabetes because it aids in weight loss and can also lower blood sugar levels.

Some research has also shown that an aerobic-exercise regimen can have psychological benefits, including improved self-esteem, lessened anxiety, and, in some cases, relief of depression. In addition, reports of exercisers indicate that they often are able to cope with psychological stress better than nonexercisers. Though such research is difficult to undertake and interpret, objective measures of stress levels (such as blood pressure and pulse rate) tend to be lower in fit people. In one study of sedentary students, for instance, half were put on an aerobic program (brisk walking or jogging for thirty-five to forty minutes, three times a week).

Activity vs. Exercise

Starting in the late 1980s, researchers began to pay more attention to what they call "moderate exercise," and found that it may offer some of the same benefits as vigorous aerobic exercise. A study at the University of Minnesota found that men who routinely engaged in activities such as gardening, strolling, household chores, or bowling had stronger hearts and a lower risk of dying from a heart attack than their sedentary counterparts. In this study—a re-evaluation of data from an earlier long-term study of almost thirteen thousand middle-aged men at risk for heart disease—benefits appeared to stabilize at about an hour's worth of physical activity daily: that is, gardening for over an hour didn't result in better health.

Another potential benefit provided by less-than-strenuous exercise is for women over forty who are concerned about osteoporosis. Any type of weight-bearing exercise that places stress on the bones can help maintain or increase bone mass. Walking, dancing, or a modest weight-training program are often recommended.

For maximum cardiovascular benefits, nothing can take the place of aerobic exercise performed at your target heart rate. Nevertheless, those who engage in moderate physical activities—which also include leisurely cycling, ballroom dancing, and softball—are doing something to improve their fitness. If you're basically sedentary and feel you can't face a program of vigorous, sweaty exercise, then include forty-five to sixty minutes of some enjoyable and/or useful activity in each day. It's the first step toward a longer, healthier life.

After fourteen weeks, all of the students were tested with a series of unsolvable anagrams and were told that their performance would predict success in college. Measurements taken during and after the exams revealed that the nonexercisers had higher blood pressure and experienced higher levels of anxiety and muscle tension than the exercisers.

Studies have also shown that age is no barrier to these and other exercise benefits. For example, a study of men and women in their sixties conducted at Washington University School of Medicine in St. Louis showed that after twelve months of endurance exercise, cardiovascular function improved by 25 to 30 percent. In another study, women aged fifty to sixty-three were put on aerobic dancing or walking programs at West Virginia University; after six months, both groups showed significant improvements in muscular strength and cardiovascular fitness.

Strength, muscular endurance, flexibility

Muscular strength is the force a muscle produces in one effort—a lift, a jump, a heave—as when you swing a mallet to ring a carnival bell. *Muscular endurance* refers to the ability to perform *repeated* muscular contractions in quick succession, as in doing twenty push-ups in a minute. Although muscular endurance requires strength, it is not a single all-out effort.

Muscular strength and endurance are interrelated. A soccer player needs endurance to sprint the length of the field; he needs strength to perform the single explosive effort to kick a goal. An athlete with great strength will necessarily have enhanced endurance: he will use a small portion of his total strength for each effort and so will be able to use his reserves to repeat the effort again and again.

Yet, interrelated as endurance and strength are, they are distinct. Endurance enables you to maintain a sustained effort, while strength will give extra force to your golf swing or tennis serve. Gains in strength come most quickly from

Everyday Activity
You can get many benefits from an activity like gardening if you pursue it regularly. Weeding, trimming, and raking can burn about 300 calories an hour; pushing a manual lawn mower burns between 420 and 480 calories an hour (as many as an hour of tennis); and spading, tilling, and lifting can improve muscle tone and strength. Try to work at a constant pace, and—as with any kind of exercise—warm up and stretch before you start. Most importantly, don't be a "weekend" gardener; you need to garden at least three or four times a week for exercise benefits.

How Fit Are You?

A twelve-minute running test, developed by Dr. Kenneth Cooper of the Aerobic Center in Dallas, Texas provides an easy and reliable way to evaluate your aerobic fitness. Thousands of men and women in the Air Force have used this test. While not as accurate as traditional treadmill tests, the running test is an excellent way for you to measure your fitness progress periodically.

If you are forty-five years old or over, unless you have been exercising regularly, don't take this or any other test requiring maximum physical exertion without first checking with your physician.

The test calls for running as far as you can in twelve minutes and then comparing the distance with the chart below. Run on an indoor or outdoor track—at a health club or high school, for instance—where you can compute the distance you've run. If a track isn't handy, run on any level terrain and later check your distance on a car odometer (although less precise, this will provide an adequate guide). If you can't run for the whole twelve minutes, walk part of the time. Stop if any unusual symptoms occur, such as chest discomfort or pain in the knees or ankles. Use this chart to evaluate your results.

Before You Begin

If you are forty-five or over, the American College of Sports Medicine recommends that you consult your doctor before beginning an exercise program. Your doctor may recommend that you take an exercise stress test (see page 447).

You should also see a doctor if you are thirty-five or older and have any risk factors for heart disease (such as recurrent chest pain, high blood pressure or cholesterol levels, smoking, or obesity). And at any age, you should consult with a physician first if you have cardiovascular or lung disease (or symptoms suggestive of these diseases).

Miles Covered in Twelve Minutes

Fitness Category	AGE (YEARS) 20-29	30-39	40-49	50-59	60+
Very Poor					
men	<1.22	<1.18	<1.14	<1.03	<0.87
women	<0.96	<0.94	<0.88	<0.84	<0.78
Poor					
men	1.22-1.31	1.18-1.30	1.14-1.24	1.03-1.16	0.87-1.02
women	0.96-1.11	0.95-1.05	0.88-0.98	0.84-0.93	0.78-0.86
Fair					
men	1.32-1.49	1.31-1.45	1.25-1.39	1.17-1.30	1.03-1.20
women	1.12-1.22	1.06-1.18	0.99-1.11	0.94-1.05	0.87-0.98
Good					
men	1.50-1.64	1.46-1.56	1.40-1.53	1.31-1.44	1.21-1.32
women	1.23-1.34	1.19-1.29	1.12-1.24	1.06-1.18	0.99-1.09
Excellent					
men	1.65-1.76	1.57-1.69	1.54-1.65	1.45-1.58	1.33-1.55
women	1.35-1.45	1.30-1.39	1.25-1.34	1.19-1.30	1.10-1.18
Superior					
men	>1.77	>1.70	>1.66	>1.59	>1.56
women	>1.46	>1.40	>1.35	>1.31	>1.19

Chart is from the The Aerobics Program for Total Well-Being by Kenneth H. Cooper, M.D., M.P.H., Copyright © 1982 by Kenneth H. Cooper, M.D., M.P.H. Used by permission of Bantam Books, a division of Bantam, Doubleday, Dell Publishing Group, Inc.

Don't be dismayed if your results are less than "good." Dr. Cooper estimates that 80 percent of all Americans fall in the "very poor," "poor," or "fair" categories. If running isn't your usual form of exercise, however, it's possible that you are in better shape than this test reflects. If you are a swimmer or cyclist, for instance, this test may not be as good a gauge of your level of fitness as it is for someone who walks or runs regularly. If your initial test results are not up to par, you can improve them by undertaking a regular aerobic conditioning program.

exercising with the maximum amount of resistance—usually weights—that you can heft comfortably in a few repetitions. The way to build endurance is through increasing repetitions—working at below your maximum level and gradually increasing the number of times you perform an exercise.

Flexibility refers to the ability of the joints to move through their full range of motion. It varies from person to person and from joint to joint. Good flexibility is thought to protect the muscles against pulls and tears, since short, tight muscles may be more likely to be overstretched. Some people find that stretching certain muscle groups helps relieve or prevent pain. For instance, stretching hamstring and lower-back muscles may alleviate lower-back pain; calf stretches may help prevent leg cramps.

(For guidelines, tips, and exercises to develop muscular strength, endurance, and flexibility, see pages 258-271.)

Maintaining fitness

The beneficial effects of exercise are transitory, so when you stop, you start to lose them—this process is known as detraining. Studies suggest that how quickly this occurs depends as much on how fit you are and whether or not you have been on a long-term exercise program as on how long you have been sedentary. It also depends in part on which type of exercise you were doing. Most research has focused on the effects of detraining on aerobic fitness. For instance, a study at Washington University School of Medicine in St. Louis looked at runners, cyclists, and swimmers who, having worked out regularly and vigorously for years, abstained from all exercise. After twelve weeks, they lost more than half their gains in aerobic conditioning (compared to a sedentary control group who hadn't exercised regularly for at least eight years). But in another study, when sedentary people undertook an eight-week cycling regimen and then stopped for eight weeks, they lost all their aerobic gains and returned to their pretraining fitness levels.

Other studies show, however, that when people merely cut back on exercise, they are often able to avoid or postpone the effects of detraining for at least several months. So if you have been exercising regularly but find that you no longer have the time or that an injury restricts you, try an abridged workout schedule—but don't quit exercising altogether.

It's hard to predict exactly how long it will take to regain the previous level of fitness after ceasing all exercise. After a three-month hiatus, a week of training won't return you to your peak condition. And if your layoff was long and total, it may take you as long to retrain as it did to become fit for the first time.

A Workout Guide

Exercise can be so involving, particularly because you are trying to push yourself, that it's easy to be carried away by the joy of the moment and to forget—or skip—certain measures that can reduce risk of injury. The following nine pages contain guidelines and tips that can protect you from injury and will make exercise itself more enjoyable.

Eight basic tips

1. Whatever activity you pursue, don't overdo it. Studies show that the most common cause of injury is exercising too aggressively—the "too much, too soon" syndrome. Even if you consider yourself in good shape, start any new exercise at a relatively low intensity and gradually increase your level of exertion over a number of weeks. In an exercise class, don't feel constrained to do any set number of repetitions or lift a predetermined amount of weight. You don't have to keep up with an instructor or other exercisers. If a class includes an exercise that is too difficult for you, substitute something easier.

2. "No pain, no gain" is a myth. Exercise should require some effort, but discomfort isn't necessary. If you are in an exercise class, beware of any instructor who says that exercise must hurt (or "burn") to do any good. Indeed, pain is a warning sign you are foolish to ignore. If you have continuing pain during an exercise, stop and don't do it again unless you can do so painlessly. (If the pain occurs in the chest or neck area, you should see a doctor immediately.)

General muscle soreness that comes after exercise is another matter: it usually indicates that you are not warming up sufficiently or that you are working too long or too hard. Sore muscles need not make you stop exercising, but they should make you slow down. (For more information on assessing exercise-related aches and pains, see pages 368-379.)

3. Use adequate footwear. Wearing improper or worn-out shoes places added stress on your hips, knees, ankles, and feet—the sites of up to 90 percent of all sports injuries. Choose a shoe suitable for your activity (see page 223) and replace them before you wear them out—with frequent use, athletic shoes can lose one-third or more of their shock-absorbing ability in a matter of months.

4. Control your movements—if you can't, slow down. Rapid, jerky movement can set the stage for injury. Flailing your arms or legs can overstress joints. Instead, as you move your limbs, keep the muscles in them contracted and move them as if you are pushing against some resistance—for instance, squeezing a beach ball or pushing a weight.

5. Watch your form and posture. In most activities, stress can result from poor form, whether it's landing on the balls of your feet (instead of your heels) when running, or constantly cycling in the highest gears. Keep your back aligned (abdominal muscles contracted, buttocks tucked in, and knees aligned over feet). This is particularly important when jumping or reaching overhead.

6. Don't bounce while stretching. "Ballistic" stretching, in which you stretch to your limit and perform quick, pulsing movements, actually shortens muscles and increases the chance of muscle tears and soreness. Instead, do "static" stretches, which call for gradually stretching through a muscle's full range of movement until you feel resistance. This gradually loosens muscles without straining them.

7. Avoid high-impact aerobics. Surveys have found that most aerobics instructors and many students suffer injuries to their shins, calves, lower back, ankles, and knees because of the repetitive, jarring movements of some aerobics routines. Fortunately, there's a less stressful form called low-impact aerobics, which substitutes marching or gliding movements for the jolting, up-and-down motion of typical aerobics (see page 228). A well-designed low-impact aerobics routine can easily raise your heart rate enough to provide cardiovascular benefits. Working out more strenuously than that isn't necessary and may cause injury.

8. Warm up and cool down. Even the best exercise routine can become risky if you don't take the time to do this properly (see below).

Keys to Maintaining Exercise

Despite the best of intentions, half of all people who take up new exercise programs drop by the wayside within six months. Here are six ways to bolster your perseverance:

Set realistic exercise goals. Adopting a plan beyond your capacities is a sure route to failure, especially if you are a perfectionist. Set definite goals rather than hazy ones ("I'll cycle ten miles this week," not "I really should get more exercise this week."). Even more important, set exercise goals that you know you can achieve.

Record your progress. Before you start, evaluate your condition. For each workout, weigh yourself, monitor your heart rate, and record both your time and achievements (such as the distance covered).

Start slow and easy. If you haven't exercised regularly in some time, working out ten minutes three times a week is just plain easier to stick to than forty-five minutes four times a week. So is starting with a moderate level of intensity, one that leaves you feeling good afterward. Gradually lengthen your workouts and step up the pace.

Seek convenience. Have you found a convenient time slot? A convenient location for your workout? If the gym, track, or pool you use isn't nearby, or if you frequently can't find parking space, you may use this as an excuse and stop going.

Find a support group. A workout partner can help keep you motivated. One recent study found that 55 percent of women who exercised with a partner stuck with a twelve-month program versus only 31 percent of those who went it alone.

Add variety. Performing one type of exercise day in, day out, can become boring; instead, try swimming one day, riding a bike the day after, and jogging the next. Indeed, there are many activities you can choose from to stay motivated and maintain or even enhance fitness benefits.

The right way to warm up

If you think that stretching is the smart way to start your workout, you're wrong. Stretching cold muscles can injure them. Whether you're running, playing a sport, doing calisthenics, or lifting weights, *it's essential to warm up first, then stretch.* Warming up prepares you for exercise by gradually increasing your heart rate and blood flow, raising the temperature of muscles and connective tissue, and improving muscle function. It may also decrease the chance of a sports injury. Sudden exertion without a gradual warm-up can lead to abnormal heart rate and inadequate blood flow to the heart along with changes in blood pressure, all of which can be dangerous, especially for older exercisers.

Fitting in Exercise
According to a Gallup poll, people who manage to exercise regularly fit workouts into their existing schedules, rather than getting up early or altering their work routine. There are many strategies for squeezing exercise into even the busiest schedule. For a moderately good aerobic workout, for instance, park your car a mile or two from your office or the train station and walk briskly to your destination. Take the stairs instead of elevators or escalators. Better yet, ride a stationary bike while you read the paper or watch the news on TV.

There are two techniques for warming up. The generic type—such as jogging in place or stationary cycling—is a full-body warm-up not necessarily geared to the particular activity you're about to perform. Because they use the large muscle groups, general warm-ups are most effective for elevating deep muscle temperature. You should always perform a general warm-up before you stretch or work with weights.

Specific warm-ups are slightly less vigorous rehearsals of the sport or exercise you're about to perform. A tennis player, for instance, would warm up by lightly hitting balls. Specific warm-ups are particularly effective in preparing both physically and psychologically for activities involving skill and coordination.

Warm-up tips

•A five- to ten-minute warm-up is usually enough to raise your body temperature. However, if you exercise in warm weather, you may not have to warm up as much, and in the cold, you may need a longer warm-up. A light sweat is a good indication that you have warmed up sufficiently.

•After exercise, cool down. Slow down gradually and take an extra lap around the track or pool; pedal the last quarter mile slowly; or stretch gently for five to ten minutes. Not only can this reduce muscle stiffness, but it can also prevent the abrupt drop in blood pressure that occurs when you suddenly halt vigorous activity. Never stand still immediately after vigorous exercise.

•In cold weather, try warming up before going outdoors; also, wind up cooling down indoors. Many exercisers find that when it's cold outside, they stretch more fully in the comfort of their homes.

Fluid replacement

When you exercise intensely, indoors or out, you need to replace fluids lost through sweating. This is particularly important in hot weather, when you can easily lose more than a quart of water in an hour. At the very least, neglecting to compensate for fluid loss can cause lethargy and nausea, interfering with your performance. In endurance activities like marathon running, long-distance cycling, strenuous hiking, or cross-country skiing, water loss can be severe, potentially producing heat exhaustion or heat stroke.

Even if you don't feel thirsty, it's important to drink at regular intervals when exercising. (Thirst is satisfied long before you have replenished lost fluids.)

•In hot weather, drink at least sixteen to twenty ounces of fluid two hours before exercising and another eight ounces fifteen to thirty minutes before. While you exercise, drink four to eight ounces every ten to twenty minutes.

•After exercising, drink enough to replace the fluid you've sweated off. In hot weather, weigh yourself before and after your workout; drink one pint for each pound lost and eat normally.

•Research shows that cool drinks (forty to fifty degrees Fahrenheit) are absorbed more quickly than lukewarm ones.

Sports drinks vs. plain water. What should you drink when working out? Most exercise physiologists have recommended water as the ideal replacement fluid because it is absorbed more efficiently than any other beverage. Over the past several years, though, specially formulated sports drinks have been widely touted as providing additional benefits. These drinks promise to replace the sodium and

Myth: Beer is a good post-exercise drink.

Fact: *It may taste good when you're thirsty, but beer is not a good way to get the fluid you need after prolonged exercise. Alcohol is a diuretic, so that rather than replenishing the water you've lost in perspiration, beer can promote dehydration.*

Some people say that beer gives them a quick shot of carbohydrates (the basic fuel for muscles) and potassium. But there's no pressing need for these nutrients immediately after a workout.

Ironically, even if you needed these nutrients, beer isn't a very good source. Compare beer to orange juice. The beer has 13 grams of carbohydrates, versus 39 in orange juice. And while the beer has just 89 milligrams of potassium, the orange juice has a whopping 700 milligrams.

potassium lost through sweating as well as supply carbohydrates—in the form of sugar—for energy. However, in a number of studies, researchers found that sugar significantly slowed the body's absorption of fluid from the digestive tract—and most sports drinks have a sugar content of 6 to 8 percent; the sugar content of fruit juices and soft drinks is even higher.

On the other hand, further research has indicated that although a drink containing 6 percent sugar may leave the stomach more slowly than water, it gets into the bloodstream just as quickly through the small intestine. Moreover, subjects performing endurance exercise experienced significantly less fatigue when they consumed the carbohydrate solution than when they drank plain water.

Other studies suggest that running and other activities that jostle the abdomen may also help to force fluids through the stomach—so that, in fact, the rate at which fluid leaves the stomach may not begin to diminish until its sugar concentration rises above 8 percent.

The companies that produce sports drinks have cited these studies to suggest that their products are superior to water for fluid replacement. *But unless you are engaging in long workouts, there is no evidence that sports drinks offer any advantage over water.* In virtually all of these studies, the subjects were trained endurance athletes who exercised two hours or more, and the researchers noted that sports drinks will probably not provide any benefit over water during shorter bouts of exercise. In hot weather, furthermore, fluid replacement is far more critical than restoring carbohydrates or sodium (which you can easily replace through your normal diet).

Studies comparing different brands of sports drinks have found no significant difference in their rate of absorption. Researchers also point out that the efficiency of fluid absorption varies tremendously among individuals. Some people's systems don't handle sports drinks well, so even when drinks are diluted, they can cause nausea in certain individuals.

If you want to spend the money on sports drinks, that's up to you. If a sports drink makes you feel bloated, try diluting it with one to three parts water. Another option is to dilute orange juice or apple juice, both of which are about 10 percent sugar—or switch completely to water.

Exercise and pregnancy

Proper exercise during pregnancy can have many benefits. For a woman who enjoyed regular workouts before becoming pregnant, it can be important psychologically to continue with a regular exercise program. Moderate exercise during pregnancy can help prevent excessive weight gain and help speed up recovery after birth.

Which kind of exercise, and how much, is safe to perform during pregnancy? Medical experts say that your exercise program must be geared to your level of fitness, medical history (particularly any problems during past pregnancies), the stage of development of the fetus, and maternal complicating factors. Therefore, it's important to consult your physician.

Generally, you should not take up *new* exercise programs during pregnancy. Stick with your usual exercise routine, but cut back on the intensity. Remember that pregnancy puts extra demands on your heart and lungs. Your oxygen consumption and heart rate goes up. As pregnancy advances, breathing becomes harder work because each breath must displace the enlarging uterus downward.

Sports Bras
According to one university study, 56 percent of women experience breast discomfort while exercising. The researchers suggested that large-breasted women in particular might benefit from sports bras. The problem is, many so-called sports bras aren't any better than regular models. Here are points to keep in mind when shopping for a sports bra:

- *Sports bras come in two types: those that compress the breasts and those that encapsulate each breast. Try on both types to find which is best for you.*
- *Simulate the motions of your activity when trying on the bra.*
- *Choose a bra with seamless cups or with seams that don't cross a nipple; avoid models with hooks, fasteners, or rough seams that may chafe.*
- *Bands at top and bottom should be slightly elastic and wide enough to control bouncing and prevent the bra from riding up. Be sure the straps don't dig into your shoulders.*

For exercise to be effective, it should be regular. Try to exercise no less than three times a week in half-hour sessions. The best exercise is an activity you enjoy. Walking and swimming are particularly good for pregnant women who have been relatively sedentary. Warming up and cooling down are especially important during pregnancy, but stretch carefully because muscles and joints are looser than usual. Cool down with leisurely walking, which helps return blood to your heart from your lower extremities.

What to avoid. Avoid bouncing, jarring, twisting, and any activity that puts your abdomen in jeopardy. Contact sports are too risky, as is any activity that requires rapid stops and starts, since your center of gravity has changed and it is easier to lose your balance. In addition, take the following precautions:

•If you feel very tired or experience discomfort, stop and rest. You should not exercise so intensely that you are unable to talk. You should recover your pre-exercise heart rate within fifteen minutes of your exercise session.

•Don't exercise while lying on your back after the fourth month. This can block the blood supply to the uterus and depress the fetal heart rate. If you need to rest during an exercise session, lie down on your side, not on your back.

•Don't exercise vigorously in hot, humid weather, and always drink plenty of water before and after exercising. This avoids the dehydration and elevated body temperature that could injure the fetus.

•Remember that your muscles and connective tissues are gradually undergoing hormonal changes that will relax them. This will facilitate the baby's birth, but it also makes you more susceptible to strains and sprains. Wear properly fitting shoes that support your feet in whichever activity you choose.

Exercise and kids

Parents shouldn't assume that schools are taking care of their kids' "physical education." On average, schools are offering fewer gym classes; only 36 percent have required daily gym classes, according to the President's Council on Physical Fitness and Sports. More important, few gym programs are effective in promoting cardiovascular fitness. Instead of aerobic activities, gym classes tend to stress competitive sports, which involve only a limited number of students who have the required abilities. All kids, though, can participate in aerobic exercise, since it requires minimal hand-eye coordination and little athletic talent. Aerobic activities are also likely to become lifelong habits. Running, for example, can be a good aerobic activity for children. Long-distance running poses an increased risk of injury for prepubescents, but if a running program is gradual and well supervised, and if the child wears good running shoes and warms up properly, the risks should be minimal. Swimming, cycling, brisk walking, and hiking are other good aerobic options that can easily be shared as family activities.

Exercise should be fun for children: the adage "no pain, no gain" is even more dangerous for kids than for adults. For example, weight lifting that calls for hefting as much weight as possible may be hazardous for youngsters. If a child over nine wishes to begin a weight-lifting program, make sure he or she works with a trained supervisor who allows only slow lifts that can be repeated twelve to fifteen times. Indeed, a child who wants to engage in any type of strenuous after-school exercise or sports program should be supervised by a qualified person—and should also have a physical exam beforehand.

Aging and Exercise
Adults of any age should basically follow the same safety guidelines for exercise. However, as you get older, it's especially important to start a workout slowly: begin with five to ten minutes of exercise at a comfortable level of exertion and increase your effort gradually. Also, there is no need to exceed 70 percent of your maximum heart rate, and 50 to 60 percent is sufficient if you are starting out or find more exertion too strenuous.

The Right Footwear

Athletic shoes

Specialized athletic shoes have proliferated during the last decade. But do you really need different shoes for running, aerobics, tennis, calisthenics, even walking?

There are two basic kinds of athletic shoes— running shoes and tennis-type shoes. Active people generally need both kinds, and athletes may require other specialized shoes for their sport as well.

Running shoes. These are good for activities that primarily involve forward movement. These light weight shoes have a durable, deeply patterned outer-sole; a thick heel wedge to tilt the body forward; a firm, shock-absorbent mid-sole; and a breathable upper.

A study at Tulane University found that all running shoes lose about 30 percent of their shock absorbability after five hundred miles of use, regardless of the brand, price, or construction. If shoes can't be repaired, replace them (see page 248).

Tennis-type shoes. Good for any activity that primarily involves side-to-side movement, such as tennis and other racquet sports. These are heavier and stiffer than running shoes, and they usually have a herringbone outer-sole and a reinforcement under the toes for stop-and-go action.

Aerobics shoes. Because aerobic dance calls for multidirectional, high-stress movement, these shoes combine the features of running and tennis-type shoes. You can use tennis-type shoes in aerobics classes, but not running shoes.

Walking shoes. Shoes for everyday walking should have a rigid shank for support. Rubber heels are a must—they absorb shock and are replaceable. Shoes specially designed for long treks may have curved soles to facilitate the rocking motion of walking and extended heel counters at the backs.

Can insoles protect your feet?

Special insoles that can be inserted in shoes are often claimed by manufacturers to provide better shock absorption than the soles normally built into athletic shoes. (These flat insoles shouldn't be confused with orthotic devices that are molded foot supports designed to correct abnormal foot motion and alignment.) But based on a number of studies, most experts don't think that these insoles significantly increase the shock-absorbing ability of good athletic shoes. Your best bet is to concentrate on choosing shoes that provide sufficient cushioning by themselves. The material used in conventional insoles (ethylene vinyl acetate, or EVA) wears out after about six hundred miles of running—by which time it's probably time to replace the shoes. Of course, if you have chronic or recurrent pain, you should consult a podiatrist or orthopedist to see whether you might benefit from an orthotic device.

A better reason to buy replacement insoles is that they may make your athletic shoes more comfortable. And if you stand for long periods in shoes that have no built-in cushioning, insoles may provide additional comfort.

If you decide to buy insoles, try different brands to see which ones feel most comfortable. Be sure to try them in the shoes they'll be worn in. Also bear in mind that some insoles may make feet feel overheated.

Sports-specific socks

For people who take their athletics seriously, there are socks designed for specific sports, including tennis, cycling, running, skiing, aerobics—even for walking and golf. These differ according to where protective padding is placed (ball, toes, instep, heel, arch, or shin), how thick the padding is, and which materials are used. For instance, aerobics socks are comparatively short and have dense padding at the heel, ball, and toes to protect against abrasion and blisters. Ski socks are high and have a protective pad along the shin, an area often irritated in downhill skiing. Nearly all of these are made of Orlon, polypropylene, or other synthetic materials that draw (or "wick") away perspiration.

Do you really need such sports-specific socks? They do provide extra cushioning and can help decrease foot abrasion. But the sock is less important than the appropriate athletic shoe, since the shoe can make up for many shortcomings of a sock. Thus, good shoes and all-purpose socks that wick away moisture will do the trick for most people.

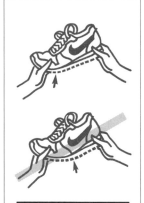

Running shoes should bend at the ball of the foot; shoes that bend at mid-foot offer no support. A mid-sole that is too soft will feel very good in the store, but can cause the foot to turn inward.

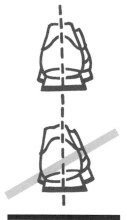

Make sure the uppers are correctly attached to the soles—they should be perpendicular to the heels, not slanted, when examined from the back.

Exercising Outdoors

Exercising in different conditions can be exhilarating, whether you are hiking in the heat of summer, cross-country skiing on a crisp winter day, or heading out for an evening run. Yet it's important to be aware of potential hazards associated with these conditions and how to sidestep them. As the following guidelines show, the trick is to combine a few simple precautions with the right gear.

Cold-weather workouts

Cold weather doesn't have to mean the end of outdoor exercise for most people. Running, cycling, or walking in winter can be as much fun as skiing. They're also good ways to get you outside in the sunlight and thus help you avoid wintertime blues. All you have to do is make allowances for the weather.

Don't overdress. The most common problem isn't that exercisers wear too little clothing in the cold, but too much. Exercise raises body temperature significantly—even a moderate workout can make you feel that it's thirty degrees warmer than it really is. So when you're about to run on a twenty-five degree day, dress for about fifty-five.

Wear several layers of loose-fitting, thin clothing. This helps insulate you by trapping the heat you generate. And you'll be able to take off layers if you become too warm. Remove layers *as soon as you start to sweat.* You can tie a garment you have shed around your waist or put it in a day pack.

First layer: Start with thermal underwear made of a fabric that draws sweat away from your skin (such as polypropylene, Capilene, or Thermax). In contrast, cotton holds moisture next to your skin, making you feel cold and clammy. Wet clothes draw heat away from you.

Middle layers: Next layer a wool sweater, synthetic turtleneck, and/or pile jacket. Keep legs warm with sweat pants, lycra tights, or leg warmers (worn over thermal long johns when it's really cold).

Outer layer: A jacket that's waterproof, wind-resistant, and yet breathable (so that moisture isn't trapped inside). Synthetics like Gore-Tex fit the bill. An ordinary windbreaker is okay for a short workout in dry weather.

Zip up. Zippers make clothes adaptable: when you get too hot, you can unzip them halfway to let in air and can remove a garment easily. Tie a small loop of string to each zipper so that you can open it without taking off your gloves or mittens.

Mittens or gloves. Mittens are warmer than gloves since they keep fingers together and have less surface area from which heat can escape. In very cold weather, the added warmth from mittens is worth the loss in dexterity. You can also wear inner liners made of polypropylene or another material that draws sweat from your skin with a second layer over them.

Head-wear. Oddly enough, one way to keep your feet warm is to wear a hat, since you lose so much heat through your head. Wear a wool or synthetic cap or a hood. Another option is a cap that folds down into a face mask in case the wind starts gusting or it begins to snow (make sure it doesn't obscure your vision or hearing).

Shoes. Wear shoes that offer good traction and shock absorption, especially when running on hard, frozen ground. Shoes should have a little extra space inside to trap warm air and, when it's really cold, let you wear an extra pair of socks.

Although you may think that snow is a good source of water during winter exercise, it isn't. It can chap your lips and irritate the lining of your mouth—and it also may contain contaminants.

Heading outdoors

Warm up and stretch. It's a good idea to warm up first (such as jogging in place) and stretch indoors, and then perhaps stretch again outside. When you've finished exercising, cool down and stretch indoors.

Drink as much water in the cold as in the heat. This is crucial. It's easy to become dehydrated in cold weather because of the water you lose from sweating and breathing (you have to warm and moisten the cold air you inhale), and because of your stepped-up urine production. And dehydration hinders your body's ability to regulate its temperature. Drink fluids before, during, and after your workout. Skip alcohol and caffeine; both dehydrate you. Drinking alcohol may give you the illusion of warmth but actually robs you of heat by dilating surface blood vessels in the skin.

Compensate for the wind. The wind can penetrate clothes and remove the insulating layer of warm air around the body. When the temperature is twenty degrees Fahrenheit, a fifteen-mph wind makes it feel like five degrees below zero (this is the wind-chill factor). Fast motion, as in cycling or skiing, has the same effect as the wind since it increases air movement past the body. Compensate for a strong wind by running or riding against it on your way out, then with it behind you on the way back—you'll do the most work before you're tired and sweaty.

Be on the defensive. Shorter daylight hours, poor visibility, plus the risk of skidding cars call for careful running, walking, and cycling.

Keep moving. If you stop exercising for any reason and remain outdoors, put on extra clothes before you start to feel cold. To stay warm, try to keep moving.

Snow and ice. Though some joggers manage to run in even the worst weather without injury, exercising on snow or ice is not worth the risk. One exception: some people are able to run reasonably well on hard, packed snow, provided they slow their pace, take smaller steps, and wear shoes with good traction.

Wear sunglasses and sunscreen. Snow-covered ground on clear days can reflect the sun and thus burn your face and obscure your vision, especially at high altitudes.

When to come in from the cold

Breathing cold air is not harmful to healthy people; you can't "freeze your lungs." However, it can be risky for those who suffer from angina, asthma, or high blood pressure—they should check with a doctor before exercising in the cold. For such people, wearing a ski mask or scarf pulled loosely in front of the face may help warm up inhaled air.

Frostbite and hypothermia. These are the two main dangers of exercising in the cold. Dressing properly and taking other precautions described here are your best safeguards. Be on guard for the numbness and white discoloration of frostbite—particularly on your hands, ears, toes, and face. Cyclists and runners have also reported cases of penile frostbite, so consider wearing an extra pair of shorts. Hypothermia, which involves a dangerous drop in body temperature, is mostly a risk when you're out in very cold weather for many hours, especially if you're wet, injured, and/or not moving around enough to stay warm.

Safeguards at night

If you exercise at night, as many do when winter days grow shorter, dress in bright colors. Reflective clothing should be part of every exerciser's attire, since even people

Is it dangerous to exercise in polluted air?
Since you breathe faster and more deeply when you exercise, you also take in more carbon monoxide, sulfur dioxide, and other atmospheric pollutants—notably ozone, smog's major component. Running or cycling during the early afternoon, for instance, when ozone levels tend to be highest, may result in chest pain, coughing, throat irritation, and difficulty in breathing deeply. Although studies haven't yet made clear whether repeated exposure to pollutants during exercise can result in permanent lung damage, it would seem wise to avoid exercising near heavy or even moderate traffic. Your best bet if air pollution is a problem in your locality (and you can't exercise indoors or away from city surroundings) is to work out early in the morning before pollution levels peak, or in the evening after rush hour, when levels fall again.

who avoid nighttime cycling or jogging occasionally find themselves out later than planned. Night cycling is fifteen to twenty times more dangerous than cycling during daylight hours. A National Safety Council study found that 54 percent of all pedestrian fatalities occur at night, and a report from Florida shows that half of all cyclists killed on that state's roads are night riders, even though they make up only 3 to 5 percent of the bike-riding population.

Wearing light-colored clothing isn't enough. A study by the National Highway Traffic Safety Administration found that at night a pedestrian in white shirt and jeans is visible at a distance of only a little more than two hundred feet, usually not enough space to allow a driver to swerve or stop. So it's essential to adopt additional safety measures, such as these:

For running and walking at night

•Wear fluorescent or reflective material as vests, headbands, wrist and ankle bands, belts, or as patches stuck on cuffs, waist, or shoes.

•Run or walk against the traffic. That way you can see oncoming cars. If you know you're approaching a blind curve, switch to the other side.

•Use lights. There are battery-operated flashing devices that clip to belts or strap onto legs. Carrying a flashlight helps. In a National Highway Traffic Safety Administration study, a pedestrian with a flashlight was visible to drivers six hundred feet farther off than one wearing reflective material.

For cycling at night

•Get a headlight and taillight, preferably halogen (brighter than incandescent) and powered by a generator or rechargeable batteries. Test them before buying. A good headlight should be visible five hundred feet away and light up potholes and other hazards. The red taillight should be visible from six hundred feet.

•Wear reflective Day-Glo clothing and patches. The most visible way to wear a reflective stripe is horizontally, across the full width of your back. Stick patches on your helmet, chest, upper arms, seat, shoes, and saddlebags or wear the special reflector for cyclists—a triangle of fluorescent fabric edged with reflective tape.

•Wear the same kinds of lights recommended for runners.

•Try a reflective spacer, a horizontal rod attached at a right angle to the rear wheel and topped with a flag or disk, to keep traffic at bay.

•Make sure your bike is equipped with front, side, rear, and pedal reflectors, which are now required by law on new bikes. They aren't enough, but they help.

•Use a rearview mirror to check for passing cars. You can also use your shadow as a gauge. Passing on the left, a car throws your shadow to the right. If your shadow remains straight in front of you, the car is on your tail: be ready to pull over.

•Ride with the traffic. Drivers expect you to follow the same rules they do.

Other nighttime safety tips

•Don't look directly at approaching headlights; they'll blind you temporarily.

•Stay off high-speed roads.

•Don't wear headphones—you may not hear a car approaching.

Reflective vest

Cycling reflector

Aerobic Activities

One of the truly pleasant aspects of exercising is that you have plenty of options. You can choose to do something as simple as walking, you can take up one or more recreational sports, or you can perform a specific routine in an exercise class or at home. In fact, variety is one of the keys to staying fit. For one thing, no single exercise adequately builds all aspects of fitness equally well. And having more than one activity to turn to keeps exercise from getting monotonous. Studies also show that people tend to stick with activities that are accessible and enjoyable.

The activities that follow provide aerobic exercise—that is, they can work your heart and lungs to promote cardiovascular fitness. In addition, they help make muscles stronger and more limber. This section spells out the benefits of each activity and basic techniques for performing it effectively and safely.

Aerobic exercise guidelines

The American College of Sports Medicine has made the following recommendations, which leave you leeway in designing a program that suits your physical condition and weekly schedule:

Frequency. Exercise three to five times a week.

Duration. Perform the activity for fifteen to sixty minutes.

Intensity. Try to raise your heart rate to 60 to 90 percent of its maximum (see page 214). Experts at the University of California, Berkeley, recommend not exceeding 80 percent of your maximum rate unless you are in peak physical condition. A schedule of low- to moderate-intensity exercise is best for most people, especially those who aren't in peak condition.

If one of these three factors is low, compensate by increasing the others. For example, if you exercise only for short periods, increase the frequency of the activity. Or increase the intensity of the exercise, but only do this gradually.

Aerobic Movement

A popular form of exercise, especially among women, aerobic dance and movement uses a wide variety of dance forms—folk, modern, jazz, ballet, and disco—and combines them with body movements such as skipping, walking, running, jumping, and toe-touching in order to tone muscles and develop cardiovascular fitness. Learning aerobic dance routines is important, but the emphasis is on exercising the heart and lungs, not giving a command performance.

Here is how a typical aerobic movement class might be divided:
- four to five minutes of stretching done to music;
- five minutes of slow aerobic movement to further stretch and limber the body;
- fifteen to thirty minutes of routines done at low, medium, or high intensity—the heart of the class;
- five minutes of slow aerobic movement to cool down.

Benefits of aerobics

Overall, aerobic movement promotes fitness through enjoyable exercise, and that is exactly what irritates its critics, who contend that it is more fun than fitness. Yet a number of studies support proponents' claims that aerobic movement builds cardiovascular fitness and develops leg muscles, and contributes to muscular endurance and flexibility. Low-intensity routines, however, are not always strenuous enough to improve cardiovascular efficiency, especially in fit, young individuals. And most controlled studies have found no evidence that aerobic dance is better than any other type of aerobic exercise at taking off pounds or inches. For those trying to lose weight, one reason aerobic dance may not prove effective appears to be the relatively short time devoted to strenuous activity—only twenty to thirty minutes out of a fifty-minute class. Most participants take only two or three classes per week. Significant weight loss, however, requires workouts of thirty to sixty minutes four to six times per week.

Tips and techniques

Like all forms of cardiovascular training, aerobic movement must be performed three to five times per week to develop cardiovascular fitness. Research has also shown that the benefits of training take at least twelve weeks to become apparent.

During the first two weeks, the heart rate should be monitored after each aerobic dance routine or about every five minutes and should usually not exceed the lower end of your training rate (that is, 60 percent of your maximum heart rate); if it does, modify the workout to make it less strenuous—for example, by lowering your jumps, pumping your arms less vigorously, or reducing the number of steps you take per beat of music.

Softening your workout

Along with the fun and fitness benefits of aerobic movement, the repetitive, jarring motions can sometimes be traumatic to your body. Exercising too often or too long, improperly warming up, wearing shoes that don't give enough support, and working out on a surface that is too hard are possible causes of injury. In fact, according to two studies published in *The Physician and Sportsmedicine,* 76 percent of aerobics instructors who responded to a questionnaire and 43 percent of their students sustained injuries from this activity. Their shins seemed most vulnerable, with calf, lower back, foot, ankle, and knee problems also reported.

Fortunately, low-impact aerobic exercises—which were initially designed for people recovering from an injury and for older people—have gained general popularity as a way of achieving the benefits of aerobic exercise without subjecting the body to excessive stress. In low-impact aerobics, at least one foot is almost always kept on the floor, and the exerciser's arms are constantly busy—swinging as well as doing biceps curls, triceps extensions, and overhead arm presses. It is important that the movements be strenuous enough to raise the heart rate sufficiently; otherwise, the exercises will not truly be aerobic.

Any kind of exercise, of course, requires reasonable caution. The side-to-side movements in low-impact aerobics, for example, could injure the feet or legs if overdone. And arm movements have to be done carefully, especially if you are using hand weights, which can be dangerous (see page 230). Also, the floor shouldn't be too hard, and your shoes should be well padded.

Exercising less than three times a week may produce only minimal benefits; exercising more than five times a week usually offers no significant additional cardiovascular improvements.

Interval Training

Exercising at a moderate pace for twenty to thirty minutes (preceded by warming up and followed by cooling down) three to five times a week is the accepted standard for boosting your body's ability to utilize oxygen and enhancing your cardiovascular system. Recent research suggests, however, that you may be able to get in shape faster with interval training—spurts of intense exertion alternating with lower-intensity recovery periods.

Benefits

Researchers at the Human Performance Laboratory at the University of Miami studied the question by having female students participate in thirty-five minute aerobic dance sessions (not including warm-up and cool-down periods) three times a week for twelve weeks. They found that interval training—three to five minutes of intense exercise alternating with up to three minutes of brisk walking or mild running—produced greater gains (18 percent) in aerobic capacity than did steady-speed dance sessions (8 percent). Both groups also lost body fat (but not weight, necessarily, since the exercise increased their muscle mass).

Researchers theorize that the recovery periods in interval training may make it easier for participants to maintain the intensity of the workout, knowing that a low-intensity period is coming up, while those attempting to work at a steady speed may gradually slow down as the workout continues. Another advantage is that interval training is less monotonous than steady-pace exercise.

How to train

Interval training can be applied to nearly any exercise. Alternate fifteen seconds to three minutes of high-intensity running, cycling, hiking, swimming, rowing, or aerobic dancing with low-intensity intervals of the same length. During the intense bouts, your heart rate should reach 80 percent of its maximum (85 to 90 percent if you are in excellent condition). (Since this puts markedly increased stress on your heart as well as on your joints and muscles, consult your doctor about interval training if you are forty-five or over, are out of shape, or have a medical condition or previous injury that restricts your ability to exercise.) During the recovery periods, don't let your heart rate drop below 60 percent of its maximum. You can also use the computerized exercise bikes, specially programmed for interval training, found in many gyms.

If you have less than twenty minutes to exercise, it appears that only interval training will give you a significant cardiovascular workout—but don't necessarily expect maximum conditioning. If you're after all the benefits of aerobic exercise, twenty- to forty-minute workouts are still recommended.

Rating an aerobics class

It's important that an exercise class be fun and that you like the teacher, but that's not enough. You will get only a fraction of the potential health benefits from a poorly run class—and you are more likely to injure yourself or drop out. In deciding on a class, consider the following factors:

The routine. Many exercise professionals recommend mixing aerobics with stretching and strengthening calisthenics. The level of the class—beginning, intermediate, or advanced—must be correct for you. The class should start with a warm-up of gentle stretching and end with a cooling-down period, each at least five minutes. At least twenty minutes worth of the exercises should be designed to get your heart to its training rate. If there are calisthenic exercises, they should work all the major muscle groups, starting with the large muscles in the legs and ending with the smaller muscles in the arms.

The workout room. The temperature shouldn't be too hot or too cold, and the ventilation should be good. A suspended wooden floor with carpeting is safest; harder floors must be covered with thick carpet. For calisthenics, there should be mats. And you should be able to move around without bumping into people.

Upper-body Aerobics

"Jarming"—a series of upper-body exercises using vigorous arm movements that can be done sitting in a chair—is based on the theory that if running or cycling works only the lower body and is effective, then upper-body exercise alone could be just as effective.

However, exercise physiologists agree that lower-body exercise is much more effective in terms of total energy expended. You use less energy when you exercise with only your arms because less muscle mass is being used. And moving upper-body muscles, especially arm muscles, increases heart rate more in proportion to the oxygen supply than do the large leg muscles; hence, raising your heart rate with jarming does not signify you are working your cardiovascular system to the same extent.

For people with heart problems, upper-body exercise can even be dangerous, since using smaller muscles appears to raise blood pressure more than using larger muscles.

The instructor. The most difficult—and perhaps most important—judgment you will have to make concerns the qualifications of the instructor. Being an athlete or dancer doesn't qualify a person to teach a class, though many athletes and dancers, with suitable training, make excellent instructors. There is no single organization that provides nationwide standards for instructors, and until legal standards are adopted, it is difficult to recommend any one program. American College of Sports Medicine certification is currently one of the best.

Even if a teacher is certified, you should ask about the requirements of the particular program that he or she was enrolled in. One sign of an instructor's in-depth involvement is a degree in an exercise-related field such as exercise physiology. Instructors may also receive excellent training from seminars and courses offered at local fitness workshops. (If you are taking an exercise class as part of a rehabilitation program after an illness, you should ask a health professional for a specific recommendation or referral.)

Still, the best way to judge an instructor is not by educational degrees or training certificates but by watching a class. Or, better yet, see if you can try a class before signing up. Notice whether the instructor tells participants how to avoid injuries and reminds them to check their pulse rates so that they reach—but don't exceed—their recommended training heart rates. Also, the instructor should not be a drill sergeant, but should let you work at your own speed. Finally, the instructor should watch the exercisers and actually instruct them—not be too busy looking at his or her own performance.

Is ballroom dancing good exercise?

At the competitive level, ballroom dancing can elevate your heart rate just as much as running or cross-country skiing. And one study showed that even beginning dance students can derive health benefits. During a twenty-minute aerobic section consisting of the cha-cha, a polka, two swing dances (the jitterbug and the lindy), a Viennese waltz, and a samba, the great majority of the subjects (aged eighteen to thirty-five) got their heart rates up to near maximum training rates, particularly in the polka, swing dancing, and the waltz. As for caloric expenditure, even moderate ballroom dancing can burn between 250 and 300 calories per hour, and fast, vigorous dancing burns upward of 400 calories per hour.

Hand and Ankle Weights: Pros and Cons

Hoping to shorten their road to fitness, thousands of people have begun doing their aerobic exercises with hand or ankle weights. Studies show that using small weights (one to five pounds) does increase oxygen consumption, heart rate, and the number of calories burned during exercise—but usually only by five to ten percent, depending on the amount and location of the weights. That's much less than the claims made by most proponents of the weights. Similar increases in energy output can easily be achieved by exercising a little longer or harder. Anyone thinking of using hand or ankle weights should first consider the following:

•The weights can increase the chance of injury during exercise, particularly traditional aerobic dance or running. Ankle weights, in particular, add to stress on the legs and feet, though they also increase energy output the most. Moreover, weights carried anywhere on the body can distort proper form, rhythm, and balance. Unless you have complete control over the weights, using them can lead to muscle sprains and damage to the ligaments and tendons.

•Weights slow down your speed, so you may build muscle strength at the expense of your aerobic workout.

•People with high blood pressure or heart disease should avoid exercising with weights, especially hand weights, because they tax the cardiovascular system.

Lifting light hand weights rapidly while standing in place can be a part of your warm-up routine; it helps raise your heart rate and tone your upper body. Moreover, hand weights may be suitable for individuals who are unable to perform running or jumping movements and wish to increase the work of the heart and upper body while walking. They should start with light weights (one pound) and, with elbows bent, briskly swing the arms from the shoulder.

For most people, however, the drawbacks of wearing weights during aerobic exercise outnumber any possible advantages. Even if you are aerobically fit and fully able to control your weight-bound movements, hand and, especially, ankle weights are not recommended for aerobics classes or other activities that involve running or jumping.

Cross-Country Skiing

Cross-country skiing has lagged behind the downhill variety in popularity in the United States, but in terms of all-around aerobic benefits, it's the front runner. Using muscles in the shoulders, back, chest, abdomen, buttocks, and legs, cross-country skiers can burn as many as six hundred to nine hundred calories per hour. Champion cross-country skiers expend upward of one thousand calories per hour and have set records for the highest levels of oxygen consumption ever, indicating excellent aerobic fitness. The kick-and-glide technique, combined with the poling motion to propel you along, can provide a more complete workout than running or cycling, both of which emphasize lower body muscles. And the activity can also help you develop coordination.

Another advantage of cross-country skiing is that it has a lower risk of serious injury than downhill skiing. Also, you can rent (or buy) skis, poles, and boots for considerably less than what you would pay for downhill gear. You don't need to make any reservations at high-priced ski resorts, because you can cross-country ski in a nearby park or even your own backyard. Most people don't need a lesson before starting out, yet a good instructor can help with advanced technique.

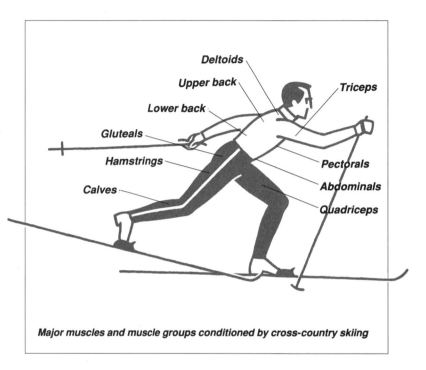

Major muscles and muscle groups conditioned by cross-country skiing

Tips and techniques

The sport combines skiing and hiking. Although a beginner may use the skis like snowshoes and tramp across the snow using the poles for balance, the right technique calls for gliding across the snow with your body at a forty-five to sixty-degree angle to the ground. The upper and lower body work together in a rhythm of kicks, long glides, and propelling poling motions.

The skis are longer than downhill skis (usually about as long as the distance between the wrist of your upstretched arm and the ground, though less experienced skiers may find slightly shorter skis more maneuverable), and they are narrower and lighter. They come either waxable or waxless. Most novices find it easier to start out with waxless skis because these require less fuss and tend to provide more control on downhill inclines. But once you've become more proficient, you may want the better overall performance and speed afforded by waxable skis. The cross-country ski boot resembles a walking shoe or hiking boot. The binding attaches only to the front of the boot, leaving the heel free to lift off the ski as you take long strides.

Burning so many calories generates a lot of heat even on the coldest days, so it's best to dress in layers that you can peel off. You can start off in jeans or knickers (which are good for mobility), long cotton underwear, a couple of shirts, and a wool sweater, but veterans of the sport know the advantages of garments made of newer fabrics. For instance, polypropylene undergarments pull sweat away from the body, and outerwear made from other synthetics provide protection against the elements while allowing moisture to escape. Don't forget a wool hat and lightweight insulated mittens or gloves. If you plan on skiing all day, bring along a light backpack or "fanny" pack to hold cast-off clothes, an extra sweater for rest stops, and food and drink.

If you are forty-five or over or not in good shape, check with your doctor before you begin skiing. Gradually build up the amount of time you spend at it. Otherwise you run the risk of overuse strains (such as tendinitis) of the shoulder, knee, and arm. To prepare for a season of cross-country skiing, it's best to combine activities that primarily strengthen the upper body (rowing, swimming) with those working the muscles in the lower body (cycling, brisk walking) to promote overall muscle tone. Cross-country ski machines, available at many gyms and health clubs, mimic the sport's motions and offer a good workout in snowless weather (though they won't help improve your technique on the snow).

Cross Training

Are you tired of running or cycling all the time? More and more people these days alternate the types of sport or exercise they do, and biathlons (two sports) and triathlons (three sports) are catching up to marathons in popularity. This combination of activities is called cross training–working out regularly at more than one physical activity. Not only is it a way to avoid the boredom of day-in, day-out routine exercise, but it can also provide good overall conditioning, while reducing the risk of injury.

The advantages of variety
Cross training allows you to exercise more muscle groups than a single activity would. For instance, cycling builds your lower body, and swimming works your upper body, so alternating them can help give you the benefits of both while you build aerobic endurance. Similarly, running strengthens the hamstring muscles (located at the rear of the thigh) far more than the quadriceps (at the front of the thigh), a muscle imbalance that may be a factor in some injuries. But by combining cycling, which strengthens the quadriceps, with running, you can work complementary muscle groups in your legs and thus achieve better muscle balance.

Overtraining at one sport or activity continually stresses the same muscles and joints, thus increasing the risk of injury. If instead of running every day, you alternate it with swimming every other day, you'll give your leg muscles and joints a needed rest between runs. And if you do hurt your knee while running, you won't have to stop exercising—you can keep on swimming to maintain your aerobic capacity. Or if you pull a shoulder muscle playing tennis, you can give it a rest while you continue to cycle.

Some sports-medicine specialists believe that cross training may also reduce the risk of injury by moderating the "addiction" to a single sport that can result in overtraining. However, competitive cross trainers may fall prey to certain overuse

Is there really a "second wind"?

For a few minutes into any relatively strenuous bout of exercise, you may feel a little breathless and your muscles may hurt. They hurt because without enough available oxygen, they're burning carbohydrates for energy anaerobically—that is, without oxygen—which increases the output of lactic acid, a by-product of muscle metabolism associated with fatique. All at once, however, you fall into stride. The muscles are now burning carbohydrates aerobically, and this is what's called getting a second wind. Getting your breath "back" this way seems to be linked to reaching a point of equilibrium at which your respiratory and circulatory systems are able to keep pace with the intensity of your physical effort. The better conditioned your body is, the sooner you can reach this aerobic "steady state."

injuries, due to insufficient muscle rest and an unbalanced training schedule.

If you're serious about one particular sport, don't expect cross training to help improve your performance. The plain fact is, you've got to run to become an outstanding runner or swim to win swimming meets. Several studies of the cross trainers who make the headlines—the triathletes who run a marathon, bike a century (one hundred miles), and swim over two miles all in one day, in heroic events like the Hawaii Ironman triathlon—show that however qualified they may be to take on three events, triathletes don't approach the competitive levels in individual events achieved by single-sport specialists. But in terms of overall fitness, top-class triathletes are some of the best-conditioned athletes in the world.

Tips for cross training

If you decide to take up cross training, start slowly, as you would any exercise program. The best method is to pair sports that train different parts of your body: swimming with cycling, rowing with running. Instead of three or more forty-minute cycling sessions per week, cycle for twenty minutes and spend the other twenty running, or swim one day and play tennis the next. If you belong to a health club that has a track, a pool, weight-training machines, and stationary bikes, you'll find cross training a snap.

Cycling

Cycling is one of the best forms of exercise around: it gives the heart and circulatory system an outstanding aerobic workout; it can burn between four and seven hundred calories per hour; and it conditions not only your legs but, if you ride a touring bike with drop handle bars, your upper back and shoulders as well. For injured runners, cycling is ideal, since it develops aerobic capacity while imposing far less stress on joints than running. You can also choose to ride indoors on an exercise bike—one of the most convenient forms of aerobic conditioning (see page 238)—or to ride outdoors, which offers considerably more variety and mobility than practically any other form of exercise.

To get the most from cycling for fitness, you need to consider both your location and your bike. If you ride in stop-and-go traffic in a suburb or a city, gaining any aerobic benefit will be difficult. Similarly, riding in the country over hilly terrain may be too strenuous for beginners. When you begin cycling, it's best if you can ride on paved roadway that ranges from level to gently rolling; this allows you to ride in low to moderate gears at a good, even pace without straining. Then, as you become stronger, you can increase your cadence—the rate at which you pedal—and also try climbing long hills.

To ride for any significant distance, especially if you will be tackling hills, you should acquire a bike that has at least ten to twelve speeds. Such bikes have sturdy but lightweight frames and are usually equipped with drop handlebars that can help alleviate stress on your back. Prices for these bikes range upward from 200 to 250 dollars, depending upon their construction, weight, quality of components, and workmanship. There are also "all-terrain" bikes available that have eighteen speeds, and while these tend to be heavier than ten-speeds, many of the newer models are suitable for riding on paved roads. Whatever type of bike you choose, it's important that the frame fit you properly; otherwise you can develop muscle soreness in your neck, lower back, and legs. (See page 235.)

Tips on pedaling and form

Many inexperienced cyclists think that the higher the gear you ride in, the better the workout. But, in fact, riding in very high gear, which increases the force you need for pedaling, can lead to overuse injuries such as biker's knee (a generic term usually referring to pain around or under the kneecap). Pushing hard on the pedals also puts a lot of stress on the sole of the foot, and may interfere with blood circulation in leg muscles. But pedaling fast at a very low gear (one with low resistance) may not be preferable since your muscles have to contract quickly, which can lead to muscle soreness.

Proper pedaling: *When you pedal, the extended leg should be slightly bent; this effectively exercises the lower body, particularly muscles in the thighs, calves, hips, and buttocks, and also reduces strain on your knees.*

After a long uphill climb on a bike, don't coast downhill without pedaling. As you climb up the hill, lactic acid builds up in your muscles and can contribute to muscle soreness; by pedaling lightly but constantly while coasting downhill (even if there's little resistance), you can help remove the lactic acid.

•Studies have found that the optimal cadence for most cyclists is sixty to eighty rpm (revolutions per minute), though racers cycle in the range of eighty to one hundred rpm and, when they sprint, even faster. Optimal cadence does vary somewhat from person to person, depending on training level, speed, and the use of accessories like toe clips.

•Save high gears for level terrain, and the highest gears for riding downhill or with a good tail wind.

•Use very low gears if you're climbing steep grades, carrying heavy gear, or if you have a knee problem that's aggravated by strenuous cycling.

You can better maintain a constant pedaling effort if your riding posture is both comfortable and efficient. When you ride, bend from the waist but don't slouch; your back should be slightly curved, not hunched (see illustration). In addition:

•Don't ride in the racing "drop" position (with your hands on the curved parts of the handlebars) for any extended period of time. Although this position does make you a bit more aerodynamic and thus makes your pedaling more efficient, it may cramp your hands and shoulders. Instead, switch hand positions frequently to the tops of the handlebars.

•Keep your arms relaxed, and don't lock your elbows. This technique helps you to absorb bumps from the road better. Also, when you see bumps ahead in the road, raise your buttocks slightly off the seat—this will prevent painful bouncing.

•Wear shoes with rigid soles. These allow for more efficient pedaling, since they transmit more power to the pedals.

Defensive riding

When you ride outdoors, road conditions, traffic, and weather can pose potential hazards. Bicycling is generally a safe activity, but more than one thousand people die annually in the United States because of cycling accidents. Here are steps you can take to improve cycling safety:

Equip yourself

•Always wear a helmet: this is the most important precaution a cyclist can take (see page 236).

•When cycling at night or when visibility is poor, wear brightly colored, reflective clothing—in fact, this is good advice at any time—and use your headlight if you have one. (For more tips on cycling at night, see page 226.)

•Don't wear headphones. They can block out most of the street sounds you need to hear to ride defensively. That's why wearing headphones while cycling is a misdemeanor in some municipalities.

•Don't wear a heavy backpack. It can throw you off balance. Carry packages only in baskets, handlebar or seat bags, or panniers (side pouches made especially for bicycles).

Braking

•For most road conditions, use both brakes; using one or the other alone can be

---

Getting a Bike That Fits

For comfort, efficiency, and safety, you have to have a bike that fits. The following tips will help you check the bike you're buying, or the one you already ride.

Frame. Handlebars, saddle, wheels, gears, and brakes can all be adjusted to match your size and riding ability, but the frame has to fit from the start. A man's frame (with a tube running from the handlebar stem to seat) is usually sturdier and is likely to have a more efficient braking system. It's the best choice for a man or woman. Bicycle frames range in size from 19 to 25 inches (the length of the seat tube). To find the right frame for your size, straddle the top tube. There should be about one inch between it and your groin.

Handlebars and stem. Drop handlebars are preferable because they allow you to change your riding position frequently. The handlebar height should be level with the saddle. To check your reach to the handlebars, stand at the side of the bike and place your elbow at the tip of the saddle and try to grab the bars— your fingertips should just touch (below). If not, the horizontal bar extension (or stem) of the handlebars is too long.

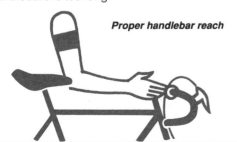

Proper handlebar reach

Another way to check this is to sit on the bike and look down at the hub of your front wheel. If the stem length is correct, the handle bars should block your view of the hub. While handlebar height can be easily adjusted, the stem length can be adjusted only by replacing the stem.

Saddle. Seats are easily replaced or improved and come in a number of different styles and materials as well as with padding. Test out a few. Your pelvic bones—those you sit on—should support your weight evenly. The seat should be firm, but also flexible enough to absorb the impact of bumps as well as the pressure of your pelvis. Saddles that are gel-filled provide form-fitting cushioning that can greatly increase riding comfort.

Adjustments. Once you've decided on a bicycle, adjust the seat height and position. First sit on the bike and pedal until one leg is extended and the pedal is at its lowest point. Your knee should be slightly bent. Check further by back-pedaling with your heels while someone holds the bike steady. If the seat is at the right height, your heels will barely remain in contact with the pedals. Adjust the seat accordingly, leaving it parallel to the top tube or tilted up slightly.

Also adjust the position of the handlebars to accommodate your preferred riding style. An upright position may help minimize back strain, while a racing position—in which you are bent over the handlebars—will help you cut wind resistance.

Cycling Helmets

More and more people are buckling up before driving and wearing helmets before riding motorcycles—so how is it that so many cyclists continue to ride without any protection for their heads? A recent study found that 80 percent of all cyclists believe that helmets offer effective protection, but only 2 to 10 percent of all cyclists, adults or children, actually wear them. As a consequence, head injuries account for 85 percent of the nation's one thousand annual cycling deaths, 34 percent of which claim the lives of children aged five to fourteen. Even if you're moving at only twenty miles an hour and your unprotected head hits something solid, you have little chance of surviving.

According to an estimate in the *American Journal of Public Health,* less than 2 percent of all schoolchildren wear helmets while cycling; yet each year seventy thousand children are treated in hospital emergency rooms for bicycle-related injuries. In California, officials have found that, in recent years, young passengers accounted for an increasingly greater proportion of all reported injuries, especially head injuries, in the state; consequently, California has passed legislation requiring children under five to wear this vital piece of equipment while cycling or riding as passengers. (Children's neck muscles are strong enough to support a helmet from the age of eight months.)

The experts—the American Academy of Pediatrics, the National Safety Council, the Bicycle Federation of America—are un-conditionally in favor of helmets. Reasons for not wearing helmets are usually based on aesthetics or comfort. But such objections don't hold up considering the attractive lightweight designs now approved by the American National Standards Institute (ANSI) or the Snell Memorial Foundation, whose test standards are accepted nationwide.

Choosing a helmet

Whichever style you choose, check for the ANSI approval sticker. This tells you that the helmet meets reasonable laboratory standards for absorbing severe blows. An ANSI sticker should be adequate for most cyclists. A Snell sticker means the helmet meets even stricter standards (though it has not been proven this makes the helmet any safer). Only about a dozen models have both stickers.

Helmets keep getting lighter. Conventional helmets with a hard outer shell and an energy-absorbing interior made of polystyrene foam liner weigh a pound or less. The popular new ultralight models weigh as little as 8½ ounces; they are made of very dense foam and have no outer shell, which makes them cool and comfortable. However, such helmets may be less able to withstand daily wear and tear over the years than helmets with hard outer shells.

Helmets should be replaced every five years. The plastics used in both their inner and outer layers deteriorate under the stress of weather and hard knocks. If you have an accident, send your helmet to the manufacturer for inspection, even if it appears undamaged. Many manufacturers will replace damaged helmets free of charge.

If you're still riding with one of the older hair-net-type-helmets or "skid-lids," you should definitely invest in something new. A good helmet may cost from thirty to seventy dollars.

Shopping tips

When you buy a helmet, look for the same features for yourself and your children:

Shock absorbency. The liner is as important as the shell. A good liner should be at least half an inch thick and made from crushable expanded polystyrene (the foam used for picnic coolers and packing material). Although it is stiff, it will give under impact, absorbing the shock of a collision or fall.

Comfort and fit. You (and your child) are less likely to wear an uncomfortable helmet. Sponge-rubber or fabric pads should hold the helmet firmly to your head. The helmet should allow for good ventilation, which is crucial on summer days.

Impenetrability. A rigid outer shell can stand up to abrasion and collision with sharp, hard objects like car doors and handles. The usual materials are polycarbonate or fiberglass.

Security. A snug-fitting chin strap, fastened with a D-ring or buckle, will keep the helmet from flying off.

Style. Kids may like brightly colored or decorated helmets and hence be more likely to wear them.

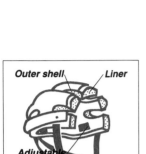

Outer shell **Liner**

Adjustable comfort pads **Strap**

Cross-section view showing components of a well-made helmet.

hazardous. Remember that each of the two hand brakes has a specific function. The front brake (the left lever) has the power to stop you more quickly than the back (the right lever) and, given enough pressure, can throw you over the handlebars. The back brake, with strong pressure, may cause the bicycle to skid.

•Brake with your hand at the end of the lever. This will allow you to exert optimal pressure.

•Don't brake abruptly when it starts to rain, since roads are especially slippery.

•On long, steep downhills, as well as in wet weather, it is safest to "feather" the brakes—that is, gently tap the brakes, applying intermittent pressure.

•For a quick stop, as you firmly press the brakes, slide your buttocks to the very back of the saddle. This will keep the rear of the bike down so that you don't flip over the handlebars. Be careful not to jam the brakes, however, or you may lose control of the bike.

Cycling road sense

•Use hand signals. This will allow the drivers of the cars around you to predict your actions.

•Learn to change gears without taking your eyes off the road so that you won't swerve into traffic.

•Watch out for storm drains, cattle guards (for country riders), and railroad tracks. They're all slippery when wet. And if you don't cross them at the right angle, your front tire may get caught, causing you to be thrown off your bike.

•Don't ride side by side with another cyclist.

Bicycle touring

As growing numbers of long-distance cyclists are discovering, bicycling allows you to combine an excellent form of exercise with a wonderful way to travel—to see the world up close, meet new people, and enjoy the flora, fauna, and geology of whichever area you choose to tour.

Beginning long-distance riders will probably find the basic ten-speed more than adequate for touring. Any reasonably healthy person with some experience in ordinary cycling can, after a few weeks of strengthening exercises, be prepared to tour. Cycling a few miles a day several times a week will build up your speed and endurance. Increase your goals 5 to 10 percent each week until you can comfortably cover the average daily distance anticipated on your bicycle-touring itinerary. When road workouts are not practical, a reasonable alternative is the stationary bicycle, which should be ridden several times a week for thirty to forty-five minutes. Precede every workout with warm-up exercises and conclude with cool-downs to increase muscle flexibility and decrease fatigue.

Tips for touring

Saddle soreness often waylays the best-prepared touring cyclist. To minimize discomfort on long rides, ride on an anatomically comfortable, padded bicycle seat, and wear shorts that do not bunch up or have seams where you sit. Take great care to set the seat and handlebars to your particular body proportions. The seat should be level, or only slightly tilted up or down, and at a height that permits your legs to be slightly bent at the bottom of the down stroke when your feet are positioned properly on the pedals, thereby lessening the strain on knee joints. Drop bars,

Myth: Women don't tolerate the heat as well as men when exercising.

Fact: *Women and men who are equally fit are likely to tolerate exercise in the heat equally well. Women do tend to sweat less than men, but this doesn't appear to affect their ability to cope with the heat or their physical performance. Furthermore, while some studies have suggested that it may take women longer to start sweating during certain phases of the menstrual cycle, most researchers have not found significant differences in heat regulation during the different phases of the cycle. Overall, sex is far less important than cardiovascular fitness when it comes to the way a person responds to heat.*

which offer three grip positions for your hands, allow you to change your upper-body position frequently, thus minimizing back and neck strain.

Footgear. Select a cycling shoe with a stiff sole that spreads the pressure of the pedal across the length of the foot. Shoes should also be comfortable for walking, have plenty of toe room, and soft, well-ventilated uppers. For maximum riding efficiency, equip pedals with toe clips that hold shoes firmly in place.

Gloves. These decrease pressure on the hands, which can cause numbness in riders who do not relax their grip. Gloves also reduce scrapes in case of falls. They should be padded, well ventilated, and made of a fast-drying material.

Helmets. A cycling helmet is a must. Tests have shown that the safest ones are fully enclosed on top with a polystyrene foam liner inside to absorb blows in case of a fall. Your helmet should also offer good peripheral vision, ventilation, light reflectance, and a visor. Shatterproof, tinted goggles or sunglasses to protect eyes from stones or other debris thrown up from the road and to reduce sun glare are another piece of safety gear no touring cyclist should fail to wear.

Lastly, riders should equip themselves with some means of carrying essentials, such as a bag (pannier) or carrying rack (a backpack is not recommended because it can cause loss of balance). Properly distributed over the front and rear wheels, racks will permit you to carry comfortably thirty to thirty-five pounds of clothing, a water bottle, food, bike and tire repair tools, first-aid equipment, maps, flashlights, camera gear, and sunscreen.

For your first long-distance trip, it may be a good idea to join an organized tour with an experienced leader. Chances are you'll have more fun, and should you need it, there will be moral and mechanical support at the end of a hard day. Your local bike shop and biking magazines can steer you to a list of congenial tours and touring organizations.

Cycling: Exercise Bicycles

Working out on an exercise bike is a great year-round conditioning program. Because it is indoor equipment, there's no need to interrupt your training just because the weather turns bad. Any well-equipped Y or health club will have exercise bicycles. Many people also have them at home. In fact, the stationary exercise bicycle is the most popular item of home exercise equipment in the United States.

Pedaling an exercise bike can be as good as swimming or running for aerobic conditioning if you follow a schedule of at least three twenty-minute workouts per week. As you get into better shape, you'll want to prolong your workouts and increase their difficulty by adjusting the resistance of the flywheel. A 170-pound man using an exercise bike at 20 mph can burn approximately 700 calories an hour. These bikes are also excellent for toning your calves, thighs, and buttocks—though they don't exercise the muscles of the upper body.

Exercise bicycles are also a great conditioning tool if you are extremely out of shape, since you can start by setting the pedaling resistance at an easy level—easier than, say, the intensity that running demands. (Some doctors recommend exercise bicycling to patients recovering from heart attacks.) Moreover, because the seat supports your weight, pedaling puts less stress on your muscles and joints than running. One limitation of a stationary bike is that it has a negligible conditioning effect on the muscles of the upper body.

There are two basic kinds of exercise bikes: standard stationary bikes and ergometers. Both kinds have just one wheel—a heavy metal flywheel at the front that spins as you pedal. The wheel turns against a strip of fabric or some other resistance that can be tightened or loosened to adjust your workload. Don't buy a bike that doesn't allow you to adjust the workload.

Ergometers have indicators that calculate your work output. Different ergometers have different types of indicators; some, for example, calculate your output in watts, others show calories consumed. Ergometers are more expensive than standard stationary bikes because you are paying for the indicating devices, which you probably don't need. An ergometer tells you exactly how much work your body is doing, which makes it possible for you to duplicate and then exceed that output in your next workout. But output is not the most important measure in aerobic fitness; your heart rate is. So even when riding an ergometer, you should take your pulse regularly as you pedal to make sure you are reaching, but not exceeding, your target heart rate.

Choosing an exercise bike

A lot of people who use an exercise bike a few times grow bored with it and give up, often because the bike is poorly designed, the seat is uncomfortable, or the pedal motion is uneven (as you hit the bottom or top of a cycling motion, the pedals will seem to stick on a poorly made bike). The two keys to a good bike are a heavy flywheel, which ensures smooth pedaling, and a comfortable seat. In the long run, a more expensive bike is a better investment than a bottom-of-the-line model. A wobbly bike that's hard to pedal will only make you quickly give up your exercise program.

To get maximum efficiency from your leg muscles while putting minimum strain on the knees, adjust the height of the seat so that, with your heels on the pedals, you can pedal backward without swaying from side to side. Keep the seat level, or tilt it up a little at the front—this takes the strain off the wrists and arms.

Start out your session at about forty-five revolutions of the pedal per minute, and work up to seventy to ninety revolutions per minute at moderate tension. Some people pedal slowly at a high tension setting, but this actually puts an excessive load on the legs, heart, and lungs that cannot be sustained very long.

Tips for beginners

•Never buy a machine without a test ride. It could turn out to be wobbly or the wrong size for your body. Some bikes are also very noisy.

•Use toe clips to prevent your feet from sliding; this keeps equal upward and downward force on the pedals.

•You can buy a padded or anatomically shaped seat and handlebar pads to make the bike more comfortable.

•Most bikes have an optional, extra-long seat post, which is important for very tall people.

•Wear lightweight absorbent clothing.

•Play a radio, read, or watch television if you find yourself getting bored. Use a fan if you get too hot while pedaling.

Adapting your own bike

If you already have a conventional bicycle, you can convert it into an indoor exercise bike—one that you know will be comfortable—and you will pay far less than you would for a good store-bought stationary bike. One option is to purchase a device outfitted with rollers that supports your bike while allowing you to pedal; you can adjust the rollers as well as the gears on your bike to control the resistance. You can also buy a wind-load simulator—a round, cage-like device that simulates the wind resistance of actual outdoor bicycling. You put your regular bike on a frame with the simulator; then the harder you pedal, the greater the resistance, just as if you were pedaling into the wind.

Downhill Skiing

The most breathtaking winter sport, downhill skiing will never be a low-risk activity, but it's a lot safer than it used to be. According to researchers at the University of Vermont, the overall rate for significant injuries dropped 50 percent during the past fifteen years on slopes at nearby Sugarbush. The lower-leg injuries most commonly associated with skiing have, in fact, become comparatively rare. Ankle sprains were down 86 percent and tibia fractures down 88 percent in the Vermont study—a reduction that is partly attributable to advances in equipment (see below). And while downhill skiing doesn't work the heart and lungs to the same extent as cross-country skiing, it does provide some cardiovascular conditioning and exercises most muscle groups of the upper and lower body. It also promotes coordination, agility, and good balance. Besides that, downhill skiing burns a healthy 420 calories an hour.

You don't need a mountain for downhill skiing. In hilly regions of most northern states, there are many small ski areas better suited to the needs of beginners than jet-set resorts. Machines that produce artificial snow make it possible to ski from Thanksgiving through Easter.

Downhill equipment

A new set of skis, boots, bindings, and poles can be expensive. Until you've developed a feel for the sport and are ready for more specialized gear, renting equipment is best. Ski shop personnel will assist you in assembling an equipment package to fit your particular height, weight, and ability. The cost of lift tickets and transportation can be cut by joining a ski club that sponsors trips to local slopes. Ski clubs also provide discounts on lessons and offer the opportunity to learn to ski within the supportive atmosphere of a group.

Once you know you want to pursue skiing, you should consider buying your own equipment—and not simply to look fashionable. The overall reduction in injury rates among downhill skiers is due in part to advances in boot and binding technology. If you already ski, but you're still using equipment you bought a dozen years ago, you may decrease your risk of injury by replacing the old equipment—especially if you're not a highly skilled skier.

To take stock of your old equipment, bring it to a well-run ski shop for evaluation. You may have to replace just the bindings, or you may have to retire all of it. Before investing in new ski gear, though, rent it first and test it on the slopes.

Here are pertinent facts about new developments in ski equipment:

Boots. Ski boots are stiffer and higher than they used to be, thus reducing the risk of twisting the lower leg and spraining an ankle. Rear-entry boots, which have a hinge in the back that closes and pushes the foot forward, are more convenient and may offer more consistent support because of their one-piece, no-buckle front. A skilled boot fitter should examine your feet carefully, measuring the foot length and width as well as instep height and calf size. A proper fit is not just a matter of comfort, but of safety, too.

To get a better fit from your ski boots:

•Use thin socks, either silk or polypropylene, for skiing and boot-fitting.

•Avoid in-the-boot ski pants: they can cause blisters.

•Avoid over-tightening ski boot buckles and other adjustment features. If boots need extreme adjustment, they don't fit.

•Let your feet adjust to ski boots: at the beginning of the season, unbuckle boots during rides up the ski lift.

Bindings. These have undergone major safety improvements over the last decade. New bindings release more quickly and reliably than old models. Bindings should hold you to your skis until you begin to fall, when you must instantly break away to prevent an injury. Premature release, however, can be as dangerous as no release.

Some new bindings release upward at the toe in case you fall backward. These may help reduce the risk of some knee injuries. If your bindings have old-fashioned "runaway" straps, have these straps replaced with modern ski brakes, which are far less likely to cause injury when the bindings release. You may need to replace the bindings as well.

Many injuries result from improperly adjusted bindings. Have the release setting on your bindings machine tested and adjusted by a certified technician at least once a year. Remember, your bindings are adjusted to your weight, so if you gain or lose lots of weight, they need to be readjusted. Practice releasing your bindings at home in order to get a better sense of their release points. Keep bindings clean and lubricated. Before each use, check them for damage and make sure they are releasing smoothly and properly.

Poles. Gone are the days when your only choice in poles was in color and size. For safety, poles today almost always have a blunt rather than pointed tip. Another feature meant to prevent potential eye injury is a grip that is wider than the eye socket. Some new poles are slightly bent near the grip to make them easier to plant and allow for greater wrist and elbow comfort. Since thumb injuries are among the most common mishaps on the slopes, one new type of pole comes with a special support to protect the thumb in a fall.

One caveat: don't let new gear make you overconfident. Even with its safety improvements, new equipment can't substitute for skiing skill, which is still your best safeguard against injury.

Skiing tips and techniques

While the fundamentals of downhill skiing are not hard to learn, they are usually learned quicker with a few short lessons from a qualified instructor. Your instructor can also help you ride the lift and teach you how to lessen the impact of falling. When you have mastered the beginner's slope and are looking for a challenge, try following a better skier, keeping your tracks on top of his. Keep your eyes open and ski only on terrain appropriate to your ability; this will reduce the risk of collisions and falls, the two basic types of skiing accidents.

When dressing for skiing, remember that speeding downhill subjects you to a great wind chill, and that the ride back to the top may be cold as well. Dress in layers that can be easily peeled off as conditions change. Sunglasses or goggles and a sunscreen lotion are essential.

While there may be no way to avoid stiffness after your first day on the skis, to minimize it prepare yourself with a conditioning program of stretching and aerobic exercise. You can also help prevent debilitating knee injuries—the number-one problem of downhill skiing today—by strengthening the muscles surrounding the knees. (While the overall rate of injuries has dropped, the incidence of debilitating knee sprains has gone up 170 percent during the last fifteen years, in part because of higher boots that protect ankles but transfer stress to knees.) Exercises that strengthen your quadriceps are also an excellent preparation for skiing (see page 375).

Ice Skating

Ice skating is an exhilarating winter activity that can be enjoyed by young and old alike. It is an excellent aerobic sport that markedly increases flexibility and uses more muscle groups than running. The stroking motion over the ice strengthens the calves, quadriceps, buttocks, and abdomen, while the back, neck, and shoulders are worked to control the position of the upper body. Surprisingly, it is also safe, having one of the lowest injury rates of any sport.

Ice skating is no longer limited to frozen lakes in northern states. With indoor rinks, it is possible to skate year round in all parts of the country under nearly ideal, controlled conditions. Most indoor rinks also rent skates, sharpen dull blades, and provide instruction for those whose legs are still a bit shaky—though it is not a hard sport to learn. Most people find that within their first few hours on the ice, they have mastered enough of the basics to both enjoy the sport and reap the principle benefits from it. Older people learning to skate for the first time or starting again after a long hiatus should take care in developing their skills. This applies especially to postmenopausal women, who may be at greater risk of incurring bone fractures. They should learn caution under the supervision of a good instructor, and they should wear protective padding until they improve their sense of balance.

Good skates are important. While beginning skaters often complain of weak ankles, their wobbliness is more likely due to loose, poorly fitted skates rather than inherent muscle weakness. A good pair of ice skates costs about a hundred dollars. So before rushing out and buying a pair, or attempting to salvage grandpa's rusted classics from the basement, you may want to experiment with rental skates until you've developed a feel for the sport.

Skate boots should hug your foot, especially around the ankle, and fit snugly without bunching up your toes. (Be sure to try on skates with the socks you will wear skating; socks made from Orlon or other synthetics that "wick" away moisture from skin are best.) Arch and toe areas should have padded support, and the tongue should be well padded. Blades should be good-quality tempered steel and be kept sharpened at all times: dull, rusty blades will not only slow you down, they'll make you fall. Lace your skates so that the toe area is loose enough for your toes to move freely, but so that the area across the instep of your foot is tight and the top of the boot is snug enough to provide support and comfort.

While the skating motion does not exactly resemble walking, skating does become a simple matter of transferring the body weight from one foot to the other in a rhythmic fashion. The trick is in learning to glide. As you gain confidence on the ice, lower your center of gravity over the foot you glide forward on, gracefully "squatting" into each stride. With practice and perhaps a few lessons from a good instructor, you'll soon be zooming around the rink, taking sometimes as few as two strides to glide from one end of the ice to the other.

As with all strenuous physical activities, a thorough loosening of stiff muscles before skating will help prevent injury and greatly increase your enjoyment of the sport. Pay particular attention to stretching your Achilles tendons and the muscles of your calves. Slacks and sweaters that are warm without being bulky are good choices for skating apparel. But since most skating injuries involve the hands—scrapped or sprained while shielding against falls—the most important piece of clothing the skater should wear is a good pair of gloves.

While it may not be possible for you to skate often enough to maintain a high level of fitness merely by skating, ice skating—as a supplementary aerobic exercise—can provide a refreshing change of pace for a runner or cyclist during inclement winter weather. And for the family in search of fun together, it can be a healthy alternative to the movies.

Jumping Rope

Jumping rope develops cardiovascular and muscular endurance along with agility, coordination, and muscular strength. You can do it virtually anywhere and it costs almost nothing for the best equipment. And it's not hard to learn.

With so much going for it, jumping rope may seem like a perfect exercise. Boxers swear by it; the St. Louis Cardinals do it both in and out of season; and forty thousand girls in Manhattan take part in yearly competitions of double Dutch jumping (that is, jumping with two ropes that are spun at the same time in eggbeater fashion).

Nonetheless, skipping rope is far from the perfect exercise, and exaggerated claims have been made for it. The most flamboyant claim made by rope skippers is that they get all the aerobic benefits of a thirty-minute jog in just ten minutes. No research backs up such a claim. Skipping rope does raise the heart rate—indeed, it raises the heart rate too high and too fast to be safe for those who are not already fit. However, a detailed study of students at Ball State University in Muncie, Indiana, showed that the aerobic-training effects of rope skipping are not quite as good as those of most other aerobic exercises. Ten minutes of fast rope skipping gives a person a brief aerobic workout; but for full aerobic benefits, strenuous skipping needs to be sustained as long as strenuous running.

For those in search of a good form of exercise, rope skipping should be used the way professional athletes use it: not as their basic workout but as a special supplement for agility, muscular strength and endurance, and for its cardiovascular

Wind Chill
Ice skaters, as well as skiers and runners, can create their own wind chill. Skating at ten miles per hour in twenty degree Fahrenheit weather is the equivalent of four degrees. If you move into the wind, it is even colder. Therefore, when possible, run or skate away from the wind. If you must face into the wind on a cold day, be sure to cover exposed flesh, including earlobes and nose, and be on the lookout for frostbite.

benefits on rainy or snowy days, when outdoor exercise such as cycling or jogging is difficult.

Some equipment is crucial. A good pair of aerobics shoes, or a supportive pair of sneakers, will save wear and tear on feet and knees. The right rope is important, too. It should be heavy enough to develop a steady rhythm and long enough for the ends to reach your armpits when you stand on the center of the rope.

The technique is simple. Your body should be erect but relaxed when you jump. You should look straight ahead, not at your feet. Land on the balls of your feet, not on your heels, and with your knees slightly bent. Try not to move your arms much; at first turn the rope just fast enough to keep its arc. As you get more comfortable, go faster. Since jumping rope raises your heart rate fairly high, alternate 30 seconds of jumping rope with 30 seconds of jogging in place for the first several weeks. Gradually build up to two-minute intervals of jumping—and be sure to warm up and cool down.

Selecting a rope of the right length

Correct jumping form

Racquet Sports

About thirty million Americans play a racquet sport regularly. Chasing a ball around a squash, tennis, or racquetball court is an excellent way to develop agility and coordination, but can it promote cardiovascular fitness? In the past, the stop-and-go nature of these activities led many researchers to believe that the aerobic benefits were few and far between. Yet studies that looked at tennis players, for instance, found them to be a fit bunch—lean and aerobically well conditioned. Could it be that these sports attract people who are already fit? Such questions have prompted researchers to look more closely at the physiological effects of racquet sports and conclude that racquet sports can indeed produce aerobic benefits similar to those of running, but these depend completely on which game you choose and how you play it.

The aerobic benefits derived from a raquet sport depend upon how long you play, how skillful you are, how hard you push yourself, how long the ball is in play, and how quickly you retrieve the ball. Two basic requirements: to get an aerobic workout from any racquet sport, you must play vigorously enough to raise your heart to its training rate for twenty minutes at least three times a week. And you should play with an opponent who is at your level of skill and fitness so that you'll have extended volleys.

Tennis

As exercise, tennis is less demanding aerobically than squash or racquetball: just watch a recreational tennis player sometime and estimate how much of the time he is inactive. Some studies have shown that tennis players reach their optimum

Does table tennis provide a workout?

For average players, a swift game of singles table tennis burns about 350 to 450 calories per hour, about the same as brisk walking, doubles tennis, or cycling at six to eight miles per hour. It also helps improve agility and coordination, and its stroking action may increase flexibility and strength in the upper body. The key to making table tennis a workout is to keep moving. Try to keep the ball in play constantly; try not to pause between points. Also, push yourself; reach, bend, and stretch for every shot. It helps if you can play with someone who is slightly above your own skill level.

exercise heart rates and maintain them despite the stop-and-go action, while other studies have found that tennis players hardly give their hearts a workout at all. One thing is sure: doubles tennis generally does little to promote cardiovascular fitness. In recreational doubles, your heart rate stays relatively low, and your caloric expenditure is much less (averaging 300 calories per hour for doubles versus 450 per hour for singles). After all, you're covering only half the court in doubles and the ball is in play less. Competitive tennis is another matter: professional tennis players can burn over 600 calories per hour during a match.

If tennis is your game, stick to singles. You can also turn the game into a better workout by trying the following techniques:

•Run as hard, as far, and as constantly as you can. Run to get behind the ball, which will increase the power of your shot. Sprint to the net for volleying shots. Run down every ball, even the wide ones you think you can't reach. And after a point, run after the ball to retrieve it.

•Exaggerate bending, reaching, and stretching. Put all of your torso into forehand and backhand shots; bend at the knees and then rise up to meet low shots; and stretch high for serves and overhead slams. These full-body strokes may also help prevent tennis elbow, the foremost injury of tennis players (see page 377).

•Play shadow tennis. Developed by former Davis Cup captain Dennis Ralston, shadow tennis is like shadow boxing; you play against an imaginary opponent, without actually hitting the ball. Work out a sequence of strokes that mixes up lobs and volleys and forces you to race around the court. Keep moving, bending, and reaching as you would in a game. Begin playing shadow tennis for one-minute stints and work up to five minutes. This not only conditions you but also makes an excellent pregame warm-up.

Squash and racquetball

Both of these games are usually faster paced than recreational tennis because the courts are contained by walls; this keeps the ball in play and minimizes the time between points. Thus, studies show that players can maintain a heart rate more than high enough for aerobic conditioning, and burn 600 to 850 calories per hour, with racquetball being slightly less demanding than squash. One study at the University of Manitoba in Canada looked at the effects on aerobic capacity in novice racquetball players. The men in the study, who played for an hour three times a week, had a significant increase in maximum oxygen consumption (a measure of aerobic fitness) as well as a decrease in percentage of body fat. The women in the study, however, showed no significant improvement in fitness level; the researchers suggested that the reason for this was that they played only twice a week.

If you're used to leisurely tennis, the additional aerobic demands of squash or racquetball may well leave you feeling winded at first. You can prepare yourself by cycling, running, or jumping rope several times a week.

You should also purchase—and use—a pair of eye protectors. Because of its speed (up to 140 miles per hour), a racquetball or squash ball can seriously damage an eye. Or, in the heat of the game, it is all too easy to get hit with an opponent's racquet, particularly a squash racquet (which has a long neck). Get protectors with plastic shields over the eyes. Some models are simply empty frames, and racquetballs have been known to squeeze through these frames. Regular eyeglasses, even those with shatterproof lenses, are no protection.

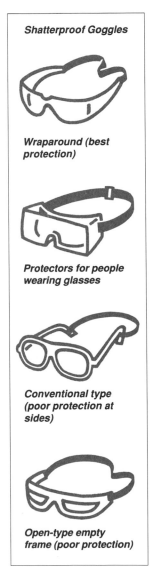

Shatterproof Goggles

Wraparound (best protection)

Protectors for people wearing glasses

Conventional type (poor protection at sides)

Open-type empty frame (poor protection)

Rowing

Among the very fittest of all athletes are members of the Olympic rowing teams. They use more muscles—not only the arms, but also the legs, abdomen, and torso—and burn more calories than anyone else except cross-country skiers. They get all the aerobic benefits of running in a workout that also effectively builds muscular strength and endurance. At the same time, rowing is a relatively stress-free exercise. The joint and muscle problems that can trouble runners are not evident among people who row regularly, and rowing also puts little strain on the back; indeed, sports physicians often prescribe it for people with lower back and disk problems. (Rowing can, however, aggravate some types of back conditions, so check with your physician if you have back trouble. People with heart trouble should also approach rowing cautiously, since it sends up the heart rate rapidly.)

Rowing machines

Nowadays rowers can work on dry land, at their own speed, in the comfort of their own homes. You can spend anywhere from one hundred and fifty to two thousand dollars for a rowing machine, but a satisfactory model can be purchased for three to four hundred dollars. A good machine will mimic a real scull. The machine will have two handles (oars) rigged with adjustable (usually hydraulic) pistons to provide variable resistance as you pull against the handles. It will have a comfortable padded or contoured seat that slides on rollers or ball bearings back along the stationary frame. It will usually have footrests that rotate as you push backward with your legs and straps to hold your feet firmly in position.

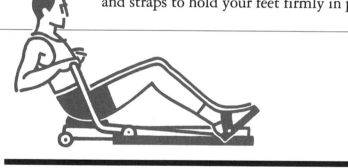

Proper rowing form: Lean back from your hips, pushing back with your legs and torso. Bend your arms until your elbows pass behind your chest and the handles are an inch from your stomach. Keep your back straight throughout.

The fanciest machines have ergometers that read out your speed and distance during your workout, or that even give you a read-out on calories expended as you work. Some even have a flywheel instead of hydraulic pistons to provide resistance, on the theory that a flywheel more closely resembles the feel of a real scull because it has a continuous momentum that approximates gliding. Less fancy but often first rate are the lightweight machines that are easy to fold up and store in a closet or put out of the way. At the least, any machine you get should sit solidly on the floor, not wobble or "jump" as you row. Its seat and oars should move smoothly and not stick. Some machines have a single bar to pull back on instead of two handles; either design is acceptable, and your choice is a matter of personal taste.

Whether you use a rowing machine or a real shell, you can begin your workouts by performing sets of strokes with the sliding seat in different positions—a routine that helps establish your sense of rhythm and also warms up the right muscles. Row for two minutes using a quarter of the slide on each stroke, then another two or three minutes using three quarters of the slide, before going on to use the full slide for your workout.

Running

For overall fitness, running is one of the easiest and least expensive activities. Running is *the* aerobic sport, and the one by which every other aerobic fitness program is measured. Running for half an hour three or four days a week will provide excellent fitness benefits very rapidly. It quickly increases the fitness of the cardiovascular system—as shown by decreased heart rate and blood pressure. Running is also good as part of a weight-reduction program, since a runner can burn a whopping four hundred calories in half an hour.

One great advantage of running over other sports is that it is accessible to virtually everyone. People of any age can run, it can be done almost anyplace, and it requires a relatively small outlay of money—well-fitting running shoes will be your chief expense. You can pass up all the costly clothes and other paraphernalia.

Because Americans are obsessed with speed and distance, many people think that the best way to run is fast and far. They start off at full speed, and when they find they can't sustain it for more than a mile, they quit. Actually, you get a far greater fitness benefit from running at a moderate pace for thirty minutes than by gunning it for fifteen. And there is no need to become obsessed about piling up mileage day after day. Dr. Kenneth Cooper, president of the Aerobics Center in Dallas, recommends running four times a week; that is sufficient for building and maintaining aerobic fitness.

Guidelines for running

The best way for people who are out of shape to start a running program is to walk. At a brisk pace, walk nonstop for thirty to forty-five minutes three days a week. As you get fitter, run for a few minutes, then walk briskly for a few more, and repeat for half an hour, increasing the running and decreasing the walking gradually until you are running steadily for half an hour.

If you want to increase your distance and running time, keep in mind that running more than twenty miles a week does not greatly increase your aerobic fitness, but it does increase your chance of injury. Running places harsh stresses on the legs and feet. Avoid hard surfaces and excessive downhill running—and whenever you experience a recurring pain, take heed.

Proper running form: *Stand tall with head up, eyes ahead, back straight, chest high, hips forward, arms and hands relaxed. Land on your heels to put less strain on feet and legs.*

Running Downhill
Contrary to popular belief, running downhill is much riskier for the joints and muscles in your feet and legs than running uphill. As you go down a hill, you speed up, your stride lengthens, and thus your impact with the ground increases. While jogging on a level surface causes your foot to strike the ground with a force equal to at least three times your body weight, running downhill can double the impact.

Because your muscles simultaneously tense up and elongate—known as "eccentric muscle contraction"—when you run downhill, there's an increased risk of muscle soreness later. Your distorted gait can also leave you with "runner's knee," a pain behind the kneecap.

To avoid injury, never run straight down a steep hill. Walk down it. Or run down in a zigzag pattern, leaning slightly forward and keeping your knees bent.

Many injuries occur because muscles are tight and joints are not prepared for stress. So before running, warm up the muscles by walking briskly and jogging slowly for ten to fifteen minutes. Then stretch, which is a crucial part of running because running tends to stiffen the muscles at the back of the leg.

The Right Running Shoes

A study at Tulane University found that all running shoes, regardless of brand, price, or type of construction, lose about 30 percent of their ability to absorb shocks after five hundred miles of use. So if you have been experiencing aches and pains and suspect that running or another type of exercise is to blame, check your shoes—you may need a new pair.

Before you discard your old shoes, however, take a good look at them. The signs of wear tell a lot about your running form, and may help explain any knee or leg pain you feel after a run. Using these clues to help select your next pair of shoes, may even prevent injuries.

Normally, when you run or walk fast, the outer part of your heel strikes the ground first, so that's where you see the most wear on your sole. Your foot then rolls inward and your weight is transferred to the inner side of the foot, causing wear on the middle of the sole in the area below the toes. The illustration at right shows areas of normal wear; the more wear, the darker the shading.

Too much rolling inward (pronation) or outward (supination) can put added strain on the feet, hips, lower legs, knees, or ankles. Many runners overpronate—that is, their feet roll too far inward—and your shoes may indicate to what extent you are doing this. When checking the signs of wear on your old shoes, here's what to look for:

Outer-sole. People who roll their feet outward (for instance, those with high arches) tend to wear down the outer side of the heel, while people who roll inward (such as those with flat feet) show more wear on the inner side. Such signs of wear are usually accompanied by damage inside the shoe, thus further reducing shock absorption and increasing stress on the lower leg and foot.

Mid-sole. This shock-absorbing layer between the outer-sole and insole can usually be seen from the side of the shoe. If one side is more compressed than the other, the mid-sole may absorb shock poorly, which could lead to foot instability and an ankle sprain or stress fracture. Rolling inward on your feet may severely compress the inside edge of the mid-soles. If your mid-soles are excessively or unevenly worn, look for firmer ones in your next shoes—and replace your shoes more frequently.

Heel counter. This rigid section at the back of the shoe stabilizes the heel. Look at the shoe from behind—does the counter bulge or lean to one side? Runners who roll their feet outward tend to force an outward bend on the counter, thus destabilizing the heel.

Upper. If both sides of the shoe extend beyond the sole, the shoe may have been too small for you. If the upper portion hangs over the sole on one side, the basic shape of the shoe (called the last) may be wrong for your foot. People who roll inward when they run need extra support on the shoe's inner side, which can be provided, in part, by a straight last. (To find a straight last, look at the soles—left and right soles should be almost indistinguishable.) In contrast, if you have high arches and your foot rolls outward, a curved last will conform better to the shape of your foot and give better support. If there's a hole or tear over the big toe, the shoe was probably too small. There should be one-half inch of space between your longest toe and the tip of the shoe when you put all your weight on that foot.

Shopping tips

•If you have an old pair of running shoes, take them with you when you shop for a new pair; a knowledgeable salesperson can evaluate the wear pattern to help you choose a suitable shoe. Run around in the store. Remember to wear your running socks.

•Examine new shoes carefully. Make sure they are the same length and width. Put the shoes side by side on a flat surface and look at them from behind: the uppers should be perpendicular to the sole; they should not lean to one side.

•Hold onto the front and back of the shoe and try to bend it. It should bend where the foot bends—at the ball; if the shoe bends at mid-foot, it will offer little support. It shouldn't bend too easily or be too stiff. Also, hold the heel and try to move the counter: it shouldn't move from side to side.

•In general, if your foot rolls outward significantly when you run (supination), you're probably better off with a shoe with a strong heel counter, a substantial yet somewhat soft mid-sole, a curved last, and a flexible sole. If your foot rolls inward (pronation), you might benefit from a shoe with a good arch support, a straight last, and a less flexible sole, especially along the inside edge.

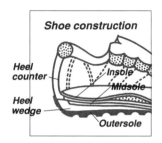

Shoe construction

Heel counter
Insole
Midsole
Heel wedge
Outersole

Areas of normal wear

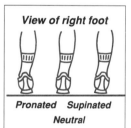

View of right foot

Pronated   Supinated
Neutral

It is also extremely important to know how to stop. If you stop running abruptly, you may faint or even suffer heart rhythm abnormalities because your blood pressure may drop sharply. The way to stop is gradually—cool down by slowing your pace and then walking briskly for five to ten minutes or so. If you do feel faint, don't remain standing—lie flat on your back.

If running has a drawback, it is the lack of a workout for the upper body—your arms and shoulders will not be strengthened by running. But running regularly can give you the discipline and confidence to undertake a broad program of exercise. And after a running program has gotten you into shape, you'll find that you get more enjoyment out of tennis, hiking, volleyball, and other recreations.

Swimming

Swimming calls into play nearly all the major muscle groups; it works out more than two-thirds of the body's total muscle mass, and so it places a vigorous demand on the heart and lungs, making it one of the very best aerobic exercises. It develops muscle strength and endurance and improves posture and flexibility. It does all this at the same time that the body is supported by water—and so stress is taken off the bones and joints. The buoyancy factor makes it especially good for people who are overweight, or who have leg or lower back problems. But it is good exercise for people of all ages and at all levels of proficiency.

The best stroke for achieving all the benefits of swimming is the forward crawl. The breast stroke and side stroke—which have long periods of gliding—will not achieve an aerobic effect (though they can be made more strenuous by reducing the glide phase). The breast stroke and side stroke can be used, however, as a change of pace between laps of the crawl, as can the back stroke. Synchronized swimming may look aerobic, but it is too stately to be aerobically beneficial.

Swimming and target heart rate
For reasons that physiologists don't yet understand, studies have shown that people have a lower maximum heart rate when swimming than when running. So if swimming is your means of training, this difference—averaging 13 beats per minute—must be subtracted from the age-related maximum heart rate (220 minus your age). Thus, a 40-year old swimmer would subtract 40 *plus* 13 from 220 and get a maximum rate of 167, and then take 60 to 80 percent of that to get a training range of 100 to 134.

Tips and techniques
You can begin a swimming program easily and build to a more rigorous workout in several steps. You will want to start out with four laps of twenty-five yards each, with a rest between each lap, and gradually add laps and decrease rest intervals. Eventually you will want to swim continuously thirty to forty minutes at least three days a week. As with all exercises, your goal is to reach a level of exertion that causes your heart to pump for twenty to thirty minutes at your target heart rate.

Taking your pulse while you are swimming can be tricky. Once you are going at cruising speed, stop between laps and take your pulse for ten seconds; multiply by six to get your heart rate, and adjust your swimming accordingly. If you are

Will swimming help you lose weight?
Researchers have suggested that swimmers tend to lose less weight than would be expected from an equivalent expenditure of energy during other aerobic activity. But studies have had inconsistent results—some found that swimmers lost weight (and body fat), others that they gained a few pounds, and some that they had no change in weight. And often, if the swimmers gained weight, it was lean body mass (muscle), not fat. If your main reason for swimming is to lose weight, it's only common sense that you should also try to cut down on calories. In addition, though, make sure you swim fast. Many overweight people don't swim fast enough or long enough. At a slow pace, twenty lengths of the pool may burn only 50 calories more than just staying afloat—hardly enough to make you lose weight.

counting calories, remember, it is the intensity and duration of your swimming that largely determines how many calories you burn. A 150-pound swimmer doing a brisk forward crawl will often burn as much as 11 calories per minute.

You shouldn't train in water that is too warm, since your body will have to work harder to throw off the heat generated by the exercise. Most pools used by swim teams are seventy to seventy-three degrees Fahrenheit, but at that temperature you need to keep moving to stay warm.

Swimmers are subject to some minor vexations. Chlorine will make your hair dry and brittle, so it is wise to wear a bathing cap in the pool. A shower after swimming in a pool or the ocean is a must. Both chlorine and salt dry out the skin. If your skin does get dry, rub moisturizing lotion into it while it is still wet.

Infection of the ear canal is another common problem for swimmers. This can sometimes be prevented by the use of alcohol or glycerin drops after a swim. If you do get an infected ear, have it treated by a physician (see page 321).

Goggles will reduce the risk of eye problems due to chlorine, salt, sand, and microorganisms—and also make it easier to see. It may take some effort to find goggles that fit properly, but it's worth the trouble.

Swimming lessons are worthwhile for beginners and are also helpful for brushing up on your technique. An inefficient stroke makes swimming both awkward and harder. A smooth stroke makes swimming not only a perfect exercise, but also a perfect way to relax.

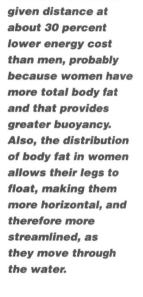

Women can swim a given distance at about 30 percent lower energy cost than men, probably because women have more total body fat and that provides greater buoyancy. Also, the distribution of body fat in women allows their legs to float, making them more horizontal, and therefore more streamlined, as they move through the water.

The key to an efficient crawl: *Keep your elbow higher than your hand as you pull back (left) and have the water break at your hairline. Don't drop your elbow (center) or straighten it (right).*

Should babies learn to swim?

Water programs designed to give babies and toddlers a head start in learning to swim and in water safety are enjoying increasing popularity around the country. Such programs should be well supervised to avoid endangering the health of youngsters. Perhaps the greatest risk is the misconception that children who learn to swim as toddlers are "drownproof." Children who can paddle around a pool will not necessarily be able to swim if they fall into the water. According to the American Academy of Pediatrics, the only way to keep children safe around the water is to supervise them. Children in boats need properly fitted flotation jackets, whether they can swim or not.

Particular attention should be paid to pool cleanliness. If a child defecates in a pool, the stool should be removed and all swimmers should leave the pool for thirty minutes or so to give the chlorine time to kill any parasites. (The chlorine concentration should also be checked to make sure that it is adequate.) In addition, the American Academy of Pediatrics has proposed the following guidelines:

• A qualified instructor trained in infant CPR should be in charge.

- Each infant should be "taught" one on one by the parent or other supervisor.
- Forced total submersion is prohibited.
- All participants must shower immediately before class.
- Any child with diarrhea should be excluded until recovery.
- All children must wear training pants or plastic pants.

Open-water swimming

Surf swimming can be a great pleasure and good exercise as well, and in summertime, many people also swim in lakes, ponds, and rivers. If you're accustomed to a pool, you'll need to approach the great outdoors with somewhat more caution. About seven thousand people drown each year, most of them in lakes, rivers, and oceans rather than pools. Most of these drownings are alcohol related, so to be safe in the water keep your outing alcohol free. In addition, take the following measures:

- Don't swim alone. Stick to areas where there's a lifeguard if possible, or at the very least, go with someone who is a capable swimmer.
- Keep children under constant observation.
- Test yourself in shallow water before swimming out. The water may be colder or rougher than it looks, or there may be currents. Locate any steep drop-offs. Discover how far out you can go and still touch bottom. Check with the lifeguard, if there is one, about water conditions.
- If you want to do long-distance swimming, swim along parallel to the shore or riverbank, and not too far out.
- Backwash from waves (undertow) is of less concern for swimmers than underwater rip currents (water moving swiftly seaward, usually in currents not more than ten or twenty feet wide). These are hard to spot and may exist even in calm-looking waters. A break in the wave pattern or discoloration (usually caused by sand) can help you spot rip currents. If you get caught in one, however, don't struggle. Swim with it, but angle toward the shore or bank. Or just ride the current seaward, and as soon as possible turn and swim to shore outside the current.
- Avoid weedy areas. If you do get tangled up, don't struggle. Tread water, and try to move with the current. You'll soon break free.
- If you get into any situation you're afraid you can't handle, call for help.

Finally, don't swim in waters that have not been tested for safety by the local board of health. Contamination isn't always visible to the naked eye.

At swimming meets and other competitions, you may see athletes inhaling oxygen from canisters during breaks in the game. However, this practice has little, if any, effect on their performance. It increases the amount of oxygen in the blood only minimally—and this small increase disappears after a minute or two of breathing normal air.

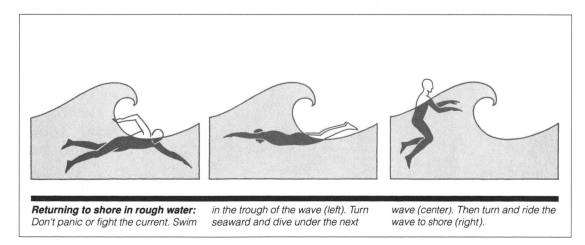

Returning to shore in rough water: Don't panic or fight the current. Swim in the trough of the wave (left). Turn seaward and dive under the next wave (center). Then turn and ride the wave to shore (right).

Walking

The simplest, safest, and least expensive exercise is walking. A long-term study of thousands of Harvard alumni has suggested that a regimen of walking (an average of nine miles a week) can significantly prolong life. Other studies have shown that walking benefits nearly everybody, regardless of previous state of fitness. At Western New Mexico University, two groups of women—one premenopausal and the other postmenopausal—improved their cardiovascular fitness and increased their percentage of lean body mass (at the expense of fat cells) through brisk treadmill walking. The older women achieved the same improvements as the younger ones. In fact, walking is particularly good for postmenopausal women, since it is a weight-bearing exercise, which may help slow down osteoporosis.

Other research has shown that walking at speeds of $3\frac{1}{2}$ to $4\frac{1}{2}$ miles an hour—that's brisk walking, not strolling—produces cardiovascular benefits. (A woman of average size can walk comfortably at brisk speeds of $3\frac{1}{2}$ to 4 miles an hour, while the average-sized man can walk at $4\frac{1}{2}$ to 5 miles per hour.) Slower walking (2 miles per hour) can be advantageous for older people, cardiac patients, or people recuperating from an illness. Walking at speeds of 5 miles an hour can burn as many calories as moderate jogging, but even slow walking can burn 60 to 80 calories per mile.

Still, walking by itself is not enough to prevent disease. It must be combined with other good habits, such as avoiding cigarettes, controlling blood pressure, and following a prudent diet. It's important to remember, too, that in order to get the maximum benefits from exercise, it must become a long-term habit. *Walking represents a particularly effective way to develop a lifelong program of exercise.*

Tips and techniques for a walking program

•If you're inactive but healthy, start with mile-long walks at a pace of three miles per hour five times a week. Over the course of a month, gradually increase your distance to three miles at a pace of four miles per hour five times a week. If you are unable to walk that fast, walk a little farther.

•You can increase the aerobic benefits of brisk walking in two ways. Swing your arms: your upper body needs a workout, too. And as you get used to walking, carry a six-pound backpack or hand weights. You can substitute a briefcase or shopping bag for the backpack.

•Don't ride when you can walk. Incorporate walking into your daily routine. If you must take public transportation, get off a few stops early and walk to your destination.

•If it's too hot or cold outdoors, you can walk for exercise in your local mall, or in any other climate-controlled

One-Mile Walking Test

If you are thirty to sixty-nine years old and want to evaluate your general aerobic fitness level, walk one mile as fast as you can and time yourself. Compare your results with the following chart, devised by Dr. James Rippe and his colleagues at the University of Massachusetts.

Category	Male (min:sec)	Female (min:sec)
Excellent	less than 10:12	less than 11:40
Good	10:13-11:42	11:41-13:08
High average	11:43-13:13	13:09-14:36
Low average	13:14-14:44	14:37-16:04
Fair	14:45-16:23	16:05-17:31
Poor	more than 16:24	more than 17:32

environment. Many malls have instituted walking programs sponsored by the American Heart Association.

•Put variety into your walking program. Take a companion along. Try a different route, particularly leading to hilly territory, which will boost the aerobic benefits. If you get tired, alternate fast walking with strolling.

•You don't need special footwear, but don't walk long distances in soft, shapeless shoes. Walking shoes should have a shank (a rigid arch), as well as some cushioning for the heel and the ball of your foot. Socks made from synthetic materials that "wick" away sweat—such as Orlon or polypropylene—will add to your comfort and absorb perspiration as well.

Hiking

Rambling through the woods has become a pre-eminent summer activity, and it's no wonder: a hike is noncompetitive, open to all ages and abilities, and provides a great variety of challenges and scenery. You can hike alone, with your family, or with friends. The equipment is minimal. And you can give yourself a first-rate workout. Hiking along a rough but level trail expends about 50 percent more energy than walking on a paved road. Caloric expenditure and aerobic benefit increase dramatically when you hike uphill: ascending a fourteen-degree slope requires nearly four times as much effort as walking on a level surface. Hence, the caloric expenditure during a day-long hike can be considerable. A 150-pound person hiking at a normal pace for eight hours over varied terrain will use up about 3,500 calories—a thousand more than a good runner expends during a marathon. Of course, even a one-hour hike can provide a good aerobic workout. There are psychological benefits as well. Passing through beautiful scenery relaxes the mind, eases stress, and stimulates creativity.

Footwear. For light hiking on smooth trails, several manufacturers make low-cut trail shoes that weigh only a bit more than running shoes but provide better support. Sturdy leather Oxford-style shoes with a treaded rubber sole are also appropriate.

For trails that are at all rough or steep, or in wet weather, ankle-high boots are best. The lightest ones are made of nylon, canvas, or breathable waterproof fabric reinforced with leather. Slightly heavier, but offering better support and durability in rough terrain, are boots with all-leather uppers. Whichever type you choose,

Walking a mile burns only about 10 to 20 percent fewer calories than jogging a mile, though obviously it takes longer. If you walk briskly, you can get nearly the same aerobic benefits provided by running.

How Fast Do You Walk?

Many people have no idea what their pace is as they're walking. One way to measure your speed is to use a pedometer. Or you can walk on a measured track. Here is another way to get a rough estimate of your speed: count how many steps you take per minute and compare the results with this table.

WALKING SPEED CONVERSION TABLE

Steps per minute	Minutes per mile	Miles per hour
70	30	2
90	24	2.5
105	20	3
120	17	3.5
140	15	4
160	13	4.5
175	12	5
190	11	5.5
210+	less than 10	more than 6

This table is based on 2.5-foot-long stride. If your stride is closer to 3-feet long, here's an easy way to estimate your walking speed: count how many steps you take in a minute and divide this number by 30. Thus, if you are taking about 105 steps per minute, you are covering about 3.5 miles per hour.

the most dependable models have these features: a treaded outer-sole of hard rubber or a composite such as Vibram; an insole and one or more mid-soles for cushioning and strength; a heel counter for stability; a padded tongue to protect your instep.

Try on several models of the boot style you prefer, starting with a half-size larger than your street shoes. A laced boot should be snug across the ball of your foot and around the ankle, but with a half inch between your toes and the boot front.

Clothing and supplies. In fair weather, wear loose cotton pants and a long-sleeved cotton shirt. Since temperatures can vary abruptly even in summer, take along extra clothes that you can add in layers if you get cold.

Other basic articles for day-long hikes include a small first-aid kit (with bandages for blisters), insect repellent, a knife, a flashlight, and matches. A container of water, iced tea, or juice is essential to avoid dehydration. Carry your gear in a day pack with wide shoulder straps. Choose a size that you can load loosely; it will be more comfortable to carry than a tightly stuffed pack.

Hiking tips. Walk upright and relaxed. Your arms should swing easily, but keep shoulders, hips, and feet straight. If you are carrying a pack, lean forward slightly so that the combined weight is centered over your feet. Maintain a steady pace, even uphill; if the slope is extreme, though, pause briefly before each step, resting your weight a second on your back foot. Walk around, not on, roots, rocks, and logs, and take your time with hills—these are the spots where injuries occur. Novice hikers should take five-minute rest stops every half hour. Use the time to drink water and stretch.

Boosting the benefits. Any recreational hike will work your heart and lungs and burn off calories. But for those who want to combine the pleasures of a jaunt through the woods with the benefits of vigorous exercise, here are some tips for making a hike more of a workout.

•Most trails are not suited for sustained sprint-walking. But on smooth stretches, try alternating one hundred yards of hiking with one hundred yards of easy jogging.

•If you are going to retrace a route, hike at a leisurely pace going in, then double your pace returning.

•If your pack is light, add some smooth stones to increase its weight. Every seven pounds will burn off about 30 calories per hour.

•Increase the distance you hike (with rest stops once an hour).

•Hike up hills. Going uphill can provide a training effect comparable to brisk running or cycling.

•Start getting in shape before your first hike of the season. Walk to work, climb stairs, and take short weekend jaunts with the gear you'll be carrying.

Race-walking

If you're one of the millions now walking a brisk mile or two a day for pleasure and health, you may occasionally have been left in the dust by someone speeding along like Roadrunner—hips swinging and arms pumping and feet barely skimming the ground. Walking isn't merely locomotion but an activity with several potential variations, including walking at the Olympic level. In 1983, the world record for a mile walk was set by Ray Sharp of the United States: 5 minutes 46.21 seconds. It takes the average person about three times as long to walk a mile. Although you may not expect to set an Olympic record, race-walking offers many benefits to the

Stair-Climbing

When you climb stairs, the effort usually doesn't last long enough to produce aerobic benefits. But it certainly burns more calories than standing on an escalator. And as a supplement to other forms of exercise, stair-climbing may help keep your weight in check, particularly if you make a point of climbing stairs instead of taking an elevator.

Of course, you can make stair-climbing an aerobic exercise simply by stair-stepping repeatedly up and down a single flight of steps. If a set of stairs isn't convenient or to your liking, many well-equipped gyms have machines that simulate stair-climbing. Because the stairs continually keep moving, you never run out of floors to climb, and thus you get an excellent workout.

walker who's gotten in good shape and is ready for a challenge. Race-walking can burn as many calories per hour as running, but with much less risk of injury. It's not an expensive sport: all you really need, besides clothing that suits the weather, is an adequate pair of shoes (see page 256). It's fun to race-walk alone or with a friend, competitively or just for company. And a companion can be very useful for checking your posture and form for you when you're learning to race-walk.

The right gait. The object of race-walking is to move your body ahead as quickly as possible (without running) and to avoid the up/down motions of regular walking. That's the point of the forward-thrusting hip swivel, which is meant to propel you more efficiently than the normal side-to-side swing of the hips. Here's how to start:

•Think of race-walking as walking a tightrope (see diagram at right). In normal walking, your feet make parallel tracks, but in race-walking, you must try to put one foot down in front of the other, almost in a straight line. Because of anatomical differences, this form may not be completely achievable for everyone, but come as close to it as you can.

•Swing your hip forward as you step forward—it's the hips and legs that act as the propulsive force.

•Feet should be close to the ground, with no wasted motion. Each foot should strike the ground solidly on the back of the heel with toes pointed up at a slight angle. (Two rules of competitive race-walking are that one foot must always be on the ground, and your knee must be straight at one point in the cycle.)

•Use long strides. Your motion should be fluid, efficient, and smooth.

•Bend your arms at a ninety-degree angle, keeping your wrist straight. With the motion coming from the shoulder, not the elbow, pump your arms rhythmically in time with your leg motion. When you pump back, your hand should go about six inches behind the hip; on the swing forward, the hand should come near the center of your chest (see illustration below). Keep your hands above your hips. The vigorous arm pumping counterbalances your leg/hip motion, allows for a quick pace, and provides a good workout for your upper body.

•Keep your torso, shoulders, and neck relaxed, and your head in line with your back. Don't bend from the waist—this can lead to back strain. Some race-walkers angle their whole body slightly forward from the ankles.

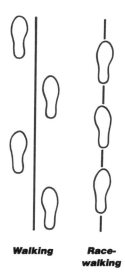

Walking   Race-walking

Since technique is important in race-walking, you will need practice. If there's an experienced race-walker around who can give you pointers, so much the better. Start with leg movement first, build up some speed, and then incorporate the arm motions. See what a difference it makes to have your arms in proper ninety-degree angle position instead of hanging at your sides. Your pace should quicken automatically as you learn to use your arms. Start slowly, walking for twenty to thirty minutes and increasing your pace gradually. Try interval walking—

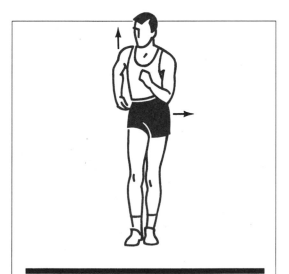

Hip and arm power: *As one arm pumps backward, swivel the opposite hip outward.*

race-walk for a few minutes, then walk normally and briskly. If you want to be sure of getting aerobic benefits, pause occasionally to check your heart rate.

Avoiding injury. Race-walking is not as hard on the body as running, but your shin muscles get much the same kind of workout, and most beginning race-walkers experience some shin soreness. To build shin muscles, try these exercises indoors:

- •Walk back and forth across a room on your heels.
- •In a sitting position or standing (balanced on one foot), rotate each foot clockwise and counterclockwise in large circles several times. This works shin and calf muscles.
- •For hip flexibility, walk a straight line, practicing hip movement. Exaggerate the movement by crisscross walking over the imaginary line.
- •Warm up and stretch before and after race-walking.

Shoes. If you already have running shoes, or any pair of walking shoes you like, you can try race-walking in them and see how you do. Ideally, your race-walking shoe should have the following qualities:

- •adequate cushioning to absorb repeated shocks;
- •flexible, curved sole to accommodate the rocking motion of walking, as opposed to the flared sole of running shoes;
- •low back tab to reduce pressure on heel tendons, and reinforced heel counter;
- •perforated upper to cool the foot.

Water Aerobics

Swimming is not the only form of exercise drawing people into the water these days. For joggers and people who take aerobic dance classes, deep-water running and other water workouts can provide fitness benefits without putting stress on joints and muscles. For people recovering from a leg or back injury, aquatic exercise is good because of the water's cushioning, supportive effect; this also makes it suitable for pregnant or obese people. For swimmers, less-conventional water aerobics can add variety to their time in the pool. Even for nonswimmers, water workouts can be an attractive option on a hot summer day.

Most studies show that as an aerobic activity, running in water is on a par with running on land, or only slightly less strenuous. (Walking in water, however, is more demanding than regular walking because of water resistance.) The most basic type of water aerobics is jogging back and forth across the pool in chest- or waist-

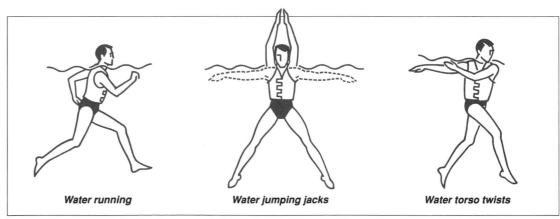

Water running   **Water jumping jacks**   **Water torso twists**

deep water, or running in place while treading water at the deep end. All you do is exaggerate the normal running movements by lifting your knees high and pumping your arms back and forth.

Vests and other devices

You can also use a flotation vest to keep you upright as you run in deep water. By wearing a vest, you can concentrate on moving your limbs through their full range of motion at a constant speed. Besides making your workout more enjoyable, the vest lets you keep an injured foot or ankle off the pool floor. To vary your aerobic workout, you can do cycling movements, jumping jacks, and torso twists while the vest supports you.

Which types of life vests are good for water workouts? One relative newcomer is a snug-fitting, nonbulky training vest called the Wet Vest. You can also use a traditional type III life jacket, the kind used by water skiers. It is bulkier but cheaper and, unlike the Wet Vest, has been approved by the United States Coast Guard. Get one with crotch straps to keep it from riding up. An advantage of the Wet Vest is that it doesn't ride up, and it keeps you more vertical than the type III vest. To decrease chafing, you may want to apply petroleum jelly under your arms or wear a T-shirt under the vest. Note: if you can't swim, don't rely on a flotation device; don't go in a pool unless a partner or lifeguard is present who knows you're a nonswimmer.

Devices such as fins, hand paddles, and inflatable rubber mitts can help strengthen your upper body or legs by enlarging the surface area you push or pull through the water. Like the vests, these can be purchased at swim shops, sporting-goods stores, and many department stores.

When exercising in water, make sure its temperature is comfortable, usually eighty-two to eighty-six degrees Fahrenheit. If it's too hot, you could become weak or even pass out; if too cool, it may cause pain in stiff or arthritic joints.

The buoyancy of water is ideal for low-impact exercise in that it effectively reduces a person's weight by about 90 percent. For example, when a 150-pound man is submerged up to his neck in water, his lower limbs have to support only 15 pounds—which means that ligaments and joints receive substantially less stress during a workout.

Strength and Flexibility

Developing strong, flexible muscles is important for everyone, not just for athletes and body builders. Well-conditioned muscles and joints help you perform better physically, assist you in maintaining good posture, and may help prevent injuries and chronic lower-back pain. The following pages show you the correct way to perform basic strengthening exercises, offer guidelines on how to start a weight-training program, and show you how to test and improve your flexibility. (If you are forty-five or over, or if you have hypertension or a cardiovascular condition, it's important to consult your doctor before beginning any strengthening routines, particularly lifting weights.)

Basic Calisthenics

You can increase both the strength and endurance of your muscles with exercises that apply resistance to normal body motion. The resistance, or load, should be sufficient so that muscles contract at tensions close to maximum. You can use adjustable weights or your own body weight, but adjustable weights allow you to progressively increase the resistance as the muscles develop.

The best way to increase strength—the maximum force a muscle can produce in a single effort—is working out with weights. Strength gains come most quickly from heavy resistance and few repetitions, and free weights (barbells or dumbbells) or weight machines allow you to continually increase the resistance. Power lifters, who are interested almost solely in building strength, train by hefting weights that are near the maximum they can lift, and doing so only three to six times.

The key to building muscular endurance—the ability to repeat an effort—is to perform many repetitions of an exercise. You can use weights and weight machines to accomplish this, using a workload that is about 55 to 75 percent of the maximum amount you can lift, and performing about fifteen or more repetitions. But for most people, calisthenics—such as sit-ups and push-ups—are quite effective and usually more convenient. This is the most basic type of resistance exercise, since you lift your own body weight: all you need is a padded surface to exercise on. You can also buy a slant board (for sit-ups), a chinning bar, or other inexpensive equipment to vary your routine.

Toning the abdominals

A trim waist and a flat stomach are goals that many of us yearn to achieve. Even in people who are not overweight, a few extra pounds often seem to accumulate around the midsection. Are there specific exercises that can help? Aerobics classes, for example, often begin with side bends and waist twists, which teachers and students believe will reduce their waistlines. And there are a hundred gadgets on the market that promise that if you bend at the waist often enough, you can flatten your abdomen, eliminate your "love handles," or whittle inches from your middle.

The truth may sound discouraging at first: there's no way to spot reduce. Exercising small muscle groups, such as those at the waist, won't burn the fat around those muscles. Moreover, limited exercise of this sort using only specific muscles burns fewer calories than exercising large muscles in dynamic activity. If you're really interested in shedding some fat, you have to perform aerobic exercises such as cycling, running, or brisk walking.

But fat may not be what worries you. Poor muscle tone can contribute to a flabby look, and exercise can improve muscle strength and firmness. *However, side bends and waist twists are not effective for strengthening abdominal muscles.* Neither exercise puts a great enough load on the muscles to promote toning. In side bends, gravity does most of the work. Bends and twists can stretch torso muscles, but they won't strengthen them significantly.

Sit-ups, on the other hand, can strengthen and tone up three sets of abdominal muscles—the *rectus abdominus* (the long muscle running vertically down the abdomen) and the external and internal obliques (the diagonal muscles that form the letter V across the lower abdomen)—which are all otherwise hard to exercise. Even more important, sit-ups can prevent or alleviate back problems, since strong abdominal muscles provide better support for the back. Strengthening these muscles will also give you more power for running, tennis, and other physical activities that involve the torso.

These benefits occur only when sit-ups are done correctly, however. Here are some variations to avoid:

•The old-fashioned straight-leg sit-ups (below left), in which you come all the way up to a vertical position, are a waste of effort and potentially dangerous. Keeping your legs flat on the floor arches the lower back, which overextends it and places it under stress. Also, there's no need to sit up fully, since the abdominal muscles work only during the first part of the movement. After that the hip flexor muscles (the ones that bend your leg at the hip) take over, and the shift to these muscles can pull the hip out of alignment and arch the lower back, which can cause back strain.

•Alternating bent-leg sit-ups (below right), in which you hold one leg straight out, produce an asymmetric pull on the pelvis, so they aren't recommended.

Muscle is denser than fat, so if you lose fat tissue but add muscle, your weight may climb. However, you will probably look like you have lost weight, since muscles are firmer and more pleasing to the eye than fat, and, even though your weight may go up, your waistline may actually shrink. Furthermore, most people will not gain more than two or three pounds of muscle from body-shaping workouts.

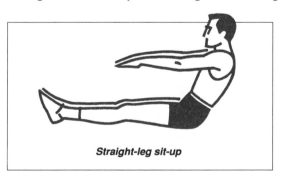

Straight-leg sit-up

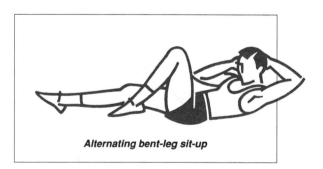

Alternating bent-leg sit-up

•Using a slant board can increase the resistance of sit-ups, but many people may find sit-ups too difficult if the slant board is set at a steep angle. Moreover, because the feet are hooked under the bar of the board, leg and hip muscles can end up doing much of the work.

•Another difficult maneuver is to keep the legs straight up in the air as you curl towards them, which keeps the abdominal muscles continually contracted. If you want to raise your legs, lean them against a wall for support, which allows the abdominal muscles to relax during the rest phase of the exercise.

The best sit-up

The safest, most effective way to do a sit-up is to lie on your back, keeping knees bent and feet on the floor. This sit-up works all the abdominal muscles as a group. The safest arm position is to cross your arms behind your head with your hands placed on the opposite shoulders; this lets your arms support your head. Holding your hands behind the head or neck tends to jerk the neck and put pressure on it, possibly causing injury. It also makes you work your arms, not your abdomen.

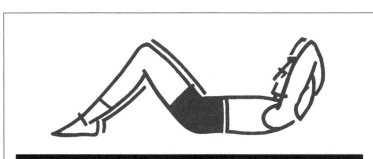

Sit-up: Contract the abdominal muscles and press your lower back into the floor, which will cause your upper body to lift up. It is necessary to come up only to a thirty- to forty-five degree angle. Always keep your lower back pressed firmly into the ground to prevent arching.

For easier sit-ups, put your hands at your sides or folded across the chest. As the hands are brought closer to the head, the exercise becomes more difficult due to a shift in the center of gravity. If you still find this too taxing, try a *curl down*, or negative sit-up, which eases the load on your muscles because you are moving in the direction of gravity.

Beginners should start with three sets of five sit-ups with a rest between sets and gradually work up to three sets of fifteen repetitions. Those in good shape can start with sets of ten. Do these at least three times a week.

If you want to *tone* the muscles that shape the sides of your waist, try *diagonal crunches*. However, stop if you feel any discomfort in the lower back.

Sit-ups by themselves won't improve your posture, and bad posture can lead to back pain. To maximize the beneficial effects of sit-ups on posture, try tightening the abdominal muscles for a few seconds while standing several times a day.

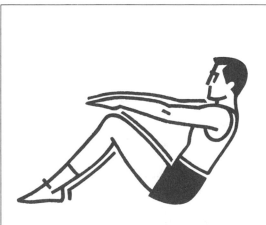

Curl down, or negative sit-up: Start by sitting with your knees bent and arms reaching forward. Slowly lower yourself to the floor, as if you could touch one vertebra at time to the floor. After you are completely down, push yourself back up with your arms. Repeat ten times.

Diagonal crunch: Starting with your head and right shoulder slightly raised, twist your right elbow toward your left knee and hold for three seconds. Repeat ten times. Then twist your left elbow to your right knee, hold, repeat ten times.

Push-ups

Push-ups put off a lot of people—especially women—in part, because of their association with military basic training and a tough, macho image. In this age of Nautilus machines, push-ups may also seem old-fashioned. Yet the push-up remains one of the best upper-body exercises around, one that can be done anywhere, requires no equipment, and is easily adapted to any level of proficiency.

Women in particular will find push-ups useful for strengthening their upper arm and shoulder muscles, which tend to be underdeveloped.

The standard push-up works muscles in the shoulders (deltoids), backs of upper arms (triceps), and chest (pectorals). The beauty of the push-up is that it also exercises muscles in the abdomen, hips, and back, which are tensed to keep the body stiff while it moves up and down. Aligning the body like this and contracting opposing muscle groups also helps promote good posture.

Standard push-up: *Place your hands slightly wider than shoulder width, feet close together, knees locked, and arms perpendicular to the floor. Most important, hold your body in a straight line—from shoulders to ankles—throughout.*

Try to touch your chest to the floor for a second, but don't rest there. Go slowly. Inhaling on the way up and exhaling on the way down makes the exercise easier. Do three or four sets of as many repetitions as you can, but don't strain.

Modified push-ups

Don't give up if your arm muscles are not strong enough to lift your body at first. There are modified push-ups that let you slowly build up your muscles. By keeping your knees on the floor, for example, you will have less body weight to lift. Still, avoid the common mistake of arching your lower back and moving only your chest up and down. Always keep your torso straight and lift your body from the knees to insure that your arms receive the maximum workout and you do not strain your back.

Let-downs. The U.S. Army has been using an updated form of push-up called the "let-down" for recruits who can't manage the traditional version. It is part of the Army's "negative strength training" program that allows you to strengthen muscles without overwhelming them. The rationale behind the let-down is that it's easier to hold your body up than to lift it up. You begin in the "up" position of the standard push-up, with your arms fully extended and body straight. Slowly lower your body a few inches at a time, keeping your body aligned, until your chest is almost on the floor; this should take ten to fifteen seconds. Relax; then, using your knees, return to the starting position and repeat. In a short time, you should be able to repeat this exercise for ten to fifteen minutes.

When the let-down becomes too easy for you, move on to the standard push-up. Once proficient at that, you can increase the difficulty with various advanced push-ups. Placing your hands close together on the floor with elbows flared out emphasizes the arm (triceps) muscles. In contrast, keeping your hands far apart works the chest (pectoral) muscles more. You can also try keeping your feet on a chair or a step as you do push-ups, which places more weight on the arms. In addition to focusing on specific muscle groups, a mixed menu of push-ups also helps prevent boredom.

Isometrics: a quick workout

Surveys show that the most common reason people give for not exercising is lack of time. But, even if you can't set aside time for an ideal fitness regimen—for instance, daily fifteen-minute stretching sessions followed by a half hour of aerobic activity or a strength-building routine—some exercise is always better than none.

Building strength on the go doesn't require carrying dumbbells or doing push-ups wherever you are. Among the best options are isometric exercises, which call for contracting muscles against a fixed resistance, such as a post or wall, or against each other. These involve little or no movement, require no equipment, and take only seconds to perform. Thus, they can be done anytime, anywhere—at the bus stop, in the office, on a plane. The exercises below will get you started.

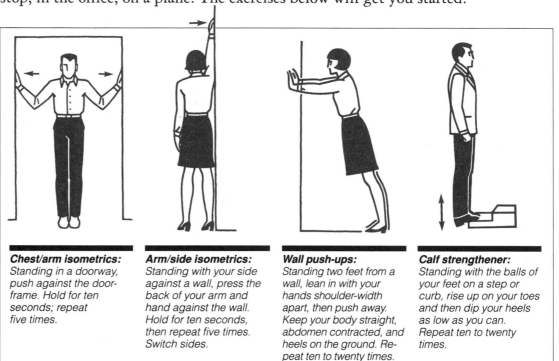

Chest/arm isometrics:
Standing in a doorway, push against the door-frame. Hold for ten seconds; repeat five times.

Arm/side isometrics:
Standing with your side against a wall, press the back of your arm and hand against the wall. Hold for ten seconds, then repeat five times. Switch sides.

Wall push-ups:
Standing two feet from a wall, lean in with your hands shoulder-width apart, then push away. Keep your body straight, abdomen contracted, and heels on the ground. Repeat ten to twenty times.

Calf strengthener:
Standing with the balls of your feet on a step or curb, rise up on your toes and then dip your heels as low as you can. Repeat ten to twenty times.

Muscle toning for two

There is an alternative to exercising alone or in a class. You can work out at home with a partner—a friend, relative, or mate. The benefits are congenial company, friendly competition, and extra motivation as you spur each other on. And you need no special equipment: instead of barbells or expensive weight machines, your partner supplies the resistance.

Many solo exercises can be adapted to two-person workouts. Partner strength-building exercises work in three different ways: one person supports the other and provides variable or fixed resistance; both partners perform the same exercise together and work against each other's resistance; or each performs a different exercise at the same time.

The exercises on the opposite page will get you and a partner started. Remember to switch roles after a few repetitions, so that you both benefit. Adjust to your partner's capabilities—for instance, one of you may be stronger, the other more flexible. Repeat each strengthening exercise five to ten times. As with any exercise, if there's any pain, stop.

Partner Routines

Shoulder/arm strengthener: Stand with your arms at your sides with your partner standing behind you and holding onto your forearms. Slowly lift your arms sideways to shoulder level while your partner provides downward pressure. This can also be done with your partner providing immovable resistance at various arm levels. Then reverse the movement: with your arms stretched out sideways, resist as your partner slowly pushes your arms down to your sides. Or have your partner try to elevate your arms as you try to keep them down at your sides.

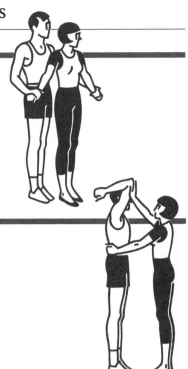

Upper-back strengthener: Raise one arm, elbow bent, above your head. Your partner faces you and puts one hand at your lower back, the other under your elbow. Using your chest and upper back muscles, push your elbow down against your partner's immovable resistance for five to ten seconds. Switch arms. Your partner can also provide movable resistance by allowing you to slowly lower your arm.

Pectoral strengthener: Sitting on the floor or in a chair, lock your fingers behind your head and point your elbows outward. Your partner kneels behind you, braced against your back, and lightly grasps the inside of each elbow. Using your chest muscles, try to pull your bent elbows together as your partner provides immovable resistance. Hold for five seconds. Repeat with elbows slightly farther back or forward. Your partner can also provide movable resistance.

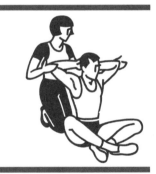

Thigh strengthener: Lie on your stomach, with your head on your hands, one leg outstretched, and the other leg bent upward. Your partner kneels and grasps the raised ankle with both hands. Try to lower your foot to the floor against your partner's immovable resistance for five to ten seconds. Switch legs. Your partner can also gradually allow you to lower your foot, thus providing variable resistance.

Inner/outer thigh press: Sit facing each other about five feet apart, with legs extended in medium straddle position. Your partner's feet are outside yours. Press your legs outward as your partner presses inward for five to ten seconds. Switch positions. Keep your arms at your sides (for support), back straight, and stomach tight.

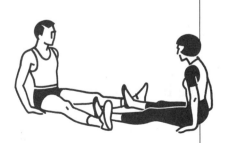

Water calisthenics

In a water workout, calisthenics that are often a sweaty chore can be soothing and sensuous, not to mention cooling on a hot day. Water calisthenics offer several other advantages as well. The water's resistance makes many exercises more efficient conditioners than nonaquatic routines. Moreover, because of your buoyancy, there is less stress on your joints and muscles and less chance of an injury. This makes water exercises particularly valuable for the obese, people recovering from injuries, and the disabled.

Unlike swimming laps, water calisthenics require little space, so they can be done in a crowded pool. And nonswimmers can also do them.

As in any exercise program, at least three workouts per week are needed for progress and sustained conditioning. Stretch before you begin and when you finish. Start slowly, gradually increase repetitions, and build to a workout of forty-five minutes to an hour. These exercises will get you started:

•Simply hold the edge of the pool and kick.

•Do jumping jacks. Stand in water up to your chest and jump up, parting your legs as you rise. Raise your arms from your sides to the surface as you jump.

•Make an X with your arms in front of you, keeping them just underwater. The water should be deep enough so that you have to bend a bit to keep your arms below the surface. With fingers slightly spread, swing your crossed arms to your left and to your right, back and forth.

•In waist-deep water, step forward, bringing your left leg, with your knee straight, to the surface. Repeat with the right leg, then alternate legs.

•Reach forward and touch your left foot with your left hand. Repeat with your opposite leg and hand, then alternate legs.

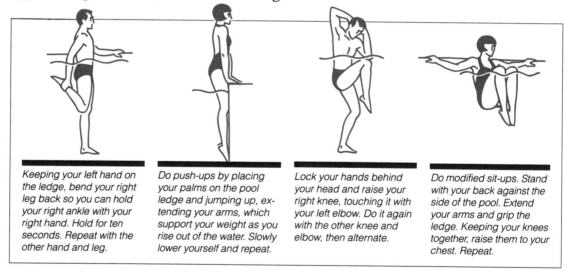

Keeping your left hand on the ledge, bend your right leg back so you can hold your right ankle with your right hand. Hold for ten seconds. Repeat with the other hand and leg.

Do push-ups by placing your palms on the pool ledge and jumping up, extending your arms, which support your weight as you rise out of the water. Slowly lower yourself and repeat.

Lock your hands behind your head and raise your right knee, touching it with your left elbow. Do it again with the other knee and elbow, then alternate.

Do modified sit-ups. Stand with your back against the side of the pool. Extend your arms and grip the ledge. Keeping your knees together, raise them to your chest. Repeat.

Weight Training

Despite the stereotype of a weight lifter—muscle-bound, hefting and grunting, big but weak—weight training can be used by everyone, not just those interested in becoming body builders. Paired with regular aerobic exercise, weight training increases your strength and muscle endurance as well as your overall feeling of fitness in ways that no other single exercise can. Bicycling develops one set of muscles, basketball another, but weight training works out a whole range of muscles in a very short amount of time. Specific weight-training routines can be used to help you develop particular muscle groups that will improve your performance in your chosen sport. True enough, nothing improves your tennis game as much as playing tennis: specificity is the iron rule of modern sports training. Nonetheless, upper-body training will give you an extra edge in tennis, and developing your leg muscles will improve your swimming kick.

The basic principle of any sort of muscle development is that of overload: contracting a muscle group against added resistance. The way a muscle grows—according to some research, at least—is by splitting, longitudinally, under the strain placed on it, and "healing" after the workout by adding protein. Over a period of time, the overload placed on the muscles is increased a step at a time (the technique is called progressive resistance), and so the muscles continue to develop.

How to overload muscles

The three modes of exercise for developing muscles are isometric, isotonic, and isokinetic. In isometric exercises, you contract a muscle group without moving the joint to which the muscles are attached—for instance, pushing steadily against an immovable wall. These exercises build muscle, but the gain occurs mainly at the angle at which the muscle is exercised. Isotonic exercises, by contrast, contract a muscle through a range of motion—as you can do with movable weights. The virtue of isotonic exercises is that they build muscle through this full range of movement, unlike the limited buildup of isometric exercises. Isokinetic exercises also consist of contracting a muscle through a range of movement. But isokinetic exercises, which are performed on machines, use equipment designed to apply maximum stress to the muscles through the whole range of movement.

Isotonic exercises use both free weights and machines. Free weights are barbells (long bars with adjustable weights at each end) and dumbbells (shortened barbells, ordinarily used in pairs, one in each hand). The advantage of free weights is that they allow movement in any direction and so lend themselves to an enormous variety of exercise routines; and they are relatively inexpensive. Their disadvantage is that they do not isolate muscles as clearly as

Comparing Equipment

FREE WEIGHTS

Advantages:
- Relatively inexpensive (as little as 100 dollars for a basic set of barbells and dumbbells).
- Can be used at home.
- Versatile—you can work virtually any muscle from any angle.
- Can help improve balance and coordination.

Disadvantages:
- Adjusting weights can take time.
- Weights can slip or be dropped, causing injury.
- Safely lifting heavy weights requires a "spotter."

MACHINES

Advantages:
- Easy to use—machines guide your movements, and the weight load can be quickly adjusted.
- Muscles are isolated more efficiently than with free weights.
- Newer machines tax muscles consistently through their full range of movement.
- Safe—weights are held in place in stacks.

Disadvantages:
- Expensive and bulky; using them usually requires joining a health club.
- A variety of machines is necessary for a good workout.
- Some machines won't "fit" all body sizes.

machines do; and the stress that they provide is not nearly as uniform over the full range of motion as that provided by some machines.

Machines can isolate muscle groups very efficiently by maintaining your body in a particular position and by making you move a weight along a predetermined path. And isokinetic machines such as those by Nautilus are also designed to provide variable resistance through the full range of motion, so that as you move a limb, the resistance stays at or close to maximum. Nautilus machines, for example, provide variable resistance with a special cam device.

The most advanced isokinetic machines—many of them hydraulic or pneumatic—work on the principle of accommodating resistance: that is, the harder you push them, the harder they push back, ensuring the absolute maximum resistance at every point along a muscle's range of movement. Such machines can isolate muscles most efficiently and tax them to the maximum.

Weight training tips

A typical workout with weights includes a warm-up of five to ten minutes followed by an exercise routine that leaves the muscles thoroughly exhausted. Your exact exercise routine should be formulated with an exercise specialist in a gym, who will tell you just how to position yourself, how to lift so as to prevent strain or injury, which weights or machines to use, and how many repetitions and sets to do. If you continue to work out with a trainer or a friend, he or she will keep your routines interesting, give you emotional support, and help see to it, through proper "spotting" techniques, that you do not injure yourself.

A good exercise routine for overall fitness will work out different parts of the body. It will consist of about a dozen exercises—six for the upper body, six for the lower body. Above all, it will be scheduled so that you give each muscle a full day's rest before you exercise it again. If you exercise the same muscle two days in a row, it won't recuperate; it will become weaker, not stronger. Therefore, you should either exercise different muscles on successive days (upper body one day, lower body the next, for example) or space workouts at least two days apart.

Circuit training

Since conventional weight training mainly involves stop-and-start movements with resting between sets, it has virtually no aerobic benefits. But you can turn lifting weights into an aerobic activity if you adopt a form of training known as circuit training—though the benefits fall far short of those you can get from running or other aerobic workouts. Circuit weight training is done on exercise machines at a gym. It calls for performing several repetitions using a moderate weight in a continual fashion, moving from station to station or machine to machine with minimal rest in between. This allows you to work on legs, arms, hips, and back in quick succession, and gives your heart and lungs a workout.

Studies show that circuit training enhances aerobic capacity by, on average, about 5 percent; this will vary according to your fitness level and how intensely you train. The evidence suggests that if you've already achieved cardiorespiratory fitness through a conventional aerobics program, you can maintain it—though you can't increase it much—with circuit weight training.

The problem is that weight lifting can raise your heart rate quickly, out of proportion to the amount of oxygen your muscles are using. So the conventional

If you are interested in using machines at a gym or health club, make sure that there is a sufficient variety to give you a full workout. You should be able to perform four to six exercises for the lower body and six to eight for the upper body. Machines should be arranged to that you can work larger muscles before smaller ones, since this is the desirable sequence for the most efficient workout.

way of gauging how hard you are working your heart and lungs—taking your pulse—can be misleading during weight training. In fact, you may raise your blood pressure precipitously, especially if you lift heavy weights, hold your breath, or work only your upper body. This can be particularly dangerous for older people.

As with all exercise programs, when you start circuit training, take things easy—start with a weight you can comfortably heft for ten to twelve repetitions. Work up gradually to ten to fifteen repetitions for each machine along the circuit. But don't necessarily take things slow: try to get to the gym at a time when people aren't lined up at the machines. For aerobic benefits, it's essential to move along the circuit quickly, making two to three rounds of the circuit with no more than a fifteen- to thirty-second rest between machines.

Stretching

In addition to just making you feel good, stretching promotes flexibility—the ability to use muscles and joints through their full range of movement. Whether you are a cyclist, runner, tennis player, or walker, being flexible is an essential part of your overall fitness. Research has suggested that good muscle elasticity lends agility, a potential for greater speed, and—since it keeps your muscles from tightening up quickly—a reduced chance of injury to muscles, tendons, and ligaments. So stretching is an excellent activity to do before and after a workout.

At the same time, stretching is not just for joggers, ballet dancers, and athletes. More than anyone, sedentary people need the relief from muscle tension and stiffness that stretching provides.

There are three basic types of stretching: ballistic, static, and contract-relax. The one to avoid is ballistic stretching, in which you stretch to your limit and perform quick, repetitive, bouncing movements. This movement may do more harm than good, by actually shortening muscles and increasing the risk of muscle tears, soreness, and injury.

In contrast to ballistic stretching, static and contract-relax stretches are highly recommended because they are slow and gentle, never sudden or drastic. A static stretch is a gradual stretch through a muscle's full range of movement until you feel resistance. You hold the maximum position for three to thirty seconds, relax, then repeat this several times. In static toe touches, for instance, you roll down slowly toward your toes and hang in the down position without bouncing, then slowly roll up. It could hardly be easier, and it is much better for your muscles.

Ten tips for stretching

1. Stretching should always be preceded by a brief warm-up, such as jogging in place or riding a stationary bicycle. This increases blood flow and raises muscle temperature, both vital for muscle elasticity. Stretching while muscles are cold may sprain or tear them.

2. If there's any pain, stop. At worst, any discomfort should be mild and brief.

3. Try to stretch three or four times a week to maintain flexibility.

4. An optimal stretching session should last ten to twenty minutes, with each stretch held at least three seconds, gradually working up to holding the stretches for twenty to thirty seconds.

It's never too late to get flexible. In a study that compared the joint stiffness of a group of twenty young men (aged fifteen to nineteen) and a group of twenty elderly men (aged sixty-three to eighty-eight), it was found that both groups could reverse joint stiffness with equal ease. A number of other studies have shown that virtually anyone, regardless of age, can improve flexibility by stretching.

5. Begin by stretching major muscle groups, then stretch the specific muscles required for your sport or activity. A tennis player, for instance, needs to stretch muscles in the upper back, shoulders, neck, and calves.

6. Stretch within an hour before exercising or playing a sport in order to help prevent muscle strain and injury.

7. Don't bounce. Stretching should be gradual and relaxed.

8. Try to isolate the muscles you want to stretch. If other parts of the body move, there will be less benefit to that muscle and a greater risk of injury.

9. Stretch *after* vigorous exercise as well as before. This prevents muscles from tightening up quickly and lessens the chance of soreness.

10. Don't give up because you are less flexible than others. Flexibility varies from person to person. It may take months for you to notice an improvement—but if you keep stretching you will.

Testing Your Flexibility

The tests below will indicate how flexible you are. Remember, however, that everyone is flexible to a different degree, and that no one test can measure your overall flexibility. For instance, you may find that your hamstrings are tight, but your shoulders flexible. Still, by focusing on several major muscle groups—shoulders, hamstrings, lower back, and hip flexors—these tests will give you a general idea of how limber you are. There is some consensus that flexibility doesn't significantly decrease with age if stretching is done regularly.

Moreover, while girls tend to be more limber than boys, in adults the gap closes. And contrary to popular belief, arm or leg length usually has little effect on flexibility.

Jog in place (while pumping your arms) for a few minutes before doing these, since warming up will bring blood to the muscles and make it easier for them to lengthen. Don't push yourself. If it hurts, stop. Poor results may motivate you to begin to stretch regularly. Once you embark on a stretching program, chart your progress from time to time.

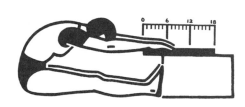

How Far You Reach (inches)	Rating
over 13	Excellent
9-13	Good
4-9	Fair
under 4	Poor

Sit and reach test: *This measures the flexibility of the hamstrings and muscles in the lower back. You need a box or step eight to twelve inches high, with a ruler taped to its top so that it extends six inches in front of it. After warming up, sit with your bare soles flat against the box, about four inches apart. Without bending your knees, gently reach as far forward as you can toward the box. Have a friend note how far your fingertips reach along the ruler. If you don't stretch regularly, you may not be able to reach the box. Compare your results with the chart above.*

Shoulder flexibility: *Raise your right arm and reach down your back as far as possible. At the same time, place your left arm behind your back and try to reach the fingers of your right hand. If your hands overlap, your arms and shoulders are fairly flexible. Repeat with arms reversed; most people are more flexible on one side than the other.*

Hip flexibility: *Lie on your back on a firm surface with your knees bent over the edge. Keeping one leg in place, pull the other knee to your chest and hold it firmly with both hands. Repeat with legs reversed. If you can't keep the lowered leg in place, or if you feel tightness or discomfort in the groin area, you should do hip-stretching exercises regularly.*

Stretching for Sports

The number of pulled muscles and strained backs after a weekend softball or volleyball game can be amazing. Unconditioned players often strain or tear tight muscles when a game calls for abrupt, forceful movements—during a hearty swing, an all-out jump or run, or a twisting stretch, for instance. You can reduce the risks of such routine injuries by starting a regular program of stretching muscles and by warming up properly before a game or workout. Pay special attention to stretching calf, groin, thigh, hamstring, and back muscles. These four basic stretches will get you started. (Hold each stretch for fifteen to twenty seconds; repeat it two or three times, then stretch the opposite arm or leg.)

Shoulders and upper back: *In a sitting or standing position, dangle a towel behind your back with one hand. With the other hand, reach behind and up as far as you comfortably, grasp the towel and pull down, holding the stretch; then pull up with the hand over your shoulder.*

Chest and arms: *Stand sideways and at arm's length from a wall or a doorframe. Reach out and slightly behind you, and place one palm on the wall (or grasp the doorframe). Keeping your hand in place, turn your body away slightly.*

Calves: *From a bit less than arm's length, lean towards a wall, supporting your weight on both hands. Keep your legs straight and your heels on the ground.*

Hamstrings: *Sit on a flat surface like a bench or table and extend a leg on it, keeping the foot flexed and knee straight. Lean over the leg, reaching toward the ankle until you feel a stretching sensation. Try to bend from your lower back, not your shoulders.*

Partner stretching

Another type of stretching—called proprioceptive neuromuscular facilitation, or PNF, stretching—is a bit more complicated. You first contract a muscle against a resistance, usually provided by another person, then relax into a static extension of the muscles, at which point your partner pushes the muscle back into a stretch that extends it farther than before. By bringing the opposing muscle into play, contract-relax stretching (as it is also known) is the best way to increase a muscle's flexibility.

Contract-relax stretching: *To stretch your hamstrings (the muscles behind the thighs), lie on your back with one leg extended upward. While your partner kneels under the raised leg, push it down against his shoulder for* five to ten seconds, which contracts the hamstring muscles. Then stretch the leg toward your head, which tenses the quadriceps (the opposing muscles) and relaxes the hamstrings.

Correcting Common Mistakes

Not all strengthening and stretching exercises performed in classes or in videotaped workouts are good for you. Some are just ineffective; others are hazardous because they are so often performed incorrectly. And even good exercises can be risky if you overdo them, especially if you're out of shape, have muscle or joint problems, or simply haven't warmed up. Realizing this shouldn't scare you off exercise. But it should tell you that you can't just walk into a fitness class or turn on an exercise tape, turn off your mind, and follow orders.

To help you take an active role in selecting exercises and deciding how to do them, here is a list of some of the most commonly done high-risk exercises, along with safer alternatives. The general categories of problems are: overflexing a joint (such as the knee or elbow), overarching the back or neck, sudden twisting or flexing, bouncing while stretching, and poor body alignment.

Double leg lifts can strain your lower back since raising both legs causes your back to arch. Leg scissors present similar risks.

Raised-leg crunches are a safe way to strengthen abdominal muscles. Keep one leg bent with the foot on the floor; raise the other leg straight up. Raise your upper back and reach toward the lifted ankle.

Locked-knee toe touches can over-stress the back, knees, and hamstring muscles, especially when done quickly with a bouncing movement.

Yoga plow can compress disks in your neck area. A shoulder stand (or bicycling position in which you rest on your shoulders and upper back) can do similar damage.

Fold-up stretch is a safer way to stretch your upper and lower back. Just sit back on your heels and press your chest to your thighs, reaching forward with your hands.

Alternating bent-leg sit-ups, in which you pump your legs and hold one straight out, put an asymmetric pull on the pelvis, which can strain the lower back. Also, in your effort to keep both legs off the floor, you may arch your back.

Knee rolls strengthen oblique abdominal muscles safely. Lie on your back, knees up toward your chest, arms out flat. Slowly lower your knees to the right side, keeping your lower back on the floor; hold for a few seconds. Slowly return to starting position. Repeat to the left.

Bent-knee hang-downs call for rolling down slowly with your knees slightly bent and abdominal muscles tight until you feel your hamstring and back muscles start to stretch. Hang over for ten to twenty seconds. Don't use force, don't try to reach the floor, and don't bounce.

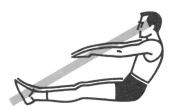

Straight-leg sit-ups *arch the back and strain it. Also, there's no need to sit up fully. The abdominal muscles work only during the first part of the movement. After that, the hip flexors take over, and the shift to these muscles can further arch the back.*

Bent-leg sit-ups *are the safest, most effective way to strengthen abdominal muscles. Keep your knees bent and come up only thirty to forty-five degrees. Always keep your lower back pressed to the ground. Cross your arms over your chest or behind your head.*

Arched push-ups *are sloppy push-ups in which you lower your hips and pelvis to the floor. Like any exercise that arches the back, these can injure the disks in the lower spine. And they do little for arm and shoulder muscles.*

Full squats, *like deep-knee bends or squat thrusts, greatly increase stress on the knees.*

Partial squats *strengthen the muscles on the front of your thigh. Squat no more than one-quarter way down: hold on to the wall for support as you extend one leg forward.*

Straight-back push-ups *give your shoulders and arms the maximum workout without straining your back. Hold your torso in a straight line and slowly lower your chest to the ground by bending your elbows.*

Donkey kicks, *in which you rapidly lift your leg as high as possible while on all fours, arch the back and also contort the shoulders and neck.*

Rear-thigh lifts *safely work your buttock muscles. Bring your thigh only parallel to your torso. Keep your back straight, and move your leg in a slow, controlled manner.*

Three-hundred-and-sixty-degree head rolls, *in which you vigorously roll your head around or bend your head back, may injure the disks in your neck.*

Swan stretches—*lying on your stomach and lifting your chest and legs—put your back in jeopardy.*

Prone arm/leg raises *strengthen back muscles safely. Lie face down with a pillow under your stomach and your arms above your head. Raise your right arm and left leg four to six inches for five seconds. Repeat, alternating sides.*

Side neck stretches *use the weight of your hand to pull your head gently to the side and then forward. Also pull it diagonally.*

SELF-CARE

Many of the common health problems that affect your well-being—from an aching back to a sunburn—often don't require expert medical attention, but can be prevented or treated effectively on your own. The chapters that follow spell out self-care measures for a wide variety of concerns, complaints, and disorders. Throughout, the focus is on what options are available and which remedies work (and which don't). The guidelines given, for the most part, are intended for individuals with no serious illness or underlying medical condition; if you have any special medical problems, you should consult your physician to find out what is right for you. The first nine chapters are organized around parts of the body; the other chapters deal with such areas of wellness as stress management, getting a good night's sleep, and how to stay healthy while traveling. In the final chapter, you will find information about choosing a doctor, diagnostic tests, medications, and other aspects of using the health care system to stay well.

Skin, Hair, and Nails

Caring for your skin, hair, and nails is more than a matter of cosmetic concern. Your skin is your largest organ. The skin—along with its glands—hair, and nails make up the body's integumentary system. The primary function of this system is to protect your body from outside elements, but it has many other functions as well.

Traditionally, skin has been thought of as just a passive envelope—a container for the more important parts of us. But it plays a more important role. The skin contains receptors for receiving the stimuli of touch, pain, pressure, and temperature, thus acting as the intermediary between the body and its external environment. It also is important in regulating body temperature, and helps prevent dehydration of the cells by deterring excessive loss of fluid.

The skin is also an essential part of the immune system. It prevents a number of harmful bacteria, viruses, and toxins from entering the body. For many years, scientists have known that the skin is laced with Langerhans cells, named for the medical student who discovered them in 1868. But not until 1978 did studies show that these cells have a major protective role. They actually "catch" microorganisms and other antigens and present them to the T-cells (a type of white blood cell), which then produce an appropriate immune response. Besides microorganisms, allergens of many kinds are also handled by the Langerhans cells. In fact, Langerhans cells may play a larger role. There is apparently some interchange between the lymphatic system and the skin and this interaction may prove to be a kind of staging ground for many immune responses—the field where the immune cells mount their strategies for dealing with all kinds of infections.

Thus, the intact human epidermis has an extremely able line of defense against harmful bacteria, fungi, viruses, and other would-be intruders. Unbroken skin is a tough terrain to penetrate, so an individual has almost no chance of catching a disease from a pay telephone, the handrails of a bus, a public toilet seat, or any of the objects people share daily. The one disease you might catch from an object is the common cold, which you can pick up by touching something that has been handled by a sick person. Even then you would have to infect yourself by touching your nose, eyes, or the inside of your mouth.

COMMON SKIN CONCERNS

Dry Skin

Skin cells need moisture to keep them smooth and flexible. Though the top layer of the skin is dead, the layers below supply it with moisture. When the cells lose too much water through evaporation, the skin becomes brittle and flakes. Dry skin is a common problem, particularly in the winter months when wind, cold, dry air, and dry indoor heat can parch your skin. Skin also becomes drier with age.

Relieving Itches

Hardly a day goes by that you don't get an itch. While there are dozens of remedies to relieve itchiness (known medically as pruritus), some of the most popular remedies are not only a waste of money, but can make the itch worse.

Itching is actually a minor form of pain transmitted by nerve fibers similar to those that transmit pain. The same stimuli that cause pain can, in a milder form, cause an itch or tickle. Though researchers don't know why, seeing someone scratching or even reading a vivid description of itching can also provoke the sensation.

Scratching an itch helps because it overstimulates the affected nerves with a more powerful sensation that overwhelms the itch. And some researchers think that scratching may stimulate the body's production of substances called endorphins, which can alleviate pain. Scratching can also remove an irritant causing an itch—but continued scratching can make an itch worse by causing secondary bacterial infection.

What does help an itch depends on what the itch comes from. Itching from dry, flaking skin can be relieved in some cases by using a moisturizer. Insect bites respond to an ice pack, a paste made from baking soda or meat tenderizer and water, cool water, or to an astringent such as witch hazel or rubbing alcohol. Creams or ointments with cortisone may effectively ease itching from a mild allergy, but they can aggravate an infection such as impetigo. Medications that contain benzocaine or other "-caine" anesthetics can cause secondary allergic reactions, and most physicians prescribe them sparingly. On the other hand, old standbys such as calamine lotion and cold compresses are safe, somewhat effective treatments for many kinds of itches. As a rule, you should use creams or ointments only on dry rashes. If the lesion is oozing, use lotion or liquids.

Does baby powder soothe skin?

Baby powder—while harmless for most infants—is unnecessary since its absorptive, lubricating, and odor-covering capabilities are small. Still, many parents like its fresh fragrance. If you choose to use it, be sure to shake it into your hand first so that there isn't a cloud of it around the baby's face. If your baby has respiratory problems, however, powder can be an irritant. A cream or lotion will be a much safer way to soothe baby's bottom.

How moisturizers can help

Moisturizers work just on the skin's surface to relieve the flaking, itching, and tightness that characterizes dry skin. Despite the claims in ads, however, these creams and lotions can't penetrate and "nourish" the deeper layers of the skin, slow the aging process, or reduce wrinkling.

Still, moisturizers can help relieve the symptoms of dry skin. There are two types of moisturizers:

Emollients (such as petroleum jelly, lanolin, and mineral oil). These work very much like your skin's natural oils; they form an oily barrier on the skin's surface that seals in moisture to some extent and thus blocks its evaporation.

Humectants (such as glycerin, sorbitol, lactic acid, and urea). These attract and hold water on your skin's surface.

Which moisturizer will work best for you? This depends on the moisturizer's ingredients and how chapped, dry, or sensitive your skin is. The simpler the moisturizer, the better. The more ingredients in a moisturizer—perfumes, colors, thickeners, emulsifiers—the greater the chance of a sensitivity reaction, especially if you have delicate skin. However, if you are prone to acne, overuse of any moisturizer may cause your skin to break out.

Other steps to relieve dry skin

In addition to using a moisturizer, you can take the following measures to prevent dry skin:

•If you bathe rather than shower, add a little bath oil to the water. (Be careful of the slippery bathtub that may result.)

•Limit bathing to ten or fifteen minutes a day, and favor a tepid shower over a hot bath. Excessive bathing, especially in hot water, and strong soaps wash away the natural oils that help trap water in the skin. Use a mild soap, and dilute it with water rather than lathering directly on your skin.

•Apply a moisturizer immediately after bathing or showering to take advantage of your skin's dampness. Apply a light rather than a heavy coating.

•In cold weather, wear gloves to limit the evaporation of moisture from your hands; cover your face with a scarf or ski mask.

Contact Dermatitis

Contact dermatitis is a term used to describe skin irritation, itching, and inflammation caused by a substance that comes in direct contact with the skin. One type of contact dermatitis, called irritant dermatitis, can occur when the skin is exposed to mild irritants—such as soaps or solvents—regularly over a long period of time, or to strong irritants, such as chemicals, that cause immediate damage to the skin. Irritant dermatitis can be particularly painful; it is characterized by red, dry, tight skin that may crack or blister.

Allergic dermatitis occurs when an individual is exposed to a substance that triggers an allergic reaction in the skin. Usually, you have no reaction when you are first exposed to the substance, but your skin becomes sensitized to it and subsequent exposures result in redness, itchiness, swelling, and often fluid-filled

Hot Tub Skin Safety
Hot tubs and heated pools that are not properly cleaned on a regular basis can be the source of a skin infection called folliculitis, an itchy red rash in and around the hair follicles, usually caused by the bacteria Pseudomonas. This rash can appear within a few hours or up to several days after exposure, often in the armpit, waist, or trunk area. The rash usually heals on its own. Over-the-counter steroid creams actually aggravate it. If you own a hot tub, be sure to clean it regularly; if you use one at your health club, ask the manager about the club's disinfectant and cleaning guidelines.

Cosmetic Claims

If you've had allergic reactions, if your skin is very dry or oily, or if you've ever suffered from acne or other skin eruptions, you probably choose your cosmetics carefully. But you may be surprised at what the claims on the label actually mean:

Fragrance free, unscented. If you've recently switched to a new moisturizer and are wondering why your face itches, suspect the fragrance first. Of all ingredients, fragrances are the most likely to produce contact dermatitis. If you prefer to avoid fragrances for any reason, remember to check the ingredients list of anything labeled "fragrance free." It can legally contain a small amount of fragrance to mask some unpleasant oily odor. Thousands of different fragrances are in use, and a single scent may contain hundreds of different substances, so it's nearly impossible to isolate the allergens, if any. Some fragrances are activated as irritants only when exposed to sunlight. Musk ambrette, a scent popular for after-shave lotions, is one such "photoallergen."

Hypoallergenic. Products with this label may be less likely to cause contact dermatitis, since "hypoallergenic" ("less allergenic") should signal some effort on the manufacturer's part to eliminate the more common irritating ingredients—but there's no guarantee. The Food and Drug Administration (FDA) has no list of allergens, nor rules governing use of this term.

Allergy-tested, dermatologist-tested. Presumably the manufacturer, or possibly a real dermatologist, will have tested the product on animals or people, but there's no FDA regulation about the use of this term. Products without the label might also have been tested for potential irritants. (It is not in cosmetic manufacturers best interests for their products to be causing rashes.)

Natural. On cosmetics, as on foods, this term is meaningless. Nearly all cosmetics (and many other products, including medications) contain preservatives to ward off bacteria and fungi. "Natural" cosmetics, the customer might assume, would necessarily be preservative-free. But this is often not the case. (A natural lotion with cucumber, milk, or other food products in it might need more preservatives, rather than less.) This may be a problem since, as is true with fragrances, some people are allergic to preservatives.

blisters on areas of the skin that came in contact with the substance. This explains why a product you have been using without problems suddenly causes a reaction. Substances that commonly trigger allergic dermatitis include cosmetics (including moisturizers), hair care products, colognes, and antiperspirants. However, only a small percentage of people (roughly 5 percent) develop adverse reactions to such products. (Poison ivy and poison oak are perhaps the most common cause of contact dermatitis. Unlike cosmetic products, however, a great many people develop a sensitivity to these plants. For more information on poison ivy and poison oak, see page 298.)

Most cases of contact dermatitis are mild and hence never get reported. While true allergic reactions to cosmetics may be few, many people may be irritated by such products as deodorant soaps, bath salts, hair removers, hair straighteners, permanent-wave solutions, and hair dyes containing ammonia. Even if you don't think of yourself as having sensitive skin, be cautious about products that promise to kill bacteria or dissolve, curl, or straighten hair. They may leave you itching and burning, so follow instructions carefully if you do decide to use them.

Caring for sensitive skin

If you tend to have allergic reactions to cosmetics, follow these tips:

•When you get cosmetics as gifts or decide to try a new line, use only one new product at a time. That way, if you have a bad reaction, you'll be able to nail the perpetrator at once.

•Don't skip the patch test whenever it's part of the instructions. If you're wary of any product, try your own patch test: put a dab of the new product on your forearm and cover it with a small bandage. Repeat daily for three or four days, and then wait another day or two. If you have no reaction, it's safe to use.

•If you do get a reaction and don't know what caused it, stop using all cosmetics. An over-the-counter hydrocortisone cream can help relieve itching or

---

Myth: Certain cosmetics can shrink your pores.

Fact: *Although some products can cause a temporary reduction in pore size, within a short period of time your skin will return to its normal state.*

Pore size is determined by heredity. People with oily skin have larger pores, and men tend to have larger pores than women. Acne can enlarge pores and squeezing pimples can permanently damage them. Since aging relaxes the skin, it tends to make pores bigger.

Astringents, fresheners, toners, bracers, and clarifiers are all designed to shrink or hide pores. The active ingredient in most of these is alcohol, which evaporates from the skin producing a cooling effect and thus a temporary tightening of the pores. Other ingredients with similar effects are witch hazel and salts.

Masks—soft ingredients that harden on the skin—are also designed to tighten pores. All of these products work temporarily—the effects last only about two hours.

Nickel Allergies

Ear piercing with a nickel-plated needle can trigger an allergy to that metal. One study showed that 95 percent of women with nickel allergy had pierced ears. Nickel is used in most costume jewelry, and is also a component of some silver, yellow gold, and platinum objects, as well as nearly all white gold.

Once sensitized to nickel, you're likely to be allergic for life. You may find that not only jewelry, but also some watchbands, snaps, and zippers can cause rashes, itching, soreness, skin discoloration, and swelling. And since perspiration easily dissolves nickel, these reactions tend to be worse in hot weather.

Here's a simple way to find out if you're allergic to nickel: tape a nickel to your skin on a hot day and see if your skin turns red. For a more definitive diagnosis, consult a dermatologist.

If you're allergic, avoid nickel-containing jewelry. Neither brass nor copper contains nickel. To test gold, silver, or platinum objects, you can use a nickel-detecting kit. The following may also help:

•Coat jewelry with clear nail polish; this may fend off allergic reactions for several hours—provided you aren't allergic to nail polish.

•Dust talc beneath a watchband or any other nickel-plated object that comes in contact with the skin. This may offer temporary protection.

•If you do have your ears pierced, make sure it's done with a stainless-steel needle. (Stainless-steel contains nickel, but it is so tightly "bound" chemically that it shouldn't cause a problem.) Use only earrings with stainless-steel posts for the first three weeks; or use nickel-free gold studs.

rash. Resume cosmetic use only after doing a series of patch tests, trying one product at a time until you find the culprit. If the irritation lasts more than ten days or is severe, see a physician.

•Remember that even a product you've used for years can suddenly turn into an irritant. The "new and improved" version of an old standby may contain an irritating surprise for your skin.

•Despite the price, expensive cosmetics are no more or less likely to cause irritation than others.

Varicose Veins

Varicose veins occur when the tiny valves that regulate blood circulation in the legs malfunction. Doctors aren't sure why some people and not others are predisposed to this condition. Hereditary and, apparently, hormonal factors are at work: "varicosities" run in families, and of the more than forty million Americans affected, women outnumber men four to one.

Causes of varicose veins

Prolonged standing or inactivity can cause varicose veins in people genetically inclined to develop them. Strain in the abdominal region—from repeated heavy lifting, pregnancy, or constipation, can also be a cause. Age is also an important factor. As the skin ages it becomes less elastic and therefore cannot support veins as firmly.

When you are standing, the heart pumps blood through the arteries to the legs with assistance from gravity. But muscle contractions are required to recirculate blood against gravity up through the veins—which lie just under the skin as well as deep in the legs—back to the heart. When the valves of the perforating veins do not work efficiently, blood accumulates, distending veins into a network of lumps that are visible just underneath the skin.

Preventing varicose veins

If you're prone to varicose veins, you may be able to head them off by avoiding prolonged sitting or standing in one position. Get up from your desk periodically and take a short walk. When standing, be sure to move around. Walking for exercise can also help control a mild case of varicose veins. You can also try wearing elastic support stockings (with your doctor's consent). Don't wear tight shoes or garters or other constricting clothing.

Medical intervention

In severe cases, varicose veins may cause swollen ankles, itching calves, and leg pain. Sensitive and prominent veins can be unsightly and uncomfortable. Fortunately, doctors can remove them safely and permanently. One surgical method is called stripping, whereby distended veins are cut out or tied off. A second option, sclerosing, calls for the injection of a solution that hardens the affected veins and blocks the blood flow. The blocked veins form a kind of scar tissue and are eventually absorbed. In both instances, blood reroutes itself through veins that lie deeper in the skin.

Warts

Warts are caused by strains of human papilloma virus that can enter the skin through tiny breaks. Ordinary warts are slightly contagious; they spread most commonly from one location to another—for example, from finger to finger—on an infected person, rather than from person to person. (The exceptions are anal and genital warts, which are highly contagious and may contribute to the development of penile and cervical cancers. Warts on the larynx can also be dangerous. These three types always require medical attention.)

Warts never spread from one species to another: that old story about toads causing warts in people is just a myth. Warts are most common among children and young adults. Of the several million people who seek treatment for warts each year, about 70 percent are under forty.

Warts can occur anywhere on the body, but they take on a different appearance depending on where they grow. On the face and tops of hands, they protrude as dry growths with a horny surface. On pressure areas such as the palms and soles, they grow inward. One of the most painful types is the plantar wart, a light-colored, flat growth on the sole of the foot, that may be spread through swimming pools or showers. Shower shoes can keep you from spreading or exposing yourself to such a wart.

Oddly enough, up to 80 percent of all warts (but not genital or anal warts) disappear by themselves, typically within two years, at least in children. This vanishing act has bred all kinds of legends and given credence to hundreds of home remedies. Huckleberry Finn recommended handling dead cats as a treatment for warts, and Tom Sawyer believed that spunk-water (stagnant water in an old tree stump) could cure warts, at least if you approached the stump backwards at midnight and recited the proper spell. Unfortunately, warts that have gone away (a process known as "spontaneous remission") can also return just as mysteriously.

Treating warts

Drugstores sell salicylic acid products for the removal of warts, and if you decide to try one of these be sure to protect the surrounding skin. Do not use these remedies on genital or anal warts. Never cut a wart yourself, as there is a risk of bleeding, infection, and scarring. If you want a wart removed, it's best to see a physician. While there's no agent known to kill the virus, surgical and other kinds of removal, such as freezing and laser treatment, are available and are usually successful. If you notice a growth and aren't sure whether it's a wart or not, seek medical advice.

Acne

Acne, bane of teenagers, also strikes adults. One study indicates that even in their fifties, 6 percent of men and 8 percent of women are affected by it.

What causes acne

Acne's causes at any age aren't completely understood. As in adolescence, acne flare-ups in adults are linked to various kinds of hormonal changes—for women, the hormonal fluctuations that accompany menstruation appear to be a factor. But contrary to conventional wisdom, you don't bring acne on yourself. It isn't a sign of poor health or the result of dietary indiscretions. Nor is it caused by masturbation or constipation.

Adult acne differs from the teenage variety. Teenagers are likely to get acne on the back, face, chest, and upper arms; in adults the outbreak is usually confined to the face. And in adult men acne is likely to be more serious. In both adult and adolescent acne the oil glands associated with the pores from which face, chest, and back hairs emerge secrete too much sebum, the waxy lubricant that acts to retain moisture. Excess sebum clogs the pores and, if it remains beneath the skin, results in whiteheads. Blackheads occur if the plugs of sebum protrude above the skin. Angry red pimples appear if excess secretions invade and inflame surrounding tissue. The more extensive the inflammation, the more likely it will form abscesses and leave permanent scars and pits.

Adults can watch out for specific conditions that seem to aggravate acne: the use of oil-based cosmetics, for example, which block sebum from reaching the skin's surface naturally. The same goes for sweaty exercise in tight-fitting, nonabsorbent clothes or sweatbands, since sweating increases oil production. There is no scientific proof that chocolate, nuts, or colas can trigger flare-ups; but if they seem to for you, there's no harm in avoiding them. Flare-ups may also be related to emotional upset and too little rest—at least in some people.

Treatment and prevention

Acne can't be cured, but you can take steps to keep symptoms under control until they go away:

•Wash daily, but not too roughly or too often, with ordinary soap and water. Don't waste money on medicated cleansers (the medication just rinses away) or granular face "scrubs" (a washcloth does the same job). Facial saunas (actually facial steam baths) may aggravate acne.

•Use a drying lotion or cream. The most effective of these over-the-counter preparations contain benzoyl peroxide.

•Wear your hair off your face to keep your complexion free of scalp oils, and avoid greasy hair dressings.

•Use water-based makeup (or skip cosmetics entirely, if acne is severe). Don't overdo moisturizing.

•Avoid prolonged exposure to sunlight and ultraviolet lamps. These sometimes work to dry up acne, but can cause long-term skin damage, which can result in skin cancer, and thus are ill-advised.

•Don't pick at your face. Squeezing and picking increase inflammation and the risks of pitting and scarring. Ask your doctor if you can use a blackhead extractor (this device is available at most drugstores). If so, soften the area with hot wet compresses for about ten minutes first. Make sure your hands and the extractor are very clean.

•Severe outbreaks need a doctor's attention. Doctors can prescribe a wide variety of therapies, including various lotions and ointments, antibiotics (taken orally or applied to the skin), and a drug called tretinoin, used only in very resistant cases. (Tretinoin cannot be used by pregnant women, or those intending to become pregnant.)

Sun Protection

Suntans are deceptive. People used to believe that a tan looked good and gave the impression of good health, but more and more people are getting the message that the sun causes skin cancer and premature aging of the skin. Exposing your unprotected body to anything but minimal amounts of direct sunlight is undeniably unhealthy, if not downright hazardous. The short-term effects of sunning yourself may be the pain and discomfort of a sunburn. In the long term the result is premature aging of the skin: the sun slowly but surely destroys the elastic fibers that keep the skin taut and young-looking, leaving it dry and wrinkled.

Myth: Tanning booths give you a safer tan.

Fact: *Tanning salons— which promise a safe tan without a burn—pose a host of known and suspected hazards.*

Tanning booths use predominantly UVA radiation, which is less likely to cause an immediate burn, than the shorter-wavelength UVB radiation. But UVA is far from safe. It penetrates into the skin more deeply and will prematurely age the skin; it may damage blood vessels and even inhibit immune reactions in the skin. It also sensitizes the skin so that sunlight will be more likely to cause skin cancers. A session under a UVA lamp can cause a severe adverse reaction if you're taking antibiotics, tranquilizers, antihistamines, birth-control pills, or oral diabetes medication.

UVA rays also increase the risk of cataracts and retinal damage. Federal guidelines require protective goggles to be issued at tanning salons, but many times their importance isn't sufficiently stressed. Keeping your eyes closed is not enough.

Skin cancer

A far more serious danger from tanning is an increased risk of skin cancer, particularly basal cell carcinoma and malignant melanoma. The skin changes that result in cancer develop cumulatively and irreversibly in an individual over the years, and so may take decades to produce a malignancy. And Americans are developing skin cancer at ever-younger ages because of increasing amounts of time spent in the sun.

Skin cancer is the most common of all cancers. Basal cell carcinoma is the most prevalent type, striking one out of every eight Americans, including people in their twenties and thirties, women as well as men, with four hundred thousand new cases reported annually. Malignant melanoma, once rare, has increased five- to sixfold worldwide over the past four decades, and some researchers expect it to double again in the 1990s. Once melanoma was a disease of the aging; now half of all those who develop it are between the ages of fifteen and fifty.

But most skin cancer is curable, when treated early. While basal cell carcinoma can be disfiguring, malignant melanoma is potentially lethal, especially if the disease is allowed to progress. Thus, for both types, prevention and early detection are vital.

Preventing skin cancer

Whatever your age, one of the major steps you can take to prevent all forms of skin cancer is to reduce direct exposure to sunlight: use adequate sunscreens and wear protective clothing. This is particularly important if you have: fair skin and hair; light-colored eyes; a high incidence of moles; a tendency to burn rather than tan; a family history of skin cancer; an outdoor job; or, for any reason, spend long periods in the sun. People with these characteristics are at high risk for developing skin cancers.

Steps to early detection

Self-examination is the key to early detection. It isn't difficult—certainly no harder than the examination for breast cancer many women have learned to do. And it is vital; in the most successfully treated cases of malignant melanoma, for example, the patients themselves brought the melanoma to their doctors' attention early on. Pay special attention to areas that are habitually exposed to sunlight: your face, neck, and hands. Don't forget your scalp and the back of your ears. Use a mirror to check areas you can't easily see. Self-examination should be performed once a month (see page 441). And don't forgo self-examination even if you habitually stay out of the sun. While it's important to avoid excess sun exposure at any age, you cannot undo damage from past exposure, which is cumulative, starting in childhood. In fact, some experts believe that by age twenty the average American has already received 80 percent of the damaging ultraviolet rays that may lead to cancer in later years. In addition to self-examination, ask your doctor to include a total skin exam as part of your routine checkup. When examining your skin, be alert for the following signs; if you have any of them, see a physician at once.

Common signs of basal cell carcinoma

•A sore that doesn't heal. Have it checked if it hasn't healed after three weeks and it crusts, bleeds, or oozes.

•A persistent reddish patch. It may be painful, or crust and itch; or it may not bother you at all.

•A smooth bump indented in the middle. The borders will be rolled, and as it grows you may notice blood vessels on the surface.

•A shiny, waxy, scar-like spot. It may be yellow or white with irregular borders.

Common signs of malignant melanoma

•A mole that begins to enlarge, thicken, or change color. Some 70 percent of early-state lesions are identified because of recent enlargement, mottled color, irregular borders, or irregular surfaces.

•A mole that bleeds or ulcerates.

•A mole that has irregular rather than round borders.

•A mole with irregular pigmentation—some portions light colored, others almost black.

Treatment of skin cancer

When caught in time, basal cell carcinoma can often be removed by a doctor on an outpatient basis leaving only a minor scar. Once malignant melanoma is detected, the treatment is prompt surgical removal. If done in the early stages, the five-year survival rate from melanoma is 95 percent; the ten-year rate, 90 percent. If done during a later stage, when a tumor has begun to invade the surrounding tissues or other areas of the body, the survival rate drops sharply.

Is there such thing as a safe tan?

A tan is damaging to your skin, whether you tan quickly or accumulate it slowly over a period of weeks. Though a suntan may protect you against sunburn, it does not protect you against accumulated radiation. All exposure to ultraviolet light is cumulative. Thus, the sun exposure you get at age ten can affect you adversely at age thirty-five.

Exposure to the sun thickens the skin while encouraging the production of melanin, a pigment that absorbs UV rays. This is the skin's defense against the sun. Blacks and other dark-skinned people probably don't need any sort of sunscreen because their high concentration of melanin protects them from UV rays. They seldom develop skin cancer and are less susceptible to sun-induced wrinkling. But in people who are not dark-skinned to begin with, repeated exposure to UV rays can result in the destruction of elastic fibers in the skin, which causes it to sag and wrinkle, and damages blood vessels. Even though people who tan easily appear to be less susceptible to skin cancer, they still need protection against ultraviolet rays.

Chronic exposure to the sun reduces the efficiency of the Langerhans cells in the skin, which play a role in the skin's immune-protecting activities. Researchers are investigating the relationship between this phenomenon and skin cancer.

Fortunately, protection is available in the form of a variety of over-the-counter sunscreen preparations. These medications minimize the damage inflicted on the skin by blocking some or most of the sun's ultraviolet rays, which cause both suntan and sunburn.

Defining SPF

Sunscreens are labeled with a Sun Protection Factor (SPF) number. This number tells you the relative length of time you can stay in the sun before you burn, compared to using no sunscreen. A product with an SPF of 8, for example, would allow you to remain in the sun without burning eight times longer, on average, than if you didn't apply sunscreen. Thus, if you're fair-skinned and would normally burn in ten minutes, a screen with SPF 8 would allow you eighty minutes before burning.

Not all sunscreens with the same SPF offer the same protection, however. Although it is a fairly reliable indicator, the SPF pertains only to ultraviolet B (UVB) rays—those mainly responsible for sunburn and skin cancer. The most commonly used ingredients in sunscreens—PABA (para-aminobenzoic acid) derivatives such as padimate O—effectively absorb UVB rays, but let through the longer-wavelength ultraviolet A (UVA) rays, which researchers once thought would help you tan without harming the skin. Now it appears that UVA rays can damage the skin's connective tissue, leading to premature aging, as well as playing a role in causing skin cancer. There is, however, no rating system to indicate the degree of UVA protection, so two screens with the same SPF can offer very different protection against UVA rays.

Products containing a group of chemical compounds, known as dibenzoyl-methanes, offer the fullest protection against UVA rays. At this time, the Food and Drug Administration (FDA) has approved only one product that contains one of these chemicals. Called Photoplex, it also contains padimate O to block UVB, thus offering protection against the full UV spectrum. It has an SPF of 15.

Sunproof Clothing

Dressing properly for summer is a concern for people who are sensitive to the sun, have malignant or premalignant skin tumors, or are taking medication that is affected by sunlight. Yet even if you don't fall into one of these categories but plan to spend a day in the sun, you might consider the following factors affecting the amount of ultraviolet radiation that penetrates fabric:

Tightness of weave. This is the most important factor. Hold a garment up to a light bulb—if it allows lots of light through, it's loosely woven and probably inadequate to guard you against ultraviolet radiation.

Color and thickness of the material. Dyed fabric usually blocks more ultraviolet rays than undyed material. And the thicker the fabric, the better the protection.

In studying these criteria, researchers at Dryburn Hospital in Durham, England, found that tightly woven cottons are better protectors against the sun than nylon/polyester knits. Specifically, they showed that tightly woven blue denim, dark needlecords, and dark cotton prints are among the most protective options. They have a sun protection factor, or SPF, of more than 1,000. That means that if you wear such tightly woven cottons you can stay in the sun 1,000 times as long as you could with unprotected bare skin before you would burn. The researchers found that blue denim, for instance, allowed through only 0.1 percent of ultraviolet B rays (the kind that is most responsible for sunburn), compared to the 24 percent that penetrated a loosely knitted nylon jersey.

Sunshine and Kids

The best time to defend against skin damage from the sun is during childhood, since the damage accumulates year after year and can't be undone. The following tips will help you protect your children:

•Cover up your children with long pants, a long-sleeved shirt, and a hat; especially if they have fair skin, blond or red hair, and light eyes.

•Keep infants and toddlers out of the sun as much as possible. Use a baby carriage with a hood or a stroller with a canopy or with an umbrella attachment.

•Try to schedule your children's outdoor activities in the early morning or later afternoon, since the sun's rays are most intense from 10 A.M. to 3 P.M.

•If your child is on medication, consult with your doctor or pharmacist to avoid possible adverse reactions to sunlight.

•Use a sunscreen with a SPF of 15 or higher. The regular use of a screen with SPF 15 during the first eighteen years of a child's life might reduce the lifetime risk of skin cancer by a whopping 78 percent. For young children choose a milky lotion or cream, since this is less irritating than a clear solution, which may contain alcohol. Test the screen on the underside of the child's forearm to see if any irritation occurs. Apply the screen at least thirty minutes before the child goes into the sun to give it time to soak in, and reapply frequently; be careful around the child's eyes.

Of the common ingredients in sunscreen, compounds called benzophenones (such as oxybenzone) offer some protection against UVA rays, but less than Photoplex. Benzophenones are used together with anti-UVB chemicals, such as a PABA derivative. Look for these name on the list of ingredients.

Whatever sunscreen you use, however, it is important to apply it liberally. Studies have shown that people tend to apply only about half the amount of sunscreen that the FDA uses to determine SPF. Thus SPF 15 could drop, in effect, to SPF 8. So if you're fair-skinned and will be outside all day, either use a high-protection sunscreen (SPF 30 or more) or better yet, plan to apply a lower SPF sunscreen at frequent intervals. According to the American Academy of Dermatology, however, some of the higher SPF formulas may cause skin irritation because their chemicals are so concentrated.

Physical blocks vs. chemical sunscreens

Creams, lotions, and oils that are SPF rated are referred to as chemical sunscreens because they contain chemicals that screen out UV rays. They are easy to apply and aren't very visible on the skin. Even though screens with an SPF above 15 are sometimes referred to as sun blocks, they still allow some UV wavelengths to pass. The only true sun blocks are the opaque creams or pastes containing zinc oxide or titanium dioxide. Properly applied, they prevent any light from reaching the skin; thus they carry no SPF rating. They are good for the nose, lips, or other sensitive areas, but they can be messy to use and unattractive. However, many brands come in a wide variety of colors (versus the original white), which may appeal to some people, particularly children and teenagers. In addition, many high-SPF chemical screens now contain a physical block, such as zinc oxide.

How to select and use a sunscreen

•Choose a screen with SPF 15. If you're fair-skinned and will be outdoors for long hours, use one with an even higher SPF. Look for the seal of approval from the

Protecting Your Lips
Your lips are one of the most sun-sensitive parts of your body. Here's a few tips geared specifically toward protecting them.

•Sun-blockers—such as zinc oxide—offer good protection for sensitive areas such as lips, but can be messy and unattractive.

•Lip sunscreens in stick form are most convenient to use, but—as they are waxy or greasy—they are generally short lasting. According to one study, the waxier or greasier a sunscreen feels on the lips, the greater the tendency to lick it off. A liquid or gel that is fully absorbed and cannot be felt on the lips will last longest.

•Colored lipstick offers partial protection against the sun for women; for full blockage, a sunscreen should be applied first. Ordinary lip lubricant such as petroleum jelly provides no protection.

Skin Cancer Foundation which tests sunscreens with SPF 15 or higher for safety and effectiveness in blocking UVB. About eighty brands now carry the seal, however, some new products may not have applied for the seal as yet.

•For greatest protection against both UVA and UVB, use Photoplex. Otherwise, look for a "broad spectrum" sunscreen which contains two or more ultraviolet absorbing ingredients. Many ingredient combinations work in concert to block a broader range of light waves and also wash off less easily.

•Apply the screen at least thirty to forty-five minutes before exposure to the sun. Studies show that this allows it to penetrate the skin for optimal effectiveness.

•Apply frequently and generously. A single application won't remain potent for long periods.

•Take into account the time of day and your location. UV rays are strongest between 10 A.M. and 3 P.M., so adjust your sunscreen strength and reapplication schedule accordingly. Intensity of the rays also increases the closer you are to the equator and the higher the altitude. If you're fair-skinned, you may need to wear protective clothing (see box on page 284), a hat, and a physical sunscreen on your nose and lips.

•If you're taking medication, ask your doctor or pharmacist about possible reactions to sunlight and interactions with sunscreens.

Just because your skin isn't red while you're outdoors doesn't mean you're not getting burned. A sunburn is most evident six to twenty-four hours after exposure.

Do you need a waterproof screen?

If you spend a lot of time going in and out of the water, or if you are participating in activities outdoors that might cause you to perspire heavily, you may want to use a sunscreen that offers protection in the water. By law, products labeled "water-resistant" must protect at their SPF level even after you spend forty minutes in the water. "Waterproof" screens must do so even after eighty minutes in water. It's a good idea to use water-resistant or waterproof screens on children, since it may not be easy to reapply sunscreen to their skins after every swim.

Treating a sunburn

The best thing you can do for a sunburn is to soak the affected area for fifteen minutes in cold water (not ice water), or apply cold compresses—the same treatment that applies to all first-degree burns, which damage only the outermost layer of the skin. This provides some immediate relief from the pain, conducts heat from the skin, and lessens the swelling. If you are sunburned all over your body, try an oatmeal bath. Scatter a cup of dry instant oatmeal in a tub of cool water and soak for awhile. The oatmeal soothes the skin and reduces inflammation. (Cornstarch works equally as well.)

Greasy substances such as baby oil or after-sun creams seal in heat. Cooling lotions containing menthol or camphor may provide temporary relief by affecting the nerve endings and constricting superficial blood vessels in the skin, but they can be quite irritating and cause allergic reactions, especially in children. If the burn is very painful, you may want to try a first-aid spray containing benzocaine, a topical anesthetic that also acts on the nerve endings in the skin. Using benzocaine, however, may sensitize the skin and lead to an allergic reaction upon subsequent applications of other medications in the "-caine" family. Do not use other "-caine" anesthetics for sunburn: they are readily absorbed into the bloodstream if the skin is broken and may cause immediate toxic or allergic reactions.

Aging Skin

Your skin changes as you grow older. With age, the skin gradually loses its elasticity and becomes thinner and dryer. Because of the effect of gravity, skin may begin to sag. When these developments affect facial skin, causing wrinkles and bags under the eyes, many people turn to moisturizers, skin compounds, and anti-aging formulas.

Do anti-aging formulas work?

Unfortunately, there is no such thing as youth in a bottle. Advertisements for skin care products may claim that they can prevent or reverse the effects of aging, but it has never been scientifically proven that they have any beneficial effect. While a moisturizer can help make the skin feel smooth, temporarily prevent moisture loss from the cells, and decrease the fine lines caused by dryness, no cream or lotion sold at the makeup counter—not even the ones that contain such exotic ingredients as grape seed or geranium oil, squalene (shark liver oil), collagen, and even human placental protein—can delay or reverse the effects of aging on the skin.

Pros and cons of Retin-A

There is one prescription drug, however, that seems to be slightly effective at erasing tiny wrinkles. The vitamin A derivative tretinoin, originally approved by the Food and Drug Administration (FDA) to treat severe acne, was found to smooth out some wrinkles and reduce blotchiness in a highly publicized 1988 study. Thirty subjects (aged thirty-five to seventy) applied tretinoin—marketed as Retin-A—to one arm and a placebo cream to the other once a day. After four months all of the treated arms had fewer fine wrinkles and rosier skin. Fifteen of the subjects also applied the drug to their faces, and the results were similar though somewhat less significant. In addition, there was some suggestion that tretinoin may retard certain potentially cancerous skin growths. Three out of four participants in the study with premalignant skin areas showed a regression of these conditions. Researchers are not sure why tretinoin works, but the treated skin apparently grew new tissue to replace sun-damaged cells.

Still, though, most of the improvement was in fine wrinkling and general complexion, with little change in deep, coarse wrinkles after four months. The effect was less evident on the face because wrinkles there tend to be deeper than those on the arm. In addition, since the study was small and short-term, it's not clear if over time more and more wrinkles smooth out, or if in time improvements cease or even reverse. Nor is it clear what happens if you stop using the product.

In almost all of the participants, tretinoin caused skin inflammation lasting two weeks to several months. Three people had to quit the study because of the severity of this side effect, and eleven had to apply a potent steroid cream to reduce the irritation. In other words, for the sake of eventual minor skin improvements, you may have to walk around with a red, swollen, peeling face for a month or more. Irritation may be worse if treatment isn't carefully supervised.

If after weighing the pros and cons you decide to go ahead and try tretinoin, remember that it is available by prescription only. "Anti-wrinkle" creams containing other forms of vitamin A won't have the same effect. (Vitamin A capsules taken orally won't work either, and can be toxic in large doses.) In

Collagen: Not a Miracle

Collagen, a type of protein, is the chief component of skin and connective tissue. Wherever it occurs it takes on the most efficient configuration, depending on its function. For example, in the tendons, which connect muscles to bones, collagen fibers arrange themselves in bundles to permit twisting and flexing, while in the skin the fibers are arranged in a flat crisscross pattern.

Some dermatologists promote collagen injections for minimizing scars and wrinkles. Performed carefully, the treatment is reasonably safe but quite expensive, and no one should expect long-lasting results. The injected collagen will be broken down by enzymes in about two years.

As an additive to cosmetics—which is one of its most common uses today—collagen is useless. Though it may come at a premium price, collagen cream is no better than any other kind. You cannot absorb the protein through your skin.

Minimizing Bags Under the Eyes

"Bags" under the eyes occur because fluid tends to accumulate there, where the skin is thinner than anywhere else on the body. With advancing age (and a little help from heredity) this puffiness may become more prominent or even permanent, since your skin gradually loses its elasticity and may begin to sag.

Other factors may be involved as well. In some people permanent bags may be due to a hereditary condition in which the fat that cushions the eyeball protrudes through weakened muscles. Certain medications, such as cortisone, and allergic reactions (to cosmetics, smoking, or air pollution, for instance) may aggravate matters. Generally, when your eyes are tired or irritated, accumulated fluids may make eyes puffy. Thyroid, kidney, or heart disease can all increase fluid retention, which may be particularly noticeable around the eyes. Not to be overlooked is the force of gravity: when you

sleep or otherwise lie flat for a while, extra fluid may pool in the upper and lower lids.

Besides avoiding cosmetics that worsen the problem, there isn't much you can do about the puffiness. Sleeping with your head elevated on an extra pillow may be enough to allow gravity to drain the eye area. In severe cases the sagging tissue or excess fat under the eyes can be removed surgically. The operation is frequently performed on an outpatient basis.

Dark circles under the eyes also tend to be a family trait and to worsen with age. They seldom are a symptom of an underlying medical problem. What appears as a bluish-black tint is the blood passing through veins just below the surface of the skin. These "rings" may be darker when your eyes are tired, and during menstruation or pregnancy. If you wish, you can cover dark circles with special cosmetic concealers or regular makeup bases.

addition, it is known that retinoic acid can cause severe congenital defects when given to pregnant animals. Since there have been no human studies on the absorption of tretinoin through the skin, don't use the drug if you are or may become pregnant during the treatment.

The best defense against aging skin

Prevention is the key, and the best preventive measure you can take is to stay out of the sun. According to estimates from dermatologists, as much as 70 percent of skin damage comes from the sun. This damage is cumulative, starting in youth. Thus much of what is considered an inevitable part of aging is preventable or modifiable. Avoid long periods in the sun; whenever you're in the sun, wear a potent sunscreen.

Soaps

Soap is simply a combination of fats and alkalis that lathers in water and cleanses dirt and oils from your skin. Manufacturers may add a wide range of ingredients to soaps—perfumes, deodorizers, lotions, extra fats, and even vitamins—and may claim that their soaps will moisturize, soften, or otherwise transform your skin. But the facts are:

•Any soap will get you clean.

•All soaps by their chemical nature may irritate the skin and remove natural oils. One way to soothe this irritation is to use a moisturizer after washing your hands or bathing.

•Deodorant soaps kill bacteria and cut down on body odor, but the antiseptics they contain may also cause dry skin or rashes as well as destroy helpful bacteria. This can increase the risk of skin infection, especially in the feet and under the arms. You are better off bathing frequently with some other kind of soap.

•Perfumed soap, though pleasant to use, may also irritate the skin. Regular perfume will last longer and smell better than the perfume in soap.

Personal soaps may cost anywhere from a few cents a bar to eight or nine dollars for a brand name in a beautiful package. The cleansing power, however, is the same, and the less expensive bar may actually contain fewer additives.

Your own preference is the best guide. If you like and can afford the soap you are presently using, stick with it, whether it is the generic bar from the supermarket or the eight dollar kind with the heavenly perfume. Either one will get you clean. Neither will make you beautiful, successful, or moist.

Bar vs. liquid

Should you worry about contamination from a bar of soap? Studies of bacterial contamination, conducted during the 1980s, showed that bar soaps, even those containing germicides, swarmed with microorganisms after a week's use in a public washroom. But these studies didn't examine whether soap actually transmits germs to humans, let alone whether disease resulted, and a newer study suggests that a sloppy bar of soap may not be as threatening as it looks. When volunteers washed with contaminated soap bars (softened and then inoculated with two highly infectious strains of bacteria), researchers found that no detectable levels of the bacteria were actually transferred to the volunteers' hands. However, this study was small, the actual number of bacteria on sludgy soap may be higher than that used here, and only two strains of bacteria were measured.

Thus, the debate is far from over. Both the newer study and the old studies found that liquid soap dispensed from plastic containers remained uncontaminated. Liquid soap dispensers are certainly neater, and you may prefer them, as do most physicians. But recommendations to avoid bar soap on health grounds may be premature. It's important to remember that potentially harmful microorganisms exist on most surfaces, including money, doorknobs, and the hands you shake every day.

To prevent the spread of disease, you're obviously better off washing your hands often (and rinsing well)—even with the sloppy looking bar you may find in a washroom—than leaving them unwashed.

Antiperspirants and Deodorants

Almost one hundred years ago the first commercial product to control body odor, Mum, was introduced on the market. Since then two kinds of preparations designed to minimize underarm sweating and odor have evolved—antiperspirants and deodorants. The first inhibit sweating; the second inhibit the bacteria that cause odor, or simply mask the smell. More recently, combination antiperspirant/deodorants—whether creams, roll-ons, sticks, or aerosols—have become prevalent on drugstore shelves.

Because antiperspirants affect the functioning of the body, the Food and Drug Administration (FDA) considers them drugs. Virtually all over-the-counter brands

Is heavy sweating a dangerous sign?

If you are in good health, chronic heavy sweating is nothing to worry about.

Most sedentary people sweat anywhere from a negligible amount to two quarts a day, but heat and physical exertion can increase this output to as much as five to ten quarts. Age, race, sex, conditioning, and sensitivity to heat also affect the amount an individual sweats.

A few people suffer from hyperhidrosis (probably a genetic condition), perspiring so profusely that their clothing can become drenched in fifteen minutes. It is generally treated with topical antiperspirants. Sweat glands can also be removed, but because of subsequent scar formation such surgery is rarely recommended.

If you normally do not sweat much but suddenly start to do so, it may be due to fever and illness, or, in women, the onset of menopause.

Sweating can be dangerous if it leads to dehydration. Drink plenty of fluids—whether or not you are thirsty—before, during, and after exercise.

sold today contain an aluminum compound as their active ingredient. No antiperspirant can stop sweating completely. As for body odor, bathing is by far the best way to control and prevent it.

The effectiveness of specific antiperspirants varies from person to person. It also depends in large part on a product's form—such as roll-on or spray—as much as on the brand, active ingredient, and/or formula. The reduction in sweating afforded by antiperspirants ranges from about 15 to 50 percent. Because they are applied directly to the skin and are rubbed in, sticks, roll-ons, and creams generally provide more protection than aerosols. Aerosols that spray on wet tend to be least effective.

Not only are aerosol antiperspirants less effective, they also have aroused safety concerns. The problem is the fine mist hangs in the air near the mouth and nose when you spray an aerosol: some of it is inhaled. For this reason, many ingredients that are allowed in roll-ons and other forms aren't permitted in aerosols. Zirconium, for instance, was banned in aerosols by the FDA because it caused lung tumors in laboratory animals. Aluminum chlorohydrate is the only aluminum compound approved by the FDA for use in aerosols. In addition, aerosols can be very irritating if accidently sprayed in the eyes. Despite these questions about safety and effectiveness, aerosols remain popular because they are quick and easy to use.

Unlike antiperspirants, deodorants control body odor without affecting sweating; the FDA considers them cosmetics. Unless you perspire very little, a combination antiperspirant/deodorant will be more effective.

The most common problems involving antiperspirants and deodorants are allergic reactions (caused, for example, by an aluminum compound, antibiotic, or perfume in a product) and skin irritation. There is no way to predict who will be allergic to what. Don't apply these preparations to broken (as immediately after shaving underarm hair) or sensitive skin, and switch to a brand with different ingredients if a rash or other irritation develops. Usually the rash will disappear as soon as you stop using the product.

Deodorants and antiperspirants have been oversold. For many people, using their regular product two or three times a week, instead of daily, works just as well.

SKIN FIRST AID

Burns

Superficial or first-degree burns—defined as a burn involving only the outer skin layer—can be the result of some minor household accident, such as grabbing the handle of a pan that's too hot or scalding yourself with hot water or steam. They are not dangerous, but can be extremely painful. The best way to treat a minor burn is not, as many people believe, butter; butter won't relieve pain and may cause infection if blisters form and then break. Cold (but not iced) water is by far the most effective first-aid treatment; it eases the pain as it cleanses. If you burn yourself, immerse the burn in cold water or hold it under cold running water for fifteen minutes. Continually applying fresh cold-water compresses will help if it's not practical to immerse the burned area. Afterwards, you can bandage it with sterile gauze pads held on by tape if you wish, but if blisters appear try not to burst them. Burn ointments are not necessary.

When to seek medical attention

A deep or extensive burn, especially one caused by hot liquids or contact with fire, electricity, or corrosive chemicals, requires immediate medical attention. Signs of a second-degree burn are blistering, pain, and swelling. Sunburn that causes blisters, swelling, and oozing of fluid is a second-degree burn and treatment by a doctor is advisable. Don't put anything on a second-degree burn: creams or lotions may interfere with medical treatment the doctor will perform. Don't break blisters or peel damaged skin—you will only encourage infection.

Signs of a third-degree burn are lack of immediate pain (nerve endings have been destroyed), whiteness, and charring. Cover the area with sterile gauze, if possible, and get professional help.

Cuts and Scrapes

What is the best way to deal with the little cuts, abrasions, and scrapes of everyday life? Many remedies—from hydrogen peroxide to mercurochrome to antiseptic sprays and ointments—have enjoyed popularity over the years. The truth is, most small wounds don't need much doctoring.

Treatment

A simple two step process is the most effective method of treating a small wound. First, stop the bleeding—if there's any amount of it—by applying pressure with a clean cloth or tissue. If possible, elevate the wounded part above heart level to slow blood flow. (Exception: a puncture wound, from a nail or needle or similar long, sharp object should be encouraged to bleed as part of the cleansing process. See page 292 for more information.)

Second, the main concern with any small wound is avoiding infection, and you can best accomplish this by cleaning the wound and keeping it clean. Cleanse a scrape or cut by swabbing gently with a clean wet cloth or holding the injured part under cold running water. Use a mild soap in the area, but try to keep it out of the wound per se. If there are dirt particles clinging to a scraped shin or elbow, remove them with tweezers (wash tweezers first and dip the tips in alcohol). If the wound is on the hand or finger and likely to get dirty, if the area needs protection from further injury, or if you'd just feel more comfortable not looking at the wound, a homemade or store-bought bandage is in order. This is really all you need to do for most wounds, which will heal in a week to ten days.

Unnecessary steps

Antiseptic solutions—rubbing alcohol, iodine, and hexylresorcinol—and hydrogen peroxide kill some microorganisms but they can also destroy skin cells. The FDA permits them to be sold for cleaning small wounds, and if you feel you have to use something, make it alcohol. Iodine can actually burn your skin under a tight bandage. Hydrogen peroxide can damage the outer layers of the skin and thus retard healing. Such solutions as mercurochrome and merthiolate (once medicine cabinet staples) contain mercury, which is highly toxic, and are not judged safe or effective by the FDA.

Antibiotic ointments—such as Bacitracin, Neomycin, Neosporin,

Myth: Aloe can heal burns.

Fact: There is no solid evidence that aloe helps heal burns, cuts, or vaginal irritations. Aloe vera is a popular houseplant, and people often treat minor burns by snapping off a leaf and applying the juice to the affected area. Many users report that this provides relief and promotes healing. A Japanese study done about twenty-five years ago suggested that aloe could speed the healing of skin damage by burns or injury by removing protein build-up from dead and injured cells. More recently, however, FDA study groups reviewed the scientific tests that have been done on aloe derivatives and concluded that there is no solid evidence for this. Manufacturers of sunburn lotions have been adding aloe to their products, but even if aloe were effective in treating burns, the amount of it in these compounds is too small to have any effect.

When a Cut Needs Medical Attention

In any of the following situations, call your doctor, or go straight to the emergency room:

•If bleeding comes in spurts. This indicates that an artery may have been cut, and that you might not be able to stop the bleeding. Cover the wound with a large soft cloth, and if possible, elevate it above heart level. Press directly on the wound to help stop blood flow; apply an additional compress on top of the first, if necessary. Don't use a tourniquet, which can damage nerves.

•If a cut looks very deep, or if the edges of the wound gap open. A jagged cut, particularly from broken glass, is likely to need medical attention. If you need stitches, you should not wait more than six hours to get them.

•If a scrape is very large (for example, the whole length of your arm or leg) and there are bits of debris in it.

•If your face is cut. You may need plastic surgery to avoid scarring.

•If you think a wound has hidden dirt or debris in it.

•If you have a deep puncture wound, especially if it was made with a dirty object (a gardening tool, for example), and if you haven't had a tetanus booster within the past five years. If more time has passed or you don't remember when you last had one, arrange to have a tetanus immunization as soon as possible. If any sign of infection (redness, pus, or fever) develops, get medical attention. You may need to soak the wound to keep the puncture open and encourage draining.

Aureomycin—may cause skin irritation and offer few benefits. Though the FDA allows first-aid antibiotic ointments to be sold over the counter, there's no evidence that they promote healing or can effectively treat an infection. Antibiotic ointments might be of some preventive value, however, if you have a cut finger and have to perform some task where its hard to keep your hands clean—or for scrapes and cuts on a child's hands and feet when the child is engaging in active outdoor play. Wash the wound first, and apply a small amount of ointment under a bandage, and repeat these steps if the wound gets dirty.

Overall, if a wound is small and is kept clean, the body's own immune system can adequately dispose of any bacteria that may be present. Be wary of any product that claims to "speed" or "promote" healing.

Treating puncture wounds

A puncture wound caused by a nail or pin or other sharp object often doesn't bleed freely, so bacteria don't wash away and may be sealed in. If such a wound is not bleeding enough, press gently around the wound to encourage bleeding. Examine the wound and remove any foreign objects from it. Clean the wound with soap and water and cover it with a sterile dressing.

If the wound is deep or was made with a dirty object and you haven't had a tetanus shot within five years, contact your doctor about tetanus immunization. For the next few days, soak the wound several times a day in warm water to keep the puncture open and to help flush out bacteria. If infection develops (severe swelling, redness, pus, and fever), consult a physician.

A deep puncture wound on the hand may lead to an infection that is hard to combat; preventive antibiotic treatment may be advisable for such a wound. Any puncture wound of the head, chest, or abdomen requires immediate medical attention because of the possibility of internal injury. Numbness or tingling may indicate nerve damage, which requires medical attention.

Do you need a bandage?

For most small wounds, keeping them dry and exposed to air will make them heal faster. A scab helps protect the area from infection and shouldn't be removed until the wound has healed. However, some studies have shown for certain serious wounds covering a large area, moisture can aid healing and preventing scabbing can decrease the risk of scarring. New, flexible, transparent, waterproof bandages (called "occlusive" from "occluded," meaning to shut out) have thus been designed to retain moisture around the wound and protect it from bacteria and dirt. However, if a wound is draining, it can become infected unless the bandage is changed at intervals and the wound is cleaned. If you have a wound serious enough to need this kind of extensive treatment, you should probably be in a doctor's care.

If you do decide to use a bandage for a wound, how can you tell which type is best? Most people like to use ready-made bandage strips and keep a supply of them on hand. These come in a wide variety of shapes and styles for different small injuries. Old-fashioned adhesive tape and sterile gauze are less convenient to use but equally as good for minor wounds, particularly for the occasional wound that a ready-made bandage won't cover. Change any bandage when it becomes soiled or wet.

You can find the transparent, waterproof, occlusive bandages mentioned above in most drug stores; this new design has the advantage of not sticking to the wound itself. Though fairly expensive, they can be useful for some small wounds and abrasions such as a heel blister subject to chafing or a cut that needs protection from water.

As soon as you can comfortably do so, leave the bandage off. The warm, moist environment under a bandage is an excellent microclimate for breeding bacteria. A white, wrinkled appearance is a sign that the skin is too moist and has been covered by a bandage too long.

Dealing with Dog Bites

If you are bitten by a dog, the first thing you should do is rinse the wound thoroughly with water to remove the animal's saliva. Then wash the wound gently with soap and water for five minutes. Rinse it again, dry it, and then cover it with a sterile gauze dressing. Even if it is a small, minor bite, it is important to check with a doctor to see if further care is warranted and to evaluate the risk of infection, rabies, and tetanus.

There is a danger of infection with dog bites, especially deep ones that mangle tissue. In such cases a doctor will usually prescribe antibiotics to prevent infection. Any dog bite carries the risk of rabies. Many states require that any incident of dog bite be reported to the local health department. The animal must be kept under observation to watch for signs of rabies: the symptoms in an animal are agitation, viciousness, paralysis, and eventually death.

Rabies shots

If an animal is not available for observation, you will need to consider rabies shots. Because of widespread immunization programs for pets, rabies is uncommon in household animals, but not unheard of. If a human contracts rabies, the disease can be fatal. Symptoms can appear from ten days to two years after a bite; the average incubation period is one month. Tetanus infection is also possible, though not very common, after an animal bite. If you have not had a tetanus shot in more than five years, you may want to get a booster to make sure you're fully protected.

Removing Cactus Spines

To remove very fine cactus spines from a child's skin:

First, use tweezers to remove as many spines as possible. Then apply a nontoxic household glue (definitely not Krazy Glue; use a glue like Elmer's Glue) to the skin with a cotton swab and top it with a single layer of gauze. Let the glue dry, then remove the gauze with the glue. The spines should come with it. It's much less upsetting for the child than extracting the spines individually, which can be difficult or impossible to do anyway. In a controlled study, this treatment worked better than any other method.

Obviously, the glue-and-gauze trick would work for grown-ups, too, and might even be worth a try for briars or multiple splinters.

Insect Bites and Stings

Insect bites and stings are a common occurrence during the summer months (year round in warm climates). And while they are usually harmless—albeit, potentially painful—they can be dangerous for some people. Some insects also carry disease. Below are suggestions for warding off and treating the most common types of insect bites.

Bees, wasps, hornets, yellow jackets, and fire ants

These insects sting with venom that produces fierce burning, swelling, redness, and sometimes welts and itching in the areas around the sting. The best way to treat a sting is to wash it with soap and water. Applying ice, calamine lotion, or a paste made by mixing baking soda or meat tenderizer and water may bring some relief.

If you've been stung by a bee, you'll have to remove the stinger as well (the bee is the only insect that leaves it behind). Don't pull at the stinger directly with tweezer or fingers, because it has a sack at the exposed end that can pump more venom into you if squeezed. Instead scrape the sack away cleanly with a sharp blade held against the skin, then remove the stinger.

Avoiding stinging insects. You can avoid being stung by taking a few preventive measures. Wear shoes and socks outdoors; when gardening, wear long-sleeved shirts, long pants, and gloves. Bees can mistake you for flowers, so avoid brightly colored clothes, floral prints, and sweetly scented perfumes, soaps, or lotions. Be cautious about eating outside, particularly sweet, drippy foods like ice cream or watermelon. If an insect is annoying you, don't swat it—either walk away or, if attacked by a swarm, lie down and cover your head.

Ticks

Ticks probably exceed all other pests in the variety of diseases they transmit to man and domestic animals. Tiny, wingless, louselike creatures, they range in color from brown to gray and from one sixteenth to one quarter inch in length. Many species are known to carry diseases such as Rocky Mountain spotted fever, Colorado tick fever, tularemia, babesiasis, and Lyme disease, to name a few. They occur in every part of the United States, though large numbers are concentrated in certain areas.

People usually pick up ticks from woodsy underbrush, tall grass, and the fur of free-ranging pets. The tick brushes against some part of the body and looks for a place to settle. It then bites the skin, embeds its head, and taps into a blood source, such as a small vein or capillary. As it feeds, the external part of its body swells to as much as three times its original size. The bite is relatively painless; the real danger is the viruses or bacteria that the tick may harbor and that may infect you.

The best way to remove a tick. If you discover a tick attached to your skin, remove it immediately. The sooner it is removed, the less likely the chance of transfer of any infectious organisms. Don't try to detach it with your bare fingers; bacteria from a crushed tick may be able to penetrate even unbroken skin. Instead use a pair of fine-tipped tweezers. In fact, if you spend much time hiking or gardening in overgrown areas, a pair of "tick tweezers" (available at many sporting-goods stores) should be part of your first aid kit. To remove a tick, grip it as close to your skin as possible and gently pull it straight away from you until it releases its hold. Don't

Allergic Reactions to Insect Stings

For most people, the reaction to a sting is harmless, but some people are so sensitive to the venom that even one sting can provoke their immune system to overreact drastically. This is known as anaphylactic shock (from the Greek ana, meaning "excessive," and phylaxis meaning "protection"); it can include nausea, flushing, depressed blood pressure, irregular heartbeat, vomiting, and difficult breathing, and may lead to a coma and even death. In fact about fifty Americans die each year as a result of being stung by bees, wasps, or hornets. No other venomous animal, even snakes, kills that many. And this figure may be too low: experts suggest that an unknown number of deaths attributed to heart failure may actually be caused by stings.

Anyone who has experienced any symptoms of anaphylactic shock or any systemic reactions after being stung should know that reactions usually become increasingly severe with successive stings. Life-threatening reactions most often occur in people over thirty.

Fortunately, there are effective long-term and short-term treatments for those who are highly allergic. In the initial moments of a serious reaction, a dose of epinephrine (adrenalin) can arrest the attack. Your doctor can prescribe an emergency kit for you that includes a syringe and epinephrine, or an EpiPen, which comes with a spring-loaded mechanism that automatically triggers the injection of epinephrine when pressed against the skin. Take the kit with you whenever you go outdoors in bee season. If you get stung and must inject yourself, rub the site vigorously after the injection in order to increase the absorption rate.

Long-term treatment involves going to an allergist for regular shots of a serum made from insect venom. This may gradually desensitize the patient until a sting poses little serious harm. Recent studies indicate that this therapy can be discontinued after about five years without posing any future risk. (Follow-ups were done for only about five years, not over a lifetime.)

Despite its name, Rocky Mountain spotted fever is most prevalent in the South and East.

twist it as you pull, and don't squeeze its bloated body—that may actually inject bacteria into your skin. Afterwards, thoroughly wash your hands and the bite area with soap and water and apply antiseptic (such as rubbing alcohol). If you must touch the tick, cover your fingers with tissue; then wash your hands thoroughly.

Home remedies for tick removal—gasoline, petroleum jelly, kerosene, nail polish remover, or a hot match—have not been shown to be effective and may actually increase your chance of becoming infected from the tick. These methods may cause the tick to respond by secreting more of the infected organism.

Save the tick in a small container or jar labeled with the date, the body location of the bite, and where you think the tick came from. This way you can show it to your doctor if necessary.

Warding off ticks. The best treatment for tick bites, however, is prevention. Take these precautions:

•Cover your body as much as possible. Wear long pants and a long-sleeved shirt with buttoned cuffs. Don't go barefoot. Tuck the shirt into your pants and your pants into your socks or shoes. Wear light-colored, tightly woven fabrics: it's easier to spot ticks on white or tan slacks than on dark ones, and the ticks may not be able to grab onto the tight weave of slippery materials such as nylon. A hat may help, too, since ticks like to settle on the scalp.

•In overgrown countryside, try to stay near the center of trails.

•Check yourself occasionally for ticks, especially when you're in underbrush or forests. Check your clothing, too; ticks often crawl around on clothing or even on the skin for a long time before they bite. Later do a thorough check of your entire body. Have someone look at your back and head if possible or use two mirrors.

Shower and shampoo after your outing; this may help remove ticks that haven't yet begun to feed. Check your clothes, too; wash them immediately to remove any ticks that may be hidden in creases. Inspect any gear you were carrying.

•Check pets after they've been outdoors. Remove ticks from them as you would from yourself.

•Inspect your children daily for ticks, perhaps before they go to bed. This is especially important during the summer, when they spend lots of time outdoors.

Stings from Sea Creatures

Stingers include jellyfish, the Portuguese man-of-war, sea anemones, and some corals, all equipped with stinging cells called nematocysts. On contact with the skin, they discharge a small barb and a dose of toxin. You're more likely to encounter jellyfish and the Portuguese man-of-war while swimming; divers should watch out for coral and sea anemones. Sea urchins, which live on the sea bottom but may show up in shallow water, have poisonous spines that can puncture the skin even through thongs or sneakers.

Jellyfish. Only about one in ten species of these translucent, bell-shaped blobs produces severe reactions in humans. But if you do come into contact with a toxic jellyfish's trailing tentacles, you'll feel mild burning and stinging; long red weals that look like the marks of a whip will develop. If you have to pull the tentacles off, protect your hand with cloth or a glove to keep the stingers off your skin. To deactivate the stinging cells, wash with sea water, then apply rubbing alcohol, vinegar, or witch hazel. If possible, apply a papain-based meat tenderizer in paste form. This appears to break down the stinging cells (and the toxins in them) attached to your skin. A paste made of talcum, baking soda, or flour mixed with sea water may also help. When the paste is scraped off, the cells come with it. *Don't* rub the affected area or rinse with fresh water: this can discharge unactivated cells. If pain persists, a nonprescription topical anesthetic (such as one containing a "-caine" ingredient) can be applied.

The Portuguese man-of-war. Bright blue or purple and red, this is actually a colony of many individual jellyfish at two stages of development. The floating colonies are easy to spot, but not so their transparent tentacles, which can trail invisibly for as far as sixty feet. Contact with skin provokes red weals similar to jellyfish stings, but the burning and pain can be far more severe. Shortness of breath, nausea, stomach cramps, and shock may ensue. Treatment is similar to that for jellyfish stings (you can also try ammonia), but in some cases you may need to see a doctor.

Coral. On contact, some corals release toxins; fragments may break off and become embedded in your skin. Apply calamine lotion or rubbing alcohol, and if there is an abrasion, remove fragments with anything at hand: for instance, a towel, a handkerchief, tweezers, or a needle. Wash with soap and water.

Sea anemones. These flowerlike creatures live fixed to the sea floor; their waving tentacles equipped with stinging cells. If you step on one, follow the same measures as for jellyfish; do not rub and do not rinse with fresh water.

Sea urchins. Also floor dwellers, sea urchins are protected with toxic spines; broken-off spines can cause secondary infections if not removed. A scrub with soap and water will get rid of some. Extract others with a sterilized needle or tweezers; a doctor may have to pull out the remainder. Hot compresses or immersion of the foot in hot water increases blood flow, which helps remove the toxins. Since the punctured foot may be numb, check the water temperature with your hand or uninjured foot.

If you're stung or stuck by any of these get out of the water as calmly as you can, and if possible identify the culprit so that you can choose appropriate first aid measures. If you didn't see what hit you, ask someone who knows the area. Check ahead of time on the hazards that may be lurking off the beaches where you plan to spend your vacation. Pack a small first aid kit with the following items: needles and tweezers, rubbing alcohol or calamine lotion, and meat tenderizer. Sea stings are rarely fatal, though when the reaction is severe, you should see a doctor right away.

•One of the best ways to ward off ticks is to use an insect repellent containing deet. For more information on insect repellents, see the box below.

For information on how to keep your yard free of ticks and on Lyme disease, see pages 499-502.

Chigger mites

In April in the northern United States (year round in warmer climes), the newly hatched mite larvae climb the nearest plant and wait for a bird, snake, small animal, or human to brush by. The mite drops off the plant and attaches itself with a pair of jawlike claws. It doesn't burrow, like a tick, but clings for about three days before dropping off. During that time it feeds by secreting enzymes that liquefy skin cells. Chigger mites do not, as ticks do, feed off blood, nor do they spread disease. But, these enzymes can provoke an allergic reaction resulting in two weeks or more of intense itching—which leads to the scratching that may result in serious bacterial infection.

If you're hiking through the underbrush, fend mites off by wearing a long-sleeved shirt secured at the wrist, waist, and throat; tuck your pants into your socks

---

Insect Repellents

There is a relatively safe, effective insect repellent to drive off the bugs of summer. It's N,N-diethyltoluamide, mercifully known as DET or deet, which will keep most chiggers, ticks, biting flies, mosquitoes, and other insects (except bees) at bay. Some popular brands of insect repellent have only a little of it; others are pure deet.

The only trouble is that some of the chemical ultimately enters the bloodstream through the skin, traces of it showing up in urine. For most people this is of no concern. But a variety of allergic reactions to deet have been reported, as well as a few cases of toxic brain disease caused by the chemical, mainly in children.

Insect repellents containing the chemical compound Repellent-11—also known as R-11 or 2,3,4,5-Bis (2 butylene) tetrahydro-2-furaldehyde—have been banned by the EPA because studies show that it causes reproductive problems and tumors in lab animals that were fed it. The risk posed to humans, however, has not been fully determined since there's no data on how much of the pesticide is absorbed through the skin.

Although you will no longer find repellents containing R-11 on store shelves, you may still have an old bottle or can of repellent in your home. Read the label carefully and don't use it if it contains R-11. Call the manufacturer to see if you can exchange it for a reformulated product or throw it away—but don't be casual about disposing it. Find out if your area has a household hazardous waste collection program. Otherwise tie several layers of newspaper around the repellent and dispose of it with other garbage.

If you want to use insect repellents, take the following precautions:

•Buy products with a lower concentration of deet; these are safer, but have to be applied more frequently. Avoid brands that are totally deet, since the risk of an adverse reaction is highest with them.

•Don't use insect repellents on broken skin, such as cuts and scratches.

•Be very careful with infants and children, in whom the greatest number of serious reactions have been reported. Don't spray them (or anybody else) repeatedly over long periods, and don't use excessive amounts.

•When possible, use clothing as protection (long-sleeved shirts, socks, shoes, and loose-fitting trousers tucked into your shoes or socks). Applying repellent to clothing may also help.

•Don't reapply until necessary. Wait until flying bugs are circling close by.

If you—or a child in your care—develop a skin rash while using a repellent, discontinue its use. Severe reactions such as breathing difficulties or seizures are extremely rare. Should they occur, seek medical aid at once and be sure to tell the physician you were using a repellent; bring the can or bottle with you.

or boots. It also helps to apply insect repellent to exposed skin and to trouser and sleeve cuffs and shirt fronts. If a mite does attach—they look like a tiny red fleck—a needle, small knife, or even your fingernail will remove it.

Starch baths and calamine lotion help relieve itching. Lindane and crotamiton (a prescription drug) kill mites; crotamiton also alleviates itching. For more serious attacks, your doctor may prescribe an oral antihistamine or topical steroid cream to control the itching. If you do develop a secondary infection due to scratching, an antibiotic may be needed.

Poison Ivy and Poison Oak

You may remember the old saying "Leaves of three, let it be." It's a reminder that poison ivy and its cousin poison oak consistently have three leaves. But beyond that these plants can vary tremendously—which is why many people don't recognize them and end up in misery each year. They can grow as woody vines or shrubs. The leaves can be dull or glossy, from one to five inches long, and have edges that are saw-toothed, lobed, or smooth. Though usually green, in autumn they can turn yellow or pink; in spring they often bear small green or white flowers that mature into berries in late summer.

The plants are widely distributed. Poison ivy grows throughout the United States except California, which is where one type of poison oak is concentrated. Another form of poison oak grows in the southeastern states. In damp areas like swamps or bogs, you may encounter poison sumac, a small tree or shrub related to poison ivy that has seven to eight leaflets on each stem.

People who think they're immune to these plants are usually inviting trouble. Often people aren't affected after their first or second exposure. But four out of five become sensitive after several exposures to urushiol—the chemical in the oil secreted by these plants—which causes itching and burning along with a red, blistery rash. Usually the rash begins a few hours after exposure, but it may not appear for several days. And you need not touch the plant itself. Urushiol is extremely hardy, and brushing an object that was contaminated months before can cause the rash. In addition, dogs and cats that have brushed against the leaves carry the irritating oils on their fur, and may transfer it to you.

Preventive steps
If you walk or hike through the woods where these plants grow, wear clothing, including gloves, that protects your extremities. Always wash the clothing afterward. If your shoes might have touched a plant, sponge them off. And if you find poison ivy on your property, don't burn it; this allows the urushiol to become airborne and can cause severe allergic reactions all over your body. Dispose of plants in sealed plastic bags, or kill them with a herbicide and then bury them.

Treating poison ivy and poison oak
If you think you've been exposed, wash your skin thoroughly within minutes, using plenty of cold water. Don't use soap, which can spread the oil. If a rash develops, don't scratch it; scratching won't spread the rash, nor will breaking the blisters (the fluid inside doesn't contain allergens), but excessive scratching can

lead to infection. To relieve the itch, try compresses soaked in cool water. Calamine lotion, baking soda, and hydrocortisone cream can also be soothing.

Frostbite

Frostbite can be insidious—if you've been out in the cold a while and your extremities already feel cold and numb, you may not notice that it has set in. Frostbite comes in three categories, from mild to serious: frostnip, superficial frostbite, and deep frostbite.

While the treatment for each type of frostbite varies, two guidelines are applicable to all three types: never massage or rub frostbitten areas (with or without snow), and do not apply any ointments.

Frostnip. The first hint of this stage of frostbite is numbness, followed by a whitening of the tissue—a change that can take place very quickly. Frostnip usually affects the nose, ears, hands, or feet. If possible, get out of the cold. The best treatment is direct application of warmth—blow on the areas, or get someone else to do so; if your nose is frostnipped, apply your warm hands. If it's your hands that are freezing, put them in your warm armpits. Your skin will probably burn and tingle as it warms, but there should be no lasting injury.

Superficial frostbite. This type of frostbite requires medical attention, but there are some steps you should take first. The area will appear very white and waxy and will feel hard on the surface, yet will have its normal resilience in the lower layers. (When checking, press very gently). Get out of the cold, and warm the areas, preferably by immersion in warm water (100 to 105 degrees—a temperature that should feel comfortably warm, but not hot to undamaged skin). Keep adding warm water as necessary, but take care that it doesn't get too hot. Avoid dry heat or uncontrolled heat sources such as campfires. Don't try to walk on frostbitten feet, and avoid the temptation to rub frostbitten hands or fingers. The warming process may be painful. On the way to the emergency room or doctor's office, keep the area warm.

Deep frostbite. In this stage, the tissues may be blotchy or blue and will be very hard, without any underlying resilience. Don't try to administer first aid or thaw the tissue. Wrap the frozen area in a blanket or other soft material to prevent bruising, and keep it elevated on the way to the hospital.

HAIR CARE

Hair is found all over the body, except on the palms of your hands and soles of your feet. A strand of hair is composed of two parts: the shaft—the part of the hair that we see—consists of dead cells; the follicle, which lies just under the skin, is composed of the root and connective tissue. Cells proliferate in the follicle and manufacture a protein called keratin. As more and more cells are produced, the other cells move up and out of the follicle and die, thus creating the shaft of the hair. As long as the follicle remains intact, new hair will be produced. Hair stops growing when the follicle is damaged.

Protecting your hair from the elements

A strand of hair is not as simple as it looks, and its very structure makes it vulnerable to such elements as the sun's ultraviolet rays, the chlorine in pools, beauty-shop chemicals, and detergent shampoos. The cells in the hair shaft's thin outer layer (the cuticle) overlap like scales to protect the shaft's inner mass of fiber (the cortex). Normally this shaft is covered with a protective lubricant, sebum. Sun, salt, and chlorinated water draw moisture from the hair shaft, strip away the sebum, and can damage the cuticle. If the cuticles' scales crack or warp, the roughened hair surface loses its natural sheen, and the unprotected fiber of the cortex frays or "splits," resulting in frizzy, dry hair.

Even worse, pool water can leave blond or gray hair green-tinted. This occurs when copper compounds found in algicides or leached from water pipes bond to the hair and penetrate the cortex, thus acting as a pigment. (People with dark and unbleached hair don't face this problem because the hair shafts' dark pigment, melanin, disguises the green.) In the past, if your hair turned green, all you could do was wait until the hair grew out. But several new gels or shampoos that may help remove discoloration have come on the market.

One way to keep your hair, dark or light, in good health despite exposure to the elements, is to use a hair conditioner. Some of the claims made for conditioners may be commercial hype, but they really do work on a temporary basis by coating the hair with a lubricant, natural or synthetic, that temporarily replaces stripped-away sebum. Other conditioner ingredients bond to the hair, helping to smooth down the cuticle (thereby restoring sheen); still others reduce the static charges that result in flyaway hair. Conditioners (which are mildly acidic) also help balance the pH of shampoos (which are usually mildly alkaline).

Keeping hair healthy

- If you swim or spend a lot of time outdoors, go easy on coloring, permanent waving, hot combs, heated rollers, and blow driers.
- Wear a hat in the sun.
- Wear a rubber bathing cap, but don't expect it to keep your hair completely dry. Before you put the cap on, comb conditioner into your hair.
- After your swim, rinse out salt or chlorine with tap water and, if it is available, use shampoo.
- Dry your hair by wrapping it in a towel. Blot and squeeze, don't rub or pull, and don't brush wet hair. Use a wide-toothed comb instead.

Dandruff

Mild dandruff isn't so much a medical problem as a cosmetic concern. Your whole body continually sheds outer layers of dead skin. Usually the process isn't noticeable, but when the scalp sheds skin, flakes can get trapped in the hair and collect with dirt and oil. The result may be unsightly, but it's generally not a cause for alarm; dandruff doesn't signal hair loss, for instance.

There's no way to prevent dandruff from forming, but frequent shampooing can help keep it under control. An ordinary shampoo may work if used often enough—usually every two to four days. Dandruff shampoos may control it for a few days longer, usually by helping to slough off the scales. Look for these effective anti-dandruff ingredients: zinc pyrithione, sulfusalicylic compounds, selenium sulfide, or coal tar. (While there is some concern that hair dyes containing coal tar—see page 302—may be carcinogenic, dandruff shampoos have much smaller concentrations of coal tar, and are considered safe and effective by the Food and Drug Administration (FDA) and dermatologists.) Use special care with products that contain any of these ingredients—they can hurt your eyes. And since continually using any shampoo may leave a residue build-up, alternate it with another dandruff shampoo, or regular shampoo.

Consult a doctor if more extreme symptoms develop. Severe flaking, crusting, itching, and redness may be signs of medically treatable problems.

Baldness

The causes of ordinary male pattern baldness are not well understood, but seem to be a normal sign of maturity. It runs in families, and occurs mainly in men. Contrary to myth, however, baldness is passed down through the genes of both parents, not just the mother's genes; therefore having a maternal grandfather with a full head of hair is no guarantee that you will be in similar circumstances at the same age. Furthermore, baldness is not induced by anxiety, zealous shampooing, or an excess of male hormones.

Products containing lanolin, vitamins, or such ingredients as wheat germ oil are harmless when applied to the head, but they won't make hair grow or prevent it from falling out. Products with large amounts of estrogen might stimulate hair growth, but almost always have unpleasant side effects.

A possible treatment

A prescription drug called minoxidil seems to stimulate hair growth. Just why, nobody can say. Its effects were discovered accidentally when patients taking the drug in tablet form to counteract high blood pressure noticed new hair growth. Now the firm that developed minoxidil is marketing the drug specifically as a hair restorer in a 2 percent solution.

But this "miracle" has definite limits. For one thing, it affects only the crown of the head, just one of the trouble spots in hereditary male pattern baldness. A receding hairline or baldness at the temples is rarely restored. Those who profit fall mainly between the ages of eighteen and thirty. In trials sponsored by the drug company that manufactures minoxidil, none of the 2,300 balding participants was over the age of forty-nine; none displayed "billiard-ball" baldness or even receding temples.

Second, only 8 percent of the men showed "dense" new hair growth after applying minoxidil twice daily for a year. And the definition of "dense" in the experiment was only about one-fifth as dense as normal hair growth. "Moderate" growth—a thin fluff—was the outcome for a further 31 percent of the men. But a large majority, 61 percent, had to settle for little or no hair growth.

Minoxidil has so far caused no serious side effects among this test population of healthy and relatively young males. But it might well pose a danger for men with cardiovascular disease, who are generally older than those in the test group. Under no circumstances should it be used by pregnant women. Users, whatever their age, should check with their physicians after a month's application of the product, and have another checkup six months later.

Finally, minoxidil means lifetime commitment. Any new hair may vanish if you discontinue the treatment (and the drug has not been shown to inhibit hair loss). Nor can you economize by cutting out one of the twice-daily applications—the benefits will be significantly reduced. One side effect may be severe itching, and the long-term side effects remain a mystery.

Other causes of baldness

Baldness can result from such abnormal conditions as a overdose of vitamin A, radiation or chemotherapy treatment, and crash dieting. This type of hair loss is usually reversed once the underlying condition is corrected and does not respond to treatment with minoxidil. Women also tend to experience hair loss as they age, and in a very few women during pregnancy, but it is usually in the form of thinning all over the head.

Hair Dyes

Some thirty million American women and an unknown number of men use hair dyes, most of which contain coal-tar dyes. Because they work better, last longer, and look more natural, coal-tar dyes have almost entirely replaced plant derivative dyes (such as henna) and metallic dyes (the kind you apply every day for gradual darkening). In spite of their superior cosmetic qualities, the use of coal-tar dyes can cause severe skin allergies in some people. Moreover, in 1978 two chemicals found in coal-tar dyes—known as 4-MMPD and 4-MMPDS—were shown to cause cancer in animals.

Curiously enough, though, the Food and Drug Administration (FDA) has no power to ban hair dyes. According to the Food and Drug Act of 1938, coal-tar dyes have a special status among cosmetics, and the FDA cannot take them off the market. The FDA does require that packages warn about possible skin irritation. In 1978 the FDA proposed that a cancer warning be posted on hair dye packages. Rather than comply, many companies "voluntarily" removed 4-MMPD and 4-MMPDS from their products. This sounded reassuring to the public, but in fact these dyes were simply replaced with similar ones whose carcinogenic qualities had never been tested.

Most of the studies evaluating hair dye safety have involved feeding large quantities of dye to laboratory animals. According to cosmetic manufacturers, this is a far cry from putting a small amount on your scalp every four weeks or so. Yet the scalp is a highly sensitive area, and hair dyes do penetrate the skin. So far human studies have been inconclusive. Some reveal no increase in the risk of breast or bladder cancer, while others do show increased risk. Still, the National Cancer Institute advises people to check hair dye labels and avoid any with the following ingredients, which have been shown to cause cancer when fed to laboratory animals: 2,4-diaminoanisole sulfate, also known as 4-MMPD and 4-MMPDS (no longer used); 4-amino-2 nitrophenol, also known as 2-nitro-p-phenylenediamine; direct black 38; direct blue 6; lead acetate.

Myth: Worry can turn hair white.

Fact: *Nothing turns hair white but the gradual decrease of pigmentation that occurs with age. Shock or stress does not affect hair color. Graying, whether it comes with the normal process of aging or prematurely, has a genetic basis. If you are Caucasian, you'll begin graying on average at about age thirty-four; the average black person begins at forty-four.*

Whenever it happens, hair turns gray or white when pigment ceases to be produced in the hair root, and new hairs grow in that are gray or white. Overnight graying rarely if ever occurs. In any case, it has never been documented. It is impossible that pigmented hair could simply shed its color without benefit of a bleach. There is, however, a rare type of scalp disorder, known as alopecia areata, which causes hair to shed rapidly. This might leave remaining unpigmented hairs looking all the whiter—hence the "overnight" myth.

Safety guidelines

If you do dye your hair, follow these suggestions:

•Women who are or might be pregnant should avoid dyes entirely, since some may pose a risk to the fetus.

•Dye your hair as infrequently as possible, and don't leave the dye on your head longer than the instructions tell you.

•Try frosting or streaking instead of methods that call for applying dye to the entire scalp.

•Wash your hair and scalp thoroughly after dyeing.

•Avoid using dyes regularly over a period of many years.

•Check the label of henna and metallic dyes. Henna can only dye hair bright red; a product that does anything else may have coal-tar supplements. Metallic dyes often contain lead acetate.

N A I L   C A R E

Fingernails are simply another form of skin, a hardened protein called keratin that has a high sulphur content. Contrary to popular belief, the calcium content of nails is very low. Fair-skinned people appear to have pinkish nails; others may have brown or black ones, according to the skin color underneath. Healthy-looking fingernails are more often than not a sign of good health. But changes in color and appearance are not necessarily a sign of illness. Although a careful physician will always look at the nails, diagnosing or predicting any generalized ailment would be impossible on the basis of nails alone.

Among the nail problems that cause anxiety from time to time are:

Brittleness. Like dry skin, this is likely to worsen in winter. Frequent immersion in water—particularly if chlorine, soap, or detergent is added—makes nails break. Wearing rubber gloves will help if dishwashing is causing the brittleness. So will wearing warm gloves outdoors in the winter.

White spots. As a rule these result from minor injury. White spots seldom indicate any vitamin or mineral deficiency; they will vanish as the nail grows.

Ridges. Longitudinal ridges are not unusual; they may be genetic, and they do become more prominent as you age. If you have transverse furrows (known as "Beau's lines") that begin at the base of the nail, one thing to suspect is excessively rigorous manicuring. Pressure with a manicure tool can cause pits or bumps in the nail; so can biting your fingers. Furrows may appear after such illnesses as measles, pneumonia, or other severe infections, but they are not symptoms of infection.

Discoloration. Cigarettes, hair dyes, and even the tints that sometimes leak out of nail polish can discolor your nails. An injury may also be the culprit.

Separation of nail from nail bed. This condition, along with alterations in the nail texture, may be a sign of psoriasis, a disorder of the skin, often mild and often confined only to fingernails. Like brittleness, it may be caused by, or aggravated by, exposure to water, detergents, soaps, and even nail hardeners. An allergic reaction to nail polish is also a possible cause.

Reversal of the normal nail curvature (spoon nail). This may indicate iron deficiency, especially in older children.

Nail Growth

•*Rate of nail growth varies from person to person and from finger to finger. The nail of the middle finger grows fastest, the thumbnail and little-fingernail lag behind.*

•*Right- or left-handedness affects nail growth— nails grow faster on the hand you use most. For unknown reasons nails grow faster in the premenstrual phase in women. Male nails grow slightly faster than female, perhaps because the nail plate is bigger. Hormones may also play a role.*

•*The nails of well-nourished people grow faster than those of the undernourished, but no specific food, mineral, or vitamin accelerates nail growth—not even that old standby gelatin.*

•*It takes 5 $\frac{1}{2}$ to 6 months for a nail to grow from cuticle to tip, so your nails are a mini-biography. A ridge caused by an injury near the cuticle line in May will still be visible in October.*

With the exception of spoon nail, none of these problems are likely to be significant. Nevertheless, your nails are one of many indicators of health. Any dramatic changes in their texture, shape, color, or growth rate may be a signal to seek medical advice.

Are nail products safe?

Under most circumstances nail enamels, hardeners, and polish removers won't do you any harm. Nevertheless, you should read the labels, as with any product, and be aware of the problems nail products can sometimes cause.

First, polish remover is very drying to nails and cuticles, so use it sparingly and as infrequently as possible. Don't remove nail enamel every day. Make repairs by reapplying enamel.

Second, nail plates (the visible nails) are very porous and dry quickly. Enamels waterproof the nail plates, so when the skin under them gets wet, it stays moist longer and thus is subject to infection, especially if you accidentally injure the nail bed. If you notice signs of infection (pain, redness, pus), see a doctor.

Third, some nail product ingredients can produce allergic reactions. One such component is called toluene-sulfonamide formaldehyde resin. This can cause rashes on the fingers or around the eyes, since buffing or filing nail enamel—or even blowing on it as it dries—can cause small particles to enter the air. For a hypo-allergenic enamel, look for one without formaldehyde resins. "Hardeners" are particularly likely to contain them.

Caution on artificial nails

What are the long term effects of artificial nails? Sculptured nails are more likely to damage nails than other products. They are formed by mixing a powder and liquid containing acrylics and peroxide; this mixture is applied to the nail plates and, after it dries, filed and shaped like a real nail. Methyl methacrylate, which can cause skin inflammation and splitting of the nail plate, was once a common ingredient of the sculpting powder, until the FDA enjoined American manufacturers from using it. However, you've really no way of knowing what's in the mix the manicurist may apply, since manufacturers seldom specify what's in wholesale nail products and, in any case, some salons may use imported products containing methyl methacrylate.

A potential hazard for manicurists is repeatedly breathing the vapor from such solvents as toluene, found in a wide range of nail products. This chemical may cause damage to the bone marrow and liver, as well as irritation to the throat and lungs. Cyanoacrylates (found in Krazy Glue, for instance), another nail-sculpting ingredient, can also produce irritation and splitting, and particles may enter the air during filing.

Stick-on nails—preformed plastic nails glued to the nail bed—are not so bad, so long as cyanoacrylates are not in the glue. However, wearing artificial nails for long periods can damage the natural nails because they form an airtight cover. Thus stick-on nails should be removed at least once a year to give the nails a breather.

Eye Care

Good eyesight isn't difficult to maintain: the great majority of eye problems that occur are relatively easy to prevent or correct. But it is important to have your eyes examined regularly. Not only do regular exams alert you to any small changes in visual acuity—how sharply you see things—but they can also detect more serious eye conditions, most of which can be controlled with early treatment. Infants eyes' should be checked during routine physicals; children between three and four should have at least one eye exam; and from age five to age eighteen you should have you eyes examined every eighteen months to two years. From ages nineteen to forty, you need eye exams only if you have symptoms of eye problems. From age forty-one to sixty, eye exams every five years with glaucoma tests are recommended. After age sixty, eye exams should be conducted every year or two.

There are three types of eye-care specialists:

Ophthalmologists are certified doctors of medicine who specialize in medical and surgical care of the eye. As such, they have the greatest range of expertise among eye-care specialists. In addition to testing vision and prescribing corrective lenses, ophthalmologists diagnose and treat all sorts of eye disorders, from minor infections to conditions like glaucoma that can lead to blindness.

Optometrists diagnose, manage, and treat conditions of the human eye and visual systems as regulated by state law. They are licensed to perform vision testing and they prescribe corrective lenses and fit contact lenses. They are not medical doctors, but they have completed a three-year university science program plus a four-year program at a school of optometry. In twenty-five states, optometrists can also diagnose and treat specified eye diseases—but if a disorder outside their expertise is apparent, an optometrist would refer you to an ophthalmologist.

Opticians do not test vision nor prescribe treatment for any sort of eye problem; rather, they are technicians who fill prescriptions for eyeglasses or contact lenses.

The most common eye problem

Most people are never troubled by anything other than faulty focusing—so-called refractive defects, which occur because light entering the eye isn't precisely focused on the retina, the "film" inside the back of the eye. In most cases the problem is either nearsightedness—in which near objects are more clearly focused and distant objects are fuzzy—or farsightedness, in which close-up vision is blurred. Another common refractive defect is astigmatism, a distortion caused by an uneven cornea or lens. Presbyopia, a fourth common condition, is caused by an impaired ability to change focus as a result of weakened eye muscles and rigidity in the lens. This problem gradually develops with age, such that most people need help in correcting their vision by their mid-forties, even if only for reading.

Fortunately, all of these focusing problems can generally be easily remedied with corrective lenses, which are now worn by about half of the population, either in the form of eyeglasses or contact lenses. You should consult with your eye specialist as to which corrective measures are best for you.

Contact Lenses

Today some 16 to 18 million Americans wear contact lenses instead of eyeglasses. For most wearers they are both comfortable and safe, and they can sometimes be superior to glasses in correcting vision problems. They are especially good for correcting severe nearsightedness and for people who have had cataract surgery. Not everyone can wear them, of course, and they won't correct all vision problems. But they are a boon to those who have complex vision problems or dislike the look of glasses or the hindrance they can pose in active sports.

How contacts work

Contact lenses are plastic disks that cling to the cornea, the transparent tissue that covers the front of the eyeball. On the surface of the cornea is a layer of tears— actually a layer of protein, water, and oil. These tears do many jobs: primarily, they serve as the medium through which oxygen passes from the atmosphere to the corneal cells; they also combat and wash away bacteria; and they lubricate the surface of the eyeball and the interior surface of the eyelid. Since the cornea has no blood supply, these tears also provide nourishment to the corneal cells. Without this fluid layer, wearing contact lenses would be impossible, for tears cushion the lenses and hold them in place. A cornea that has become dry will quickly make the lens uncomfortable and may lead to scratches and irritation of the eye.

The key of contact lens design is allowing the cornea to "breathe." The lenses must either fit loosely enough so that the oxygen, carried by the tears, can circulate beneath them, as with the older type of hard contacts (no longer used), or else the plastic itself must be gas-permeable, as with soft contacts or the newer rigid gas permeable hard contacts that have replaced the old hard lenses.

Types of lenses

Most contact lenses are made of plastic, a few of silicone. There are hundreds of brands and types, including highly specialized lenses for patients who have had cataract surgery, lenses that appear to change the color of the eye, and even bifocal lenses. But for most people, there are three types on the market to be considered. Two types are intended for daily wear only (that is, they must be removed for sleep): rigid gas permeable lenses and soft lenses. The third type is extended-wear lenses, soft lenses that are designed to be worn for longer periods. Disposable lenses are a new type of soft extended-wear lens.

Daily-wear lenses: rigid gas permeable

There is much to be said for rigid gas permeable lenses. They cover less eye area than the other types. They generally provide better vision than soft contacts and can correct certain refractive errors that soft lenses cannot. They are the least expensive lenses and with reasonable care can last for years. They are also the easiest lenses to care for (see box on page 308).

But they do have some disadvantages: even the best may be somewhat uncomfortable at first, and not everyone can adapt to them. Dust particles can slip under them and be painful. And because they are small, they may occasionally pop out, which reduces their value for sports and physical activities. Therefore, while

Over-the-Counter Eye Drops

Most are safe, but they are rarely necessary. Normal eyes do not need "cleansing," "soothing," or "refreshing" solutions. Your tears, which contain anti-bacterial agents, are the most effective eye cleansers of all. Though they may be soothing, over-the-counter drops can mask symptoms of serious eye infection and diseases. If there's irritation or redness for more than a day or two, seek professional advice. In no case should you continue using eye drops for more than a day or two.

Nonprescription eye drops come in three types: artificial tears to soothe dry eyes (such as Aqua Tears, Tears Plus, Muro Tears); decongestants, which whiten the eyeball (Visine, Murine Plus); and eyewashes (usually a mixture of boric acid and salt), which "irrigate" the eye.

Artificial tears can temporarily soothe eyes, but are needed only by people with serious eye problems. Most contain preservatives that can cause allergic reactions. Dr. Richard L. Abbott, a specialist in eye diseases at Pacific Presbyterian Medical Center in San Francisco, recommends that people with dry eyes humidify their houses and avoid dry environments—two steps that can reduce the need for artificial tears.

Decongestants, too, can provide temporary relief to eyes irritated by air pollution, chlorinated pool water, or fatigue. But they can have an irritating effect all their own. Don't use them more than three times a day.

As for eyewashes, they may feel refreshing, but they have no medicinal effect and are no more effective than cold tap water.

If you wear contact lenses, use eye drops recommended by your eye-care specialist.

proper fitting is important with all types of contact lenses, it is even more so with rigid gas permeable lenses.

Daily-wear lenses: soft

Soft lenses, which are permeable and hydrophilic (consisting of anywhere from 38 to 79 percent water), have accounted for the big upsurge in sales of contact lenses. They are usually comfortable from the first day of wear and require no break-in period. Because they cover a larger area of the eyes, they are unlikely to pop out. Dust particles are also less likely to become trapped under soft lenses.

But they, too, have their disadvantages. They tear easily, and a torn lens can irritate the eye as well as interfere with vision. Even with meticulous care, they usually don't last longer than a year or, at the outside, eighteen months. Because they contain water, they can act as a breeding ground for bacteria, and since they are often worn for twelve or more hours a day, the protein and salts from tears gradually build up on them. Thus they require careful daily cleaning as well as overnight disinfection and soaking. If allowed to dry out, soft lenses can be ruined. All this upkeep is expensive, and you must use only the brands of lens solution prescribed. If your prescribed solution is not available, check with your eye specialist before switching, since brands are not always interchangeable. Some are made for specific kinds of lenses, and what works for one person may cause another person's eyes to redden. But to most users the cost and nuisance of maintaining soft lenses is a fair price to pay for their comfort and convenience.

Extended-wear contacts: real problems

In recent years extended-wear lenses have become very popular—about four million Americans now wear them. Often extremely thin and fragile, they are advertised as sufficiently permeable to oxygen to be worn while sleeping—and so

---

Caring for Contacts

Lens care—a daily job with most types of lenses—demands a commitment of time and money. Many different kinds of lens solutions and several systems of lens care are available. Some products may contain preservatives (to keep them sterile) and other potentially irritating ingredients. What works for one person may produce an allergic reaction in another. Not all brands of solution are interchangeable, so don't experiment without professional advice.

Rigid gas permeable lenses

Clean with a lens cleaner, rinse in sterile saline before and after wearing (or, if advised, a special rinsing solution), and store in a disinfecting solution overnight. Since the fluid is susceptible to contamination, the lens case must be cleaned and refilled each night. These lenses may also need cleaning once or twice a week with enzyme cleaner to remove protein deposits that the lens picks up from the eye.

Soft lenses (daily and extended-wear)

As many as five products may be necessary:
1. Special lens cleaner for cleansing lenses after wear.
2. Saline solution for rinsing.
3. Soaking solution for disinfecting.
4. Enzyme tablets to combat protein build-up.
5. "Wetting" eye drops for lubricating lenses every so often.

To ensure that solutions are bacteria-free, users can buy solutions with preservatives (which may cause allergic reaction) or sterile solutions without preservatives

All soft lenses—including extended wear—must be disinfected daily by storing them in special disinfecting solutions or in electrically heated disinfecting units. Again, professional advice is always necessary.

---

you can supposedly leave them in your eyes for several weeks, clean and disinfect them, then put them back in your eyes. However, the Food and Drug Administration has advised that no lens be worn for that length of time. And even one night may in fact be too long.

Studies have shown that extended-wear lenses put great stress on the eyes if worn for long periods—to the extent that they are three to five times more likely to cause infection of the cornea than daily-wear contacts. Though permeable, extended-wear lenses still limit the amount of oxygen that gets through to the cornea—and when you're sleeping with your lenses on, the oxygen supply is cut down even further. Oxygen deprivation affects the metabolism of the outer layer of the cornea, which may thin and more become prone to infection. Lack of oxygen may also encourage the formation of superficial blood vessels, which can interfere with clarity of vision. The degree of infection or damage is usually related to the length of time the lens is in the eye.

Wearing contacts while sleeping also causes edema in the cornea. During sleep the cornea normally swells slightly—and harmlessly—but the lenses aggravate the condition. One possible complication of this is the development of corneal ulcers as a result of bacteria growing in the oxygen-deprived area under the lenses. In two studies at Harvard's Massachusetts Eye and Ear Infirmary, people who wore contact lenses while they slept were found to be ten to fifteen times more likely to develop a corneal ulcer than those who took their lenses out. The ulcers can result in permanent loss of vision. Initial symptoms include burning, red eyes, and sometimes fluid discharge. The risk of infection appears to increase by at least 5 percent with each consecutive day that you wear the lenses without removing and cleaning them.

Disposable contacts: similar risks

Disposable extended-wear contact lenses sound great: you wear them day and night for a week (or occasionally longer) and then discard them. You never have to clean them, and never touch them except when you first put them in and then throw them out. This is an advantage because not only is lens cleaning and disinfecting a time-consuming inconvenience, but it can be a cause of eye infection if done less than scrupulously. Unfortunately, disposable contact lenses still have many of the problems of ordinary extended- or daily-wear soft lenses:

•Disposables, like other soft lenses and contacts in general, limit the amount of oxygen that gets through to the cornea, increasing the risk of corneal infection.

•Like other soft lenses, disposables accumulate bacteria and debris.

•They are particularly delicate and prone to tearing.

•Though many advances are expected, they aren't currently suitable for all vision problems. They may correct moderate nearsightedness and farsightedness, but not astigmatism or severe nearsightedness. Like other extended-wear lenses, disposables will probably be irritating if your eyes tend to be dry.

"Disposable" doesn't mean cheap. True, you don't have to buy lens-cleaning supplies. But for a year's supply plus fittings and checkups, disposable contacts cost about twice as much as ordinary extended-wear lenses, depending on how often you replace them.

Choosing lenses

Your best bet is to avoid all extended-wear lenses, disposable or not. Stick to daily-wear lenses. If you already own extended-wear lenses, you don't have to give them up—just never wear them overnight, and clean and disinfect them daily before reinsertion, like other lenses. Since every person is different, it is best to follow the recommendations of your optometrist or ophthalmologist regarding the type of lens that is best for you.

Clean and disinfect daily-wear lenses carefully with commercially prepared solutions (see box on page 308), and be sure to keep your follow-up appointments with your eye-care professional. Whatever type of lens you wear, if you notice any unusual redness (especially in just one eye), blurring or other sudden change in

---

Trouble Spots

The following conditions, situations, and products may make wearing lenses temporarily impractical:

Very low humidity. Dry heat, air conditioning, or extremely dry weather can make lenses uncomfortable. So can airplane cabins, wind, and blow-dryers.

Slowed blinking rate, for instance, while watching television. This may dry out eyes.

Cold pills and diuretics. They decrease the amount of tears.

Colds. Watery eyes can make contact lenses uncomfortable.

Pregnancy, menstruation, or birth control pills. In some women these can cause dry eyes.

Tobacco smoke and other types of airborne irritants.

Eye makeup. Apply eye makeup carefully after inserting lenses, and don't use cosmetics that are likely to run into the eye. Avoid putting makeup on the inside edge of the eyelid.

Aerosol sprays. Avoid using while wearing lenses.

All contact lens wearers should have one pair of properly prescribed glasses. If you experience minor eye fatigue, especially toward the end of the day, change to your regular glasses. It never hurts to give your eyes a rest.

Eyes and Eye Makeup: What to Avoid

•Don't use saliva to wet eye makeup. Mouth bacteria can be carried to the eye, where they can cause infection.

•Don't buy an open package that may have been sampled.

•Don't use eye makeup if you already have an eye infection.

•Don't share eye makeup, even with a family member. Another woman's bacteria may be harmless for her but not for you.

•Don't try out eye products from testers in department stores. One survey showed that 67 percent of such samples were contaminated. Test the shade on your hand.

---

your vision, or persistent pain in or around your eye, remove the lenses and consult an optometrist or ophthalmologist.

Special note: People with cataracts or certain other eye disorders may need to wear extended-wear lenses as prescribed by their ophthalmologists.

Where to buy lenses

Recently, chains of discount optical stores have sprung up all over the country, some offering huge stocks and low prices. Be leery of commercial stores that advertise cut rates. The lenses they offer may be of older design, acquired at bargain rates. In some cases, discount stores offer no follow-up care at all beyond a booklet and a kit of solutions.

The way to judge a practitioner is not by price but by the time he devotes to the eye exam, to prescribing and fitting lenses, and particularly to follow-up care. A first consultation and fitting should take at least an hour, and the practitioner should give you precise instructions for inserting and removing the lenses, as well as a demonstration of proper lens care. Follow-up visits are a necessary part of professional care.

One way to find a contact lens specialist is by a referral from your physician or a friend. Find out about the schedule of follow-up care and ask about initial and ongoing costs. Don't be afraid to shop around. And remember that lenses, by themselves, cost relatively little. What you pay for—and should insist on—is continuing professional care, supervision, and advice.

In addition to sunglasses, a hat with a brim is an important protection against harmful UV radiation and blue light.

Sunglasses

Sunglasses are no mere fashion statement: good ones provide safe, comfortable vision, especially on the beach, in a boat, or driving. The main purpose of sunglasses is to reduce the amount of visible light that reaches the eye. In addition, some people will want protection from glare, and others may need protection from ultraviolet (UV) rays.

If you wear prescription glasses, it is probably best to have sunglasses made according to your prescription. Clip-on shades may offer protection, but generally are not as comfortable or reliable as a custom-made, prescription pair of sunglasses. People who wear contact lenses and those with normal vision can get nonprescription sunglasses. But choose sunglasses carefully—many "over-the-counter" sunglasses, even some very expensive designer models, are of poor quality.

What your sunglasses should do

If you think that the best sunglasses are the darkest ones, you may be looking for trouble. Unless they have a coating to absorb UV light and blue light, dark lenses still allow damaging radiation to enter the eyes. While most sunglasses provide comfort in the sun—that is, they block high-intensity visible light and reduce glare sufficiently—nearly half don't provide adequate UV protection. Exposure to UV rays over the years can damage the lens, potentially leading to cataracts, and has been implicated in damage to the cornea and retina. Of the million cataracts removed each year in the United States, it's estimated that up to one hundred thousand may be sun-related and thus preventable. That's why eye specialists now recommend that everyone wear UV-absorbing sunglasses whenever they are in the sun—not just during the summer or at the beach.

Even fewer sunglasses block blue light, which recent research suggests may be a potential danger to the eyes over the long term. So if you're looking for maximum protection, the best sunglasses are those that block most or all blue light along with all UV rays. How do you find such glasses? While you usually get what you pay for, a high-price, high-tech model is no guarantee of protection. Here are factors to consider when buying sunglasses:

UV protection. Unless specially treated, sunglasses usually don't provide complete protection from UV rays, which extend from 290 to 400 nanometers (a unit of measure for wavelengths of light) in the light spectrum. A label claiming blockage of "100% UV" may be referring only to radiation up to 380 nanometers. The only industry standards for UV absorption are those of the American National Standard Institute (ANSI), but they are voluntary, are only for nonprescription glasses, and aren't regulated. Glasses that conform to ANSI standards have "Z-80.3" printed on the frame.

Do they block enough visible light? Excess light can damage the retina. Lenses should block 75 to 90 percent of visible light, thus transmitting only 10 to 25 percent of it. Some brands bear labels stating this "transmission factor." If this information isn't stated on the label, try on the glasses and look in the mirror—if they're dark enough, you won't be able to see your eyes.

Do they block blue light? Beyond UV rays on the spectrum is violet/blue light (400 to 510 nanometers), which may play a role in degeneration of the macula (the area

Labels and Standards for Sunglasses

Labeling for UV light and visible light blockage is voluntary, and there are no government standards. Some glasses now carry labels indicating that they meet the standards of the American National Standard Institute (ANSI). But if your sport or occupation keeps you in very bright environments, especially where sunlight is reflected off water, sand, or snow, it's best to see an eye-care professional, who can recommend special-purpose lenses to give you the maximum protection you need (see box).

You should also see an eye-care professional if you've had cataract surgery (which removes the eye's UV aborbent lens) or you're taking a drug (such as tetracycline) that increases sensitivity to UV light.

Special Needs, Special Lenses

If you do a lot of driving, are an avid cyclist or fisherman, or spend long hours at certain other outdoor activities or sports, the following types of lenses offer special characteristics that may best suit you.

Polarized lenses. These are usually made by sandwiching a polarizing filter between pieces of tinted plastic or glass to block glare reflected at certain angles from water, wet or sunlit roads, a car hood, or any other horizontal surface. They are good for fishermen, boating enthusiasts, and drivers; however, polarized lenses may bring out distracting patterns in some windshields. Unless specially treated, polarized lenses provide little protection against UV rays and blue light.

Mirrored lenses. The thin metallic coating (over a tinted lens) on mirrored lenses acts as an extra buffer against strong light and offers excellent protection against overall glare. This makes them useful for water and snow sports. Some mirrored lenses block more than 90 percent of all visible light, but not necessarily 100 percent of UV rays. The mirrored coating scratches easily.

Photochromic lenses. Made of light-sensitive glass (rarely plastic) that adjusts to light conditions, photochromic lenses are good for cyclists, golfers, and other people who are in constantly changing light. They don't work well in a car, however, since the interior isn't that bright and the windshield blocks much of the UV radiation that stimulates them. If you're considering sun-sensitive lenses, make sure they get dark enough when you go outside, and remember they may take several minutes to adjust to light conditions. How dark they become largely depends on their thickness and the temperature. Photochromic treatment is not by itself effective against all UV rays and blue light.

Gradient lenses. Many drivers and pilots prefer single-gradient lenses (darker at top than at bottom), which allow them to see the dashboard or instrument panel easily. Because of the glare reflecting off the snow or water, skiers and fishermen often prefer double-gradient lenses, which are darker at the top and bottom than in the middle. Gradient lenses can be polarized, photochromic, or mirrored.

of the retina with greatest acuity) over a long period of time. Some eye-care experts believe that everybody should wear lenses protective against all UV rays plus most blue rays, just as everybody should wear a potent sunscreen whenever in the sun. This is especially important if you:

•Spend much of your time outdoors, especially where the effect of the sun's rays is most intense—at high altitudes or where sunlight is reflected off water, sand, or snow.

•Are fair-skinned and blue-eyed.

•Have had cataract surgery, which removes the eye's UV-absorbing lens. You need to be especially careful if you have had a lens implanted that has no UV protection.

•Have a personal or family history of macular degeneration.

•Are regularly taking medication, such as tetracycline, that increases your sensitivity to UV rays.

Lenses that absorb blue light are tinted yellow, brown, or amber. Generally, these also provide comfort from glare, particularly for older people. However, since lenses that block all blue light distort some colors, you may prefer a partial block. The amount of protection a particular brand offers may be indicated on the label; otherwise, you should consult your eye-care professional.

Size. Make sure that the lenses are large enough to protect against light coming in from the sides, top, and bottom of the frames. Wraparound sunglasses can be particularly effective.

Fit. Sunglasses shouldn't slip down your nose. A study from the University of Massachusetts Medical Center has shown that when glasses slipped even just one quarter inch from the forehead about 20 percent more UV rays entered the eyes.

Color. Gray, followed by green, lenses have traditionally been considered best because they distort colors least. Brown and amber lenses are now gaining favor for certain sports or activities; not only can they help block blue light, they may also enhance contrasts in haze or fog. Fashion tints such as purple can greatly distort colors, particularly traffic lights. Check color accuracy by looking outdoors.

Glass or plastic. There are pluses and minuses for each type. If you toss your glasses around, glass may be better because it resists scratching, but thick glass lenses can be heavy. Plastic is lightweight and doesn't fog up much, but it scratches, and scratch-resistant coatings are easy to smudge. Both materials need to be specially treated for adequate protection against UV rays. Lenses made from polycarbonate (a special plastic) are often used by cyclists since they have improved impact resistance.

No distortion. Distorting lenses won't harm your eyes, but they may give you a headache. You can test sunglasses for distortion in the store. When shopping for nonprescription sunglasses, hold them at arm's length and look at a straight line in the distance. Slowly move the lenses across that line; if the line sways or bends, the lenses are imperfect. Look through the periphery as well as the center of the lenses. (This test will not work for most prescription lenses, some of which cause a straight line to waver or curve.)

How to choose. Your best bet, particularly if you have special needs, is to talk to an eye-care professional, who will have technical data from manufacturers. However, you can buy protective sunglasses at other retail outlets, provided you ask the right questions about the amount of visible light, UV rays, and blue light absorbed by various brands. Don't go just by how the glasses look on you.

Reading Glasses

Most people over forty-five begin to need glasses to read small print, even those who still have excellent distance vision. This perfectly normal condition, called presbyopia (meaning "old eyes"), occurs when the lens of the eye becomes less flexible and thus less able to change shape and focus on close objects.

All that's needed to correct presbyopia is a set of reading glasses. These can cost one hundred dollars or more if prescribed by a specialist; yet over-the-counter glasses, which cost around twenty dollars, may be just as effective. These glasses must meet the requirements of the American National Standards Institute (ANSI) and of the Food and Drug Administration (FDA), including impact resistance tests.

There's an important caution, however: over-the-counter reading glasses won't correct nearsightedness, astigmatism, or other refractive defects, and buying a pair of them is no substitute for an eye exam. If your vision is changing rapidly, consult an optometrist or ophthalmologist to make sure that a magnifier is all you need.

When you pick out nonprescription reading glasses, be sure you have the time to try on several pairs and read the test cards provided. You might also carry along a book or newspaper for testing. Glasses will usually be marked with a number ranging from 1.00 to 4.00, indicating the magnifying power. (Low magnification would be 1.25 or 1.50, high would be 3.00 and above.) Start at the low end and work your way up, holding the card at a comfortable reading distance. (In New York, only lenses up to 2.75 can be sold without a prescription.)

Eyestrain and Computers

By 1990 some seventy million people will be working at video display terminals (VDTs), and that does not include those who use computers at home. Many people who spend their workdays in front of terminals suffer from eyestrain (visual fatigue, headache, eye irritation, and similar symptoms). But some studies show that these problems were judged no worse than those caused by any close work and were not unique to video display terminals. However, clinical findings at the School of Optometry at the University of California, Berkeley, suggest that working regularly at a video display terminal may cause a premature loss in the eye's ability to focus. Dr. James Sheedy, chief of the VDT clinic at the university, emphasized that his evidence was preliminary and that his conclusions were based on people who had come to the clinic with eye problems—not on a controlled study.

Still, of 153 patients who averaged six hours a day at a video display terminal for four or more years, more than half had difficulty changing focus. Presbyopia, or loss of ability to focus with advancing age, accounted for half of these problems. The other patients, though, were in their twenties and thirties and should have had good focusing mechanisms. Eyeglasses corrected the problem. The conclusion is: if you work at a computer screen, you should have your eyes checked annually. (And when you do, tell your eye-care professional that you work at a screen.) Also:

•If you already have corrective lenses, you may need a special prescription for work at a terminal. Regular reading glasses, designed to focus at about eighteen inches, may not be right for terminal work if the screen is farther away.

Myth: Eyeglasses that are too strong can make your vision worse.

Fact: Eyeglasses can't worsen your vision or damage your eyes. If you think your reading glasses are too strong or if you have difficulty with a new prescription, you should certainly see your ophthalmologist or optometrist. It makes no sense to wear glasses that seem too strong or otherwise unsatisfactory—they're uncomfortable and can interfere with your daily life, and might cause you to have an accident. But they won't actually hurt your eyes. Going without your glasses doesn't hurt them either (unless you have a special eye problem for which glasses are part of the treatment).

•Bifocals may not be well suited for video display terminal work because the near-vision part of the lens is designed for looking down. Even trifocals may not help, since the field of vision in the medium-distance range will be too narrow to take in the whole screen. If you wear glasses and use a video display terminal, you'll probably find that single-vision lenses are best for this distance.

There are other ways as well to cut down on VDT eyestrain:

•Choose nonreflective glass screens, and eliminate reflected glare from windows or light fixtures. Overly bright light can be worse than inadequate lighting.

•Keep the reference document as close to the screen as possible and at the same level, so that you needn't change reading focus as you work. Light it at the same intensity as the screen.

•Keep your screen ten to fifteen degrees below the straight-ahead eye position.

•Take regular breaks—fifteen minutes every hour or two—to perform other work. Frequently look away from the screen to rest your eyes momentarily.

Glaucoma

Glaucoma, a disease of the eyes marked by increased pressure within the eyeball that can ultimately damage the optic nerve, currently affects about two million Americans. It cannot be prevented, but it can be treated and sometimes cured by surgery or laser treatment. If it is caught early, it need not result in blindness.

Open-angle glaucoma, the most common type, has nearly no symptoms in its early stages; its earliest sign is a painless increase in eyeball pressure, which can only be measured by an eye-care specialist. Side or peripheral vision may be affected, but only gradually. Those at high risk for developing glaucoma are:

•anyone with a family history of the disease;
•blacks;
•the severely nearsighted;
•diabetics;
•anyone over age sixty-five (up to 3 percent of whom may have the disease);
•anyone taking certain blood-pressure medications or cortisone.

Accurate screening for glaucoma is best done by ophthalmologists or optometrists, who can perform a specialized type of measurement of the pressure within the eye called tonometry; dilate the pupil for a complete look inside the eye; and carry out measurements to detect subtle losses of peripheral vision. Studies have shown that a combination of screening procedures is more likely to uncover early glaucoma than the simple hand-held tonometer used by many primary care physicians. According to the American Academy of Ophthalmology, a complete ocular examination should be done at least once between age thirty-five and forty-five and repeated every five years after age fifty. Those who fall into any of the risk groups should begin routine testing at an early age.

While open-angle glaucoma at first has no symptoms, there is a rarer type that manifests itself by a sudden blurring of vision, a halo effect around objects, redness of the eye, and possibly nausea and vomiting. Anyone with these symptoms should immediately seek medical help, since glaucoma of this type can quickly damage the optic nerve.

Floaters

Floaters—those spots or lines that drift across your eyeball from time to time—are generally nothing to worry about. Called "entoptic phenomena," they are sloughed off retinal cells "floating" in the vitreous—the jellylike substance that fills much of your eyeball. Floaters tend to appear when you tilt your head or suddenly glance up or down, causing cellular debris to cross the center of the retina.

But, in rare instances, floaters can be a danger sign. Flashing lights, a sudden onset of floaters, or a rapid increase in them (especially if they are confined to one eye or appear in large clumps), blurry vision, or partial shading of your visual field may indicate that your retina has—or is about to—come loose. If you have such symptoms, call an eye doctor or go to the emergency room at once. Don't wait until the next morning, as a detached retina, when untreated, can lead to blindness.

Ear, Nose, and Throat

Disorders of the ear, nose, and throat—such as hay fever, the common cold, hoarseness, and hearing loss—are troublesome afflictions that affect nearly everyone at one time or another. While not life threatening, such problems can cause considerable distress and discomfort. Fortunately, there is much that you can do yourself to prevent or alleviate them.

Colds

Though people don't die of colds and seldom develop serious complications from them, the discomfort can be debilitating. A cold is by definition temporary and self-limiting. The symptoms vary but usually include a runny nose, sneezing, a sore or scratchy throat, hoarseness, coughing, and general malaise, as well as occasional low-grade fever (more often found in children than adults), and muscle aches and pains. Inflamed membranes in the nose and throat may cause discomfort day and night, making normal life (including sleep) difficult.

What causes colds

Researchers know more than they used to about how colds are transmitted and about the viruses that cause them. At least two hundred different cold viruses exist, the most common being the rhinoviruses ("nose viruses"), which are estimated to cause 30 percent of all colds. Rhinoviruses tend to infect people in late summer and early autumn. Other types of viruses, not so well understood, are more likely to cause winter and early spring colds.

A sure way to "catch" a cold virus to which you are not already immune is to get a dose of it directly in the upper nose, where the temperature and humidity are ideal for its growth. In laboratory experiments, putting rhinovirus in the noses of volunteers almost always gives them a cold, no matter what their state of physical or emotional resistance or whether they are cold and wet or warm and dry. Three possibilities exist for getting cold viruses into your nasal passages: they may travel through the air (from the sneezing or coughing of others); they may be transmitted through direct contact (shaking hands with a cold sufferer, for example, and then touching your eyes or nose); or they may spread via a telephone, toy, or cup used by a cold sufferer. One study has found that airborne transmission is common in adults, whereas children tend to transmit secretions directly.

But, in fact, unless the virus gains access to the upper nose, the body has many lines of defense against it. Simply putting a cold virus near the nose usually has no effect, because it cannot penetrate the skin. The mucous membranes of the mouth are usually an effective barrier, so kissing is not an efficient way to spread a cold. Simply being in the same room with a cold sufferer won't do it. Workers in the same office usually don't share colds. They may have colds at the same time, but they are due to different viruses. Family members, though, do tend to share their colds. The three factors that primarily influence transmission are the amount of time spent around the cold sufferer, the volume of his secretions, and the amount of virus in them.

Who is most susceptible

No one knows what makes a person prone to colds in general or to any particular cold. Although newborns are thought to be immune to 20 percent of rhinoviruses (they get the antibodies from their mothers), they quickly lose their immunity. Small children are the most susceptible to colds, and can have six or eight a year. People who spend a lot of time with children, such as teachers, also tend to have numerous colds. Most people believe that being overtired or under emotional stress can "bring on" a cold. Others blame industrial pollution. There's no proof one way or another. There is evidence, though, that smokers are more likely to catch colds and to have longer-lasting symptoms than nonsmokers. Tobacco smoke paralyzes the hairlike projections that line the nose and throat. Thus, these cilia are less efficient at moving mucus out.

A flu shot won't help ward off colds. Influenza and colds are caused by different viruses.

Because of the great variety of viruses, no one vaccine could ever be effective against all colds. To track down every virus type and make a "magic bullet" for each would be a horrendous and probably futile task. (Through genetic technology it may one day be possible to identify a common genetic component in all cold viruses so that one vaccine would cover all of them.)

Yet in one sense, every cold is your last—from that particular virus. One compensation for growing older is that you develop immunity to a progressively larger number of viruses and thus catch fewer colds. By age sixty, most people have one cold per year, if any.

The weather factor

Colds do occur seasonally—peak periods in the United States are September, October, and early spring—and it is hard to keep from blaming them on the weather. Puzzlingly enough, researchers have never been able to connect cold viruses with the weather. (One theory says that people catch colds in September because the schools open then, and the most susceptible population—that is, children—begins transmitting viruses.) Getting chilled or undergoing rapid weather changes cannot cause you to catch cold. At least in the laboratory, low temperatures do not seem to increase susceptibility. In one study reported in *The New England Journal of Medicine*, one group of volunteers in a forty-degree temperature was exposed to cold viruses, while another group received its viruses in an environment warmed to eighty-six degrees. Both groups caught colds at about the same rate.

Some people believe winter is a prime time for colds because indoor heat removes humidity from the air, which dries out your nasal passages and makes you more susceptible. But while dry air may make you feel more uncomfortable if you already have a cold, there's no evidence that it increases your susceptibility to them.

The best way to avoid colds

The most effective way to keep a cold from spreading is hand washing. If you have a cold, remember that it spreads via your fingers, so wash them often in soap and warm water. If you are around people with colds, wash your hands often and try to avoid putting your fingers to your nose and eyes. Try not to share objects with cold sufferers—their telephones, pencils, typewriters and other tools, drinking glasses, towels, or bars of soap. Paper towels and paper cups are worthwhile investments during cold season. See that used tissues are disposed of promptly and properly. They should be discarded in a plastic-lined receptacle or paper bag, or in any manner that makes rehandling them unnecessary.

Though megadoses of vitamin C have been highly touted as a means of "heading off" a cold, no clinical trial has ever shown vitamin C to be more than marginally useful; there's really no reason to think that it will prevent or cure a cold or noticeably relieve symptoms. Megadoses of vitamin C—defined as more than ten times the Recommended Dietary Allowance (RDA) of sixty milligrams—can cause nausea, abdominal cramps, and diarrhea. Chewable vitamin C tablets can erode tooth enamel.

Managing a cold

There is little or nothing that a doctor can do for the common cold. Antibiotics, including penicillin, cannot cure or alleviate a cold, nor is it wise to take antibiotics in an attempt to prevent later bacterial infection. Most colds last a week or less, but two-week colds are not unheard of. (See box on page 318 for how to tell if it is more than a cold.) Your symptoms, however uncomfortable, are a sign that your body's defenses are working against the virus. A fever, for example, may represent one way of killing viruses, so there is no need to take measures to bring down a mild fever. Keep the following pointers in mind for your general well-being:

•Don't automatically "take something" for a cold or insist on giving medicine or vitamins to a child. Many over-the-counter cold medications made for adults

Cold Products

Decongestants. Available in pill form, nose drops, or inhalers, decongestants constrict blood vessels in the lining of the nose, open nasal passages temporarily, and may dry up mucus. They can also have a rebound effect—an increase in swelling and more congestion than ever if overused. In some people they can increase heart rate, induce insomnia, and elevate blood pressure.

Pain relievers. Aspirin and acetaminophen can relieve fever and muscle aches. Ibuprofen relieves muscle aches but not fever. Children under sixteen should not take aspirin, which may cause Reye's Syndrome. Pregnant women, especially in the last trimester, should avoid aspirin as well as ibuprofen. Alcoholics or those with liver or kidney disease should avoid acetaminophen. In treating a sore throat, avoid aspirin-containing chewing gum and aspirin gargles. Aspirin applied directly to the mucous membranes won't reduce pain and can act as an irritant.

Antihistamines. These drugs are effective against hay fever but may make cold congestion worse; they can dry up secretions, but may also make mucus too thick, and thus difficult to expel by coughing up. They can also induce drowsiness.

Cough syrups. Coughing serves a useful purpose by clearing secretions from your throat. Thus cough suppressants should not be used for wet productive coughs, unless the cough prevents you from sleeping. Try hot drinks, steam, or hard candies instead. For a dry, nonproductive cough, suppressants may help you get a good night's sleep. Cough medicines that are expectorants can help to loosen mucus.

Combination cold medicines. Both children and adults should avoid those drugs that combine a variety of ingredients for "fast" relief of a whole range of symptoms. The active ingredients may work against each other, and none is likely to do much good.

Ear, Nose, and Throat

The Right Way to Blow Your Nose
Despite popular belief, it's not possible to rupture the eardrum by blowing your nose too hard. The sensations you may feel in your ears while blowing are due to vibrations resulting from pressure changes. But you can give yourself a bloody nose if you blow hard enough, by breaking blood vessels in your nose. And if you're suffering from an upper respiratory infection and have heavy nasal discharge, forcefully blowing your nose may send bacteria from the nose to your ears and so contribute to an ear infection. The best advice is still to blow gently.

Is It More Than a Cold?

There's nothing a doctor can do for a cold. Some symptoms, however, should tip you off that what seems to be a cold may be something more serious requiring professional care:

- Oral temperature above 103 degrees.
- Severe pain in the chest, head, stomach, or ears.
- Enlarged neck glands.
- In a child, shortness of breath or wheezing (particularly difficult breathing), marked irritability or lethargy.
- Sore throat combined with oral temperature that remains above 101 degrees for twenty-four hours.
- Oral temperature that remains above 100 degrees for three days.
- A fever, sore throat, or severe runny nose that persists for more than a week.

contain ingredients that are harmful when taken by children.

- A salt- or sugar-water gargle (one-quarter teaspoon of salt or one tablespoon of Karo syrup added to eight ounces of water) can be helpful in relieving sore throat symptoms.
- Saline nose drops (also one-quarter teaspoon of salt to eight ounces of water) may clear your nasal passages.
- "Drink plenty of fluids" is time-honored advice, but there is no evidence that an increase in fluid intake will do anything but increase the need to urinate. Drink as many fluids as you want. They ease a dry throat. You need not force them on yourself or any other cold sufferer.
- Hot drinks, on the other hand, are definitely comforting. In one study, chicken soup (as compared with cold water and hot water) was shown to increase the flow of nasal secretions. The taste and aroma was thought to be part of the therapy, as well as inhalation of the vapor. Some other hot soup might do as well, depending on your preferences and the availability of the soup. Tea with honey is not bad, either.
- Hot alcoholic beverages or a shot of brandy may sound tempting, but alcohol dilates blood vessels and may produce more nasal congestion. Overindulgence, obviously, may bring on stomach upset and headache. Pregnant women are advised never to drink.
- Bed rest will not cure a cold or even alleviate symptoms, but if you feel exhausted or your symptoms are distractingly painful, rest at home—either in bed or just around the house.
- If a child has a cold, going to school will do him no harm. But for the protection of other children, a child in the first stages who has a severe runny nose should probably stay at home. The most infectious period generally begins about a day before symptoms appear and lasts only another day or two.
- Increased humidity in the air you breathe can sometimes make you feel better, at least temporarily. Hot-water vaporizers offer some advantages but can cause burns and scalding. Use a cold-mist vaporizer or humidifier if you wish. There is no value in adding medications to the water. Remember that humidifiers can harbor molds, which may cause allergic reactions. Clean the tank daily, rinsing with a mild solution of chlorine bleach and refilling with fresh water.
- There's no harm in exercising if you feel up to it, but you should never force yourself if you feel too tired or unfit, or if you have a fever. A break of two or three days in your exercise program won't be a significant setback.
- A red and sore nose and lips, caused by mucous secretions and aggravated by nose blowing, can often be relieved with a light application of petroleum jelly or skin lotion.

Hay Fever

According to the Asthma and Allergy Foundation of America, about one in every thirteen Americans has the seasonal runny nose, itchy eyes, sneezing, and throat congestion that hay fever produces. What most people call a cold is actually hay fever, and it usually vanishes with the first frost. The term hay fever is ill-chosen, since hay does not cause the disorder, nor is it characterized by a fever. It is a form of allergy, usually to some seasonal airborne pollen, such as spring grasses or autumnal ragweed. Other allergens can also cause hay fever symptoms—mold spores, animal dander, foods, feathers, or cosmetics.

The first step in preventing hay fever is to find out what you are allergic to. You may be able to determine this yourself by noticing when the symptoms occur in relation to a specific allergen. If you are unable to pinpoint the cause, consult a physician or allergy specialist. Besides determining what substance is bothering you, a specialist may also be able to prescribe antihistamines or other medication to relieve symptoms.

How do you avoid the allergen, once you identify it? If the problem is a cosmetic, feather pillow, household pet, or food, the solution may be relatively simple. If the problem is ragweed, you might—during the worst of the ragweed season—vacation in some region that is free of ragweed. Almost any place outside of North America will do, except the western coast of France. The Pacific coast has almost no ragweed but does have other pollens. Very dry regions and high altitudes may be helpful, and you may also find relief at the seashore, but it is hard to find a place that is really pollen-free. If you are allergic to common trees or grass, escape may not be possible.

If you have to stay at home during hay fever season, keep your windows closed. If possible, stay in an air-conditioned room and use an air-purifying machine (an electrostatic precipitator). Drive with your car windows closed. Pollen is likely to be worse in rural and suburban areas than in cities, and less troublesome near the water. Nights are better than days. Rain may improve the condition, unless you are overly susceptible to cold and damp.

If all else fails, you may respond to a series of desensitizing immunizations after suitable testing under the care of a good allergist.

If you're allergic to molds, raking leaves can cause itchy eyes, nasal congestion, and difficult breathing. The risk of allergic reaction is less if you rake freshly fallen leaves, since it takes a day or two for leaves to decompose and for molds and mildew to develop.

Hoarseness

It has long been known that high noise levels can cause hearing loss over time. But the noisy modern world may have an effect on your speaking voice, too. As the noise around you increases, you tend to shout over it and thus alter the quality of your voice. In addition, more people these days work in jobs requiring heavy telephone use. Trying to sound authoritative, people sometimes unconsciously pitch their voices lower than is really comfortable.

Your vocal cords react just like any other tissue strained by overuse: they resist. Typical symptoms are hoarseness, dry cough, and increasing difficulty in producing normal sound. Continued irritation can result in small benign growths—known as vocal nodes or polyps—on your vocal cords.

Protecting your voice

How can you head off these problems or minimize the damage and get your natural voice back? One way is to follow some of the rules professional entertainers follow to protect their voices:

•Avoid talking over background noise. Wait until the hubbub subsides.

•When using the telephone, speak softly. If you have to be on the telephone for long periods, a phone rest or a headset may lessen the strain on muscles in your face, throat, and neck, thus relieving some vocal cord tension. Try to rest your voice between telephone calls.

•Be aware of voice pitch. Don't pitch your voice unnaturally high or low.

•If you are hoarse or your voice is squeaky, rest your vocal cords. This means that for two or three days you should speak only when absolutely necessary and in a soft, breathy voice. Don't whisper. That puts more pressure on your vocal cords than speaking softly.

•Keep your vocal cords well lubricated. Increase your fluid intake. Increase the humidity in your surroundings. Avoid alcohol and cigarettes. A glycerine throat lozenge may be helpful, but avoid cold pills containing decongestants or antihistamines, which may dry your throat.

If hoarseness, voice change, or discomfort lasts more than two weeks (and you don't have a cold or allergy), check with your doctor. When all other measures fail, surgical treatment for polyps may be an option. Many chronic voice problems can be solved with the help of a speech-language therapist. Such therapists are usually certified by the American Speech-Language-Hearing Association and licensed by the state; your throat specialist should be able to refer you to one.

Nosebleeds

Unless you've had a blow to the nose, a nosebleed usually starts and stops spontaneously. The dry air of wintertime can be a major factor. So can the low humidity of an airplane cabin. The septum (nose partition) is the most common site of bleeding. When the fragile nasal membranes in the forward part of the nose dry out, they crack easily, and it doesn't take much to damage the blood vessels that lie just beneath their surface. These thin membranes offer very little supporting tissue, especially as they grow more delicate with age. Inflammation from a cold, an allergy, or sinusitis can also weaken the tissue.

Thus blowing your nose hard can set off a nosebleed; so can picking or hard rubbing—and, of course, a bump or blow. If you have a history of nosebleeds, it may help to use a home humidifier. Avoid repeated rubbing or picking.

The following measures usually stop a nosebleed quickly:

•Sit up so that gravity will lower pressure in the veins. To keep blood from running back into the throat, tilt your head forward a little.

•Pinch the fleshy part of the nose (between the bridge and the nostril) with your thumb and index finger for five to ten minutes. Applying ice probably won't help, since it's really pressure, not temperature, that stops the bleeding.

•After the bleeding stops, don't blow your nose too hard or too often. Sneeze through an open mouth, and avoid strenuous sports for a few days. Apply a little petroleum jelly with your fingertip or a small cotton swab just inside the nostrils several times a day for a week to keep membranes moist. If your nose bleeds on plane trips, try using petroleum jelly before you depart.

In people past middle age, nosebleeds sometimes start farther back in the nose, beyond the fleshy area. And a blow to the nose can also result in bleeding farther back in the nose. Since it may be harder to stop, this type of nosebleed is a potentially serious problem that may result in significant blood loss and require medical help.

A nosebleed doesn't herald a stroke, nor does it necessarily signal hypertension, as some people believe. Of course, those with hypertension who take aspirin or other blood-thinning drugs may have more frequent episodes of nosebleed. If the bleeding doesn't cease with simple remedies, you should see a doctor.

Swimmer's Ear

A common plight of those who swim competitively, for exercise, or just for fun is swimmer's ear. This painful, itchy infection of the external ear canal most often develops after long periods of swimming or bathing. Water gets trapped in the ear canal, where it softens and breaks down the skin lining, making it an ideal breeding ground for bacteria.

To prevent swimmer's ear, take these simple precautions:

• After swimming, shake your head to remove water trapped in your ears.

• Gently dry the external ear with a corner of a towel. Don't insert cotton swabs or anything else into the canal to dry or clean your ears. This could cause injury, remove protective earwax, and encourage infection.

• If you are prone to swimmer's ear, try this home remedy. After swimming, insert one or two drops of a one part white vinegar and one part rubbing alcohol mixture into each ear and let them remain there for thirty seconds. Before inserting, warm the drops to body temperature by holding the container in your hand for a few minutes. This solution will restore the normal acid balance of the ear canal as well as help dry it out. People who are sensitive to alcohol can substitute water.

If, despite these precautions, you do develop swimmer's ear, don't scratch—use the vinegar/alcohol drops three times a day. Scratching or inserting cotton swabs will only encourage the infection. One expert estimates that vinegar/alcohol drops cure 80 percent of external ear infections. Keep your ear dry until the infection has cleared; this usually means no swimming for two weeks. If your symptoms persist for several days, or if they get worse, see your physician. If you have or suspect you have a ruptured eardrum, do not swim or use ear drops without consulting your doctor. If you get a burning sensation or a sharp pain in your ear when you use the vinegar/alcohol drops, it may be a sign of a perforated eardrum; stop using the drops and see a doctor immediately.

Hearing Loss

The ear is a remarkable piece of sound-receiving equipment, designed to last for decades without repair or replacement parts. With age, this receiver inevitably

The Right Way to Clean Your Ears
Some people use cotton swabs or even bobby pins to clean wax from their ear canal (the tube leading to the eardrum). Such objects can push wax up against the eardrum and temporarily impair hearing. They can also irritate the delicate skin of the canal or, far worse, perforate the drum.

Wax build-up isn't a problem for most people, since the ear canal is basically self-cleaning. Wax accumulates, dries up, and falls out of the ear or is washed off. It's okay to use your well-washed little finger to wipe off wax near the outer part of the canal.

If wax does accumulate in your ear canal, you can try an over-the-counter wax softener. Follow directions carefully. Don't use any medication that causes fizzing in your ear, since this may perforate your eardrum. (Don't put any liquid in your ear if you have a perforated drum.) If your ear remains blocked because of impacted wax, consult your doctor.

grows less acute; hearing loss makes social communication a chore for half of all men and a third of all women over sixty-five. But some of this hearing loss is preventable and much of it is modifiable.

Excessive noise: a common cause of hearing loss

Few people realize that excessive noise can accelerate age-related hearing loss. Currently, the Department of Labor sets some limits for allowable exposure to noise in the workplace, or at least requires that workers be given protective devices, but no government agency protects us from the din of the casual environment or from the recreational noise we inflict on ourselves.

A decibel is a physical measurement used to express the relative intensity of sound; a whisper produces 20 decibels (dB), an ordinary conversation, 60. The decibel scale is logarithmic—each rise of 10 dB represents a tenfold increase in physical energy; a rise of 20 dB, a hundredfold increase. However the perception of sound does not follow the same logarithmic scale. For example, at a moderate sound level, an increase of 10 dB may be perceived as only a doubling of volume. Sounds become annoying around 70 dB (a vacuum cleaner), and potentially damaging at 85 or 90 dB (a motorcycle close by). Electronically boosted Mozart isn't any easier on the ears than rock music. Headphones mercifully shield innocent bystanders, but they can damage the user's hearing over the long haul. Millions of people now use headphones—while working, while exercising, or on long plane flights—and even a cheap set can put out more than 110 dB. (The Environmental Protection Agency has proposed that industrial workers be exposed to no more than 85 dB for eight hours and recommends that exposure time be cut in half for every 3 dB over this amount. Thus enduring 106 dB for three minutes is the equivalent of eight hours at the recommended maximum level.) Studies have suggested that people tend to listen at high volume, but it's hard to specify at what point hearing loss begins, for the decibel level interacts with the length of exposure. Decreasing one but increasing the other keeps the risk more or less constant. The longer you're subjected to the noise, the harder it is on your ears.

Reducing noise

There are many common sense ways of avoiding hearing loss:

•When wearing headphones, never use the music to drown out other noise. If you want to use headphones while your companion watches the ball game on television, perhaps you should move to another room rather than compete with the television noise. If you're in a bus that is making a deafening racket, lay your headphones aside. If you can't hear any sounds around you, you've got the volume too high.

•If background noise in any setting drowns out a normal conversational voice, you should try to escape or reduce the noise as soon as you can. If you have to shout to be heard, something is wrong.

•If you must be exposed to high noise levels while you are working or commuting, give your ears a break during leisure time. Don't go to the noisiest restaurant or nightclub in town.

•If you have to be in noisy environments frequently, carry a pair of earplugs and use them. They won't keep you from hearing a concert, for example; they'll just keep the decibels from damaging your ears.

Combating hearing loss

Even with precautions, however, age-related hearing loss is still a problem for many people. Most hearing problems can be alleviated by a hearing aid, yet only about one-third of those who need hearing aids actually have them.

It isn't easy to admit to hearing impairment; it's too often taken as an embarrassing sign of "old age." But the truth is that *most* people suffer some degree of hearing loss after age fifty. This age-related degeneration of the inner ear—called presbycusis, from the Greek meaning "old hearing"—results in lowered sensitivity to high frequencies (you don't catch those high notes or the doorbell the way you used to) and a loss in the ability to discriminate among speech sounds (it seems that people mumble). Or you may be aware of a persistent low hiss or ringing in the ears.

Any one of these symptoms should send you to your doctor for advice. Don't go first to a hearing-aid dealer. If your doctor recommends a hearing aid, you'll need his written prescription, and you should take your hearing test results along so that the dealer can match the hearing aid to your particular problem.

Medicare will pay for an evaluation of your hearing loss if requested by a physician, but not for the aid itself. It pays to shop around. Look for a dealer who'll give disinterested advice and reliable after-sales service. Most dealers also offer a thirty-day free trial of any aid you select. All hearing aids consist of a microphone, amplifier, speaker, volume control, and battery. Most people want a model worn behind or in the ear, or fitted to a pair of glasses. Some people may be able to wear an aid that fits entirely inside the ear or even in the ear canal. (These smaller devices tend to distort sound and are useful only for mild hearing loss, but new technology offers marked improvements.) People with severe hearing loss may still need the type worn in a shirt pocket with a wire connection to an ear receiver. Many newer types of assisted hearing devices are being developed, one of which should be able to help you even if your hearing loss is marked. Don't assume, however, that only the most expensive model will do. Get one that seems to meet your needs, and ask your doctor to check it.

Tips for coping

If you know someone with hearing loss (with or without a hearing aid) there are many ways to make life easier for him. Indeed, a little thoughtfulness in this domain can counteract the tendency among some elderly people to withdraw from normal conversational give-and-take into depressed isolation.

When you talk to someone with a hearing problem:

•Speak a little louder, more distinctly, and in short, simple sentences. Don't shout; shouting distorts.

•Don't overarticulate. Just be sure to face your listener squarely.

•Make sure your mouth isn't obstructed by food, chewing gum, a cigarette, or your hands.

•Make an extra effort to bring hearing-impaired persons into the conversation.

If you have difficulty hearing:

•Don't be shy. Ask people to repeat or slow down if you don't understand.

•Cut out background noise. Turn off the radio or TV during conversation.

•In noisy places, station yourself near sound-absorbent surfaces (curtains, books, or upholstered seating) and stay clear of echoing expanses of plaster and glass.

• Above all, don't ignore even mild hearing loss. Delay in dealing with it can only intensify it, sometimes irreversibly. And it could be a sign of another medical problem that needs attention. Let your physician decide.

Tinnitus

Most of us hear faint ringing sounds occasionally when there's no external noise. Usually such sounds last a few minutes or, at most, several hours. But if ringing or other noises in your head are persistent, you have tinnitus. Though the term is from a Latin word meaning "to ring like a bell," people with tinnitus may actually hear many sounds, from buzzing, tinkling, and humming to popping and clanging.

Researchers estimate that about thirty-six million Americans have occasional or constant tinnitus. About ten million have such severe symptoms that they have sought medical help. The rest experience a low level of noise—usually in both ears but sometimes in just one—which can still be a nuisance, interfering with work, social life, and sleep. The onset of tinnitus doesn't signify that you will become seriously or permanently deaf, but tinnitus is often associated with some hearing loss—though it does not cause it. About 80 percent of Americans who have some hearing loss also experience tinnitus.

Tinnitus has been described by one expert as someone "listening to old age sneaking up on him," since the great majority of tinnitus sufferers are middle-aged or older. It usually comes on slowly, with intermittent episodes that may become chronic as you age. But some young people also experience tinnitus.

Causes of tinnitus
While it's true that the sounds of tinnitus are all "in your head," they are nevertheless real. The physiological or neurological cause of such subjective sounds isn't always known, but they are a symptom of something that has gone awry in the auditory system. For example, infections of the middle ear or a perforated eardrum can provoke tinnitus, as can a build-up of wax or dirt in the outer ear. One of the most common causes is exposure to loud noises such as gunshots, jet engines, jackhammers, chain saws, rock music, or industrial machinery. Tinnitus has also been linked to tumors of certain cranial nerves, head injuries, and excessive use of alcohol and aspirin.

There is a less common form of tinnitus—"objective" tinnitus—in which the sounds you hear can also be heard by your doctor listening with a stethoscope. Usually these sounds are produced by either the movement of the jaw (the temporomandibular joint) or the flow of blood in major blood vessels of the head and neck.

Medical treatment
There is no standard drug or medical procedure to relieve tinnitus. If you hear persistent ringing or other noises, you should see an otologist (ear specialist) or an otorhinolaryngologist (ear, nose, and throat specialist). He can determine if it is due primarily to an ear condition or to other medical conditions. For instance, if the underlying cause is otosclerosis (a fusing of minute bones in the ear), surgery may help relieve tinnitus. If a middle-ear infection is involved, it may be treated

with antibiotics. When conductive hearing loss, such as that caused by wax in the ear canal, is involved, treatment is almost always successful. However, when the cause is unknown—which is generally the case—the chances of medically correcting tinnitus are quite small.

Nonmedical treatment

There are nonmedical ways of relieving tinnitus that have proven effective. Perhaps the most promising method is to drown out the sounds of tinnitus with less bothersome sounds. For the many tinnitus sufferers with hearing loss, the ambient sounds picked up by a hearing aid can reduce or even eliminate tinnitus of medium or low pitch. A newer device that has been quite successful is the tinnitus masker, which is worn like a hearing aid and emits a steady, monotonous noise like wind in trees or the hum of an electric fan—a sound that quickly becomes familiar and can be easily ignored. One benefit of such a device is psychological: one of the most disturbing aspects of tinnitus is your lack of control over the noise, and a masker gives you back that sense of control. Masking devices must be approved by the Food and Drug Administration (FDA) because of the potential risk they pose if too loud. They are sometimes combined with hearing aids.

One expert estimates that almost 60 percent of patients with severe tinnitus can be helped by using a hearing aid, masking device, or combination device.

Self-help

Alcohol, caffeine, nicotine, and aspirin can all make tinnitus worse, so reducing your intake of them can help alleviate the condition. One of the only preventive steps you can take is to avoid loud noise; use ear plugs when necessary.

Since stressful situations often seem to aggravate tinnitus—and tinnitus in turn is stressful—almost any type of relaxation technique may help you cope. Some tinnitus sufferers have reported that biofeedback helped them temporarily. Claims have also been made for hypnosis and acupuncture.

Another way to deal with tinnitus is to join a self-help group, which can offer support as well as information about new techniques and treatments.

Dental Care

There is more to good dental hygiene than simply brushing your teeth every day. If you pay only superficial attention to your teeth and gums—or ignore them altogether—you risk developing a dental disorder that can require expensive and time-consuming treatment, or worse, can result in the loss of one or more teeth. Most tooth decay and subsequent tooth loss is preventable with proper oral hygiene (along with regular visits to the dentist). This chapter covers the right way to take care of your teeth at home and addresses other topics of dental care that may require professional intervention.

Basic Self-Care

The aim of dental self-care is to prevent the buildup of plaque—a gummy film made up of polysaccharides and bacteria that adheres to your teeth, especially along your gum line. Plaque control is the best way to avoid tooth decay and periodontal disease as well as bad breath. Not only does plaque lead to cavities, it also eventually combines with certain minerals in saliva to form tartar (also called calculus). These deposits, above and below the gums, lead to periodontal disease—called gingivitis in its earlier reversible stage. Symptoms of periodontal disease are bleeding, swollen and receding gums, bad breath, and, ultimately, loose teeth. Destruction of the underlying bone and loss of teeth occur in advanced stages. Obviously, it's worth taking every possible step to prevent all this.

Steps for clean, healthy teeth and gums

Here are the essentials of good oral hygiene:

•Your first line of defense is brushing thoroughly at least twice a day, and flossing once a day. *Total time: five minutes a day minimum* for the brushing and flossing, in order to thoroughly clean all tooth surfaces, especially those between the teeth. (For more detailed advice on toothbrushes and other dental equipment, see page 327.)

•Use a fluoridated toothpaste.

•Use a brush with soft bristles (hard bristles can damage the gums), and hold it at an angle pointed toward the junction of teeth and gums. For your upper teeth, point your toothbrush up at a 45 degree angle to the gum line; for the bottom teeth, point the brush down. That will help clean out plaque that may lurk at the gum line. Remember that the goal is not so much to polish flat surfaces as to clean between the teeth and in the spaces where teeth meet gums. Use enough pressure so that you feel the bristles against your gums, but don't press so hard that you do damage, particularly if you have periodontal disease. Brush back and forth on the outside and inside of your teeth, using short, gentle strokes, then brush the biting surfaces.

•Besides floss, you may find interdental brushes and special soft toothpicks (sold

Dental Anxiety

An estimated thirty-five million Americans suffer from some degree of anxiety over visiting the dentist, and another twelve million can be classified as true phobics. Fortunately, dentists are becoming more and more aware of the problem and have developed many ways to help patients relax—everything from fish tanks in the waiting room to video games to be played while in the dental chair. According to the American Dental Association, most dental squeamishness can be traced to an unpleasant childhood experience. Making a child comfortable with dental treatment from the outset can do much to eliminate anxiety in adulthood. The following tips will show you how to make your child's dental visits more pleasant.

•Don't put off a child's first dental visit until a painful condition has occurred. This will only teach the child to associate the dentist with pain. Your child's primary teeth are important, so have them examined as early as your dentist and pediatrician recommend.

•Emphasize to your child that the dentist is a friendly doctor. Never threaten a child with a visit to the dentist as punishment.

•Avoid passing on any fears about dental treatment you may have to your child. Studies have shown that parents and other family members often provide negative reinforcement about dentists. Dental treatment is not as painful as it used to be. In fact, thanks to widespread fluoridation and new developments such as dental sealants, many kids today have no cavities at all. And when dental work is necessary, modern equipment and techniques minimize the discomfort.

•Many dentists will postpone treatment until the second visit so that the child can become familiar with the surroundings. Ask the dentist to explain to your child what is being done and why it is necessary, and to use the "tell, show, do" technique—where the dentist demonstrates the procedure first—with your child during any treatment.

•To help your child relax, play a cassette tape of a favorite story at the dentist's office.

Is chewing gum an aid to dental hygiene?
It can be. Gum-chewing stimulates copious secretions of saliva, and saliva helps neutralize tooth-decaying acids in dental plaque. The chewing action also helps squeeze the saliva into the spaces between the teeth.

Frequent chewing, however, can inflict harmful stress on jawbone and gum tissue. Since most chewers favor one side of the mouth over the other, the favored side is overdeveloped, which can lead to jaw pain. Constant chewing can also erode biting surfaces, crack fillings, and loosen inlays, allowing the possibility of recurrent decay.

For dental health, the key to chewing is moderation: chew on a piece of sugarless gum within five minutes of finishing a meal, and chew for fifteen to twenty minutes, no more.

---

at the drugstore in matchbook packs) useful and effective for removing plaque between teeth.

•Nonfluoridated mouthwashes are not usually necessary. However, a fluoride rinse may be useful.

•See your dentist twice a year—or more often if recommended—for a thorough cleaning and removal of accumulated tartar.

•Finally, don't rely on the "magic" in any dental product to protect your teeth. There's no magic in dental hygiene. The most effective plaque fighter and tartar controller is you.

Brushes and floss

The key instruments for removing plaque and preventing gum disease are still the toothbrush and floss.

Toothbrushes. Look for soft nylon bristles with rounded or tapered ends rather than stiff natural bristles, which are much more likely to fray, damage gums, and become contaminated with food particles. Flexible, water-repellent nylon bristles are also smaller in diameter and able to remove plaque between teeth and around gums more efficiently. When you buy a new brush (every three or four months, or sooner if the bristles begin to mat), choose a compact head that can be maneuvered to any part of the mouth, particularly if your jaw is small. The shape of the handle doesn't really matter in most cases—use a bent or straight one, as you prefer.

Electric toothbrushes. These are not necessarily more effective. They may, however, save you time and may be useful for people with certain physical handicaps.

One special type of electric toothbrush is Interplak, which has ten soft bristle tufts that rotate at high speed, continually reversing direction. The bristles can get between teeth and reach most, if not all, tooth surfaces. Some dentists and periodontists recommend it, especially for heavy plaque formers. It may be possible to get the same cleaning from a manual toothbrush, but it would take more time and more work. Interplak isn't cheap, but it costs far less than dental visits for gum problems that result from chronic plaque buildup. Some dental insurance policies will pay for the device.

Floss. Though flossing is as important as brushing for healthy teeth and gums, surveys show that most Americans don't do it. Waxed floss is designed to glide easily between tightly aligned teeth, but most studies have found no difference between it and the unwaxed variety in terms of plaque-removing efficiency. Some brands of waxed floss use "natural" components: beeswax, aromatic oils, spices. These added substances provide no advantage over plain floss, other than possibly providing you with incentive to adhere more faithfully to a daily flossing routine.

Follow these tips for quick, safe, effective flossing:

•Break off about a foot and a half of floss. Wind most of it around the middle finger of one hand and then wind the other end around the same finger of the other hand. Unwind from the full "spool" as you work.

•Hold the floss taut between thumb and forefinger, with about an inch of floss between them.

•Don't snap the floss into your gums. Use a gentle sawing motion. Remember, you're after plaque on the side of the tooth.

•When you reach the gum line, curve the floss into a C-shape and slide it very carefully between tooth and gum until you feel resistance. Pull the floss down against the side of one tooth, then reinsert and repeat for the adjacent tooth.

•Don't forget the far side of your rearmost teeth.

•If you are just starting to floss, your gums may bleed for the first few days. As the plaque is removed, your gums will heal and bleeding should stop. If it doesn't, see your dentist.

Toothpastes

Though it's theoretically possible to get your teeth clean without toothpaste, it's still better to use toothpaste. Any toothpaste, or even baking soda, acts as an abrasive and cleans tooth surfaces. Thorough flossing and brushing with any toothpaste will remove plaque. The plaque-removing ability of one toothpaste is no greater than any other; a toothpaste's pleasant taste and clean aftertaste, however, can be an incentive to brush.

The benefit of fluoride. Fluoride really does reduce tooth decay—a fact established long ago in studies of children's teeth. And according to research published in the *Journal of the American Dental Association*, fluoridated toothpaste also reduces cavities in adults. Though older people tend to get fewer cavities than kids, gums recede with age, exposing the softer root surfaces to decay. You don't outgrow your need for toothpastes containing fluoride—even if the drinking water in your community is fluoridated. Fluoride toothpastes most commonly contain sodium fluoride or sodium monofluorophosphate. Both are effective. Any fluoride toothpaste with the American Dental Association (ADA) seal will do the job.

"Tartar-control." Toothpastes containing zinc chloride or pyrophosphates decrease tartar build-up on the tooth's exposed surface, according to several studies. One

Myth: Young children don't need to floss.

Fact: According to the American Dental Association, parents should floss their children's teeth from age one and a half until the children are eight years old, when they will probably be able to do it themselves. Children should be supervised, however, so that they do not injure their gums.

study suggested that a toothpaste with pyrophosphate, used twice a day, decreased tartar build-up on tooth surfaces by 36 percent over a three-month period, and by 46 percent over six months, compared with a regular fluoride paste. Even if a "tartar control" toothpaste bears the ADA seal on its label, this is only a partial endorsement stating that while such toothpastes may reduce the formation of tartar above the gum line, they have not as yet been shown to affect tartar formation below the gum line. Thus manufacturers cannot claim that these toothpastes have any therapeutic effect on periodontal disease. They are not a substitute for dental care and regular professional cleanings. Furthermore, any agent that cleans away plaque will reduce new tartar, whether it's marked "tartar control" or not. *Indeed, dental floss is still the best plaque remover and "tartar-control" agent.*

Another potential antiplaque weapon is sanguinaria or bloodroot (an herb with antibacterial properties), which is the active ingredient in some rinses. So far, there's no conclusive evidence that products with sanguinaria are any more effective than regular toothpastes.

Desensitizing toothpastes. Dental hypersensitivity is not a disease but a symptom—of a root exposed by receding gums, or possibly of a fractured tooth or a cavity. If a tooth or teeth become sensitive to heat and cold, you should check with your dentist. But if you have chronic hypersensitivity with no underlying cause, you may need a special desensitizing toothpaste containing potassium nitrate, sodium citrate, or strontium, for instance. Four or five brands are available with the ADA seal. To get fluoride protection when you're using a desensitizing toothpaste, look for a brand with added fluoride and use a fluoride rinse.

Dental rinses

Brushing thoroughly twice daily with a fluoride toothpaste and flossing once a day will be adequate dental hygiene for most people. But if you want added protection against decay, you can use a fluoride rinse after brushing. The ADA recommends a fluoride rinse for everyone (except children under six). Rinsing once a week seems to be effective for children. The benefits for adults, however, haven't been as well studied. Rinses contain either stannous or sodium fluoride—both effective in preventing decay.

Keep in mind, though, that a fluoride rinse is only extra insurance. No rinse or mouthwash can take the place of brushing with a fluoride toothpaste and daily flossing of your teeth.

If you are taking good care of your teeth, you don't need an antiplaque mouthwash any more than you need a "tartar-control" toothpaste. Studies have shown that antiplaque rinses do decrease plaque to some extent. But brushing and flossing do a better job.

A prescription rinse. Peridex, a prescription rinse that bears the ADA seal, is usually prescribed for those with symptoms of gum disease. It contains chlorhexidine, an antibacterial agent that sticks to the teeth and provides a longer antiplaque action than most other ingredients, which lose their effect after you spit out the rinse. Peridex is particularly useful for people with trench mouth or other infections; for those who have just had gum surgery; and for handicapped people who can't adequately clean their teeth. However, some patients may develop unpleasant side effects—discolored teeth and fillings, along with a brown film on the tongue. Professional cleaning can correct these.

Accessory aids

Nothing can replace brushing and flossing, but there are a few new implements that make flossing easier and more effective, plus other devices that take up where toothbrushes leave off. These are particularly useful if you have crowns, bridges, other orthodontic elements, or any hard-to-reach tooth surfaces.

Filament floss. Marketed under the trade name Super Floss, this improved floss has been given the seal of acceptance by the ADA. Each length has three parts: a stiff threader section, a fatter central section of nylon-mesh filaments, and a final section of regular floss. The threader gets under bridgework and other orthodontic work so that you can pull the filament "brush" after it. You gently move this section back and forth to get rid of debris and plaque. Then using the third section, you finish with a regular flossing.

Floss handle. This useful plastic device looks like a miniature coping saw and is a good utensil for people who lack the dexterity needed for normal flossing. You simply thread your floss through its two ends. Ready-threaded, throwaway, miniature versions are also available.

Floss threaders. These small plastic loops help you thread regular floss through the space between connected crowns and under bridges. First you pass the threader between your teeth, put the floss through the loop, then pull the floss through.

Interdental brushes. These look like tiny bottle brushes, and they're excellent for cleaning between widely spaced teeth, between teeth and bridges or crowns, and areas where the gum has formed a pocket because of some degree of gum disease. Studies show them to be more efficient than floss for removing plaque between widely spaced teeth. You either throw them away when they become matted, or fit replacement brushes to toothbrush-shaped handles. They come in a variety of sizes, so you can shop around for the one right for your teeth.

Rubber tips. You can buy toothbrushes with pointed soft rubber tips affixed to the ends of their handles. Or look for replaceable tips fitted to the end of a handle; some devices have a rubber tip at one end and an interdental brush at the other. The tips are useful for routine plaque removal, for gently stimulating the gums, and for removing debris trapped in orthodontic bands, around the margin of a crown, or around bridgework. Note, however, that studies show that in most cases regular use of an interdental brush or floss can accomplish these jobs equally well.

Toothpicks. These old reliables have been upgraded from the round, hard, splintery picks that are a standby in some restaurants, to flatter, round-tipped versions that soften in contact with saliva, massage gums, and remove trapped debris. Sold in matchbook-style packs, they're a useful adjunct to a brush and floss in getting rid of plaque.

Whatever dental aids you adopt, remember never to force anything between your teeth or into bridgework or other dental work. This can damage gums.

Special Concerns

Cleaning crowns and bridges

If you have had to replace a tooth, or teeth, with a crown or a bridge, you may have assumed that since the new "tooth" is artificial, you need not be so particular about dental hygiene. After all, a crown or a bridge can't get cavities. But, though a crown covers most of a tooth (usually one that has undergone root canal or has had extensive decay), what remains of the original tooth is still subject to decay, and your gums are still subject to periodontal problems. If you have a bridge (an artificial tooth attached to two abutting teeth), it is essential to keep both bridge and adjoining teeth free of plaque. If periodontal disease develops (signaled by gum swelling, inflammation, and bleeding), it could lead to bone loss and the destruction of the bridge support. A perfect fit in crowns and bridges is vital to good dental health. If the crown is too large, or if its base does not fit smoothly and continuously around the tooth, trapped food and plaque can collect under it.

Crowns, like teeth, need to be cleaned at least twice daily, after meals and especially at bedtime. A number of dental aids are available for cleaning around crowns and bridges. Besides floss and a soft-bristled toothbrush, you may need a floss-threader (see page 330). There are also special toothbrushes that go between the bridge and adjoining tooth. An oral irrigating device such as a Water Pik may help remove food debris. Wooden dental toothpicks that soften with saliva can be used to remove plaque from around crown margins. A rubber tip can also be useful along the gum margin. With crowns or bridges, pay particular attention to cleaning in that area.

Avoiding gum problems. Because they are slightly more difficult to keep clean at the margins than natural teeth, crowns and bridges have the potential for increasing gum problems, but good care can offset this tendency. Several studies have indicated that patients with restored teeth had no significant problems with them, so long as they were given (and followed) good instruction in dental care and had their teeth cleaned regularly by a dentist. If you are undergoing restorative dentistry, be sure to ask your dentist for suggestions and instructions for special care. Anything that exerts undue pressure on a crown or bridge, such as nail-biting and tooth grinding, can displace a restored tooth. Be sure your dentist checks for fit and stability at your regular visits.

Dental sealants

Sealants are a plastic-like coating applied to the biting surface of the teeth. When applied to children's teeth, they can prevent up to 80 percent of all cavities. Some dentists are prejudiced against sealants because the earliest sealants, which appeared in the mid-1970s, produced a fragile and easily dislodged coating. But today's sealants are far more advanced in design and execution.

Why are sealants helpful? Fluoride and brushing are effective against cavities on the smooth surfaces of the teeth, but they have little effect in preventing cavities on the biting surfaces—and that's where 80 percent of the cavities in children under fifteen occur. Dental sealants that are brushed on the pits and fissures of the teeth form a tight protective seal against decay. In combination with fluoride, sealants virtually guarantee a cavity-free mouth.

Teeth to be sealed are first cleaned with a mild abrasive, dried, and then etched with acid to improve the bonding of the plastic to the surface. The liquid sealant is applied with a fine brush and exposed to ultraviolet light or high-intensity white light to harden the bonding material. The procedure is painless and takes about half an hour to seal three teeth. The cost varies, but is usually less than half the cost of fillings. The sealant should last seven to eight years, and if it wears away or falls off, it is easily replaced without damage to the teeth.

Mercury in Dental Fillings

According to the American Dental Association, "For the vast majority of dental patients, mercury-containing amalgams present no health hazard." There's no evidence to support the claim that the mercury used as a hardener in silver dental amalgams can leach into your bloodstream in significant amounts and thus, supposedly, cause a variety of conditions, ranging from insomnia to multiple sclerosis. Researchers conducting tests on 1,100 people with amalgams found levels of mercury in their urine of less than 20 micrograms per liter; according to the American Conference of Governmental Industrial Hygienists, there's no need to be concerned unless levels exceed 150 micrograms.

Sensitive teeth

Does eating a bite of a frozen dessert or drinking something hot make your teeth ache? Dental hypersensitivity is a problem for an estimated one out of seven adults. It's usually caused by a thinning of the enamel on the crown or exposure of the root of the tooth. The receding gums that may occur as you get older can make your teeth hypersensitive to heat and cold; so can grinding your teeth at night or brushing with too stiff a toothbrush. Another aggravating factor can be brushing your teeth right after you have eaten or drunk some highly acidic food. For example, if you are in the habit of eating grapefruit for breakfast and brushing your teeth vigorously right afterward, the combination of citric acid and the abrasion of brushing may erode the enamel and bring on hypersensitivity.

Severe and persistent dental hypersensitivity can be a symptom of underlying tooth or periodontal disease. It's a sign that you need to see your dentist. If you have gum disease, cavities, or cracked enamel, a dentist can diagnose and treat them. At the same time, you can take preventive measures:

• If you suspect that you grind your teeth at night, ask your dentist to recommend a mouth guard.

• Don't brush your teeth immediately after drinking fruit juices or eating acidic foods (such as citrus fruits or tomatoes).

• Use a toothbrush that has soft bristles, not hard ones. Brush teeth thoroughly but gently.

• Use a special desensitizing toothpaste that has been approved by the ADA. These products usually contain potassium nitrate, sodium citrate, or strontium; some also have fluoride.

Wisdom teeth

At one time apparently the jaw had room for three sets of molars. But today the third molars, or wisdom teeth—dens sapientiae—often cause trouble. Sometimes they are badly positioned and crowd the second molars. Sometimes they fail to grow through the gums, a condition called impaction. A partially exposed wisdom tooth may decay because of overlying gum tissue that makes it hard to clean. Impacted wisdom teeth can also cause pain and swelling.

No wonder that removal of wisdom teeth is one of the most common forms of dental surgery today. It is often prescribed even for young patients before the roots of their wisdom teeth have fully formed. But if you have a wisdom tooth (impacted or not) that doesn't cause you any trouble, don't assume you should have it removed.

One school of dentistry says any wisdom teeth should be extracted to ward off future problems. But there is no evidence that a dormant wisdom tooth will necessarily harm the alignment of your teeth. A consensus report from the National Institute of Dental Research counsels general caution instead. Remove wisdom teeth only when there is clear evidence of trouble: infection, pain, a cyst, nonreparable cavities, or a threat to the second molars. (If you engage in contact sports, you should consider extraction, since there is some evidence that an impacted wisdom tooth seriously increases the risk of jaw fractures during such sports as football or boxing.)

If your dentist recommends extraction and you have any doubts, you should seek a second opinion.

Canker sores

Canker sores, those small crater-like lesions that can occur on or under the tongue or inside the cheeks, have not been proved to have a viral origin, nor are they contagious or a sign of disease. Painful and irritating as they are, they usually go away in about a week, with or without treatment. That's the good news. The bad news is that doctors aren't sure what causes them, or how to cure them.

Canker sores have bothered humanity since ancient times. Hippocrates coined the medical term for them—*aphthous stomatitis*—in the fourth century BC. Canker sores seem to be brought on by stress in some people; stress can also be a side effect. Heredity may play a role, and some women find that the sores recur with menstrual periods. Some people believe that food allergies can cause an outbreak. There's no proof, but it certainly won't hurt to follow your hunches.

Another suspect is trauma—the kind that comes from biting your tongue or the inside of your cheek. But again, trauma does not produce a canker sore. If you unconsciously bite the inside of your cheek, try to kick the habit. Any mouth injury can get infected. If you are prone to canker sores, stay away from anything that can hurt the lining of the mouth, such as hard-bristled toothbrushes and bones in meats. If canker sores become very painful, ask a pharmacist to recommend an over-the-counter medication. And if the lesions don't heal fully within two weeks, see your doctor.

TMJ

At one time or another most people have mild trouble with the hinge of their jaw. It may grind or click, feel as if it is about to unhinge itself, or even get sore enough to make eating chewy or hard foods—like a piece of steak or an apple— uncomfortable, even painful. Usually the condition goes away by itself, but in some people it persists painfully. TMJ is an abbreviation for this condition— Temperomandibular Joint Syndrome.

What causes jawbone pain and soreness in the muscles you use when chewing? TMJ is often related to stress. That certainly doesn't mean the symptoms are imaginary, but it does mean that such signs of emotional stress as muscle tension, clenching your teeth or grinding them at night, facial muscle fatigue or spasm, or such nervous habits as nail-biting or chewing the inside of your cheek can contribute to TMJ.

Correcting TMJ. First, try to pinpoint what's making you tense and do something about it. If you're under pressure at work or in your personal life, do what you can to alleviate the problem for the moment, and plan some breaks in your schedule. Make time for exercise and for conversation with friends. Do something you enjoy.

Second, even if you can't control the source of your emotional stress, try to be aware of your facial habits. If you're clenching your teeth or tensing your facial muscles, make a conscious effort to relax. Don't let teeth-clenching or chewing the inside of your cheek turn into a habit. Other helpful measures: give your jaw a break by switching temporarily to a soft, easy-to-chew diet, or by cutting your food into very small pieces. Try to suppress yawns. Stifle them by ducking your head and pressing your chin against your chest momentarily. If nocturnal tooth grinding is part of your problem, see your dentist. He can prescribe an orthopedic appliance or "splint"—a device fitted over the biting surface of your back teeth. Worn at night or occasionally in the day, it can keep you from grinding your teeth.

The Causes of Bad Breath

Chronic halitosis, or bad breath, is most often caused by periodontal disease (infection of the gums). It can also stem from a multitude of sources ranging from something as simple as food particles lodged between the teeth or a dry mouth to more serious conditions like respiratory or gastrointestinal disorders. Other contributing factors include smoking, alcoholic drinks, and such foods as garlic and onions. Mints and mouthwashes will only temporarily quell bad breath; they cannot cure anything.

If you practice good dental hygiene (brushing and flossing daily) and still have chronic bad breath, consult your dentist to make sure that periodontal disease is not the reason. And if it's not, see a physician to eliminate the possibility of lung or gastric disorders.

If your sore jaw persists for more than two or three days, you should consult your dentist. He can check for, and if necessary treat, an impacted wisdom tooth, swollen glands, or any mouth infection that might prove to be complicating your problem. If his diagnosis is TMJ he will probably recommend remedies like those listed above. He may also suggest applications of moist heat twice daily, as well as gentle massage of the painful area. Aspirin and other over-the-counter painkillers can also be useful. In severe cases prescription drugs such as muscle relaxants may help.

TMJ may also be caused by internal derangement of the jaw or other orthopedic problems of the joint, such as arthritis, disk degeneration, injury, or developmental disorders. If your dentist can't alleviate the pain, and the above measures offer no relief, he should refer you to a TMJ center or specialist.

If you have headaches, dizziness, ringing in your ears, eye pain, or other symptoms with no immediately evident cause, be wary of a diagnosis that attributes these symptoms to TMJ. For symptoms besides jaw soreness, see your doctor, not your dentist. Be cautious about any recommendations for surgery or other irreversible treatment for TMJ. At least get a second opinion from a dental surgeon.

In most cases TMJ is not totally curable. You may have recurrences throughout your life. But simple remedies at the first sign of trouble can help you manage the problem on your own.

Saving a knocked-out tooth

If you or a child of yours knocks out a tooth, the last thing you should do is throw it away. Pick it up, replace it in the socket if possible, call your dentist, and get to his office as soon as you can. Research shows that you have a 50 percent chance of a successful replantation if you get to the dentist within thirty minutes. Accomplishing this may not sound difficult, but don't underestimate the trauma of the situation: blood and confusion may delay you. Try to remain calm and rational—saving a tooth is definitely worth the effort. And even if more than thirty minutes elapse, take the tooth to the dentist anyway and let him decide what to do.

Follow this step-by-step post-accident procedure:

• After finding the tooth, rinse the it gently in tepid tap water, holding it by the crown (nonroot) surface. *Don't scrub the tooth*—this could injure the surface root tissue needed for successful replantation.

• Call the dentist to inform him of your imminent visit. Unless he tells you not to, gently insert the tooth in the socket. To seat the tooth properly, bite down firmly on a clean handkerchief or piece of cloth for at least five minutes; keep biting down with moderate pressure until you get to the dentist's office.

• If reinsertion at the scene of the accident isn't possible, place the tooth, bathed in saliva, under your tongue or inside your cheek until you get to the dentist's office. If a child is so young that he may swallow the tooth, transport it in a plastic cup or bag filled with milk or tap water and a pinch of salt.

Digestive Disorders

The digestive system is divided into a number of sections: the mouth, the esophagus, the stomach, the small and large intestines, and the rectum. The digestive organs and glands—the liver, gall bladder, and pancreas—are also part of this system. It is the job of the digestive system to take in food; to break it down so the nutrients can be absorbed by the body; and to eliminate waste.

Disorders of the digestive system afflict nearly everyone at one time or another. This section covers the most common digestive disorders—many of which are preventable or are treatable at home.

Heartburn

The most common cause of heartburn is "gastroesophageal reflux"—the backup of stomach contents into the lower esophagus, where gastric acids produce a burning sensation and discomfort. This can occur when there's too much pressure in your stomach—or sometimes a loosening of the muscle band (sphincter) separating the esophagus from the stomach—during the digestive process.

Occasional heartburn is no cause for concern. Repeated reflux can, however, lead to injury of the esophageal lining. If you frequently have heartburn, the following steps can help prevent or alleviate it:

•Don't overeat.

•Avoid tight clothing, especially waist-pinching belts.

•Try to avoid constipation by increasing your fluid and fiber intake. This will help prevent straining during bowel movements, which can increase abdominal pressure and encourage heartburn.

•Don't eat just before retiring, or lie down for a nap right after a meal. It helps to stay upright for at least several hours after eating.

•Put the force of gravity to work—don't sleep flat. Try elevating the head of your bed by at least six inches or more. (Wood blocks or a couple of fat phone books under the bed frame legs should do the trick.) This may be the single most important mechanical alteration that heartburn sufferers can make.

•Limit your fat intake, since fat slows the emptying of the stomach.

•If you're prone to heartburn or have eaten a heavy meal, avoid chocolate, alcohol, peppermint, and spearmint. Highly flavored after-dinner liqueurs, often thought of as aids to digestion, may make you feel worse. Caffeine may be an irritant, as may tomatoes and citrus fruits and juices.

•Birth control pills, antihistamines (often found in over-the-counter cold remedies), valium, and other drugs can promote heartburn. If you are taking any type of drug regularly, ask your doctor if it might be the cause of your heartburn.

•Don't smoke. Nicotine adversely affects the tone of your esophageal sphincter and thus can contribute directly to heartburn.

•If discomfort continues or recurs frequently, see your doctor.

Flatulence

Although most belching is due to swallowing air, most gas passed from the rectum is produced in the bowel. There's no need to fret about passing gas occasionally—everyone does it. Though on occasion it can be an acute social embarrassment, it's not a symptom of bowel cancer or other serious disease.

The offending gases, including hydrogen, methane, and carbon dioxide, are produced when bacteria that are normally present in the large intestine cause incompletely digested carbohydrates to ferment. The only real way to cut down on flatulence is to cut down on foods that contain these indigestible carbohydrate residues—particularly legumes like beans and lentils. Intestinal gas is also common in people who can't digest the lactose in milk and some dairy products. If you are bothered by excess flatulence, simply cut down on, or avoid, the foods that intensify the problem for you.

How to reduce gas

•Soak beans before cooking to remove some of the carbohydrates that cause gas. You must discard the soaking water and then boil the beans in fresh water.

•Chew food thoroughly. If you gulp it, you swallow harder-to-digest lumps that remain longer in the intestine, where their residue may ferment.

•Avoid constipation, which slows down the passage of food through the gastrointestinal tract, thereby stepping up fermentation. Eat high-fiber foods and drink plenty of fluids.

•If you have problems digesting lactose, avoid regular milk. Stick to cheese, yogurt, and special lactase-treated milk.

•Don't expect relief from over-the-counter remedies. Antifoaming agents (such as simethicone), found in some "antacid-antigas" preparations, merely change large gas bubbles into smaller ones—hardly a remedy for flatulence. Bulk-forming laxatives can actually promote the kind of fermented residues that cause the problem in the first place. As for products containing "activated charcoal," there's little or no evidence that they can actually absorb gas in humans, as claimed. They can, however, interfere with the absorption of some medicines.

Constipation

Constipation, defined as failure to have a bowel movement after three days or more, can usually be alleviated or prevented altogether by drinking plenty of fluids, exercising regularly, and eating a diet that features high-fiber foods—grains (including unprocessed wheat bran), fruits, vegetables, and legumes. Fiber provides bulk in the intestine and absorbs water, thus making bowel movements easier. As your grandmother may have told you, prunes are particularly effective in preventing constipation, as are raisins and figs. Besides drinking an adequate amount of fluids and forming good dietary and exercise habits, you should allow yourself time for bowel movements. Medical authorities advise that you never ignore the urge to defecate, even when it may not be convenient to interrupt your routine. If you follow these guidelines, constipation should not be a problem for you.

Laxatives are not the answer

In spite of what the laxative advertisements say, the human intestine does not have to function according to an exact schedule. It is okay for a person to have a bowel movement once a day, twice a day, every other day, or perhaps only three times a week, according to most doctors and the National Institutes of Health. What is normal for one person may not be normal for another.

Worry about "irregularity" leads many people to rely unnecessarily on laxatives or enemas. Recently an Food and Drug Administration Advisory Review Panel on laxatives and similar products expressed the view that Americans are too concerned about the health implications of bowel movements. We spend almost four hundred million dollars annually on laxatives—a mostly useless expenditure that fails to promote normal bowel movements or accomplish any health objective.

While a mild laxative may occasionally be appropriate if your eating or exercise habits have been altered by travel or some other circumstance, relying on laxatives can actually cause irritable bowel syndrome or other problems that will intensify constipation rather than cure it. A laxative is a drug and it should not have a permanent place in your medicine cabinet.

Constipation that lasts longer than a week is a signal to consult a doctor, for it can occasionally be a symptom of some underlying disorder.

Diarrhea

Simple diarrhea is common and has many causes; it can result from bacterial or viral infection or from eating contaminated food or drinking water. In addition, specific types of diarrhea can occur after taking antibiotics and with excessive use of certain over-the-counter antacids. People who are lactose-intolerant—that is, they have trouble digesting milk products—may also suffer from diarrhea if they eat dairy products.

Diarrhea occurs when too much water is passed along with the stool during a bowel movement. Normally, fluids in the digestive tract are mostly reabsorbed through the intestinal walls, so that fecal matter solidifies as it travels through the digestive tract. If something interferes with the effectiveness of that process, you'll pass excess fluid as you defecate. Fortunately, simple diarrhea is usually self-limiting—it gets better without treatment in a day or two. However, diarrhea can be serious, particular for children and the elderly, because of the risk of dehydration. And, at any age, diarrhea requires prompt medical attention if it lasts more than forty-eight hours or is accompanied by any of these symptoms: severe abdominal cramping, blood in your stool, or lightheadedness or dizziness (indicating dehydration). You should consult a physician if you get frequent bouts of diarrhea or if you have alternate bouts of diarrhea and constipation since this may be a sign of a potentially serious underlying disorder.

Prevention

Food poisoning is the most easily prevented cause of diarrhea. It's simply a matter of taking precautions when preparing, cooking, and storing food. (For information on how to prevent food poisoning, see pages 341-347.) People who are lactose intolerant should avoid the dairy products that seem to trigger symptoms or drink

Myth: Carbonated beverages relieve nausea.

Fact: Fluids—especially carbonated ones—are hard to keep down on a queasy stomach. What often works best for nausea is eating a cracker (or other dry food) and lying down for a while.

Drinking cola or ginger ale may be a good way to restart the eating cycle and to replenish any fluids lost through vomiting. But these beverages must be at room temperature and flat, and you should drink them in small sips. Carbonation bloats an already upset stomach and may actually cause more vomiting.

Apple and grape juices at room temperature are also good choices. Avoid citrus juices, however, since their acidity can further irritate the lining of the esophagus, and they often contain hard-to-digest pulpy solids.

milk treated with lactase. Avoid taking megadoses of vitamin C; too much vitamin C can cause diarrhea.

Treatment

First and foremost, drink water, fruit juices, or clear broth to help restore fluid balance. In addition, avoid alcohol, caffeine, milk and dairy products, and any products containing the sweeteners sorbitol, xylitol, and mannitol, most commonly found in sugarless gums, vitamins, and diet foods. If you suspect a drug you are taking could be the cause, stop using it—unless it is a prescription drug. In that case, consult your doctor.

Some over-the-counter medications to alleviate diarrhea can be useful in certain cases. Products containing loperamide (brand name Imodium), diphenoxylate hydrochloride, or bismuth subsalicylate can be helpful for run-of-the-mill diarrhea (Products containing tincture of opium, attapulgite, or kaolin, pectin, and atropine-like substances are not effective.) If you suspect food poisoning, however, you are probably better off letting it run its course; you want to get the harmful bacteria out of your system. But in that case, consult your doctor just to be sure.

(Traveler's diarrhea is a separate issue and is discussed on pages 427-428.)

Irritable Bowel Syndrome

Irritable bowel syndrome—also known as irritable or spastic colon—is a common condition that primarily affects women and usually begins in early adulthood. It occurs when the regular rhythmic contractions that normally propel waste through the intestines to the rectum, are disrupted by irregular contractions resulting in either constipation or diarrhea, or sometimes alternating bouts of both. Other symptoms include nausea, abdominal pain, abdominal distension, an uncomfortable feeling of fullness, gas, painful bowel movements, and sometimes heartburn or indigestion.

Treatment

No one really knows what causes irritable bowel syndrome, so there is no proven cure. If you frequently suffer from the symptoms of irritable bowel, you should make an appointment with your doctor who can rule out more serious disorders. If you are diagnosed as having irritable bowel syndrome, there are many things you can do to help keep it under control.

•Reduce the amount of anxiety in your life. Anxiety seems to be the most common condition associated with attacks. Try using relaxation techniques and regular exercise. (For more information on stress, see pages 401-409.)

•Keep a record of the foods you eat and drink, and pay special attention to the ones that seem to exacerbate symptoms.

•Many sufferers of irritable bowel have found that gradually increasing the fiber in their diets is helpful in reducing the frequency of attacks. However, when symptoms strike, some people respond better to a lower-fiber bland diet. You will have to experiment to see which one is right for you.

•If you smoke, stop. Smoking can bring on attacks.

•If none of these self-help measures work, your doctor may prescribe a bulk

Your stomach growling is the sound of your digestive juices mixing with gas as they move through the digestive tract. You are more likely to hear this noise when you're hungry because you tend to salivate more then and swallow more air.

laxative to stimulate muscle contractions and add volume to your feces or a drug to alleviate the abdominal pain and control muscle spasms.

Diverticulosis

Diverticulosis is a condition, not a disease. It occurs when tiny pouches (diverticula) form in the wall of the colon. These are small, self-contained hernias that appear to be related to aging, not diet or life style. People under thirty-five seldom have them, but one in ten Americans over forty does, and about one in every two by age sixty. The colon wall thickens as we age, and the pressure inside increases, causing small protrusions. The condition has no symptoms and is not usually serious.

However, in a small number of people diverticulosis can turn into diverticulitis, an inflammation of the colon that may have dangerous side effects. Caused by blockage of the diverticula and a subsequent overgrowth of bacteria, diverticulitis may cause severe pain and requires prompt medical treatment.

The best way to head off diverticulitis is to avoid constipation and straining during bowel movements. Don't take laxatives, however, which can irritate the large bowel. Keep your dietary fiber at the recommended level of thirty to forty-five grams daily, or even higher if constipation remains a problem. Eat fruits, vegetables, and whole grains. Wheat bran, which you can add to casseroles and baked goods, is especially helpful. These are good practices for the health of your digestive tract, whether you have diverticulosis or not.

Hemorrhoids

Hemorrhoids are cushions of a combination of blood vessels and muscle and connective tissue, normally present in the rectum and anus. Increased pressure on the hemorrhoidal veins, most commonly caused by constipation and subsequent straining on the toilet, pregnancy, or obesity, can result in a pooling of blood. These dilated veins are more susceptible to abrasion and hemorrhage.

In general there are two types of hemorrhoids, internal and external. Internal hemorrhoids lie within the rectum and are often painless. External hemorrhoids lie at the outer edge of the anal opening. Internal hemorrhoids sometimes protrude (or prolapse) through it, particularly during a bowel movement. Both types differ in degree of severity, from barely noticeable to large and protruding.

Bleeding is the most common symptom of both types of hemorrhoids. Pain results when thrombosis (clotting) occurs in one of the veins. The blood is usually bright red and visible on the toilet tissue when wiping, (rather than dark and mixed with the stool, which can be a sign of a more serious disorder). In addition, you may experience discomfort or even some pain when you have a bowel movement. Prolapsed hemorrhoids may produce a mucous discharge and can also cause anal itching.

While hemorrhoids can be painful, they are rarely dangerous. However, their symptoms can mimic those of more serious gastrointestinal illnesses. Therefore, *any* blood in your stool warrants a doctor's prompt evaluation.

Self-help

The best way to avoid hemorrhoids or ease the symptoms of those you may already have is to avoid constipation (see section on pages 336-337). Drink plenty of fluids and eat foods high in fiber, such as fruits, vegetables, legumes, and whole grains. If you already have hemorrhoids, gently clean the anal area after each bowel movement with moistened toilet tissue and dry yourself thoroughly afterwards. A particularly painful attack can be treated with warm sitz baths or an ice pack.

In general, over-the-counter anorectal preparations designed to provide relief of mild pain and burning can be used on a temporary basis, but avoid regular use unless ordered by your doctor.

Medical help

Hemorrhoids that become so enlarged that they are extremely painful or permanently protrude out of the anal opening may require treatment by a doctor. If removal of the hemorrhoid is warranted, a doctor may use an in-office procedure, such as rubber-band ligation, where a rubber band is placed around the hemorrhoid to cut off its blood supply so that the tissue will shrink and fall off. More serious protrusions may require other therapy, including surgical removal.

Laser treatment

Laser therapy is another form of surgical removal for hemorrhoids. Advertisements for walk-in clinics may make laser therapy sound like a miracle cure, promising quick removal with less pain than traditional methods, but laser therapy isn't for everyone and often isn't as pain-free as the ads may suggest. Laser therapy should never be undertaken without consultation with a physician who has no vested interest in such a clinic.

Anal Itching

Anal itching—known medically as pruritus ani—is generally regarded by physicians as a simple problem that home remedies can alleviate. Very rarely, persistent anal or rectal itching may be a sign of serious infection, so if it does not respond to simple treatments or the passage of time, you should see a doctor. Pinworms, rare in families without small children, are one possible cause that requires a doctor's advice.

Common causes

The majority of cases are caused by skin irritation from fecal soilage. In older people or in anybody with a touch of diarrhea, seepage of fecal matter may occur. As people grow older, anal skin becomes more irregular and harder to clean; people with hemorrhoids (which may trap small fecal particles) are more prone to itching. At any age haste may contribute to bad hygiene. One doctor blames pruritus ani on dispensers that give out toilet tissue one sheet at a time. Too much hygiene, such as rubbing energetically with dry toilet paper, can injure the skin, too. Another precipitating factor may be constipation.

Once the itch starts, many factors can exacerbate it. Such as walking, sitting—particularly prolonged sitting on a plastic seat—and such activities as bike riding.

Myth: Decaffeinated coffee is safe for people with digestive problems.

Fact: Decaffeinated coffee stimulates the flow of stomach acid almost as much as regular coffee. Though caffeine is a mild stimulant of stomach acid and digestive juices, the principal components in coffee that provoke this flow (with consequent irritation of stomach ulcers) are apparently introduced during the roasting process whether the beans have been decaffeinated or not. Increased acid flow can also exacerbate heartburn, so people with ulcers or chronic heartburn should avoid regular coffee and decaf. Other coffee substitutes include caffeine-free herbal teas and grain-based beverages such as Postum, Pero, and Cafix. These, unfortunately, may also stimulate stomach acid.

Hot weather and sweating, tight clothes that compress the buttocks, and nonabsorbent nylon panty hose and underpants may make matters worse. Some experts think stress may be a factor in anal itch.

Self-help

Don't scratch; it only causes further irritation and invites infection. Meticulous, gentle cleaning provides relief. A bidet would be a convenience, but a shower is just as efficient. Wash the area gently with soap and water, taking care to rinse thoroughly, and don't wipe with dry tissue. Pat yourself dry with cotton. When away from home, carry a few premoistened, individually packaged wipes—the kind you'd use for a baby. If leakage is your problem, wear a small cotton pad against the anal opening and change it frequently. Wear under garments with cotton crotches, and generally avoid tight clothing. Go easy on cycling activities until you feel better. Corticoid lotions or creams can be effective if used for a short time. Avoid the "-caine" creams sold for topical relief, since they can often further inflame sensitive skin.

Anal Fissure

An anal fissure is an elongated ulcer—or crack—in the skin lining the anal canal. Fissures usually result from constipation and the passage of hard stool, stool that is inadequately emptied, or in association with hemorrhoids. Subsequent bowel movements can irritate the fissure and cause spasms of the sphincter muscle—which can be extremely painful—and sometimes bleeding.

Prevention and treatment

The best way to prevent anal fissures is to avoid constipation by eating a diet high in fiber along with drinking plenty of fluids.

If you experience pain during bowel movements, or notice any bleeding, don't simply assume it is an anal fissure. See your doctor to rule out potentially more serious conditions. If your doctor diagnoses anal fissure, avoiding constipation can help make them less likely to cause pain. Warm sitz baths can help ease the pain of spasms. Your doctor may prescribe stool softeners. A fissure will usually heal within two to three weeks.

Food Poisoning

It is estimated that 33 to 50 million Americans get sick each year from foodborne bacteria, yeasts, molds, or viruses. Every home, and every person, is host to a variety of bacteria that can cause serious illness if they get into food and multiply. You can get mild food poisoning without realizing it. When people come down with a "bug" accompanied by symptoms such as headache and stomach distress, it's often dismissed as "stomach flu" or "twenty-four-hour virus"—but it may be food poisoning. Food poisoning is more than just a stomach ache; some types of bacteria and viruses can cause severe illness which can be fatal in the elderly, in children, in diabetics, in alcoholics, and in individuals whose immune systems are depressed, such as cancer patients. Anyone with prolonged symptoms should be seen by a doctor.

Food poisoning is primarily caused by a number of different bacteria and some viruses, with bacteria being responsible for the majority of cases. Just about every type of food—unless it has been sterilized—has bacteria in or on it, but most of them are harmless. In addition, bacteria can be introduced into foods from external sources. For example, some types of bacteria are always present on the skin; others are found around sores, pimples, or infected wounds. Soil and dust are also homes to bacteria. Household pets, insects, individuals with poor sanitary habits (such as not washing their hands after going to the bathroom) and those who are ill and handle food can all transmit bacteria, as well as viruses, into food.

Still the mere presence of bacteria or viruses in food isn't enough to make you sick. They cause problems only when the food is improperly handled and prepared. Heat inactivates most viruses, and bacteria are relatively harmless unless they are allowed to multiply. Bacteria begin to multiply quickly in food left at room temperature and thrive on food that is kept warm on a stove. Moist foods, such as stuffing or cooked rice, are especially susceptible to bacterial growth. Refrigeration retards the growth of bacteria, and cooking at high temperature kills most of them. But if food has been left out long enough, some types of bacteria can form a toxin that will survive heat or freezing.

The most common type of food poisoning

The bacterium salmonella is by far the most frequent cause of foodborne illness and it is rapidly becoming even more prevalent. In the 1970s, poisoning by salmonella, called salmonellosis, accounted for about 740,000 reported cases of food poisoning each year; researchers now project that estimates could be upward of four million cases annually. The number of cases may actually be higher, since many individuals and even doctors mistake salmonellosis for intestinal flu.

When is it safe to eat food from a dented can?

As a general rule, if the seal of the dented can isn't broken—that is, if the contents aren't exposed to air—the food is safe to eat. However, the following signs should tell you when not to buy a damaged can:

The can is leaky. *A stained label, a dented seam, or rust should make you suspicious.*

The ends bulge. *This is a possible sign of botulism.*

Odor. *If the food has an off odor, or spurts out of the can when you open it, don't eat it.*

Microwaving Microbes

While microwave ovens cook foods quickly and tend to destroy fewer vitamins than conventional cooking methods, they also may heat foods unevenly and leave some parts undercooked. This leaves open the possibility that bacteria may survive cooking. To be sure that your microwaved food doesn't cause food poisoning, follow these guidelines:

•To be sure that foods cook evenly, rotate all foods at various intervals during cooking.

•Check the internal temperature of meat and poultry to be sure that they are cooked all the way through.

•Wrap plastic made to be used in microwave ovens around the dish, or cover it with glass or ceramic. The trapped steam will help decrease evaporation and will heat the surface. Prick a hole in the plastic wrap to vent steam. The plastic wrap shouldn't touch the food.

•Allow microwaved food to stand covered after cooking. Heat concentrated on the inside will radiate outward through the food, cooking the exterior and equalizing the temperature throughout. Food will taste better this way, too, since it will be consistently hot.

•Thaw meats before cooking in a microwave oven; most models have defrost settings for this purpose. Ice crystals in frozen foods are not heated well by microwaves and can leave cold spots.

•If you're used to conventional cooking, remember that the more food you're microwaving, the longer it will take. For example, four baked potatoes will take much longer than two.

Types of Food Poisoning

Disease/Organism	Sources of Infection	When Symptoms Begin	Symptoms
Campylobacteriosis (*Campylobacter jejuni*)	Food can become contaminated during processing of meat and poultry. Sources of infection include raw or undercooked beef and poultry and raw milk. Can also be present in untreated water and in shellfish.	2 to 5 days	Fever, diarrhea, abdominal cramps, and bloody stool
Botulism (*Clostridium botulinum*)	Improperly processed, low acid canned goods (usually home canned products), such as green beans; foods contaminated by soil and then left in an oxygen-free environment, such as potatoes coated with oil or butter, at room temperature.	8 to 36 hours	Nervous system affected: double vision, problems swallowing, trouble breathing. Can be fatal.
Perfringens food poisoning (*Clostridium perfringins*)	Grows rapidly in large portions of food that are cooling slowly or at room temperature. Can grown in any dish made with meat or poultry as well.	8 to 24 hours	Abdominal pain and diarrhea. Sometimes nausea and vomiting. Symptoms are usually mild, but can be more severe in the ill and the elderly.
Salmonellosis (*Salmonella*)	Raw or undercooked beef and poultry, or foods contaminated by coming into contact with them. Raw or undercooked eggs or products made with them. Food handlers with poor hygiene.	12 to 48 hours	Nausea, vomiting, abdominal cramps, fever. Can be fatal in infants, the elderly, and individuals with depressed immune systems.
Shigellosis (*Shigella*)	Food can become infected by a food handler with poor hygiene and can cause illness if the food is not cooked properly. Multiplies when food is kept at room temperature for long periods.	1 to 7 days	Abdominal cramps and pain, nausea, vomiting, diarrhea, bloody stool, fever. Can be serious in infants, the elderly, and those with depressed immune systems.
Staphylococcal food poisoning (*Staphylococcus*)	Food that has been coughed or sneezed on or otherwise handled in an unsanitary manner. Staph is present on the skin, around pimples and boils, and thus can be introduced into foods by a food handler with a skin infection. It is particularly common in foods that require a lot of handling, such as tuna or potato salad. Multiplies rapidly at room temperature.	1 to 8 hours	Nausea, vomiting, abdominal cramps, diarrhea.
Cholera (*Vibrio cholera*)	Fish and shellfish from waters infected with sewage.	1 to 3 days	Diarrhea and abdominal pain. Can be mild or severe. Cholera can be fatal.
Parahaemolyticus food poisoning (*Vibrio parahaemolyticus*)	Fish and shellfish. Proliferates in warm weather.	15 to 24 hours	Abdominal pain, diarrhea, nausea, fever, headaches, chills, bloody stool.
Gastroenteritis (*Enteroviruses, rotaviruses, parvoviruses, and norwalk*)	Viruses present in human intestine. Can be passed on by food handlers with poor hygiene. Also in shellfish from waters contaminated with sewage.	12 to 48 hours	Vomiting, nausea, diarrhea.
Infectious hepatitis (*Hepatitis A*)	Can be passed on by a food handler who has the disease. Also in shellfish from contaminated waters.	15 to 50 days	Fatigue, jaundice, nausea. Can cause liver damage. Can be fatal.

The increase in salmonellosis has been attributed to the widespread practice in the meat industry of feeding antibiotics to cattle, pigs, and poultry. Also, high-speed mechanical methods of slaughtering and eviscerating animals, especially poultry, further increase the risk that salmonella (present in feces) will be introduced into the meat. Antibiotics—most frequently tetracycline and penicillin—are fed to animals to enhance their growth. While the antibiotics kill off some microorganisms in the animals, they allow antibiotic-resistant strains of salmonella to flourish. Then, unless the meat is handled with utmost care and thoroughly cooked to kill all microorganisms, these super-salmonella strains can make people ill. The danger increases if a person has been taking antibiotics before consuming the tainted meat; a number of bacteria that normally grow in the intestine will not be present and the resistant salmonella will be able to reproduce more rapidly.

Take special precautions with vacuum packed prepared foods. These sous-vide foods, as they are called, are fresh, raw ingredients that are packaged in a plastic pouch from which all the air has been removed. Because these foods are in an oxygen-poor environment they carry a risk of botulism if they are not kept cold during shipping and storage.

Raw eggs, too, can be a source of salmonella. But in these cases, poor handling may not be the cause. Researchers suggest that the bacteria come from inside the hen, rather than by the usual route of cracked or dirty eggshells. While raw or soft-cooked eggs—or foods made with them such as eggnog or Caesar salad—are potentially risky, commercial products made with eggs, such as mayonnaise, are safe because the eggs have been pasteurized.

Common symptoms

Contaminated food can look, smell, and taste perfectly fine. The only way you know you've eaten it is when you experience the symptoms (of course, if a food looks off, throw it away). Never test to see if leftovers—or any food—have spoiled by tasting them. Even a small taste of contaminated food could contain enough bacteria or toxin to make you sick. The most common symptom of food poisoning is diarrhea. Other symptoms include abdominal pain, nausea, vomiting (sometimes severe), and sometimes fever. The onset of symptoms can occur anywhere from one hour to seven days after eating contaminating food, depending on the infectious agent. (Hepatitis A, however, has a longer incubating period.)

Botulism—rare but dangerous

Botulism is caused by potent toxins produced by the spore-forming bacterium Clostridium botulinum, which is common in soil. Any food that is contaminated by soil and is subsequently carelessly washed or mishandled may be a source of botulism. However, this microbe produces poisons only at temperatures above 38 degrees Fahrenheit and under certain conditions—notably an almost complete lack of oxygen—and therefore is quite rare, especially in this country.

Canned foods are a potential source of botulism. Modern commercial canning methods have gone far toward eliminating botulism from canned foods, but outbreaks still occur as a result of home canning. Though contamination usually causes cans to swell, the absence of swelling does not guarantee safety. Other possible warning signs of botulism in canned foods are gas bubbles, discoloration, and milky liquids that normally should be clear.

While botulism is generally associated with canned foods, studies have found evidence of new trends. In one case, for example, onions sauteed in butter carried the toxin and in another, potato salad was the culprit. The salad had been made from leftover baked potatoes, which had sat unrefrigerated overnight and had been wrapped tightly in aluminum foil, thus creating the airless environment the spores require. With the onions, the butter coating deprived them of oxygen, and in addition the dish had been left at room temperature for several hours.

Even if the spores are present, however, toxin won't be produced unless food is left at room temperature for long periods (at least twelve to twenty-four hours) *and* under relatively airless conditions—for example, a tight wrap or a coating of fat.

Honey should never be fed to children less than a year old. It may contain dormant Clostridium botulinum spores, which can grow in an infant's less mature digestive tract and produce the toxin that causes botulism. Honey is safe for older children, since it has never been shown to contain the toxin itself.

Safety for Mail-Order Food

Americans send about one billion dollars worth of mail-order food each year, especially as holiday gifts. Many of these foods—from baked turkeys and hams to smoked fish and cheesecakes—are highly perishable. Large shippers use sophisticated packaging systems to keep food from spoiling, but sometimes goods arrive in an unsafe condition. People who receive food in questionable shape may simply throw it away, not wanting to complain about a gift (anyway, it didn't cost them anything). Worse yet, they may take a chance and eat the spoiled food and get sick. By thinking ahead you can avoid many of the problems that may arise with mail-order food.

When ordering a gift

•Set a workable delivery date for any perishable food you're sending. Find out how long the mailing should take and make sure someone will be home on or around that date to receive it. If people are out of town, the food may end up sitting and spoiling at the Post Office or parcel-delivery office.

•Unless there's no other option, don't send perishable food to a friend's office, where it may be left unrefrigerated for many additional hours.

•Make sure the package will be labeled "perishable" on the outside. It will stand a better chance of being handled properly.

When receiving a gift

•If it was frozen when shipped, then raw, cooked, or smoked meat, poultry, and fish should arrive frozen or at least hard in the middle. If it has never been frozen, it should be firm and cold—at or below 40 degrees Fahrenheit. The same is true for canned or processed foods (including most vacuum-packed foods) that are labeled "keep refrigerated." Some smoked fish, if highly salted, doesn't need to be refrigerated.

•Baked hams (except dry-cured hams) should arrive cold. Many canned hams must be kept cold even when unopened because they are only pasteurized and not sterile; their labels say "keep refrigerated."

•Cheese should have no mold—unless, like Roquefort and other ripened cheeses, it is supposed to. If mold has grown, cut it off along with a thick slice underneath.

•Cheesecake should arrive fully frozen.

If you have a question about food you receive, or think you deserve a replacement delivery or refund, call the mail-order company. Most reputable firms have customer-service telephone numbers and offer money-back guarantees. Remember, it's the company's responsibility to deliver food in good condition, but it's your responsibility to make sure someone is there to receive it.

The spores can be destroyed only by moist heat at 248 degrees Fahrenheit under pressure (in a pressure cooker, for instance) for thirty minutes, but the toxin will be inactivated if the food is brought to the boiling point (212 degrees Fahrenheit) for ten minutes. Thus if the onions or potatoes had been thoroughly reheated, they would not have made anybody sick.

The symptoms of botulism poisoning do not involve the digestive tract, as with most food poisoning, but the nervous system: sudden marked weakness, difficulty in breathing, swallowing, or speaking, and double or blurred vision. Seek medical aid at once if such symptoms occur, and try to bring any of the offending food that may be left. Botulism need not be fatal if diagnosed early.

If the Power Fails

Power outages are common and, if they last long enough, can cause havoc in the freezer and refrigerator. According to guidelines from the U.S. Department of Agriculture, first of all, do not open appliance doors. A well-stocked freezer provides its own insulation and should stay at a safe temperature for up to two days without power; a half-full freezer may last up to twenty-four hours.

If dry ice is available for the freezer, you can bring it home in a cardboard box or picnic cooler. Don't touch dry ice—it will instantly freeze your skin. Handle it with gloves or tongs in a well-ventilated area, and avoid inhaling the fumes. Don't lean into a freezer in which dry ice has been stored; there is no oxygen left to breathe. Twenty-five pounds should keep a full freezer (ten cubic feet) safe for three or four days, and a half-full freezer for two or three days. Dry ice will stick to plastic wrap, so put it on an empty shelf, or insulate packages of food with pieces of cardboard.

A nonfunctioning refrigerator will hold food safely for up to six hours in a cool room. You can add block ice to the main compartment and dry ice to the freezing compartment. (Do not put dry ice in the main compartment: it might freeze the contents.)

FROZEN FOODS

Frozen food	Thawed but cold (under 40°)	Thawed and held above 40° for up to two hours
Meat, poultry	refreeze	cook and serve, or cook and refreeze
Casseroles, stews	cook and serve	cook and serve
Dishes made with cream, milk, eggs	cook and serve	discard
Hard cheese, butter, margarine	refreeze	refreeze or refrigerate
Vegetables	refreeze (may lose quality)	cook and serve
Juices	refreeze (may lose quality)	refreeze

If frozen food is thawed and held for over two hours, treat it like refrigerated food—see below.

REFRIGERATED FOODS

Discard after eight hours above forty degrees:	milk, cream, soft cheese, mayonnaise, raw meat or poultry, lunch meat, hot dogs
Discard after one day:	fruit juice
Discard after five to seven days:	fresh eggs
Keep as long as they look and smell okay:	fresh fruits and vegetables, hard cheese, butter, margarine, open containers of

Preventing food poisoning

There are a number of simple steps you can take to prevent food contamination and reduce your risk of getting sick from tainted food:

- Keep your refrigerator below 40 degrees Fahrenheit and the freezer below zero.
- Wash your hands thoroughly before you handle food. The proper way is to use soap and warm water for at least twenty seconds, working the soap into the hands, including the fingernail area and between the fingers.
- Use a fresh dish towel every time you cook.
- Keep pets away from food preparation areas.
- Defrost frozen foods only in the refrigerator, in the microwave, or under cold running water.
- Ask your butcher or supermarket manager to stock meats obtained from growers who use no antibiotics. Such meats are currently available, though you must expect to pay premium prices. Nevertheless, marketers are usually sensitive to public demand for healthier foods.
- After preparing raw meat or poultry wash the utensils, counter, cutting board, and your hands—anything that touched it—thoroughly in hot soapy water before making a salad or handling vegetables.
- Marinate meats and poultry only under refrigeration. And don't put cooked meat back into an uncooked marinade or serve the used marinade as a sauce unless you heat it to a rolling boil for several minutes.
- Cook rare beef to at least 145 degrees Fahrenheit (pink, not red). Pork and chicken should, of course, be thoroughly cooked—not pink at all.
- Don't serve barbecued meat on the same plate you used for the raw meat and don't use the cooking utensils for serving.
- When eating out, pass up the steak tartare and any other uncooked meat.
- Hold foods at room temperature no longer than an hour before or after cooking. Don't leave normally refrigerated foods sitting out. Given the right conditions, the bacterial content in some foods can double in twenty minutes.
- Promptly refrigerate leftovers, particularly anything with a coating (bread or fat) or a tight wrapping. Divide large amounts of leftovers—such as sauces, soups, stews, and casseroles—into smaller containers so that they cool faster.
- Store all starchy stuffing (rice, bread) separately from the poultry in which it was cooked.
- If you can fruits and vegetables at home, ask your county health department for guidelines about safe procedures to protect against botulism.

Steam tables and chafing dishes are often not hot enough to prevent dangerous bacteria from growing. Hot food has to be kept at a temperature of about 140 to 165 degrees Fahrenheit to prevent food poisoning, so beware of food that has been kept warm for more than two hours.

Sexuality and Reproduction

Topics concerning sexuality and reproduction are discussed more openly than ever before. And yet, despite—or at times because of—changing attitudes and scientific advances in this area, many people are confused or misinformed about choices that can directly affect their health, particularly with regard to birth control and sexually transmitted diseases. This section includes essential information on these two topics and other concerns that can be self-managed. (You should consult your doctor for any type of sexual dysfunction; likewise, you should see your doctor or gynecologist if you become pregnant and for any problem related to pregnancy.)

Birth Control

The ideal contraceptive is 100 percent safe, 100 percent effective, convenient, and yet doesn't interfere with the sex act or hamper the potential to reproduce. To date, no birth-control method meets all of those conditions. At the same time, the variety of contraceptives is greater than ever and there are additional variables to consider when choosing among them. Condoms, for example, are widely promoted because they also reduce the chance of contracting sexually transmitted diseases (STDs) such as gonorrhea and chlamydial infection as well as AIDS and herpes. And oral contraceptives, which pose some risks for certain women, particularly those who smoke, are now known to protect against some types of cancer and other disorders.

More than half of all American women between the ages of fifteen and forty-four use some form of contraception.Unfortunately, American women have more unplanned pregnancies and more abortions than women in most industrialized nations, according to a study by the Alan Guttmacher Institute in New York, a nonprofit organization that studies population issues. Moreover, the most common method of preventing unwanted pregnancies in the United States, especially after age thirty, is not contraception but sterilization, which is largely irreversible.

Our national reluctance about using contraceptives stems partly from the belief that all available methods pose medical risks, an apprehension based on the early problems associated with birth-control pills and an awareness of the pelvic infections caused by the Dalkon shield (an intrauterine device, or IUD, that was withdrawn from the market). There are additional reasons: in many other industrialized countries women have easier access to advice about contraceptives. Also, Americans have fewer methods of contraception to choose from than do women abroad. (Most western European countries market IUDs and birth-control pills not available in the United States.) Since not every type of contraceptive is appropriate for every woman, nor for every stage of her reproductive life, the more choices available, the more likely she is to find one she is comfortable enough with to use regularly—the only way birth-control devices can be effective.

Since the introduction of the "pill" and the IUD in the 1960s, no revolutionary new advances in birth control have come on the market. However, available methods have, in some cases, undergone improvement. And users have come to realize that contraceptives have advantages in addition to preventing unwanted pregnancies (see chart below).

So far, the only definitely reversible contraceptive for men is the condom. Women, who are more often responsible for choosing and using a contraceptive, have wider choices. Permanent sterilization (tubal ligation for women and

Comparing Contraceptives

Type and Estimated Effectiveness	Advantages	Disadvantages	Comments
Birth-control pill (oral contraceptive) 98% (combination) 97% (mini)	Most effective reversible contraceptive. Results in lighter, more regular periods. Protects against cancer of the ovaries and uterine lining. Decreases risk of pelvic inflammatory disease, fibrocystic breast disease, and benign ovarian cysts.	Minor side effects similar to early pregnancy (nausea, breast tenderness, fluid retention) during first three months of use. Major complications (blood clots, hypertension) may occur in smokers and those over 35. Must be taken on a regular daily schedule.	Combination types contain both synthetic estrogen and progesterone (female hormones). Mini-pill contains only progesterone and may produce irregular bleeding. Available by prescription only.
Intrauterine device (IUD) 95%	Once inserted, usually stays in place. Remains effective for one to four years, depending on type.	May cause bleeding and cramping. Increased risk of pelvic inflammatory disease. If pregnancy occurs, increased risk that it may be ectopic.	Only two types available in the United States: Progestasert (which requires annual replacement) and ParaGard (effective for up to four years). Should be used by women who are over 25, have had a child, and have no history of pelvic inflammatory disease or tubal pregnancy. Available by prescription only.
Condom (rubber, prophylactic, sheath) 90%	Protects against STDs, including AIDS and herpes. May protect against cervical cancer.	Must be applied immediately before intercourse. Rare cases of allergy to rubber. May break, may blunt sensation.	More effective when the woman uses a spermicide.
Vaginal spermicide (used alone) 70-80%	Available over the counter as jellies, foams, creams, and suppositories.	Messiness. Must be applied no more than one hour before intercourse.	Best results occur when used with a barrier method (condom or diaphragm).
Diaphragm (with spermicide) 82-90%	No side effects. Can be inserted up to two hours before—rather than during—intercourse.	Increased risk of urinary tract infection. Rare cases of allergy to rubber.	Must be used with spermicide. Available by prescription only.
Cervical cap (with spermicide) 82-90%	Less fragile than diaphragm; can be left in place for up to 48 hours; spermicide needn't be replaced for subsequent intercourse.	Can be hard to insert or remove; may cause unpleasant odor.	Approved only for women with a normal Pap smear prior to use and after three months of use. Available by prescription only.
Vaginal sponge 85-90%	Easy to use because spermicide is self-contained. May be inserted as much as (but no more than) 24 hours prior to intercourse.	May be hard to remove; may fragment. Higher failure rate in women who have given birth.	Must be left in for 6 hours after intercourse.

vasectomy for men) is now available at comparatively low cost and offers the advantages of efficacy, safety, and convenience. Its only drawback is its significant degree of irreversibility. Methods such as coitus interruptus and periodic abstinence from sexual intercourse (rhythm method) are not included in this chapter because of their high failure rate.

Oral contraceptives: benefits and risks

Oral contraceptives for women are easier to use and more reliable than any other method of birth control. Yet surveys show that Americans tend to overestimate the risks of the pill and underestimate its benefits. The following information should help you put the pill into perspective—though, naturally, new research on the pill will probably continue to raise issues about its use. As a basic safeguard, you should always consult your physician before you decide to start—or stop—taking an oral contraceptive.

Oral contraceptives contain compounds chemically related (but not identical) to both estrogen and progesterone, the two major female hormones that define a woman's reproductive cycle. Estrogen and progesterone, if taken orally, go from the digestive tract into the liver, which breaks them down. Synthetic hormones used in oral contraceptives travel intact through the liver into the main circulatory system, where they effectively shut down the reproductive cycle. Because of the presence of these hormones in the blood, the hypothalamus—a gland in the brain—doesn't stimulate the production of FSH and LH (sex hormones involved in ovarian function). Ovulation ceases and pregnancy cannot occur. Even if ovulation should occur (and some experts think it may), implantation of the ovum is impossible because the uterus is unprepared.

The cancer risk. Though estrogen alone may promote cancer, today's oral contraceptives contain progesterone as well, and the combination is known to be protective against cancers of the cervix and uterine lining (endometrium). An additional advantage is that women who take oral contraceptives are more likely to have annual pelvic examinations and Pap smears—a proven method of detecting reproductive cancers at a more curable stage.

So far, the evidence on oral contraceptives as a promoter of breast cancer is unclear or unconvincing; some studies show oral contraceptives not to be linked to breast cancer, others suggest they might be. A further difficulty in gathering accurate evidence is the advent of the low-dose pill. Since breast cancer develops slowly, and its causes are unknown, scientists have to survey many women over many years to answer the question. Thus there's been time to study women using the old, high-dosage pill (with inconclusive results, as noted), but not those on low-dose oral contraceptives. Studies of low-dose oral contraceptives, it's thought, will fail to demonstrate any link with breast cancer. But some women with particular risk factors should proceed with caution (see next page).

Heart disease and stroke. In the 1960s the pill was shown to have another potentially hazardous side effect—an increased likelihood of heart attacks and blood clots. While a woman is using high-dose oral contraceptives, her risk of coronary artery disease is 4.7 times higher. But this is far less serious than it sounds, because for women in their twenties the risk of heart disease is extremely small: less than 1 in 500,000. A fivefold increase in that age group brings the odds to 1 in 100,000. Even this small risk has been markedly reduced by low-dose

The Low-Dose Pill

In the 1960s and 1970s, oral contraceptives contained up to three times as much estrogen and ten times as much progesterone as the pill of the 1980s. The low-dose pill has been proven as effective and is much less likely to cause side effects or increase long-term risk of disease. Properly used, low-dose oral contraceptives are almost 100 percent effective. (One note of caution: while oral contraceptives prevent pregnancy very effectively, they cannot protect you from any of the sexually transmitted diseases—AIDS, herpes, chlamydia, syphilis, gonorrhea, or genital warts.)

oral contraceptives, so that the increased risk of heart disease among pill users has been shown to be negligible.

Moreover, a recent major study indicates that women who have stopped taking the pill, even if they took it for a decade or more, are at no more risk for heart disease or stroke than women who never took the pill at all. This reassuring news is based on an eight-year follow-up of the subjects of the Harvard Nurses' Health Study, conducted on a group of nearly 120,000 nurses aged thirty to fifty-five when the follow-up began. About 7,000 were taking the pill at the time; about 50,000 had taken it in the past.

Previously, researchers focused on women who were currently taking the pill. This was the first major study to examine the residual cardiac effects on long-term pill users, many of whom took the original "big pill" of the 1960s.

Who should avoid using oral contraceptives? Smokers, diabetics, and women with high blood cholesterol levels or high blood pressure (since all these factors increase the risk of coronary artery disease) and women who have had cancer of the reproductive system or breast cancer should avoid oral contraceptives. Women who have a family history of breast cancer, who have had surgery for benign breast disease, or have other risk factors for breast cancer should consider using other methods. In addition, women are generally advised not to use oral contraceptives throughout their reproductive lives, as such complications as blood clots are more likely to occur after thirty-five. At this age, switching to another method is advised.

Condoms

As a birth-control device, condoms fell in popularity as other methods improved. Condoms can be distracting, some people complain that they dull sensation, and occasionally they also break or leak, reducing their effectiveness. But a condom is the only inexpensive and easy method of birth control for men. And it offers potentially excellent protection against most sexually transmitted diseases (STDs). Indeed, unless you choose abstinence as the way to protect yourself from the sexual transmission of AIDS and other STDs—and that isn't a solution many people are likely to adopt—the alternative is to use condoms consistently during sexual intercourse.

Laboratory studies show that an intact latex condom prevents the passage of the AIDS virus along with other viruses and bacteria that cause various STDs. However, there are no human studies to show conclusively that condoms prevent the transmission of AIDS during sexual intercourse—nor are there likely to be, given the unacceptable risk of exposing someone to a fatal disease during controlled trials. Still, there's enough evidence in favor of the condom to convince most health officials and physicians that condoms play a crucial role in "safer sex."

Reliability. While in theory condoms should be 100 percent effective, in reality they aren't. How reliable they are is hotly debated. As a contraceptive, they are about 90 percent effective, which is substantial protection, but hardly guaranteed. However, you can take steps to enhance condom effectiveness.

Three potential problems can undermine condom effectiveness: breakage, leakage, and improper use. Breakage rates depend on the type of sexual activity; for instance, anal sex is harder on a condom than vaginal sex; lack of lubrication (or use of an oil-based lubricant) also increases the chance that a condom will break. According to a survey published in *Consumer Reports*, about one latex

Myth: Douching is part of good feminine hygiene.

Fact: Vaginal tissue is self-cleaning. Douching is not necessary after a menstrual period or after intercourse, and—another myth—postcoital douching should never be relied on as a contraceptive. Indeed, if you use a spermicidal foam, a douche can wash it away. Some vaginal discharge is normal, and odors, if any, probably originate from the external genitals; both can be taken care of with soap and water. If an unusual odor, a discharge, itching, or other discomfort leads you to suspect an infection, you should see your doctor.

At least one major study has linked douching to ectopic (tubal) pregnancy, a potentially life-threatening condition. Moreover, some douches contain chemicals that may seriously endanger the health of a fetus if absorbed. Thus, pregnant or potentially pregnant women should not douche.

condom in 140 breaks. As for leakage, standard water tests revealed that the major brands' leakage rates met the Food and Drug Administration (FDA) requirement of fewer than four failures per one thousand condoms. In addition, air-burst tests have found that most brands have a low failure rate. Though these results are somewhat reassuring, many health officials are calling for the FDA to adopt tougher quality-control standards.

Most of the time, however, condom ineffectiveness is due to human failure, not product defects. Researchers estimate that *when condoms are used properly, failure rates can be as low as 1 to 2 percent.* That's why education about how to use condoms is crucial. Some condom packages provide inadequate instructions.

The most effective condom

Whatever your age, use a condom every time you have intercourse if there is any risk of sexually transmitted disease. Even if you or your partner has been sterilized, so that pregnancy is not a concern, you still need to use a condom to protect yourselves against STDs.

Latex. About 5 percent of condoms are made from "lambskin" (actually lamb gut), which is more porous than latex. Though such condoms block sperm, at least one study has shown that some viruses can find their way through the skin. Thus manufacturers of skin condoms aren't allowed to claim that these protect against STDs. People allergic to latex can try wearing a lambskin condom under a latex one.

Fresh. When stored in a cool, dark, dry place, condoms can last three to five years. Latex deteriorates faster when exposed to light, temperatures over 100 degrees Fahrenheit, humidity, and air pollution. Glove compartments and hip pockets do not provide ideal storage conditions. Most brands now bear expiration dates. Buy from a busy, reputable pharmacy, where the stock is likely to be fresh. Remove the condom from its individual sealed wrapper only when you're ready to use it. If it looks dried-out or discolored, throw it away.

Lubricated. Adequate lubrication helps lessen the chance of breakage. Use only a water-based lubricant. Oil-based products, including petroleum jelly, mineral oil, cold cream, and hand lotion, can cause latex to deteriorate rapidly and thus break. (Remember, "water-soluble" isn't necessarily water-based.) The package should say that the lubricant is safe for use on latex.

Nonoxynol-9. This spermicide has been shown to kill the AIDS virus in lab studies. If you use prelubricated condoms, look for ones with nonoxynol-9. However, prelubricated condoms contain only small amounts of the compound, so you should probably also use a vaginal spermicide containing nonoxynol-9 for added protection.

Reservoir tips. A well-designed condom has a reservoir tip, a bubble or nipple that provides a place for semen to collect. If your condom doesn't have this feature, don't pull it snug; leave a quarter- to half-inch space at the tip when you put it on. The condom should be long enough so that a surplus of rubber at the open end forms a rolled rim or seal at the base of the penis.

The most effective use

•Roll the condom down over the penis as soon as it's erect and before you continue foreplay; don't wait until the last minute.

•If you aren't circumcised, pull back the foreskin before putting on the condom.

•Squeeze out the air from the reservoir end or the space you've left at the tip.

•Remove it after ejaculation before the penis becomes flaccid. Otherwise, it could slip off and leakage could occur. Handle the used condom carefully by the rim and discard in a tissue.

•Use a new condom for each act of intercourse.

Sexually Transmitted Diseases

Sexually transmitted diseases, or STDs, are among the most prevalent kinds of infections in the United States, with millions of new cases reported every year. The incidence of syphilis, for example, which is highly curable with penicillin, began rising in the 1980s after years of declining. Researchers have identified more than twenty sexually transmitted diseases, and the most common ones—which are listed in the chart on page 354—are estimated to affect more than thirty million Americans.

Sexually transmitted diseases, including AIDS (see pages 355-361), are so-called because they are transmitted by sexual contact, usually sexual intercourse. Syphilis, like AIDS, can also be spread by infected blood. And the herpes virus, if mouth sores exist, can be transmitted by kissing. But sexually transmitted diseases are not transmitted by toilet seats, towels, dishes or other objects; by ordinary contact such as shaking hands, sharing meals, or using the same telephone; or by mosquitoes or other insects. Organisms that cause sexually transmitted diseases usually die within a minute outside the body.

If you have been in a mutually monogamous sexual relationship, sexually transmitted diseases are very likely not something you need to worry about. But anyone who has had multiple sexual partners, or has a relationship with someone who has multiple partners, may be at risk. *All of the diseases covered here are preventable.* Most are also treatable. Syphilis, gonorrhea, and chlamydia can be cured with antibiotics. Genital herpes, genital warts, and AIDS cannot be cured, but they can be treated or managed. However, no sexually transmitted disease can be accurately diagnosed and treated without professional help. *There are no home remedies.*

Preventing sexually transmitted diseases

Apart from abstinence, the most reliable preventive is long-term monogamy with a partner who is also monogamous. If you're healthy now and have a long-term monogamous relationship with a healthy partner, you're at no risk. But if you have not had a long-standing monogamous relationship, always take the following protective measures:

Use latex condoms and a spermicide containing nonoxynol-9. These provide protection—though not infallible—against infection (see pages 351-352). Jellies, foams, creams, and condoms containing nonoxynol-9 are recommended, since this chemical appears to kill many microorganisms. Remember that nonbarrier forms of birth control (oral contraceptives, IUDs) offer no protection against sexually transmitted diseases. While a diaphragm and cervical cap protect against pregnancy, they are *not* reliable against infection. Use a condom and spermicide in addition. Note: Condoms may not offer adequate protection against genital warts if, for example, they are in the anal area.

•Know who your partner is. It's risky to have sexual intercourse with someone you have just met, or someone you won't be able to locate later.

•Don't have sexual contact with anyone who has genital or anal sores, a visible rash, a discharge, or any other sign of venereal disease. But being observant is not a substitute for knowing your partner.

•Recognize the symptoms of STDs and seek medical treatment at once if you

Sexually Transmitted Diseases

Disease	Symptoms and Course	Complications	Treatment
Syphilis. Bacterial infection. Treatable and curable in its early stage. Historians argue whether it originated in the Americas or Europe and Asia; written records of the disease go back to the time of Columbus's voyage. After declining in this century in the United States, the number of cases began rising in the 1980s. If untreated, it is chronic and ultimately fatal.	Up to twelve weeks after infection, a painless sore (chancre) appears on genitals, mouth, or elsewhere. Lymph nodes may enlarge. Chancre more obvious in men; if vaginal, rarely noticed; heals without scarring. About 6 weeks later, fever, rash, and flu-like symptoms may occur, then disappear and later reappear. Symptoms may vanish but the infection will not.	Years later, brain and spinal chord damage, blindness, insanity, and death may result. Can cause miscarriage and birth defects; can be contracted by fetus in utero.	Even if no symptoms are present, diagnosis can be made by a blood test, but results may be negative for up to twelve weeks after exposure. Antibiotics, taken as prescribed, are a dependable and relatively inexpensive cure.
Gonorrhea. Bacterial infection. May not have immediately detectable symptoms. Known since ancient times. Chronic and progressive. If untreated, can result in physical disability and infertility. Spreads by direct contact with infected mucous membranes in genitals, mouth, and throat. Estimated one to two million new cases each year.	Symptoms (if any) noticeable within two to ten days of infection: painful urination, vaginal or penile discharge, sore throat (if contracted through oral sex), rectal pain or discharge (if contracted through anal sex). Possibly heavy menstrual bleeding or bleeding between periods..	If untreated, may cause arthritis, skin sores, and heart or brain infection. Common cause of pelvic inflammatory disease (PID), which may damage Fallopian tubes, leading to ectopic pregnancy (potentially fatal to the mother). Can cause permanent sterility in both women and men. Infants infected during birth may become blind.	Diagnosed by a smear or culture. Antibiotics, taken as prescribed, are a reliable cure; some strains resistant to standard antibiotics can be treated by newer drugs.
Herpes. Caused by two types of herpes virus: type I commonly produces cold sores around mouth; type II produces genital outbreaks. But both viruses can infect either area, causing roughly the same symptoms. Chronic but not progressive or fatal. No cure. Transmitted by direct contact with an active sore or virus-containing genital secretions. Virus establishes itself permanently in nervous system, staying dormant for months or years. Can spread silently, since some people may shed viruses while asymptomatic. An estimated thirty million people are infected.	Within ten days after infection, flu-like symptoms—muscle aches, swollen glands, fever, and sometimes shooting pains in legs or abdomen; followed by painful blisters and sores, usually on genitals or mouth. Symptoms subside without treatment, but sores recur at unpredictable intervals in 90 percent of cases. First outbreak is usually most severe, but in some cases may be so mild as to go unnoticed.	Frequent recurrences can result in depression. Infants may acquire herpes during birth, resulting in central nervous system damage or death. Caesarian delivery may be necessary for infected mothers.	Diagnosis confirmed by a scraping or culture. Does not respond to antibiotics. Acyclovir, a relatively new, expensive drug (ointment or capsule) is not a cure but can ease symptoms and may reduce length of attack. If taken continually, this drug usually prevents recurrences. Herpes support groups may be helpful in combatting depression and other emotional problems that sometimes result from the disease.
Chlamydia. A bacterial infection. Thought to be the most common curable sexually transmitted disease in America today (estimated four million cases annually). Chronic if untreated. Like other sexually transmitted diseases, spreads by contact with infected mucous membranes. Can occur simultaneously with gonorrhea.	Similar to gonorrhea: within twenty-one days painful urination, vaginal or penile discharge, abdominal pain, possibly urethral itching. Symptoms may be very mild (possibly going unnoticed) and can go away without treatment, only to produce later complications. High percentage of women have no symptoms.	In women, leading cause of pelvic inflammatory disease (PID), which may result in ectopic pregnancy or sterility. In men, can lead to diseases of the urinary tract and sterility. Babies born to infected mothers are subject to eye infection and pneumonia.	Diagnosed by lab test. Antibiotic treatment, taken as prescribed, is a reliable cure.
Genital warts. Caused by human papilloma virus (HPV). Warts appear on, in, and around the genitals, or in the mouth and throat. Highly contagious, spread by intimate bodily contact. HPV is a recent discovery as a cause of cancer in humans.	Within eight months of infection, local irritation and itching, followed by soft, flat, irregularly surfaced wartlike growths that may increase in size. May cause no symptoms. If inside vagina or cervix, usually detectable only by physician.	Strongly associated with cancer (cervical and possibly penile). Infants born to mothers with human papilloma virus may develop warts.	Immediate treatment is essential. Can be removed chemically or surgically. Virus remains latent: warts often recur. Infected women should have annual Pap smear. Drugstore remedies for other kinds of warts are useless and may be harmful.

notice them in yourself. A lesion, blister, sore, discharge, or rash in the genital or anal area should be a signal to seek medical help. If you're at risk for STDs, persistent unexplained flu-like symptoms and abdominal pain are other signals to see your doctor.

•If you think you may have been exposed to a sexually transmitted disease, don't have sex again until you've seen a doctor and been diagnosed and, if necessary, treated. If you are infected, inform your partner or partners and advise them to seek medical help. Remember, no sexually transmitted disease confers immunity: *you can be reinfected with the same disease.* Refrain from all sexual activity (even if you have no symptoms) until your doctor tells you you're cured—and until your partner has sought treatment and been given the same assurance. (See chart opposite for more detailed advice about herpes and genital warts, which are not curable.)

Remember that syphilis, like AIDS, can be transmitted by contaminated needles. Make sure such instruments used in tattooing, acupuncture, even ear piercing are sterile (or, better yet, disposable). And, of course, intravenous drug users should never share needles.

Inform others. If you have adolescent children, make sure they understand what sexually transmitted diseases are and how they can be transmitted and prevented. If they are not sexually active now, don't assume they'll remain inactive. Sex education classes in school can help, but don't rely on them exclusively. There's no substitute for parent-child discussions about sexuality.

AIDS

Acquired Immune Deficiency Syndrome—AIDS—is the clinical name of a disease now recognized as a worldwide epidemic and one of the most dangerous health problems of modern times. AIDS is caused by a bloodborne virus that attacks and eventually destroys the body's immune system. It is a sexually transmitted disease, and although the virus is most likely to pass from one person to another during anal intercourse, it can also be transmitted during vaginal intercourse and possibly—though so far not definitively—during oral sex. AIDS can also be spread via contaminated hypodermic needles and syringes, and—if donated blood is contaminated—blood transfusions. In addition, an infected mother can pass the virus to her child in utero or during delivery.

In Africa, AIDS is primarily a heterosexual disease, but in the United States it has been confined primarily to certain well-defined risk groups—male homosexuals, intravenous drug users, and hemophiliacs (because they need frequent transfusions). AIDS can be transmitted between heterosexuals by vaginal intercourse, but the rate of infection by this route seems to be low—although it increases with frequency of intercourse and especially with multiple partners. Once AIDS develops it is fatal. So far there is no cure, and no vaccine to prevent it.

What we know so far

Not all the news about AIDS is bleak. First of all, we know what causes it. In 1983, only three years after the disease was first fully described, scientists discovered its cause. The virus, known originally as HTLV III and now simply as HIV (Human Immunodeficiency Virus), is an infectious agent known as a retrovirus, which has the ability to take over certain cells and interrupt their normal genetic functioning. While none of this may sound particularly hopeful, what is amazing is how much scientists already know about the virus. None of the deadly infectious diseases of modern times, has so quickly met scientific understanding. The AIDS virus can already be cultured in the laboratory; scientists have devised reliable tests to detect its presence in blood samples.

Secondly, we know that the disease is hard to catch. The virus is not transmitted through air or water. Nor does it travel easily from person to person, as other infections may. Until a vaccine can be developed, halting the spread of AIDS must depend solely on educating those at risk — all sexually active people, particularly those who have not lived in strict, long-term monogamy. Though education may not be the ultimate weapon, it is an effective and powerful means of controlling the spread of the disease. If AIDS advances at its present rate, by the end of 1992 an estimated 365,000 cases will have occurred, with 263,000 deaths. Yet these predictions need not come true, since some of those people are not yet infected, and education could save many of their lives. In addition, new therapies such as the drug AZT could positively affect the survival rate.

Unfortunately, though, misconceptions about AIDS have spread faster than AIDS itself. Here are some of the leading myths about AIDS and the facts established at present.

MYTH: AIDS is a disease of male homosexuals and intravenous drug addicts. Other people have nothing to worry about.

FACT: Of the nearly 122,000 cases of AIDS in the United States as of January, 1990, the vast majority were homosexual or bisexual men or intravenous drug users; the rest were hemophiliacs and others who had received contaminated blood, or heterosexual sex partners of infected persons. Of the more than 2,000 children under age thirteen diagnosed as having AIDS, most were born to AIDS-infected parents, and the rest had hemophilia. *But while the two main risk groups remain for the moment well defined, anybody who participates in unprotected sex can get AIDS.*

In this country, male homosexuals still run the highest risk of contracting the disease sexually. Less than 5 percent of newly diagnosed AIDS cases in the United States can be traced to heterosexual transmission and the disease is far less likely to

---

AIDS Terms

AIDS-related complex (ARC): Milder clinical symptoms (such as fever, weight loss, diarrhea, and swollen glands) caused by the AIDS virus. About 25 percent of people with AIDS-related complex will develop full blown AIDS within three years. Also, a substantial number of people have died from ARC without developing AIDS.

ELISA: (enzyme-linked immuno-absorbent assay): a simple test for detecting the antibodies that form in the blood in response to an invasion by the AIDS virus. If antibodies are present, the patient is "AIDS positive." The results of ELISA need to be confirmed by the Western blot assay.

Opportunistic infections: Once AIDS destroys the body's immune system, certain otherwise controllable infections, such as a specific type of pneumonia, may gain a foothold and eventually cause death.

High risk sex: Any unprotected sexual contact with a person who might be carrying the AIDS virus.

pass from woman to man during conventional intercourse than from man to woman. The frequency of sexual contact appears to be more important than the form. Though a single contact can spread AIDS, people who have multiple sexual partners are in considerably more danger than those with fewer partners. Prostitutes, both male and female, are more likely to be infected by AIDS and to transmit it, since in addition to frequent exposure, many use intravenous drugs.

In Africa, AIDS has been spread primarily by heterosexual transmission. In one study in Africa, 340 heterosexual subjects were tested for HIV antibodies, a sign of infection; all of the subjects had reported frequent sexual contact with prostitutes among whom HIV infection was known to be rampant. Of these men, 11.2 percent (38 men) tested positive for the antibodies, all of them infected through vaginal intercourse. Significantly, among this group, nearly two out of three had a previous history of genital ulcers, compared with just under one out of five of the 302 who tested negative. This suggests venereal diseases, such as herpes, that cause genital ulceration may predispose to HIV infection. Indeed, a higher rate of AIDS transmission in people with genital ulcers has been confirmed by studies in the United States.

MYTH: AIDS could spread rapidly through the general population.

FACT: Based on a number of recent studies, the estimated risk of becoming infected with the AIDS virus from a single sexual encounter can be as low as one in five million. This assumes the person you have sex with is not in any known risk group for AIDS (but whose infection status is unknown). If a condom is used, the odds rise to one in fifty million—far greater than winning a lottery or being struck by lightning.

At the other end of the spectrum, one sexual encounter with a person infected with HIV poses a risk of infection of one in five thousand if you use a condom, and one in five hundred if you don't. This margin diminishes sharply as the number of sexual encounters rises: five hundred sexual encounters with an infected person would pose a 9 percent risk of infection if condoms are used, and a 66 percent risk without condoms. Therefore, in their efforts to contain the spread of AIDS, health experts emphasize the need to limit the number of sexual partners and to choose them carefully. Unless you and your sex partner are both sure you are not infected, you need to take precautions: use condoms and a spermicide, and avoid high-risk practices such as anal intercourse. Couples who have not been monogamous for at least ten years may wish to consider testing (see page 360).

MYTH: AIDS can be transmitted by casual contact with an infected person—a handshake, a cough, or sharing bathrooms, toilets, and bathing facilities.

FACT: The AIDS virus has never been transmitted via food and drink, and cannot penetrate intact human skin. It can only be spread by sexual intercourse or the exchange of blood or blood products with an infected person, or by an infected mother to her unborn child. There is no known risk of nonsexual infection in daily life. In numerous studies of families caring for AIDS patients here and abroad, not one case of AIDS occurred in a family member who was not the sexual partner of the victim or the newborn child of an infected woman.

Why not mandatory screening?
Mandatory programs would very likely drive infected people underground and delay their seeking medical care. Since AIDS is not a disease spread like tuberculosis or measles, quarantine is not likely to be helpful, either. Depriving AIDS-infected people of jobs, medical attention, medical insurance, access to public facilities or to education would not protect the healthy. Keeping people in lifelong quarantine—even if no civil rights issues were involved—would also divert tax money that could better be spent on scientific research.

**MYTH: The AIDS virus is something new—
probably a product of the lax sexual
mores of modern times.**

FACT: Our knowledge of the AIDS virus is new, but retroviruses are a part of the natural world and are no more likely to manifest divine wrath than any other infectious agent. As early as 1910 an American scientist isolated and studied a retrovirus that causes cancer in chickens. Dr. Robert C. Gallo, head of the team that discovered the first human retrovirus (the agent responsible for a form of leukemia), theorizes that it may have originated in Africa centuries ago and have been spread around the globe by the slave trade and other commercial ventures in the period after the discovery of America. Nor are sexually transmitted diseases anything new; they have been carried around the world for centuries. Syphilis, once regarded as retribution for sinful habits, can now be completely cured with adequate penicillin. AIDS, too, may one day be curable with proper treatment.

**MYTH: Children with AIDS should be barred
from schools to protect other children.**

FACT: So far as is known, no case of AIDS has ever been transmitted from one child to another at school. Some parents fear that a bite from an AIDS-infected child might transmit the virus. But the virus only rarely appears in saliva, and even then not in sufficient quantities to cause infection. The Centers for Disease Control in Atlanta has stated that "casual person-to-person contact as would occur among school children appears to pose no risk." Similarly, the noninfected siblings of an infected child will not acquire the virus from him.

MYTH: AIDS can be spread by mosquitoes and bedbugs.

FACT: No case of AIDS has ever been traced to insect bites, and there is every reason to think such transmittal is impossible. AIDS viruses are scarce even in infected blood, and the amount of blood on a mosquito's proboscis is minuscule.

The Highest Risks

Groups now at highest risk of infection in the United States are homosexual men (unless they have been celibate or living in a monogamous relationship for the past ten years), bisexual men, and intravenous drug users of both sexes (and their sexual partners), simply because these groups have the highest infection rate. *But it's not who you are, but what you do and with whom you do it that puts you at risk for contracting AIDS.* The following are high-risk practices:

• Sharing drug needles or syringes.

• Anal sex (with or without a condom) with someone who might carry HIV antibodies. The virus is passed easily during anal sex.

• Unprotected vaginal or oral sex (without a condom) with someone who might carry HIV

antibodies. Obviously, the more times you have unprotected sex, the greater your risk. Sex with prostitutes, especially in big cities, is particularly risky.

In addition, some recipients of blood transfusions between the fall of 1978 (when HIV first appeared in the United States) and May 1985 (when blood donor screening became routine) may have been at risk for infection, particularly if they received the blood in San Francisco or New York City or if they had multiple transfusions. Hemophiliacs, who also receive donated blood products, may also have been at risk during those years. Since 1985 the risk of infection from transfusions has been minimized thanks to rigorous screening (see page 359).

Furthermore, if insect bites could spread AIDS, the whole population would now be randomly infected—children and the elderly, the celibate and the promiscuous—since mosquitoes don't confine their attentions to groups with any particular sexual profiles and practices.

MYTH: You can get AIDS by donating blood.

FACT: There is no AIDS risk in giving blood. Part of the confusion arises from the potential risk of getting the virus through blood transfusions (see marginal at right)—and unfortunately, fear of getting AIDS through donating blood has created serious shortages in blood banks across the nation. When you donate blood, however, no substance enters your veins, so there is no way a donor could be exposed to the AIDS virus or any other infectious agent. The sterile needle used to draw your blood is immediately discarded after this one use. No donor has ever used it before, nor ever uses it again.

MYTH: In hospitals that treat people with AIDS, staff and other patients alike are in danger of getting the disease.

FACT: For the same reasons that AIDS is not transmitted in a family setting, it is unlikely to be spread in a hospital setting. AIDS patients are mainly admitted to hospitals because they are suffering from "opportunistic" infections that are life-threatening. As with other infected patients, the hospital staff uses special isolation procedures for blood and tissue samples, as well as for hospital equipment. Accidental self-puncture with an AIDS-infected needle is a possible danger for health-care workers. However, in a survey of 2,500 health care workers who had been carefully tested for AIDS, about 750 of them had experienced accidental spills of bodily fluids of AIDS patients or had been stuck accidentally by contaminated needles; of these, only three—all of them stuck by needles—had developed AIDS antibodies.

MYTH: Everyone who tests "AIDS positive" currently has the disease.

FACT: Testing positive (after a confirmatory test) simply means that a person has been exposed to the AIDS virus and has developed antibodies to it. No one knows what percentage of antibody-positive people will develop the disease. And because the disease can be so slow to develop, it will be years before scientists have the answer to this question.

MYTH: Sexual abstinence is the only sure way to protect yourself against AIDS.

FACT: If you have had a lifetime sexual partner, and both of you have been monogamous, you are not at risk for AIDS. Any person who has multiple partners, or has a sexual relationship with someone who has multiple partners, may be at risk. Fortunately, condoms provide a nearly foolproof AIDS preventive: the AIDS virus cannot penetrate an intact condom. Unless you are certain that you and your sexual partner have not been exposed to AIDS, the use of condoms must be habitual for any intimate sexual encounter.

AIDS and Blood Transfusions
Before blood screening was possible, a small number of people receiving blood transfusions did contract AIDS. But blood banks in the United States are now as safe as modern science can make them. People who might be at risk for AIDS are discouraged from donating. All blood is tested for the AIDS antibody; infected blood is not used for transfusions or the manufacture of blood products. The chances of contaminated blood slipping through this net are estimated at 1 in 100,000 transfusions.

Who needs an AIDS test?

Dread of AIDS is universal, and many Americans (with or without good reason) now wonder whether they or someone in their families or among their friends has been infected with the AIDS virus. How can they find out? Should everybody be tested? Or only those in high-risk groups? Or nobody?

The test is fairly simple. A blood sample from the arm is analyzed in a laboratory. What the test detects is not the presence of the AIDS virus—the human immunodeficiency virus, or HIV—but of antibodies that the immune system produces after the virus enters the bloodstream. The first stage of the testing is known as ELISA (enzyme-linked immunoabsorbent assay). Should it prove positive, it is followed by a confirmatory test known as the Western blot assay.

The accuracy of the combined tests is high. In a high-risk population, virtually all people who test positive will truly be infected, but among people at low risk the false positives will outnumber the true positives. Thus for every infected person correctly identified in a low-risk population, an estimated ten noncarriers will test positive. Such testing of low-risk groups creates more problems than it solves. False negatives may occur, too. Indeed, it has been recently discovered that in rare instances carriers of the virus may not start to produce antibodies for years.

Testing positive: benefits and drawbacks

Many people have resisted testing, in large part because all they could do if they tested positive was wait helplessly for symptoms to occur. However, evidence has been accumulating that the antivirial drug zidovudine (commonly known as AZT) may delay the progression to AIDS in symptomless individuals infected with the HIV virus. Furthermore, researchers have found that a lower dose of the drug works as well as a high dose, and that neither dose produced significant side effects. (In contrast, many people who don't start taking AZT until they have AIDS symptoms suffer serious side effects, notably anemia.)

The improved prospects afforded by early treatment with AZT (as well as drugs to reduce the risk of the type of pneumonia that eventually strikes most AIDS patients) *offers people who think they may have been infected the best reason yet to be tested for HIV.*

People in high-risk groups would also seem to have much to gain from being tested. One situation is fairly clear: anyone who is at high risk and is contemplating parenthood should certainly consider being tested. The chances of an infected mother transmitting the AIDS virus to a fetus or a newborn run from one in three to one in two; and infected babies almost always develop the disease and die. Besides, pregnancy may accelerate the disease in an infected but still healthy woman. No one infected with HIV should become pregnant or father a child, and thus a test can be of crucial importance.

It is true those who test positive will often need extensive counseling; some have become chronically depressed or even suicidal. Thus people should undergo testing only where adequate counseling is available. And there are social and financial risks in getting a positive result. According to a report in the *Journal of the American Medical Association,* in a small Midwestern town, one young man tested positive, only to learn that his doctor had notified the local health department, which did not keep the information confidential. The man was then fired from his job, and the loss of his job meant loss of health insurance.

However, in addition to the benefits offered by AZT (and with the expectation of other drugs to come), there are two good reasons to be tested. First, if you know you are infected you can avoid passing the virus to others. This means either abstaining from sex or limiting sexual activity to safer practices. Second, you can inform your sexual partner or partners and encourage them to protect others. These two reasons should be motivation enough for people at high risk to be tested. Also, a doctor can monitor you, administer drugs, and perhaps offer preventive treatment for some opportunistic diseases.

But a person willing to abstain from sex or practice safer sex in order to protect others can do so without having the AIDS test. Indeed, anyone not in a long-term and strictly monogamous relationship should practice safer sex. For some people, it may be easier psychologically to alter behavior without taking the test. Others may want to know. Some people may refuse to change their practices even if they know they carry HIV, although this is morally (and perhaps legally) unjustifiable.

Negative test—potential risks

If the test result is negative, everyone involved will be relieved, but there are pitfalls here, too. A person who does not wait at least twelve weeks after his last possible exposure to the virus may test negative but develop antibodies later. So to be absolutely certain, some people who test negative feel obliged to repeat the test. A negative test can be damaging, too, if it leads to a sense of invulnerability: the fallacy "I've taken risks and didn't get it, so this proves I'll be okay" could be deadly. Whether the test result is negative or positive, the practical result has to be the same: safer sexual practices. That's why the so-called "AIDS-free singles' clubs" that have sprung up around the country are so dangerous. To join you have to test negative for AIDS and then promise to refrain from sex with nonmembers. But people who are infected could test negative if they take the test too soon. And testing negative does not guarantee that a person is safe forever.

Getting an AIDS test

If you decide in favor of testing, try to ensure confidentiality, and make certain that counseling will be available. If you live in New York City, Washington, D.C., or San Francisco, you can be tested at a clinic where anonymity is the rule: you will be required to fabricate a name or use a number. In a number of states, you have to give your correct name and show identification, though confidentiality requirements are specified. In others, positive tests are usually reported to the health department. And in a few, contact tracing is mandatory. That is, you will be asked for the names of your past sexual partners, who will then be notified if your test is positive.

To find out where to be tested and to discuss other issues, you can start by calling your doctor, your local or state health department, an AIDS hotline, or the the American Social Health Association hotline, which can give you the number of your state's AIDS coordinator. In big cities, you can locate so-called alternate test sites (which provide free or low-cost testing) through your local health department. Do not have your insurance company billed for the test, whatever the result may be. Insurance companies "bank" such information, and you may, in effect, be blacklisted for future life or health insurance. If you are at low risk and test positive, have the test repeated at another lab.

Menstruation and Menopause

For most women, menstruation and menopause create no medical problems: even the most uncomfortable symptoms are not permanent, nor do they usually indicate any serious underlying condition. Yet both these stages of life can create physical and emotional problems, and few women escape some form of discomfort or anxiety at one stage or another—in part because patterns of menstruation and menopause are as unique as each individual. Here are the problems you are most likely to encounter and the remedies that are most effective.

Dysmenorrhea

The Greek-derived word dysmenorrhea, meaning painful menstrual flow, is a term for what most women call "cramps." Besides pain in the lower abdomen or back, women may also experience nausea, diarrhea, vomiting, and jumpiness. When it occurs, menstrual pain always comes at the beginning of a period and may last up to three days. It chiefly affects women twenty-five and under; for reasons not well understood, dysmenorrhea tends to vanish as women grow older, especially after the birth of a child.

Although it can cause emotional distress, dysmenorrhea is not psychological in origin. The discomfort comes from uterine spasms, which temporarily deprive the muscle of oxygen. These spasms are triggered by prostaglandins, hormone-like substances that the body sometimes releases in excess. The high level of progesterone characteristic of ovulation is what triggers the prostaglandins. Thus cramps are a fairly sure sign that ovulation has taken place.

Remedies. For centuries women have relied on home cures for cramps—hot drinks, massage, stretching exercises, keeping warm. No specific exercise for relieving dysmenorrhea exists, and there is no scientific evidence that any of the old tried-and-true remedies really work. Yet personal experience cannot be discounted; different things work (or don't work) for different people.

Effective, inexpensive medications that suppress prostaglandins are available without prescription. They include aspirin and ibuprofen, the same drugs that are useful for headaches. If you usually have cramps, you may want to begin taking such an anti-prostaglandin the day before you expect a period and to continue for a day or two. (For more information on these pain relievers, see pages 454-457).

Oral contraceptives are another highly effective treatment for cramps, since they prevent ovulation and hence high levels of progesterone and prostaglandin production. They are available only by prescription and must be taken on a regular basis, not just when symptoms appear. Smokers and women over thirty-five have to consider other risks in taking oral contraceptives (see page 350). Nevertheless, when cramps are truly incapacitating, oral contraceptives may be a practical option.

Premenstrual syndrome

Most women can tell when a period is about to start: tension, increased irritability, and breast soreness are common symptoms, as are a small weight gain, headaches, a craving for certain foods, and a feeling of fatigue. For many women, the tension evaporates in a burst of energy and feeling of well-being just before a period starts. Others find premenstrual symptoms minor nuisances that vanish after a few days.

But for some women, the problems remain and may intensify throughout a two-week period.

Thus from ovulation until the start of a period, some women's emotional tension and physical symptoms may severely disrupt their personal and professional lives. Premenstrual syndrome (PMS) has received a great deal of attention in recent years: courts in France and England have accepted it as a mitigating factor in criminal cases, and some people even cite it as evidence that women ought not to hold high political office. Yet doctors have never agreed on what it is, what causes it, how many women suffer from it, or how to treat it. One difficulty in diagnosing PMS is that some of the more disturbing emotional symptoms (irritability, depression, binge eating, and wide emotional swings) may in some cases not be tied to the menstrual cycle at all.

Is Postponing Pregnancy Risky?

Since 1977 the number of women having their first babies after thirty has been rising. Some studies have seemed to show that as women grow older, they run a greater risk of three problems develping: miscarriage, premature birth, and having a low-birth-weight baby. Yet other research suggests that the risks of delaying pregnancy until late in the reproductive years (after thirty-five) are not related to age at all but to pre-existing disorders such as high blood pressure or diabetes that may worsen with age.

Several studies, however, have been solidly reassuring, finding no evidence of increased risk of low birth weight or of premature delivery in women having their first pregnancy after age thirty compared with younger women. One study, performed at the Mount Sinai School of Medicine in New York, followed 3,917 women who were pregnant for the first time. The researchers found that mothers over thirty were no more likely to deliver a baby prematurely or to have stillbirths than younger first-time mothers, and that mothers thirty-five and older had only a slightly higher risk of producing low-birth-weight babies.

The increased risk of low birth weight and premature births that has showed up in earlier studies came about because women whose general health was poor or who had a history of reproductive problems were included. The subjects in the Mount Sinai study were largely white, well-educated nonsmokers who had private insurance, received prenatal care and were on private wards when they delivered their babies—these women may have had more education and more financial resources than older mothers had in the past; thus they

may be able to deal more effectively with the problems of pregnancy.

However, the risk of miscarriage and of congenital abnormalities increases with age, and rises very dramatically after age thirty-five, while fertility declines. Moreover, in the Mount Sinai study as well as in other studies, women over thirty-five were twice as likely as younger women to have health complications such as diabetes and high blood pressure (conditions that are frequently age-related).

In short, if you are a healthy woman attempting a first pregnancy at age thirty-five or older, you should be reassured as to the likelihood of having a healthy baby—provided that you take the following precautions:

•Avoid using oral contraceptives in your thirties. These may delay conception even after they are discontinued.

•Avoid cigarette smoking and alcohol consumption before and during pregnancy, since both of these increase the risk of miscarriage. Smoking can also adversely affect birth weight.

•Women over thirty-five should undergo amniocentesis and other procedures in order to determine whether there are genetic abnormalities in the fetus.

•If pregnancy does not occur readily, seek professional advice early. If either partner needs treatment for infertility, the sooner it is begun the better.

•Try to embark on pregnancy before the age of forty, since fertility declines quickly after that, and the chances of abnormalities in the fetus increase. Nevertheless, women in their early forties can still conceive and bear healthy babies.

Remedies. Treatment with diuretics and the same anti-prostaglandin drugs that are known to relieve dysmenorrhea have helped some women but not others. Women may also find it helpful to keep a daily diary of their cycles, noting what the symptoms are and exactly when they occur and disappear. If these symptoms do not fall within the two weeks preceding a period, they are probably not connected with menstruation. Women who tend to have swelling in the hands, ankles, and abdomen can predict this by means of their diary.

Since salt intensifies the tendency to retain water, you can head off this symptom by going on a reduced-sodium diet. Increasing water intake will help as well, since water is a diuretic.

As with dysmenorrhea, no specific exercise will relieve PMS. Nevertheless, in at least one study, a small group of women with PMS had fewer symptoms after they began a weekly running program. They averaged only forty-one miles per menstrual cycle (about $1\frac{1}{2}$ miles a day), but the subjects reported improvement in a wide range of problems from breast soreness to irritability. As investigators pointed out, the therapy had beneficial effects, although more research is needed to prove why.

Menopause

Because of their life expectancy—up to age seventy-eight currently—women can now expect to live half their adult lives in the postmenopausal years. As a woman approaches midlife, her estrogen production declines, and she gradually stops ovulating. The body never entirely stops making estrogen, but production does fall off to levels insufficient to cause menstruation. This is a normal physiological phenomenon: half of all women will stop menstruating by age forty-eight; at age fifty-two, 85 percent will have reached menopause. Smoking is a factor: women who smoke reach menopause one to two years earlier than nonsmokers.

One out of five women experience no unusual symptoms at menopause; their periods simply stop. Others may have irregular or very heavy periods. For some women, mild headaches, backaches, and fatigue are also a problem. About 49 percent will suffer hot flashes, and of these women 15 percent will find them so severe that they will seek medical relief.

The hot flash or hot flush, that classic menopausal symptom, is a sudden feeling that the body's temperature has risen. The upper torso may flush, along with the face, and sweat breaks out. Hot flashes at night—"hot sweats"—can interrupt sleep and cause insomnia. These episodes are causes by fluctuating hormone levels, which through some poorly understood mechanism dilate the blood vessels.

In addition, lower estrogen levels can cause the lining of the vagina to thin out, and vaginal lubrication to decline, leading to difficulty in intercourse. Mood swings or depression may also occur, though the influence of hormone deficiencies on emotions is a matter of debate. Lack of estrogen may also increase a woman's risk of heart attack (though of course by no means all postmenopausal women suffer from heart disease). Of greater concern is that all women do experience some loss of bone density at menopause. Particularly in women who have small frames and lower bone density, this may lead to clinical osteoporosis.

Remedies. In many cases hot flashes will slack off markedly and occur less frequently a year or so after they begin. But some women have them for years, long after menstruation stops. One way to deal with them is to avoid overheated rooms and heavy fabrics, especially synthetics; wear cotton or other soft clothing and dress in layers with a jacket or cardigan that can be easily and quickly removed. For heading off discomfort at night, try cotton nightwear and sheets as well as lightweight thermal blankets. Though a hot flash can make you self-conscious, it is nothing to be embarrassed about, and in any case it is usually more noticeable to the person suffering from one than to her companions.

To cope with any difficulty in sexual activity due to vaginal dryness, a non-hormonal lubricating cream can be helpful; if it doesn't ease the problem, a physician may prescribe estrogen creams or oral hormones.

Hormone therapy. Years ago, estrogen replacement therapy (ERT) was often prescribed for the side effects of menopause, including hot flashes, vaginal dryness, and menopausal bone loss. Some of these are caused by lack of estrogen and progesterone, but the traditional therapy replaced only the estrogen. This not only increased the risk of uterine and breast cancer but also caused blood clots and uterine bleeding. Since the mid-1970s, however, ERT has been superseded by hormone replacement therapy (HRT), consisting of low doses of both estrogen and progesterone, administered in the form of pills or by a skin patch.

Studies have shown that HRT not only reduces hot flashes and other symptoms but protects women against heart attacks and may actually reduce the risk of uterine cancer. It may work similarly against breast cancer, but the evidence (as with oral contraceptives) is not clear. Like ERT, HRT can effectively slow down bone loss. Indeed, women with one or more risk factors for osteoporosis— sedentary women, heavy smokers and drinkers, small-boned, fair-skinned women, and women with low-calcium diets—are most likely to benefit from HRT. (For other factors that can help prevent osteoporosis, see pages 384-385.)

Not everybody, though, is a candidate for HRT:

• Women who have had breast cancer should not take HRT.

• Women who have migraine headaches, diabetes, asthma, heart disease and other disorders may also be advised not to undertake HRT.

In addition, HRT may have minor drawbacks: it can cause premenstrual symptoms and short periods of bleeding, similar to menstruation. At least in the first stages, HRT requires careful medical follow-up to evaluate potential side effects and ensure that dosage levels are correct.

Even if you think you are a candidate for HRT, you should discuss your own situation carefully with your doctor before deciding. Some women do very well without it; menopause is *not* a medical condition requiring drugs. Also bear in mind that HRT will not help keep you looking young. Though estrogen loss may be involved in changes in skin appearance, many other factors also influence it—exposure to sun, genetics, and general health and nutrition.

Sex and Arthritis

For arthritics, sex can actually be a pain reliever. Sexual orgasm can stimulate the production of hormones from the adrenal gland, which may help reduce arthritic discomfort for up to six hours. If arthritis pain interferes with certain physical movements or positions you use during sex, try taking a hot bath or shower beforehand to relax your joints and muscles. Experiment to find comfortable, enjoyable positions.

Sex and Aging

We live in a culture that until quite recently has disapproved of sexuality in people past their reproductive years, viewed it as distasteful, or preferred to think it nonexistent. And yet experts in the field indicate that, in the absence of disease, sexual expression may endure throughout life. At Duke University ongoing research into sexual activity among the aging found that 80 percent of men in their late sixties continue to be interested in sex. At the age of seventy-eight or older, one in four men continues to be sexually active.

Researchers have found that women, too, retain their sexual abilities and interests throughout life. Decreased sexual activity in older women quite often arises from the lack of a partner rather than a lack of interest. While the *intensity* of sexual interest may generally decline with age, individuals may continue to be sexually active at age sixty, seventy, and beyond.

Whether sexual expression is heterosexual or homosexual, a person with a happy sex life in youth and middle age is more likely to maintain it in old age. This does not mean, however, that sexuality cannot be developed later in life. The physiological and biological changes of midlife may change the nature and possibly the frequency of sexual activity. Some of these changes may be decidedly for the better: a postmenopausal woman no longer has to worry about contraceptives, menstrual periods, and the possibility of pregnancy. After children leave home, couples may have more privacy and more time for sex. In middle age and after, people can be interested in the quality rather than the quantity of sex. Nevertheless, sexual capabilities do alter with time, and remaining sexually satisfied is largely a matter of knowing what changes to expect as you age, and how to adjust.

What to expect as you get older

Postmenopausal women may find intercourse painful at times due to a decrease in vaginal lubrication. The vaginal wall thins and may be less elastic. As discussed on page 365, a lubricating jelly or cream—or hormones prescribed by your doctor—may be helpful in correcting diminished vaginal lubrication.

Older men may find that they feel less sexual urgency, that erections are sometimes delayed or partial, and that the moment of ejaculation is less well defined. This is neither a reflection of decreased sexuality, nor a symptom of impending impotence. Rather, it is the result of physiological changes: your body secretes less testosterone (the hormone that regulates sexual performance and desire) and conducts nerve impulses more slowly. In addition, the arteries in the penis are less able to maintain the blood pressure necessary for a full erection.

These changes needn't be alarming; indeed, they can be turned to advantage since they can allow a man to prolong foreplay, sustain intercourse longer, and delay orgasm until the moment when both partners will be most satisfied. Many people find that more leisurely lovemaking is a bonus. A woman of any age requires on average thirteen minutes of arousal and direct stimulation before climaxing, but only three minutes may elapse between arousal and orgasm in a young man. Aging lengthens this time between your sexual arousal and climax, bringing it closer to your partner's timetable.

Problems that are sexual

Nearly everyone experiences a diminished sexual response from time to time, due to such routine difficulties as fatigue, stress, or acute illness. For some people, however, this becomes a chronic problem.

Impotence. Whether occasional or frequent, impotence—the inability to achieve and maintain an erection—is not the inevitable result of aging, but the reported rate of impotence does increase with age. More than ten million American men are chronically impotent. By the age of fifty-five, 18 percent of men report the

How to Find Sexual Counseling

Since the vast majority of sexual problems have a psychological basis, psychotherapy is often suggested to help solve them. If you are having sexual problems, turn to your doctor first, since he will be in the best position to assess your physical condition. If counseling is in order, a referral from your doctor is probably the best way to find a properly certified sex therapist, although some family practitioners may have training in sexual therapy.

problem; by age sixty-five, that figure increases to 30 percent; and by the age of seventy-five, 55 percent of men report suffering from impotence.

Up until just a decade ago, more than 90 percent of all cases of impotence were blamed simply on emotional causes. During the past ten years, however, doctors have come to believe that at least half, and perhaps as many as three quarters, of all cases have a physiological basis as well. Medical problems such as diabetes, Parkinson's disease, liver or kidney disease, and lower back problems have been linked to impotence. Other causes are medications, including prescription drugs (especially those for hypertension) and some antihistamines and decongestants, which may cause temporary impotence; and life-style habits such as excessive alcohol consumption, drug abuse, and smoking. When a medication or habit is the cause, the remedy is fairly straightforward. Most cases of impotence, however, have a psychological component—anxiety, depression, or marital problems are common causes—and about 80 percent of these cases can be overcome with psychotherapy.

When a man who experiences impotence awakes at night or in the morning with a full, firm erection, the cause of the impotence is most likely psychological. But for any case of chronic impotence, a doctor should first be consulted to rule out any physiological causes. If the doctor suspects a physiological cause, he can perform tests to see if blood flow into the penis is adequate and check whether spinal cord problems might be involved. Nearly all forms of impotence can be at least partially corrected by various methods ranging from a special vacuum device that draws blood into the penis to surgically implanted prosthetic devices. And as research on impotence continues, treatments that are equally or even more effective, and less intrusive, may become available.

Sexual dysfunction in women. Frigidity is the label used for a wide range of sexual dysfunctions in women. The term misleadingly implies coldness, and has been inappropriately used to describe women who become sexually excited but are unable to achieve orgasm through intercourse alone. This "failure" is in fact the norm: surveys indicate that an estimated 70 percent of women fall into this category; most women need direct stimulation of the clitoris to have an orgasm. True frigidity, a lifelong inability to become excited, may be the result of sexual repression, anxiety, or guilt, and can often be treated by psychotherapy. As with male impotence, however, frigidity may have organic causes that can be medically treated.

Maintaining sexual satisfaction

None of the changes that you go through as you age need limit your sexuality. However, as people grow older they may find it wise to emphasize other aspects of sexuality (kissing, affectionate behavior, new positions) and to remember that coital performance is not the inevitable, or the only, expression of sexual love. Another point to bear in mind: according to William Masters of the Masters & Johnson Institute in St. Louis, continuing sexual activity as you get older helps to slow sexual changes that are physiological. Indeed, the best predictor of a satisfying sex life in later years is a satisfying sex life in the middle years. Even if you are currently without a sexual partner, experts say that if you stay physically active in general, and take other steps to keep in good health, you should be able to resume a rewarding sex life in the future.

Counteracting Impotence

•*Avoid drinking too much alcohol. Impotence among men in their late forties and early fifties is associated more often with excessive alcohol consumption than with any other single factor.*

•*Maintain an active and regular sex life. In one study of men over sixty, those who engaged in more frequent sex had significantly greater levels of testosterone in their blood.*

•*Not every sexual experience has to end with orgasm. Thinking that you must achieve a climax can make you anxious, which can result in impotence. Instead, you and your partner can agree to focus on caressing and kissing rather than having an orgasm. This may relieve performance anxiety.*

Muscles and Joints

Nearly everyone has experienced stresses and strains to those parts of the body responsible for movement: the bones and muscles; major joints like the knee and ankle; and the tendons and ligaments—the soft connective tissues that transmit movement among muscles and joints. Though sometimes referred to as sports injuries, these mishaps can occur not only during sports and exercise, but during such everyday activities as brisk walking, climbing stairs, housework or gardening. The injuries range in severity from minor bouts of muscle soreness to tears or sprains that may take weeks to heal. Fortunately, the likelihood of injury can be reduced through conditioning exercises and by observing certain precautions.

In the following pages you will find an overview of activity-related problems: the steps you can take to protect specific body parts; what to do if you sustain a muscle or joint injury; and how exercise can help you cope with two problems related to aging—arthritis and osteoporosis. This section doesn't discuss the injuries that physicians refer to as "direct trauma," such as broken bones and severe cuts and bruises, which usually require first aid and, often, a doctor's care. The injuries covered here can often be managed without professional help.

Preventing Aches and Pains

From runner's ankle and biker's knee to tennis elbow and swimmer's shoulder, there is hardly a sport or exercise that doesn't have some type of aggravating problem associated with it. Despite the proliferation of names, most injuries associated with exercise fall into a few broad categories. An understanding of these basic types may help you avoid injury, minimize the damage when you are hurt, and speed your recovery. Don't let concern about injuries keep you from exercising, though. A number of studies show that the benefits of exercise far exceed the risk of injury.

Muscle soreness

When you exercise, you intentionally use certain muscles to increase their strength and endurance. As your body adapts to these efforts (depending on their intensity), you are likely to experience minor aches, twinges, and soreness. For example, one type of discomfort, called ischemic pain, occurs when muscle tissue doesn't have enough oxygen to continue working. This is the ache you feel when you attempt to perform more sit-ups or lift more weights than you are accustomed to, and it disappears when you stop exerting yourself or when you reduce the intensity of the workout, such as by slowing down or using lighter weights.

After any unaccustomed, strenuous exercise, you may experience a painful stiffness called *delayed-onset muscle soreness* (or DOMS, as it is sometimes referred to by physiologists). This type of discomfort occurs most often to weekend athletes who exercise only occasionally or among frequent exercisers who suddenly increase the intensity of their workouts. Typically, it sets in a day or two after a game or workout and can last a week or more.

Physiologists believe that this soreness may be a symptom of microscopic injury to muscle tissue, but there is no evidence that it leads to long-term damage. Often the injury appears to be brought on by activity that has an "eccentric component"—that is, one requiring your muscles to produce a force while lengthening. Ordinarily, muscles shorten when they contract, as when you lift a weight; this is called a concentric contraction. In contrast, when muscles lengthen, as when you lower a weight, the action is called eccentric. Running downhill, when your legs must extend in stride, and, at the same time, resist gravity, is another example. Most exercise—running, brisk walking, aerobic dance, calisthenics—has an eccentric component to it, during which some muscles are elongating and at the same time producing enough force to slow down a movement.

Prevention. Unfortunately, there is no proven way to prevent delayed-onset muscle soreness. Some people believe that stretching after exercise can help prevent it, but studies have failed to confirm it. (Still, you should not forego stretching since it has other benefits.)

What does work to minimize muscle soreness from unusually hard activity, according to research, is to do some mild training beforehand. If you plan a hiking trip, do some exercise with an eccentric component—for example, walk down long flights of stairs every day during the preceding week or two.

Relief. Once your muscles are stiff and sore, resting for five to seven days can ease the discomfort. However, "active" rest may be better: according to recent research, relief from delayed-onset muscle soreness may be best achieved by repeating the activity that caused the soreness at a much lighter intensity.

If you become very uncomfortable and you want to take a pain reliever, don't use aspirin or ibuprofen. New evidence suggests that aspirin and ibuprofen (for instance, Advil or Motrin), block the production of prostaglandins, which help stimulate muscle repair. Acetaminophen (Tylenol), which has no anti-prostaglandin effect, is probably your best choice for relief.

Muscle cramps

Though they are harmless and do not involve injury, few things are as painful as the common muscle cramp. Cramps, also called spasms, can occur in any muscle at any time, but they most often occur in the calf or foot, and usually while you are lying in bed or playing sports or exercising. Cramps remain something of a mystery, and it's seldom possible to pinpoint why they occur. Still, some general facts about cramps can help prevent or alleviate them.

Nighttime calf cramps usually strike in bed at night as a result of contracting the calf muscles by suddenly pointing your toes or by lying with the feet in that position. (Swimmers, who kick with their toes sharply pointed, can suffer calf spasms similar to nocturnal leg cramps.) If you exercised strenuously earlier in the day, your muscles may tighten while you sleep and thus cramp. Similarly, if you're not used to them, wearing high heels may cause cramps. In general, as you age you may find that you experience leg cramps more frequently. Certain medications, notably diuretics, may also promote cramps.

Athletes' cramps occur during exercise for a number of reasons. The imbalance of minerals called electrolytes (potassium and sodium) in the blood, which often

Can liniments help?
Liniments and balms are popular, convenient methods for producing a feeling of heat or cold in muscles. But their effect is only superficial—the active ingredients stimulate sensory nerve endings in the skin just enough to produce sensations of heat or cold that may temporarily mask the pain of sore muscles. The massaging action can increase blood flow and help relax muscles. But since the heating action isn't real, it does little or nothing to promote healing. Never put a liniment over a wound or cover it with a heating pad or elastic bandage. Severe burning or blistering can result.

results from excess sweating and dehydration may cause muscles to cramp. Another common cause is overexertion or muscle fatigue, marked by excessive tightening of the muscles and/or a build-up of lactic acid in them. Poor conditioning may also contribute to cramps.

Prevention. If you seem predisposed to nocturnal calf cramps, don't point your toes while stretching, and try not to sleep with your toes pointed. Sleep on your side, and don't tuck in your blankets and sheets too tightly, since these can bend down your toes.

Stretching your calf muscles can also help (see page 374), as can drinking plenty of water before and during exercise, especially in hot weather. Quinine also appears to reduce the likelihood of cramps, but it must be prescribed by your doctor. (There's not enough quinine in tonic water to have any beneficial effect.)

Relief. Though medication is sometimes used to alleviate calf cramps, your best bet is massage and stretching. To halt the cramp, flex your foot by pointing your toes upward. Lying down and grabbing the toes and ball of your foot and pulling them toward your knee may help. At the same time, massage the muscle gently to relax it fully. Ice packs can reduce blood flow to the muscles and thus relax them. Walking may help, too, particularly if you put your full weight on your heels.

In addition, if you get the cramp during a workout, especially if you are participating in a long athletic event in the heat, drink water. This can help correct any fluid loss from excessive sweating. If a mineral imbalance—too little potassium or sodium, for instance—is contributing to the cramping, a sports drink may help. Don't take salt tablets; these can be counter productive.

Strains and sprains

These are the most common type of acute injury—that is, an injury that usually results from a single, abrupt incident causing sharp pain, often accompanied by swelling. Strains and sprains are especially common among eager weekend athletes who don't know the limitations of their unconditioned muscles and joints.

Strains. Also called "muscle pulls," these occur when muscles or their tendons are stretched to the point their fibers actually start to tear. This can happen when you lift a heavy weight or suddenly overextend a muscle—for instance, when swinging a golf club or stretching to catch a baseball. The most common sites for strains are the hamstring and quadriceps muscles in the thigh and the muscles in the groin and shoulder—all large muscles that are used for sudden powerful movements.

Mild strains are usually only a nuisance; the tears are microscopic and, with rest, repair themselves easily. More severe strains involve a greater degree of fiber destruction and produce not only sharp pain but also loss of power and movement.

Cold, fatigue, or immobilization reduces blood flow and lessens muscle elasticity, increasing the risk of strains. The best way to prevent them is to warm up, then stretch all the muscles involved in your upcoming activity. A full-body warm-up, such as jogging in place or stationary cycling for five to ten minutes, increases blood flow and raises the temperature of large muscle groups. You can also warm up by slowly rehearsing the sport or exercise you're about to perform. A light sweat usually indicates that you've warmed up sufficiently.

Sprains. Whereas strains occur to muscles, sprains damage ligaments (the bands connecting bones) and joint capsules. They are most often the result of a sudden force, typically a twisting motion, that the surrounding muscles aren't strong

Myth: You can "run through" pain.

Fact: *If you feel pain (beyond mild discomfort), stop exercising and rest.*

It may seem that many professional athletes bounce right back after an injury. But they usually have the benefit of care by experts who diagnose and treat their injuries quickly. Moreover, they are usually in better condition than the rest of us and are highly motivated to recover.

The surest way to speed recovery is to treat any recurring ache or pain right away, even if you're able to continue exercising in spite of them.

enough to control. As a result, the ligaments, which usually wrap around a joint, get stretched or torn. Like strains, sprains can range from minor tears to complete ruptures. But sprains tend to be more serious than strains: not only do they often take longer to heal, but a torn ligament can throw bones out of alignment, causing damage to surrounding tissues. A ruptured ligament requires medical attention.

Because of its construction and the fact that it must support your entire body weight, the ankle is the most frequently sprained joint—in fact, a sprained ankle is probably the most common sports injury. The knee, too, is vulnerable because it must absorb twisting stresses every time the body rotates from the hips. Ankle and knee sprains are most likely to occur during activities involving sudden twists or stop-and-start movements, such as dancing, tennis, soccer, hiking on rough terrain, and downhill skiing.

Strong, flexible muscles help protect against sprains. To safeguard your ankles, strengthen the muscles surrounding them and stretch your calf muscles (see pages 373-374). To protect your knees, strengthen your quadriceps, the muscle group along the front of the thigh (see page 375).

Overuse injuries

Also known as chronic or stress injuries, overuse injuries are brought on gradually as a result of wear-and-tear from a repetitive activity such as cycling, running, or playing tennis. Although a weekend athlete can experience overuse soreness, it is far more of a problem for people who do the same exercise repeatedly and/or often. In one survey of athletes, overuse injuries outnumbered acute injuries in all activities except basketball and skiing. In two of the most popular activities, running and tennis, almost 80 percent of all injuries were of the overuse variety.

Whereas you can almost always pinpoint the incident that caused an acute injury, an overuse injury may have no obvious cause. For instance, you suddenly increase the intensity or duration of your normal workout and feel a dull, annoying pain. Over the next few days, the pain recurs intermittently, but isn't bad enough to stop you from exercising. In effect, you have pushed your body beyond its ability to absorb the force of exercise effectively. As a result, muscle tissue has gradually developed microscopic tears that can cause pain, tenderness, and swelling. Initially, an overuse injury may seem less serious than an acute one. But as time passes, you usually feel pain during and after exercise. If you ignore the damage, it can worsen—and you may suffer a strain or other acute injury at the site of the weakened tissue.

Tendinitis. This condition is the problem behind many common overuse injuries. Tendons—the fibrous cords that anchor muscles to bones—are vulnerable, since the force of muscle contractions is transmitted through them. People who exercise regularly are especially at risk because of the strong forces produced by their well-conditioned muscles. These increase tension on the tendons, which can then rub against bones, ligaments, and other tendons, causing irritation. The suffix "itis" means inflammation (characterized by pain, swelling, warmth, and redness).

Tendinitis is deceptive: the pain can be severe when you start exercising, then diminish as you continue—only to return sharply once you've stopped. Perhaps the most common form of tendinitis is tennis elbow (see page 377). In sports and activities that involve running and jumping, tendinitis is most likely to develop in the knee, foot, and the Achilles tendon at the back of the ankle. For cyclists, knees

A study of three thousand U.S. Marines examined the relationship between common running injuries and the use of different shoes and insoles. The researchers found that special shock-absorbing insoles were no more effective in preventing running injuries than normal insoles. Much more important was a subject's level of conditioning: subjects who were out of shape were much more likely to sustain an injury than those who were more active.

are most vulnerable. Shoulder tendinitis can develop from pitching a ball, swinging a golf club, or swimming.

Stretching and strengthening routines can help prevent tendinitis, but equipment and technique may be equally important. For example, an improperly executed backhand is often the cause of tennis elbow, and running shoes with worn-down heels contribute to Achilles tendinitis.

Stress fractures. These microscopic breaks in bone, usually in the foot, shin, or thigh are another form of overuse injury. Common among long-distance runners, aerobic dancers, and basketball players, the fractures are caused by the repeated impact of running or jumping. Often the pain is mild at first, occurring during or right after exercising. If you continue to exercise it gradually worsens, but for the first few weeks such fractures are usually too small to be detected, even by X-ray. Fortunately, the fractures rarely break through the bone, so they don't require splints or casts to heal, only rest.

Prevent stress fractures by increasing the intensity of your workouts gradually, not dramatically. Try to minimize impact on your legs: run and jump on soft or resilient surfaces—grass, carpet, mats, or suspended wooden gym floors—rather than concrete. Wear well-cushioned exercise shoes.

Injury Sites

The following pages contain tips and exercises that are geared primarily to help prevent injuries to a joint. The exercises can also be used to condition muscles during recovery from an injury, but only after an initial stretching regimen has restored full range of motion to the joint.

Ankles

For athlete and nonathlete alike, the most frequently injured joint is the ankle. A single anklebone, the talus, supports your entire body weight, with the help of

---

Sneakers for Weak Ankles

Though originally designed for basketball—nearly all college and professional players now wear them—high-topped sport shoes are moving into other sports. That's because, according to some researchers, high tops may help protect your ankles. (These aren't the old-fashioned floppy canvas high tops—today most high tops are higher, more stable, well padded, and yet flexible.)

High tops may protect against ankle sprains by stabilizing the ankles and preventing a roll-over, or inversion, onto the side of the foot. Inversion injuries frequently occur when people jump up and then land awkwardly to one side. People who can benefit most from high-top sneakers are those who suffer from recurrent ankle sprains and play basketball, tennis, racquetball, volleyball, soccer or any sport where there is a tendency to roll over on the ankle.

If walking is your preferred form of exercise, and you have ankle problems or travel on rugged terrain, lightweight hiking boots or other high-top shoes are good options. High-top aerobic dance shoes are also available. Of course, if you're a serious athlete and have ankle problems, your trainer or physical therapist may also recommend lace-up ankle stabilizers or athletic tape.

When shopping for high-top shoes, try them on and make sure they're supportive enough to prevent your feet from rolling over; look for a pair with an ankle collar high enough to support your ankles well.

small ligaments and long tendons. And when you run or jump, the ankle must transmit the force of impact (equal to more than three times your body weight) from your foot to your leg. Moreover, since the ankle is designed to move like a hinge in one plane, the joint and its supporting ligaments and musculature resist lateral movement. Most ankle injuries occur when the foot inverts, or rolls over to the side, causing a sprain on the outside of the ankle. Activities that are likely to put added stress on the ankle include running, racquet sports, bowling, dancing, ice skating, or skiing.

Weak muscles, tendons, and ligaments are one cause of ankle sprains. Many sprains, though, result not from "weak ankles" but from tight calf muscles, the two major ones being the soleus and the gastrocnemius. These muscles pull on the Achilles tendon, the strongest, thickest tendon in the body, which is attached to your heel bone. Tight calf muscles prevent you from raising the front of your foot fully, so if you step in a pothole or land awkwardly during a jump, your foot may be brought up short and twist to the side, possibly resulting in a sprained ankle.

Tight calf muscles can also cause stress injuries, notably Achilles tendinitis (a common affliction among runners, which, in extreme cases, can result in a rupture of the tendon) and plantar fascitis (pain or discomfort at the heel, often radiating along the sole).

You can guard against ankle injuries with the exercises below, which will help strengthen muscles surrounding the joint; perform them at least three times a week if you are starting any new activity that may stress your ankles. The calf stretches on page 374 will promote a more complete range of ankle motion; perform them before and after you work out or take part in a sport.

Heel raises. *Stand with your feet comfortably apart. Rise on the balls of your feet as far as possible, hold for a few seconds, then lower. Gradually work up to twenty repetitions. Eventually try this exercise while standing with the balls of your feet on the edge of a step, so that you dip your heels lower than your toes.*

Toe raises. *Wearing flat shoes with smooth soles, stand on your heels and keep your toes as high off the ground as possible; walk like this, keeping your toes elevated, for three to five minutes. Next walk on your toes with your heels elevated. Also try walking on the insides of your feet, then the outsides.*

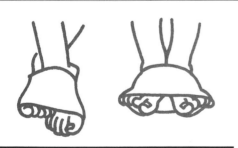

Strengtheners. Sit with your knees, ankles, and feet together. Wrap bicycle inner tubing or surgical tubing (available at surgical supply stores) around your feet. Pull the front of your feet apart, pushing against the tubing, then pull your heels apart; repeat ten times. Next try pointing one foot at a time, up and down, ten times each. Then cross your ankles and push the top foot outward (right); repeat ten times, then switch feet.

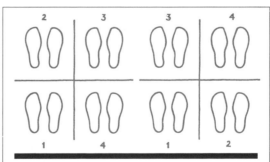

Sprints and hops. After warming up (such as jogging in place), and stretching, run ten- and forty-yard sprints at half and three-quarter speed. Run in circles, figure eights, and zigzags. Hop slowly with both feet together in a square pattern (left), then reverse direction. Hop in an X pattern (right), then reverse. Eventually try hopping on one foot in these patterns.

Calf stretches. *To stretch the gastrocnemius, stand about two feet from a wall and place your hands against it (left). Extend one leg behind you with the knee straight. Keep your heel on the floor and lean forward until you feel a stretch in the rear leg. To stretch the soleus, assume the same position but keep the back knee slightly bent (right). Hold each stretch for twenty to thirty seconds, then repeat two or three times. Do each stretch in three positions: rear foot pointed straight ahead, pointed in, and pointed out. Keep the front foot flat, and make sure your knee is in line with it.*

Variation. *To further stretch your calf, place the ball of your foot on a book, lean into the wall and slowly lower your heel.*

Knees

One out of every four sports injuries involves the knee. Even people who don't play a sport, but are just active—ride a bike, dance, hike, or climb stairs frequently—can develop knee problems. This is the largest joint in the body, one of the most complex, and one of the most mobile. Functioning simultaneously as a hinge, lever, and shock absorber, the knee is the key to the ability to stand up, walk, climb, and kick.

Because of its complexity and the great forces to which it is routinely subjected, the knee is susceptible to a host of injuries. Most common is runner's knee, an overuse syndrome characterized by dull, aching pain under or around the kneecap and usually most noticeable when descending stairs or hills. It is estimated that nearly 30 percent of the 15 million runners in this country develop this disorder. But, in addition to runners, skiers, cyclists, soccer players, and people who participate in high-impact aerobics classes are also prone. Another frequent complaint is "jumper's knee," a form of tendinitis common among basketball and volleyball players.

You can reduce the likelihood of knee injury with the following precautions and conditioning exercises:

•Beware of suddenly intensifying or lengthening your workouts. A sudden burst of training can create additional friction in the joint and increase the risk of an overuse injury.

•Check your exercise shoes. If they are worn or don't fit well, they may put your knees at risk.

•To minimize knee stress when cycling, make sure the seat is at the proper height and avoid high gears.

•The knee sometimes pays the price for foot abnormalities (such as flat feet) or poor leg alignment (such as knock-knees), which can put greater stress on the joint. An orthotic device—a custom-made arch support—may help correct some foot or alignment problems.

•Perform exercises to strengthen the quadriceps, the large four-part muscle group on the front of the thigh that, along with the hamstrings (located behind the

Wellness Body Atlas

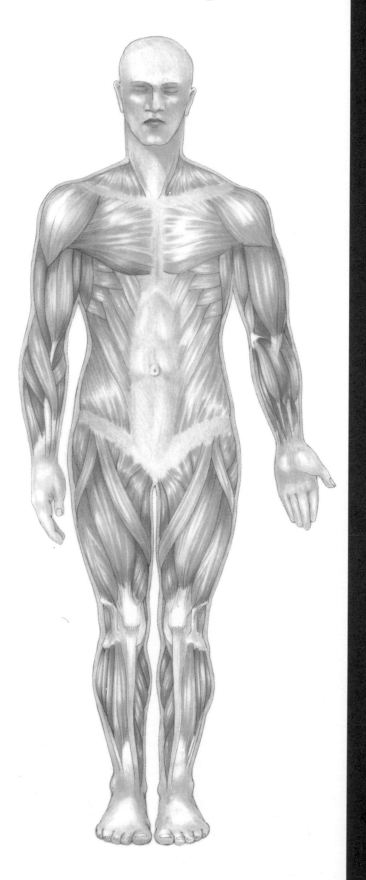

Knowing how joints and muscles operate can help you safeguard them. Basically, joints permit movement, while skeletal muscles create and control movement. Aided by fibrous bands called ligaments, joints bind two or more bones together in a variety of ways to give your limbs, torso, and neck flexibility. Muscles, which are attached to bones by tendons, operate around a joint in a seesaw pattern, working in pairs to pull the joint in one direction or another. By virtue of the body's sophisticated nervous system, many muscles can be coordinated to perform complex actions—for example, consider the variety of movements in a tennis game, which involves almost every area of the body.

The following seven pages illustrate principal joints and muscle groups, explain how they function, and indicate some of the ways in which these body parts are vulnerable to injury. The text also refers to specific conditioning exercises elsewhere in the book that can help prevent undue stresses and strains.

The Back

The mainstay of the back is the spine (illustrated below). Forming an S-shaped curve from the base of your head to your pelvis, this mechanical marvel is sturdy enough to support the upper body, yet pliable enough to allow the trunk and neck to bend, stretch, and rotate. The spine is involved in almost every movement you make, from walking to serving a tennis ball to opening a door. It must also provide adequate stiffness and stability to protect the bundle of nerves that makes up the spinal cord.

The spinal column, or backbone, is composed of twenty-four separate spool-shaped bones called vertebrae, plus the sacrum (a triangular bone located between the hipbones), and the tailbone (coccyx). These are all stacked like a flexible tower with three curves—in the neck, chest, and lower back. The vertebrae are connected and held erect by ligaments and muscles that act much like the guy wires that hold up a ship's mast. In addition, much support for the lower back comes from the muscles in the abdomen. (When you lift a heavy weight, your abdominal muscles tighten.) Sandwiched between the vertebrae are gel-filled pads of tough connective tissue called discs, which act as shock absorbers. Discs contribute to the spine's flexibility, as do facet joints, which help stabilize the spine while contributing to spinal movement.

A healthy spine is capable of great strength: a single disc in the lower back has been shown to bear loads in excess of 2,500 pounds. While wear and tear on discs and joints can cause back pain, as can a number of structural problems, most cases of pain in the lower back stem from sprains to ligaments. These are usually aggravated or even caused by muscular weakness, particularly in the abdominal muscles. Strengthening this supporting musculature (illustrated on the next two pages) is the best way to spare yourself back pain and strain. When well conditioned, these muscles act like a protective girdle to keep the spine properly aligned and to distribute stresses placed upon it. (See page 388.)

Cervical vertebrae
Slender, highly flexible section of seven vertebrae that allows movement of the head.

Thoracic vertebrae
Larger, more rigid section of twelve vetebrae that is partially supported by the ribs. This part of the spine helps anchor the chest and protect the lungs.

Lumbar Vertebrae
Largest, sturdiest vertebral section that acts as the pivot point for most movements of the trunk and supports heavy loads.

Sacrum
Triangular bone that holds the pelvic arch in place with a network of ligaments. The sacrum serves as the base for the spinal column.

Coccyx
Four small segments of bone that fuse together to form the tailbone.

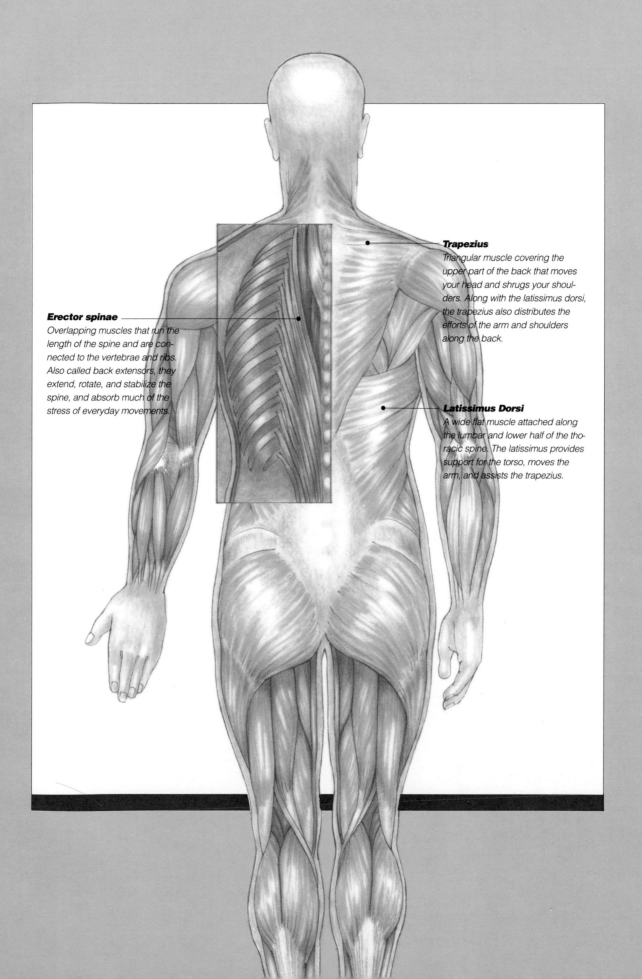

Trapezius
Triangular muscle covering the upper part of the back that moves your head and shrugs your shoulders. Along with the latissimus dorsi, the trapezius also distributes the efforts of the arm and shoulders along the back.

Erector spinae
Overlapping muscles that run the length of the spine and are connected to the vertebrae and ribs. Also called back extensors, they extend, rotate, and stabilize the spine, and absorb much of the stress of everyday movements.

Latissimus Dorsi
A wide flat muscle attached along the lumbar and lower half of the thoracic spine. The latissimus provides support for the torso, moves the arm, and assists the trapezius.

The Midsection and Upper Body

Several sets of muscles support and propel your torso and arms. The abdominals (illustrated below) help transfer force between your upper and lower body, and they also protect your internal organs. But their most crucial function is to support your back. Running in several directions, these muscles help maintain your posture and aid your spinal muscles when you bend, twist, and perform other everyday movements. Most activities do little to exercise the abdominals; hence, if these muscles are not toned and strengthened regularly, they will weaken, and the result can be increasingly "swaybacked" posture and chronic lower back pain.

Muscles also play a key role in the functioning of the shoulder (illustrated opposite). Compared to a joint like the knee or elbow, the shoulder is highly mobile. Indeed, it is the body's most flexible joint, allowing you to throw a ball, swing a golf club, perform a backstroke, or swing your arm in a full circle. But whereas the knee and elbow are secured by their ball-and-socket structures and by a network of strong ligaments, the shoulder's socket is more like a shallow dish upon which the ball rests—an arrangement that makes it comparatively unstable. Moreover, the ligaments that keep the shoulder in place are weak, and it depends for stability on muscles and tendons running across the joint. If some of these muscles are weak or out of balance with other muscles, the risk of strains or sprains increases. Hence, to safely meet the demands of swimming, rowing, golf, and other activities that involve throwing, lifting, pulling, and stroking, it is important to strengthen this array of musculature, which includes the biceps, triceps, deltoid, latissimus dorsi, and pectoralis major as well as a deeper layer of four small muscles (and their tendons) called the rotator cuff. (See page 376.)

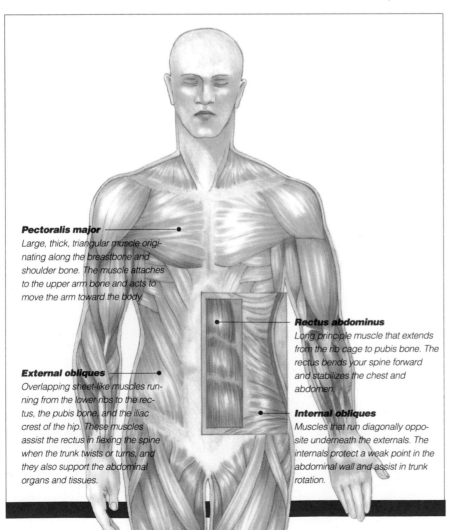

Pectoralis major
Large, thick, triangular muscle originating along the breastbone and shoulder bone. The muscle attaches to the upper arm bone and acts to move the arm toward the body.

External obliques
Overlapping sheet-like muscles running from the lower ribs to the rectus, the pubis bone, and the iliac crest of the hip. These muscles assist the rectus in flexing the spine when the trunk twists or turns, and they also support the abdominal organs and tissues.

Rectus abdominus
Long principle muscle that extends from the rib cage to pubis bone. The rectus bends your spine forward and stabilizes the chest and abdomen.

Internal obliques
Muscles that run diagonally opposite underneath the externals. The internals protect a weak point in the abdominal wall and assist in trunk rotation.

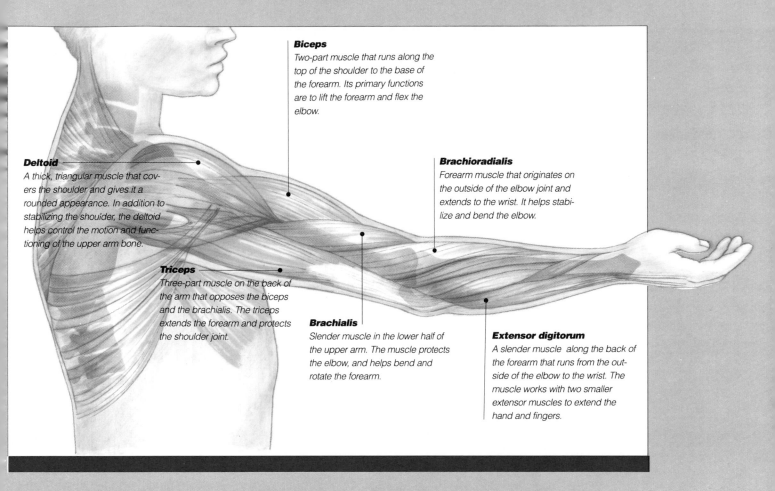

Biceps
Two-part muscle that runs along the top of the shoulder to the base of the forearm. Its primary functions are to lift the forearm and flex the elbow.

Deltoid
A thick, triangular muscle that covers the shoulder and gives it a rounded appearance. In addition to stabilizing the shoulder, the deltoid helps control the motion and functioning of the upper arm bone.

Brachioradialis
Forearm muscle that originates on the outside of the elbow joint and extends to the wrist. It helps stabilize and bend the elbow.

Triceps
Three-part muscle on the back of the arm that opposes the biceps and the brachialis. The triceps extends the forearm and protects the shoulder joint.

Brachialis
Slender muscle in the lower half of the upper arm. The muscle protects the elbow, and helps bend and rotate the forearm.

Extensor digitorum
A slender muscle along the back of the forearm that runs from the outside of the elbow to the wrist. The muscle works with two smaller extensor muscles to extend the hand and fingers.

The shoulder forms a base for the arm, the most versatile, mobile part of the body. In the upper arm, the biceps and triceps are arranged to give the forearm power to thrust and bend. The two muscles join at the elbow, a hinge-like joint that allows you to bend and straighten your arm, and also rotate your wrist and hand. Forearm muscles transmit power to the wrist, hands, and fingers. The wrist, despite its vulnerable location and delicate structure, is a relatively sturdy joint due to strong interlocking ligaments and tendons that run through the forearm. Unlike the shoulder, the wrist is rarely dislocated, but both it and the elbow may be strained by performing activities that involve repetitive or excessive use of the forearm. (See pages 377-379.)

The Thigh and Knee

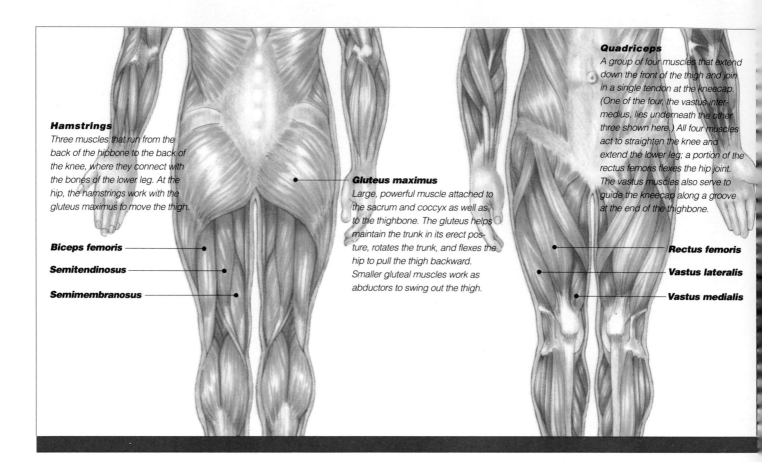

Hamstrings
Three muscles that run from the back of the hipbone to the back of the knee, where they connect with the bones of the lower leg. At the hip, the hamstrings work with the gluteus maximus to move the thigh.

Biceps femoris
Semitendinosus
Semimembranosus

Gluteus maximus
Large, powerful muscle attached to the sacrum and coccyx as well as to the thighbone. The gluteus helps maintain the trunk in its erect posture, rotates the trunk, and flexes the hip to pull the thigh backward. Smaller gluteal muscles work as abductors to swing out the thigh.

Quadriceps
A group of four muscles that extend down the front of the thigh and join in a single tendon at the kneecap. (One of the four, the vastus intermedius, lies underneath the other three shown here.) All four muscles act to straighten the knee and extend the lower leg; a portion of the rectus femoris flexes the hip joint. The vastus muscles also serve to guide the kneecap along a groove at the end of the thighbone.

Rectus femoris
Vastus lateralis
Vastus medialis

Your legs provide the power for such common activities as walking, running, and jumping, they absorb the cumulative impact of those activities, and they also bear much of your body weight. Not surprisingly, then, the leg's muscles and joints are strong and relatively stable. The thigh consists of the body's largest bone—the femur—which is girded on all sides by sets of powerful muscles that allow it to bend and straighten (also referred to as flexion and extension) as well as move outward and inward (or abduction and adduction). Some of these muscles are relatively long and participate in more than one type of movement—for example, the rectus femoris, a quadriceps muscle, flexes the hip and also extends the knee.

The hip is an exceptionally solid joint held intact largely by a round ball that is form-fitted into a deep socket. The knee stands midway between the hip and the shoulder in terms of stability. Although its ball-and-socket arrangement is not as secure as the hip's, the knee is held together by an elaborate system of strong ligaments and tendons that function like stays and pulleys. They not only allow the joint to twist, bend, and push, but also keep the kneecap properly aligned during these movements, and help the knee withstand the pressure of running and jumping.

By virtue of its engineering, the knee is the most complex joint in the body and also the one most frequently injured during exercise and athletic activities—mainly because it is subjected to a good deal of stress and because there are so many places where it is vulnerable. Strengthening the muscles in the thigh, particularly in the quadriceps, goes a long way toward preventing these problems. (See pages 374-375.)

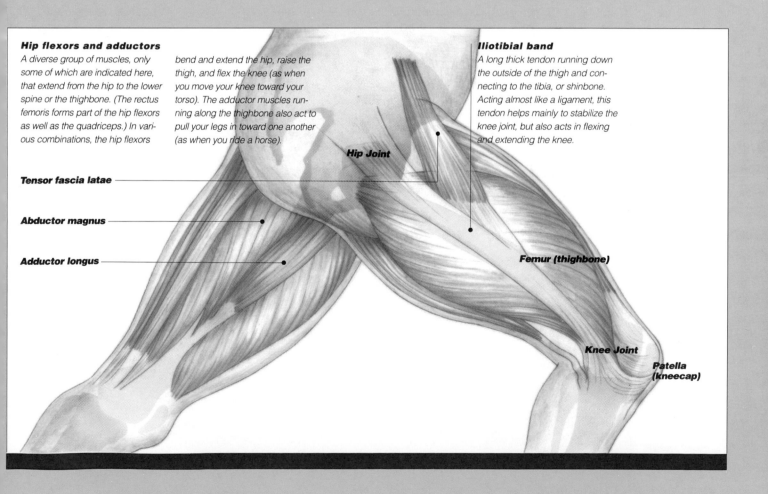

Hip flexors and adductors
A diverse group of muscles, only some of which are indicated here, that extend from the hip to the lower spine or the thighbone. (The rectus femoris forms part of the hip flexors as well as the quadriceps.) In various combinations, the hip flexors bend and extend the hip, raise the thigh, and flex the knee (as when you move your knee toward your torso). The adductor muscles running along the thighbone also act to pull your legs in toward one another (as when you ride a horse).

Iliotibial band
A long thick tendon running down the outside of the thigh and connecting to the tibia, or shinbone. Acting almost like a ligament, this tendon helps mainly to stabilize the knee joint, but also acts in flexing and extending the knee.

Hip Joint

Tensor fascia latae

Abductor magnus

Adductor longus

Femur (thighbone)

Knee Joint

Patella (kneecap)

The Lower Leg

The calf, ankle, and foot are controlled largely by a series of muscles and tendons that function as a single biomechanical unit. Acting like a sling and lever system, the calf muscles, Achilles tendon, heel bone, and plantar fascia—which runs from the heel bone to the toes—work to lift or lower the heel for virtually any activity that involves locomotion. All of these parts in the lower leg are interconnected: for example, when you stand on your toes, you can feel the muscles in back of your calf doing most of the work. If you flex your foot, muscles along the front of the calf are brought into play.

Because of its structure, and because it absorbs the impact from activities like running and jumping, the lower leg is subject to more exercise-related injuries than any other area of the body. These problems range from bunions and blisters to stress fractures—microscopic cracks in bone—to sprained ankles, the most common sports injury of all. The construction of the ankle is straightforward compared to the knee or shoulder—the main ankle bone (the talus) fits into the concave surfaces of the lower leg bones (the tibia and fibula), and is held in place by a set of ligaments. But the borders of the leg bones are not parallel, which allows the ankle bone to roll more easily toward the outside of the joint. Moreover, the musculature around the ankle is relatively weak, affording minimum stability. Therefore, if you turn or twist your ankle, the ligaments often cannot withstand the stress, and they stretch or tear. An excellent defense against an ankle sprain is to strengthen and stretch the muscles in the lower leg. (See pages 372-374.)

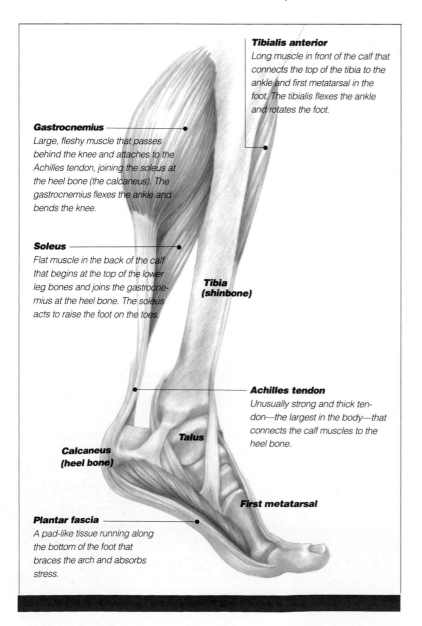

Tibialis anterior
Long muscle in front of the calf that connects the top of the tibia to the ankle and first metatarsal in the foot. The tibialis flexes the ankle and rotates the foot.

Gastrocnemius
Large, fleshy muscle that passes behind the knee and attaches to the Achilles tendon, joining the soleus at the heel bone (the calcaneus). The gastrocnemius flexes the ankle and bends the knee.

Soleus
Flat muscle in the back of the calf that begins at the top of the lower leg bones and joins the gastrocnemius at the heel bone. The soleus acts to raise the foot on the toes.

Tibia (shinbone)

Achilles tendon
Unusually strong and thick tendon—the largest in the body—that connects the calf muscles to the heel bone.

Talus

Calcaneus (heel bone)

First metatarsal

Plantar fascia
A pad-like tissue running along the bottom of the foot that braces the arch and absorbs stress.

thigh), power knee movements; the quadriceps also guide the kneecap (patella) in its groove at the end of the thighbone.

•In many runners the quadriceps are much weaker and less developed than the hamstrings. Cycling is an excellent way to strengthen the quadriceps, so it's a good idea to alternate running and cycling. Walking up stairs or hills will also help strengthen these muscles. However, if you have an injured knee, avoid hills and stairs; also avoid kneeling and full squats, which stress the knee.

In the following exercises, work up gradually to the suggested number of repetitions. If you are recovering from a knee injury, avoid doing the knee bends and knee extensions.

One-quarter knee bends: *Holding on to a wall, lift and extend one leg forward and slowly lower yourself by bending the other knee. Don't go more than one-quarter of the way down. Hold for five seconds, then slowly straighten up. Repeat ten times, then switch legs.*

Knee extensions: *Sit on a desk or counter and hold onto the edge. Slowly straighten one leg, extending the knee completely. Hold for five seconds, then lower slowly. Repeat ten times, then switch legs. You can also do this with a light weight.*

Straight leg lifts: *Lie on your back and bend one knee, keeping your foot on the floor. Slowly lift the straight leg about twelve inches off the floor; keep hips and lower back on the floor. Hold for five seconds, then lower slowly. Repeat ten times, then switch legs. You can also do this with a light weight around your ankle. Avoid this exercise if you have back problems.*

Lower leg

The catch-all term "shin splint" refers to a family of overuse injuries causing inflammation of muscles and tendons of the lower leg. Pounding the feet on hard surfaces in aerobic dance class or jogging is a common cause. The pain generally starts during exercise and continues during daily activities, but sometimes begins several hours later. Only a physician can diagnose the exact type of injury and prescribe proper treatment.

Shin splints are referred to as "posterior" or "anterior," depending on the location of the injury. A posterior shin splint is characterized by aching pain on the inner side of the calf due to inflammation of the muscles that roll the foot inward and support the arch. People with flat feet are the likeliest candidates for posterior shin splints. An anterior shin splint causes pain along the outer side of the calf.

To lessen your risk of shin splints:

•Wear well-cushioned running shoes with good support.

•Don't run on hard surfaces.

•Don't suddenly increase the intensity of your workout.

•Stretch calf muscles before running (see page 374).

•Begin a regular routine of stretching and strengthening leg muscles. Do toe raises and foot rolls several times a day; lie on your back and flex your feet; sit on the edge of a table and flex your foot with a weight attached to it.

•Check with a podiatrist to see if you need an orthotic device to improve your posture and gait. If so, wear it in all your shoes.

Shoulders

Driving a golf ball, throwing a baseball, serving a tennis ball, doing the butterfly stroke, or any other activity requiring overhead arm motion can put undue stress on the muscles that allow you to rotate or raise your arms, which can result in pain and tenderness in the shoulder and upper arm.

One of the many attractions of an activity like golf or swimming is that it produces fewer sprains, strains, and fractures than more vigorous sports. Yet both golfers and swimmers are prone to what is technically called a rotator cuff injury, named after the group of shoulder muscles that are involved.

The four muscles of the rotator cuff, located on or near the shoulder blade, stabilize the upper arm bone (humerus) in the shoulder socket. Repeated overuse of the shoulder in golf or other sports can cause microscopic tears in the tendons of these muscles, leading to swelling and inflammation (tendinitis). With repeated injury, you can actually tear the tendon. Older golfers are particularly at risk, since the rotator cuff can degenerate with age.

In the past it had been thought that golfers primarily used the deltoid muscle (located on top of the shoulder) during a swing. Thus many players did conditioning exercises to strengthen that muscle. But one study of professional golfers found that the rotator cuff muscles, not the deltoids, are key muscles throughout the golf swing.

When your rotator cuff muscles are weak, the deltoids take over the action during your swing, leaving the upper arm unstable and increasing the risk of injury. If you do suffer shoulder pain, apply ice and stop playing for a while, or at least reduce your playing time.

By keeping your rotator cuff muscles strong and flexible, you may prevent injury—and improve your game at the same time. (Flexibility not only helps muscles reduce stress, but also puts distance into throwing or hitting a ball by permitting better extension during the "cocking" phase and the follow-through.) The following exercises will help keep your shoulders in shape.

Shoulder stretch: Stretch the back of your shoulder by reaching with one arm under your chin and across the opposite shoulder; gently push the arm back with the other hand. Hold for fifteen seconds. Repeat five times, then switch sides.

Another stretch: Raise one arm and bend it behind your head to touch the opposite shoulder. Use the other hand to gently pull the elbow downward. Hold for fifteen seconds. Repeat five times, then switch sides.

Rotator cuff strengthener: Holding light weights, lift your arms out horizontally and slightly forward. Keeping your thumbs toward the floor, slowly lower your arms halfway, then return to shoulder level. Repeat ten times.

Another strengthener: Lie on your side with your head supported. Keeping your elbow against your side, and your arm bent at a ninety-degree angle, lift a light weight toward the ceiling. Slowly lower the weight forward, not moving the elbow from your side. Repeat ten times.

Elbows

One of the most common stress injuries of the arm is tennis elbow, a type of tendinitis that at some point afflicts almost one-third of the 32 million Americans who play tennis. Yet tennis players aren't the only ones at risk—any activity that calls for forceful, repeated contraction of the arm muscles can bring on tennis elbow (the medical term is epicondylitis). Working with carpentry tools, gardening, raking leaves, or even tightly gripping a heavy briefcase are only a few of the activities that can cause tennis elbow. Baseball, golf, bowling, racquet sports, even darts can also bring it on.

The injury occurs when you flex, extend, twist, or contract your wrist or forearm excessively or improperly, and thus strain the tendons that connect muscles to the elbow joint. In time, the overstressed tendons develop microscopic tears, producing tendinitis (painful inflammation of the tendons) centered around the epicondyle, the point at which the tendons attach to the elbow. The pain can radiate down to the wrist and up to the shoulder. Moving your arm or gripping something aggravates the pain.

Most recreational tennis players who are afflicted feel pain in the lateral part (the outer part, when your palm is up) of the elbow. Experts often attribute this to poor backhand technique, improper serving, and a late forehand stroke. Advanced players tend to feel pain on the inside (medial part) of the elbow, usually because of strain from hitting powerful serves.

What determines who gets tennis elbow? To some extent it depends on the condition of your muscles and how much they are overused. In tennis, the injury occurs most frequently among recreational players who are thirty-five to fifty years old—when muscles have begun to lose their resiliency—and who play at least two or three times a week. In a study of 2,600 amateurs, almost half of those who played daily got tennis elbow. Occasional players are less vulnerable as they tend not to play often enough or hard enough to overstress their arms. And pros are generally protected by superior conditioning and stroking technique, though they too can develop tennis elbow as they grow older.

If you play tennis regularly, here are the keys to avoiding tennis elbow:

•Work on your form. Power your serve and backhand with your legs, torso, and shoulder muscles rather than with your forearm and wrist. During a stroke, your elbow should be almost fully extended but not locked, and your grip should be firm but not viselike, so that force is transferred to your shoulder.

•Some teaching pros recommend that beginners learn a two-handed backhand; players who use this technique seldom develop tennis elbow, since the second hand provides additional support.

•Using a lighter, midsized graphite racquet that is loosely strung may also reduce strain. The racket frame should be neither too stiff nor too flexible; make sure you are carefully measured for proper grip size.

If you develop tennis elbow, reduce your playing time or stop completely until the pain lessens. For players persistently troubled by tennis elbow, some sports physiologists recommend the use of an elbow brace, which supports and protects the muscles and tendons of the forearm; this offers some pain relief without restricting movement.

For athlete and nonathlete, the best defense against tennis elbow is to strengthen muscles in the forearm. One of the most effective forearm strengtheners

Favoring one sport can cause problems: you are likely to strengthen certain muscles at the expense of others, leaving tendons and ligaments unbalanced and thus vulnerable. Varying your activities is one way to prevent this; another precaution is to strengthen the muscle groups you underuse, and stretch all muscles involved in your workout.

is simply to squeeze a ball forty or fifty times with your arm extended horizontally in front of you. Start with a racquet ball and progress to a tennis ball, which is larger and firmer. The three exercises illustrated below should be performed daily for at least three months to build strength, then two or three times weekly to maintain it.

Arm rotation: *Sitting or standing, hold a light weight (two or three pounds) in front of you with your elbow bent at a ninety-degree angle and your palm up. Slowly roll your forearm to palm-down position, then return to the starting position. Repeat twenty to thirty times. Switch arms and repeat.*

Wrist curls: *Lay your forearm on a table with your hand hanging over the edge and your palm up. Holding a five-pound weight, slowly flex your wrist ten to twenty times. Then turn your hand over so the palm faces down and repeat ten to twenty times. Switch arms and repeat.*

Finger stretches: *Twist a thick rubber band around all five fingers. Keeping your elbow straight, try to straighten and spread your fingers. Hold for three seconds, then relax your fingers. Repeat until fatigued. Switch hands and repeat.*

Wrists

If you put in long hours at a repetitive hand-intensive task—working on an assembly-line or in the garment-industry, typing or computer keyboarding, or a hobby like knitting or piano playing—you could develop carpal tunnel syndrome (CTS). The symptoms begin with pins and needles and numbness in the hand, and can worsen, extending to wasted thumb muscles, a weakened grip, and severe hand pain that sometimes radiates to the forearm or shoulder. Known by other names, the syndrome has been around a long time, but the spread of automation into industry and offices has stepped up the risk for thousands of people. Estimates of the number of industrial workers afflicted annually range from 23,000 to ten times that. Women are two to six times more likely to develop the syndrome than men, probably because their carpal tunnel space is smaller and because more women have small-part assembly and keyboarding jobs.

"Carpal" comes from the Greek word for wrist, *karpos.* The tunnel is the passageway in which the median nerve and the tendons that flex your fingers pass through the wrist and enter the hand. Bones and ligaments form its floor, sides, and roof. The discomfort of carpal tunnel syndrome results when repeated movement thickens the tendons' lubricating membranes, squeezing soft nerve tissue up against inflexible bone and ligament. This process, called nerve entrapment, can also occur as a result of a bone dislocation or fracture, arthritic inflammation, or diabetes. In addition, fluid retention associated with pregnancy or menopause can narrow the tunnel and compress the nerve.

Usually symptoms first occur in the early morning: sufferers suddenly waken to burning, tingling, and numbness in their hands. Shaking or kneading it may improve matters temporarily. But the symptoms should serve as a warning to get to a doctor for a diagnosis. If, after testing for the speed of nerve transmission and the electrical activity of certain muscles, he diagnoses CTS, he may prescribe medication, a splint to immobilize the wrist, or both. In unrelenting cases he may advise surgery to "release" the ligament roofing the tunnel and ease pressure. The operation can often be done on an outpatient basis.

A few simple precautions can help minimize the risk of CTS:

•While working with your hands, keep your wrists straight. Flexing, extending, or twisting them stresses the carpal tunnel.

•Use your whole hand and fingers when you grip an object.

•Cut down on repetitive gestures as much as possible, and take a break from handwork every half hour or so.

Side stitches

While running or walking briskly, nearly everyone has experienced the sharp pain in the side known as a stitch. No one knows what causes a stitch, though there's no shortage of educated guesses. One theory is that the diaphragm (the large muscle that separates the chest from the abdominal cavity) sometimes fails to receive enough blood during its contractions, and, much like a leg cramp, this results in spasm and pain. Another theory is that a stitch is caused by trapped gas pockets brought on by exercising right after a meal.

To prevent stitches:

•If stitches seem to hit you after a meal, wait thirty to ninety minutes after eating before exercising.

•Warm up before exercising—a good policy in any case.

•Work out at lower intensity for longer periods, rather than suddenly increasing the intensity of the workout. If you are going to increase intensity, do so gradually.

•Well-conditioned runners and walkers don't seem to get stitches as often, so work at increasing your aerobic capacity.

If you get a stitch:

•First stop or slow down, then bend forward and push your fingers into the painful area.

•Breathe deeply and exhale slowly through pursed lips. This should help relax the diaphragm.

•Stretch the abdominal muscles by raising your arms and reaching above your head.

Treating Injuries

Unfortunately, no matter how careful people are, injuries do occur. And injured tendons, muscles, ligaments, and cartilage—the soft tissue involved in most sports injuries—can take a long time to heal, longer in fact than broken bones. What follows are guidelines on the most effective home remedies, which are aimed at assisting the healing process.

Stages of healing

Here is how the natural healing process works:

Inflammation. In this initial response to injury, blood vessels in surrounding tissues dilate and release a variety of substances. White blood cells arrive to remove dead tissue and other debris. These and other vascular changes produce heat, swelling, and redness. The subsequent pain and stiffness had the beneficial effect of keeping you from moving and aggravating the injured muscles or other body parts.

Regeneration. After twenty-four to forty-eight hours, the body begins replacing injured tissue. Damaged cells are flushed from the area, then a network of capillaries forms that allows a greater flow of oxygen and nutrients into the injury site. Two to three days after the initial damage, strands of collagen—a protein that is the major component of connective tissue—begin forming scar tissue over the damaged areas, a process that lasts two to three weeks.

Remodeling. If you don't move the injured body part at all, the collagen will grow into a puckered, inelastic scar that remains weak and can cause tightness and discomfort—particularly in muscles, which are normally far more elastic than tendons or

Should You See a Doctor?

There is no hard and fast rule—it depends both on the type of injury and especially on how severe it is. A severe acute injury such as a pulled muscle or a sprained ankle may require a cast or surgery. *Call a doctor if any of the following symptoms persist:*
- severe or persistent muscle pain, swelling or spasm;
- pain centered in a bone or joint;
- stiffness or decreased mobility of a joint or inability to move it at all;
- stabbing or radiating pain;
- numbness or tingling.

If dealt with properly, overuse injuries such as tennis elbow or runner's knee—which are due to the cumulative wear and tear of a repetitive movement—probably won't require a doctor's care. In fact, self-treatment is generally just what the doctor recommends. However, if pain persists for more than ten days in spite of self-care measures, or if it is severe or is growing worse, consult a doctor.

ligaments. That's why you should gently stretch and strengthen damaged tissue. When it recovers properly, the affected muscle or tendon usually regains 80 to 95 percent of its original strength within three to six months. (There will always be at least a slight residual loss in strength.)

Ice: the first step of treatment

Ice is the most effective, safest, and cheapest form of treating an exercise or sports injury. With acute injuries such as torn ligaments, muscle strains, and bruises, *the key is to start icing as soon possible.* Even if you plan to go to the doctor immediately, icing the injury right away will help speed recovery. Not only does ice relieve pain, but it also slows blood flow, thereby reducing internal bleeding and swelling. This in turn helps limit tissue damage and hastens the healing process. Follow these steps for icing:

- Although commercial ice packs are available, plain ice is fine: simply put ice cubes or crushed ice in a heavy plastic bag or hot-water bottle, or wrap the ice in a thick towel.
- Apply the ice on the injured area for ten to twenty minutes, then reapply it every two waking hours for the next two days. Be sure not to go over the twenty-minute limit; longer than that may damage skin and nerves.
- If you start to feel *mild* discomfort when exercising and think it may be the first sign of an overuse injury, such as tendinitis, you may well be able to finish your activity—a set of tennis, for example. But apply ice over tender areas right after you finish, and reapply it several times a day for the next forty-eight hours.

•If swelling occurs, which is likely with acute injuries, use ice in conjunction with these other measures that are often referred to as RICE:

Rest the injured body part;

apply **I**ce;

apply **C**ompression;

Elevate the injured extremity above heart level.

Resting not only reduces pain, but also prevents aggravating the injury, compression and elevation help keep excess fluids from accumulating in tissues. To apply compression, wrap a towel or an Ace-type elastic bandage around the injury (don't wrap it so tightly that you cut off circulation). You can often combine ice and compression by holding the ice pack in place with a bandage.

When to apply heat

Traditionally people started applying heat to an injury soon after icing it. But heat actually stimulates blood flow and so increases inflammation. Most sports physicians and trainers now recommend that you stick with ice for at least the first forty-eight hours after an injury, and only then, *after swelling has subsided,* try heating. At that point, heat can speed up healing, help relieve pain, relax muscles, and reduce joint stiffness.

You can apply either dry heat (using a heating pad or lamp) or moist heat (a hot bath, whirlpool, hot-water bottle, heat pack, or damp towel wrapped around a waterproof heating pad). There's much debate about whether dry or moist heat is best, and for what type of injury, so check with your doctor about which is appropriate for you. If you have a heart condition, for instance, he may tell you to avoid using a hot bath or whirlpool. He will probably also advise against these if you have a fever or infection, or if the injury is bleeding. Also call your doctor if pain or inflammation gets worse after heating an injury.

The key word is "warm," not "hot." Use heating pads on low or medium settings, and keep the water in baths between 98 and 105 degrees Fahrenheit. (It should feel comfortable when you dip your wrist in.) Apply the heat twenty to thirty minutes, two to three times a day. You can also use it for five to ten minutes before exercising to reduce stiffness.

Pain-relief medication

Taking over-the-counter pain relievers such as aspirin or ibuprofen (for instance, Advil or Motrin) can indeed help ease the pain and reduce inflammation of minor sprains, strains and tendinitis. The other major over-the-counter pain reliever, acetaminophen (such as Tylenol), is good for relief of muscle soreness, as discussed on page 456. However, it is less helpful for these other injuries since it has no anti-inflammatory effect.

There are more potent prescription medications, widely recommended by athletic trainers, which can eliminate pain and swelling very quickly in many cases. But these drugs—which include cortisone (or its derivatives), the strongest of all anti-inflammatory medications—can produce serious adverse side effects. Another potential problem: they can let you ignore the pain—which is a warning sign that you are doing damage to your body—and allow you to exercise vigorously and perhaps cause permanent damage to the injured tissue. Hence, such drugs should be used only under medical supervision and for brief periods of time.

Whirlpool Treatments

By providing an underwater massage, whirlpool baths can help soothe stiff, sore muscles. But whirlpools (and hot tubs, for that matter) are also associated with certain hazards. The hot, agitated water simultaneously breaks down chlorine and promotes the growth of a bacteria that causes folliculitis, an itchy red rash that usually lasts about a week. Therefore, make sure that chlorine levels in any whirlpool you use are properly maintained. In addition, women who are pregnant should be especially careful: the high temperature and agitation tend to raise a person's core body temperature, which can lead to birth defects. With men, hot water can cause temporary infertility. To reduce these risks, be sure that the water temperature does not exceed 105 degrees Fahrenheit.

How long to rest

For most overuse injuries, rest a day or two and then try to exercise the affected area at an intensity that doesn't cause pain. You can try to gradually return to your usual workout routine, initially decreasing your speed, duration, and/or frequency by at least 25 percent. Don't work out, though, if persistent pain returns, and don't resume your full level until you are free of pain both during and after exercise. It's also important to identify the cause of the injury—poor equipment, poor technique, or some other factor—and correct it.

For minor strains and sprains—if you turn your ankle slightly while hiking, for example—staying off the injured part for a day or two is often enough. More serious injuries will require a longer rest period, and you may have to immobilize the injured part—keeping weight off a wrenched knee, for example, or supporting an injured wrist or elbow in a sling. Check with your doctor.

Unless an injury is severe, however, absolute rest should not exceed forty-eight hours. Otherwise, muscles may weaken, joints may get stiff, and scar tissue that forms around the injury may start to tighten. Activity helps prevent this and, by increasing blood flow, also encourages healing.

As soon as the initial pain and swelling of a sprain or other acute injury subside, therefore, you should begin to exercise the injured area *gently*. (If you have any doubts, consult your doctor). Start with isometric exercises. Then do stretching and strengthening exercises that move the affected muscles through their full range of motion. To maintain aerobic fitness, you can substitute another activity that puts less stress on the injured part. So if you're a jogger with a sprained ankle, for instance, try cycling or swimming until you recover.

Arthritis

Osteoarthritis is so common that nearly everyone over forty shows some signs of it on X-rays—a gradual loss of the soft, smooth cartilage at joint surfaces, and frequently a compensatory overgrowth of bone at the joints. It's estimated that 20 million Americans have symptoms of this joint disease at any given time. Unlike rheumatoid arthritis, which is a totally different disease, osteoarthritis causes minimal inflammation. There are two types of osteoarthritis. Primary osteoarthritis, resulting from normal wear and tear, most commonly affects thumb joints and the end joints of other fingers, the hips, knees, neck, and lower spine. Secondary osteoarthritis can occur after injury to a joint; from disease (such as diabetes); or as a result of chronic trauma (due to obesity, poor posture, or occupational overuse).

Because of the pain and stiffness, the natural tendency is to minimize movement of arthritic joints. Unfortunately, this can simply lead to stiffer joints—and thus more pain—since inactivity weakens the muscles that stabilize joints. Studies have shown that many people with osteoarthritis can maintain flexibility, and even restore it to some degree, through a well-designed exercise program that is gradually implemented and followed regularly. Specialists have devised scores of exercises (such as the ones below) to stretch muscles or strengthen important joints. Exercise may cause you some pain at first, but the discomfort should diminish.

Osteoarthritis sufferers will benefit from three general types of exercise:

Stretching exercises limber up muscles and help increase joint mobility.

Strengthening exercises tone muscles that support vulnerable joints, making them more stable. If you're having an intense flare-up, isometric exercises—which are static and thus move muscles, not joints—are safest and easiest.

Endurance activities enhance aerobic capacity (the ability of the cardiovascular system to carry oxygen to the muscles) and thereby improve overall fitness, provided they are done at least three times a week for twenty minutes at your training heart rate. Swimming, particularly in a heated pool, is excellent because the water supports the body as you take your joints gently through their full range of movement. Walking is another good choice; if you're able to, gradually work up

Warning Signs of Arthritis

You should see your doctor if any of the following symptoms persist:
- *early morning stiffness;*
- *swelling;*
- *recurring pain or tenderness in one or more joints;*
- *changes in joint mobility;*
- *redness or warmth in joints;*
- *unexplained weight loss, fever, or loss of strength in association with joint pain.*

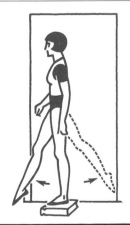

Hip swing: *Stand with one foot on a thick book or low stool; for stability hold on to a door handle or chair back. Slowly swing the free leg forward and backward like a pendulum 10 or 20 times, keeping your foot pointed; then switch legs. As a variation, swing the leg in a semi-circular motion.*

Finger stretches: *1. Try to form a letter O with your thumb and index finger, then spread your fingers as wide as you can. Then touch the thumb to the tip of each of your other fingers, spreading your fingers wide after each attempt. If you can't bring the fingers together, use your other hand to help. 2. Squeeze a soft rubber ball. 3. Twist a large rubber band around all five fingers of your hand. Gently spread the fingers apart, using the rubber band as resistance.*

to a brisk, heart-healthy pace. As a general rule, it's wise to avoid high-impact activities like tennis, aerobic dance, or running, which can overload sore joints.

Exercises must be individualized, depending on the joints involved and the degree of pain. Your doctor or physical therapist will help you develop an exercise program that focuses on your most painful joints and takes into consideration your overall level of fitness. Whatever exercises you do, there are some general rules:

Start gradually and never overdo it. Follow the instructions of your doctor or physical therapist. There will probably be some pain or discomfort, but stop that particular exercise if there's unusual or severe pain. Cut back if need be, but don't stop exercising entirely.

Always warm up first. After walking in place for a few minutes, do some gentle stretches. Gently massaging stiff joints may help, as may heat (a warm bath or shower, an infrared lamp). Wear a sweat suit, or leg or arm warmers.

Repeat stretching and strengthening exercises daily. Don't rely on one long, strenuous (and painful) session a week. Begin with as few as three repetitions of each exercise. Over the course of several weeks try to work up to ten repetitions, or as many as your doctor recommends.

Osteoporosis

One of the inevitable consequences of aging is that our bones tend to lose mass, gradually becoming thinner and more fragile, and at times collapsing—a process that is responsible for the fact that people tend to shrink in height as they grow older. Osteoporosis is a condition in which the amount of bone tissue has diminished to the point where bones can fracture easily from a fall, a jarring movement, or even from an effort to lift something. The condition afflicts some 25 million Americans, most of them women. Both men and women lose bone mass as they age, but in women the process accelerates dramatically with the onset of menopause. Estrogen is crucial for the ability of bones to absorb calcium from the diet, and as a woman's estrogen levels drop during menopause, bone loss increases. In women who develop osteoporosis, the condition usually becomes apparent during their sixties or seventies. Among the earliest observable signs may be a decrease in height. But for many people, unfortunately, the first indication is the occurrence of fractures, especially of the hip and spine. The beginning of a disfiguring "dowager's hump," for example, is not due to poor posture, but is a permanent collapse of bone resulting from osteoporotic fractures of the cervical vertebrae.

Who is at risk for osteoporosis
About 25 percent of women are considered to be most susceptible to osteoporosis. The following risk factors—most of which are hereditary—can't be modified:
- being a Caucasian or Asian female;
- having close relatives with osteoporosis;
- having light skin;
- having a delicate frame;
- experiencing previous bone loss due to illness or medications;
- experiencing early menopause.

Other risk factors, some the result of life-style habits, can be modified:
- being sedentary;
- inadequate calcium intake;
- smoking cigarettes;
- consuming more than two alcoholic drinks daily;
- being underweight;
- a deficiency of vitamin D;
- undergoing surgical removal of the ovaries before menopause.

Preventing osteoporosis

Even though osteoporosis afflicts the elderly, women should not wait until they are older to do something about it. Rather, it's important that prevention start early in life. The growth of bone mass occurs most rapidly during childhood and adolescence, and peaks in the twenties and thirties in most people. By building strong bones during those years, you help insure that your body's bone stores will be at their maximum when bone density begins to decline.

Once bone is lost, it can't be restored with tissue of equal strength. Nevertheless, studies show that preventive measures can help retard or even halt bone loss in people over thirty-five. But if you are under thirty-five, the key is to start now, particularly if two or more of the above risk factors apply to you. (Each of the following steps is covered in more detail elsewhere in the book.)

Get an adequate supply of calcium. Calcium is critical for building strong bones. Children and young adults should consume 1,200 milligrams a day; for postmenopausal women, the National Institutes of Health recommends a daily intake of 1,200 to 1,500 milligrams.

Maintain a balanced diet. A number of nutrients in addition to calcium—particularly vitamin D, manganese, fluoride, and protein—help the body build bone and absorb calcium. Consuming other substances in excess—including sodium, phosphorus, caffeine, and alcohol—has been shown to interfere with calcium absorption. Very-low-calorie diets can also hinder calcium absorption as well as increase urinary excretion of calcium. So if you are trying to lose weight, plan your diet to make sure you are getting a balanced supply of nutrients.

Exercise. Bones are similar to muscles in that they shrink from inactivity and benefit from exercise. Weight-bearing exercise—such as walking, running, cross-country skiing, cycling, racquet sports—has been shown to increase bone mass. Whatever activities you choose, exercise regularly for twenty to sixty minutes three to five times a week.

Don't smoke. Women who smoke undergo menopause early, which may result in a longer period of estrogen deficiency and, therefore, more years of bone loss. Cigarettes may also reduce calcium absorption and may affect estrogen metabolism. (Women who take estrogen have lower blood levels of estrogen if they smoke.)

Consider hormone replacement therapy. A number of studies have proven that estrogen replacement prevents bone loss and protects against osteoporotic fractures. Menopausal and postmenopausal women, particularly those with any risk factors for osteoporosis, should consult their doctors about the benefits and possible side effects of taking estrogen. Any woman whose ovaries have been surgically removed before natural menopause should also consider hormone replacement.

Diagnostic Testing
Women approaching menopause who are at risk for osteoporosis should consult their doctor about getting a bone density study to assess their skeletal status. Several scanning techniques can be used to measure bone density at the hip, spine, or wrist, though many physicians are uncomfortable with the predictive value of wrist bone diagnosis. You can be tested at selected hospitals as well as at specialized diagnostic centers. Your doctor can help you decide whether a test is necessary and refer you to a reliable test unit in your area.

Back Care

About 80 percent of all Americans will have at least one backache during their lifetime. Every year articles and books about back pain appear, espousing new and old theories about its causes and how to treat it. However, there's room for controversy because the back is such a complicated, sophisticated structure, and while we can name all the bones, joints, nerves, muscles, and ligaments that comprise it, the sum total remains something of a mystery. Fortunately, most backaches aren't serious and generally go away in a few weeks, with or without medical attention. And they are usually preventable.

Back trouble is so common because the human spine hasn't evolved to the point where we can walk upright without some risk. Being erect puts extra pressure on the vertebrae of the lower back, or lumbar region, where the back curves most and where pain most often strikes. Backache becomes more common between the ages of thirty and fifty, as the disks—the fibrous pads that cushion the vertebrae—start to lose water and elasticity and thus some of their ability to absorb shock. In middle age, too, people tend to become less active and their muscles grow lax, contributing to back instability.

Sprain, strain, or spasm

A small portion of all backaches do have clear causes—for instance, a ruptured disk or some underlying disease. But in the great majority of cases the exact diagnosis isn't known. Is the cause of your backache that sudden movement yesterday when you bent to pick up the newspaper, or is the problem that you get too little (or too much) exercise? Or could it be your poor posture, or just everyday wear and tear? In fact, it's probably a combination of all these things. A backache can range from mild discomfort to sudden excruciating pain. Usually X-rays show nothing wrong despite the pain—but in some cases there's dramatic damage to disks but no pain whatsoever.

The terms back strain or sprain are often loosely applied to a broad spectrum of back disorders. *Strain* is generally used when a muscle is overstretched, and *sprain* when a ligament is partially torn. However, it is seldom clear whether it's a muscle or ligament that's been damaged, let alone whether it has been torn or not. Two other terms, muscle spasm and ruptured disk, are more clearly defined.

Muscle spasm. The most common form of spasm is a sudden onset of sustained, painful, involuntary contractions of muscles in the back. This may serve to immobilize irritated back muscles, thereby protecting them and spinal nerves. A spasm usually results from a back injury, but may also be caused or aggravated by poor posture, lots of sitting in the same position, tense back muscles, and weak abdominal muscles. Many researchers claim that psychological stress can also trigger spasms.

Disk problems. These are actually relatively uncommon. Only 2 to 4 percent of back ailments are due to what is commonly called a "slipped" disk. The term "slipped" is a misnomer, since the disk actually bulges (herniates) from between two vertebrae and may eventually rupture. If a displaced disk presses on a spinal nerve, the nerve can send shooting pains to the legs or arms, or create a tingling or sensation of numbness in them. If, as is common, the affected nerve is the sciatic, the condition is called sciatica and causes pain along the back of the hip and outer side of the leg.

Underlying diseases and structural problems. A small percentage of all backaches are related to identifiable medical problems such as kidney disease, cancer, arthritis, osteoporosis, or spinal infection. Sideways curvature (scoliosis), sway back (lordosis, or excessive curve in the lower back), or other structural defects may also be at the root of back pain.

When to see a doctor

Call your doctor if you have any of the following symptoms: pain, numbness, or tingling that radiates down an arm or leg; back pain that continues unabated when you're lying down; back pain that doesn't improve after two days of complete bed rest; back pain after a fall or car accident; vomiting or fever associated with back pain; or backache in an elderly person or child. Any of these may indicate a more serious problem.

That leaves the great majority of backaches (less serious strains, sprains, or spasms), which usually don't require a doctor's attention. For soreness and minor pain in the back, avoiding physically demanding activity may be sufficient. But if the pain is more severe, lie down and rest. Reclining may relieve the pain, and takes mechanical pressure off the stressed back during the first day or two of injury. Allowing the inflamed tissue to repair itself, can prevent a chronic cycle of back injury. According to research by the Swedish orthopedist Alf Nachemson, compared to standing, reclining reduces pressure on the lumbar disks by 70 percent, while unsupported sitting increases it by 40 percent.

The current trend in treating common backaches is to get people out of bed as soon as they can get up comfortably. While doctors traditionally recommended a week or two of bed rest, a study at the University of Texas Health Science Center at San Antonio found that two days in bed were usually sufficient for run-of-the-mill backaches and suggested longer bed rest only for disk problems. Moreover, shorter periods of bed rest tend to reduce the potentially adverse effects of prolonged bed rest, such as weakening of muscles from inactivity, that can lead to further back injury. (As patients bedridden for other reasons often discover, a couple weeks of bed rest can actually produce a painful back.)

But remember, if severe pain recurs when you get up, go back to bed and consult your doctor. And any resumption of activity must be gradual, since your back needs time to heal completely. Once the pain is gone, take it easy for a week, and avoid heavy chores and sports for at least two weeks. Aspirin or ibuprofen will help reduce the intensity of pain and inhibit inflammation. Do not use a corset or back brace unless your doctor prescribes it.

Ice or heat?

Though icing is best for many types of injury, there is some disagreement when it comes to the back. Most physical therapists now recommend icing immediately after a sudden, wrenching back injury that causes localized pain. This can both relieve a spasm and minimize swelling. Ice for ten to twenty minutes several times

Exercises for a Better Back

The key to a pain-free back is strong, supple abdominal and lower back muscles, which can be developed through calisthenics and stretching routines. The following exercises can form the core of a back-strengthening program. They should be done at least four times a week. Start any exercise program slowly, especially if you have ever had back pain. Stop if you feel any pain. Avoid exercises that increase the stress on the spine, such as straight-leg toe touches or backward bends. And always warm up and stretch before working out.

Begin an exercise routine *before* you feel any back pain. If your back currently hurts, do not do these or any other exercises. What type of exercise is best for people with back pain remains controversial, so before beginning an exercise program you should first consult a physical therapist or doctor.

Pelvic tilt. *Lie on your back, with knees bent. Hold in your stomach and tighten your buttock muscles. Lift your hips off the floor and hold for 10 seconds, keeping your lower back on the floor. Release. Repeat 20 times.*

Lower back stretch. *Lie on your back. Grasp one knee and pull it toward your chin, keeping your other leg straight. Hold for 10 seconds, then perform 10 times, alternating knees.*

Abdominal strengthener. *Sit with your knees bent, feet flat on the floor, and arms folded. Keeping your back straight, slowly lean back about 30 degrees until your abdominal muscles tighten. Hold for 5 seconds, then slowly sit up. Turn your head occasionally to prevent neck strain. Repeat 10 to 15 times.*

Cat stretch. *Start on all fours, with hands and knees shoulder-width apart. Slowly curve your lower back downward, pressing your stomach down and lifting your head. Then gently arch your back and lower your head. Hold each position for 5 seconds. Alternate positions, 5 to 10 times each.*

Fold-up stretch. *Sit back with your legs folded underneath you and reach as far forward as you can. Gently press your chest into your thighs, trying to rest your elbows and forehead on the floor. Breathe deeply as you stretch. Hold for a minute or two.*

a day during the first forty-eight hours. On the other hand, for a widespread backache that gradually sets in hours after an injury, or for chronic back discomfort, a hot bath or moist heat may be soothing and can promote healing. The ultimate criterion is which treatment works for you: if cold therapy feels uncomfortable or doesn't offer relief, try heat.

Back schools

For many people, self-help is the key to the prevention or relief of back pain, and some of the best places to learn how are the hundreds of "back schools" that have sprung up around the country since the mid-1970s. They range from classes set up by hospitals, corporations, and YMCAs to postsurgical rehabilitation groups at leading spine centers. Most are run by a physical therapist, often in conjunction with a physician. The general concept gets high ratings from back specialists, since such programs are inexpensive, safe, and, when complied with faithfully, highly effective.

The typical back school includes three or four weekly sessions plus a follow-up meeting a month later. You'll learn how the back works and what can go wrong with it, as well as analyzing your living, sleeping, and work habits and their effect on your back. Most important, the program should help you design an exercise program suited to your physical condition and life style. Many courses also emphasize relaxation techniques in an effort to keep tension from compounding back problems.

For information on back schools near you, check with your doctor, a local hospital, or an orthopedist or physical therapist in your area.

A Swedish study comparing the various amounts of stress to the back showed some surprising results. A good belly laugh and coughing are more stressful than either walking or twisting. Lying down was the least stressful activity; the worst was lifting an object without bending at the knees.

Preventing back pain

There is much you can do to prevent backache. In more than half of all cases back pain eventually recurs, so it's a good idea to take some preventive measures, especially if you have a history of back problems. Most backaches are due at least in part to excessive strain or to weak or tense muscles. To protect your back, consider the following:

Extra weight. A paunch can strain back muscles, distort posture, and overly compress the disks in the lower back. Not surprisingly, then, most obese people have chronic back problems. Excess weight, particularly if it has been recently gained, puts increased strain on back muscles and ligaments. Being pregnant can have a similar adverse effect because it alters your center of gravity.

Poor posture. Sitting and standing puts considerable pressure on the lower back. Correct posture keeps the head and chest high, neck straight, pelvis forward, and stomach and buttocks tucked in (see page 392).

Sleeping. Don't lie on your stomach, since that makes the stomach muscles sag and increases sway back. Instead, lie on your side with your knees bent to relieve pressure on the disks. For the same reason, if you lie on your back, keep your knees slightly bent by putting a pillow under them. For most people, the ideal mattress has firm inner support but adequate surface cushioning. If your mattress is too soft, insert a board under it.

Exercise. Regular exercise is vital to the health of your back. Calisthenics and stretching routines (such as those opposite) can help strengthen the back. In addition, low-impact activities like walking, swimming (but not the butterfly or breast stroke, which can put excessive strain on the lower back), and cycling (with an upright posture) are good for the back. For information on the effect of other sports on the back, see the box below.

Lifting and carrying. Bending to pick up an object puts maximum strain on your back and is probably the number one cause of backaches. When you lift, bend at the knees, not at the waist, making your leg muscles do most of the work. To pick up something heavy, squat with your legs apart, tighten your stomach muscles, keep your back straight, and hold the object close to your body. Better yet, push a

---

Back Pain and Sports

Regular exercise is essential for maintaining a strong back and protecting it from injury. Exercise also promotes weight control and good posture, and helps reduce muscle tension—important factors in maintaining a healthy back. Sports can be excellent back conditioners, too, but some forms of physical activity carry high risks of back injury, particularly if carelessly performed. The best way to avoid back injuries is to play regularly and stay within your physical limits. Begin any new activity gradually, and supplement it with exercises specifically for strengthening the back. Remember, always warm up, stretch, and cool down to minimize any risks to your back.

Good for the back
The following sports reduce stress on the back and, in some instances, help tone and stretch key muscles.

Walking. This is the perfect exercise for promoting a healthy back. According to Swedish back expert Dr. Alf Nachemson, walking puts less strain on the spine than does unsupported sitting, and only a little more than plain standing.

Swimming. Since the water supports the spine, thus relieving pressure on it, swimming is the best activity for relieving back pain. The back stroke and side stroke are best for the back; avoid the butterfly and breast stroke, which cause you to arch your back.

Cycling. This is an excellent aerobic exercise if you have back problems, provided you maintain an upright posture.

Jogging. The great impact running places on your body is normally absorbed by your shoes, feet, legs, and spinal disks. Jogging with poorly cushioned shoes, on hills, or on hard surfaces increases the jarring impact on the back. If you are in good condition and have a smooth stride, jogging will probably not put your back at risk. Still, runners with bad backs should swim and/or do exercises to strengthen muscles in the back and abdomen.

Rowing. Proper posture is vital, since rowing places great stress on the lower back. If done correctly, rowing can strengthen muscles in the lower back. Always keep your back straight; avoid hunching over or swaying.

High-risk sports
Activities that involve lifting, twisting, arching of the spine, sudden starts and stops, and falls or collisions with other players are most risky for people with back problems.

Golf. One survey found that 25 percent of golf pros suffer from lower back injuries. If you have a weak back, you may have to learn to minimize the twisting movement of your swing. Teeing the ball, removing the ball from the cup, and prolonged putting practice all involve bending forward at the waist, which strains the lower spine. When bending, keep your knees bent and try to keep your back straight.

Tennis and racquet sports. These activities can strain the back because of their twisting and quick stop-and-go movements. Work with a pro to modify your serve and backhand if you are straining your back.

Bowling. Lifting a heavy weight while twisting and bending your upper body can easily aggravate back problems. Try to develop a smooth delivery, and don't use too heavy a ball.

Football, basketball, baseball. Because they involve twisting, jarring movements, jumping, bending, and, often, contact with other players, these sports are potentially hazardous for a weak back.

Weight lifting. If not done properly, this can put immense stress on the lower back. The worst thing you can do to your back is to bend over with your legs straight, twist to one side, and pick up something heavy like a dumbbell or bag of groceries. Keep your back as straight as possible when hefting a weight, and bend your knees so that your legs help you lift it. Avoid jerky movements. A weight lifting belt may help maintain correct, back-preserving posture when hefting a heavy load.

heavy object instead of lifting it. Pulling is more likely to injure your back. When carrying a heavy load, don't arch your back or twist your body—try to let your arms and abdominal muscles bear the weight. Because a heavy purse or briefcase can pull your back out of alignment, alternate the load from side to side.

Dress. Prolonged use of tight pants and girdles may induce weak abdominal muscles and result in back trouble. Avoid high heels since they tend to increase the curvature of the back and increase the risk of a fall.

Desk Stress

Anyone who sits at a desk or computer terminal all day is subject to the physical stress induced by static as opposed to dynamic muscular effort. Static effort, in which muscle groups are contracted for long periods in an unvarying position, may obstruct blood flow, possibly inducing fatigue in oxygen-deprived muscles. It generally constrains the way you hold your back, arms, head, and shoulders—encouraging overall poor posture. Think a moment about the position in which most desks and chairs force you to work: perched on the edge of your seat, leaning forward, your neck bent as you scrutinize documents, your shoulders hunched as you type. All of this requires strenuous static effort, and causes office workers to complain about back, knee, neck, and shoulder pain, usually in that order.

A properly chosen chair and desk or work table can go far to alleviate aches and pains due to the strain of static effort. Much of this misery is due to poorly designed office furniture: desks and work surfaces that are too

low or too high, chairs that are at the wrong height and whose backs fail to offer support where it's needed. Adjustability can provide the first line of protection against static-effort fatigue. A study of AT&T operators showed that switching to easily adjustable tables and chairs resulted in a significant decrease in reported discomforts, particularly in the shoulders, back, and legs. The table used in the study could be adjusted for both computer-screen and keyboard height; chair heights could easily be adjusted while the occupant remained seated. Similarly, a study of computer operators showed that adjustable terminal heights and flexible backrests helped reduce pressure on the spine.

If you often feel discomfort or muscle strain after long hours at your desk and chair, measure their dimensions and compare them to those illustrated below. Adjust them where possible. If you are shopping for a desk or chair designed to minimize stress, look for these features and optimal dimensions.

Full-length, adjustable backrest, slightly concave and able to move back and forth

Center of keyboard 27-35" above floor (approximately at elbow level, when seated)

Padded support for lower back

18-20"

7-12"

Adjustable table height

Adjustable seat height, 15-22"

Room under desk to stretch or cross legs (no drawers)

Foot rest, if you are short

Stress and Back Pain
The role of psychological stress in backaches (and pain in general) is much debated. Since emotional stress can generate muscle tension, and tense muscles are more susceptible to injury, some back specialists claim that stress is the major cause of many backaches. In some people anxiety and back pain become a vicious cycle: they worry about recurrent backache, which in turn leads to more anxiety, more muscle tension, and eventually more back pain. Depression, too, may contribute to back pain by magnifying it. Try to recognize when stress is building up. To reduce tension—emotional and physical—try exercise or relaxation techniques.

Good posture

Sitting and standing put considerable pressure on the lower back; standing exerts five times more pressure than lying down, and sitting, surprisingly, is even more strenuous. So good posture isn't just a matter of making you look and feel better; it can also help you distribute that pressure so it doesn't put added stress on your back.

Sitting. The extra pressure that sitting exerts on your lower back comes from the upper body shifting forward, forcing the back muscles to strain to hold you upright. Slouching increases the pressure on your lower back to about *ten to fifteen times* as much as when you're lying down. And hunching over tenses the muscles in the neck and upper back. Good sitting posture involves the same slight forward curve in your lower back that's also the key to good standing posture. The following steps can help improve your sitting posture:

•Keep your shoulders back, with your head centered over them; your knees slightly higher than your hips; and your feet either flat on the floor or on a stool. Cross your legs at the ankles, if at all, since crossing them above the knee can pull your pelvis out of alignment. And try not to keep a bulging wallet in your hip pocket; when you sit, the wallet can press on your sciatic nerve and lead to leg pain.

•Choose a chair that firmly supports your lower back. The chair shouldn't be heavily padded, since that can cause excess curving of your back. It should fit under your desk or table so that you maintain your upright posture (see illustration, page 391). Chair armrests are a plus, too, since you can support some of your weight on them, especially when you shift positions in the chair. Propping up reading matter also helps.

•When driving, move your car seat forward so that your knees are bent. A small pillow or piece of foam placed at your lower back may be helpful.

•Sitting for long periods—even with the very best posture—can become uncomfortable. Be sure to stand up every once in a while and do some stretches.

Standing. Take a look in the mirror for these signs: a protruding abdomen, slumped or rounded shoulders, or swayback (an excessive forward curve in the lower back). Any of these could be putting extra pressure on the muscles and ligaments of your spine. *A slight* hollow in the lower back is natural and desirable; in fact, good standing posture maintains this and the two other natural curves that are visible from a side view—a gentle forward curve in the neck area and backward curve in the upper back. The goal is to avoid exaggerating these curves. Even the "military" stance, with chest thrust forward and shoulders and derriere pushed way back, isn't conducive to a healthy back, since it creates a sway back.

•Simply stand tall with your head held over your shoulders, your chin

---

Improving Posture

A simple test can make you more aware of what constitutes good posture and help improve your spinal flexibility. Stand in a normal, relaxed posture with your back against a wall—upper back and buttocks touching the wall. Slip your hand into the space between your lower back and the wall; it should slide in easily and almost touch both your back and the wall. If there's extra space, you may have a sway back. To correct it, imagine that a string is tied to the top of your head and is pulling you straight up; then tuck in your abdomen and tilt your hips so that the space between your lower back and the wall is lessened. When you walk away from the wall, try to maintain the stance and the mental image of the string.

parallel to the floor, and your neck straight. Your shoulders should be level without any slumping, and in front your chest, waist, and hips should all line up (see illustration, page 392).

•To avoid fatigue when you're standing, occasionally shift your weight from one foot to the other; or prop one foot up on a low stool or a chair rung, which helps to flatten out any excess arch in your lower back.

•Don't stand too long in one position.

Relieving neck tension

The head of an adult weighs ten to twelve pounds, and it's the job of the neck and shoulder muscles to hold it upright as well as allow it easy movement. No wonder these muscles sometimes develop kinks and become painful. Poor posture is the most common cause of neck pain. If you habitually thrust your chin forward or tilt your head to one side, your muscles may start aching under the strain. But many daily activities can also stress your neck and shoulder muscles. How to avoid neck stress? One key is to work on your posture. Here are some other corrective actions you can take:

•Whether in a movie or an airline terminal, don't stare for long periods at screens above eye level. Avoid the first few rows of a movie house or theater. When you watch television, make sure the screen is at or below eye level.

Neck Stretches

If you are prone to neck pain, start a regular routine of neck stretches and exercises; those below will get you started. If you feel pain when exercising your neck muscles, cut back on repetitions and resistance. Stop if you feel any sharp pain or one that radiates down your arms. If you've had any serious injury to your neck, such as a whiplash, or if you have persistent neck pain, consult your doctor before beginning a neck-exercise program.

Side neck stretch. *Tilt your head to the left, keeping your shoulders down. Place your left hand on the right top side of your head. Gently pull your head toward your left shoulder for 20 seconds. Reverse position and stretch to the right.*

Neck pull-down. *Clasp your hands behind your head and let it lean forward. Hold for 15 seconds. Then pull down gently on your head for another 15 seconds. Breathe and relax in this position, keeping your back straight. Rest briefly, repeat.*

Isometric exercise. *To strengthen neck muscles, place your left hand against the side of your head. Without moving your head or arm, push head against hand for 10 seconds. Repeat three times, then reverse exercise and use your right hand.*

•When you sleep, on your back or side, use a small synthetic or feather pillow under your head and neck. When sleeping on your back, make sure your head is not pushed forward toward your chest by your pillow. You can use a rolled-up towel instead of a pillow, if you prefer. Keep your neck and shoulders covered if sleeping in a drafty or chilly room. Feeling cold may cause you to hunch up and the resulting muscle tension can produce a neck ache.

•Don't read or write with your chin on your chest, or your neck tilted backward. If you watch TV in bed, don't lie on your stomach.

•When cycling, make sure your bike helmet fits. A helmet that slips back and forth can cause neck strain. See that your handlebars are at a comfortable distance—if they're out of reach, you'll assume a neck-straining position. You can move your seat forward to correct this or you can get a repair shop to install a different handlebar stem.

•When doing any kind of activity that puts stress on the neck—cycling, driving, or typing—for long periods, stop at intervals to stretch.

•Don't use your shoulder to cradle the telephone receiver, especially during long conversations.

•Routinely perform the neck stretches in the box on page 393.

Protecting Your Feet

The foot consists of some twenty-six bones laced together with many layers of ligaments, tendons, and muscles—a remarkable piece of engineering that functions as a stable structure when we stand on it, yet adapts to any kind of terrain as we walk. The foot is built to absorb shock. Like a suspension bridge, the arching bones of the foot (the metatarsals) distribute weight from the heel bones toward the toes. The sole is designed for protection: it is thicker than other skin, and beneath it lies a thick pad of fat and fibrous tissue known as the plantar fascia.

Though much has been said about the punishment feet take in the course of a lifetime, feet are healthier with vigorous use than without it. Healthy feet are an indispensable asset—equipment for a healthy life and the basis of physical as well as mental well-being.

Unfortunately, four out of five adults have painful feet, and accept it as a fact of life. Some medical conditions such as obesity, poor circulation, arthritis, or diabetes can cause or intensify foot problems, and some common foot abnormalities, such as flat feet, are inherited, as are many idiosyncrasies of gait and stance.

At the same time, much of the everyday agony people experience stems from ill-fitting shoes, socks, and stockings, or from footgear that is not appropriate to the activity it is being used for. This kind of foot pain is preventable. Moreover, many problems of the feet that do develop can be treated effectively at home.

Proper footwear: the key to healthy feet

Your first line of defense is to buy shoes that fit; ill-fitting shoes, it is thought, cause 80 percent of all foot problems. Besides causing corns, bunions, nail deformities, and other problems, painful shoes can alter your gait.

Yet a good fit can be hard to find, and the problem has gotten worse because 77 percent of all shoes sold in America today are imports—often from countries where the ethnic mix is not as diverse as it is here. While American-made shoes, in their heyday, offered the largest selection of sizes and widths found anywhere in the world, the range of available lasts (the metal, wooden or plastic forms over which the shoes are made) and sizes are not as varied in imported shoes. Inexpensive imports in particular tend to be made in one wide width.

Another complicating factor is that feet are as individual as fingerprints, and no two (not even your own two) are exactly the same. Your feet continue to change throughout your adult life. Your shoe size may change when your weight or your pattern of activity changes. The pads on your feet get thinner as you grow older.

While numerical sizes can serve as a guide, they aren't what matter most. More important to your foot and to your comfort is the shape. Sneakers, loafers, moccasins, and most men's shoes are made on a straight last, by far the most comfortable. Many shoes, however, are shaped for style. Elegant as they may look, these can cause problems if worn over a long period.

As well as fitting your foot, your shoe should fit your life. If you stand up several hours each day, or if you walk or run on hard surfaces, you need shoes with a thick sole and a soft upper. If you run for exercise, you need a running shoe. But practicality need not rule every shoe decision. Most people also want dress shoes, which is fine, so long as they fit.

Because stylish shoes for women are often high-heeled and pointy-toed, women have far more foot problems than men. If you wear high heels, save them for special occasions or times of day when you know you'll be sitting down—at your desk, for example. Then change into walking shoes for other activities. If you wear high heels most of the time, your calf muscles may ache when you do put on low heels.

Finally, if you buy a pair of shoes that prove painful, don't wear them. Throw them out and buy another pair. And if the heels of your shoes wear down, replace them or throw away the worn shoes. Unevenly worn heels can decrease foot stability and make you tired.

About one billion people world wide wear no shoes at all. The few surveys of barefoot populations tend to show that they have fewer foot problems.

Shopping tips

•Ask to have both feet measured (the metal Brannock device is more accurate than a wooden ruler) and always put your full weight on the foot being measured. Try the size that fits the larger foot. Remember, sizes indicate very little: size $8^{1}/_{2}$ C in one brand may be a 9 B in another. Imported shoes are likely to run small.

•When testing new shoes, stand on one foot at a time. Wiggle your toes. Stand on tiptoe. The shoe should bend where your foot bends.

•Never buy a shoe with the idea of breaking it in. Your foot may alter in an uncomfortable shoe, but the shoe won't.

•Check to see that you have one half inch of space between the end of your big toe and the tip of the shoe.

•Make sure the widest part of your foot—the metatarsal joint—fits comfortably in the widest part of the shoe.

•Try to shop for shoes in the middle of a normal day, not early in the morning, since your feet swell as the day progresses. Wear the kind of socks or stockings that you intend to wear with the shoes.

(See page 223 for information on choosing athletic shoes.)

Common Foot Problems

Ingrown toenails

Perhaps the most common of all foot afflictions, ingrown toenails usually occur on the big toe. The edge of the nail cuts into the soft toe tissue, causing swelling and redness. Besides being painful, ingrown toenails can lead to infection. They have two causes: tight shoes or stockings that press the nail into the tissue and improper trimming of the toenail. When trimming toenails, follow these directions to avoid ingrown toenails:

•Use heavy long-handled scissors or nail clippers to cut the nail neatly.

•Never try to tear away the nail with your fingers.

•Always trim the nail straight across—the end of the nail should be a square, not a half moon. Don't trim too close. Finish the edge with an emery board or nail file, and clean the grooves with an orange stick.

Contrary to myth, making a V-shaped cut in the middle of your toenail won't make it grow toward the middle and thus won't prevent an ingrown toenail.

Treatment. If you have an ingrown toenail, try to determine and eliminate the cause. Soak the toe in warm water to soften the nail, and then press a few strands of absorbent cotton under the nail to keep it from cutting the skin. Wear open shoes, if possible. If pus, bleeding, or painful swelling occurs, get medical advice.

Athlete's foot

Prevention is the best treatment for athlete's foot, which basically means keeping your feet clean and dry. Despite the popular name for this usually harmless infection, it can develop in places other than locker rooms or gym showers. The fungus that causes it thrives best in warm, moist, enclosed environments: snug, poorly ventilated shoes and damp, sweaty socks provide an ideal breeding ground. (Your chances of catching athlete's foot from another person is slight, but the fungus can be spread by shed fragments of affected skin.)

You'll know when athlete's foot strikes. Your toes, soles, or sides of your feet will itch, tiny blisters may appear, and there may be red scaling in these areas and between your toes.

The usual treatment is one of the over-the-counter antifungal preparations. Things should clear up in a week or two. If they don't, or if the area turns red and swollen, see your doctor.

Treatment. Some people are more susceptible to the fungus than others. If you are susceptible, follow these commonsense rules especially in hot weather, and anytime you're very active and your feet tend to perspire:

•Keep your feet clean. Daily washing with soap and water is a good idea, but be sure you dry thoroughly, especially between the toes.

•When you can, go barefoot. Next best thing to bare feet is sandals. But when you wear shoes, wear socks, too.

•Wear socks that "wick" away moisture and keep your feet dry. Change your socks daily.

•Cornstarch or baking powder can also help keep feet dry.

•Choose shoes that let your feet breathe and don't wear the same pair every day. Air them between wearings.

Toenail fungus

The same fungus responsible for athlete's foot or other related yeastlike fungi can grow under and within a toenail given the right environment—such as sweaty socks, shoes with poor ventilation, or a bandage worn around a toe for an extended period of time. Less commonly, trauma to the nail may also increase the risk of fungal growth. The fungus may cause the toenail to thicken and become brittle, discolored, and distorted.

Treatment. There is no sure way to prevent the growth of toenail fungus, but keeping your feet dry and clean may help. The same guidelines for preventing athlete's foot apply here: dry your feet completely after bathing, and wear dry socks and well-ventilated shoes.

Curing chronic toenail fungus is difficult, or, in many cases, impossible. To control it, file or sandpaper the thickened nail and apply an antifungal product (over-the-counter or by prescription); the solution form can cover the nail more thoroughly. If you can't control the fungus, or if your nail becomes red or painful, seek medical attention.

Blisters

Friction or pressure from ill-fitting shoes, socks, or stockings—either too big or little—causes blisters. Going without socks or stockings in normally well-fitting shoes can also blister heels and toes, particularly in hot weather, when feet are likely to swell and sweat. Sandals and other shoes with straps are particularly likely to blister bare skin. A small blister (less than one-half inch in diameter) will usually heal by itself.

Treatment. Make sure the area is clean, and avoid breaking the blister, if possible. Cover it with a thin foam pad with a hole in the center, or a light bandage. Leaving the blister uncovered and going barefoot indoors, if practical, is a good idea. Large blisters and any blister that breaks should be cleaned with soap and water and protected with a light bandage. Watch carefully for signs of infection—reddening, swelling, or pus—and see a doctor if infection occurs.

The average person takes from 5,000 to 10,000 steps a day, mostly on hard surfaces.

Corns and calluses

Corns and calluses are similar manifestations of the skin's response to pressure and chafing. People with flat feet are particularly susceptible to them. Corns, which usually appear on the toes, come in two varieties—hard and soft. Both are thickenings of skin around a core, whose apex points inward. Most hard corns appear on the little toe; soft corns appear on the web between toes. A callus has the same causes as a corn but is a protective mechanism formed of dead skin, usually on or under the heel or on the ball of the foot.

Treatment. Treat corns and calluses at home by soaking the foot in warm water until the hardened skin softens, then gently applying a pumice stone. Don't rub the area raw; it may take several treatments to soften. Try to determine which shoes or socks are causing them, and switch to other footgear. A bony growth beneath the skin may be the cause, so if self-treatment doesn't work and pain is persistent, consult a doctor. After treating a corn, protect the area with a light pad or bandage. Adhesive-backed moleskin can be trimmed to fit the spot.

Orthoses

In theory, the human foot is a perfect piece of design, but in practice some people's feet don't hit the ground in quite the right way. The resulting condition can be painful for the knees, hips, and the feet themselves, and the pain may be particularly noticeable for those embarking on a fitness program.

To correct for abnormal foot motion and alignment, many people buy devices called "orthoses," popularly (but incorrectly) known as "orthotics." Made of foam, leather, plastic, fiberglass, graphite, or some combination thereof, orthoses are foot supports that fit in your shoes. A podiatrist or orthopedist should prescribe and fit them, since they must be specially cast or designed. Improperly constructed orthotic devices can do more harm than good. They are expensive—they can cost up to six hundred dollars for the examination, casting, X-rays, and lab fees. Fortunately, some medical insurance plans cover them.

Orthoses can't change the shape of your foot, but they can make its motion more efficient and can correct certain structural imbalances that may lead to pain in the hips, knees, back, or feet. Some athletes—for example, certain runners, cyclists, and skiers—have been shown to benefit from them. And for people with alignment or imbalance problems, orthotic devices can relieve discomfort and reduce the risk of foot injury. They are, however, an aid, not a cure; if you need therapy for structural foot problems, orthotic devices can be one part of the total treatment program.

Over-the-counter corn remedies are available, most containing salicylic acid, which removes dead skin. Though the Food and Drug Administration (FDA) has approved these products, most doctors advise using them with caution, if at all. They can burn the skin and result in additional discomfort and possibly infection. If you choose to use such a preparation, be careful not to apply it to surrounding normal skin.

Bunions and hammertoes

When the large metatarsal bone angles outward at the big toe joint, thus forcing the toe inward, pressure over this distended joint can cause swelling and eventually a bony outgrowth. This is a bunion, which is not only disfiguring but painful, and can seriously interfere with standing and walking if neglected over the years. (Smaller bunions—bunionettes—may occasionally appear on the fifth metatarsal bone and the little toe joint.) The tendency to develop bunions may be hereditary, and flat-footed people are more likely to get bunions than others. But poorly fitting shoes—especially those with high heels and narrow toes—are undoubtedly the worst bunion-makers. Thus women are more prone to bunions.

Treatment. If you think you are developing a bunion, switch to shoes with a low heel and an ample toe box; avoid any shoes or stockings with seams that put pressure on the big toe joint. Wearing open shoes, if practical, may be a good idea. Soaking your feet in warm water at night and gentle massage may also relieve some symptoms.

Hammertoes and mallet toes are deformities of the toe bones, usually of the second, third, or fourth toes, whereby the toes grow in a bent position. This can be painful and even disabling and can keep shoes from fitting properly. Shoes, particularly high-heels with pointed toes, are almost always to blame for these deformities, which occur most commonly in women. Well-fitting shoes are often the best treatment, and corrective pads can help as well. If the deformity is painful or hinders walking, seek professional advice.

Painful heel syndrome

If you are over forty, you could well find yourself among the three million new cases of painful heel syndrome reported each year. Fortunately, this syndrome is eminently treatable—without surgery. You may need a doctor to diagnose the condition, but the treatment is self-administered and simple.

Because the shock-absorbing pads of fatty tissue on the heel of your foot get thinner as you grown older, repeated pressure on the bone and muscle in the heel can bring on painful heel syndrome. Being overweight can add to the pressure; so can prolonged standing. One cause of pain is plantar fasciitis, an inflammation of the plantar fascia—the tough band of fibrous protective tissue in the sole of the foot. Inflammation occurs when the flexor muscles, which are attached to the plantar fascia at the heel, tear or pull away under stress, the type often associated with minute bone fractures. While X-rays may show a small spur of bone near the site of stress injury, orthopedic surgeons no longer think this causes the heel pain or needs to be removed. Bone spurs show in about half of all cases of painful heel syndrome, but also occur among 15 percent of people without heel pain.

Though pain builds up gradually in this syndrome, you'll know when it hits its stride. It is particularly severe when you swing your weight onto your feet first thing in the morning, or when you get up after a long period of sitting. Keep moving, and in about a half hour the pain will lessen. But it can recur intermittently for three to eighteen months; the average episode lasts nine months.

Nerve, joint, and tendon inflammation (neuritis, arthritis, and tendinitis, respectively) can also cause heel pain. If one of these is the culprit, your doctor will diagnose and treat it accordingly. But for plantar fascitis he is likely to prescribe self help.

Treatment. The best treatment may be rest, a sure way to take the pressure off your heel. You may have to modify your exercise program. If you jog, switch to an exercise that doesn't stress the heel, such as swimming or cycling. You can also do special exercises designed to stretch the Achilles tendon for five to ten minutes twice a day. (See pages 373-374.)

Shoes are also important. A good walking shoe with rubber heels or thickly cushioned heels can bring relief; women should shun both thin-soled flats and high heels. If the painful heel persists, try shock-absorbing heel pads .

When severe pain hits, relieve it by massaging your heel with ice for five minutes or so. Over-the-counter pain relievers are helpful. If you don't get relief, consult your doctor. But in most cases the syndrome heals itself.

When you can't treat it at home

If you have any medical or inherited problems—or if any of the problems described in the sections above do not respond to home treatment, you need professional advice. Two kinds of professionals specialize in foot care: the orthopedist and the podiatrist. Orthopedists are MDs who treat bone disorders, both medically and surgically. Podiatrists treat foot disorders and in some states can prescribe for ankle disorders as well, but they are not MDs. Like orthopedists, they can perform surgery and prescribe medications, but only for problems of the foot and ankle.

Stress

Stress has never been adequately defined, beyond such vague generalizations as "Stress is how people respond to demands." Once stress became a popular concept, old terms such as "worry," "anxiety," "fear," "impatience," and "anger," gave way to "stress" and its offshoots, "stressful," "stress-related," and "stressed-out." "Stressors" have been defined as everything from war and famine to job loss, family arguments, and encounters with the IRS. Further complicating matters is the fact that different people react to the same "stress" in unpredictable ways. In addition, when put to the test of scientific proof, it's been hard to demonstrate that specific attitudes lead to specific illnesses.

In fact, according to some experts the psychological concept of "stress" (as something originating in a person's mind) should be retired. The idea that emotional anguish arises from personality or individual flaws beclouds the fact that many physical and psychological problems come from social conditions not always within an individual's control. Many problems arise specifically from problems relating to a person's occupation and financial security—or the lack of them. (Not having a job at all can be at least as painful as having the wrong one.) Of course, the workplace is not the only source of human happiness and misery: we all live within society and with our friends and families. Still, most of the important research on stress so far has been conducted in the workplace, and the theory that has developed there may apply to other situations.

Stress and the sense of control

Most of us dread intense demands in the workplace, but sometimes such demands can lead to a sense of control and indeed exhilaration. Many occupations (including even some that are unpaid, such as raising children or doing community work or playing an instrument for pleasure), can, under ideal circumstances, provide great challenges and intense satisfactions—a sense of cohesion, accomplishment, and control. A sense of personal control may, in fact, be a critical factor in maintaining health. The evidence is strong, and growing, that *people whose lives or jobs make high demands on them but allow little latitude for decision-making have higher rates of many diseases.*

Indeed, the risk of illness for such people is two to four times what it is for others, independent of all other risk factors. Though it's not known exactly how unsatisfying jobs and unhappy lives might make people sick, one possibility is by interfering with some general integrating system of the body—the nervous or hormonal or immune system. But there is solid evidence that social support (i.e., involvement with family, friends, and community) can buffer social stress.

Researchers Robert Karasek of the University of Southern California and Töres Theorell of Sweden's National Institute for Psychosocial Factors and Health, divide occupations into four categories:

Active jobs. Heavy pressure to perform, but leeway allowed for problem solving. Examples: doctors, engineers, farmers, executives, other professionals. Hours may be long, but are partly at the worker's discretion. Job provides chances to advance and to learn new skills. Initiative is part of job description.

Low-strain jobs. Self-paced occupations. Examples are tenured professors, carpenters, repairmen, successful artists, naturalists, or any occupation with low demands and high decision latitude. (This idyllic category seems somewhat underpopulated in this research, no doubt because few such jobs exist in an industrial society. Professors, carpenters, artists, and others can certainly experience high strain.)

Passive jobs. Low demands on skills and mental processes, little leeway for learning or decision-making. Examples: billing clerks, nightwatchmen, janitors, dispatchers, key-punchers. These jobs offer almost no latitude for innovation; sometimes worker skills actually atrophy.

High-strain jobs. Heavy pressure to perform but little control over decisions. Examples: assembly line workers, waiters, waitresses, nurse's aides, telephone operators. Includes any job where hours and procedures are rigid, where the threat of layoff may loom, where no new skills are learned from day to day, and where it may be difficult to take time out, or off, for personal needs.

Who is subject to stress

Studies in the United States and Europe have consistently shown that people in high-strain jobs (that is, those at the bottom of the job ladder) have the highest rate of heart attacks, while those in active jobs have the lowest. Passive jobs and low-strain jobs were in between. Those in high-strain, low-echelon jobs also exhibited the highest levels of psychological stress (including depression and exhaustion), and they took the most medications for depression—while those at the top of the job ladder were by far the best-off in this category. In short, though "executive stress" exists, it's the bossed, not the bosses, who experience the most stress on the job.

A study conducted at the Volvo plant in Goteborg, Sweden, showed that those who saw themselves as influential (usually managers, men, and white-collar workers) were much more highly motivated and less subject to stress-related medical complaints than those who saw themselves as cogs in the wheel (nonmanagers, women, and blue-collar workers). In another area, studies of older people living in nursing homes, indicate that a sense of self-management (expressed even in such small ways as the ability to choose one menu over another) can strongly contribute to psychological as well as physical well-being.

Stereotypical "high stress" jobs such as manager, electrical engineer, and architect have proved not to be associated with health risks, because professionals get to make more of their own decisions and thus feel more in control. Even when such risk factors as age, race, education, and smoking were factored into the equation, those in the bottom tenth of the job echelon turned out to be in the top tenth for stress. They had four to five times the risk of heart attack as those at the top tenth of the ladder whose jobs gave them a high sense of control.

Since there are still few occupations with large proportions of both sexes, much of this type of research has focused on men. Nevertheless, according to Karasek and Theorell, "Women's average level of decision latitude is markedly lower than men's." Women fill more than their share of high-strain jobs, less than their share of active ones. Many of the high-strain jobs for women are newly created clerical

Researchers at the University of Massachusetts Center for Health and Fitness found that after subjects worked out by taking a brisk forty-minute walk, they experienced a 14 percent average drop in anxiety levels.

jobs (such as computer operators in highly automated offices). This might have some impact on women's health in the future.

Regaining control

In the workplace, supervisors are recognizing that people do better work if they have some say over what they do. If your job is managing others, you can reduce the stress of your own responsibilities by asking others to share them. If those who report to you seem bored, uninterested, and all too willing to vanish at quitting time, remember that powerlessness is a bad motivator. Provide some on-the-job training and some real responsibilities that lead to a sense of control.

If you feel that your job does not provide you with enough input, try either to change the way you feel or change the situation. For a start, try to analyze what bothers you and come up with one or two possible solutions. Then see whether you can discuss these matters with a co-worker. Next, try to talk to your supervisor. If you can spot problems and discover solutions, your supervisor may like your suggestions and give you more responsible work to do. Work toward the goal of being an active participant at your job, rather than a passive observer.

At the same time, be willing, if necessary, to conclude that you're in the wrong place. Some bad work situations just can't be changed. If you know you're in the wrong job, consider improving your skills in your leisure time and looking for something new. You can also simultaneously try to improve your life outside the workplace. Some people dissatisfied with their jobs can find a sense of effectiveness and control by becoming more active outside their jobs—in community organizations for instance.

The benefits of social support

Support of co-workers and supervisors may be one of the most important factors ameliorating workplace stress. Social support at work acts as a palliative, mitigating the bad health effects of even high-strain jobs. A variety of circumstances can provide social support on the job: a comradely atmosphere among co-workers and between workers and management; a boss who treats his staff with respect; and the feeling of making a creditable contribution in a team effort. Labor unions and other kinds of employee organizations also provide social support. Indeed, depending on the circumstances, some high-strain jobs (in restaurants or factories or hospitals) can have some support built in—a good supervisor, regular job breaks, or a sense that customers or patients appreciate the service rendered.

If a job is lonely or a person's colleagues are unhelpful or even actively hostile, there is some evidence that social interactions with family and friends, as well as with the community can be a factor in maintaining health. Studies have shown that people who enjoy the companionship of friends or family live longer and are healthier than people who are socially isolated. Dr. Leonard Syme of the University of California, Berkeley and Dr. Lisa Berkman of Yale University followed the health and social habits of seven thousand individuals for nine years. They found that lonely women have nearly three times greater risk and lonely men a doubled risk of illness and death than people who can count on family or friends. Earlier studies indicated that married people are healthier and live longer than single people, but this study suggested that marriage per se is not essential for health but

The Ideal Job
According to researchers Robert Karasek and Töres Theorell, a satisfying job provides:

Skill discretion. The job requires maximum use of skills and offers chances to increase them.

Autonomy. Workers are in control of machines; they can participate in long-term planning; flexible hours are available.

Psychological demands. Routine demands are mixed with new but predictable challenges. Workers have some say-so over magnitude of demands.

Social relations. Workers can collaborate.

Social rights. Democratic procedures rule the workplace. Some way exists to settle grievances.

Meaningfulness. Workers understand what they are producing and for whom. Feedback from customers is provided.

Integration of family and community life with work. Working men and women are able to share family responsibilities. The job also allows time and energy for activities outside of work-related ones.

that the companionship and emotional support associated with marriage are. However, a study of Swedish workers did suggest that in some circumstances "the psychosocial situation at work appears to have a greater impact on psychological well-being than do family situations." Nevertheless, since high demand coupled with a low sense of control appear to create the most damaging strain in the workplace, it's reasonable to wonder whether the same principle wouldn't apply to family life and to many situations outside the workplace.

Stress and illness

More than two decades of research into the relationship between personality and disease has found little of significance, and indeed has created a lot of confusion. People who get ulcers have a wide range of personalities and habits. Some appear to live under extreme emotional stress; others are calm and contented. Optimists and pessimists, extroverts and introverts get cancer—and recover from it (or do not).

The theory that Type As (aggressive, competitive, tense, time-conscious, and generally hostile men) were at higher risk for coronary heart disease emerged from early research, and for several years was treated almost as dogma. But careful study has stripped away aggressiveness, tenseness, and competitiveness as risk factors for heart attacks. A recent twenty-two-year follow-up study of some three thousand middle-aged men by Dr. David Ragland and Dr. Richard Brand from the University of California, Berkeley, indicated that Type A behavior was not related to heart attack deaths. Smoking and high blood pressure were still far more important risks than personality or behavior.

But the one personality trait that may be linked to heart disease is chronic hostility or cynicism. Several studies suggest that the chronically angry, suspicious, and mistrustful (as measured by objective tests) are twice as likely to have coronary artery blockages. Still, it's not clear what the connection is. Maybe cynical hostility somehow does physical damage. But perhaps mistrustful people adopt a "why bother" attitude and thus fail to take care of their health.

The idea that a positive attitude can help keep you from getting sick has been studied in individuals with cancer. Some researchers have suggested that patients with a positive attitude are likely to get well. For example, a study conducted in London showed that a "fighting spirit" as opposed to helplessness and hopelessness," may help women with breast cancer survive, but only if the disease has not spread. These people, of course, have the best prognosis, whatever their state of mind. But other studies have been unable to find a relationship between attitudes and cancer survival.

Still, many doctors believe that a strong desire to stay alive and well is an asset to anybody. If nothing else, it will give you the incentive to take care of yourself. In cancer patients, a courageous attitude and a willingness to follow a prescribed course of therapy is an advantage, not only for them but for their doctors, friends, and families.

Personality and health habits

According to researcher Suzanne Kobasa of the City University of New York, some people weather adversity with fewer side effects than others. She terms these people "hardy" personalities. According to her surveys, the hardy enjoy better physical health as well as more satisfying personal lives.

According to one Swedish study, commuters who board a train twenty miles outside of their destination were found to have significantly higher stress levels than those traveling twice the distance. Apparently the more control the commuter has over his surroundings (such as being able to get a seat), the less stressful the journey. This suggests that commuters may be better off trading a short, stressful ride for a longer but calmer one.

Supporting Friends in Times of Crisis

It is hard to say which is the more difficult position: to be needing reassurance and support, or to be trying to help a friend or family member and not knowing what to say. Perhaps you grope for the right words and end up saying nothing, or manage to say exactly the wrong thing.

Most of us (including many doctors) are convinced that grief always follows the same patterns: the bereaved person first experiences deep distress and depression, then begins to "work through" and adjust to the new situation, and finally resolves the loss and resumes functioning. All this is supposed to happen pretty quickly—and any deviation is generally interpreted as "bad."

But according to some researchers people don't always conform to this pattern. Those who don't mourn openly may find themselves accused of "denial." Those who can't recover quickly may be categorized as morbid or self-indulgent. But, in fact, there are really no definitions for "normal" grieving or "working through." Even health-care professionals have been known to recommend "a pat on the back and kick in the pants" for people who seem to be grieving too deeply or too long. But given how little is known about grieving, pats and kicks may not be approriate at all.

Because mourning is so personal, comments on a person's method of dealing with loss may do more harm than good. Thus when you offer support to someone who's having a hard time, it's always a good idea to stop and think about

what you would want to hear yourself, or how you would want to be listened to. Though much depends on the individual you're dealing with, a few general pointers may apply:

•Make sure there's no implicit criticism in any suggestions you make. Instead of "you're brooding too much," try "I wish you'd be our fourth for bridge" or some similar invitation.

•Compassionate listening can often accomplish more than talking. Allow the other person to take the lead in conversation. Instead of making assumptions about how he is feeling, find out what is really on his mind. If your widowed aunt still needs to talk about her husband two years after his death, you can help by listening sympathetically.

•On the other hand, remember that people who are bereaved or ill don't want to talk about their problems all the time. It's all right to bring up other subjects. It may be the most helpful thing for them.

•Just be there. A report by psychologists Gayle Dakof and Shelley Taylor of UCLA, who asked fifty-five cancer patients what they perceived as helpful support, has a similar theme. Love, emotional support, and calm concern turned out to be the most helpful contributions from family members and friends. Such acts of service as coming along for a doctor's appointment, providing transportation to and from treatments, or other kinds of practical aid were also cited. "Just being there" turned out to be the strongest supportive factor for a spouse.

Exercise relieves anxiety.
Aerobic exercise not only reduces anxiety and muscle tension, but can improve your coping skills with anxiety-provoking situations as well. In one study, two groups of college students—one that exercised and one that did not—were given a test consisting of problems, most of which could not be solved, and told that the test was a good indicator of how they were likely to perform in college. The nonexercising students showed increased blood pressure, muscle tension, and anxiety when told they did poorly on the test. The exercising group also showed increased muscle tension and anxiety over the poor test results, but not as much as the non-exercisers and showed no increase in blood pressure.

One way to spot the hardy personality is in the workplace. For example, Kobasa studied middle- and upper-level executives at a large Illinois corporation, which was undergoing upheavals at the time. The men who coped best with the strains were likely to:

•Consider new developments and problems to be exciting challenges rather than threats.

•Display a sense of commitment to work.

•Find a sense of control in the job, and take part in outside activities (perhaps community affairs) which offer other responsibilities.

•Accept change optimistically and see it as a normal life process, rather than interpreting it as a source of stress.

A person who exhibits such qualities will probably also be "hardy" in personal relationships. Interesting as this research may be, its value as practical advice applicable to the individual is probably limited.

If you aren't hardy, it's difficult to alter personality (as any one knows who has

Watching television is a favorite relaxation method of 34 percent of American adults, but studies show that time spent watching television programs with a violent theme does little to reduce anxiety. One study found that heavy television watchers tend to express mistrust of others and to view themselves as living in a hostile world.

Pet Therapy

Studies suggest that pets can be a significant source of comfort for the ill, the elderly, and the very young. If nothing else, animals provide a sense of normalcy in what otherwise might be a frightening or a depressing situation. In one experiment conducted at the University of Pennsylvania School of Veterinary Medicine, children were brought into an unfamiliar room and interviewed by a stranger—a situation designed to make them nervous. Researchers found that the presence of a friendly dog helped put the children at ease, as indicated by a slight decrease in their blood pressure. Other investigators have reported that pets have been effectively used to allay the fears of children undergoing psychotherapy and of nursing home residents.

Nevertheless, despite some extravagant claims made for the health-enhancing potential of pets, no pet can lower the blood pressure of a hypertensive or otherwise take the place of preventive health care. The real therapeutic usefulness of pets may be as an adjunct to psychotherapy, particularly with disturbed children or people recovering from illnesses. Pet therapy reinforces what many people want to believe anyway—that pets are intrinsically good for people. If walking your dog makes you happy, or you love coming home to your cat, the health benefits are self-explanatory. No scientific studies are necessary. As one researcher in the veterinary field has written, "pets are active members of human social systems." The benefits they bring to normal life at home may be translated into therapy for those whose normal life has been interrupted.

ever tried). However, Kobasa suggests that the hardy are likely to do the following and perhaps the "unhardy" could make some gains by following similar policies:

- Maintain good health habits, such as exercising and eating a healthy diet.
- Engage in open discussion with others, particularly when crises arise.
- Seek social support.

Learning to relax

Although it is not clear what effect your emotional state has on your health, it is clear that when some people are anxious, angry, or tense they experience physiological effects such as increased blood pressure and heart rate, muscle tension, and intestinal upset. These physical responses to emotional situations seem to be the result of the "fight or flight" response—your body's reaction to a perceived threat. This response seems to be a holdover from the time when man had to deal with physical threats to his well-being either by staying and fighting or running away. In order to give man the extra energy and alertness needed, the body responded to emergency situations by releasing two hormones—epinephrine (also known as adrenaline) and norepinephrine (also known as noradrenaline)—which caused the heart to beat faster (thereby pumping more blood to the muscles and brain), increased respiration rate and blood pressure, and activated blood-clotting mechanisms to prepare for physical injury. In today's modern world, this response is rarely needed, but is activated frequently by emotional upsets—arguments with friends and family, excessive demands on your time, irritation with traffic, long lines, and rude people.

It has been a truism in western civilization for centuries that we can control all sorts of physical functions that are under our conscious influence—walking, swallowing, writing, even crying—but that we cannot control that wide range of involuntary functions that go on in our bodies without our conscious thought: the regulation of our bodies' temperatures, our heart rate, our blood pressure, or even the tension in our muscles Yet eastern mystics have long studied and practiced control of autonomous functions—not necessarily for reasons of health, but in order to achieve a certain composure conducive to meditation and spiritual communion.

Among the western scientists to study just how eastern mystics went about achieving this composure were Herbert Benson, of the Harvard Medical School, and his colleagues. Benson's group focused on Transcendental Meditation—a simplified version of several eastern meditation techniques. In TM, as it is popularly called, a subject is given a mantra—a personal, secret word, sound or phrase—by his instructor. The subject then sits in a comfortable position and repeats this mantra over and over again to drive out all distracting thoughts and to think about nothing at all. Subjects are advised to meditate in this way twenty minutes every morning and evening.

The Benson group monitored several bodily functions of volunteers trained in this technique, before, during, and after meditation. The experiments showed that during meditation there was a marked decrease in the body's oxygen consumption and a corresponding slowing of metabolism. At the same time there was a marked increase in alpha waves, the slow brain waves associated with relaxation. Also there was a sharp decrease in blood lactate—a by-product of metabolism in the skeletal muscles that is associated with muscle tension and physical activity. And finally, both heart rate and respiration rate slowed down. What did not change in these volunteers was blood pressure. And, indeed, later research has shown that blood pressure is lowered only in people who have mildly elevated blood pressure to to begin with.

The relaxation response

These results led Benson's group to the next step of their experiments; what if volunteers were taught simple physical relaxation techniques that were stripped of any mystical or religious aura or purpose? Benson outlined four elements necessary to achieve what he called the "relaxation response" and had his subjects learn and practice these techniques over four consecutive days:

A mental device. There needs to be a constant stimulus of some sort—a word, a sound, a phrase repeated silently or audibly, or fixed gazing at some stationary objects—to shift the mind from logical, externally oriented thoughts.

A passive attitude. If distracting thoughts do intrude they should be disregarded, and attention redirected by repetition of the word or phrase, but redirected without worry about how well one is doing.

Decreased muscle tension. The subject should be in a comfortable position so that minimal muscle work is needed.

A quiet environment. The subject should choose a quiet place, with few environmental distractions. A place of worship or a quiet room is good; sometimes closing your eyes helps.

Using these four simple guidelines, Benson's group was able to measure the very same alternations in bodily functions among untrained volunteers that they had measured among those schooled in Transcendental Meditation. In short, though some experienced meditators may use these techniques as avenues toward spiritual experiences, the techniques can be used for simple physical reduction of some symptoms of tension as well.

Writing about traumatic events may be at least as helpful as conversation in easing emotional upset. It seems that the mere act of disclosure in writing is helpful. Writing may be a particularly good emotional outlet for people who find it hard to speak about deep emotion, who have suffered experiences they are reluctant to discuss, or who have no ready listener.

Benson and his associates used the relaxation response in numerous and varied studies. In one, they showed that people with mildly elevated blood pressure were able to significantly reduce pressure by regular practice of the relaxation response. In quite a different study, Benson found that a group of subjects dramatically reduced their alcohol intake. The alcohol they had used to reduce anxiety and tension had become a problem in itself; invoking the relaxation response reduced general stress levels as well as the need for alcohol.

Progressive muscle relaxation

Benson's technique for achieving the relaxation response is not, however, the only stress reduction technique. Another technique known as progressive muscle relaxation seems especially well suited to reducing muscle tension—and so alleviating the pain of some forms of headache and backache as well as high blood pressure. This simple technique was developed back in the thirties by Dr. Edmund Jacobson, a physiologist/physician. Subjects are instructed to lie down in a quiet room and let their minds drift into as passive a state as possible. Then, one by one, muscle groups are singled out—tensed to their ultimate extent and then relaxed. A subject works his way from toes to head in this way, several times if necessary, until he has achieved deep relaxation, particularly in the muscles of the face and eyes. Coupled with this training, subjects are instructed to tense a muscle halfway, or a quarter of the way, or as little as possible—so that they recognize even the slightest evidence of muscle tension in their bodies.

Eventually subjects are instructed to relax their muscles without going through any of the tensing routines at all. A study at the Utah Medical Center found that progressive muscle relaxation can reduce blood pressure in some hypertensives by 8 or 9 percent.

Biofeedback

The most "scientific" of all relaxation techniques—or in any event, the most technological—is biofeedback. The technique of biofeedback could not be more direct and simple. A subject is brought into a laboratory and hooked up to a machine that measures systolic blood pressure, the temperature of the fingers, and/or the tension of the muscles in the forehead. The measurements taken by these machines are then continuously displayed on a monitor—either as numbers or as the sound of high or low pitch. The subject is then told to relax, be quiet, and lower the number, or change the pitch. The subject, using whatever sensations, thoughts, or feelings work for him, is not told how to lower the number or pitch—just to do it. One well-designed study found that biofeedback successfully lowered mild hypertension, and other studies have confirmed these findings.

Pros and cons of relaxation techniques

Just how to evaluate the relative merits of all these techniques is difficult to say. While all these phenomena of lowered respiration and metabolic rates are interesting, it is not clear just what significance they have for the health of any individual. The principal clinical benefits of meditation, relaxation, and biofeedback techniques would seem to be in the reduction of headaches, muscle aches, and hypertension. In people who conscientiously practice biofeedback techniques over a long period of time, such maneuvers seem to help headaches.

A study at Pennsylvania State University suggests that people who identified themselves as chronic worriers were able to reduce anxiety by setting aside a "worry period" everyday. Subjects set aside a half-hour a day to worry and when they caught themselves worrying at other times during the day, they postponed it.

Quick Relaxation Techniques

Here are four ways to relax in twenty minutes or less. They require only a little practice and aren't seriously disruptive.

Countdown. With eyes closed, count backward from ten or twenty, saying each number silently as you exhale. You must concentrate and call your imagination into play. Imagine you are going down a stairway, or past the floors in a building as an elevator descends. Count down from your age, and imagine that you are traveling briefly into your past. When you have reached zero and want to resume your normal routine, inhale and count to three.

Imagery. Stop what you are doing and close your eyes. Imagine a beautiful scene, perhaps something you saw on your last vacation. Spend five minutes examining and enjoying every detail of the picture. If you are by a lake, listen to the water lapping. Count the trees and flowers. See, hear, and smell things.

The turtle. This simple exercise, adapted from a yoga practice, is designed to relax the muscles of your neck and back. Sit up straight and let your chin fall to your chest as you exhale. Inhale and move your head back slowly as though trying to touch the back of your neck with your head. Then pull your shoulders up as though trying to touch them to your ears. Then release. You can do this anytime, anywhere. It doesn't even look all that odd.

Scanning. At your desk, during your coffee break, or even while you are riding a bus or waiting at a traffic light, inhale and slowly "scan" your body. Think about each muscle group—face and neck, shoulders, arms, abdomen, legs, and feet—and seek out tense muscles. As you exhale, relax all the muscles that are tense. It may help, as you scan your body, to recite silently some phrase that has a calming effect.

So called "stress vitamins," which claim to help you deal with emotional stress, serve no pupose. Although your body may need more vitamins during periods of physical stress (after surgery for instance), there's no evidence that these special formulas (usually vitamins C, E and B-complex) will help you if you're facing psychological stess.

However, it is wrong to look at biofeedback as the new health panacea. There are no licensing guidelines for biofeedback personnel and it can be very expensive. The American College of Physicians concluded in a position paper that there was no evidence that biofeedback was more effective than less expensive types of relaxation techniques.

Muscle relaxation techniques clearly help muscle tension. Whether any of the techniques has a sufficient impact on blood pressure, however, and whether patients will sustain their biofeedback or relaxation techniques for a long enough duration to make the sort of difference that drugs demonstrably do is still an open question. In the treatment of mild hypertension, these methods are most likely to be effective when they are combined with a change in life style—that is, with weight reduction, sodium reduction, exercise, cessation of smoking, and moderation in the use of alcohol.

At the same time, some studies have indicated that some people even have increased anxiety as a result of relaxation training. Evidently, the varieties of individual response to such forms of psychological manipulation are a reflection of individual temperament. For some people such techniques may be of profound and lasting benefit; for others they may be a mere escape mechanism from the normal strains of daily life; for others they may be misleading substitutes for proven medical drug therapies.

For most people, though, relaxation techniques rarely harm and may help. If you are under a doctor's care for hypertension, heart disease, or headaches, you can try adding relaxation techniques to your daily routine, but certainly don't discard medication without your physician's approval. If you are healthy, you may want to try relaxation techniques to reduce daily tension.

Memory

Memory lapses can happen to anybody, and they occur more frequently with age. People often make offhand remarks about forgetting names, dates, or where they've left their keys or glasses, but unfortunately, they're often really worried—a negative approach to the problem of memory loss that won't bring about an improvement. For more often than not, such benign hitches in remembering are symptoms of neither disease nor encroaching senility. They do indicate an age-related slowdown of the memory's information-processing functions, which include the short-term memory you need to find your glasses, and the search and retrieval functions needed to recall names.

How memory works

Our senses are continually bombarded with stimuli—all potential memories. Fortunately, we do not keep every item on short-term recall. The S-shaped ridge of the brain called the hippocampus (from the Greek for "seahorse," which it resembles) appears to play an important role in registering this sensory data and screening it for discard or storage.

Yet memories can't be said to be "located" in the hippocampus or in any other easy-to-pinpoint part of the brain. Research indicates that they are also stored throughout the cells of the cortex, the mass of wrinkled tissue that forms the surface of the brain, and in the cerebellum, a structure situated beneath the cortex at the rear of the brain, that coordinates movement and balance. Electrical stimulus of specific brain areas can occasionally provoke vivid "you-are-there" memories (childhood scenes, music) almost like switching on a radio. But the exact storage points of more abstract memories (stories, mathematical formulas) have yet to be determined.

Prior to storage, sensory information passes in the form of patterns of electrical impulses into your short-term memory, which processes it for immediate use, then discards or retains it. It allows you to remember a number, for instance, just long enough to make a phone call. If you rehearse it—repeat and memorize it because you know you'll need it again—the number is processed for long-term storage. Memorization and studying are forms of rehearsal, but so are more casual moments when you ponder something you've just read in the newspaper or seen on television. Items that are rehearsed or that carry emotional impact win a secure niche in our long-term memories.

This stored information is received through the interaction of recognition and recall. Both depend on the mind's power to make associations. Recollections of your high-school prom may surge into consciousness unbidden when someone describes the gardenias you wore. Even the scent of gardenias on its own could summon up such memories.

Multiple-choice tests are largely based on the faculty of recognition. Other tests, and daily life, ask for answers to direct questions, answers that depend on the employment of recall, a more conscious scanning of memory files. "Who was in the

White House during the First World War?" "How did you make that delicious stew you served last night?"

If you've trained your memory by developing a solid system for associating one memory with another, the answers may pop into your head immediately. On the other hand, in your search for Woodrow Wilson you may have had to consider and reject Theodore Roosevelt and William Howard Taft. As you go through the list of ingredients for your stew, you might forget to include turnips if you've always relied on a cookbook and have never rehearsed the recipe.

The processes involved in short-term memory and storage and retrieval depend on a chain of electrical, chemical, and physical changes to some of the brain's more than one hundred billion nerve cells, or neurons. Under the stimulus of incoming sensory information, received as electrical impulses, projections called axons (transmitters) and dendrites (receivers) branch out from each neuron to form electrical circuits with neighboring neurons. The axons and dendrites transmit the information they carry through synapses, the junctions between the cells. In addition, chemicals called neurotransmitters are produced at neuron junctions to facilitate the passage of these impulses. They also stimulate an increase in the size of the cell bodies and the number of their smaller dendrites. Training increases the amount of neurotransmitters and synapses. But the impulses rapidly disappear from the neuron circuits unless they are reinforced by repetition or rehearsal.

Memory and aging

Because an aging brain produces smaller amounts of neurotransmitters (and because neurons die), growing older affects our ability to process incoming information rapidly, and in the case of long-term memory, to retrieve the appropriate recollection as quickly as we used to. Our store of memories expands enormously with the passing of time. An obvious example is our vocabulary. At college age most of us have command of twenty thousand words or so; by age sixty our vocabularies have doubled. Access to that stored information remains unblocked. It is the act of remembering—the process of retrieval—that may slow down with age, but the fact is that age usually enhances "intelligence," in part because our store of memories has become so vast.

In terms of short-term memory, some psychologists suggest, however, that we may institute a kind of unconscious screening process as we get older: at fifty or seventy we may discard facts and observations that would have been retained as fresh and new at an impressionable eighteen or twenty-five. Selectivity could be one factor in short-term memory slowdown, but the aging process looms larger. Even so, studies repeatedly show that older people who make a poorer showing than college students on timed tests actually do as well or better than the students when they are allowed to pace themselves. It's not so surprising, given their far larger stores of experience.

Forgetting is not necessarily a sign of senility. According to the National Institute on Aging, senility "is not even a disease," and the term should not be used, as it commonly is, to cover everything from Alzheimer's disease to more widespread and reversible conditions that mimic symptoms of Alzheimer's such as memory loss. Memory problems are eminently treatable when triggered by minor head injuries, high fever, poor nutrition, adverse reactions to medication, or the emotional problems common to old age—depression, loneliness, boredom.

Memory loss in Alzheimer's disease is irreversible, however, though it is benign in the early stages—when victims begin to forget appointments or friends' names. As millions of brain cells die, it worsens inexorably to a malignant state in which sufferers don't even remember that they have friends. While only a small percentage of the population over sixty-five will come down with true Alzheimer's, it is the apparent triviality of those early symptoms that provokes anxiety among the not-so-silent majority of the "normally" forgetful.

It's true that, despite continuing research, the outlook at the moment is bleak for the victims of Alzheimer's and those who care for them. But most people don't get the disease. Indeed, it's reassuring to look at the statistics. It's estimated that only about 7 percent of Americans over sixty-five get Alzheimer's or other degenerative brain diseases. Of those over eighty, one out of every four or five get Alzheimer's or another form of dementia. For the majority of healthy people who, according to one estimate, do suffer a degree of memory loss after the age of sixty-five, the culprit is simply the normal aging process.

The fear of any slowdown as a symptom of degenerative brain disease can often provoke a self-defeating attack of the very forgetfulness we dread. Fortunately, there is little for most of us to worry about, and plenty we can do to improve our memory. Studies have shown that, like physical exercise, we can take steps to train our memories even late in life.

Exercising your memory

Mnemonics, the art of improving short-term recall and ferreting out stored facts, depends on strong visual images and meaningful associations: it's a system for cross-indexing stored information in arresting ways. These methods take only a little time to master. They work because they seize the attention and demand concentration. The more outrageous the connections you set up, the better.

Use "loci" (Latin for "places"). Take a string of facts to be remembered: for instance, points you want to cover in a talk. Match each one to a specific site you can visualize easily—your living room, perhaps, or your street. If you're giving a talk on substance abuse, make a tour of the living room, stationing your introductory remarks on drug cartels on the table left of the fireplace. On the mantel, store what you're planning to say about government policy. To the right of the fireplace, in the bookcase, situate drug education, and beyond that, on the television set, leave your notes on police enforcement—and so forth, around the room. When you give your talk, make another mental tour of the room and "pick up" your notes. Adopt the same loci to something more innocuous, like a grocery list: pasta on the table, tomato sauce on the mantel, salad greens in the bookcase, dressing on the television.

Make up rhymes. Nobody ever forgets the useful "I before E, except after C." But to remember home chores, make up your own rhymes: "Skitty, skat, let in the cat," for instance. The cornier the better.

Compose mental pictures, particularly when you're trying to remember a name: Helen Decker, say, might conjure up a vision of Helen of Troy on shipboard.

Repeat or rehearse new facts. "How do you do, Helen," you say when introduced at a party. A few minutes later you say to yourself, "That's Helen Decker." And a minute or so after that, "Can I get you anything to drink, Helen?" You probably won't forget Helen's name.

Make up acronyms or sentences. "Maple" could help an out-of-towner in New York remember the order of Madison, Park, and Lexington Avenues. "The postman at Sutter's Mill was bushed from pining for California" could help a visitor remember the order of five San Francisco streets, Post, Sutter, Bush, Pine, and California.

Chunk or regroup clusters of data to give them a pattern. Telephone numbers are already partially grouped, but you can give them further meaning. Helen's three-number exchange, 744, is easy to remember, but you won't forget the rest of the number either, 4591, when you reflect that she looks to be about 45, almost halfway to 91.

Write things down. Writing notes and making lists will fix things in your mind. You may not even have to refer to your notes or lists.

Structure your life. The hook for the house keys by the back door is a mnemonic device: you'll always look there first. For example, keep your checkbook in the third drawer of your desk, or park your reading glasses on the night table.

Ease your mind. This advice has less to do with mnemonics than your frame of mind. If you feel you are forgetting too much, consider the following:

•Give yourself time. The sky won't fall in if you forget a name or a number, and if you employ a few delaying tactics (don't rush right up to the friend whose name you've forgotten), the missing data may surface. If they don't, don't make a big fuss over it. Just admit you've forgotten.

•Don't expect too much. If you're nervous about forgetting, you usually do.

•Play games. Crossword puzzles, Scrabble, and card games are all good exercises for improving memory.

•Improve your mind. Going to lectures, taking night classes, and joining groups will introduce new stimuli and keep your neurons transmitting.

Headaches

Headaches are one of the most common human ailments. For most people a headache is merely an infrequent annoyance, a passing discomfort that results from lack of sleep, sitting in a smoky room, or having an argument with someone. With aspirin, rest, and maybe a gentle massage, the pain goes away. But for millions of others the pain does not go away; they suffer from chronic headaches. Americans spend about three hundred million dollars a year on headache remedies, leading researchers to estimate that twelve to twenty million Americans suffer from severe chronic headaches.

There are many different types of headaches. Some more often afflict women, others tend to strike males. Like the common cold, headaches are not completely understood by medical science, and researchers have advanced numerous theories to explain them. Tension, personality traits, heredity, and diet are a few of the factors that may play a role in chronic headaches.

Headaches have been divided into three main types: muscle contraction (or tension); vascular—caused by the constriction or dilation of blood vessels in the brain; and organic headaches that are related to other health problems.

Muscle contraction headaches

Muscle contraction headaches are often called a tension headaches and are usually associated with stress, exhaustion, or repressed anger. These emotional and physical states can cause muscles in the head and neck to contract, putting painful pressure on nerves and blood vessels. Poor sitting posture and bad lighting often lead to headaches at the office. The pain is relatively mild (compared to a migraine or cluster headache) and can be localized in the forehead, the back of the neck, or on the sides of the head. Usually there is a feeling of tightness in the head. The muscles of the head and neck may feel knotted and tender to the touch.

Until recently it was thought that muscle contractions caused 80 to 90 percent of all headaches, but now specialists are not so sure. Researchers have found that some people do not show any abnormal muscle tension in the head and neck during what is presumed to be a tension headache. Muscle contraction does play a role in many headaches, but headaches caused by dilation of blood vessels may be more common than specialists once thought.

Depression headaches. Some people who have daily headaches have been found to be suffering from depression as well. Usually they are muscle contraction headaches. Persistent headaches accompanied by lethargy, insomnia, or suicidal thoughts are signs of clinical depression. Researchers do not understand the connection between depression and headaches, though some have suggested that the depression and the headaches may have a common biochemical cause. In some cases it may be the persistent headaches that cause the depression. And in some cases treating the depression makes the headaches go away.

Vascular headaches

A variety of circumstances that affect blood vessels in the brain can cause headaches. Blood pulsating through the vessels may the basis of the throbbing associated with many headaches. Headaches from hangovers and hunger are due to vascular changes. Certain substances in foods have been shown to trigger headaches in sensitive individuals because they cause blood vessels to dilate or constrict. For example, drinking red wine can cause some people to develop headaches because it contains tyramine, a strong vascular dilator. Tyramine is one of a group of natural substances called amines, which are produced in the body and are present in many foods (see box below). In addition, the very painful migraine, cluster, and probably exertion headaches as well, are vascular in origin.

Migraines. The word migraine, derived from French and Greek, means "half a head"—an apt description of these headaches, which usually attack one side of the head. Migraines often start with a hazy light, called an aura, which may interfere with the vision of one eye. Some sufferers see zig-zag patterns of shooting lights or have a blind spot. Migraines can last up to eighteen hours, with severe pain sometimes accompanied by nausea, blurred vision, and numbness or tingling in the limbs.

Migraines tend to run in families, and 70 percent of the victims are women. Female migraine sufferers often have more frequent and more severe attacks around the time of menstruation, but a decrease during pregnancy and after menopause. Oral contraceptives may also increase the incidence of these headaches.

Migraines may be related to personality traits: sufferers are often perfectionists in their work and personal lives. They are usually careful about their appearance—dressing well and keeping trim—and demand a lot of themselves. Research has found a possible biochemical factor in migraines as well: sufferers often have abnormal levels of brain chemicals that may affect the dilation and contraction of blood vessels.

Cluster headaches. These extremely painful headaches strike in a group: the victim comes down with several headaches a day, for days on end. Sometimes the clusters last for weeks, but there can be months of freedom from them. Cluster headaches are variations of migraines. Most cluster-headache sufferers are men. Heavy drinking and smoking have been implicated as factors contributing to cluster headaches.

Exertion headaches. Some physical activities, including sexual intercourse and strenuous sports, have led to so-called exertion headaches. Football players and joggers are the athletes most frequently struck by them. These attacks are probably vascular, caused by

It may seem that a headache causes your brain to hurt, but actually brain tissue contains no sensory nerves—it's immune to pain.

Tyramine-Containing Foods

Tyramine, a chemical that occurs naturally in many foods, may lead to vascular headaches because it causes your blood vessels to dilate. The evidence is not definitive, but if you suffer from frequent headaches you may want to see if eliminating some of the foods and beverages listed here from your diet makes the headaches stop.

- Alcoholic beverages
- Bananas
- Caffeine-rich drinks
- Canned figs
- Chicken livers
- Chocolate
- Citrus fruits
- Cured cold cuts
- Herring
- Onions
- Peanut butter
- Pork
- Ripe cheese
- Sour cream
- Vinegar
- Yeast products, freshly baked
- Yogurt

the abrupt dilation or constriction of blood vessels, but researchers have not been able to pinpoint the exact cause of the pain. These headaches often hit just after exercise and are so painful that some sufferers have been rushed to emergency rooms. This is a prudent precaution in sports such as football where a head injury is possible. But in almost all cases exertion headaches are neither harmful nor symptomatic of other ailments. With rest the pain goes away.

Organic headaches: headaches as symptoms

The sudden onset of severe headaches in a person who previously had been free of headaches can indicate a serious disorder. The most common disease that causes persistent headaches—often as the only symptom—is high blood pressure. If you suffer from frequent headaches, get your blood pressure checked, especially if you are over forty. A lot of people think first of a brain tumor as an important cause, but that is very rare. Of all the people who seek treatment for headaches, less than one-half of one percent have been found to have a brain tumor.

Eyestrain can cause a headache but it will go away as soon as you rest your eyes. Poor lighting or posture may also lead to a headache.

Sinus headache. The advertising industry virtually invented the notion of sinus headache. Persistent headaches due to chronic sinus problems or allergies are very rare. The congestion and swelling that come with these ailments can touch off a headache, but sinusitis or allergies are almost never the cause of frequent headaches. One sign of a real sinus headache is that it gets worse if you bend over.

Treating headaches with medication

Aspirin, acetaminophen, and ibuprofen are all effective in relieving occasional headache pain, but prolonged use of these drugs for frequent headaches can have bad side effects on the liver and kidneys. Aspirin can irritate the stomach.

Narcotics. Drugs such as codeine, Demerol, and Percodan are stronger pain relievers than aspirin, but these medications don't deal with the origins of the pain and are habit forming.

Mood-altering drugs. For headaches considered to be due to underlying emotional problems, some physicians have prescribed tranquilizers for anxiety and antidepressants for depression. Mood-altering drugs may act by raising the body's pain threshold. However, many doctors are reluctant to prescribe them because of possible side effects and the risk of dependency. Muscle contraction headaches can be alleviated by muscle relaxants, such as Valium, but the use of these drugs can also lead to dependency.

Medication for migraines

For infrequent migraines (one or two a year) a strong analgesic such as codeine or Percodan can help a sufferer sleep until the migraine has run its course. But frequent attacks may call for specialized medicine designed to deal with the mechanisms of the migraine pain. Some drugs used for migraines are:

Inderal. Widely used for high blood pressure and angina, inderal must be taken regularly to prevent migraines. Unfortunately, it can lead to diarrhea, fatigue, and in some cases, impotence.

Ergot and its derivatives. These drugs, which are obtained from a fungus that grows on wheat are used to abort acute attacks by constricting blood vessels. They must be used at the very start of a migraine, otherwise, they're or not effective. Serious side effects—including nausea, vomiting, and gangrene—are possible.

Sansert. This is a substitute for serotonin, a brain chemical that drops sharply at the onset of a migraine. Sansert doesn't stop migraines, but prevents them when taken on a daily basis. It can have a harmful effect on the kidneys and cause scar tissue to develop around the heart and lungs and should not be taken for more than several months without a break.

Nondrug treatments

Because almost all headache drugs have undesirable side effects, and because in some people headaches are a long term problem, many doctors look for nondrug treatments. Although not scientifically established, several measures have been reported to be of value:

•Hot or cold pads placed around the neck or head can help muscle-contraction headaches. Hot baths also soothe contracted muscle. Vascular headache suffers have been able to stop the pain by running cold water over their heads—the cold constricts swollen blood vessels. Migraine victims have also found relief by putting their hands in hot water (but not hot enough to burn), which causes blood to rush to the hands, relieving the blood pressure in the head.

•Massaging tense muscles also brings relief. Gently massage your forehead with your fingertips, moving from the center to the sides, then upward at the side of the head to the hairline. Compress tight neck and shoulder muscles with the thumb and forefinger. If muscles feel knotted, rub them with circular motions.

•Relaxation techniques—exercise, meditation, yoga, and biofeedback—are considered by some to be effective alternatives to drugs. (See pages 406-409 and page 458.)

Sleep

Everyone needs to sleep, and a sound sleep can leave us feeling wonderfully refreshed. For many people, going to bed is among the day's most pleasant experiences. At the same time, there are many others who worry about not getting enough sleep. Yet how much sleep is enough and if not sleeping enough is harmful in any way remains unclear. The truth about sleep's relationship to health has been difficult for scientists to trace: for example, we still do not know why sleep is necessary. However, researchers have uncovered a great deal about what takes place during sleep, what disturbs sleep, and how to improve sleeping habits.

The sleep cycle

A person's sleep alternates through two phases of sleep, which researchers have called REM (Rapid Eye Movement) and non-REM. Non-REM, the first phase, is called "the quiet sleep"—there is a general absence of body movement, brain activity is slow and regular, and the five senses shut down. The non-REM phase moves through four stages as sleep gets progressively deeper and the sleeper becomes more difficult to arouse. The deepest sleep—called delta sleep—appears to be the most restorative stage. People deprived of sleep will spend more time in delta sleep during subsequent nights.

About seventy to ninety minutes after falling asleep, having moved through the non-REM stages, the brain switches into the second phase of sleep, REM. Abruptly the sleeper's eyes begin to dart behind closed lids; heartbeat and metabolism speed up; and breathing gets faster and more irregular, as do the brain waves. Toes and fingers twitch, yet large muscles are practically immobile. And the sleeper dreams, often vividly.

The first episode of REM ends after about ten minutes, completing a sleep cycle of about ninety minutes which will recur four or five times during the night. The first few hours of sleep are dominated by deep sleep, however, in the final sleep cycle, REM can last thirty to forty minutes. An adult who sleeps seven and a half hours will spend one and a half to two hours in REM sleep.

The benefits of sleep

There seems to be little doubt that sleep rests and restores our bodies. Delta sleep is the time for releasing most of our growth hormone, which some researchers credit with the renewal of worn-out tissues. More specifically, researchers at the University of Goteborg in Sweden found that growth hormone enhances bone synthesis, while a study at the University of California School of Medicine linked it to the formation of red blood cells.

The most important benefit of sleep may be that it restores us mentally. Without it our minds seem to suffer more than our bodies. A person kept up twenty-four hours, studies have shown, feels fatigued, his attention wanders, and he has difficulty performing simple routine tasks. The psychological effects are even more dramatic. In a study at the Walter Reed Hospital, volunteers who

Napping for Energy

About half the people in the world take a nap each day—the afternoon siesta is part of life in most tropical and subtropical regions. And in our own society, those who have the time to nap indulge in it: one study of college students found that 55 percent of them nap one or more times a week.

If you want to try renewing your energy and reducing everyday stress by taking a nap, there is sound evidence that the ideal nap time is indeed mid-afternoon, between 2:00 and 3:00 P.M.

•For most of us, the urge to nap strikes in the afternoon. We tend to attribute this drowsiness to eating and digesting lunch, or in warm climates, to the heat of midday. But in fact, our bodies experience a slight drop in temperature—part of our internal biorhythms—that probably promotes sleepiness.

•Afternoons are also optimal because napping early or late in the day can interfere with your nighttime sleep. It's all right to use a nap for catching up on lost sleep—but naps shouldn't become a substitute for sleep.

•Afternoon naps also give you just enough deep sleep to feel refreshed. Morning naps are mainly light sleep, while evening naps put you into an overly sound deep sleep; either way, you end up feeling fatigued or groggy after the nap rather than invigorated.

•Keep your nap under an hour—more than that won't increase the benefits.

---

stayed up beyond sixty hours experienced distortion, mood shifts, headaches, and blurred vision.

Yet in spite of such consequences, the ability to perform complex tasks—such as taking examinations—does not diminish significantly with short-term sleep loss, nor is physiological performance impaired. In an Indiana University study, researchers tested subjects who stayed awake for thirty hours and then exercised. They found that heart rate, oxygen intake, carbon dioxide production, and other measures of physical exertion were not affected by the sleep loss. However, subjects perceived that their exertion was greater after sleep loss than after a period of sleep. Perhaps most remarkable is how efficiently we make up for drastic amounts of lost sleep. Studies have confirmed that, even after being awake for days, most people need only one long night's sleep to recover.

How much sleep do we need?

The notion that we all need eight hours a night—or any other fixed amount—is nonsense. A good night's sleep is whatever allows us to feel refreshed, alert, and in good spirits the next day. And there are wide individual differences in how much sleep people need to achieve that. Some need nine or ten hours, others only six.

But how solidly you sleep is as important as the amount of sleep. Most people feel more rested when they consolidate sleep than when they parcel it out over five or six periods in a day.

Sleep and age

Age is the most important trait affecting sleep. Infants sleep roughly twice as much as adults, slumbering fourteen to eighteen hours a day. After six months, sleep time dwindles and increasingly takes place at night. By age twelve, sleep patterns approximate those of adults.

The next dramatic shift appears in the elderly. In about 80 percent of people over sixty, sleep becomes more fragmented. They tend to wake up more often (and for longer periods) during the night, and earlier in the morning, with generally less

Myth: You yawn to increase oxygen intake.

Fact: Yawning is universal—and oddly contagious—yet nobody is sure why it happens. Some people think it plays some role in stepping up alertness. However, the notion that we yawn to increase oxygen intake has never been proven. In fact, studies have shown that high oxygen levels in the blood do not inhibit yawning.

Both humans and animals yawn, and in humans it appears that situations short on stimuli favor yawning—a long wait, a monotonous job. We are more likely to succumb to a yawn when we're tired or bored.

Researchers have theorized that a yawn may force blood through cerebral blood vessels to increase alertness. At the moment, though, only one thing is certain about its physical benefits: on a plane, a yawn is an excellent way to balance the air pressure between your middle ear and the cabin air during ascent or descent.

Circadian Rhythms

Science has discovered that human beings—indeed all living things on earth—operate according to an inborn circadian (from the Latin words *circa* and *dies,* meaning around the day) rhythm. This inner body clock regulates practically all physiological functions including your hormone levels.

But human beings are out of sync with the turning of the planet: the human internal "day" does not last twenty-four hours, but twenty-five. Experimental subjects confined for several days to a clockless room and given no clues about the actual time of day tend to go to bed an hour later each night and wake up an hour later each morning. That's why it is easier for us to lengthen our days than to shorten them and why we feel all right after a plane flight westward across two or three time zones, but exhausted after flying the same distance eastward. That's also why we happily adapt to a new bedtime in the fall when we switch to standard time and gain an hour, but complain about the springtime switch. This may also help explain why it's hard to get up on Monday morning since on the weekend you may have drifted toward your natural twenty-five hour cycle.

Circadian rhythms and work

These circadian rhythms can have major economic and health consequences. It is estimated that some 27 percent of American working men and 16 percent of working women rotate between day and night shifts. These people work in round-the-clock manufacturing, in the military, on airlines and other forms of transportation, in radio and television, or as health care professionals. According to a study in *The New England Journal of Medicine,* over 80 percent of these people have serious sleep disruption (insomnia at home and sleepiness at work), which lowers their productivity as well as the quality of their lives. The study also cites a higher risk of cardiovascular and digestive tract diseases among these workers.

Adjusting Circadian rhythms

These problems, however, can be alleviated by applying our knowledge of the circadian rhythms. In one experiment at a Utah potash mine and processing plant, workers had been advancing from day to evening to night shifts on a weekly basis, a grueling procedure that would have affected them rather like flying eastward around the world in three hops, departing every Monday. But when they were allowed to stay on one shift for three-week periods and to rotate in the other direction—night to evening to day—their circadian rhythms were disrupted less. Productivity improved and so did health.

Can light help?

Another study has suggested that light affects the inner clock independent of its influence on our sleep/wake patterns. Researchers were repeatedly able to readjust the biological clocks of fourteen men aged eighteen to twenty-four by exposing them to light (equal to sunlight in brightness) for three five-hour sessions at various stages of their circadian cycles over the course of three days. Circadian rhythms were reset by as much as twelve hours, backwards and forwards.

These findings may have practical applications. For instance, after a jet trip across many time zones, or after a sudden change from a daytime to nighttime work shift, it may take as long as nine days for the body to fully readjust. (As a rule of thumb, for each one-hour time zone you cross, it takes roughly one day to recuperate.) But properly timed exposure to bright sunlight and/or artificial light may be able to reset the biological clock much more quickly.

While this research is encouraging, more studies will need to be done before scientists can prescribe specific amounts of light for people with circadian disorders. Meanwhile, after a long jet trip, try to get some sunlight during the first few mornings and afternoons. Just walk around, sit, or even run outside; wearing sunscreen won't cancel out the beneficial effect of the light. If you travel on business and will have to spend all your daylight hours indoors, try to arrive a day early so that you can recover from your flight by getting some light. Despite tiredness or wakefulness, try to go to sleep and awaken at the usual local times.

The average man in his twenties awakens ten times during the night. By the time he reaches forty, the number of wakenings increases to fifteen. By age sixty, it may be as many as twenty-two times. Sleep interruptions among women follow a similar upward curve, though frequency is somewhat less at every age.

deep sleep and more light sleep. Though the amount of time in bed stays fairly constant, sleep time usually lessens—averaging six and a half hours a night.

Though increasingly fragmented and interrupted sleep is normal in older people, in some cases poor sleep results from a sleep disorder. For instance, sleep apnea—a potentially dangerous condition in which you stop breathing temporarily and then snore loudly as you struggle to recover—can prevent restful sleep (see box on page 422). In addition, the elderly consume an abnormally high proportion of sleeping medications—drugs which often do not improve sleep and may be harmful (see box below).

Troubled sleep

The elderly are not the only ones with sleeping problems. According to several national surveys, between 15 and 25 percent of the adult population complain about insomnia—a general term that refers to difficulty falling or staying asleep. In one survey of some seven thousand San Francisco residents, 30 percent across a broad age range reported insomnia-related problems.

Insomnia is not a disorder but a symptom with many causes. For example, temporary insomnia can be caused by jet lag, which upsets the body's biological clock, or by some specific stressful situation like a divorce or change in job. Once these situations have been resolved, sleep returns to normal.

Persistent insomnia is more difficult to diagnose. The Association of Sleep Disorders Centers has suggested causes ranging from psychological and medical conditions to environmental factors like noise and room temperature. There have also been many studies to determine if personality differences make one a good or poor sleeper. Some researchers found that poor sleepers are more anxious, depressed, and introspective, and tend to internalize psychological conflicts. But other studies have found no personality differences between the two groups.

Many experts are convinced that in the majority of cases, the original cause becomes secondary; instead, the insomnia persists because of behavioral factors that reinforce it, such as excessive time in bed, drug dependency, and napping. Also, the harder you try to fall asleep, the more anxious you become, which makes success all the more difficult.

Nightmares are most common among children aged three to seven. But some adults are also prone to them. Researchers have isolated the characteristics of these chronic nightmare sufferers—sensitive, open, and vulnerable. Creative people, who are in touch with imagery and fantasy, seem to have more nightmares than others.

Sleeping Pills

Prescription sleeping pills—which are called hypnotics—are among the most frequently taken drugs in America. Yet rather than aid sleep, they end up disrupting the body's natural sleep cycle. Barbituates, for example, suppress REM sleep—the period when we dream. When drug use stops, REM sleep rebounds, taking up abnormally long portions of sleep time and decreasing the periods of deep, restful sleep. This results in fragmented sleep, disturbing dreams, and daytime fatigue. Similarly, Dalmane, the most widely used hypnotic and the one considered most effective, reduces deep sleep. It also stays in the body for well into the next day, which may result in daytime fatigue.

If hypnotics are taken nightly, their effect diminishes markedly in less than a week. Increasing the dosage only accustoms the body to a higher level of the drug, and increases the side effects and risk of an overdose.

At best a hypnotic should be used occasionally, and never more than three nights in a row. Pregnant women, people with kidney or liver problems, those on medication, and older people (whose systems are more sensitive to the side effects) should not take sleeping pills. Never combine sleeping pills with alcohol.

Snoring

Over one hundred million Americans snore, which can seriously disrupt sleep or annoy a sleeping partner. Snoring occurs mostly during non-REM sleep and is caused by the rattling of the walls of air passages, which can happen when nasal passages dry out or when the sleeper lies on his back. If you are getting a good night's sleep, your snoring is probably harmless. But if it annoys your bedmate, try these techniques to stop it.

•Attach a rolled up sock to the back of your sleepwear to keep you from lying on your back when you sleep.

•Check the bedroom's humidity level. Low humidity dries out mucous membranes, so consider getting a humidifier.

•See a specialist to determine if you have a nasal obstruction, adenoids, a deviated septum, or enlarged tonsils, all of which can cause snoring.

Snorers who are chronically sleepy may have sleep apnea, a potentially dangerous condition that afflicts fifty thousand or more Americans. Sleepers with apnea stop breathing temporarily and snore loudly struggling to recover. New surgical techniques have been used to treat apnea. if you suspect you have it, visit a sleep disorders clinic.

A nightcap might lull you to sleep, but it won't be a sound sleep. Alcohol typically produces light, unsettled sleep, and often the sleeper will suddenly snap awake.

Getting a good night's sleep

Try the following methods to enhance your sleep:

•It is best to avoid overexertion and muscle fatigue immediately before bedtime. Exercise in the afternoon or early evening.

•Don't drink coffee, tea, or colas within two to four hours of bedtime, since they contain caffeine.

•Avoid cigarettes—the nicotine in them is a stimulant. Heavy smokers experience less deep sleep and REM sleep. Similarly, alcohol distorts sleep stages.

•Relax a hour or so before getting in bed; read, listen to music, take a warm bath (not a hot bath, which is actually invigorating).

•Your bedroom should be quiet, dark, and at a moderate temperature—for most people, sixty to sixty-five degrees.

•Get into bed and progressively relax each muscle area, starting at your toes and then traveling slowly up to your head. Or try the old standby, do a repetitive, boring routine, such as counting sheep, which helps you slow down and relax.

•If possible, have sex in the evening before going to sleep.

For those who have difficulty falling asleep:

•Try to establish a regular sleeping schedule, but don't go to bed until you are sleepy. If you can't fall asleep in fifteen to twenty minutes, leave the bedroom and return only when you are sleepy. If possible, do not use the bedroom for anything but sleeping and sex.

•No matter when you go to sleep, get up at the same time—and avoid naps during the day.

•If you have trouble sleeping, cut your time in bed by an hour or more until 90 percent of of it is spent sleeping. Then gradually increase your time in bed by fifteen-minute increments. This technique increases sleep efficiency; you should fall asleep more quickly and sleep more soundly.

•If you suffer from chronic or severe insomnia, you should also visit a doctor or sleep disorders clinic to see if there is an underlying medical condition.

Travel Health

Leisure travel is one of life's greatest pleasures—but only if you stay well. Illness cuts into vacation time, and several large surveys of international travelers have indicated that, depending on destination, 25 to 75 percent of them had one or more symptoms of illness. In a foreign country, not knowing what is safe to eat or drink or where to turn for help with medical problems is especially upsetting. Some health risks may be encountered only in exotic locales, while other problems, such as motion sickness, can occur virtually anywhere. But wherever you wander, the key to a healthy trip is planning ahead.

Coping with flying

As anyone who flies is aware, traveling by jet can be stressful. Conditions on board the plane disrupt your system, as does flying across time zones. The resulting symptoms are such that, after a flight of, say, ten hours, it can take days to recover your sense of well-being.

One potential problem is the cabin atmosphere. While air quality is regulated in airport buildings and ground facilities, federal regulations do not apply to the air in planes—and provisions to ensure air quality can be lacking. According to a report from the National Academy of Sciences, basic design standards for ventilation in airplane cabins are minimal. Allowable levels of carbon monoxide in airplanes are, according to the Academy, much higher than standards for other confined environments. Cabins are tightly sealed, and fresh air is drawn inside and then conditioned by an "environmental control unit"—at great loss in fuel efficiency. Ironically, because of efforts to achieve greater fuel efficiency in aircraft, newer planes are likely to have the worst ventilation, especially wide-body jets. When the plane is on the ground, there is little ventilation; in the air it may not be much better. Moreover, cabin airflow and air quality are seldom measured once the aircraft is in service.

The main contaminant of cabin air is cigarette smoke. According to the Academy's report, the concentration of smokers in airplane cabins and their patterns of smoking result in higher concentrations of cigarette smoke than other public places where smoking is permitted. These concentrations occur all over the cabin, not just in the smoking sections. Fortunately, smoking is now banned on most domestic commercial flights as well as on some international flights, and it is quite possible that, in the near future, all flights will be smoke free.

How can you assure yourself of better air quality in the plane? Ventilation is five times better in first class than in coach, if you can afford the fare. Anywhere you sit, you can ask the flight attendant to ask the captain to increase the airflow. Because maximum ventilation consumes additional fuel, fresh air is expensive; still, the crew can improve air quality to some extent.

In addition to air quality, there are other cabin conditions that can cause discomfort and fatigue, and things you can do to alleviate them:

•Aircraft aren't perfectly pressurized, so the air is thin, like that at about five

Altitude Adjustment

Travelers coming by plane from sea level to such high elevations as Denver, Aspen, Mexico City, or Lake Tahoe may suddenly experience shortness of breath, fatigue, headaches, nausea, and other symptoms resembling flu. This disablement, called Acute Mountain Sickness (AMS), is usually mild and, at levels around 5,000 feet, likely to last only a day or so. As mountain climbers know, it results from a lack of oxygen. Barometric pressure decreases as you go higher—that is, the air gets thinner—and you inhale less oxygen per usual breath. Trying to compensate for this, you breathe more deeply.

Not everyone feels sick at increased altitudes, and there is no way of predicting what a person's highest comfortable altitude is. Being physically fit is not necessarily a protection. Indeed, athletes accustomed to working out daily at low altitudes may be the first to get ill if they continue intense workouts at high altitudes. Susceptibility to AMS is greater in those under forty.

Skiers, hikers, and others who go above 8,000 feet risk getting more severe symptoms of AMS and at higher altitudes may even develop a serious condition known as High-Altitude Pulmonary Edema (HAPE). This life-threatening condition is due to an accumulation of fluids in the lungs. Those afflicted must immediately descend at least 2,000 to 3,000 feet. People with chronic lung or heart ailments should avoid extreme altitudes, and anyone planning to travel to altitudes of 8,000 feet or more should seek medical advice in advance. Acetazolamide, a diuretic, may reduce the incidence and severity of AMS, but this drug is not recommended in place of acclimatization.

If you are going to the Rockies or other mountain regions (see chart below), you can probably avoid high-altitude symptoms—or get rid of them quickly—by simply taking the following precautions:

1. Spend your first day at high altitudes relaxing. Avoid even moderate exercise until you get used to the new heights.

2. Drink extra water and avoid alcoholic beverages. The fast, deep breathing you must do at higher altitudes will tend to dehydrate you—an effect that alcohol intensifies.

3. If your destination is above 8,000 feet, spend a day acclimatizing at a lower level, or climb to a new level at a rate of 500 to 1,000 feet daily with an occasional day of rest.

An Altitude Sampler

Albuquerque, NM	4,950 ft
Denver, CO	5,280 ft
Lake Tahoe, NV	6,200 ft
Aspen, CO	7,930 ft
Yosemite National Park	4,000 to 8,850 ft
Banff, Alberta	4,540 ft
Mexico City	7,440 ft

thousand feet. At that altitude the effect of alcohol is almost twice as great, so have one drink at most. When descending, ease sinus and ear discomfort by pinching your nostrils, closing your mouth, and trying to blow out slowly (a procedure called the Valsalva maneuver).

•Cabin air is much drier than normal air. Relative humidity at flight altitudes falls into the 5-to-10 percent range—a desert climate that can cause dryness of the eyes, mouth, and throat. Consuming fluids will help counteract the dryness, so drink plenty of nonalcoholic fluids, even if you are not thirsty. Also, avoid smoking; it further dries out sinuses and depletes oxygen intake.

•Long periods of sitting can hamper digestion, circulation, and flexibility, and cause feet to swell. To loosen up, walk around the cabin once an hour and do some light stretching.

(For information on airplane safety, see pages 507-508.)

Overcoming jet lag

Fatigue, insomnia, and general malaise are common problems that may affect anyone who crosses more than three time zones in a flight. Jet lag is caused by a disruption of sleep/wake patterns: your biological clock is disrupted. Flying westward lengthens your day, and flying eastward shortens it. Because it compresses the day/night cycle, the eastward flight is most likely to produce jet lag.

•One preventive is to start shifting your sleep/wake cycle to the new time in advance. If traveling east to west, go to bed—and get up—an hour later each day for three days before departure. For a west-to-east trip, move your sleep time an hour earlier each day. If traveling great distances, schedule a stopover if you can.

•Changes in diet may also be helpful. The principle behind the so-called "jet lag diet" is to eat high-protein meals when you are trying to stay awake and high-carbohydrate meals when you want to sleep. A study of U.S. military travelers found that this system alleviated jet lag. Start this diet three days before departure, alternating feast days (high-protein breakfast and lunch, high-carbohydrate dinner) with fast days (salads, soup, fruits in small quantities). If you don't want to upset your dietary habits in this manner, you may do as well by getting plenty of rest before the trip, and by assuming local eating and sleeping times as soon as you arrive.

•Sunlight may help reset your biological clock. Try to spend some time outdoors your first few days after arrival. (See page 420 for more information.)

Individuals vary greatly in how they respond to time changes, and these procedures may not be especially helpful. Thus far, the most reliable aid in adjusting to a new time zone is simply the passage of time.

Traveling abroad

Medical standards and practices can differ in other countries, sometimes dramatically. Before you travel abroad, review your medical records and insurance. If you have not had recent medical or dental checkups, see your doctor and dentist before you leave—particularly before a long trip. Pregnant women, people on prescription medications, those recovering from illnesses, and those with chronic

---

Easing Motion Sickness

In a ship's cabin during rough weather, your eyes may not register much movement, but your inner ear does. Such conflicting sensory input often leads to motion sickness. *Mal de mer*, or seasickness, can strike the traveler by land and by air as well. The principal symptoms are nausea and vomiting, as well as dizziness and a cold sweat. Once you are seasick, there is no relief except getting away from the cause. But if you act in advance, you may be able to prevent it. Experts recommend the following steps:

•Avoid eating heavy meals and drinking alcohol before traveling.

•On a boat or in a car, focus on the horizon or some other fixed point in the distance.

•At sea, stay amidship and topside.

•Small children who get carsick in the back seat may be helped by being elevated on a car seat or cushion (rather than by being moved to the front seat). This will allow them to focus on distant points. Make sure their seat belts are in place.

•If you always suffer from motion sickness, the best plan is to head it off with medication. Some over-the-counter antihistamines (such as Bonine, Marezine, Dramamine, and Benadryl) have been approved by the Food and Drug Administration for motion sickness. Start taking them thirty to sixty minutes before you leave, but remember, they may cause drowsiness. If simple remedies don't help, ask your doctor for a prescription. Scopolamine (sold under the name of Transderm Scop) is highly effective. Administered via a skin patch, which is usually placed behind the ear, scopolamine is not likely to produce any side effects beyond dry mouth.

health problems should discuss their travel needs with a doctor. If it seems likely that you'll need medical attention during your trip, your doctor may wish to give you a letter of explanation. If you do fall ill or have an accident abroad, the nearest U.S. Embassy or Consulate should be able to refer you to reliable medical care.

Carry a written summary of your health history with your passport: an immunization record (the Government Printing Office or local health department can supply a form for this); a list of current medications by brand and generic name; a list of all medical problems; a list of any drug allergies; and your doctor's telephone number. Heart patients should bring a copy of their latest electrocardiogram (ECG). Anyone with serious allergies or special conditions such as epilepsy or diabetes should have a health identification bracelet giving the diagnosis and medical precautions.

You might also wish to find out whether your regular medical insurance will cover illness and hospitalization abroad. Many policies, including Medicare, do not. Blue Cross/Blue Shield is good worldwide, but most hospitals abroad won't bill them: you will have to pay cash and save receipts for reimbursement. If you decide you need additional coverage during a long or hazardous trip, start by consulting the latest edition of *Health Information for International Travel* (available from the Government Printing Office in Washington, DC), an indispensable reference for foreign travel. Credit card companies also offer medical insurance abroad. And for travel information of all kinds, get in touch with the International Association for Medical Assistance to Travelers (IAMAT, in Lewiston, New York). This organization provides a number of excellent traveling aids, including a world immunization chart, world malaria charts, and a world-wide directory of physicians, many of them English-speaking.

Immunization

If you are traveling outside the "developed" world, get proper immunization. Since the risk of disease changes around the world, so do requirements for immunizations. Check with your doctor or local health department, or consult Health Information for International Travel, which annually lists immunization requirements for all countries. You can also check with the Centers for Disease Control in Atlanta, Georgia. Typhoid immunization is not legally required anywhere, but many countries suggest it. Vaccines for cholera and typhoid are not entirely effective, so you should be sure to observe strict sanitary precautions when eating and drinking (see opposite).

Allow six weeks minimum before your trip for immunizations. (If you have to make a trip on short notice, the process can be speeded up, but the risk of unpleasant side effects from the vaccines increases.) Some countries require an "International Certificate of Vaccination" to prove that you have had yellow fever and cholera immunizations (available from the Government Printing Office).

There's no immunization against the types of hepatitis transmitted by food or drink, but a shot of gamma globulin may be useful if you're going to areas with poor sanitation for any length of time. While there is no vaccine against malaria, anyone who might be exposed—the disease now infects parts of about one hundred countries—should start taking chloroquine, the most common antimalarial drug, two weeks before entering a malarial area. In some part of Latin America, East Africa, India, Southeast Asia, and the South Pacific, chloroquine must be

Airline Food Options
Airlines are required to offer special meals. Usually you need only place your order twenty-four hours before your flight. You can often get low-calorie, low-cholesterol, low-sodium, vegetarian, diabetic, kosher, Hindu or Moslem meals—just ask what's available. On some airlines you can get a "healthy heart" meal developed in cooperation with the American Heart Association. It is also perfectly all right to bring your own low-fat meal on the plane; pack it in disposable cartons or plastic bags. And ask the flight attendant for low-fat milk in your coffee. The nondairy powdered creamer routinely handed out has more saturated fat than milk.

supplemented with another drug, Fansidar, because chloroquine-resistant strains of malaria are increasing. A traveler must continue taking the medication for six weeks after leaving an infected region. And wherever you are going, make sure your booster shots are up to date, especially for polio and tetanus.

Unfortunately, no immunization exists against AIDS (see pages 355-361). This disease is not transmitted casually: not by ordinary human contact, by swimming pools, or via food handlers. However, infection may be a risk anywhere hypodermics and other medical equipment are reused without sterilization. To be safe, follow these precautions when traveling:

•Don't get tattooed, have your ears pierced, or undergo acupuncture.

•Avoid injections, immunizations, or vaccinations in underdeveloped regions.

•Except in life-or-death situations, refuse blood transfusions and blood products.

•Wherever you are—here or abroad—remember that casual sex can be dangerous. If you do take a new sexual partner, use all precautions for safer sex.

Food and drink

Water and food are generally safe in most of Europe, Australia, New Zealand, Canada, and Japan. Elsewhere—even in rural areas of southern Europe— haphazard refrigeration and poorly regulated water supplies may expose travelers to parasites and bacteria. Contaminated water and food can cause traveler's diarrhea as well as more serious diseases such as cholera and hepatitis. Take the following precautions when you are in a rural or undeveloped area:

•Don't drink hotel or restaurant water, brush your teeth with it, or eat raw foods that were washed in it. Be prepared to purify water in one of two ways. Boil it for two or three minutes (take along an immersion heater for this purpose). Or, add purifying tablets such as Halzone or iodine to the water. Tincture of iodine can also be used, three drops per quart if water is clear, six drops if cloudy; let water stand thirty minutes before drinking.

•Safe beverages include coffee and tea (provided that the water for them has been boiled), bottled wine and beer, and canned soft drinks. Beware of locally bottled waters, since they may just be unpurified tap water, and bottled soft drinks. Drink only beverages kept in closed containers. Wipe the top well and, if possible, use a straw that has a paper wrapping. Avoid ice cubes as explained at right.

•Since raw vegetables may be contaminated, don't eat them. Vegetables are safe when cooked. Eat fresh fruits only if they are intact, with no breaks in the skin. Wash them with soap and water, rinse them with boiled water if possible, then peel them.

•All meat and fish dishes should be thoroughly cooked and eaten hot to avoid bacteria or other contamination. Unless it is refrigerated, fish should be cooked and eaten within two hours of being caught. Don't eat large predatory fish (sharks and barracuda) or fish liver or roe. Shellfish anywhere in the world may carry hepatitis, so don't eat it raw.

•Be cautious about milk and dairy products. When in doubt, avoid them.

•Don't eat custards, pastries, cold cuts, meat salads, or other perishables that are sold unrefrigerated.

Traveler's diarrhea

Of the millions of Americans who travel to developing countries, one out of three will have to cope with diarrhea—typically two to five loose stools a day, possibly

Drinking Water
"Don't drink the water" is a warning usually heeded by travelers in Mexico and other developing countries. In addition, though, studies suggest that ice cubes made from contaminated water be treated with equal caution. When contaminated cubes are allowed to melt in a variety of liquids—alcoholic and otherwise—enough bacteria survive to cause traveler's diarrhea.

Therefore, it's best to avoid any ice cubes you are offered. If you are making your own ice cubes and safe water is unavailable, boil tap water for two to three minutes.

accompanied by nausea, cramps, and fever. The most frequent cause for this distress are strains of E. coli, an infectious microorganism that is particularly troublesome in Africa, Latin America, the Middle East, Mediterrean countries, and Southeast Asia.

The best way to avoid diarrhea is to be prudent in what you eat and drink, since it is mainly acquired from contaminated food and water. Popular medications—among them Pepto-Bismol and several antibiotics—have been used as preventives, but most physicians advise against using medications before the onset of diarrhea because of the risk of gastrointestinal upset. (Preventive use may be valid in special instances where travelers cannot afford to be sick, such as business meetings or athletic events.) The following steps should help alleviate an attack:

•The most serious consequence of diarrhea is fluid loss. Hence, the best treatment for mild diarrhea is to drink plenty of clear liquids such as tea, fruit juice, and purified water. Do not consume milk or other dairy products.

•In more severe cases (five or more stools a day), try the following rehydration formula prepared by the U.S. Public Health Service. Prepare two glasses of liquids: in the first glass mix eight ounces of fruit juice with one-half teaspoon of honey or sugar and a pinch of salt; in the second glass mix eight ounces of carbonated or purified water with one-half teaspoon of baking soda. Drink alternately from each glass until your thirst is quenched.

•Pepto-Bismol, two ounces taken four times a day, taken with the prescription drug diphenoxylate (Lomotil) may also help. Prior to your departure a doctor can provide you with additional prescription drugs to take in case of severe diarrhea.

•Diarrhea is rarely life-threatening. But if severe diarrhea is accompanied by blood in the stool and fever, it may indicate dysentery—a far more serious bacterial infection that requires immediate medical attention.

Traveling with medications

You'll travel lighter if you pack medications in pill or capsule form rather than as liquids. On any trip, be sure to pack a full supply of any prescription drug you take; abroad, you may not be able to obtain the identical drug. But in case of need, take along an extra prescription. Ask your doctor to print or type it, and to specify brand, as well as the generic and Latin name of the drug. Pack a supply of any contraceptives you may use. A small kit of over-the-counter medications will also be useful, particularly for a long or potentially trying journey. Be sure to include a pain-reliever such as aspirin, an antihistamine, and an anti-diarrheal such as Pepto-Bismol in tablet form. Pack an extra pair of glasses or contact lenses, and if you are traveling far and wide or plan to be away for a long period, take along an extra eyeglass prescription from your optometrist or ophthalmologist.

Pack at least a small supply of needed medications in a carry-on bag; checked luggage may not always arrive when you do. Be sure to take everything in the original pharmacy containers. This may save delay and trouble at customs. To protect pills from breakage, keep (or replace) the wad of cotton in the top. A small medicine cup can be a handy addition to the kit.

Watch where you swim.

In some countries, water for swimming as well as drinking can be hazardous. In Africa, the Philippines, parts of the Caribbean, and much of Asia, freshwater lakes often contain a parasite that penetrates the skin and causes schistosomiasis, a serious worm infestation that is second only to malaria as a worldwide health problem. Since it is difficult to treat, stay out of fresh water in the tropics—don't even wash your face in it—unless it has been purified.

Using the Health Care System

No matter how much attention you pay to your health, there comes a time when you need to seek professional advice. But even at those times, you can still take an active role in your health care by becoming an informed patient. This chapter provides you with information that will enable you to become a working partner with your doctor or other health care professional and help you to understand the various elements of the health care system.

CHOOSING A HEALTH CARE PRACTITIONER

Doctors

Everyone should have a good, reliable doctor for the ordinary medical problems that come up from time to time. Using a specialist such as a gynecologist or a cardiologist for basic medical care is a mistake—and can be costly. Going to an emergency room is also a mistake, since emergency rooms will not have access to your medical records and are, in any case, oriented to handle emergencies, not ordinary medical problems. A primary care physician ought to be competent to recognize and handle the full range of problems that individuals usually encounter, know your medical history, and keep your records on file. For adults, there are three basic types of such physicians to choose from:

General practitioners. At the turn of the century, most doctors were general practitioners—able to deliver a baby, set a broken bone, and even perform surgery. Then the age of specialization hit, and the number of general practitioners (GPs) fell from 112,000 in 1910 to just over 24,000 in 1988. Yet, there are still some general practitioners in business—usually older men who went into practice after only a year of postgraduate training, and who often make up in clinical experience for what they lack in formal education. General practitioners still treat the full range of medical problems, though they usually refer patients to specialists for consultation and sometimes ongoing care for such conditions as heart disease, diabetes, arthritis, asthma, cancer, and most surgical procedures. They are usually associated with community hospitals.

Family practitioners. Because of the decline in the number of general practitioners, the American Medical Association in 1969 recognized family practice as a specialty. To qualify, a physician must complete a three-year residency that covers certain aspects of internal medicine, pediatrics, obstetrics, and orthopedics, and then pass a comprehensive examination. Family practitioners handle a wide range of problems for people of all ages, treating most acute and chronic illness, and even offering psychological counseling for such family problems as alcoholism. For complicated ailments and diseases, they refer individuals to appropriate specialists.

Internists. These doctors specialize in adult medical problems. Internists must take a three-year residency after medical school and pass a rigorous examination to receive specialty certification. They have more advanced training in the diagnosis and management of such common medical problems such as heart disease, diabetes, arthritis, and cancer. Some internists will take further training in one of these or other subspecialities. A general internist may refer a patient to a subspecialist for evaluation, but will usually continue to see the patient for supervision of treatment.

When you need a specialist

Primary care physicians (except GPs) are, in effect, specialists. But since the whole science of medicine has become so complex, many doctors specialize even further. Specialties in medicine can range from the broad—for example, a pediatrician, who

---

Medical Checkups: Your Examination Timetable

The following are general recommendations for screening tests for healthy individuals. Because of your life-style, occupation, or family history some additional tests or more frequent screening may be indicated. Discuss with your doctor a schedule that meets your needs.

Age	Sex	Test	Frequency
18 and over	M/F	Complete physical	Every 1 to 3 years
	M/F	Blood pressure	Every 1 to 3 years
	M/F	Total cholesterol	Every 1 to 3 years
	M/F	Tetanus and diphtheria booster (Td)	Every 10 years
	F	Pelvic exam	Annually
	F	Pap smear[1]	Every 1 to 3 years
	F	Breast exam	Annually
35 and over	M/F	Base-line mammogram	Repeat in 5 years
	F	Kidney function: BUN and creatinine clearance	Every 5 years
40 and over	M/F	Visual acuity, glaucoma	Every 3 years
	M/F	Digital rectal[2]	Annually
	M/F	Hearing test	Every 3 years
	F	Mammogram	Annually
45 and over	M/F	Exercise electrocardiogram (Stress test)	Every 5 years
50 and over	M/F	Base-line sigmoidoscopy	Repeat every 3 years
	M/F	Fecal occult blood	Annually
65 and over	M/F	Visual acuity, with glaucoma	Annually
	M/F	Hearing	Annually
	M/F	Dipstick urinalysis	Annually
	M/F	Influenza vaccine	Annually
	M/F	Pneumococcal vaccine	One time only
	F	Thyroid function tests	Annually

[1]*After a woman between the ages of 18 and 40 has had negative Pap smears for three consecutive years, the test may be performed less frequently at the discretion of her doctor. Starting at age 40, she should have a Pap smear annually.*

[2]*An examination of the lower bowel and, in men, the prostate, in which the physician inserts a gloved finger into the anal opening.*

A Glossary of Specialists

The following are some of the most common types of specialists:

Anesthesiologist. Decides which type of anesthesia will be used, administers it during surgery, and monitors its effects after surgery.

Cardiologist. Specializes in diagnosing and treating abnormalities of the heart and the blood vessels.

Dermatologist. Diagnoses and treats disorders of the skin, hair, and nails.

Emergency medicine specialist. Practices emergency medicine in a trauma center.

Gastroenterologist. Diagnoses and treats disorders of the digestive system and liver.

Geneticist. Specializes in diagnosing and predicting inherited disorders, such as some forms of mental retardation, cystic fibrosis, hemophilia, and many metabolic disorders.

Hematologist. Diagnoses and treats disorders of the blood.

Internist. Specializes in the nonsurgical treatment of adults. Some internists obtain subspecialities, such as cardiology, gastroenterology, hematology, and oncology.

Neurologist. Diagnoses and treats disorders of the brain and nervous system as well as of the muscles.

Neurosurgeon. Specializes in operating on disorders of the brain and the blood vessels that supply it, the spinal cord, and the peripheral nerves.

Obstetrician/gynecologist. Specializes in the treatment of the reproductive systems of women. A gynecologist can treat diseases of the reproductive organs with or without surgery. An obstetrician specializes in the treatment of pregnant women and delivering babies.

Oncologist. Diagnoses and recommends treatment for cancer.

Otorhinolaryngologist. Specializes in the ear, nose, and throat.

Pediatrician. Specializes in treating children and adolescents. Like internists, pediatricians may choose to develop subspecialties, such as pediatric cardiology.

Physiatrist. Specializes in physical medicine and rehabilitation.

Psychiatrist. Treats behavior disorders. Psychiatrists often use psychotherapy in helping patients, but as medical doctors they also are able to prescribe medications.

Radiologist. Administers multiple imaging technology, such as X-rays and ultrasound. A diagnostic radiologist uses radiology to diagnose medical problems. A therapeutic radiologist uses radiation for the treatment of certain forms of cancer.

Surgeon. Specializes in the diagnosis and the surgical treatment of a wide range of diseases. A general surgeon may choose to specialize further, choosing, for example, to be a thoracic and cardiovascular, pediatric, colon and rectal, or plastic surgeon.

Urologist. Diagnoses and treats disorders of the urinary-tract organs, and in men, problems in the reproductive system.

---

treats only children, or an obstetrician, who provides care during pregnancy and delivers babies—to the very narrow, such as a gynecological oncologist, who treats cancers of the female reproductive system. When you have a specific problem or condition that your primary care physician is not equipped to handle, a specialist's experience and knowledge in that area can be invaluable. The most common types of specialists are listed in the box above.

How do you know if you need a specialist? The best way is to ask your primary care physician. If he or she says you have a particular medical problem, ask if there is anyone who specializes in that area, and if you would benefit from consulting with that type of physician. How narrowly specialized the specialist should be depends on the nature of your problem. It's important to remember that many insurance companies will not completely cover the cost of visits to very specialized physicians, which is why it's not a good idea to see a specialist for routine problems. In addition, some carriers require that you get prior authorization before seeing a specialist.

If you have determined that you need to see a specialist, remember that any doctor can legally use the title specialist without having completed any official training or gaining certification from the American Board of Medical Specialties. (Certification guarantees minimum competence, and shows that the physician has had the requisite training.) Therefore, you should ask for a referral from your primary care physician. Other good sources include local hospitals and professional organizations such as the American College of Surgeons. The reference department of a local public library or the library of a large hospital or medical school should have a copy of either the *AMA Directory of Physicians* (which lists all licensed doctors and indicates if they are board certified) or the Marquis *Directory of Medical Specialists* (which lists only board certified physicians).

Selecting a doctor

Whether you're choosing a primary care physician or a specialist, you should do some investigating before selecting one. In making your choice, you will want to consider the following factors:

•The most difficult—and yet most important—task is to make some judgment of a physician's technical abilities. Check educational background and professional associations, including hospital privileges and board certification. Ask friends and other physicians for recommendations.

•Is the physician easily available? If you have an emergency, he or she should be able to make time to see you the day you call, as well as be available to talk to you by phone and return your calls promptly.

•Is the doctor in a solo or group practice? If alone, are there other doctors available who will cover when your doctor is away—and who will have access to your medical records? If in a group practice, does the group represent a range of subspecialists? Do you have confidence in these associates?

•What is the physician's medical philosophy? Does he dismiss all your problems—or prescribe medication every time you have a complaint?

•What kind of payment is required? Do you have to pay the fee directly, or will the doctor's office bill the insurance company or accept Medicare.

•Finally, do you feel you can confide in the doctor completely and can you expect an informed and considered opinion?

Improving communication

Competence, knowledge, and expertise are important qualities in a physician, but the rapport between doctor and patient also plays a crucial role in the quality and effectiveness of treatment. Surveys have indicated that many people are dissatisfied with their physicians, not because they doubt their medical expertise, but because they are unhappy with their "bedside" manner.

The time to establish a relationship with a doctor is before you need treatment. Opening lines of communication with someone you see infrequently and usually only in times of stress isn't easy. Here are some guidelines for getting the most from your visit to the doctor.

Emergency Rooms

In case of accident or sudden illness, most people don't call a doctor. Instead, they head for the nearest emergency room. It makes sense to investigate emergency rooms in your area beforehand, particularly if you have small children in the house or anyone with a chronic condition that might require attention in a hurry. You can't always judge the quality of an emergency room by the reputation of a hospital. A certain hospital in your area may have a good reputation, but it doesn't necessarily follow that its emergency room is the best, since many emergency rooms are operated on a contract basis. Obviously, if there's a fine hospital nearby, you should investigate its emergency services as part of your research. For starters, it's a good idea to ask your doctor and your neighbors about local emergency rooms. You can also write or phone the local health department. And keep the following criteria in mind:

Location. Pick a nearby facility and check how long it takes you to get there by car or taxi. If you are driving, notice where the entrance is and where you can park. Go inside the hospital and look around.

Service. By phone or in person, find out what the hours are, whether there's always a physician on duty, and whether there's a surgical team that could treat severe injuries.

Cost. Are they willing to bill you or do they want immediate payment? Would they bill your insurance company? Would they accept a credit card? Would the physician's bill be included in the emergency room fee, or should you expect a separate charge?

Transportation. In some emergencies (if you or the person you are caring for has chest pain, severe bleeding, or some other condition that rules out driving), you'll need to call your local paramedics, who may not be able to allow you a choice of facilities. You may want to keep the number of a private ambulance service close to your telephone, so that you can be taken to the hospital of your choice. But in any life-threatening situation, you should, of course, go to the nearest hospital. (If you're not satisfied, you can always arrange for a transfer later.)

What is an emergency?

Emergency rooms should not be used for nonemergency situations or in place of routine medical care. In fact, many insurance companies will not pay for nonessential visits to emergency rooms. The following is a list of what doctors generally consider emergencies:

- severe chest pain
- difficulty breathing or shortness of breath
- severe abdominal pain
- slurring or loss of speech
- convulsions
- unconsciousness
- uncontrollable bleeding
- bullet or stab wounds
- broken bones
- head injuries
- eye injuries, sudden loss of vision, or foreign substances in eyes
- poisoning
- drug overdose
- choking
- smoke inhalation
- gaseous fume inhalation
- heat stroke or dehydration
- hypothermia
- temperature over 103 degrees
- prolonged vomiting or diarrhea
- snake or animal bites
- insect stings resulting in shortness of breath

Prepare for your appointment. An analysis by the American Society of Internal Medicine concluded that 70 percent of correct diagnoses depend solely on what you tell your doctor. Be as detailed and specific as possible when describing your condition—jot down your symptoms and concerns if it will help you. If it's your first visit to a doctor, be well versed in your own and your family's medical history. Bring along any medications you are taking, and mention any treatments you are undergoing. Try not to leave anything out; what you think is a minor detail could be important.

Become an educated patient. No question is a dumb question. You are entitled to a diagnosis given in terms you understand. You should also get a full explanation of treatments, expected outcomes, as well as the risks and benefits of the various alternatives. Your doctor should encourage you to make an informed decision about your treatment. If you want details about your condition, ask the doctor to recommend reading material. If there is a medical school nearby, you can do research in their library.

Take part in your own health care. Your doctor's advice can only help if you follow it. Listen attentively to instructions and ask when would be the best time to call if you have additional questions. If lab tests or X-rays are required, have them done promptly, and be sure the doctor reports the results to you—by telephone, mail, or in person.

Be flexible. If you have tried to make the relationship work but still feel uncomfortable, it may be time to find an other doctor. Make sure your records, including X-rays and lab work, are forwarded to your new doctor. Don't stay with a doctor just to protect his or her feelings, or because you were referred to the doctor and think you can't make the decision to switch on your own.

When to seek a second opinion

It's common for patients facing surgery to seek a second opinion. Many insurance plans now require you to get a confirming opinion before some kinds of elective surgery—for example, surgical repair of a hernia or removal of tonsils, uterus, gallbladder, or enlarged prostate. Medicare and Medicaid may require a confirming opinion, too.

There are many strong arguments for seeking a second opinion. Even though the second surgeon may only confirm the opinion of the first one, the patient can benefit. Sometimes it's the only way a person can be reconciled to having surgery. And someone who is more confident that the procedure he's undergoing is the right one will be a better patient and more likely to comply with instructions. Finally, although it may be rare for the second surgeon to disagree with the first, it does happen, and thus some unnecessary surgery can be avoided. If this occurs, you'll be happy you took that extra step. Keep these pointers in mind:

•Consultation has always been part of good medical practice, and no competent doctor should be insulted if you decide to get a second opinion, even if your insurance company does not require you to do so. Be tactful about it, however.

•Seek out the most highly qualified consultant available. At the very least, make sure that the second physician has been certified by the American Board of Medical Specialties. If you are uncomfortable with asking direct questions about a doctor's qualifications when you make the appointment, ask your family doctor, a local medical society, or the surgical department of your nearest medical school.

•A consultation allows you to compare medical opinions about how an operation will affect the quality of your life, the risks involved, and which treatments might be available. It gives you a chance to ask additional questions that might occur to you. Perhaps the most important reason to seek a second opinion is that it puts the final decision in your hands.

Midwives

Most pregnant women are at low risk for complications during childbirth: for them, a birth is not a cause for medical intervention. For such women, there's an alternative to relying solely on an obstetrician: the certified nurse-midwife. Midwifery, the art of assisting at childbirth, is an ancient practice that has seen a revival. Qualified nurse-midwives (they may be women or men) are always registered nurses and must have advanced training in midwifery as well. They work as colleagues of an obstetrician and offer up-to-date prenatal care as well as attended childbirth in a relaxed setting that will appeal to many prospective mothers and fathers. In addition, because nurse-midwives use fewer hospital facilities and charge less money than doctors, their bills will run 30 to 40 percent less than standard obstetrical care.

About 85 percent of nurse-midwives currently practice in hospitals and 11 percent in independent birthing centers, with ready and quick access to nearby hospitals should an emergency arise. In either setting, nurse-midwives usually work in birthing rooms, which are combined labor and delivery rooms that make moving from one room to another unnecessary. A nurse-midwife stays at the mother's side during labor and may encourage the mother to walk around, sit, stand, curl up, or otherwise make herself comfortable. The rooms are usually furnished to create a pleasant, homelike atmosphere, and family members are usually encouraged to be present. If labor proceeds normally, the woman may be able to avoid electronic fetal monitoring and other high-tech procedures, as well as anesthesia.

Nurse-midwives are licensed by state boards of nursing or medicine; many states require certification by the American College of Nurse-Midwives.

If the idea of a nurse-midwife appeals to you, remember the following:

•Make arrangements with the person you select as early in your pregnancy as possible. Choose one who has been licensed by your state and certified by the American College of Nurse-Midwives.

•Choose a person with whom you feel comfortable. The nurse-midwife will supervise your prenatal care as well as your labor. Choose someone with whom you are able to talk freely, who is able to answer any questions you may have, and can address your special needs.

•Find out what the backup system is in case you need medical help at any time during pregnancy or childbirth. Where would you be taken and who would take charge if an emergency should arise? If you should need pain relief, will it be available? Which kind would it be? Be sure to meet the obstetrician who will be on call.

•If you want to give birth in a hospital rather than in a birthing center, choose a nurse-midwife who practices in one. If you prefer a birthing center, that's fine, but be sure it has hospital access.

•Although nurse-midwives have become popular (and deservedly so) in many areas, don't feel pressured to use one if you'd really prefer an obstetrician and a regular hospital delivery room. The point is to feel confident about the kind of care you choose.

Nutritionists

Chances are, you don't need a nutritionist. Still, if you are overweight and unable to lose pounds on your own, or if you have some medical problem—such as diabetes, elevated cholesterol, hypertension, or a high-risk pregnancy—requiring a special diet, your physician may suggest that you get a specialist to design a diet for you.

Since there is no licensing requirement, anyone can hang out a sign saying "nutritionist." Thus, it pays to choose carefully. Ask for a referral from your doctor, the dietician at a local hospital, the department of nutrition at the nearest university, your local health department, local chapters of the American Heart Association or the American Cancer Society, or your state dietetic association.

The nutritionist to whom you will be referred will probably have "R.D." after his or her name—identifying a registered dietician, certified by the American Dietetic Association—although many competent nutritionists are not registered. A registered dietician has at least a bachelor's degree in nutrition or a related science, has done an internship at a hospital or other professional setting and has passed a comprehensive examination. He or she is likely to be a member of the American Dietetic Association; nutritionists who are PhDs or MDs may also be members of other professional groups, such as the American Society of Clinical Nutrition, the American Institute of Nutrition, and the Society for Nutrition Education.

A nutritionist should review your medical history provided by your doctor (with your written permission), and consult with you about your food preferences, level of physical activity, and general life style. He or she will help you translate basic nutritional advice into customized menus and provide follow-up support to make any needed adjustments in your diet. This could involve as few as two visits; fees vary depending on the area of the country and whether a computer-based dietary analysis is used.

When consulting with a nutritionist, be wary of anyone whose dietary recommendations lean heavily on "special" foods or megadoses of vitamins or minerals, unless it has been medically established that you have a deficiency. Don't trust a nutritionist who guarantees results or who recommends hair, nail, or saliva analysis—procedures for which there is no proven merit.

Pharmacists

Drugstores no longer double as social centers and ice cream parlors, and friendly pharmacists may seem to be an endangered species. But if you need prescriptions fairly often, try to have one pharmacist fill them all. A good pharmacist should get to know you. A conscientious pharmacist will keep your "drug profile" on record: a confidential rundown of medications prescribed, food and drug allergies, and your doctor's name and address. If you're seeing more than one doctor, the pharmacist can spot drug incompatibilities that they, or you, may not be aware of. Even if you're only buying aspirin, you may need expert advice.

Shop for a pharmacist who's willing to keep records for you and also is available—not only for filling prescriptions but for answering questions. Suppose you didn't quite understand what your doctor said. Are you sure you know whether to take the drug before, with, or after meals? If you miss a dose, is it advisable to take two the next time? Should you take all the medication, or quit when you feel better? Your pharmacist may know the answers to the questions, or at least be willing to telephone your doctor to find out.

Keep the following points in mind:

Professional qualifications. Pharmacists must be registered with the state pharmaceutical board; a certificate should be prominently displayed.

Generic drugs. These can often be substituted effectively for brand-name products and will usually cost less. Your pharmacist should stock them and be willing to use them. (Laws on generics vary from state to state. First, ask your doctor about using them.)

Customer services. Find out whether your pharmacist offers such conveniences as charge accounts, home delivery, and yearly statements for tax and insurance purposes, and whether these cost extra. Some drugstores offer discounts to senior citizens and other groups.

Emergency services. A phone number for after-hours and weekend emergency service should be displayed.

Packaging. Lots of adults can't deal with child-proof containers; don't be shy about asking for a different kind of cap, as long as there are no children in your home. If the print on the label is hard to read, say so. A good pharmacist will package the prescription to suit you—for example, by providing different-colored containers for multiple medications so that you don't confuse them.

Health aids. If the store stocks such items as crutches or braces, the pharmacist should be qualified to give advice on their use and fitting.

Even at a large chain or discount drugstore, it's worthwhile getting acquainted with the pharmacist. Find somebody with the time to get to know you. Relaxed, informed advice can save time, complications, money, and possibly even your life.

COMMON DIAGNOSTIC TESTS

Although many people think of diagnostic tests being performed only when there is a suspicion that something is wrong, many of them are conducted as part of a physical exam or as screening procedures. The tests that are listed below may be done on healthy individuals as part of routine examinations.

Blood Chemistry Tests

The following tests are conducted to determine the levels of circulating chemicals in your blood to detect whether you have higher or lower levels of substances normally present. They are simple procedures done in a doctor's office that involve drawing blood either from a vein or by a finger or ear-lobe prick. Although you can have each test performed individually, the tests listed below are often done in panels—a group of different tests taken from one sample of blood—because it is generally less expensive than conducting each test separately.

Blood glucose. Blood glucose tests determine the amount of glucose, or sugar, in the blood, which can help a physician diagnose diabetes or hypoglycemia (low blood sugar). It is usually performed if an individual experiences any symptoms of diabetes (such as excessive thirst or urination), hypoglycemia (such as light-headedness or unexplained loss of consciousness), or it may be part of a routine physical exam. Blood glucose tests are also performed by diabetics themselves to test the effect of their treatment. Generally, the blood is drawn in the morning after a twelve- to fourteen-hour fast to determine the basal levels—that is, those not influenced by food or activity.

If the results show that a blood sugar level is abnormal, a more extensive test called a glucose tolerance test may be performed. This determines the cause of high or low blood sugar and also offers insight into how the body deals with an overload of sugar. The individual being tested eats a high carbohydrate diet for several days, and then drinks a concentrated sugar solution before the test. Blood glucose levels are then measured at regular intervals over the next several hours.

Blood creatinine. This test measures kidney function. Creatinine is a waste product of muscle metabolism; kidneys that are working properly adequately filter creatinine from the blood. A high level may indicate kidney damage.

Blood urea nitrogen (BUN). This is another test to evaluate kidney function. Blood urea is an end product of protein metabolism. An excess amount in the blood may

Assessing Test Laboratories

The labs that your doctor sends your tests to should either be accredited or licensed. The difference between the two categories is that accreditation is voluntary whereas licensing is mandatory, although the requirements may vary from state to state.

Accreditation. A lab that wants a professional society's seal of approval must have certain prescribed personnel on staff and must pass whatever tests and inspections the organization specifies. But this can be an expensive process, and many labs may not be able to qualify. This does not mean, however, that the lab is not reliable.

Licensing. Most states usually call for proficiency tests and conduct on-site inspections. In addition, the Clinical Laboratories Improvement Act passed by Congress in 1967 provides that any lab receiving samples of biological material from out of state must be licensed by the Department of Health and Human Services. Such licensing requires a quality control program and Centers for Disease Control proficiency testing. Amendments to this act—to be implemented over the early 1990s—require labs to be federally certified, either directly by the Department of Health and Human Services or by approved accrediting agencies except in states where licensing laws are at least as stringent. In a state with strict licensing requirements, accreditation may not matter. California, Connecticut, Florida, Illinois, Maryland, New York, and Pennsylvania are all known as stringent states, but this does not mean that labs in other states are inferior.

Does licensing then assure you of accurate test results? Licensing and/or accreditation means that the lab may be doing high-quality work, but there are no guarantees. And even though the new laws—once they are in

widespread practice—should markedly improve the quality of laboratory procedures, at least in the mean time, you still may want to consider the following:

•Talk first to your doctor or the health practitioner doing the test. Ask if the lab is licensed by the state or the Department of Health and Human Services, and if it is accredited. It's likely that the doctor knows about the lab's quality control program and the results of the lab's proficiency tests.

•Lab work done in the doctor's office on his own patients does not have to be licensed. Studies have generally shown that the results of such tests aren't as accurate as those of licensed labs.

•You might also ask whether the lab ever returns specimens as being inadequate. Well-run labs will occasionally ask for a redo. Lab work can be only as good as the specimen sent out.

•Ask your doctor about previous experiences with the lab. Some doctors will test labs by dividing a sample in two and sending them off under different names. If the results are significantly different, a doctor will know that the lab isn't accurate or well controlled. Or the batches can be sent to different labs and then the results compared.

•Check with your state health department for information about licensed labs.

•If you are especially concerned you can contact the lab directly. Large ones publish their credentials and are willing to supply the results of proficiency tests and to provide tours—but usually only to physicians and hospital representatives.

•There isn't necessarily anything suspicious about a physician sending a sample to an out-of-state lab. Some complicated tests can be done only by specialized labs.

indicate kidney disease, impaired kidney function, or a very high protein intake.

Blood electrolytes. A test for blood electrolytes—sodium, potassium, chloride, and bicarbonate—is not usually ordered individually unless there is an indication of an electrolyte problem, such as water retention or weakness. In addition, tests for blood electrolytes are routinely performed in diabetics or individuals who have a history of heart, liver, or kidney disease, since these conditions can lead to electrolyte imbalances. This test may also be performed if a person is taking diuretics or experiencing such symptoms as dehydration or excessive vomiting or diarrhea that may deplete the body of electrolytes. (*Text continued on page 442.*)

Although many diagnostic tests are performed in a doctor's office, there are examinations that you can do at home to check for cancer. In fact, individuals—not doctors—more often find their own cancers. Therefore, regular self-examination is one of the best preventive measures you can take to significantly increase your chances of detecting cancer at an early stage. Below, are instructions for the most common self-exams.

Breast Exam

One out of every eleven women will get breast cancer in her life—it's the second leading cause of death in women after lung cancer, and it kills more women in their forties than any other illness. But if breast cancer is diagnosed early enough, women have a much greater chance of recovery.

Since 90 percent of all breast tumors are discovered by women themselves, it's a good idea to develop the habit of examining your breasts. The key is being able to detect changes in your breasts. Regular examination is necessary to familiarize yourself with what your breasts are normally like.

Monthly exams are recommended; any more often can be confusing, since your breasts change throughout the month. Do the exam at the same time each month—within a week after your menstrual period, since that is the time when breast swelling is at a minimum. Follow these steps:

1. Begin with a visual exam. Stand in front of the mirror with your arms at your sides. Familiarize yourself with the appearance of your breasts and nipples, including their shape, texture, and any normal asymmetry. Lean over to see breast contour in that position. After learning what's usual for you, look for any of these changes: bulging or flattening in one breast but not the other; puckering or redness of the skin; or reddening, crustiness, or unusual hardening or inversion of the nipples.

2. Raise your arms over your head and check for the same signs. Inspect your breasts while pressing your palms together over your head, and then again with your hands on your hips. Both of these positions contract chest muscles and may make it easier to spot any changes in your breasts.

3. Gently squeeze each nipple to check for any blood-tinged discharge.

4. The next part of the exam—feeling, or "palpation"—can be done while lying down, or in the shower or bath. Water and soap make it easier to slide your fingers over your breasts, but to examine the lower half of them, you should be lying flat. Lie down on your back with your right hand under your head. You can put a small pillow under your shoulder to help flatten your breast against your chest. Using the flat part of the fingers of your left hand, start pressing the right breast lightly against the rib cage. Begin at the outside edge of the breast, and rotate in a spiral toward the nipple, without lifting your fingers, until you have covered the entire area of the breast.

5. Then move your arm down to your side and feel the upper and inner part of your armpit, the area between your armpit and your nipple, and finally between the outer lower part of your breast and the nipple.

6. Repeat these steps for your other breast, using the opposite hand to examine it.

7. Expect to feel many normal lumps and textures; try to get to know these so you can detect changes, such as thickening or hardening of tissue, or pea- to grape-sized lumps. At first, you may want to make a chart recording where normal gland tissue is found. Any changes should be reported to your doctor, but they don't necessarily mean you have breast cancer. Studies indicate that 80 to 90 percent of all breast lumps are benign.

Keep in mind that self-exams are not a substitute for regular examinations by your physician and mammograms (breast X-rays). Mammograms are still the most effective method for early breast cancer detection. The American Cancer Society recommends a mammogram when a woman reaches thirty-five, then repeated mammograms as needed, depending on such risk factors as family history, until age fifty, when they should be performed annually.

Men can get breast cancer, too. Although they get it much less frequently than women, it's fatal more often, since it's not usually detected until it's in an advanced stage. It's a good idea for men to examine themselves occasionally, too.

Testicular Exam

This type of cancer is rare, accounting for only one percent of all cancers, but because the early symptoms of testicular cancer often go undetected, 88 percent of all cases have spread by the time they are diagnosed. Although it can strike at any age, it is one of the most common forms of cancer in young men; in fact, it's the leading form of cancer in men between the ages of twenty-nine and thirty-five. Fortunately, the survival rate approaches 100 percent if the cancer is detected early enough. Otherwise, the survival rate drops dramatically.

A monthly self-exam is the best way to detect it in its earliest stages. After a warm bath or shower, when the scrotal skin is relaxed, gently roll each testicle between the thumb and fingers of both hands. Make sure you cover the entire area of each testicle. Feel for lumps, nodules, swelling, or a change in consistency. Be sure to examine the ropelike part called the epididymis.

Each man is different and it may take a few examinations to know what is normal for you, but if you feel anything unusual, consult your physician right away—even though the odds are that it's not cancer. Symptoms of testicular cancer include a slight enlargement of one of the testes and a change in its consistency. There may be no pain, but often there's a dull ache in the lower abdomen and groin area.

There is evidence that men with an undescended or partially undescended testicle have a greater risk of testicular cancer. Normally, the testes descend soon after birth; male infants should be checked to make sure the testes have descended properly. An undescended testicle is easily corrected; boys or men with this condition should be checked by a physician.

Skin Exam

Skin cancer is one of the most prevalent forms of cancer. Fortunately, it's also one of the easiest types to detect and treat. Examining your skin is primarily up to you, since most doctors do not perform an overall check of their patients' skin on a regular basis. A skin exam is a simple process that should take no more than fifteen minutes, and should be performed monthly.

When you examine your skin, you are looking for any change from what's normal for you. Spend some time looking at your skin, noticing where you have moles or birthmarks and the color, shape, and size of them. Then each month, perform the following steps:

1. Undress completely, and look at yourself in a full-length mirror in a well-lit room. Scan your skin overall (have a hand mirror handy to check places you can't easily see; you may also wish to have a friend or spouse help you examine these areas). Look for any changes in color, size, or shape of moles and birthmarks, or the appearance of new ones; any rough or waxy-looking patches; or any sores or scabs that are crusting, oozing, or bleeding or have not healed within a week or two. Pay special attention to areas where you have been sunburned in the past.

2. Begin a head-to-toe examination of your skin. Run your fingers over your scalp feeling for any bumps or rough or scaly spots. Lift your hair and visually examine the skin underneath. Pay special attention to bald spots.

3. Closely examine your face and the front of your neck in the mirror. Be sure to check your ears and the skin underneath your jaw line and chin. Men with facial hair should be sure to check the skin underneath. These areas are very susceptible to damage from the sun.

4. Look at your hands and arms, turning them over so that you can examine ever side. Look for dark spots under your fingernails, which may be an early sign of melanoma. Run your hands across your arms and shoulders to feel for any rough spots you cannot see. These are also high-risk areas.

5. Use a hand mirror to examine the back of your neck and shoulders, also areas that are susceptible to sun damage.

6. Examine your back, buttocks, and the backs of your legs with a hand mirror.

7. Examine your chest and your abdomen in the mirror.

8. Look carefully at the fronts of your thighs, legs, and feet. Be sure to check the bottoms of your feet and between your toes. As with your fingernails, check for dark spots under your toenails.

(For more information on skin cancer, see page 282-283.)

Complete Blood Count

A complete blood count is safe, inexpensive, and practically painless, and it probably provides you with more information than any other single laboratory screening procedure. Less than two teaspoons of blood are necessary for a complete blood count. Although the blood sample is analyzed in a number of ways, four measurements—hemoglobin concentration, red blood cell count, hematocrit, and white blood cell count—are the most important ones. Here is the information each of these tests reveals to a physician.

Hemoglobin concentration. Hemoglobin is the chemical substance that transports oxygen through the bloodstream to all the cells of the body. It imparts the red color to blood and is normally contained within the red blood cells. This measurement determines the level of hemoglobin per unit of blood.

Red blood cell count. The primary function of red blood cells is to carry oxygen to all parts of the body. The presence of too few red blood cells often indicates simple anemia, usually the result of a diet deficient in iron. But it may also be an early clue to a more serious problem such as leukemia, kidney malfunction, internal bleeding, or inherited forms of anemia such as sickle cell anemia. Too many red blood cells may indicate that the body is having a difficult time supplying itself with oxygen and is an early clue to the existence of congenital heart disease, respiratory disease, or polycythemia vera, a disease in which there is an overproduction of red blood cells.

Hematocrit. The hematocrit essentially measures the ratio of red blood cells to plasma in the blood. It is also a sensitive indicator of the blood's capacity to carry oxygen to various parts of the body. Abnormal hematocrit readings indicate the presence of the same disease that abnormal red blood cell levels do. Although hemoglobin, hematocrit, and red blood cell counts all give similar information, and any one may be used to determine anemia, the combination of all three measurements aid in diagnosing the specific type or cause of anemia, if it exists.

White blood cell count. White blood cells are the body's primary defense against disease, so their presence or sparsity tells a great deal about health. An elevated white blood cell count indicates the presence of an infection, stress, a major injury, or even leukemia. A depressed level may be a sign of poor diet, certain infections (especially viruses) that have begun to overwhelm the body's defenses, or a failure of the body to produce enough white blood cells (another type of leukemia).

White blood cells are analyzed in two ways: one method is to count the total number present in a given amount of blood; the other is to look at the percentage of different kinds of white blood cells. An increased number of the kind that kill disease-causing organisms can indicate an infection. A greater than normal number of monocytes could suggest the presence of a chronic disease such as arthritis.

Electrocardiogram

The electrocardiogram (also known as an ECG or EKG) is a diagnostic tool that measures heart activity by detecting electric current flowing in the heart. The procedure is simple, safe, and takes five to ten minutes to perform. Ordinarily, you receive a resting ECG: you lie on your back, and your doctor or a technician places metal sensors at your wrists, ankles, and various parts of the chest. The sensors detect the heart's electric impulses, which are recorded as tracings on strips of special graph paper. There is no discomfort, since the current is always coming only from the patient.

A normally beating heart produces basically the same pattern of waves in all people. Variations from this pattern can indicate a number of potential problems: dysrhythmias (irregular heart rhythms), which may or may not be a sign of heart disease; damage to the heart muscle; enlargement of the heart's chambers; mineral imbalances in the blood; and whether the patient has had, or is having, a heart attack. For most people with signs of heart disease, an ECG can help reveal the source of trouble.

However, the electrocardiogram is far from perfect. Some people with normal ECGs have heart trouble, and the graph may also show abnormalities where none exist. The resting ECG doesn't necessarily reveal atherosclerosis—the buildup of fat in artery walls that causes blocked or narrowed coronary arteries—because the heart at rest is receiving enough oxygen. For this reason your physician may want to evaluate the status of your heart vessels with a stress ECG, which is taken while you are exercising on a treadmill or stationary bicycle. (For more information on stress ECGs, see pages 447- 448.)

ECGs are usually a routine part of a physical checkup after age forty; before forty, have at least one ECG to use for later comparison.

Mammogram

Mammograms, which are X-rays of the breast done to detect breast cancer, are one of the most valuable diagnostic tests available. It is estimated that yearly mammograms for women over fifty could lead to a one-third reduction in the number of deaths from breast cancer. This procedure is a highly reliable way to detect breast cancer in its earliest, most treatable stage—long before tumors can be felt during a clinical breast examination. Yet only 15 to 20 percent of women over fifty have annual mammograms.

The American Cancer Society recommends the following mammogram schedule for woman:

• Have a single base-line mammogram (for later comparison) between ages thirty-five and forty.

• Between ages forty and forty-nine, have a screening mammogram every one to two years.

• After age fifty, have a screening mammogram once a year.

• Don't stop having mammograms after age sixty-five. Although the risk of breast cancer decreases with age, approximately 45 percent of all breast cancer cases occur in women over sixty-five. Therefore, regular screening is valuable at least through age seventy-five.

Of course, at any age, if you have a personal or family history of breast cancer, you should consult your physician about the need for more frequent mammograms.

Getting an accurate mammogram requires a trained X-ray technician and equipment designed specifically for mammograms. There are two methods: film

Should you be concerned about extra heartbeats?
Perhaps as many as 75 percent of us experience occasional extra heartbeats, which usually go undetected but sometimes are felt as a brief flutter in the chest. They may also show up on ECGs, and the discovery often causes the patient alarm, even though the physician may say that nothing is wrong.

One group of scientists studied extra heartbeats—"ectopic beats," as they are called—in seventy-three people in good health without symptoms of heart disease. The subjects experienced anywhere from seventy-eight extra heartbeats per hour to a high of almost two thousand. However, not one of these people developed heart disease, and the group had a lower mortality rate than the general population. It's worth getting a checkup if you begin to feel extra beats, but if your physician tells you not to worry about it, take the advice.

and xero-mammography, both of which are equally accurate. A breast compression device—trays that hold the breasts and compress them for one second—is crucial: if the technician does not use compression, the mammogram will be inaccurate. Ultrasound scans are an adjunct to mammography; they can help to refine a diagnosis in some cases. But ultrasound is not a substitute for mammography.

Occult Blood Test

Colon cancer is the second most common form of cancer in the United States; it kills more people each year than automobile accidents. And yet, the American Cancer Society estimates that fully three-quarters of all colon cancer patients could be saved by early diagnosis and treatment.

Early diagnosis of colon cancer requires discovering occult or "hidden" blood in the stool—that is, the merest trace of blood, which shows up in the earliest stages of the disorder. Since diagnosis requires examining a stool sample, and many people find it embarrassing or unpleasant to bring one to a doctor, many simply avoid being tested. Yet everyone over age fifty—certainly anyone whose family has a history of colon cancer—should be tested every year.

The proper test requires taking a sample from three consecutive stools, which are tested for blood quickly and easily. Before collecting the samples a person must avoid eating red meat, turnips, horseradish, and high doses of vitamin C, while consuming more fruits, vegetables, and fibrous foods beginning three days before the first test and until the last sample is taken.

The key ingredient of the most common type of test is guaiac, a chemical substance that turns bluish in the presence of blood. The stool sample is placed on slides, and if the slide turns blue when processed, the test is positive, indicating blood in the stool. If blood is found, the doctor will call for further testing to determine the cause.

Guaiac tests are also available for home use. These have been approved by the Food and Drug Administration and are based on the same principles as the doctor's exam. But some experts fear that the untrained may not recognize the presence of blood. If you are particularly squeamish about taking samples to a doctor, these home kits are certainly an option, but don't hesitate to be retested by a doctor if there is any question in your mind about the results.

While guaiac tests are frequently reliable, studies have shown that for about one-third of patients with colon cancer, the tests fail to detect the disease. There are several reasons for this: some cancers bleed only intermittently; the presence of vitamin C or other compounds contained in the foods to be avoided appears to interfere with the reaction of blood and guaiac; and intestinal bacteria can alter the blood so that it doesn't react with guaiac. The test can also be positive for patients who do not have colon cancer, either because of intestinal bleeding from other causes—such as noncancerous polyps, duodenal ulcers, colitis, diverticulosis, or hemorrhoids—or because the patients have ingested something, such as red meat, that contains traces of blood.

However, another type of test for occult blood called HemoQuant may be able to detect hidden blood even after bacteria have altered it, which means it may be better at detecting hard-to-find colon cancers. This test is also able to register smaller levels of blood more exactly and seems to be less influenced by substances that cause guaiac tests to yield false results. You should discuss with your doctor which test is right for you, or whether both should be used together.

Still, no test is 100 percent reliable. Even if nothing is wrong, be on the lookout for these other signs of colon cancer:
- unexplained weakness, fatigue, paleness, or fainting;
- diarrhea or constipation lasting more than two weeks;
- unexplained weight loss lasting more than two weeks.

Pap Smear

The Pap smear was developed by Dr. George Papanicolaou in the 1940s as a screening device to detect cervical cancer. About 2 percent of all women over forty will develop cervical cancer, but 95 percent of these can be cured if the cancer is detected early.

A Pap smear consists of cells obtained from the vaginal walls and the cervix that are placed on a slide and examined under a microscope for abnormalities. Since the Pap smear was developed, the death rate from cervical cancer has steadily decreased. And among women who have regular Pap smears, the death rate is almost zero. This is because cervical cancer generally develops far more slowly than most other cancers, progressing through a long "pre-invasive" stage, during which it grows but does not invade healthy tissue. This stage typically lasts ten to fifteen years—and if the cancer is detected during this period, it can often be completely cured with relatively simple surgery.

How often should you be tested?
Because cervical cancer takes a long time to develop to the invasive stage, experts have argued about how often a woman should have a Pap smear. In 1980, the American Cancer Society decided that annual screenings aren't really necessary in most cases, and women whose Pap smears had been normal for two consecutive years could drop to three-year intervals. However, the American College of Obstetricians and Gynecologists (ACOG) disagreed, continuing to recommend an annual Pap smear for women between the ages of twenty-five and sixty. However, in 1988 the ACOG adjusted its position and recommended that when a woman turns eighteen or becomes sexually active (whichever occurs first), she should have Pap smears for three consecutive years. If they are negative, she can then be tested less frequently at the discretion of her doctor. Women at risk for cervical cancer should have the test annually: risk factors include the presence of genital warts or other sexually transmitted diseases, frequent sex with many partners, early sexual activity, and cigarette smoking.

What test results mean
The results of a Pap smear are a description of what the cytologist—a physician specializing in studying cells—sees while examining the cells under a microscope. He then prepares a report that provides the doctor with his interpretation. The original system of reporting Pap smear results—the Papanicolau classifications—are now considered outdated because they are not specific enough. Under

that system, Pap smears are categorized according to class on a scale from one to five. A class I reading represents normal cells. (This is also spoken of as a negative Pap smear.) Class II indicates some nonmalignant abnormality or inflammation from an underlying infection in the cervix or vagina. Class III readings mean that there are abnormal cells present, which are termed dysplastic (dysplasia is a disturbance in the usual organization of cells) and are considered pre-cancerous. A class IV result is indicative of carcinoma *in situ*—that is, preinvasive cancer affecting only the outer layer of the cervix. A class V finding is conclusive of cancer that has spread beyond the outer layer of the cervix. These are no longer appropriate diagnoses because, while there is clear agreement that a class I smear is normal and a class V smear is cancer, the meanings of classes II through IV are more ambiguous and vary from laboratory to laboratory.

In order to standardize the terminology used in describing Pap smear results, a group of experts at the National Cancer Institute developed a more specific and accurate system of diagnosis called the Bethesda system. In addition to providing uniform terminology, the Bethesda system provides guidelines for identifying noncancerous cervical and vaginal abnormalities, such as infections.

Under the Bethesda system, the report sent back to your doctor covers the following areas:

Adequacy of the specimen. The laboratory will report to the doctor on the quality of the Pap smear sent. If a Pap smear does not contain enough cervical cells, or if some other substance (such as a lubricant) is present, or if the specimen is not properly "fixed" on the glass slide, the interpretation given by the laboratory may not be accurate. The Bethesda system groups Pap smears into one of these three categories: satisfactory, indicating that it can be interpreted adequately; less than optimal, indicating that the smear may provide useful information, but it is not the best smear possible; and unsatisfactory, indicating that the smear is not useful for diagnosis. Unsatisfactory smears, and sometimes less than optimal smears, should be repeated.

Descriptive diagnosis: If the smear is adequate, the laboratory will provide a diagnosis using the following categories:

Within normal limits. A Pap smear with no abnormalities.

Infection. Signs of a bacterial, fungal, or viral infection, such as chlamydia, candidia, or herpes simplex. A definitive diagnosis of which type of infection may depend on follow-up tests.

Cell abnormalities. The Bethesda system divides abnormal smears into three broad categories: low-grade squamous intraepithelial lesion (SIL); high-grade squamous intraepithelial lesion; and squamous cell carcinoma. Once assigned to one of these categories, a more specific diagnosis is given using descriptive terminology—such as the system of categorization based on levels of dysplasia referred to as grades of cervical intraepithelial neoplasia (CIN). (A reading of CIN 1 indicates mild dysplasia; CIN 2, moderate dysplasia; CIN 3, severe dysplasia or carcinoma *in situ*—depending on the cause of the abnormality. For example, low-grade squamous intraepithelial lesion indicates mild changes in the cervical cells, so a diagnosis in this category may read as follows: "Low-grade SIL cellular changes associated with human papilloma virus" (the virus that causes genital warts) or "Low-grade SIL: CIN 1." A reading of high-grade SIL includes moderate or severe dysplasia (CIN 2 and CIN 3) or carcinoma *in situ* (CIN 3). Squamous cell carcinoma indicates cancer;

the lab report in each instance would require that the referring doctor be given a specific written evaluation, not merely the abbreviated clarification.

The Bethesda system is not used by all laboratories, but that doesn't mean that the labs that don't use it provide inaccurate diagnoses. Some laboratories still use the class system, but combine it with descriptive terminology. The best thing to do is to ask your doctor about the quality of the lab that will analyze the samples, and let him know that you are concerned about the quality of the specimen. Possible laboratory error is another reason to consider annual Pap smears; if the test is done every three years, six years could pass between accurate screenings.

Sigmoidoscopy

A sigmoidoscopy is a screening procedure to detect colon cancer and other abnormalities of the lower ten to twelve inches of the large intestine and the rectum (where the majority of cancerous polyps occur). The American Cancer Society recommends that everyone get a base-line sigmoidoscopy at age fifty (at forty, if there is a family history of colon cancer) and once every three years after that.

Although a sigmoidoscopy may be uncomfortable, it should not be painful. Sedation is not necessary, but a person can request a mild tranquilizer to help induce relaxation. Since a clean intestine is essential for accurate results, people will probably be asked to prepare for the test by following a special diet—frequently an all-liquid diet—for a few days prior to the test, followed by laxatives the night before and an enema on the day of the test. During the test, a thin, lubricated tube is gently inserted into the rectum and slowly advanced along the large intestine. This tube contains optical filaments through which light can pass and transmit an internal image to a microscope or monitor for a doctor to view. It may also contain small instruments that enable a doctor to take tissue samples. Air may be forced through the tube to expand the large intestine to make viewing and insertion easier. This may cause an uncomfortable feeling of gas or fullness, or simulate the urge to defecate. If a doctor sees any abnormalities as the tube travels through the intestine, he may take a tissue sample; if any polyps are present, they will be removed with the scope for analysis. Once the examination is complete, the tube is slowly withdrawn. The whole process takes about fifteen minutes to a half hour.

Stress Test

An exercise stress test is one of several techniques used for uncovering cardiac problems. It is frequently used as a screening device for older people about to begin an exercise program; if the test indicates a heart disorder, an appropriate program can be designed. The procedure is usually done in a physician's office or a local hospital, but some health clubs provide them as well.

The test is a trouble-shooting procedure designed to reveal problems that a resting electrocardiogram (ECG) does not. At rest, an ECG may indicate that the heart is receiving sufficient oxygen; but with exertion, as the heart's workload increases, the ECG may reveal signs of an inadequate oxygen supply to certain areas of the heart muscle. The most common cause is narrowing of coronary arteries caused by the build-up of plaque. Thus, the stress test can help identify an abnormality that might otherwise go undetected until a person experiences chest pain while exercising.

Who should have a stress test?

You should undergo a stress test before starting an exercise program if you are included in the following categories:

•You are forty-five or over. (Even if you have been exercising for years, its wise to have a stress test when you turn forty-five.)

•You are between thirty-five and forty-four and have at least one risk factor for coronary artery disease. These include an immediate family member (parent, brother, or sister) who developed coronary artery disease before age fifty, smoking, obesity, and an elevated blood pressure or cholesterol level.

•You have cardiovascular or lung disease at any age, or a metabolic disorder such as diabetes or hyperthyroidism. Since the test itself may entail some risk in these cases, you should first consult your physician.

According to the American College of Sports Medicine, you don't need a test if you're under forty-five, are in apparent good health, and have no risk factors for coronary artery disease. Even if you have risk factors, if you're under thirty-five and have no symptoms of coronary artery disease, you don't need this test. Even when a stress test isn't required for health reasons, some people wish to have it done so that an exercise physiologist can design an individualized workout program for them.

How the test works

During an exercise stress test, your heart's activity is monitored on an electro-cardiography while you work out on an automated treadmill or stationary bicycle, usually for ten to fifteen minutes. Before the test begins, sensors are placed on your chest to transmit signals to the machine; generally, the more sensors the better, with twelve "leads" being preferable. While your pace gradually speeds up, the ECG monitors the changes that occur in the rhythm and electrical activity of your heart; your blood pressure and pulse are also monitored continually. Generally, in a stress test, you exercise until fatigue prevents you from continuing, or until warning symptoms show up. (These may include abnormalities of blood pressure, heart rate or rhythm, or the onset of chest pain, shortness of breath, dizziness, or nausea.)

Administered correctly by a physician or another trained professional, a stress test poses few risks. But the results can be inaccurate, largely because of procedural problems. About 10 to 20 percent of stress tests result in false positives (erroneously indicating heart disease). Even more disturbing, false negatives also occur, and in much higher proportions: 20 to 40 percent. Thus, the results of a stress test shouldn't be analyzed in isolation; they must be evaluated in relation to your age, sex, and medical history.

Urinalysis

Routine urinalysis is a simple, yet very important test in terms of overall health screening. It provides vital information about an array of bodily functions and, most importantly, helps diagnose kidney disease, diabetes, and infections of the urinary tract. The procedure for routine urine testing—the type usually included in a complete physical examination—is performed quickly and easily. A fresh sample collected at any time of day is adequate for the test, and the patient need not take any special steps beforehand. Your doctor will probably instruct you to discard the specimen from the beginning of the urination and to collect a "midstream" sample, which yields the most accurate data. The specimen is then tested with a chemically coated strip of paper, which performs up to ten tests simultaneously. An instrument called an urinometer is used to measure concentration (specific gravity). And the sample is usually examined under a microscope for bacteria and other visible signs of kidney disorders or urinary tract infections.

Potential signs of kidney malfunction that may be indicated by urinalysis include excessive or diminished acidity and the presence of abnormal particles, protein, blood cells, or crystals. The presence of glucose (sugar) and/or ketones (chemicals that are the result of the breakdown of fatty acids) in the urine are likely indications of diabetes; a sweet or fruity odor may be another warning sign. Bacteria or a high level of white blood cells in the urine are often indicators of urinary tract infection.

Many of these and other findings from urine testing can be attributed to any of a number of diseases or dysfunctions, or even to temporary, harmless conditions. A reddish color, for instance, may simply occur because the tested person ate beets the night before, not because of internal bleeding. In general, the color, odor, and concentration of urine are strongly affected by the foods and liquids consumed before the sample was taken. For these reasons, the discovery of abnormal results from urinalysis almost always calls for further testing.

X-rays

Diagnostic X-rays have been one of the real lifesaving tools in medicine. These "pictures" allow a doctor to see the inside of your body without actually cutting you open. X-rays are performed to detect abnormalities in all parts of the body, including the bones, brain, gastrointestinal tract, and lungs.

How X-rays work
You are placed between a machine that beams X-rays—which are a form of electromagnetic radiation—and an X-ray film. The machine is pointed at the area to be X-rayed and the radiation passes through your body; as this occurs, different types of tissue absorb different amounts of radiation. Tissues that absorb the least, like bone, show up as white on the X-ray film, while tissues that absorb the most, like the lungs, show up as black. X-rays of areas that have a lot of bone, such as the skull or teeth, expose your body to very little radiation; X-rays of fleshy areas, such as the lower back, expose you to relatively high amounts of radiation.

Safer X-rays
X-rays account for about half the estimated lifetime exposure to radiation for the average person (the other half comes from natural background sources). While each individual X-ray is not harmful by itself, exposure to radiation is cumulative;

thus a series of X-rays over a lifetime can result in an increased risk of cancer. Aware of the problems caused by excess exposure to radiation from X-rays, physicians have sharply limited their use. And radiologists have adopted the concept of "as low as reasonably achievable" with regard to doses. Although you should never refuse an X-ray that can provide essential medical information, the following steps will help you maximize your benefits from diagnostic X-rays while minimizing radiation risks:

•Keep a written record or diary of all X-ray exposures—what was done and when, and where the film was stored. This can sometimes keep you from having to repeat an X-ray.

•If the X-ray is being done in your doctor's office, ask if the X-ray technician has an appropriate license, and if the equipment has passed an annual inspection.

•See that the parts of your body not involved in the X-ray are shielded. For example, if you are getting a dental X-ray, you should be given a lead apron and collar to wear.

•Ask if the procedure is being done with "state-of-the-art" equipment—that is, high-speed cassettes using the lowest-possible dosage. Many dentists, for example, have switched to E-speed film, which reduces your exposure significantly.

•Try to avoid unnecessary diagnostic X-rays. A routine chest X-ray is a good example; while these may be useful for examining workers exposed to asbestos or pulmonary irritants, as a routine procedure to detect lung cancer and heart disease—especially in an individual with no symptoms—it is of little value.

•When scheduled for a mammogram, ask that it be done on a "dedicated" machine, which means that it's not used for any other kind of X-ray.

X-rays are not the only types of imaging procedures. In recent years, new techniques of examining the interior of the body have been developed. These are noninvasive and do not appear to have any potential adverse effects. They cannot substitute for X-rays in most cases, but can complement them, and often be as good or better diagnostic tools. Examples of these procedures include sonograms and magnetic resonance imaging (MRIs).

IMMUNIZATION

In this century, immunization with vaccines has had greater impact on contagious diseases than all other health services available to us. Smallpox, once the most widespread disease in the world, has been virtually eradicated. And in the United States and other developed countries, diseases such as diphtheria, tetanus, polio, and whooping cough—which fifty years ago were killing or crippling hundreds of thousands of people—have been largely been brought under control. Yet as long as even a few cases of disease occur within a population, people who are not immunized are at a risk of catching it. Moreover, when immunization coverage drops, diseases can return with a vengeance, as has happened with whooping cough and measles.

How does immunization work? It prevents diseases caused by microbes—bacteria and viruses—that for the most part cannot be effectively treated. The body builds immunity naturally when it catches some infectious diseases and responds by forming antibodies, which kill the invading microbes or render them harmless. Vaccines create immunity artificially—and more safely—because they contain modified microbes or toxins that aren't strong enough to cause diseases, yet can still stimulate the system to produce antibodies. Once a person is vaccinated with a particular microbe for which there is a vaccine, he will fend off a particular infection by the same microbe with an immediate outpouring of antibodies.

American children are supposed to be routinely immunized against the leading contagious diseases—and for the most part they are. According to recent estimates, 90 percent of preschoolers have now been immunized. However, this makes many adults complacent about immunization, which is dangerous because they need to maintain certain types of immunity. For example, even if you were immunized against tetanus and diphtheria as a child, you need to receive booster shots periodically to remain fully protected. Yet nearly half of American adults are not up to date on their boosters.

Some 40 million adults should get a flu vaccine each fall. Outbreaks of influenza occur virtually every year, usually in winter, and can cause thousands of people to be hospitalized. But only about 20 percent of the people who should be receiving flu shots are getting them. The same figures apply to a new bacterial pneumonia vaccine. Also, adults in certain occupational and life-style groups, such as college students and health care workers, may be at high risk and should be immunized.

Along with being complacent, many adults are skeptical about the effectiveness and safety of the vaccines intended to protect them. For example, the influenza vaccine, although advocated by health officials, has never been widely accepted by the public. Resistance to it was especially strong after the winter of 1976-77, when a vaccine for combating swine flu was associated with about five hundred cases of a rare paralytic condition called Guillain-Barre syndrome. Because of the wide publicity this received, the safety of the flu vaccine was seriously challenged—even though nearly 48 million people got vaccinated that winter without serious consequences. What is most reassuring is that the influenza vaccines used since have not been associated with Guillain-Barre syndrome or other substantial side effects. Yet a majority of the people who could benefit from the flu vaccine ignore it.

Based on a wide number of studies, however, modern vaccines have been judged to be extremely safe and effective by the American Academy of Pediatrics, the American College of Physicians, and the Centers for Disease Control in Atlanta. This does not mean that the adverse effects from vaccines have been eliminated. But the chances of a severe reaction occurring in a healthy adult are extremely slim. For most individuals, as well as for the society at large, there is no doubt that the benefits of immunization far outweigh the risks.

Guidelines for Immunization

Because of the confusion concerning adult vaccinations, the American College of Physicians has issued a set of guidelines on the subject. Their key recommendations are given on page 452. To determine whether you should obtain a vaccination, you need to review your immunization history. If in doubt about whether you have been sufficiently immunized, the safest bet is to assume that you haven't and to consult your doctor for the appropriate vaccine. Be sure to keep a record of current and future vaccines.

All vaccines produce some side effects, though not every time and not in all people. Most of these reactions are temporary and relatively mild, ranging from local soreness and redness to fever and discomfort in the joints. Unusual adverse reactions can take the form of convulsions and paralysis, but these are extremely rare. Individuals with allergies may be hypersensitive to a vaccine, so discuss any allergies with your physician beforehand.

Diphtheria. A disease that typically produces a severe sore throat, diphtheria is spread by airborne bacteria that release toxins that in turn can attack the heart and other internal organs. Because of widespread immunization with a toxoid vaccine, diphtheria has almost disappeared in the United States, but a few cases appear yearly. Most adults received primary immunization during childhood; if you did not, do so without delay. To remain immune, all adults require a booster shot every ten years, which is ordinarily combined with tetanus toxoid in a vaccine called Td. Since many students receive a booster by age fourteen or fifteen, try to establish a mid-decade birthday (twenty-five, thirty-five, etc.) as the time for subsequent boosters.

Tetanus. The bacteria that cause tetanus enter the body through a contaminated wound that can cause painful muscular contractions, which may prove fatal. Despite a dramatic decrease, there are still about one hundred cases a year, most of them in older people. After primary immunization, adults should receive a tetanus booster (combined with diphtheria) every ten years. If you sustain a heavily contaminated wound, see a doctor: a booster may be appropriate if you have not received one within the preceding five years.

Influenza. To be effective, the flu vaccine must be administered yearly: strains of influenza constantly shift and are never the same from year to year, so the vaccine is adjusted annually to contain viruses that are expected to be prevalent. The vaccine is strongly recommended for anyone sixty-five and over, since severity and risk of death increase with age. Anyone with chronic pulmonary, heart, or kidney disease or with diabetes is also at high risk and should get annual flu shots. Those at high risk of exposure, such as health care workers and college students, should also be immunized annually. (Flu shots are not recommended for healthy adults under sixty-five, for whom influenza is almost never fatal.)

Pneumococcal pneumonia. A vaccine is now available that offers protection against the twenty-three strains that cause about 80 percent of pneumococcal diseases in this country. The same groups immunized for influenza should be immunized with pneumococcal vaccine, but only once. Yearly or booster doses should definitely not be given.

Measles and mumps. Most adults are likely to have been infected naturally with these diseases. But a substantial number of young adults born after 1957 have not been vaccinated and have not had the diseases, so they may be susceptible. (In the first half of 1985, 18.5 percent of reported cases of measles were among college students.) Furthermore, people vaccinated for measles between 1963 and 1967 may have gotten a short-lasting vaccine and should be revaccinated.

Rubella. Injury to a fetus and miscarriage are the major consequences of rubella (German measles) in adults, and an estimated 10 to 15 percent of young adults remain susceptible to this disease. Therefore, all women of childbearing age who have no history of vaccination should be tested for antibodies, and, in their absence, be immunized. Following immunization, a woman should wait for at least three months before becoming pregnant. Combined vaccines for measles, mumps, and rubella are available.

Special situations. A person's health status may determine whether a particular vaccine should be taken. Pregnant women, diabetics, cardiopulmonary patients, and people with other chronic diseases are among those to whom special considerations apply. Also, some people are in environments where there is an increased risk of contracting vaccine-preventable infections. These include college students, military personal, health care workers, veterinarians, and community workers such as teachers, policemen, firemen, and sanitation workers. Individuals in these groups should check with their doctors or medical departments on guidelines for the above diseases as well as for hepatitis B, rabies, typhoid, and meningococcal disease. Finally, travelers going to developing countries should check on recommendations for the places they will visit. (For more information, see pages 425-427.)

Children. The principle immunizations for children are: 1) combined vaccines known as DPT for diphtheria, pertussis, and tetanus; 2) a triple oral polio virus vaccine, or TOPV; 3) vaccines for measles, mumps, and rubella, which can be given separately or combined (MMR). For infants who start immunization during their first year, the American Academy of Pediatrics Committee on Infectious Diseases recommends the following schedule: DPT and TOPV at two months, four months, six months, eighteen months, and four to six years; MMR at fifteen months; tetanus and diphtheria (Td) booster at fourteen to sixteen years. Pertussis vaccine should be withheld or moderated for children with convulsive disorders or adverse reactions to the first shot of DPT. It's not given to children over six, since fatalities from pertussis occur almost exclusively before that age.

The case for DPT

American children have been getting immunized against pertussis, or whooping cough, since the 1920s. The disease, which causes violent fits of coughing, is especially damaging, even fatal, to very young children. Thanks to immunization, it has declined drastically. But starting in 1982, the media dramatically publicized instances of serious adverse reactions to the DPT vaccine. The reported reactions included convulsions, physical collapse, and occasional brain damage. Some critics contended that vaccination should be halted because the disease itself no longer posed a threat, so the benefits didn't warrant the risks involved.

Health experts have persuasively defended the vaccine. First, attributing serious reactions to the vaccine is complicated, since the same effects often occur in children without vaccinations. Second, in methodical studies of the vaccine's side effects, serious reactions have been rare. In a University of California at Los Angeles study that involved 15,000 injections, only eighteen children had serious reactions, and all recovered. A British study of 310,000 immunizations found only one case of brain damage.

But the most convincing evidence for continued widespread use of the vaccine showed up in the late 1970s, when routine vaccination declined in Great Britain and Japan as a result of vaccine scares. Within two years, one hundred thousand cases of pertussis (with twenty-eight deaths) appeared in Great Britain and thirteen thousand cases (with forty-one deaths) in Japan. Even in the U.S., the disease has by no means been wiped out; there are still about fifteen hundred to two thousand cases (with four to ten deaths) each year. That is why virtually all health care authorities recommend that we keep using this vaccine.

PAIN RELIEF

For most physicians and patients, the primary method of pain control is the use of analgesic medications (see box on page 456). Unfortunately, some people, particularly those with unremitting chronic pain, go from one pain medication to another with little relief. Others refuse to use any drug over long periods for fear of addiction. When conventional treatments don't work, alternative therapies can offer relief for some people.

Alternative treatments

Pain is a very individual matter, involving complex physical and psychological variables. Your backache may be relieved by massage or acupuncture, while someone else's may not be helped by dozens of different kinds of treatment. No therapy will work for all people, all types of pain, or even for all people with the same complaint or apparent underlying condition. Thus, trial and error is usually unavoidable.

It's safest to think of alternative treatments as adjunct therapy. Don't give up your regular medical care. Even if pain-relieving drugs have failed you, don't stop taking other prescription drugs that you may need. Talk to your physician about the new approaches you're considering, and make sure he or she continues to keep an eye on your condition. There's little potential harm in an alternative treatment for pain relief—unless it keeps you from getting a correct diagnosis of a treatable or curable condition. The effectiveness of alternative therapies has been difficult to demonstrate in controlled studies; evidence about them is frequently based on anecdotes from people who have gotten relief. Each therapy has its advocates and critics among patients, physicians, and researchers.

The body's own painkillers

In recent years, scientists have discovered that just as body chemistry creates pain, it may also supply a mechanism to control it. They theorize that some methods of pain control, such as acupuncture and electrical nerve stimulation, reduce pain by activating the body's own pain relief system. Opiate-like substances (such as endorphins and enkephalins) produced in the spinal cord and brain appear to operate in the same manner as opiate drugs. Certain sufferers of chronic pain, in fact, may have lower levels of these natural pain relievers.

Placebo effect

Another way alternative treatments may work is through what is called (sometimes derisively) the placebo effect. This phenomenon provides fascinating proof that, when it comes to pain, the mind and body work together. A placebo is any substance or procedure having an effect (usually beneficial) on a patient that, paradoxically, can't be attributed to the specific properties or actions of the drug or

Opiates and Other Drugs

Pain relievers, called analgesics (from the Greek word for "no sense of pain"), vary greatly in how they work and consequently in the type of pain for which they are most effective. In practical terms, there are two general types of pain. Acute pain is short term, may be mild or severe, and is caused by an identifiable injury or disorder, such as a broken arm or surgery. Chronic pain is long term, can be continual or intermittent, and can be of varying severity.

Analgesic drugs are narcotic or non-narcotic: Narcotic analgesics (such as Percodan, Demerol, and codeine) act like morphine—by inhibiting pain impulses in certain centers of the brain. These are useful in treating acute pain, since it is short term, and as a temporary measure in some cases of chronic pain. However, narcotic analgesics (also called opiates, though not all are opium derivatives) are usually not suitable for chronic pain because the body may develop tolerance to them—that is, experience a diminished effect with prolonged use. Another danger is addiction, the most dramatic component of which is physical dependence. Narcotics also impair physical and mental function.

The main non-narcotic analgesics are aspirin, ibuprofen, and other nonsteroidal anti-inflammatory drugs (NSAIDs), as well as acetaminophen. Most of these inhibit the body's production of inflammatory compounds, called prostaglandins, and are especially useful for bone pain (including dental), some types of arthritis, and headaches. There is a "ceiling effect"—that is, increasing the dose beyond a certain point doesn't result in greater benefit. There's no risk of addiction. Still, continual high doses of non-narcotic analgesics may entail adverse side effects (see box on page 456).

procedure itself. Typically, it's an inactive substance like a sugar pill that's given as if it were an effective treatment for the patient's pain or disease, but it can be any treatment, especially when the patient expects it to work. Since the 1950s, scientists have consistently found that 30 to 40 percent of all patients given a placebo show improvement for a wide variety of conditions—whether it's coughing or seasickness, dental or postoperative pain, angina, migraine, or pain from an ulcer. Even more surprising, about 10 percent of people given a placebo report side effects normally associated with a chemically active drug, and others even experience withdrawal symptoms when they stop taking the fake drug.

Contrary to myth, there appears to be no "placebo personality." Placebos can work for anybody (not merely suggestible people) in the right circumstances—namely, if the patient believes that someone is trying to help him and thus expects relief, and especially if the helper is an optimistic physician in a clinical setting. But also contrary to myth, the relief of pain or illness by placebo effect does not mean that the problem was feigned or just in the patient's mind.

There are possible biochemical explanations for the placebo effect. Some researchers suggest that placebos may help activate the internal pain-relief mechanism. To investigate this, they have given naloxone (a drug that blocks the effects of opiate painkillers like morphine) to patients whose pain was reduced by a placebo. Just as naloxone reverses morphine's action, so it canceled out the analgesic effect of the placebo and thus increased the pain—suggesting that placebos do indeed cause opiate-like substances to be released into the blood. On another level, the expectation of relief may itself reduce anxiety, and this calming effect can reduce muscle tension and increase the tolerance of pain.

The placebo effect can play a part in the success of any treatment. Your belief, hope, or anticipation that a drug or procedure will heal you may add considerably to its effectiveness. While it's important for scientists to know whether the

Over-the-Counter Pain Relievers

The most common forms of nonprescription pain relievers—aspirin, acetaminophen, and ibuprofen—all have one trait in common: they inhibit the production of prostaglandins, hormonelike substances that trigger inflammation, fever, and dull pain. While aspirin works against prostaglandins that set off all three phenomena, acetaminophen inhibits only those that trigger pain and fever. Ibuprofen works against the full array of prostaglandins, and especially well against those formed in the uterus. Which type of pain reliever you choose depends basically on what your problem is and how you react to the three medications. Aspirin has the widest range of applications but also the largest number of side effects. Acetaminophen has far fewer side effects and is safe for children, but it is not effective against inflammation. Ibuprofen is highly effective for pain and is better tolerated than aspirin, but it can sometimes cause stomach pain. And if you have allergic reactions to aspirin (rashes, hives, breathing problems), you may react similarly to ibuprofen. The chart below shows the advantages and drawbacks of each type.

Comparing Pain Relievers

	Aspirin	Acetaminophen	Ibuprofen
When effective	Pain, fever, inflammation	Pain, fever	Pain, fever, inflammation
Allergic reactions and side effects	About 2 to 3 percent of the population, especially asthmatics, have allergic reactions, ranging from itching to asthma attacks. Common side effects of excessive doses include stomach upset and ringing ears. At least 40 percent of people have some stomach bleeding (usually inconsequential). Frequent use can lead to ulcers or anemia.	Produces far fewer side effects and allergic reactions than aspirin. Rare reactions include skin rashes and painful urination. High doses over periods may damage liver or kidneys.	Produces fewer side effects and allergic reactions than aspirin. Can cause skin rashes, itching, digestive upsets, stomach distress, and dizziness. May interfere with diuretic and antihypertensive drugs.
Who should not take	Pregnant women (can cause bleeding in mother and child); lactating women; people with aspirin allergies, ulcers, gout, or stomach bleeding; children under sixteen with fever, chicken pox, or flu, because of risk of Reye's Syndrome; patients on anticoagulants.	Alcoholics; people with liver or kidney disease (such as hepatitis) or kidney infections; pregnant and lactating women.	Individuals suffering from gout, ulcers, or aspirin allergies (there may be cross-sensitivity); children under fourteen; pregnant and lactating women.
When to use	For relief of joint pain, fever, stiffness, inflammation of arthritis, toothaches, tension headaches, backaches, and sprains. Because it inhibits clotting, it may help prevent heart attacks.	To reduce pain and fever in people who react badly to aspirin; children under sixteen with chicken pox or flu. Because it does not affect blood clotting, safe after oral surgery.	Same as aspirin, except better for menstrual cramps. Has similar affects as aspirin in reducing blood clotting.
Comment	Highly effective and inexpensive drug for pain, fever, and inflammation, but with minor or serious side effects in many people. A good choice if it causes no adverse effects.	Probably not as effective as aspirin or ibuprofen in reducing pain and fever, but helpful for individuals who cannot take aspirin.	Fewer side effects than aspirin, but more than acetaminophen. Good for those bothered by aspirin-caused gastric problems. Less toxic in large doses than the other two types. More expensive.

efficacy of a treatment or drug is due solely to a placebo effect (which is why placebos are usually used in clinical trials of new drugs), all that matters to a patient in pain and his physician is that the treatment works. So one goal for both physician (or other practitioner) and patient is to maximize the placebo potential of any treatment.

Acupuncture

Practiced in China for more than two thousand years, acupuncture involves inserting needles into specific points on the skin and rotating them; the needles may be left in place for a period of time. Some acupuncturists transmit electrical stimulation through the needles, while others employ low-intensity laser beams instead of needles.

How acupuncture may work is speculative. One theory is that it inhibits painful stimuli by activating the body's pain control system. This theory is supported by the fact that in some studies, when patients are given naloxone, the analgesic effect of acupuncture is reversed; others question these results. Or acupuncture may stimulate nerve fibers that compete with fibers transmitting the pain messages.

Acupuncture has been used to treat a variety of kinds of pain—from backaches and headaches to dental problems. In China, it's even used as anesthesia for some patients undergoing surgery. It appears to be effective as a short-term treatment; few studies have looked at its long-term effectiveness. Several studies indicate that 40 to 80 percent of subjects may benefit. Researchers have reported that acupuncture can be effective even for animals in pain. However, there has been no conclusive, controlled study that rates the results of acupuncture beyond that of a placebo effect.

Special risks are involved, however. Incorrectly inserted needles can cause tissue swelling or even organ damage. If the needles are not sterilized and the skin not adequately cleaned, infection or hepatitis may result. Because of the risk of AIDS and hepatitis, disposable needles are recommended. Electric stimulation, either from needles or a Transcutaneous Electrical Nerve Stimulation (TENS) device, should not be used on a person with a pacemaker, a fever, or irregular heartbeat. Choose a state licensed, board certified practitioner (if your state has certification).

Hypnosis

One of the most widespread uses of medical hypnosis is for pain control. Despite popular notions, a hypnotherapist doesn't put a person to sleep and then simply command him not to feel pain. Instead, the therapist establishes a rapport with the subject, promotes muscle relaxation, produces a trancelike state, and, through suggestion, tries to shift the subject's attention away from the pain. One way or another, pain is tuned out and thus reduced in some people. Individuals vary greatly in their ability to be hypnotized, however; it's estimated that about half of all people can maintain a moderate trance. Temperament, imagination, motivation, and trust in the therapist are vital. With training, some can practice self-hypnosis.

Studies have found hypnosis most effective in lessening acute pain—for instance, pain caused by a dental procedure or burns. In a small number of people, hypnosis has even served as the sole anesthesia during surgery. It may also help control persistent pain, as in certain cancers.

Relaxation techniques and biofeedback

Although typically used to relieve day-to-day anxiety and tensions, relaxation techniques can also play a role in the management of pain. They help reduce muscle tension and, like hypnosis, shift attention away from pain. In one study, patients who were taught relaxation methods required half the painkillers after abdominal surgery compared to a control group, and were able to leave the hospital earlier.

Progressive muscle relaxation, described in 1938 by Dr. Edmund Jacobson, is a frequently used technique. It calls for tensing and then relaxing specific muscle groups, working from the feet to the head, while focusing on deep, regular breathing. Another technique, called the relaxation response, requires you to select a word or phrase and repeat it until the mind is empty and the body relaxed. This method is, in fact, a form of meditation.

The most technical of all relaxation methods is biofeedback. This calls for hooking a subject up to a device that continuously measures a physiological variable—muscle tension, for instance, or skin temperature. Meter readouts or tones tell whether the tension or temperature is increasing or decreasing—this is the feedback. The subject then tries to lower the number or change the pitch by focusing on the painful area, or on whichever sensations, thoughts, or feelings work for him. When successful, biofeedback produces muscle relaxation, reduced anxiety, and an increased sense of control, all of which may contribute to pain relief, particularly for headaches and muscle contraction pain.

Pain clinics

For persistent, intractable pain—especially in the lower back—when other treatments haven't worked, the next step may be one of the hundreds of pain clinics now operating across the country. As part of a coordinated program of treatments, a clinic may offer psychological counseling, hypnosis, or acupuncture, along with such traditional medical therapies as surgery, orthopedics, physical therapy, and drugs. The regimen usually includes a program of aerobic exercise. Exercise may help reduce pain by raising endorphin levels, increasing self-confidence, reducing tension, and/or simply distracting people from their pain.

Pain clinics employ various strategies to deal with the self-perpetuating psychological aspects often associated with chronic pain syndrome. A person's lack of self-esteem, sense of helplessness, chronic depression, or desire for attention can all help perpetuate pain and suffering. At a clinic, a patient may be allowed to discuss pain for only a set amount of time; and the staff tries to reinforce the patient's constructive behavior, such as talking about other topics and participating in group projects. The family is taught to understand the needs that the patient's pain may serve and to help him satisfy these needs without using pain as a lever.

MEDICATIONS

According to a survey done for the Food and Drug Administration (FDA), fewer than 5 percent of patients question their doctors about prescriptions. Yet prescription drugs can be ineffective or even harmful when used in the wrong way.

Before your doctor prescribes anything for you, be sure he knows about any special restrictions that apply to you, such as the following:

Allergies or dietary restrictions. A prescription drug may contain any number of substances in addition to medicine, such as a binder to hold a tablet together, coloring, or preservatives. Liquid medications often contain alcohol. Be sure your doctor knows about any drugs to which you are allergic—especially if this is your first visit.

Health conditions for which the drug could be harmful. Be sure your doctor is aware of all your health conditions, and certainly tell him if you are pregnant, planning to become pregnant soon, or are breast-feeding.

Also ask your doctor—or pharmacist—about the following:

What you are taking. Find out the name of the medication. When you pick up the prescription, check the label to first make sure that it is yours, and second that the drug named on the label is the one the doctor prescribed. Accidents do happen.

When you should take the medication. Must you take it during the night to maintain a proper blood level of the drug, or would taking it at bedtime and on awakening suffice? If you miss a dose, should you double up the next time you are scheduled to take it, or simply forget it?

How you should take the medicine. On a full or empty stomach? With water, milk, or citrus juices? Can you crush large pills or open capsules and mix them with food? Drugs that have been coated to prevent stomach upset or to provide release over a long period must be taken whole. Should you keep the drug in your refrigerator or away from sunlight?

How long you should take the drug. Just until the symptoms stop? Or, as with many antibiotics, should you finish the prescription? The label frequently says whether—and how often—the prescription can be refilled. If it's refillable, should you call the doctor before refilling it? Also, find out how long the drug takes to work, and what effect to expect, so that you can tell your doctor if it's not working.

Possible side effects. For example, should you immediately discontinue the medication if you experience some mild stomach upset? Or is it likely to pass? Will the drug make you drowsy, like some tranquilizers? Should you avoid driving or operating machinery while on the prescription? Are there any side effects that require that the drug be halted immediately?

Interactions between your prescription and other medicine you are taking. Make sure your doctor knows which other drugs (including over-the-counter medications) you currently take. Mixing over-the-counter antihistamines found in cold remedies with tranquilizers, for example, could make you very drowsy. Can you drink alcohol while taking the medication? Some drugs, such as Valium, can be dangerous when combined with alcohol. A good pharmacist will track all your prescription drugs and notify your physician and you of any incompatibilities.

When the drug will expire. If possible, have the pharmacist write an expiration date on the label for you.

Generic vs. brand-name drugs

More than eight thousand generic drugs are currently manufactured and sold with FDA approval, and millions of people use them daily. All Veterans Administration hospitals use generics, and when the U.S. President gets medications at Walter Reed Hospital, he gets generics. The FDA estimates that 70 to 80 percent of all

---

Should medication be taken on an empty stomach?

It depends on the medication. Certain types of medication are irritating to the stomach (such as aspirin, erythromycin, prednizone, doxycycline, indomethacin, and ibuprofen) and should be taken with meals to diminish or prevent digestive problems. Some other drugs (such as antibiotics) are poorly absorbed in the presence of certain foods, especially dairy products, and thus should be taken between meals—or at least one hour before or two hours after eating. Still other medications (such as diuretics and acetaminophen) can be taken any time. You should check with your doctor or pharmacist each time you receive a prescription to see which conditions apply.

Medicine Cabinet Safety

Most medicine cabinets are far too ample: the point of stocking drugs and medical supplies is to have essential items on hand in case of any emergency.

Medicine chests tend to become an elephant's graveyard of drugs. Out-of-date drugs pile up, making you think that you're better stocked than you really are. Drugs and supplies usually have a limited shelf life, so check expiration dates every few months. Out-of-date drugs may not only lose potency, they may also be dangerous, particularly antibiotics. If a drug doesn't have an expiration date, write the purchase date on the label. Then check with your doctor or pharmacist before using a drug that is more than a year old. Discard old drugs by flushing them down the toilet; children or pets could discover them in a wastebasket.

Here are some likely signs that a drug has deteriorated and should be discarded:

•aspirin that has developed a vinegary smell or crumbles when touched;

•antiseptic solutions that have become cloudy, changed color, or formed a solid residue at the bottom of the bottle;

•ointments or salves that have become spotted, changed color, hardened, or separated.

If you have any questions about the condition or potency of a drug, call your doctor or pharmacist. Since medicines don't last forever, it may be a waste of money to buy large, family-sized bottles of drugs. They may go bad before you use them.

Remember, too, that a bathroom is actually a poor place to store drugs because the high heat and humidity from the bath or shower causes pills and powders to deteriorate quickly. Choose a cool, dry spot instead—a closet shelf might be a good place, for instance. If a drug needs to be kept in a refrigerator, it will be indicated on the label.

If there are children in the house or coming to visit, be sure that potentially toxic medicines are in child-proof containers or in a locked box. Keeping them out of reach is not good enough—children are remarkably persistent in searching for colorful things to eat and drink.

---

generics are made by the same manufacturers licensed to make the brand-name drugs. A pharmaceutical company that develops a drug can patent it and sell it exclusively for seventeen years (this may be extended by five years in some cases); after that, any company can make and sell the drug competitively, provided the copy proves as good as the original—that's what a generic is. All drug manufacturers, whether they're producing brand-name or generic products, must comply with the same FDA-mandated standards.

Generics generally retail for 30 to 80 percent less than their brand-name equivalents, so many people ask their doctors to specify them. In 1984, Congress passed a law that eases the approval process for generic drugs at the FDA, and during the past decade, sales of generics have increased rapidly from one billion to seven billion dollars a year. Many large insurers and health maintenance organizations, as well as Medicare and Medicaid, favor or require the use of generics as an economical measure.

Some professionals question the efficacy and potency of generic drugs, claiming that if one drug is bio-equivalent it doesn't mean it's necessarily therapeutically equivalent to the brand name. But this is simply not true: if a drug is bio-equivalent, it must be therapeutically equivalent. Even brand names may have side effects or occasionally fail to perform as expected. Of course, the choice of prescription drug is up to a physician's best judgment, and your doctor is the person to consult if you are worried about any drug you are taking. If you do plan to discuss your medication with your doctor, keep taking it meanwhile. It can be dangerous to make changes on your own. Keep the following points in mind:

•If you're taking a prescription generic and both you and your doctor are satisfied with your progress, you have no reason to worry.

•Know what you're taking. If your doctor says a brand-name drug is a must, follow his advice but try price shopping. Some pharmacies charge less than others.

•Over-the-counter generics (aspirin, ibuprofen, steroid ointments, and the like) are also safe, and are often much less expensive than brand names.

Over-the-counter drugs

There are over three hundred thousand nonprescription drugs available in the United States. Medicines that can be obtained over the counter, by law, must be safe for use without the supervision of a physician. They are not addictive if used correctly, and they must have clear warnings and instructions printed on the labels for consumer use and protection. And yet, there's a difference between "safe" and "harmless." Over-the-counter drugs can do damage if used incorrectly, and some can lead to physical dependence if overused. Some nonprescription drugs should not be taken by children, pregnant or lactating women, the elderly, or in combination with other drugs.

To use over-the-counter drugs safely, read the label on any product you buy. It's good policy to reread labels on a new bottle or package even if it's something you've taken before. Manufacturers can and do reformulate their products at higher or lower strengths, or there may be new warnings about side effects. Always follow directions to the letter. The rate at which your body eliminates drugs is fixed, and if you take too much, or even take the recommended amount over too long a period, the drug might build to dangerous levels. Four common kinds of nonprescription drugs are especially likely to produce adverse side effects or dependence.

Nasal sprays. After several days' use, your nose may be more congested than ever. Sprays, which contain a decongestant, work by constricting blood vessels, but with repeated use the vessels no longer constrict, leading to the opposite effect—a rebound of swelling or congestion. If you use one, limit it to one or two days. Don't spray more often than the label recommends.

Laxatives. Their labels remind you that "frequent or continued use may result in dependency." The most habit-forming laxatives are the so-called "stimulants," which work by irritating the walls of the intestine. Laxatives that increase stool bulk (such as Metamucil) are less dangerous, but any laxative can cause dependency. If you feel in constant need of one, consult your doctor. To kick the habit, increase your intake of fluid and fiber. A diet high in fruits, vegetables, and grains, plus two quarts of fluids a day, will almost always alleviate constipation.

Eye drops. These blood vessel constrictors will whiten bloodshot eyes, but like nasal sprays, they can produce a rebound effect. After a day or two, blood vessels may dilate. If your eyes are red for more than a day or two, you may need medical advice. Eye-drop use can mask serious eye infections and other diseases.

Codeine cough syrups. Codeine, a narcotic, works directly on the part of the brain that controls coughing. In about two-thirds of the United States, codeine-containing cough suppressants are available simply by signing a register in the drugstore. The potential for addiction is small, but you should follow dosage limits carefully. In addition, this drug frequently causes constipation. Don't use such cough syrups for more than three days without the advice of your doctor.

Swallowing Pills
Always stand up to swallow medicine. If you're confined to bed and cannot stand, at least sit as upright as possible. Pills taken lying down or even sitting may lodge in the esophagus and dissolve there producing inflammation or injury. Even if it causes no harm, a stuck aspirin, for instance, can take an hour or more to reach the source of pain. To help the pill along, follow these guidelines:

•Before you put the pill in your mouth, always drink a swallow of water.

•Put the pill or capsule as far back on your tongue as possible.

•Wash it down with at least four ounces of water. If possible, drink another half-glass in five minutes.

•Stay on your feet for at least two or three minutes afterward.

Try drinking your water from a bottle; the sucking action helps. If you think a pill is stuck, eat several bites of banana and then drink some water.

ENVIRONMENT AND SAFETY

Injuries and illness stemming from either accidents or environmental hazards may seem to be beyond the average person's control. Accidents— which are the fourth most common cause of death in the United States— often appear to be a matter of "chance." But, in fact, the risks you are exposed to while driving a car, hiking in the woods, or cooking on an outdoor barbecue can be substantially reduced by heeding basic safety precautions. Similarly, many people believe that, as individuals, they have no control over risks to their health due to large-scale environmental problems such as acid rain or industrial pollutants. While it is true that many environmental issues require national or global policies to be dealt with effectively, you can act to control risks in your immediate environment—in your home, workplace, and local community. This part of the book covers potential problems you may encounter, puts these problems into perspective, and provides safeguards you can adopt to protect yourself and your family.

Home and Workplace

Familiar surroundings are often viewed as safe havens, yet on average about 350 injuries and three fatal accidents occur in the home every hour. This section deals with common safety and environmental hazards in the home and workplace and shows you how to guard against them.

Aerosol Cans

Although in 1978 the Environmental Protection Agency (EPA) banned the use of chlorofluorocarbons (CFCs) as propellants in most aerosol sprays because they endanger the earth's protective ozone layer, they are still used in some sprays. In addition—whether they contain CFCs or not—spray cans present potential hazards to individuals using them. The most common injuries result from heated cans that explode, and from misdirected sprays that get into eyes. Symptoms of overexposure to aerosol sprays—including headaches, dizziness, nausea, skin rashes, and shortness of breath—depend on the active ingredients involved.

Aerosol sprays are prepared from substances that are gaseous at room temperature under normal pressure but become liquid when pressurized; such propellants include petroleum or inert gases such as carbon dioxide. The active ingredient is dissolved or suspended in this pressurized material, and when the button is pressed, the liquid vaporizes and is sprayed through a small hole. The particles in the spray are so small that they are easily inhaled into the lungs where they are absorbed into the bloodstream. This can be extremely dangerous. In addition, some ingredients, such as the propane found in many hair sprays, are flammable and thus hazardous when used near a lit cigarette, match, or open flame.

A safer alternative
Manufacturers are increasingly packaging their products in pump spray containers. Compared to aerosols, these are safer for consumers and not harmful to the environment because they do not use pressurized chemicals; instead, their active ingredients are dissolved or dispersed in water and simply sprayed through a pump mechanism. Still, even though the chemical molecules in spray pumps are larger, and therefore not as easily inhaled, and the spray is more precise, be cautious about using spray pumps around the face and eyes.

Art Supplies

Nearly half of American adults occasionally practice some craft or hobby requiring the use of art materials, and many use art materials at work. Yet few people are aware that many of these materials contain toxins that can be absorbed through the skin or lungs. Most know about the hazards of lead, for example, and may assume that it was also banned from artists' paints at the same time it was banned in house paints. But art materials are exempt from this regulation, and oil paints may contain other highly toxic heavy metals, too, such as cadmium and mercury.

Besides oil-based paints, the most hazardous art supplies are found in the following categories:

Solvents. These are products used to dissolve paints and inks and to clean brushes and other tools.

Concentrated acids and alkalis. This category includes chemicals used to etch glass, to clean and etch metals, and as photochemicals.

Dry clay powders. Powdered materials such as silicates and talc may contain asbestos particles that could be inhaled.

Aerosol sprays. Products propelled in this way deliver a fine mist that may hang in the air and be easily inhaled; in addition, they often contain highly flammable solvents and propellants.

Shopping for art materials

Ask your supplier for alternatives. Instead of oil-based paints, for example, choose water-based, which can be cleaned up without toxic solvents. If possible, avoid any product containing lead, benzene, or carbon tetrachloride. All are poisonous and when used over long periods can promote liver, bone marrow, and kidney damage. The Federal Hazardous Substances Act requires manufacturers to label anything that may be *acutely* hazardous—that is, a single exposure can be dangerous. Manufacturers of fine arts supplies use a *chronic* hazard label certified by the Arts and Crafts Materials Institute on products that can be dangerous if used repeatedly. Be aware that labeling on imported products may not conform to U.S. regulations.

Homemade Play-dough

Commercial play-dough may contain preservatives that are not good for children to ingest. For an alternative to store-bought dough, try making a batch of your own—which will keep in the refrigerator in a tightly covered coffee can for a few days.

2 cups flour
1 cup salt
2 tablespoons cooking oil

Mix ingredients in a large bowl. Add water until the mixture feels right for modeling. (It should have a smooth, silky feel, but not stick to your hands.) Then add a squirt of food coloring.

Art Safety for Children

Because growing tissues can be more susceptible to toxins, young artists are in need of extra protection. Rubber cement, permanent felt-tip markers, spray fixatives, powdered clays, and instant papier-mâché are standard equipment in classrooms and playrooms, yet all of these materials contain chemicals that are hazardous if inhaled, absorbed, or swallowed. Children tend not to follow safety instructions consistently. Toddlers, or even older children, may simply not comprehend the dangers and may chew, swallow, suck, and inhale art materials or decorate their hands and faces with them.

There are many safe art materials for children on the market. Follow these pointers:

•Read labels carefully, and don't buy unlabeled products. Children's craft supplies should ideally bear the seal of the Arts and Crafts Materials Institute—your guarantee that the contents are safe, even if swallowed.

•Don't allow a child to use old art materials that may not meet modern standards.

•Remember that "nontoxic" on a label may simply mean "not acutely toxic." The product can still make a child sick if swallowed. Even wheat-based pastes and Play-doh should not be eaten, since they may contain preservatives or other elements that should not be ingested.

•Use talc-free, premixed clay. Powdered clay may contain asbestos and is easily inhaled.

•When possible, use vegetable and plant dyes instead of powdered tempera colors.

•Choose water-based ink or paints. Use only watercolor markers.

•White glue and school pastes are fine to use. Try to avoid epoxies, instant glues, or solvent-based adhesives.

If your child uses art supplies in school, check with your child's teacher, the school's principal, a member of the school board, or the president of the Parent Teachers Association (PTA) about the guidelines used for purchasing art supplies.

Whatever you buy, read the labels carefully and follow all safety instructions meticulously.

Safety measures
The following general precautions may reduce your risks:

•Always work in a well-ventilated area. One open window does not make the air flow, and an air conditioner just recirculates air. Set up a cross draft; use a fan.

•Don't set up shop in your kitchen or any room that must be used for other purposes. Reserve one area for art materials only. Keep children away from the site.

•If you must use aerosols, air brushes, or spray guns in a confined area, protect your nose and mouth with a face respirator (available in hardware stores), and wear gloves and goggles. Outdoor spraying is safer. Stay upwind of the spraying.

•Protect your hands with plastic or vinyl gloves when working with strong chemicals. Remember that many toxins can be absorbed through the skin.

•Don't eat, drink, or smoke while you work; don't bring food or drink into the work area.

•Always wash your hands thoroughly when you finish working. Be sure to clean around your cuticles and under your nails. Never use turpentine, thinner, or other solvents on your hands—they can be absorbed through the skin. Try scrubbing with mechanic's soap or a safe waterless cleanser. Rubbing alcohol, which cannot be absorbed, may also help.

•Wear special clothes when doing art work, and keep them in the art area. Wash them separately, not in the same water with your other clothing.

•Accumulated dust in your work area should be wet-mopped or vacuumed. Don't sweep—it only sends particles into the air.

Asbestos

Widely used since 1940 in the building construction trades and in some home products because of its excellent insulating properties, asbestos has been linked with respiratory diseases and some cancers of the lung, lung lining, and stomach. Most vulnerable are people who mine, process, or work with the mineral, especially if they are cigarette smokers. The fiber masses tend to break into a dust of nearly invisible particles that float in the air, adhere to clothing, and are easily inhaled. The more asbestos fibers inhaled and the longer the period of exposure, the greater the danger of lung damage.

Because asbestos is bonded with other materials in many home products, asbestos researchers do not consider households to be high-risk environments. But a damaged or loosely bonded asbestos product may release fibers into the air. Even though a brief or low-level exposure is unlikely to be harmful, no one knows exactly how much inhaled asbestos is necessary to cause disease. Consequently, it is important to understand the potential dangers from home products and take any necessary corrective measures.

Where asbestos is found
Asbestos is used to strengthen materials, as fireproofing, and as heat and sound insulation. Home-related materials that may contain asbestos include vinyl floor

tiles and sheet flooring; patching compounds (prior to 1977); textured paint (prior to 1978); ceiling and wall insulation (especially in homes built between 1930 and 1970); oil-, coal-, and wood-burning stoves as well as their door gaskets and surrounding floor and walls; insulation material covering hot water and steam pipes or furnace ducts; fireplace insulation and radiator covers; siding, roofing shingles, and roofing felt typically found on flat roofs; and some appliances—toasters, broilers, ovens, and refrigerators. Most of these products are not harmful if intact and if not disturbed by sanding, scraping, sawing, drilling, or removal without proper safeguards.

To determine whether a suspect product contains asbestos, contact the installer or manufacturer. If this is not possible, you may ask an asbestos-monitoring company or licensed abatement contractor for an evaluation. These companies will inspect and test questionable materials for you at costs ranging from about 50 to 350 dollars.

Sealing in asbestos

Most asbestos-containing materials, if intact, are best left untouched. Attempts to rip out or alter insulation, tiles, pipe coverings, etc. may so damage the materials that asbestos is released. When a product is slightly damaged or beginning to show signs of wear, opt to cover over rather than tamper. For example, if you have heating pipes encased with asbestos insulation with small punctures or minor flaking, wrap protective tape around the damaged areas and coat with a latex paint. When possible, lay new flooring over damaged asbestos tiles or sheets, and avoid sanding or disrupting the under layer. In the case of damaged asbestos roofing and siding shingles, spray painting will seal in the fibers. Apply wood, aluminum, or vinyl siding over asbestos-containing shingles; avoid cracking brittle shingles. A high-temperature paint applied to cement sheets around wood-burning stoves will seal in the asbestos.

Asbestos removal

An asbestos-containing material so deteriorated that sections are falling off or crumbling may be releasing fibers into the air. In this case, or if renovation plans will disturb asbestos materials, contact a licensed asbestos-removal contractor. Attempting removal on your own is unwise; safe equipment may be difficult to acquire, and if improperly done, removal may further contaminate the air. Neither should you dust, sweep, or vacuum any collected debris. Leave that to the contractor. Ordinary dust masks (such as those made by 3M) will not protect you from inhaling asbestos dust.

Be sure to screen any contractor you consider. Ask for a work history résumé, insurance certificates, a written proposal with a price quote, a work procedure outline (including locations of removals), references, and a copy of the notification of removal form that is required by some states. The contractor's job is not complete until air-quality tests—that are performed by the contractor after removal—give safe readings.

Many states require accreditation of asbestos-removal contractors. Your state or city environmental agency may provide a list of licensed contractors. If your state lacks a licensing program, contact your Regional Asbestos Coordinator (a branch of the Environmental Protection Agency) for assistance.

Computer Screens

Computer screens, also known as video display terminals or VDTs, are almost as common as telephones. In 1990, an estimated 70 million people worked at VDTs, and that does not include those who used computers at home or the millions of children who played at them. What are the health effects? According to research conducted by the Food and Drug Administration (FDA), VDTs do not endanger the health of their users. Other researchers, however, offer conflicting results. And many users complain of eyestrain, blurred vision, sore necks and backs, fatigue, insomnia, headaches, nausea, irritability, and tension. Some believe VDTs can even cause cataracts and birth defects. Often, according to the FDA, the problem is not the computer but environmental factors such as poor lighting or seating, and perhaps increased worker tension because of heightened workload. Concerns about the health effects of VDTs, however, persist.

A stick-on clipboard— a device that attaches to your computer terminal by a Velcro strip—can help prevent eyestrain and neck cramping.

Can video display terminals cause birth defects?

One question not yet wholly laid to rest is whether long hours at a VDT may cause miscarriages or birth defects. A study of over four thousand pregnant women recently conducted at the University of Michigan showed that those who work at VDTs less than twenty hours per week do not increase their risk of miscarriage. Among full-time VDT workers, however, there was a very slight, but not significant, increase in the number of miscarriages, but researchers emphasized that their findings should relieve the concern for many women who currently use VDTs at their jobs.

Other concerns

With a mandate from the World Health Organization (WHO), a group of Canadian experts concluded that VDTs are safe. At the same time, they made the following useful points:

Radiation. VDTs emit the same kind of low-level radiation as soil, rocks, fluorescent lights, or electrical appliances in the home. These emissions are not believed to harm humans in any way.

Room comfort. VDTs are a considerable source of heat. You may need to adjust room temperature accordingly. When operating a computer, keep room humidity at 30 percent or more.

Chairs. A stable chair, preferably with a five-legged base, good back support, a footrest, and adjustable seat height, is a necessity. A seat that curves downward at the front edge will help relieve excess pressure on the sitter's legs. A lumbar cushion—a log-shaped round pillow that is placed between the small of your lower back and the chair when you are sitting—may also be worthwhile.

Stress. Although the authors of the review were concerned chiefly with physical aspects of VDTs, they emphasized that the psychological welfare of VDT operators is important, too. People who are satisfied with their jobs are less likely to suffer from VDT-related symptoms. To compensate for the tension that may be caused by working at a VDT, it is important to take breaks every forty minutes or so: get up, walk around, or do simple stretching or relaxation exercises such as deep breathing (see page 409).

Copying Machines

According to experts at the National Institute for Occupational Safety and Health, a properly designed and maintained copying machine does not pose any health hazard. However, insufficient ventilation and lack of maintenance can cause some health problems.

Air quality

The most significant potential problem is that some photocopiers generate ozone, an irritant gas given off by high-voltage machines. While ozone in the ozone layer is good, ozone in the air we breathe irritates the respiratory system and can cause sore throats and labored breathing. It can also produce biochemical changes in the blood, and several animal studies indicate that ozone may increase susceptibility to infection—but its long-range effects are still unknown.

There are two reasons for excessively high ozone levels: poor ventilation and poor maintenance. You can ensure proper ventilation by following the recommendations of manufacturers, most of whom publish ventilation requirements for their machines. Some companies also offer filters that trap ozone. Maintenance is just as important. In one study of photocopiers, excessive ozone emissions dropped to nondetectable levels after routine maintenance. Workers should also avoid breathing the exhaust of a copier, which could occur when sitting next to the copying machine.

Avoiding chemical exposure

Because toners contain chemicals that can be hazardous, workers should watch out for toner dust—loose particles of toner either on copies or around the machine. Toner can be a source of eye irritation for people who wear contact lenses. If you spot toner dust, turn off the machine and have it serviced. Also, don't handle the photocopier's drum, another source of toxic chemicals; leave it to a technician who is trained to handle it safely.

Eyestrain and noise

In addition, copiers can cause eyestrain if they are operated with the cover up. All manufacturers recommend that a photocopier's glass be covered during exposures because the light is extremely intense. If you must keep the cover up, avert your eyes. Many large copying machines also produce noise at levels high enough to interfere with speech or telephone use in the area near the machine. This is another reason why, to be on the safe side, or simply in the interest of worker comfort, a copying machine should have its own well-ventilated room or at least ample space to itself.

Electrical Fields

Scientists have known for many years that electrical fields can affect living cells in various ways. But only in the last fifteen years or so have researchers begun to ask whether exposure to low-frequency electromagnetic fields—the kind generated

No Dangers from Fluorescent Lights

Fluorescent lights emit a very small amount of ultraviolet radiation, but this is no cause for concern for most people. The only people who are at risk from fluorescent lights are those who are endangered by sunlight. There are certain rare skin diseases that make people susceptible to skin cancer. One of these is xeroderma pigmentosum, which occurs when the skin lacks the enzyme that repairs DNA in skin damaged by ultraviolet radiation. For most people, fluorescent lights actually offer a health benefit: their ultraviolet radiation helps the body synthesize vitamin D.

by high-voltage power lines, for example, or ordinary overhead wires, or even electric blankets—causes illness in humans. Research so far is inconclusive, but at least two areas of health concern have emerged, those are: the electric fields generated by electric blankets and heated water beds, as well as those that exist near power lines.

Electric blankets and heated water beds

The use of electric blankets, or of electrically heated water beds, both of which expose the user to a low-frequency electromagnetic field for hours at a time, may be associated with miscarriages or low birth weights. This finding was reported by researchers at the University of Colorado Medical School in Denver, who studied over 1,200 users and nonusers of electrically heated beds. The annual miscarriage rate was higher among women who slept in such beds, and their miscarriages tended to occur during the winter months when they would have been using their heaters. These results were preliminary, however, and the study did not rule out the chance that excess heat (or some other factors) rather than the electrical field itself might have been the significant factor.

There's no reason to throw out your electric blanket, or to feel anxious about using it—unless you are planning a pregnancy or are currently in the early stages of one. If that is the case, avoid electric blankets and electrically heated water beds, or use them only to warm up the covers *before* you get into bed—then turn them off.

Power lines

Perhaps more important, in a study published in 1979, the University of Colorado Medical School researchers reported that living close to high-voltage power transmission lines appeared to be a risk factor for the development of childhood leukemia and other childhood cancers. Children who died of these cancers were two to three times more likely to have lived near high-voltage power lines and transformers—and thus been exposed to intense magnetic fields for long periods—than other children.

Research in Rhode Island failed to find a similar link, but in the early 1980s, when the New York Power Authority sought permission to construct a huge power line, the state ordered the utilities to put up 5 million dollars for research into the health effects of power lines, thus giving rise to a group of studies known as the New York Power Line Project. One researcher reported that there was evidence suggesting that prolonged exposure to high-voltage power lines could double the rate of childhood cancer—from one in 10,000 to one in 5,000. But because as-yet-unidentified factors might have been at work, his findings were not considered definitive.

So far—and perhaps understandably in light of the inconclusive evidence at present—there are no federal standards for human exposure to electric fields, but several states have established some limits on how strong electric fields can be around transmission lines. Researchers hope to see new studies on the health effects of exposure to both high-voltage and ordinary power lines. (In any case, you needn't be worried about possible ill effects from your household appliances; they generate weak fields and exposure to them tends to be brief, so they are thought to be harmless.)

Fires

Each year about six thousand Americans die in fires. The leading causes of home fires are heating equipment, cooking mishaps, arson, and improper electrical distribution. Smoking is the leading cause of death from home fires (30 percent of these deaths are attributable to smoking), and cooking fires are the number-one cause of nonfatal home fire injury. But many of these fires can be prevented, and precautions can be taken to protect you in case of a fire.

Beware of vines entangled in your firewood— they may be poison ivy, which can be hard to identify if the distinctive leaves are gone. Touching dried-out poison ivy can cause a rash.

Preventing home fires

Use the following guidelines to help prevent fires in your home:

Home heating equipment. Purchase equipment that has been labeled and tested by one of the many independent testing laboratories. Check with your fire department to make sure that it complies with local fire and building codes. Have your furnace inspected by a professional annually. Place portable heaters at least three feet away from combustible materials such as paper, clothing, bedding, and curtains. Inspect the cords of electric heaters—do not use the heater if the cords are frayed, split, or overheat when the heater is on. Turn off the heater before leaving the house or going to bed.

Kerosene heaters. If you use a kerosene heater—or any other heater that uses liquid fuel—do not add fuel when the heater is hot. Let it cool completely first. Use only the fuel recommended by the manufacturer with liquid-fuel heaters. *Never* use gasoline.

Wood-burning stoves. These should be installed at least three feet away from a wall and away from any combustible materials. Place approved heat shields under a wood-burning stove to protect the floor from heat and stray hot embers.

Fireplaces. If you use a fireplace, have the chimney inspected annually. Always use a screen with a fireplace.

Fireplace Safety

If you build fires in a fireplace or heat your home with a wood-burning stove, you should check your chimney annually and take steps to keep fumes and fire from entering the room.

Creosote, a black tarlike substance, can build up in a chimney and catch fire. This can crack the chimney or set fire to the house. If you've just moved in, have the chimney checked and cleaned before you use it. In expert hands, it should be a quick, clean, relatively inexpensive procedure.

A cleaner burn

To cut down on creosote build-up, build small, hot fires rather that large smoky ones. Use seasoned woods (stored and dried for at least six months). Hardwoods (maple, oak, elm, or other trees that lose their leaves in the fall) make an even, long-lasting fire. Softwoods (pine, spruce, or fir) burn faster and hotter. If you want to use softwood, combine it with hardwood for a better fire.

Be selective about other things you burn in the fireplace. Colored paper or plastic can produce harmful fumes. Christmas trees make poor firewood because they produce wild sparks. If you use man-made logs, put them on a grate and burn only one of them at a time. Don't poke them apart. They contain wax and coloring agents and thus make a dirtier fire that will clog your chimney faster, possibly contributing to chimney fires.

Electric blankets. Tucking in an electric blanket can cause excessive heat that will start a fire. Don't put anything on top of an electric blanket while it's on, either. This includes other blankets, comforters, and sleeping pets.

Cooking. Never leave food cooking on the stove unattended. Keep stoves and ovens clean; bits of food or grease can catch fire. While cooking, wear clothing with tight-fitting sleeves and avoid wearing frilly aprons. Don't store pot holders on the stove. Heat oil slowly. Never leave oil heating unattended and never heat oil on high—it can catch fire.

Smoking. Keep matches and lighters away from children and teach them that these items are not toys to be played with. Properly extinguish all smoking materials and never smoke in bed.

Home appliances. Check all electrical appliances for broken, frayed, or split wires. Have broken appliances repaired before using. Make sure that televisions and stereos have some space around them. These appliances can easily overheat.

Flammable liquids. Store all flammable liquids—such as kerosene or gasoline—outside of the house in clearly labeled, tightly closed metal safety cans away from heat and other sources of ignition.

Smoke detectors

Deaths and injuries from home fires most often occur at night. Thousands of lives could have been saved if the victims had been awakened in time to flee. Even though most states require smoke-detector installation in new homes, most fire deaths still occur in homes that have no detectors or those that have detectors that are not working. Surveys have found that one-third to one-half of all detectors are not being used, or are not working because of poor maintenance.

There are three basic types of smoke detectors, powered either by house current or batteries:

Ionization devices. The most common type, these contain a trace of radioactive material that produces a continuous flow of electric current between two electrodes. When smoke particles waft across the current, they break the circuit and set off the alarm. Ionization detectors are sensitive to fast-burning fires and react quickly to cooking smoke.

Photoelectric devices. These more expensive detectors emit a beam of light received by a photocell. If smoke interrupts the beam, it triggers the alarm. These react faster to the kind of smoldering fire that begins, for example, in wiring or upholstery and less quickly to cooking smoke.

Combination units. These combine ionization and photoelectric mechanisms, and thus respond to all kinds of fires. If you're buying only one unit, this is the type of unit to buy.

If your house is large or has more than one floor, it may be best to install some of each basic type in order to get the advantages of all of them. For instance, you can put a photoelectric detector in or near the kitchen (it's less likely to scream an alarm every time you burn toast) and combination or ionization detectors in most other areas. Make sure the units you buy have been approved by Underwriters Laboratories (UL) or another testing organization.

Install detectors in the hallway outside bedrooms and on *every level of the house,* basement and attic included. You can install additional detectors inside each bedroom, especially if you sleep with the bedroom door closed or if you smoke. If you're hard of hearing or a heavy sleeper, look for a model with a loud alarm. Since smoke rises, mount detectors high on a wall or on the ceiling, but no closer than four inches from where wall and ceiling meet. Also, don't put one within three feet of a window, door, or vent, since drafts can prevent smoke from reaching the device, as can water vapor, so avoid bathrooms, too.

Vacuum the detectors at least once a year to avoid dust-related false alarms or reduced sensitivity. Replace the batteries yearly (choose a model that emits a beep when batteries are low), and test them regularly, following the manufacturer's instructions. It's also a good idea to plan escape routes in case of fire and discuss them, or even rehearse them, with your family. Set off the detector so that everybody knows what it sounds like.

Some insurance companies will reduce your household premiums if you install smoke detectors—it's worth inquiring.

Fire extinguishers

Every household should have an extinguisher—probably more than one, since they all don't do precisely the same job. Don't count on water to fight a home fire. Because many fires originate in faulty or overloaded wiring, water can be

Hotel Fires

Whenever you stay in a hotel, investigate fire-safety measures. In hotels, as at home, smoke detectors are vital. Most people who die in hotel fires die from inhaling smoke or toxic fumes, not from burns. Adequate detection systems can save many lives; more widespread use of fire-resistant materials might save others.

Fortunately, more and more hotels have installed wireless alarms and sprinkler systems. Sensors placed in rooms, corridors, stairways, and all public spaces send radio signals to a central monitoring station, which can then alert guests, fire fighters, and police. Because the sensors are battery powered, they continue to operate even if the hotel's power is knocked out. And more hotels are decorating rooms with wall coverings and fabrics that are highly fire-resistant and, if they do burn, give off low-toxicity fumes.

Realistically, your chances of getting caught in a hotel fire are very small; chances of injury or death, even smaller. But it's only prudent to take certain precautions:

• Know your surroundings. Check the location of the floor's fire alarm in case you need to sound it, and verify escape routes. Make sure fire stairs are not locked or blocked. Count the number of doors from your room to the nearest exit; this may sound silly, but it will allow you to feel your way there through darkness or smoke. It's also wise to know where the second nearest exit is.

• Pack a small flashlight; keep it and your room key on the night table—and if there's a fire, take them along. That way if flames force you to return to your room, you won't be locked out.

• Most important, do not smoke in bed. Half of all hotel-fire fatalities are the result of careless smoking.

If there's a fire, every second may count:

• If you hear an alarm or smell smoke, get out of your room, but not before you've felt the back of the door and knob. If they're cool, open the door slowly and take the nearest escape route. If they're hot, don't open the door; fire is probably raging in the corridor, so you're safer in your room. Call the management and/or fire department to report your location, and seal the door cracks with wet towels. Shut off fans and air conditioners and wait by your window where rescuers can see you.

• If the corridor or staircase is smoky, crawl. The air will be clearer at floor level. If smoke is thick at lower levels, go back to your room. Never try to run for it through heavy smoke—you won't make it.

• If the fire is in your room, get out, close the door, set off the floor alarm, and report it to the management.

• Don't waste precious time gathering your possessions.

• Don't use the elevator.

dangerous, due to the risk of electrocution. You should fight a fire yourself only when you've made sure that everybody has fled the house and someone has called the fire department. Then resort to an extinguisher if the fire is still small and your back is to a safe exit. If any one of these conditions isn't met, or you're simply not sure whether you should stay and fight the fire, leave the house immediately, closing the door behind you.

Extinguishers are labeled A, B, or C (or combinations of these), based on the three types of fires defined by Underwriters Laboratories (UL):

Class A. These are effective against fires fueled by "ordinary combustibles," such as wood, paper, cloth, plastic, or rubber.

Class B. These work on fires fueled by fast-burning liquids, such as gasoline, cooking oils, or paints, as well as grease and tar.

Class C. These are extinguishers with nonconducting contents and therefore are used to fight electrical fires.

The UL label should also include a number indicating how big a fire the extinguisher can handle. Thus, a "2" rating means twice as much extinguishing capability as a "1." The higher the rating, the heavier the extinguisher—but it doesn't pay to buy a model too big to handle. The C models have no number rating.

A good choice to hang near the kitchen door is an extinguisher labeled BC. This is better than an "all-purpose" extinguisher (labeled ABC and filled with ammonium phosphate) because the sodium bicarbonate it contains works best against most kitchen fires. All-purpose extinguishers are smart choices for garages, workshops, and basements.

Another type of extinguisher filled with halon gas leaves far less residue than other types, and is effective against all classes of fires. But halon is much more expensive than dry-chemical models, less effective against kitchen grease fires, and harder to recharge. Even more important, halon (like its chemical relatives the chlorofluorocarbons) contributes to the depletion of the ozone layer—thus the United States and many other nations have limited its production. Don't buy a halon extinguisher for home use.

Make sure any extinguisher you buy will be easy for you and your family to lift and remove from its wall mounting, and simple to aim and trigger without your having to pause to read instructions. It should have some kind of safety catch to avoid accidental firing. Make sure there's an easy-to-read pressure gauge—and remember to check it frequently. Most models have a gauge indicating when the pressure has dropped too low. For recharging, check the instructions on the side, or look in the yellow pages under "fire extinguishers."

Formaldehyde

Formaldehyde, a colorless gas with a pungent odor, is so commonly used today that virtually everyone is likely to be exposed to at least small amounts of it, and a significant number of people are developing symptoms due to exposure to large amounts of formaldehyde in their homes or workplaces. It was an integral component of the urea formaldehyde foam insulation (UFFI) that was installed in more than five hundred thousand homes in the 1970s. (The use of formaldehyde in insulation was banned by the Consumer Product Safety Commission in 1982, but this ruling was overturned by a federal court in 1983.) In addition, it is present in a large variety of consumer products. It is a major part of the resins used as glue in particle board, plywood, and other wood products used extensively in the construction of homes and furniture. Some cosmetics, upholstery, permanent press fabrics, carpets, and pesticides contain it, too. Formaldehyde is also present in the exhaust from some appliances and in tobacco smoke.

The most common symptoms of excessive formaldehyde exposure are burning eyes, itching, shortness of breath, tightness in the chest, coughing, headaches, nausea, and asthma attacks. Large amounts of the gas have produced cancer in laboratory animals, and government policy assumes that any substance that can cause cancer in animals may also cause it in humans.

Reducing the risk

People who live in mobile homes or in homes that have been "tightened" for maximum energy conservation are most likely to suffer from the effects of formaldehyde gas. Mobile homes have particularly high levels because they contain large quantities of plywood and particle board. The formaldehyde gas seeps from the walls or furniture into the air, building up to high levels, which can be irritating, particularly to sensitive people.

To minimize your exposure to formaldehyde, ventilate your home—don't shut the windows all the way. You can seal exposed, raw surfaces of particle board and plywood with paint, varnish, wallpaper, or vinyl floor coverings. If you have UFFI insulation, make certain it is completely sealed in the walls or, as a last resort, have it removed.

Gas Stoves

About 60 percent of American families cook with gas. Although gas appliances are often called "clean burning," they can emit invisible and odorless by-products of combustion—nitrogen oxides and carbon monoxide. These compounds can irritate the respiratory system and may have long-term effects on lung function. Studies have suggested that children living in homes with unvented gas stoves are somewhat more susceptible to colds and respiratory ailments than those in homes with electric stoves.

Although gas ranges are by far the major sources of nitrogen oxides in the home, unvented kerosene and gas heaters can also be major sources if used more than occasionally. Gas furnaces, clothes dryers, and other vented gas-burning appliances usually do not pollute the air unless the vent flue is blocked or broken.

Safety measures

If you do have gas appliances or a kerosene heater, take the following precautions:
- Be sure that your stove hood vents gases outdoors. Some hood fans simply filter out grease and then recirculate gases. Installing a hood that vents properly can be expensive but is definitely worthwhile.
- If a venting hood is impossible to install, you can use an exhaust fan in a nearby window, provided you turn it on every time you cook.
- When buying a new gas range, choose a model with a pilotless ignition system

rather than a conventional pilot light. This cuts fuel consumption—and the amount of combustion by-products released—by one-third.

• Make sure that gas-burning furnaces and clothes dryers are vented to the outside and that the vents are clear.

• Check the pilot light and the flames on the kitchen range now and then. They should burn blue. If they are yellow, gas combustion is incomplete and pollutants are forming. Make sure that the burners are clear and that the gas jets are unblocked. If the yellow flame persists, call a service person or the utility company.

• Don't use unvented kerosene or gas space heaters except as emergency heat for short periods. Follow the manufacturer's instructions as to the grade of kerosene you should use.

• Leave some windows slightly open to allow ventilation.

• Discourage smoking. Cigarette smoke contributes to the level of nitrogen oxides and other toxic chemicals in the air.

Hair Dryers

Hair dryers can cause electrocution if a plugged-in dryer falls into a bathtub while someone is bathing, or the hair dryer falls into a full sink or tub and an unthinking person reaches in to get it. These incidents can be fatal *even if the switch is in the "off" position.*

Safety standards, set by Underwriters Laboratories (UL) in October of 1987, require that hair dryers be designed so they won't produce a dangerous shock if they fall in water when the power switch is in the "off" position. Some recent models also have a feature that will protect you from shocks when a dryer that's turned on falls in water.

If you have a hair dryer made before October 1987, you may want to replace it, especially if you have young children. But even if you buy a model with every safety device, no hair dryer is 100 percent safe. Take these precautions:

• Never use a dryer or other electrical device near a sink or tub filled with water.

• After you're finished using it, *unplug it immediately,* and hang or store it in a secure place.

• If you do drop it in water, unplug it—first making sure your hands are dry—before retrieving it.

If you do not already have one, you might also consider installing a ground-fault interrupter outlet in your bathroom. This special outlet contains a circuit breaker that cuts off power if any device produces an electrical surge. It costs 30 to 50 dollars at hardware stores, and you may have to hire someone to install it. But it comes closer than anything else to making you and your family shockproof.

Household Toxins

"Hazardous waste" is a term more readily associated with atomic power plants than with our storerooms and basements. Yet many home projects such as car maintenance and gardening involve chemicals that are extremely hazardous to your health or that of your neighbor. These substances can be hard to dispose of responsibly: if dumped, they can seep into the water supply; if incinerated, they can pollute the air. Many municipalities are tightening the rules on what may be sent to the local garbage dump.

Ideally every community should have collection centers equipped to handle hazardous wastes. (If your community has none, you can inquire about starting such a center through your state's hazardous waste agency.) Meanwhile, remember that it is dangerous—and in many localities illegal—to dispose of liquid wastes by pouring them into storm drains or into sewage systems.

Alternatives to Common Cleaning Materials

The average kitchen and bathroom cabinets are filled with assorted cleansers and disinfectants for almost every part of the house, but many home fixtures can be cleaned just as effectively with only six common household ingredients—salt, baking soda, white vinegar, borax,* washing soda,* and liquid soap.*†

Household Product	Substitute
Air freshener	Find the source of the odor and eliminate it. Put small bowls of baking soda in the refrigerator and around the house. Also sprinkle baking soda into the bottoms of trash cans.
Ammonia- or chlorine-based cleaners	Mix 2 teaspoons borax with 1 teaspoon liquid soap in 1 quart water. (This solution can be stored in a spray bottle.)
Carpet deodorizer	Sprinkle baking soda or cornmeal (approximately 1 cup per room) on the carpets. Let stand 30 minutes, and then vacuum.
Disinfectants	Add ¼ cup borax to ½ cup hot water. (This mixture also deodorizes.) Or sponge isopropyl alcohol onto surfaces and allow to dry.**
Drain cleaner and unclogger	*To avoid clogs:* Always use the drain sieve. *To prevent clogs:* Once a week, pour ¼ cup salt, ½ cup baking soda, and ½ cup vinegar down the drain and cover it. Allow to stand for several minutes, then pour a pot of boiling water down the drain. *To unclog a drain:* Use a plunger (or plumber's snake if the plunger is ineffective) to break up the clog, and then flush the drain with the baking soda method mentioned above.
Glass cleaner	Add 5 tablespoons vinegar to 1 quart warm water. (You can store the solution in a spray bottle.) Stubborn spots can be removed with undiluted vinegar.
Metal polish, brass	Make a paste of equal parts flour, salt, and vinegar. Apply the paste, allow to sit an hour, then rub off, rinse, and polish with a soft, damp cloth.
Metal polish, chrome	Apply undiluted apple cider vinegar. Wipe with a soft, dry cloth.
Metal polish, copper	Make a paste of salt and hot vinegar. Rub, rinse, and polish with soft, damp cloth. Or use a paste of salt and lemon juice. Rub, rinse, and polish with soft, damp cloth.
Metal polish, silver and stainless steel	Make a paste of baking soda and water. Rub with the paste, rinse, and polish with a soft, damp cloth.
Scouring powder	Combine equal parts of vinegar and salt, and scrub with a firm-bristled brush. Or sprinkle borax or baking soda on a damp sponge for a less abrasive cleanser.
Shoe polish	Rub any nut or olive oil into shoe leather and buff with a soft cloth.
Wood floor and furniture polish	Use 2 to 3 parts vegetable oil with 1 part lemon juice. Apply a small amount and rub into the wood with a soft cloth.

 * *Found in supermarkets or hardware stores.*
 ** *Use in a well-ventilated area and wear gloves.*
 † *Use only those liquid soaps that contain no added artificial fragrance or color.*

Disposal tips

Here are some examples and suggestions for safely discarding common types of household waste:

Automotive supplies (motor oils, antifreeze, transmission fluids, car wax). Many automotive chemicals are toxic if absorbed through the skin or if their vapors are inhaled. See if your gas station or automotive store will accept labeled containers of old fluids. If not, try to get the address of an oil-recycling station from your state highway department. As a last resort, pour the fluids into a container filled with sawdust or cat litter, seal it, and put it in the trash.

Painting supplies (paint, thinner, turpentine, mineral spirits). Try to give paint to someone who can use it. Latex or oil paint can be allowed to dry out in an open can and disposed of as trash. Thinners and many other painting supplies are highly poisonous, may contain cancer-causing chemicals, and are usually flammable. Seal them tightly in their original containers and hold them for delivery to a hazardous waste collection program.

Asbestos. Inhaled asbestos fibers can cause serious lung disease. Get professional help in removing and disposing of duct-wrapping and other possible sources of asbestos. Deteriorating asbestos materials can release thousands of invisible particles, which cannot be swept up with a broom or household vacuum cleaner. (For more information, see pages 467-468.)

Insecticides. These can kill pets or people; some contain cancer-causing chemicals. Unless you can get a neighbor to take your unused insecticides and use them up, store them until you can deliver them to a hazardous waste collection program. Rinse empty containers three times before discarding them.

Batteries. Battery acids are corrosive and can burn your skin. Trade in old auto batteries or return them to the battery dealer. Small batteries contain mercury or lead, both highly toxic, and should not be incinerated. If you have a number of those small button batteries that come out of watches or cameras, you may be able to dispose of them at a hospital or a hearing aid center. Keep these small batteries out of children's hands, since they may swallow them.

Outdated medicines. Flush unused medicine down the toilet; rinse the bottles before discarding them.

Household cleaners containing sodium hydroxide (lye) or ammonia. If you have a large sewage system, these can be washed down the drain with lots of water. Rinse the containers well. (Be careful whenever you mix lye with water—it can spatter in your eyes.) Take care not to mix ammonia-containing products with chlorine bleaches when you dispose of them. Combining ammonia and chlorine releases a toxic nerve gas.

Humidifiers

Indoor heat dries out the air, and dry air in turn reabsorbs the moisture from wherever it can—your skin, your throat, the interior of your nose, as well as from your furniture and houseplants. Dry throats and noses are uncomfortable in themselves, can make a cold more annoying, and can cause lung irritation. Moreover, dry mucous membranes may make you more susceptible to colds. There are several remedies for dry air—the traditional pot of water on the steam radiator, hot-air humidifiers or vaporizers, cool-air or console humidifiers, and ultrasonic humidifiers, which use high-frequency sound to turn water into mist. No humidifier will cure a cold or prevent it, but it can make you more comfortable in the dry winter air.

The best humidifier

A pot of water on a radiator is inexpensive and easy to clean, but it does not propel moisture into the air. Vaporizers are often used to relieve a cough or cold, but they pose the danger of burns and electrical shock. Cool-air humidifiers are safer to use. Because bacteria and molds can grow in the reservoir, both vaporizers and humidfiers need frequent and thorough washing with mild soap. While a steam vaporizer usually gets hot enough to kill these microorganisms, a cool-air humidifier will simply spray them into the air, where they can cause allergic reactions or more serious lung infections. Therefore, if you use a cool-air humidifier, you should wash it daily. That should keep anything from growing in it. If you choose to add a small amount of bleach to the water, it will kill molds and bacteria, but it could also be irritating or cause allergic reactions as well as create an unpleasant smell.

Don't leave a pot of water boiling on a gas flame all day to boost humidity. You don't want to breathe the continuous emission of fumes from a burning gas flame.

Ultrasonic humidifiers

Ultrasonic humidifiers use high-frequency vibrations to turn water into mist, so they eject no live molds and very few bacteria into the air you breathe. They also have the advantages of operating more quietly then other types and being able to humidify large areas.

Tests, however, have indicated that the ultrasonic humidifiers have their own drawbacks. When they are filled with ordinary tap water—and most people fill their humidifiers with just that, even if instructions call for distilled water—the humidifiers throw tiny particles of the minerals dissolved in the water into the air. Eventually these form a white dust that can coat furniture. When inhaled, these airborne particles are small enough to penetrate into the deepest part of the lungs, where they may increase susceptibility to colds and flu as well as aggravate chronic respiratory diseases like asthma and bronchitis. Besides the minerals that naturally occur even in soft water, tap water may contain lead and asbestos as well as dissolved gases such as radon that can adhere to the dust or water particles and "piggy-back" into the lungs.

How significant is the problem? Research by the Environmental Protection Agency (EPA) found that within twenty-four hours, ultrasonic humidifiers using tap water of average hardness filled a test room with a concentration of particulate matter forty times the recommended limit for outdoor air. Outdoor air regulations are the only standard of comparison available, as there are no criteria established for indoor air.

So if you use tap water in your ultrasonic humidifier, be sure to run it through a demineralizing filter first. In fact, some humidifiers come with such devices or offer them as options. If you have very hard water, it is probably cheaper to use distilled water than to keep replacing filters. In any case, ultrasonic humidifiers, like cool-air humidifiers, still have to be cleaned regularly, following manufacturer's instructions, to prevent extensive bacterial growth over time that may cause allergic reactions in some individuals.

Indoor Air Quality

There are many substances that can contribute to a decline in indoor air quality both at home and in the workplace. One possible pollutant of indoor air is carbon monoxide, produced by incomplete combustion of a solid, liquid, or gaseous fuel. Gas ranges, furnaces, and automobiles are all possible sources. Breathing small amounts won't kill you, but can make you sick. Some symptoms of chronic exposure are constant headaches, tiredness, and sleepiness. The problem becomes particularly urgent in the winter when storm windows, weather stripping, and sealers are in regular use and windows are rarely opened.

Other potential pollutants of indoor air are formaldehyde (see page 475-476); radon (see page 491); nitrogen oxides (see page 476); and passive cigarette smoke (see page 488-489). Pollen, mold spores, and dust mites can also contribute to poor indoor air quality and cause problems for allergy sufferers.

Do air purifiers help?

Although air purifiers can remove airborne smoke and dust, they're useless against gas molecules that are too small to be trapped by the filters. These gases include

Allergies and Car Air Conditioners

Air conditioners are usually a godsend to allergy sufferers, reducing indoor pollens, spore counts, and dust. Sometimes, however, a car's air conditioner (or even one in a home or office) is itself the cause of an allergy or asthma attack. The culprits are fungi that produce airborne mold spores and grow deep within the car's air conditioner, where moisture (from condensation), engine heat, and darkness combine to make a perfect environment for molds. And the close confines of the passenger compartment make matters worse.

A study conducted at Louisiana State University found that one out of five allergy or asthma sufferers experienced a worsening of symptoms (sneezing, coughing, wheezing, difficulty in breathing) because of car air conditioning, despite the continued use of medications. Up to one-third of all auto air conditioners are infected with quick-growing fungi, especially those in hot, humid regions like Louisiana.

Most people don't suffer ill effects from the organisms that hitch a ride in the air conditioner. They just notice an unpleasant musty odor when they first turn on the air conditioner. *If, however, you're allergic to the molds, try the following:*

Air it out. Keep the car windows open partway for ten to fifteen minutes after you turn on the air conditioner; if necessary, wear an appropriate mask (it must not block your vision) until most of the molds are expelled. Don't direct the vents toward your face. And, if your air conditioner gives you the choice, press the button for "fresh air" rather than recirculated air.

The disinfectant route. If these steps don't help, have your car treated with the EPA-registered disinfectant called RenNew-A/C (containing Alcide, a formulation of chlorous acid), available at a variety of outlets, including car dealer service departments, some service stations, and most auto air conditioner shops. The compound, sprayed into the core of the system, is supposed to keep the car mold-free for about six months, though in humid climates it may last only three months. A study presented at the 1988 meeting of the American Thoracic Society found that this disinfectant was as effective as hydrogen peroxide, without that compound's corrosive effect on metals. The treatment must be done by a trained, equipped mechanic. It usually costs 50 to 100 dollars and takes about one hour. Some shops offer it as part of an annual air conditioner checkup.

By the way, do-it-yourself applications of other kinds of disinfectants are unlikely to have any long-lasting effect, since the sprays don't get into the system's core. Deodorizers merely mask the odor—they don't kill mold spores.

paint and chemical fumes, radon, and formaldehyde from insulation. Air purifiers work by using a fan to draw room air past a filter to remove particles, or by electrically charging airborne particles and using polarized metal plates to pull them out of the air. How effective purifiers are depends not only on how much air they can circulate, but also on the type of filter used. The most effective filter is the HEPA filter (high-efficiency particulate arresting)—which was developed during World War II to remove radioactive dust in atomic energy plants. HEPA filters are manufactured to a high standard and are durable, but they're expensive (anywhere from 250 to 650 dollars). Some electrostatic filters treat more air per minute and may thus be just as effective.

The few controlled studies on air purifiers have shown that they have little or no effect on allergens. A purifier is ineffective against these particles because they don't remain airborne for long. Once they settle, even the most powerful air purifier can do nothing to eliminate them. One study found that the machines were helpful when placed directly above the heads of allergic children while they slept, because the particles did not have a chance to settle. These children had some decrease in their symptoms, or at least needed less medication for their allergies. However, not all steps had been taken to make the rooms dust-free; such steps might have done as much good as the filters.

Eliminating indoor pollutants

Outdoor air ventilation is most effective in alleviating many home and office pollution problems, but it's still worth taking these precautions in your home:

•Have a reputable heating company inspect your furnace, the flue, and the vent connector pipe. Replace any rusted or damaged parts. If converting from one type of fuel to another, get a qualified technician to do the work.

•Make sure your gas range has an exhaust fan vented to the outside. Use the fan every time you cook.

•Vent all fuel-burning heaters to the outside.

If you go to an indoor skating rink, remember that the ice resurfacing machines are usually gasoline-powered and can be a significant source of carbon monoxide. While resurfacing is going on, the rink management should operate an exhaust system and keep rink barrier doors open.

Houseplants and Air Quality

In addition to their aesthetic value, houseplants are good to have around since they "breathe" in carbon dioxide and return a small amount of oxygen and moisture to the air. A NASA scientist looking for ways to cleanse the air in space stations discovered that some plants—in particular, the hardy spider plant—actually remove certain pollutants from the air in enclosed environments.

Indoor pollution may result from carbon monoxide and nitrogen dioxide released from gas stoves. formaldehyde, and smoke from cooking or tobacco. (According to NASA experiments, the foliage of the common spider plant reduced the formaldehyde content of the air by about 85 percent in a six-hour period (the microbes in the plant soil also helped).

While spider plants are good at "eating" carbon monoxide and nitrogen dioxide too, they are not effective against smoke and have not been tested against other pollutants.

The catch is that an average home might need as many as seventy plants to really rid the air of all formaldehyde, carbon monoxide, and nitrogen dioxide. (As few as fifteen plants would have some positive effect, but the plants would work best if kept in a solarium through which air from the central heat/air conditioning system is pulled.) Not many houses or apartments could offer this option.

Good ventilation remains your best protection against bad indoor air. If you have room for a few spider plants, they might help, too. But don't rely on them to purify the air.

•Never use a gas range or oven to heat a room, even in a power outage.

•Do not use a charcoal grill inside the house: burning charcoal generates carbon monoxide. Even in a fireplace, fumes may back up into the room.

•When warming up your car in the garage, keep the outer door open. Carbon monoxide levels can build up quickly, and if your garage is attached to your house, fumes can seep into it.

Controlling allergens

Some of the steps above will help control pollen, mold spores, and dust. What additional steps you take depends on whether you have hay fever, are asthmatic, or merely have a sensitive nose. But here are some commonsense steps:

•In warm weather an air conditioner can help, especially if you have hay fever. Most systems reuse the air already in the room, taking in very little from the outside, thus admitting little pollen and few spores. However, in humid climates mold can grow inside the air conditioner itself. (For more information on mold, see box on page 481.)

•Vacuum, mop, and dust frequently. Remember, however, cleaning may temporarily stir up dust. Use a damp, not dry, mop or cloth, and change your vacuum's dust bag often. Or get someone else to clean for you, and for about an hour try to stay out of a room that's been vacuumed, until the dust has settled. Minimize the dust-collecting clutter in your home. Wood or linoleum floors are easier to keep dust-free than carpet.

•Clean or replace the filter in a forced-air heater every month. You can also cover vent ducts with filters.

•Keep your pets out of your bedroom in order to keep dander levels down where you are sleeping.

•Use allergenproof casings for pillows, mattresses, and box springs. Use washable blankets and bedspreads, and wash bedclothes often (use hot water to kill dust mites). Feather pillows create dust, and foam can harbor molds, so use pillows made of Dacron or other hypoallergenic polyester materials.

Ladders

Nearly one hundred thousand Americans are treated in emergency rooms each year for ladder- or stool-related injuries. Most ladder injuries are caused by falls, though some result from electric shock when a metal ladder touches power lines. While using a ladder is safer than climbing on a chair or counter, it is a risky activity and requires care and caution.

Choosing an appropriate ladder

Not all ladders are alike. Most ladders sold for household use are type III light-duty ladders, which can hold a maximum of 200 pounds (including both user and materials). If you expect to do heavier work—or are heavier yourself—get a ladder with a more heavy-duty rating (type II will hold about 225 pounds; type I about 250 pounds).

Make sure your ladder is long enough for the job. The length of a ladder is not the same as its usable length. The top three rungs of a straight ladder are not

The distance between the base of a ladder and the wall should be one-quarter the ladder's usable length. Don't count the top three rungs of a straight ladder and the top two steps of a step ladder—they are not meant to be used.

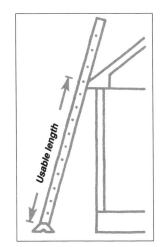

Usable length

meant to be stood on; similarly, the top two steps of a step ladder are not meant to be used. Metal ladders conduct electricity, so if you plan to use a ladder near power lines, with electrical equipment, or to change a light bulb, a wooden or fiberglass ladder is best. If you must use electrical tools on a metal ladder, make sure the tools are properly grounded.

In addition, take the following precautions:

•Never use a ladder in a strong wind, and never put one in front of a door that is not locked, blocked, or guarded.

•Put the ladder on firm and level ground or on a flat wooden board for firm support; best of all, have a helper hold the bottom of the ladder.

•Always check the eaves for wasps nests; you don't want to discover the nest when you are on top of the ladder.

•Always face the ladder when you climb it, and use both hands. Don't lean too far to the side while you are working on the ladder. Carry tools in pockets or in a bag attached to your belt, or have them attached to a rope you can raise and lower. Be sure the soles of your shoes are clean and dry.

•Avoid metal ladders with sharp edges, dents, or bent steps or rails.

•All metal ladders should have slip-resistant rubber or plastic feet and slip-resistant steps.

•On wooden ladders, watch out for cracks and any large, weak-looking knots. The steps of wooden ladders should be reinforced with metal rods or angle braces.

•Never paint a wooden ladder; the paint will hide defects.

Lead

Real progress has been made in reducing the level of lead in the environment through the government's phasing out of leaded gasoline and its ban on lead-based house paint. According to the Environmental Protection Agency (EPA), nationwide data show that blood lead levels have declined—they now stand at approximately 5 micrograms per deciliter of blood—and there is every reason to hope that blood lead levels will decline even further. The phasing out of leaded gasoline between 1975 and 1980 was a major contributor to the decline in blood lead levels. Yet lead still finds its way into our bodies, especially from tap water contaminated by lead plumbing materials. Moreover, as testing procedures become more sophisticated, it is becoming evident that even small amounts of lead can adversely affect the body. The "maximum safe levels" of lead may not be safe enough.

Assessing the risks

Elevated levels of this highly toxic metal in the body can damage the nervous system, blood-forming processes, kidneys, and reproductive system. Children and fetuses are at greatest risk. Toxicologists worry that chronic exposure of children to low doses of lead may cause learning and behavioral disorders and stunted growth. In addition, studies have shown that lead can raise blood pressure in adults. Many of these ill effects have been known since antiquity. In fact, some historians claim that the fall of the Roman Empire was due in part to the ruling class's heavy exposure to lead from pots and plumbing, which, the theory goes, caused infertility and mental disorders.

According to the EPA, nearly one-fifth of all Americans live in homes with the potential for excessive lead levels in their water supply. The problem is twofold: first, lead can come from the old lead service pipes and mains of water systems. Water suppliers must comply with the EPA's maximum level for lead—fifty parts per billion. The EPA plans to propose a lower limit of ten parts per billion—but this has not gone into effect yet.

Second, household plumbing poses special problems. Homes built over eighty years ago may still contain lead or lead alloy pipes. If your house is that old and has dull gray pipes instead of copper ones, they may be galvanized or lead. If they are lead, you should consider replacing them. A far more widespread—and usually less serious—contaminant is lead solder, which until recently was used to join copper pipes. Newly installed lead solder, which is shinier than old solder, is most hazardous, since the lead dissolves most easily during its first five years. Lead contamination is most serious in areas with soft water, which is slightly acidic and thus corrodes the lead pipes and solder. Your water supply company can tell you if your water is corrosive.

Nearly 94 percent of all cans contain no lead solder, so the risk of lead leaching into foods is minimal.

Basic precautions

Since lead in water is invisible and, even in moderate amounts, tasteless, you need special testing to find out if you have unacceptable levels of lead in your water. Your supplier or local health department may be willing to test your tap water for lead and other contaminants; or they can refer you to a private lab that will test your water.

If you find out—or have strong suspicions—that your tap water contains high lead levels, taking the following precautions may save you the great expense of ripping out your plumbing:

•Run water for three to five minutes first thing in the morning or any time the faucet hasn't been used for several hours or more. This will flush out standing water that has been in contact with any lead plumbing materials for a long time.

•Don't drink, cook with, or prepare baby formulas with hot tap water. Hot water dissolves lead more quickly than cold.

•If any new plumbing is installed or repairs made, insist that nonlead materials be used. In June 1988, Congress began enforcing a ban on the use of pipe with more than 8 percent lead and solder with more than 0.2 percent lead in new plumbing or repairs to plumbing that supplies drinking water. There are good—though usually more expensive—alternatives to lead. For instance, tin-antimony solder is a good substitute for tin-lead solder.

•Even if your plumbing system contains lots of lead, think twice before installing a water filter. Charcoal filters won't remove lead; the only type recommended by the EPA for lead is a reverse osmosis device. But such filters are expensive, energy intensive, and difficult to maintain. Though initially they may be cheaper than replacing your plumbing, that may not hold true in the long run.

Lead in pottery

Water is not the only source of lead. Nearly every American household has some lead-glazed earthenware pottery, recognizable by its bright rich colors and glossy sheen. Unfortunately, some lead-glazed pottery imported from Mexico, China, and many developing nations—and, much less frequently, from Europe—has not been fired at sufficiently high temperatures to keep the lead from leaching out into foods. Continued use of a defectively glazed object can expose a person to hazardous, possibly life-threatening, doses of lead.

Since 1971, American manufacturers have been required to fire their earthenware pottery at temperatures that make the lead glazes relatively impervious. European and Japanese wares are also usually well fired. There are occasional exceptions, however, and lead sometimes may leach out of old lead-glazed American wares.

The Food and Drug Administration (FDA) tests only a fraction of all earthenware imports. Studies have shown that even when pottery has been tested and found to be safe initially, repeated washings can cause the lead glaze to deteriorate and release several times the allowable limit of lead. You don't have to worry about stoneware (usually marked "ovenproof" or "dishwasher-proof") or porcelain, since they are both fired at very high temperatures.

The seepage of lead is most severe when acidic foods—wine, orange juice, coffee, tomato juice, spaghetti sauce, pickles, salad dressings—are stored, cooked, or served in lead-glazed jugs, mugs, and dishes. For instance, the lead content of one glass of orange juice stored for twenty-four hours in a defective pitcher can well exceed the FDA's ceiling for total daily intake of lead for an adult. The same dose of lead is more than four times the daily maximum for children.

To be perfectly safe, do not use glazed earthenware pottery—especially brightly colored imported ceramics—except for ornamental purposes. Above all, do not store acidic foods in glazed earthenware. If you are concerned about your pottery, you can have it tested at a private or university chemical laboratory to make sure it leaches only minimal amounts of lead. Home kits for lead testing aren't very accurate or sensitive, but if you test pottery with one and it is positive, don't use the pottery.

Noise Pollution

Excessive noise takes a heavy toll on your total health, not just on your eardrums. If you live or work in a noisy environment, you may be at risk from such tension-related ailments as high blood pressure and fatigue, in addition to possibly suffering some hearing loss. According to government statistics, one out of every ten Americans is exposed to noise of sufficient intensity and duration to cause permanent hearing loss.

Noise does not have to be painful to damage the ears or cause symptoms of anxiety. The EPA defines excessive noise as sounds that force individuals to raise their voices for normal conversation. Round-the-clock noise in a few urban neighborhoods approaches the maximum legal noise level to which workers may be exposed for eight hours (90 decibels). Traffic, radios, passing trains, lawn mowers, sirens, and jackhammers can add up to a nightmare for the inner ear.

Humans have the capacity to adapt to almost anything, and with noise this capability is both an asset and a liability. We can block out the noise consciously; but our bodies don't adapt physically or psychologically. Noise is like an alarm bell to the body—it signals danger and stimulates alertness. When noise is constant, the body is reacting to an alarm we are no longer aware of. In a study at a sleep center in Strasbourg, France, sleepers were bombarded with traffic noises for fifteen nights. After a few nights the subjects said they were no longer bothered by the sounds. Unknown to them, however, their bodies were still responding to the noise with increases in heart rate, blood pressure, respiration, muscle tension, hormone levels, and perspiration. Their bodies did not adjust with time: on the fifteenth night these effects remained identical to those observed by the researchers on the first night. Besides the physiological impact, there's a psychological effect. A Munich study found that after one night's exposure to noise, subjects were irritable for about ten minutes. After additional noisy nights, their bad moods lasted until the late morning or early afternoon.

Researchers at the University of Amsterdam uncovered troubling links between airport noise and hypertension. They compared the incidence of high blood pressure among people who lived near an airport to that of people from a quiet area. They found that among airport neighbors the incidence of hypertension was 72 percent higher. In another study, the Dutch researchers found that in one area, the sale of antihypertension drugs doubled in the six years following the opening of a new airport runway. People who live near airports are particularly endangered, as shown by a study of children living along the air corridor of the Los Angeles International Airport. Compared to children living outside the flight path, they had significantly higher blood pressure and greater difficulty in solving puzzles and math problems.

Reducing noise

There are many ways to reduce noise in your immediate environment: hang overlapping, double drapes over the windows; upholstered furniture will absorb sounds from inside and outside the house; if the kitchen is noisy, put in sound-absorbing ceiling tiles and place a rubber pad under noisy appliances, such as blenders; install wooden cabinets, which vibrate less than metal ones; to protect your neighbors' health, operate loud machinery such as power saws and mowers at reasonable hours; if background noise is intolerable, you can try using earplugs or protective muffs like those worn by people in factories and rifle ranges.

If you are moving into a new neighborhood, find out if the residents have had problems with traffic noise, airplanes overhead, or loud businesses. Restaurants with noisy ventilators or air conditioners are a common source of complaints in cities. If the area seems noisy, check the sound level by using the "walk away" test, developed by the Department of Housing and Urban Development. Stand outdoors with a friend and have him read aloud in a normal voice. You should be able to walk away from him and comprehend his words at least twenty-five feet away for the background sound level to be considered acceptable.

Prolonged exposure to noise levels over 80 decibels can cause hearing loss, and many everyday noises are even higher than 100 decibels. The noise level from a rock concert can reach over 120 decibels; people wearing headphones on the street typically turn them up to about 115 decibels; and customized car stereos with several speakers are often played at their maximum levels—130 decibels, roughly the sound of a jet engine taking off.

Oven Cleaners

Unless you have a self-cleaning oven, you probably resort to oven cleaners from the supermarket. Most do the job well enough, but they require the user to take special safety precautions.

The ingredient to watch out for is lye (sodium hydroxide), also known as caustic soda. Lye-impregnated cleaning pads have recently come on the market, and lye is the active ingredient in most of the aerosol and brush-on cleaners. While it can clean efficiently, it can also irritate and burn the skin and, if inhaled in quantity, the nasal passages and lungs. If swallowed, it can cause burns in the esophagus and mouth.

When using an oven cleaner containing lye, read the package carefully and be prepared to follow first-aid instructions if necessary. Always wear rubber gloves as you work. When applying an aerosol or pump spray, wear a face mask and goggles. When finishing the job, be sure that you really have wiped all the cleaner off the oven. Otherwise, unpleasant and unhealthy fumes will occur the next time you turn it on.

There are some reasonably effective "lye-free" cleaners on the market that contain a combination of metallo-organic salts. These cleaners are relatively innocuous when applied, but the heat of the oven, which makes the cleaners work, converts the material into lye. When it reacts with oven grease, the lye produces irritating fumes. It may also leave a dangerous residue that needs to be completely removed from the oven; wear rubber gloves while you work.

Most cleaners come scented, usually with lemon, but that does not minimize their danger. Even if the oven cleaner is in a childproof package, it—and other cleaning materials—should be kept in a locked cabinet well out of the reach of young children.

Passive Smoke

Smokers who switch to low-tar cigarettes may actually increase the health risk for their friends and family, according to a recent study from the United States Department of Agriculture. The secondhand smoke released from the burning end of low-tar cigarettes proved to contain up to 30 percent more cancer-causing substances than the smoke from high-tar cigarettes.

The dangers of passive smoking—that is, inhaling cigarette smoke from the air—have long been under investigation, and the evidence is now clear that these dangers are real. Secondhand smoke contains large amounts of all the dangerous chemicals released in a smoker's lungs, such as tar, nicotine, benzopyrene, and carbon dioxide. One troublesome aspect of passive smoking is the differing levels of toxic substances in different kinds of smoke. "Mainstream" smoke—the smoke inhaled by the smoker from the butt end of the cigarette and then exhaled into the air—may actually be lower in tar and nicotine than "sidestream smoke" drifting up from the hot end of a lit cigarette. That's because sidestream smoke is hotter and has not been filtered through the cigarette itself. Nearly 85 percent of the smoke in a room is sidestream smoke—much of it cooled and diluted. Exhaled smoke has fewer toxins, but it is still a significant pollutant of indoor air. In fact, one report concluded that the toxins that smokers and nonsmokers are exposed to are not dramatically different. The smoker, of course, gets more of them.

Asthmatics and those suffering from angina or heart disease can clearly be harmed by passive smoking. And passive smoke has been demonstrated to be a health risk for healthy nonsmokers as well. In addition to the immediate effects of continued exposure—such as eye, nose, and throat irritation along with acute respiratory irritation, headaches, and coughing—passive smoke increases the chances of developing both lung cancer and heart disease. According to the Environmental Protection Agency, passive smoke causes 3,800 lung cancer deaths each year. And other studies have estimated that about 50,000 Americans die each year as a result of passive smoke, 75 percent of them from heart disease. The risks are greatest for individuals who live with someone who smokes; for example, according to a study conducted by Dr. K.J. Helsing of Johns Hopkins University and his colleagues, a nonsmoker living with a smoker has a 20 to 30 percent increase in risk of death from heart disease (the heavier the smoker, the greater the risk). But even those who are exposed to passive smoke for shorter periods may be at increased risk. One study found that rabbits exposed to sidestream smoke for fifteen minutes a day for just twenty days developed lung damage. Another study of humans showed that just twenty minutes of exposure to sidestream smoke can increase the stickiness of the platelets in the blood, thus making it more likely to clot.

The harmful effects of passive smoking are particularly critical for children. Children—especially young children—who have one or both parents (particularly the mother) who smoke have an increased risk of chronic respiratory symptoms (such as wheezing and chronic coughing), respiratory problems, decreased lung capacity, and middle ear infections. Several studies have shown that infants under age one have a significantly greater incidence of bronchitis and other lower respiratory disease when one or both parents smoke. However, the cause is not perfectly clear: it has not been determined whether the illness comes from passive smoking or is the result of maternal smoking during pregnancy. As for older children, a body of research has built up showing that parental smoking (especially maternal smoking) can reduce a child's lung capacity and perhaps predispose a child to chronic lung disease later in life. However, the study that showed the greatest adverse health consequences included mostly teenagers, who may not have been forthcoming about their own smoking habits. And of course, one of the greatest risks associated with parental smoking is that children with parents who smoke are more likely to become smokers themselves.

Poisoning

There are nearly three million cases of accidental child poisoning each year, and in the majority of cases, parents were at home or nearby at the time of the poisoning. Almost 69 percent of accidental poisonings occur in children under six. Children in this age group usually mistake household cleaners for beverages, or prescription and over-the-counter drugs for candy. Often they playfully emulate adult drug taking, which sometimes leads to serious or even fatal results.

Nearly half of all accidental poisonings in the United States are caused by a limited group of items: aspirin and acetaminophen, insecticides, household bleach, detergents, fragrance products, soaps and cleaners, furniture polish, kerosene, iron and vitamin compounds, disinfectants and deodorizers, lye and corrosives, and laxatives.

To determine a pattern in childhood poisonings, researchers at the Karolinska Institute in Sweden interviewed parents of six hundred children who had suffered from accidental poisoning. Results showed that most accidents occurred in the kitchen between four and six P.M. This led doctors to speculate that the children eager for lunch or dinner selected a bottle or container they thought held food.

The second most likely site of poisoning is the bathroom. It takes just a moment for a toddler to climb from the toilet seat onto the sink and then open the medicine chest. All medicine, even aspirin, should be kept in childproof containers in a locked cabinet.

Poisons are not just swallowed.
Poisons can also cause trouble if they get in the eyes, on the skin, or are inhaled. You should seek medical help immediately for these episodes as well, but you may have to deal with the situation before going to the emergency room. Here's how to cope with these emergencies:

__Eyes.__ Flood the eye with lukewarm or cold water for at least fifteen minutes. Encourage the victim to blink while flushing the eye, but do not force the eyelid open.

__Skin.__ Remove contaminated clothing without contaminating yourself. Flood the area with water and follow with a mild soap and a final rinse.

__Inhaled.__ Move the victim to fresh air immediately or open all the doors and windows. If the person has stopped breathing, perform artificial respiration; if the heart has stopped, perform CPR (cardio-pulmonary resuscitation).

Safety precautions

To prevent poisoning, use the following guidelines. (Remember, adults are also susceptible to accidental poisonings.)

- Remove all poisonous substances from the kitchen and dining areas.
- Keep household cleaners and other potential poisons out of children's reach, preferably in a locked cabinet.
- Keep all hazardous substances and medicines in their original containers. Do not store them in food containers.
- When using toxic substances around children, don't leave a child alone with the product—not even for a minute. If you have to leave the room to answer the phone or the doorbell, take the product with you.
- Buy household cleaners and medicines in child-resistant packaging, although you should not rely solely on this packaging. Continue to store these items out of a child's reach.
- Never refer to medicine or vitamins for children as candy.
- Even if no children live in your house, take precautions when they come to visit. More than one-third of all cases of childhood poisoning from toxic prescription drugs involve a grandparent's medication.
- Avoid taking any medication in front of children, since they tend to imitate what adults do.
- Flush all old medications down the toilet instead of throwing them away in the garbage where children or pets may find them.

Toxic plants

According to the Consumer Product Safety Commission, the ingestion of toxic plants in homes and gardens is common, especially among young children. Since many cases go unreported, no precise figures on plant poisoning exist, but in 1989 some 62,000 children were exposed to toxic plants. Fortunately, few, if any, deaths occur. A child tasting a toxic leaf, for example, will usually be deterred from eating a lethal amount by his own adverse reaction. Still, parents and grandparents childproofing their homes should not overlook the dangers of plants.

Philodendron, the green and leafy vine that is probably the most popular indoor plant, is highly toxic when ingested and can also cause skin irritation. Dieffenbachia, or dumbcane, with its pointed, variegated leaves is almost as familiar and can have similar effects. A leaf of either plant, if chewed, produces severe mouth pain, swelling of the tongue, and difficulty in speaking. If you have children, the following points are worth keeping in mind:

- With infants or toddlers in the house, don't keep plants where they can reach them. Don't keep philodendron or dieffenbachia plants in your home at all if you have preschool children.
- Teach children not to sample plant leaves of any kind, and not to experiment with wild plants for food.

Where to get help

Poison control centers exist in every state. Find the number of your local regional center and keep it near your phone *before* you need it. If you discover that your child has swallowed a poisonous substance, call your poison control center immediately (unless he or she is unconscious or having convulsions; in that case call 911 or your

---

Children's Vitamins and Poisoning
According to the National Capital Poison Center, children's vitamins shaped like cartoon characters are among the most common agents of childhood poisonings. By banging and rolling around the supposedly childproof bottle, a small child can open what appears to be a jar of little candies. A bottle of one hundred or so vitamin tablets contains enough vitamin A to cause hypervitaminosis A, a vitamin-A toxicity. Iron-enriched vitamins are even more toxic and can be fatal if taken in large quantities.

local emergency number). Be ready to tell them: the age and weight of the child, what was ingested (have the bottle or container with you), when it was ingested, how much was taken, how the victim is feeling or acting at that moment, and your name and phone number. If you are instructed to go to the emergency room, bring the container of the poison or a sample of the plant with you.

You should keep a bottle of syrup of ipecac on hand to induce vomiting—it is available over the counter at pharmacies—but you should not use it unless instructed to do so by the poison control center or a physician. Some corrosive chemicals, such as bleach, and petroleum products, such as gasoline, can cause more harm if they are brought up.

Radon

Radon is a colorless, odorless, tasteless, and radioactive gas that can seep through the foundations and cracks of buildings. It is naturally occurring and comes from uranium in the soil, water that runs through uranium-bearing rock, and materials made from such soil or rock. Radon infiltration can occur in all housing. Its concentration in the air depends on the radon source strength in the ground, soil permeability, and air flow. Concentrations tend to be higher in single-story than in multiple-story buildings.

In the atmosphere, radon is diluted and therefore harmless. However, in enclosed spaces, such as mines or houses, radon may reach significant levels. And at these levels it can increase your risk of getting lung cancer. Indeed, according to a study carried out at the Lawrence Berkeley Laboratory at the University of California, radon gas exposure in American homes may be related to some ten thousand deaths from lung cancer each year. Radon may be the most common cancer-causing agent after cigarette smoking.

Radon testing

Testing for radon is now fairly easy. A reasonably accurate reading can be made with an alpha-track detector, but you can get accurate readings only if you leave the device in place for long periods—up to a year. Radon levels fluctuate so radically from week to week and season to season that a single test is meaningless. The quickest and cheapest test, with an activated-charcoal detector (often referred to as a "grab sampler"), takes a reading of radon levels in three to seven days. You might want to take a quick test just to see if you have a very high reading, which may be an immediate problem. A low reading, though, doesn't mean there's no radon, so you'll need to take the longer-term reading with an alpha-track detector before deciding what to do.

If you have a problem, modifications to your house (such as installing ventilators and sealing your house's foundations) may cost anywhere from one thousand to two thousand dollars. Be wary of anybody who comes to your home offering to do a quick radon test for you.

But meanwhile, the best thing you can do is quit smoking if you smoke: radon interacts with smoking in such a way that the combined risk of smoking and radon exposure is greater than the sum of the individual risks. Indeed, the combination may account for most radon-related lung cancer deaths.

Water

The body needs to replace about two and a half to three quarts of water every day to keep functioning. Without a supply of fresh water, we will die in only a few days. Some of this water supply comes from the water in foods. But about six to eight glasses of water are needed to make up the balance. You can fulfill this requirement with juice, milk, or other beverages; however, alcoholic drinks, coffee, tea, and colas have a diuretic effect—they wash water from the body by way of urination. Still, the best source of that essential liquid for our bodies is plain, pure water.

Water comes from rain and snow, which runs off into rivers, lakes, and oceans or seeps into the ground to form part of the underground water table. Half of our drinking water comes from the surface water in rivers and lakes and reservoirs, the other half from groundwater.

Historically, the primary public health concern with drinking water has been the possibility of contamination by infectious disease agents associated with human and animal wastes. This concern about contamination was largely confined to surface water; groundwater tended to remain pure, since infectious agents were filtered out by the seepage of the water down through the earth and aquifer (a water-bearing layer of permeable rock, gravel, or sand). And then, with the advent of chlorination of surface water—first introduced in New Jersey in 1908—along with improved general sanitation, epidemics of cholera, dysentery, typhoid, and other waterborne bacterial diseases became exceedingly rare in the United States. Chlorination is one of the most successful environmental health control measures ever.

If your water is polluted
Of all the sources of water available, your best choice is still probably your tap. The evidence suggests that tap water is predominantly safe, even though problems with seepage of chemical wastes can occur in some areas. In the short term, in these cases, alternative drinking-water sources may be needed.

If your drinking water fails to meet the Environmental Protection Agency (EPA) guidelines, the community is obliged to notify you, usually through press conferences. Although seven hundred chemicals have been recognized—and in California, for example, forty have been assigned recommended levels—the EPA guidelines have set maximum contaminant levels for only ten chemicals, six pesticides, bacteria, radioactivity, and turbidity (or cloudiness):

Coliform bacteria from human and animal wastes are still found on occasion in improperly treated drinking water. These indicate the potential presence of water-associated disease-causing microorganisms.

Nitrate poses an immediate threat to children under three months of age. In some infants excessive levels of nitrate react with hemoglobin in the blood and cause the rare anemic condition known as "blue-baby" syndrome. If you receive notice that your water contains nitrate, do not give it to infants. Do not boil it—that will only increase the nitrate levels. Follow the instructions you receive with the notice.

Arsenic is used in insecticides and can enter water from run-off. It can lead to fatigue and loss of energy if consumed over a long period of time, and high levels can even cause poisoning. It is commonly found at very low levels as a natural contaminant of water.

The average American uses anywhere from 50 to 150 gallons of water each day: 39 percent for bathing, dish washing, and laundry; 30 percent for swimming pools and lawn and garden watering; 29 percent for flushing the toilet; and only 1.5 percent for drinking and cooking. Per capita, Europeans and Japanese use about half as much water as Americans.

Barium is rarely found in drinking water. It can be a natural contaminant or can enter the water through industrial waste discharges. It is not harmful in small doses, but large doses can raise blood pressure and cause nerve damage.

Cadmium can enter the water from insecticides and the waste discharges from metallurgical industries, though the most common source is galvanized pipes and plumbing fixtures. Kidney and lung diseases are caused by heavy exposure to cadmium, the principal health hazard coming from occupational exposure.

Chromium is found in cigarettes, some foods, and the air. Some studies suggest that minute amounts may be essential for glucose metabolism, but high doses can be toxic.

Fluoride in the proper amounts prevents tooth decay. The excessive amounts occasionally found naturally in some water sources may cause brown spots or mottling on teeth. (See box on page 494.)

Lead from lead pipes causes damage to the kidneys and the nervous system.

Mercury can come from industrial and agricultural use and can cause acute poisoning at high levels, and chronic poisoning at lower levels. It is rarely found in drinking water, but more commonly in fish that come from waters that are high in mercury.

Selenium may be toxic at high levels, and studies are currently underway to determine the exact levels that may be toxic. However, there is considerable evidence that low levels of selenium may protect against cancer.

Silver is often present in water and should pose no problem.

Pesticides seep into groundwater from use on croplands, forests, lawns, and gardens. Many may cause no problem, but the EPA has set standards for endrin, lindane, methoxychlor, toxephene, 2,4-D and 2,4,5-TP Silvex.

Radioactivity is the only contaminant for which standards have been set that is known to cause cancer in humans. There are no risks of radioactivity in community water supplies, except in unusual circumstances or accidents.

Turbidity is just another word for muddiness or cloudiness. If your water looks dirty, don't drink it. Not only is it full of some sort of unidentified contaminant, but even if the cloudiness is due only to harmless dirt, it can interfere with proper disinfection and bacteria-testing of the water and can thus hide the presence of some harmful contaminant.

Obviously, this list of contaminants is very limited. Your water may contain other pollutants about which the EPA and local water authorities do not have to inform you—including, at the very least, those twenty-two chemicals the EPA has said are cancer-causing but has not adequately covered in its list of pollutants. If you have any reason to believe that your water is contaminated, you may want to check with your local environmental agencies.

Bottled water

Most people purchase bottled water not because their tap water is polluted, but because they like the taste or they feel bottled water confers health benefits. Supermarket shelves are packed with literally hundreds of brands of deluxe mineral waters, "bulk" waters, club sodas, seltzers, and the newest variant—flavored seltzers.

Bottled water, unfortunately, is not universally healthful. Some bottled waters come from sources high in sodium, for example. Three-quarters of the bottled water sold in the United States is simply processed tap water from local taps, with

Fluoridation

Fluoride in the water sometimes occurs naturally, as in Colorado Springs and other communities. And sometimes local governments, usually cities, add it to the water in controlled quantities. As medical science has known for decades, fluoride interacts with tooth enamel and hardens it, making it less susceptible to decay—50 to 70 percent less susceptible. In the generations born since the 1950s, when fluoridation came into wide use, toothaches and tooth extractions are almost an oddity.

Fluoridated water may also play a role in building strong bones, and warding off osteoporosis, a disease that decreases bone mass, weakens bones, and increases the likelihood of fractures, particularly among post-menopausal women. Studies have shown that women who live in areas with naturally fluoridated water suffer fewer osteoporotic fractures and have generally greater bone strength than those who drink nonfluoridated water.

Classified as a nutrient, fluoride occurs naturally in water and in soil. It is one of many elements that make up human tissue. As early as 1908, its properties as a tooth-decay preventive were deduced from observing dental health patterns in communities where the water supply was naturally fluoridated. According to a number of long-term studies, such communities have no greater incidence of cancer, heart disease, liver disease, or other ills than other places. One well-known side effect of fluoride, however, is dental fluorosis, a light mottling of the tooth enamel that may be cosmetically unappealing. This occurs in some people in areas where the natural fluoride content is very high.

Bottled water that has a plastic taste may contain materials such as plasticizers—used to keep the bottle flexible—or compounds used in manufacturing to get the bottle out of its mold. If your bottled water tastes like plastic, you might be wise to either switch brands or go back to the tap.

or without added carbonation. Some bottled waters are processed and bottled under conditions that actually give them higher bacteria counts than your own tap water (if bottled according to Food and Drug Administration (FDA) standards, however, bacteria must be very low). Some contain the same pollutants from pesticides and organic chemicals that your tap water may. The mineral content of any water is *not* nutritionally significant, except for the tooth-protecting fluoride that is either naturally present or added to the water supplies in most communities. Unfortunately, most bottled waters lack fluoride, and some are comparatively high in sodium. On the plus side, bottled waters are not allowed to contain appreciable amounts of lead or any other heavy metal.

Price is another factor when selecting bottled water; an eight-ounce glass of mineral water can cost 25 to 50 cents, and even more in a restaurant.

The labels on bottled water generally provide little information about chemical content. Moreover, labeling terminology can be confusing. Here are some definitions and choices:

Distilled water is definitely the purest since it contains no solid matter of any kind and is essentially free of sodium. The water is first evaporated into steam, which leaves many impurities behind, and then is recondensed. However, it is the minerals that give water its satisfying taste: distilled water tastes flat and dead. In addition, distillation does not remove many of the suspect organic chemicals.

Mineral water is simply water that contains minerals—which is true of virtually all water except distilled water. "Natural mineral water" contains just the minerals present in the water as it comes from the ground. Simple "mineral water" may have been processed and had minerals added or removed. Most mineral water, whether or not it is identified as such, comes from a spring.

Seltzer is usually tap water that is filtered and carbonated, with no minerals or mineral salts added. Oddly enough, a few so-called "seltzers" contain sweeteners such as sucrose or corn syrup, giving them up to 100 calories per eight ounces. Diabetics and other people trying to avoid sugar should therefore always read the ingredients list of any seltzer. In contrast, flavored seltzer contains a minuscule amount, or "essence," of fruit juice, usually equal to one-tenth of one percent of total volume. It contains no calories, sugar, or mineral salts. You can, of course, make your own by squeezing a little fruit juice into plain seltzer.

Sparkling water is a generic term for any carbonated water. The carbonization can be "natural" (the gases are captured as they escape from water and later reinjected during bottling) or be added artificially. The results are the same. Most are relatively high in sodium.

Club soda is usually simple tap water, filtered and carbonated, to which a mix of minerals and mineral salts have been added to give it the distinctive taste associated with its brand. Many distributers, for instance, sell their special mineral mixes to local bottling companies, which then add the local water to the mix. Most are fairly high in sodium—30 to 65 milligrams per eight ounces. People on sodium-restricted diets should stick to seltzer.

Spring water is water that has risen naturally to the earth's surface. Water labeled "natural spring water" must not have been processed in any way before bottling, whereas simple "spring water" may or may not have been processed. As with any groundwater, spring water may be contaminated. The best choice is spring water that is bottled directly from a spring in a nonindustrial area where few pollutants can reach the water. Such water would be labeled something on the order of "natural spring water bottled directly from the source." It may or may not be called mineral water, and may or may not be carbonated.

Outdoors

In addition to your home and workplace, your immediate environment also includes your yard, your community, and the places you travel to frequently. From barbecuing safely to preventing Lyme disease to ways you can help preserve the ozone layer, this chapter discusses some of the common environmental and safety concerns in the great outdoors.

Barbecues

Every summer about ten thousand Americans burn themselves at the backyard barbecue—by having the lighter fluid explode in their hands, being splashed by grease, or being caught by a flare-up from the fire. Here are some rules to help you avoid these hazards:

•Set up the grill away from the house and away from bushes or dry leaves. Never set it up in a tent, trailer, or garage or inside the house. In addition to the fire hazard, there is danger of carbon monoxide build-up.

•Don't wear clothes with hanging shirttails or frilly aprons.

•Pile the briquettes in a pyramid to start them. They'll light faster.

•Use only lighter fluid specifically designed for barbecues, never gasoline or kerosene. Let the fluid soak in before lighting it. Never add more liquid once the briquettes are lit or smoking. Better yet, use an electric starter or metal chimney starter that requires only a lit piece of newspaper to start the briquettes; these work quickly, are safe, and eliminate the chemical taste of fluids.

•Use long-handled utensils and gloves or mitts to avoid burns and spatters.

•Keep a spray bottle of water nearby so you can subdue flare-ups with a light mist of water. You might also keep a box of baking soda handy to sprinkle on a resistant grease fire. Also, a covered grill will minimize the chance of flare-ups.

•If you use a gas grill, reread the instructions the first time you use it each season in order to refresh your memory.

•Before each use and after a new gas tank is connected, apply soapy water around the connections and along the hose. If you see bubbles, you have a gas leak, which could lead to an explosion.

•Light gas grills with the lid open to prevent gas build-up and explosion.

Beach Pollution

By and large the public health danger of debris—even medical waste—washed up on the beaches has been blown out of proportion. While floating waste has been washing up on beaches for well over a century, the character of the waste has changed. Now there's more plastic and disposable waste, some of which is medical. This same waste is, of course, also turning up in municipal trash bins and landfills.

Most medical experts and health officials don't look on medical waste, however unattractive it may be, as a major public health threat. It's unlikely that anything in the ocean for any length of time could still be infectious. The chances of getting AIDS or any other illness by stepping on a used needle at a beach are virtually nil.

As for bacterial contamination, New Jersey's Department of Health looked into water quality for the summers of 1987 and 1988 and published figures concerning the incidence of illness reported by swimmers. Aside from one serious sewage spill, most water samplings were "excellent." Symptoms such as itchy eyes, sore throat, skin rash, stomach upset, and ear infections, the study concluded, are primarily the result of person-to-person transmission of viruses. Many people who get sick at the beach, the report implied, shouldn't necessarily blame pollution, but rather factors such as poor food handling at beach picnics or concessions.

Taking precautions

Pollution problems obviously vary from region to region. But wherever you are, the following commonsense measures can minimize any risks beach pollution may pose to your health:

•Stay out of the water when warnings or closings are posted. In some areas, bacterial counts may rise after heavy rains because of raw sewage overflows and run-offs of storm waters.

•Avoid touching debris that looks like medical waste. Report it to lifeguards or other officials.

•Clean up your own act, if need be. Refrigerate picnic food; don't litter. Use public toilets instead of the ocean.

Sales of old-fashioned push mowers have risen in recent years. Not only are they less expensive and less likely to break down, but they don't pollute the air. They also provide good exercise: pushing a manual mower burns between 420 and 480 calories an hour—as many calories as an hour of playing tennis.

Lawn Mowers

According to the National Safety Council, 74,683 people were injured by lawn mowers and other powered lawn equipment in 1987. Most of those injuries were incurred by those using power mowers. If you use a power mower, here are a few pointers to keep you safe:

•When mowing, wear close-fitting trousers and shoes that both protect your feet and give you traction. Sandals or cloth sneakers are not adequate. Avoid voluminous sleeves, dangling jewelry, or anything likely to get caught in the mower. Since a riding mower may hoist you up to tree branch level, safety goggles are a good idea.

•Clear the area of stones, large twigs, and other debris. These can break the blades—or can become high-speed missiles if the blades pick them up.

•Don't pull any mower backward. You may pull it too close to your feet.

•Store gasoline in an Underwriters Laboratories (UL)-labeled container. Fill the mower while the engine is cool, and always handle gasoline outdoors.

•Use an electric mower only on dry grass. Choose an extension cord with a UL seal that is intended for outdoor use.

•If it's a walk-behind mower, cut across slopes, not up and down them, to minimize the risk of the mower rolling back on you. But do the opposite with a riding mower to reduce the risk of tipping sideways.

•Keep children and pets out of the area where you are mowing, and don't offer rides on a riding mower. If children are outdoors while you are mowing, insist that they wear shoes.

• When buying a mower, look for the triangular emblem with the letters OPEI (Outdoor Power Equipment Institute). It's usually affixed to the mower near the discharge chute. This assures you that the mower meets minimum safety standards for machines with revolving parts and blades.

Lightning

At any moment there are about 1,800 lightning storms occurring on earth. Here is what happens: in a thunderstorm, air turbulence causes a negative charge to build up in the underside of a thundercloud, while positive charges build up on the earth below. Streamers of positive charges constantly flow up from the earth—from tips of trees, the edges of the eaves of houses, from poles, even from people as they walk through a large open space. Eventually the thundercloud sends a nearly invisible, negatively charged jagged streamer down toward the earth. As it approaches the ground, at least one positively charged streamer shoots up to meet it.

When the two streamers join, thus creating an ionized air channel between cloud and earth, a blinding positive stroke of lightning flashes *upward,* from the earth to the cloud. In four-tenths of a second, several strokes will rise up from the earth to create a bolt of lightning of as much as 30 million volts (compared to household current of 110 to 220 volts). The heat that such a bolt creates can run as high as 30,000 to 50,000 degrees Fahrenheit. This causes an explosion of superheated air in the ionized channel, and thus a crack of thunder.

A direct hit by a lightning bolt is usually fatal. A sideflash—a bolt of lightning splashing off a tree or other object—can be fatal. Conducted current—a bolt of lightning sending its electrical charge through the telephone wire or the plumbing—can be fatal, or just stunning. Step voltage—the charge that radiation sends out into the ground around a struck tree—is often fatal to cattle or horses, but usually only jolts a person.

Protecting lives and property

Not much will protect a house except a properly installed lightning rod. If you are in a house without a lightning rod, you will be safest if you stay away from metal objects, the telephone, plumbing, the fireplace, and open doors and windows during a thunderstorm.

Outside, stay away from lone trees, unprotected shelters, open fields, open boats, and wire fences. Anything that sticks up from the landscape can be the lightning rod from which a positive streamer rises to meet the negative streamer. In a grove of trees, stay out from under the taller trees. Get off your bike, horse, golf cart, or tractor. Don't swim. Look for a ravine or other low-lying spot, a small tree, or the underside of a cliff. If you are caught in the open, kneel down, bend low, and touch the ground only with your knees and feet.

If someone near you is struck, immediately perform cardiopulmonary resuscitation (CPR), even if the person appears to be dead. Although you may think a person has no chance of surviving a bolt of lightning, people do survive an indirect hit—even sometimes a direct hit.

Lyme Disease

With each passing summer, Lyme disease becomes an increasing cause of concern. Nearly fourteen thousand cases have been reported in the United States. Lyme disease poses a double bind for doctors and health officials: many people who have it don't know it, and many others are convinced they have it but don't. Although there's much debate about exactly how prevalent this tickborne disease is, more cases of it are reported each year. The Centers for Disease Control has provisionally reported 7,400 cases in 1989, compared to 4,574 verified in 1988. Yet despite the media hype and sensationalistic ads for tick repellents and testing kits, there is no reason to panic or, as some people are doing, avoid spending time outdoors. There is good reason, nonetheless, to take steps to protect yourself if you live in or visit an area where the disease is common.

How Lyme disease spreads
The infection, caused by a corkscrew-shaped bacterium known as a spirochete (*Borrelia burgdorferi*), is transmitted primarily via certain species of deer ticks. These are smaller than the common dog tick, though it's often difficult for any but a trained eye to tell them apart. A deer tick, before it becomes engorged with blood, looks like a mole or blood blister. While the flat, eight-legged adults are less than one-tenth of an inch long, immature ticks (called nymphs) are about the size of a pinhead, and the larvae are nearly invisible. The male is black and the female is dark red and black. When filled with blood, the tick becomes gray and increases in size three- to fivefold.

Although deer can become infected, in the eastern United States, white-footed field mice serve as the main host for both the bacteria and the young ticks. In the West, where different species of deer ticks carry the disease, lizards and jackrabbits are the main hosts. The adult ticks usually feed and mate on deer, then drop off to lay eggs. These in turn hatch into minuscule larvae, which become infected by feeding on white-footed mice in the East. The larvae molt and become infected nymphs. Both nymphs and adult ticks feed on a variety of animals. *The nymphs are the chief threat to humans—about 70 to 90 percent of all cases are caused by nymph bites.* Adult ticks are generally less of a threat to humans because they're large enough to be seen and removed before they transfer the bacteria.

The nymphs and adults wait on low vegetation in wooded areas and adjacent grasslands and transfer themselves to whatever brushes by; they don't fly or jump. Dogs and cats can carry the ticks to your home and property.

Geographical distribution
Lyme disease was first identified as a form of arthritis in 1975 in the woodlands around Lyme, Connecticut (hence its name). Cases are known to have occurred in at least forty states. Those with the highest reported incidence in 1989 were, in descending order, Connecticut, Rhode Island, New York, Georgia, New Jersey, Wisconsin, and Pennsylvania. The ticks tend to thrive in those areas where suburban lawns meet woodlands. Deer, whose population has grown in the East in recent years, help spread infected ticks to new areas. Migratory birds have brought Lyme disease to the South.

Even city dwellers may be susceptible to Lyme disease. All it takes is a weekend excursion to the countryside for you—or your dog—to meet up with a tick.

Although this disease has received the most publicity in the United States, it has existed in Europe at least since the beginning of the century (though its assorted symptoms were often not attributed to a single disorder). Lyme disease is found today in all continents except Antarctica.

While the peak periods may vary from region to region, this is primarily a summer disease. You're most likely to be bitten by a deer tick between May and September, when the nymphs are active. And that's also when people are outdoors most. The risk of being bitten is lower in April, October, and November, and lowest from December through March.

Symptoms

Lyme disease is hard to diagnose because its symptoms can vary greatly from person to person. No single symptom appears in all cases, and there's no predictable time frame or sequence of symptoms. And the problem is complicated by the lack of a reliable test for the disease. So far the available blood tests for Lyme disease have been neither sensitive nor specific enough, yielding an unacceptable number of false positives and false negatives. The results of the tests vary from lab to lab, and the meaning of the results is not standardized. This greatly compounds the problems of diagnosis. In particular, during the first four weeks after someone becomes infected, the test is unlikely to detect the small amount of antibodies the body has produced in response to the bacteria. Even in the later stages of the disease, the current tests, as routinely performed, are so unreliable that they're virtually useless. (Newer, more reliable tests are in the experimental stage, but it will probably be several years before they are available for clinical use.) Still, three general phases have been identified:

Phase one. Most often, within thirty days of being bitten by an infected tick, you'll develop a small red bump at the site of the bite surrounded by a rash that gradually grows for several weeks and then fades. The rash may have a firm center area, feel warm to the touch, and disappear briefly only to reappear elsewhere on your body. At the same time, you may develop flulike symptoms: fatigue, chills, headache, muscle and joint aches, and a low fever. Remember, however, that you may not develop a rash but just the flulike symptoms—or you may have none of these early symptoms at all. In some people, Lyme disease doesn't progress beyond this early stage. But if it goes untreated, more severe symptoms may develop, sometimes many months later.

Phase two. About 20 percent of untreated people develop neurological or cardiac disorders weeks or months after the bite. These range from heart rhythm abnormalities to impaired motor coordination and even partial facial paralysis. These symptoms also usually disappear within a few weeks.

Phase three. About half of untreated people develop recurring or chronic arthritis after a latent period of up to two years. Thus the disease was first called "Lyme arthritis." The knees are almost always affected.

If in doubt, antibiotics?

Lyme disease is treatable and almost always curable, especially in its early stage. If you have—or had—the characteristic rash, your doctor will probably put you on

You don't need a special, costly tick repellent to ward off Lyme disease. Use insect repellents that contain the chemical deet; they will do the job just as well.

antibiotics. Similarly, if you live in an area with a high incidence of the disease and find a tick on you, which your doctor or the local health department identifies as a deer tick, you'll probably be put on antibiotics.

What if you have only the flulike symptoms, fatigue, or joint pain, but no memory of a tick bite? Some people may shop around till they find a physician who will treat them with antibiotics just in case. But overuse of antibiotics has a serious downside. All antibiotics can have adverse effects in sensitive individuals. Pregnant women, in particular, shouldn't be stampeded into unwarranted antibiotic treatment by overblown news reports of birth defects caused by Lyme disease. And the overuse of these drugs can also produce antibiotic-resistant organisms.

Preventing Lyme disease

To lessen the risks of contracting Lyme disease and free yourself from worry in the fields or woods, take these precautions:

•Wear a long-sleeved shirt with buttoned cuffs. Tuck the shirt into your pants and your pants into your socks or boots. Wear hard-finished, light-colored fabrics. It's easier to spot ticks on white or tan trousers than on black ones.

A Tick-Free Yard

Ticks appear to be stubbornly embedded in our ecosystem, and there's not much we can do about it. Spraying the landscape with pesticides is apparently not an effective way to destroy them. Many ticks are underground in animal burrows, and others hide on the underside of leaves—either way, they may escape the spray. Moreover, pesticide sprays are indiscriminate and endanger all insects and perhaps other creatures on your land as well. What about killing or removing the mice or deer that feed and transport the ticks? Even if this were desirable and feasible, it might not do much to prevent Lyme disease, since the ticks could find other host animals.

There may be a way, however. Scientists are intrigued by a product called Damminix, which was developed by researchers at Harvard's School of Public Health. These cardboard tubes filled with insecticide-impregnated cotton are "roach motels" with a twist. They don't attract the ticks themselves, but rather the mice that serve as host to both the young ticks and the Lyme disease bacteria in the eastern United States. The mice bring the cotton back to their burrows and thus become covered with the pesticide. The young ticks die when they come to feed on a treated mouse or when the mouse brings them back to its burrow (the pesticide is "relatively nontoxic" to mice, according to the manufacturer).

Usage Tips

You place the tubes at ten-yard intervals on your property wherever mice may be living; lawns don't need to be treated. Preliminary tests in infested areas have found that use of Damminix can drastically reduce the number of infected ticks. But further independent studies are needed to confirm these findings.

Damminix is not cheap: a box of twenty-four tubes, a year's supply (two applications are recommended, one in spring and one in summer) for a typical half-acre property, costs about 90 dollars. The manufacturer points out that since ticks don't travel far and mice are territorial (that is, they tend to stay in a certain area), Damminix will work even if neighboring land isn't treated. Obviously, it would help if your neighbors treated their property, too.

This product won't be of any use if you live in the West, however, since lizards and jackrabbits—not mice—are the primary hosts for the deer ticks there. But permethrin, the pesticide in Damminix, is also available in an aerosol spray called Permanone. Studies have found that permethrin may be an even more effective tick repellent than deet. Though not yet approved by the EPA as a repellent, it is available in hardware stores in many states (federal law allows states with "special need" to sell unapproved pesticides). Make sure you use it only on clothing, not on your skin.

- Use insect repellent on your pants, socks, and shoes.
- Try to stay near the center of trails in overgrown country.
- Check occasionally for ticks when you're in underbrush or wooded areas. Later do a thorough check of your entire body. Have someone look at your back and head if possible.

(For information on how to remove ticks, see pages 294-296.)

Ozone Layer

The depletion of the earth's protective ozone layer is a health issue for all of us. While most of the measures needed to safeguard the ozone layer involve nations and industries, there are significant steps you can take—as an individual consumer and as a member of society.

There's good and bad ozone, depending on where it is, though both are chemically identical. Ozone is a gas formed when three atoms of oxygen, rather than the normal two, bind together. The ozone found at ground level, a by-product of car and factory pollution, is one of the more dangerous components of smog. But in the earth's stratosphere, about 10 to 25 miles above us, ozone functions as a natural screen against the sun's most damaging ultraviolet (UV) rays. Unfortunately, the ozone that pollutes our air cannot reach the stratosphere's ozone layer.

Chlorofluorocarbons—the largest contributor

The stratospheric ozone layer is being destroyed in large part by manmade compounds called chlorofluorocarbons, or CFCs. These versatile chemicals, in liquid or gaseous form, have helped shape modern society. CFCs are used as coolants in our homes, cars, and refrigerators, as foaming agents (in foam insulation, mattresses, and food packaging), and as solvents that remove impurities from computer microchips and electronic equipment. The same properties that make CFCs efficient and safe for so many industrial uses also make them destructive to the environment. Their great stability ensures that when they are released into the air (during manufacturing processes, from leaky cooling systems, or upon disposal) CFCs eventually rise intact to the stratosphere, where intense radiation breaks them down into component atoms. One of these atoms, chlorine, has a devastating effect on ozone. Other compounds called halons, used in some fire extinguishers, are even more destructive of ozone.

Scientists predict that by allowing more UV radiation to reach the earth, the depletion of the ozone layer will lead to an increase in the number of cases of skin cancer (especially melanoma) and cataracts. In addition, they postulate that the increased UV radiation may damage crops, kill plankton that serve as a food source for marine life, and even have adverse effects on the human immune system. CFCs may also trap heat in the atmosphere and thus contribute to the global warming trend (greenhouse effect).

For all these reasons, an international agreement in Montreal in 1987 called for accelerating the phasing out of CFC and halon production. Recent reports by NASA that the ozone layer is being depleted even more rapidly than was previously projected, and the discovery of vast holes in the layer over Antarctica and the Arctic, have prompted scientists and environmental groups to call for a complete and rapid phase-out of CFCs. But even if we stopped using CFCs tomorrow, the damage to the ozone layer will continue, since those CFCs already released in the air will still be making their way to the stratosphere a decade from now and destroying ozone for up to a century.

Substitutes have already been found for certain uses of CFCs. For instance, the EPA banned the use of CFCs as propellants in most, but not all, aerosol sprays in 1978. CFCs can be modified so that they do much less damage to the ozone layer, or so that they break down quickly in the lower atmosphere. Industries are also seeking ways to recycle the chemicals so that they aren't released into the air. Du Pont, the world's largest manufacturer of CFCs, announced that it would phase out production by the end of the century. The European Economic Community followed suit.

Seven ways you can help

The United States remains the leading producer and consumer of CFCs. By following these steps, you can help reduce the American contribution to the destruction of the ozone layer:

1. Have your car's air conditioner carefully serviced. *Auto air conditioners are the single largest source of CFC emissions in the United States.* Don't simply refill your leaky air conditioner; if you don't have the leak fixed, the CFCs you add will end up in the air. Go to a service station equipped to recycle the refrigerant (this costs an additional 35 to 55 dollars); otherwise the CFCs will be vented into the atmosphere. In Los Angeles, an ordinance requiring service stations to recycle CFCs has been proposed; it will also ban the sale of small cans of refrigerant, which allow people to "top off" their air conditioners instead of repairing leaks. Car air conditioners using less-harmful refrigerants are expected to be available in the mid-1990s. (Home air conditioners, by and large, contain coolants that are far less ozone-depleting.)

2. Avoid products made of plastic foam (polystyrene), such as fast-food containers, egg cartons, Styrofoam cups, and foam trays for meats. Although many of these products are now made from less-damaging compounds, you can't tell which are which, so limit your use of them.

3. Don't use foam plastic insulation in your home, unless it is made with ozone-safe agents. Instead use fiberglass, gypsum, fiberboard, or cellulose insulation.

4. Don't buy a halon fire extinguisher for home use.

5. Check labels on aerosol cans. VCR-head cleaners, boat horns, spray confetti, photo-negative cleaners, and drain plungers may still contain the most dangerous CFCs. Many cans say if they contain CFCs, but such labeling isn't required.

6. When buying a new refrigerator, choose an energy-efficient model: it may contain as little as half the CFCs. Thus, when the refrigerator wears out and you discard it, less CFCs will be released. All refrigerators on the American market today contain CFCs. To keep your fridge in the best working order, clean the coils regularly; that way it may last until models with CFC-free coolants are developed, or at least until recycling programs for CFCs are available.

7. Write to your senator and representative and to the president urging them to help protect the ozone layer by tightening regulations on CFCs and halons, speeding up their elimination, mandating warning labels on products containing them, and pressing other nations to take similar steps.

According to one estimate from the Environmental Protection Agency, for every one percent decrease in the ozone layer, the incidence of common skin cancers will increase between 3 and 6 percent.

Pesticides

Developed in the late 1930s and introduced in 1945 as a heaven-sent boon to farmers, the pesticide DDT was outlawed twenty-seven years later in the United States as "environmentally persistent." Its toxic residues in food were found to be a threat to animal and human, as well as insect, life. Even now, however, the residues of scores of other insecticides remain on or in the food we eat, while their toxic effects remain in question.

The availability and variety of fruits and vegetables have increased tenfold in ten years—in large measure, due to pesticides and other agrichemicals that increase crop yield and ward off spoilage during storing and shipping. The residues of these compounds constitute a universal environmental and health hazard whose full scope remains to be determined. No one really knows how to address this problem at this time.

Apples have been found to contain the residues of as many as 43 of a total of 110 pesticides registered by the Environmental Protection Agency (EPA) for use on apples. Yet the Food and Drug Administration (FDA), which sets tolerance levels for such chemicals, tests only one percent of the fruits and vegetables (domestic and imported) marketed in the United States. Some experts feel that such skimpy testing provides an adequate basis for predicting the long-term effects of pesticides on humans. Is consumption of fruits and vegetables—laden, after all, with vital nutrients as well as potentially dangerous agrichemicals—worth the risk, then? Some researchers imply that it is. In 1986, a report by researchers at the University of California, Berkeley, published in the *Annual Review of Public Health,* concluded: "With few exceptions, the delayed effects of pesticides on human health have been difficult to detect. Perhaps the health risks are sufficiently small that they are below the power of epidemiologic studies to detect."

While the Berkeley conclusions are correct, in 1988 the National Academy of Science, utilizing different assumptions, estimated the national risk of cancer from pesticide use at as many as twenty thousand cases a year. The academy's report noted further: "some allowed levels [of pesticide residues in food] are being challenged by scientists as being too high." EPA-acceptable intake figures, for instance, are based on a diet that includes only 7.5 ounces of foods like cantaloupe, avocado, or squash a year. Most of us eat much more.

Despite the gaps in current research, there is enough evidence of toxicity to justify concern about the effects of these residues. Fortunately, there are a number of sensible protective measures you can adopt—some in the nature of short-term first aid, others with long-term aims in view. Abide by them, and what you eat may not only be safer, but better-tasting, too.

Eat a wide variety of foods. This helps minimize your exposure to any one pesticide.

Eat what's in season. Buy strawberries and cherries in June primarily, not December, and chances are you'll get more delicious fruit grown under optimum conditions. In the right season, there's less need for chemicals.

Eat local or at least domestic produce. Obviously, if you eat seasonal produce, it's more likely to be domestically grown. In this regard, FDA figures are significant; they show that 64 percent of imported produce contains pesticide residues, against 38 percent of domestic produce.

Wash carefully. Many water-soluble residues float away with thorough washing. Use a vegetable brush to scrub hard vegetables and fruits.

Peel anything that has a wax coating. Some nutrients may be tossed out with your apple or cucumber peelings, but so are the surface residues. The wax coating, harmless in itself, not only fends off the hard knocks of shipping and storage but seals in residues, including those left by fungicides.

Trim vegetables and fruits. Based on federal and California state data, more celery samples contain toxic residues than any other of the twenty-six fruits and vegetables analyzed. But trimming celery tops and leaves gets rid of as much as 50 to 90 percent of some of these. Similarly, careful pruning of the outside layers of other leafy vegetables like lettuces and cabbages removes residues.

In states where the term means anything, you may wish to buy "organic" foods. Buying produce raised without chemicals isn't easy to do in many cities or states, and "organically grown" doesn't always mean "pesticide-free." A certification plan is in force in many states to ensure that foods labeled "organic" must not have been raised with pesticides. Even big grocery chains are beginning to stock organically grown produce. Since you'll probably have to pay a 10 to 20 percent premium for organic fruits and vegetables, try to be sure they really are grown without the aid of chemical fertilizers or pesticides, although this can be difficult to ascertain. You can ask your supermarket produce manager, but be aware that while he may reassure you, he may not really know.

The home garden—no longer a chemical battlefield

Most gardeners are now aware that chemical pesticides can endanger human health as well as kill insects. The trend in gardening is away from chemical use and back to safer and more pleasant alternatives. According to experts at the University of California, Berkeley, the rationale for using pesticides in home gardens is so weak that you should probably not use them at all. You can adopt gardening methods that will reduce the number of insects and thus the need for pesticides. Spring is the time to begin—but what you do in the fall is important, too.

•Choose a garden site in a well-drained area, and don't overwater. Practice crop rotation. Even in a small garden, this will help keep down specific pests.

•Use a high-quality fertilizer. Healthy plants are more likely to resist diseases and insects. Pull weeds regularly.

•Plant garlic, nasturtiums, onions, or chives around the garden border. They help repel some insects.

•Buy insect- and disease-resistant seedlings when possible.

•If you buy a pesticide, be just as wary of so-called "botanicals," "biologicals," or "natural pesticides" as of manmade chemicals. Whether it occurs in nature or not, a pesticide is a pesticide and can be harmful to people and animals. Pyrethrum and rotenone, for example, classified as natural, are both toxic and not very selective. Be wary of nonselective pesticides and herbicides—the ones that kill a broad spectrum of organisms.

•Neatness counts. Harvest produce as soon as it is ripe. After you've harvested the last vegetable, promptly dispose of all crop residues—vines, roots, stems, and leaves. If you have fruit trees, dispose of shriveled fruit on the ground or on branches. Be sure the garden area is free of boards, boxes, stones, and other potential hiding places for insect eggs. Deep tilling in spring and fall will kill many residual pests.

Although produce grown without pesticides may not look as appetizing—apples may have small blemishes or lettuce may have tiny holes in the leaves—it is not harmful. These fruits and vegetables are usually picked ripe and don't travel well, and may have more imperfections.

Tornadoes

According to meteorologists, clashing air masses fueled by warm, moist air from the Gulf of Mexico cause tornadoes in the United States. Tornadoes most commonly strike west Texas, Oklahoma, Arkansas, Missouri, and Kansas. But other areas have also experienced serious tornado outbreaks—Ohio, Illinois, Michigan, Pennsylvania, New York, New England, the Carolinas, the Gulf states, and even parts of Canada. Tornadoes are almost unknown west of the Rockies. An average of 773 tornadoes occur in the United States each year, killing about eighty people and injuring two hundred more—one of the highest tolls of all natural disasters. April, May, and June are the prime times with May the peak. But tornadoes occasionally strike in summer or fall and out of their customary area.

Unlike hurricanes, tornadoes often arrive with little warning—the first sign being high winds, flying debris, or the roar of the approaching funnel. A study of a series of tornadoes that killed ninety-one people in the northeastern United States and Canada in 1985 found that only a third of the injured (in one Pennsylvania locality) had known a tornado was on the way. Among survivors interviewed in Ontario, fewer than 10 percent had as much as a five-minute warning that a twister was coming. Most of these people had telephones, television sets, and radios, but because of a power failure, local stations were unable to issue warnings. However, these and other studies have revealed that people caught in a tornado or violent windstorm can take protective action, if they know in advance what to do.

A tornado can travel up to seventy miles an hour, and not even the best of meteorologists can predict the course of its winding path.

The right shelter

The main danger in a tornado is being picked up by the wind or hit by flying objects. Thus a basement or cellar is the safest place. Stay away from windows, and if there is no basement or cellar available, go to an interior room on the lowest level of the building you're in. Crouch down and try to protect your head: dragging a mattress over you is a good idea. A closet is a good place to hide, and people have survived by seeking shelter in the bathtub. If you're caught on the street, go to the interior of the nearest building. Staying in a car or truck is not safe. Get out and use whatever time you have to run for cover indoors. If no shelter is in sight, lie flat in a nearby ditch or ravine. Cover your head with your hands. You're better off on the ground than in a vehicle, which might become airborne.

Mobile homes and other poorly anchored houses are the most dangerous locales in severe storms. Government authorities have urged local agencies in tornado-prone states to provide residents of mobile home parks with accessible tornado shelters. If you live in the tornado belt in a mobile home or a house that might easily be pulled off its moorings, find out where the nearest shelter would be—perhaps an office building or nearby school. Ask the local health or police department what tornado safety provisions have been made.

If there's hail or a bad thunderstorm, find out if the weather bureau has declared a tornado watch (the first stage) or issued a tornado warning. Keep a small battery radio in the house; you shouldn't turn on the TV if there's heavy lightning. If you live in a trailer, go to a shelter when warnings are issued—never try to wait it out. If there's no better solution, leave the trailer and lie in the nearest ditch.

Transportation

You may think that you have no control over your safety when traveling by car, plane, or boat. But there is a lot you can do to prevent accidents or to lessen your chance of injury should an accident occur. For example, simply by wearing a seat belt every time you get into a car, you can reduce your risk of being injured or killed in an automobile accident by more than half. This chapter begins with a discussion of how to protect yourself in airplanes and boats, and ends with an in-depth look at driving safety.

Airplane Safety

Despite sensational headlines, few people are killed in airplane accidents, and in most cases lives might have been saved if the victims had been ready for an emergency. Unfortunately, many experienced travelers may turn a deaf ear to safety instructions or take a fatalistic attitude toward crashes. You are as safe or safer in a plane than on the highway, yet accidents do happen—usually on takeoff or landing. (In the United States, an air accident is defined as any incident that damages a plane or seriously injures any occupant.) And according to statistics collected by the National Transportation Safety Board, passengers who think systematically in advance about their own safety are more likely to come out of an accident alive and uninjured.

As with any other emergency, the best advice is to be as well informed as possible and to stay calm. Use the first few minutes on a plane to avail yourself of all safety instructions, make a plan, and commit it to memory. The following steps will keep you prepared for an emergency:

•After you take your seat, find the nearest exit and mentally rehearse the path you would take to get there. Count the number of rows to the exit so you could find it if the lights were out. According to the National Transportation Safety Board, fifty people who died in a post-crash fire in a DC-10 at Malaga, Spain, in 1982 were sitting in the back of the plane and had failed to move up the aisle to the nearest available exit.

•When you sit down, fasten your seat belt as tight as tolerable around your hips. Make sure that you can unfasten it easily. Remember that a loose seat belt will not keep you from lunging forward during an abrupt stop. Instead, the belt may slide over your stomach and cause internal injuries. As the pilot may remind you, it pays to keep your belt fastened throughout the flight. A National Transportation Safety Board study showed that in thirty-five turbulence accidents from 1977 to 1983, no injuries occurred to those who were snugly buckled in.

•Although it may not be exciting reading, study the seat-pocket card. No matter how many times you've heard them before, listen to the flight attendant's instructions. Different airplanes may have different safety procedures.

•If you are traveling with a small child, ask the airline in advance whether you are permitted to bring a regulation car safety seat on board. Check the label on your car seat: it should specify that the seat is adequate for use on an aircraft.

•If possible, wear comfortable clothing, including shoes that you can easily walk or run in. High heels reduce your stability in the aisles, even on an uneventful flight, and could seriously hamper a quick getaway via the exit door and chute.

•If your oxygen mask drops during the flight, don't wait to be told to use it. If cabin pressure is dropping at forty thousand feet, you'll have only about fifteen seconds to put on the mask before the reduced pressure will begin to affect you. You must pull the tube to start the flow of oxygen. If traveling with children, put your own mask on before you assist them with theirs.

•In any kind of airplane accident, the greatest danger is fire. Don't stop to gather your belongings. Proceed toward the exit door as quickly as possible and, since smoke rises, keep your head low.

•In an emergency landing, brace yourself against impact. If the seats are close together, cross your arms on the top of the seat in front of you and put your head on your arms; if the seats are well apart, place your head on your knees and wrap your arms around your legs. In both cases keep your feet flat on the floor, slightly ahead of the seat edge.

Boating Safety

Careless handling, oversized motors, overloading, hazardous water conditions, and alcohol consumption can all turn a boating outing into an accident. The National Safe Boating Council estimates that alcohol is involved in more than half of all boating accidents. In most cases in which a boating accident results in death, the victim could have been saved by a life preserver. Federal law requires life preservers—personal flotation devices—on all recreational boats. Unfortunately, too many people don't have the proper flotation devices or don't use them.

There are two basic types of life preservers: wearable models and models designed for throwing and grasping. The law requires that boats sixteen feet long and over must carry one wearable for each passenger, and at least one throwable per boat. Boats less than sixteen feet long are not required to carry wearable models—but they should, since nearly half of the fatalities involve smaller boats.

Test the buoyancy of your life preserver in shallow water before setting out; it should keep your head above the surface. On board, wear it at all times. And follow these other tips to avoid falling overboard: cross other boats' wakes at a right angle; crouch, don't stand up when changing position; don't hang over the sides or ends of a boat. Above all, limit your alcohol intake.

Driving Safety

Driving an automobile, or even riding in one, may be the most dangerous thing you can do. At some point in their lives, according to the National Traffic Safety Institute, half of all Americans will be involved in a serious car crash, or will have an immediate family member involved in one.

When you hear the words "car crash," you probably picture a car smashing head-

Driving a boat when you're drunk is just as dangerous as driving a car while intoxicated, and will often incur the same penalty. Many states consider a boating DWI (driving while intoxicated) conviction to be the same as a DWI motor vehicle offense.

The Low-Risk Driver

According to statistics, driving is on average about ten times more dangerous than traveling by plane or train. But that's average: if you are a low-risk driver, according to General Motors researchers, you are more than one thousand times less likely to die in a car crash than a high-risk driver. Thus automobile travel for a low-risk driver may be no more risky than travel by plane or train.

Who is a low-risk driver? The researchers defined him or her as a forty-year-old who is sober when driving and wears a seat belt. Travel on rural interstate highways in a heavy car lowers the risk even more, though these factors are less important than, for instance, age, sobriety, or wearing a seat belt.

The high-risk driver, in contrast, was defined as an eighteen-year-old, intoxicated male traveling on average roads in a light-weight car without wearing a seat belt. Of course, luck is always involved: anyone could be hit by a car driven by a drunk teenager. Even then, though, you would be more likely to survive if you take care of the factors that are in your control, such as wearing a seat belt and driving only when sober.

Be extra careful driving during the first half hour of a rainfall. A little water plus the oil and dirt on the road form a slick film. This film is eventually washed away in a heavy rain.

on into something, perhaps a telephone pole. But side-impact crashes—usually one in which a car runs a traffic light or stop sign at an intersection and barrels into another auto—are also common, especially in drivers over age fifty. Such side-impact crashes cause nearly half of all serious or fatal automobile injuries, and account for some eight thousand deaths in the United States each year. Side-impact and frontal crashes are very different. Knowing which kind you're most likely to be in may help you be on your guard and take precautions.

Side-impact crashes. About 76 percent of these involve drivers over the age of fifty, and 28 percent of the drivers are over seventy. Two reasons that may account for the higher risk in older drivers are age-related vision and reflex changes and unfamiliarity with traffic safety rules. Side crashes most often occur during the day and infrequently involve alcohol or drug use. In 69 percent of the crashes, the driver of the struck car was at fault because of a driving error; in 17 percent of the cases, this driver committed a traffic violation. Slightly more than half of the resulting injuries involve the chest and abdomen.

Frontal crashes (single vehicle). These generally involve young drivers; only 26 percent of the resulting fatalities occur in people over age fifty, and only 8 percent in those over age seventy. Most of these crashes are alcohol or drug related. The majority occur at night, and often involve head injuries.

How to handle troublesome situations

Driving defensively means that you avoid putting yourself in dangerous situations, and you know how to react intelligently in a crisis, should one develop. Learning to drive defensively could be one of the most important actions you could take. Think of it this way: the safest driver of all may well be the professional racer. Although he's going well over 150 miles per hour, he's wearing several seat belts, the chassis in his vehicle is a cage of steel tubing, and most importantly, he's trained to react to danger up ahead. We can't all be race-car drivers; yet we could be better drivers than we are. Below are some common situations that routinely give people trouble:

Braking. The safest way to brake is to do so as far in advance as possible. A basic principle of defensive driving is never to get into a situation that calls for slamming on the brakes. This can throw you into a skid (see page 510) that may injure you and your passengers. Good breaking technique is to pump the brakes repeatedly until you come to a full stop. If you are forced to brake fast, "threshold" braking is the best technique: push the brake just short of locking and hold it there.

Antilock brakes can make braking quickly safer. Activated by a sensor attached to each car wheel, these brakes detect potential skids and react accordingly, pulsing the brake power and bringing the vehicle to a faster, safer stop than conventional brakes, especially in hazardous road conditions such as ice and snow. Antilock brakes are standard equipment on some cars in the luxury category and are optional on some others.

Skidding. The first thing to do is to keep calm and not panic. The second thing is not to slam on the brakes. Take your foot off the accelerator and steer in the direction that the rear of the car is skidding. When the car is again under your control, pump the brakes gently and softly to slow down.

Tailgating. Following the car in front of you at a safe distance gives you room to stop in case of an unforeseen emergency. To be sure you're following at a safe distance, pick out some definite marker (a driveway, a bridge abutment, a sign) on the road ahead, and when the car in front of you passes it, start counting seconds, "one thousand and one, one thousand and two." Two seconds should elapse before your own car reaches the marker. In bad weather, when it's harder to stop, make it four seconds. That gives you a safety cushion of space.

If someone is tailgating you and the car in front of you is at a safe distance away, tap the brakes and start to slow down—gradually, keeping an eye on the rearview mirror. If the tailgater is daydreaming, tapping your brakes (and activating the brake lights) should wake him up. If he's being aggressive, you've politely signaled him to let up. If he doesn't stop tailgating, pull over as soon as you can and let him pass.

Highway driving. Contrary to popular opinion, statistics show that six-lane highways are safer than smaller roads. Many people find highways intimidating simply because they use them infrequently. Gaining experience will boost your confidence. Ask an experienced highway driver to accompany you and advise you about any weak points in your driving skills.

Changing lanes. When preparing to change lanes on a multilane highway, you should turn on your directional signal, check your mirrors, be aware of the traffic in front of you, and take your eyes off the road momentarily to glance over your shoulder at the lane you're planning to move into. Many people forget this last step, but it's essential. You always have a blind spot (about a car length behind you on either side) and may not be able to see an overtaking vehicle in either mirror.

Two out of three motor vehicle crashes occur at night, according to the National Safety Council. And death rates at night are more than three times greater than day rates.

Avoiding Animals

Each year more than ten thousand Americans are injured and 120 are killed in collisions with animals. In many states across the country, deer have become a special problem because their population has risen in recent years—not just in rural areas but in many suburban areas as well.

If you're coming up on an animal in the road, don't assume that it will get out of your way. The American Automobile Association recommends that you tap lightly on the horn well in advance when approaching a large animal. And, if traveling at night, flick your lights from bright to dim, since animals are attracted to—and often become immobilized by—headlights. Slamming on the brakes and swerving to avoid the animal is especially dangerous at night and on a wet or icy road; you may crash into another car or a tree. Under these conditions, travel at low speeds so that you can safely steer clear of the animal if need be.

Older drivers often fail to look to the rear when changing lanes because of stiffness in the neck or upper body. If you have problems looking behind you, it may be wise to invest in a large, wide-angle rearview mirror and a right-side exterior mirror. Flexibility exercises may also help relieve stiffness.

Inclement weather. At least one out of every ten automobile accidents can be attributed to adverse weather conditions. Many of these accidents occur because drivers fail to prepare their cars for winter driving or are unfamiliar with winter driving techniques. It doesn't have to snow for the road to be slippery—rain can create treacherous conditions, especially on heavily used roads. The main precautions you can take involve your driving skills. Adjust your speed according to the road conditions. Even if the speed limit is fifty-five, drive at forty-five or even slower if conditions are bad. The best rule is to not do anything suddenly. That includes changing lanes, slamming on the brakes, and jackrabbit starts. In slippery conditions, avoid braking on a curve. When you have to slow down, shift to a lower gear instead of braking. When you must use the brakes on a slippery surface, depress and release the brake pedal repeatedly and gently. In fog or snow, don't use your high beams; the light just reflects back at you. You'll see farther with low beams.

In addition, take these precautions:

Use snow tires. Radial tires are not snow tires. You can get away with so-called "all-weather radials" only if you live in an area that doesn't get much snow. If there's a heavy snowfall, you need snow tires. It's best to put them on all four wheels, but you must put them at least on the drive wheels. Check tire pressure periodically. Air contracts in cold weather and tires lose about one pound of pressure for every drop of ten degrees, so you may have to add air in very cold weather to maintain the right pressure. Some people let a little air out of their tires, thinking mistakenly that this improves traction because more tire surface will come in contact with the road. It's the worst thing you can do. (This goes for very hot weather as well.) Keep tires at the recommended maximum air pressure, and check them weekly.

Clean off snow. If it snows, clear off the car completely, including all lights and windows, the hood, and roof, so that blowing snow will not obscure your vision. If your car has recessed wipers, make sure they are not frozen in place. You can burn out the wiper motor or blow a fuse if you turn on the wipers when they're frozen.

Driving and alcohol and drugs

Most people are aware of the dangers of driving after drinking alcohol. But they may not know how alcohol affects your driving abilities, or how other drugs—such as marijuana, cocaine, and even some prescription and over-the-counter drugs, such as cold preparations—can significantly decrease driving performance.

Alcohol. Alcohol does not affect your abilities equally. Simple perception—seeing and hearing—is affected least of all, at least at low levels of alcohol consumption. But your ability to process the information you receive and to perform complex tasks based on that information begins to be impaired at blood alcohol levels slightly above 0.05 percent (more than one drink per hour for a 160-pound man). At slightly higher levels, up to 0.10 percent (two or three drinks an hour), your vigilance and accuracy are reduced, your reaction time is significantly lengthened, and your short-term memory is impaired. While alcohol may not immediately affect your simple skills, it quite quickly and insidiously impairs your ability to make quick decisions.

Alcohol affects different parts of your body at different rates because of variations in the way alcohol is distributed by the blood. Blood-rich organs, such as the brain and lungs, get the highest dose earliest, and the central nervous system is affected faster than the muscles and skeleton. If you think of your brain as a computer, alcohol doesn't shut the whole mechanism down until you've drunk a lot, but simply short-circuits it—usually without your being aware of what's happening to you. Thus you may not be the best judge of whether you are able to drive or not.

Just as alcohol affects your brain and body at different rates, the level in your blood is not entirely predictable. Factors such as body size, alcohol concentration per drink, other drugs used, how well you feel, how tired you are, if you ate while you drank, and how fast you drank are all important, too. People with the same blood alcohol level will behave differently. And remember, any level of alcohol in your blood will lead to some deterioration of your driving ability.

If you think you may have to drive after drinking, follow these rules:

•Don't drink on an empty stomach. Milk and cheese, or any large or especially fatty meal, can lengthen the time the alcohol takes to get into the blood.

•Don't consume more than one drink per hour. Intersperse the alcohol with something nonalcoholic.

•Don't depend on caffeine to counteract the effects of alcohol. It won't.

•Don't mix alcohol with marijuana or other drugs.

Even if you've followed the four rules above, you should still wait at least an hour after your last drink before driving. Be honest: if you don't succeed in following this plan, don't drive. Best plan of all: if you're driving, drink no alcohol at all.

Marijuana. The effect of marijuana on the smoker's ability to drive or operate machinery is harder to gauge than that of alcohol. The principal mind-altering ingredient in marijuana, known as THC (tetrahydrocannabinol), passes rapidly from the bloodstream into the brain and fatty tissue. But unlike alcohol, which is flushed out of the system fairly quickly, THC may linger for days or even weeks. Studies have shown that intoxication can return—for no apparent reason—even when a person has not recently smoked.

Marijuana definitely decreases performance, but not in any consistent relationship to THC blood levels. Unlike testing for blood alcohol levels, there's no way to tell if someone has been using marijuana or to measure THC blood levels. The marijuana user won't have a telltale breath or slurred speech. Rather than disturbing the simple motor skills involved in driving, marijuana seems to interfere with perception and attention processes. In combination with alcohol, it can be extremely deleterious to judgment and performance.

Thus, though the effects of marijuana on driver performance are hard to measure precisely, they can certainly endanger human life. And these effects may even be delayed and unpredictable. Anyone who has recently smoked marijuana—let alone a habitual user—should not drive.

Legal medications. Some prescription drugs—such as some blood pressure medications and sleeping pills (even one taken the night before) and many over-the-counter drugs, such as cold, sinus, or hay fever preparations—can cause drowsiness and greatly reduce your driving ability. If you take any medication, even occasionally, discuss the possible effects on your driving with your physician or pharmacist.

Staying awake and alert

Falling asleep while driving is a leading cause of car crashes and, after alcohol, the second most common cause of vehicle fatalities. Fatigue, the monotony of the road, the drone of the engine, an uncomfortably warm or stuffy environment, an alcoholic drink (even one you might have had many hours before driving), lack of sleep, and some medications can all produce drowsiness. Some drivers believe that using the cruise control makes them drowsy, though there's no scientific evidence for this.

Your first reaction to feeling drowsy should be to pull safely over to the roadside and take stock. Obviously, if you have a passenger who's also a qualified driver, change drivers. If not, consider stopping for the night. Or find a secure place (a roadside rest area, for example, but not the shoulder of an expressway) and take a nap in the locked car. When you wake up, take a walk if possible, or do some stretching or other simple exercises in the car. Have something to eat and drink (nonalcoholic) as soon as you can. Music can be helpful if you play it loudly and sing along, and so can opening the window and letting fresh air hit your face.

Don't drive if you've gotten drunk—not even the next morning. One study found that driving ability is still impaired the following day. Performance results of a driving test declined 20 percent even after participants had a chance to sleep it off. Even those who said they didn't have a hangover performed as poorly as those who said they felt awful.

Planning Trips

The following tips will help keep long car trips safe and enjoyable:

Give your car a complete physical. Check your tires for tread depth and keep them inflated to the required tire pressure. Don't forget to check the spare tire, too. Make sure your windshield wipers are in good condition and that you have plenty of wiper fluid. Clean your car windows inside and out—dirty windows greatly impair your vision. Have a mechanic give your car a good once-over, paying special attention to the braking system. In cold weather, keep at least a half tank of gas in your car at all times. If the gas tank is less full, the gas line can freeze.

Take along emergency provisions. In winter, pack a blanket, first-aid supplies, a flashlight, an ice scraper, some crackers, chocolate bars, or other high-energy foods, and some bottled water in case bad weather strikes and you have to stay in your car. Keep these items in your back seat—you may not be able to reach your trunk in a storm. In your trunk, you may want to have the following on hand: a shovel, emergency flares, sand or tracking mats, and jumper cables.

Make sure you are well rested. Get enough sleep the night before you drive. Stop every two or three hours to stretch your muscles. Trying to cover too much distance in one day causes tension and fatigue. The National Safety Council recommends that you drive no more than seven or eight hours a day.

Avoid taking any over-the-counter cold remedies when driving. These medications often contain antihistamines, which can cause drowsiness. Indeed, any medication may affect your driving skills. If you're taking a new medication, avoid driving until you know how it will affect you.

Keep the car properly ventilated. Carbon monoxide from the car's exhaust can cause drowsiness. Even on the coldest days, leave your car windows open a crack. Fresh air will help keep you awake.

Stay alert. "Highway hypnosis"—the trance-like state caused by the monotony of driving over miles of roadway—impairs your judgment and cuts down on your reaction time. Avoid continuously staring at the road ahead—look in your rearview and sideview mirrors frequently. Listen to the radio, sing, or carry on a conversation with others in the car. Be aware of your surroundings.

Avoid arguing with your car mates. Anger and frustration can temporarily impair your driving ability and may cause you to take risks you normally would not take. If heavy traffic is getting to you, pull off the highway and take a breather.

Generally speaking, it's good policy not to drive long hours after dark, or to leave for a long drive Friday night after work. If you do plan to drive long distances, don't drink alcohol—even the day before. Don't drive at all if you're taking medications that induce drowsiness. Don't rely on any kind of drug to keep you awake; if you're really tired, even caffeine won't keep you from falling asleep. Whether you feel sleepy or not, it's always wise to break up a long drive with rest stops, occasional snacks, and some stretching or walking outside the car.

Check your night vision

Few people realize that even though they may have 20/20 vision in daytime, their nighttime vision will have considerably lessened by the time they turn forty, and this is something that the motor vehicle department seldom tests. According to the latest figures from the National Safety Council, nighttime accidents account for about 25 percent more fatalities than daytime accidents. Although factors such as exhaustion and alcohol play a role in this, no driver can see as well at night as in the day. One study has shown that 87 percent of all drivers who hit a pedestrian at night said they didn't see the person in time—while only 11 percent of daytime drivers made the same claim.

The speed with which the eye accommodates itself to darkness starts decreasing in young adulthood. In daytime, the retina resolves visual data primarily by means of a specialized set of cells called cones, but at nighttime, it relies chiefly on another, more sensitive set called rods. The older you are, the longer it may take to make the switch, which could make driving more difficult along a road where light conditions are changing rapidly. Along with a decline in the eye's ability to accommodate itself to darkness comes a drop in visual acuity in early adulthood, and night vision deteriorates faster than daytime vision. It is possible your ability to perceive a pedestrian or some potential hazard in the darkness up ahead on a country road may start to decline when you are in your twenties. It will be greatly reduced by the time you are fifty or so. Most people become aware of this at about age forty.

This need not be a disaster, however, for driver awareness of reduced night vision is thought to be the best protection of all. Research shows that drivers who realize they have poor night vision voluntarily reduce night driving trips or eliminate them completely.

If you must drive at night, drive more slowly and carefully. Even under ideal conditions no one can spot a pedestrian at night much farther away than three hundred feet—and if you are driving fifty-five miles per hour, it will take more than three hundred feet to bring your car to a stop. Unless there is an approaching car, use your high beams—but remember that your headlights may temporarily blind a pedestrian. And keep your dashboard lights low so that your eyes are not constantly readjusting from light to darkness.

Protecting yourself in a crash

Even the best driver in the world needs to protect himself in case of a car crash; your driving skills may be first rate, but you cannot always avoid a driver who isn't in your league. Other drivers may not pay attention to the road, ignore traffic signals, loose control of their car, or drive while intoxicated. The two best ways to prevent injury and protect your life are wearing a seat belt and driving a car with an airbag.

One defensive driving tip comes from a course for individuals over age fifty sponsored by the American Association for Retired Persons: it is safer to drive a white, beige, or yellow car because it is easier for other drivers to see it.

Seat belts

There is no doubt: if you are in a car crash, a properly worn seat belt can reduce the severity of injury and indeed may save your life. According to the National Highway Traffic Safety Administration, in the event of a crash, wearing a lap-shoulder belt reduces your chances of being injured or killed by 57 percent. If everyone wore a seat belt every time they drove or rode in a car, about seventeen thousand lives would be saved every year.

And yet, despite the overwhelming evidence in their favor, many people still do not wear seat belts. Even in states with mandatory seat belt laws, front seat belts are used only about half the time.

Despite the benefits of seat belts, however, they must be worn properly to be effective. The following tips will help ensure correct seat belt use:

•Wear the seat belt low across the pelvis, not the abdomen. In a crash, the belt can exert a pressure equal to twenty to fifty times your body weight, and only the pelvis can withstand this load. If the belt is worn higher (across the abdomen) and the car stops suddenly, the belt can cause serious injury to internal organs.

•Sit upright. If you slump, the belt can slide up the pelvis onto the soft abdominal wall.

•Keep the belt tight. Some people wear belts loosely just to comply with seat belt laws. A loose belt offers little protection and may, in fact, compound injuries in a crash. An occupant can be thrown forcefully against the belt itself, or can slide forward under the loose belt and suffer head or neck injuries from the shoulder strap.

•Never wear the shoulder strap under your arm or across your neck. Some people complain about neck, shoulder, or breast irritation because of the shoulder strap and find that they can avoid this by wearing the strap under the arm instead of over the shoulder. However, in a crash, wearing the strap under the arm can concentrate pressure on the abdomen, diaphragm, and lungs. In many cases in which fatal injuries were caused by underarm positioning of shoulder straps, the victims probably would have survived had they worn the straps correctly.

When properly worn, the strap rests on the middle of the collarbone and the upper chest, both of which are better suited to absorb the strap's pressure. It must never cross at the neck. It's essential for short people to have the shoulder portion of the three-point strap lowered so that it doesn't choke them. This can easily be done by the dealer who sold you your car.

If the shoulder strap causes irritation, try keeping a little slack in it—no more than two inches of slack, however—just enough to allow you to place your fist between the strap and your chest. Or place a piece of foam rubber under the strap where it's bothering you.

Rear seat belts. Controversy has continued about the safety of using seat belts without shoulder straps in the rear seat, ever since the National Transportation Safety Board reported that lap-only belts can cause severe and fatal injuries in serious head-on collisions. No one doubts that combination lap-shoulder straps are safer than lap-only belts, and therefore the major auto makers are planning to phase in rear-seat shoulder harnesses as standard equipment. Some auto companies now offer to refit cars with shoulder strap units. However, these units aren't available for all makes and models, and some dealers don't stock them. In the meantime, most evidence suggests that you're better off wearing lap-only belts than wearing no belt

It's not true that you are safer being thrown clear of a car rather than being strapped into it by a seat belt. You are twenty-five times more likely to be fatally injured if ejected than if you stay inside and are buckled up.

Seat Belts: Special Concerns

Pregnant women

Use of a seat belt is imperative for the safety of both the woman and her fetus. There's no evidence that a seat belt increases the risk of injury to the fetus or uterus, even in an accident, according to the American College of Obstetricians and Gynecologists. The fetus is well protected in a fluid-filled sac in a very elastic uterus, which is cushioned by surrounding organs, muscle, and bones. In a crash the fetus may be squeezed by the seat belt for a short time, but it almost always recovers quickly.

The fetus is at much greater risk when the mother doesn't wear a seat belt. *The leading cause of fetal death or injury in a crash is death or injury of the mother.* Since a seat belt ensures the safety of the mother, doctors strongly recommend wearing one during the entire pregnancy—including the ride to the hospital for the birth.

For maximum protection, wear the belt under your abdomen—across your upper thighs and as low on your hips as possible—and wear the shoulder strap across your shoulder and chest. Never wear the lap belt above your abdomen or too loosely, which may injure your ribs or abdomen. Place the strap between your breasts; there should be less than three inches of slack between the strap and chest.

Children

Automobile accidents are the leading cause of death and serious injury for children over six months old. All states now require children to ride buckled up—yet surveys show that many children travel without any restraints at all.

Children over age four who have outgrown infant or toddler safety seats pose a special problem. As with adults, the complete protection provided by lap-shoulder straps is better than lap-only belts, but shoulder straps tend to cross over young children's necks or faces. In any case, few cars have rear-seat shoulder straps. The solution is to put a child (four to eight years old, forty to sixty-five pounds) in a restraining device called a "booster seat," such as the two below.

If your car's rear seat doesn't have shoulder straps, place your child in a booster seat equipped with a shield and/or harness. A large shield provides better protection than a small one.

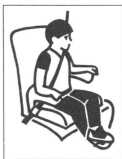

If your rear seat has shoulder straps, or if your child is riding in the front seat—which is generally not advised—use the kind of booster seat that raises him so that the strap crosses his chest, not his neck.

at all. Using the belt properly, as described on page 515, should minimize the risk of belt-induced injury.

Airbags

The experts know that the death and serious injury rate from head-on automobile crashes could be halved if all motorists used three-point lap-shoulder belts in combination with an airbag that inflates automatically in head-on collisions. Indeed, if everyone used seat belts and all cars were equipped with airbags, it would save an estimated 9,000 lives and prevent 150,000 serious injuries each year.

Until recently, airbags were available only in the most expensive European imports. But federal regulations require that all new cars be equipped with passive restraints—that is, belts that automatically protect the occupant once the door is closed—or airbags. Ford and General Motors decided to make airbags an option on some models starting in 1987, and Chrysler announced that airbags on the driver's side would be standard equipment in six models by 1990. Insurers have always been enthusiastic about the safety advantages of airbags, and some now offer significant reductions in premiums and other incentives for customers who buy airbag-equipped cars.

At a speed of only thirty miles per hour, a 150-pound passenger involved in a car crash will hit the dashboard or steering wheel with a force of 4,500 pounds. A combination lap-shoulder belt does something to soften the blow, but an airbag can do more. An airbag is a tough cloth bag usually concealed in the steering wheel. Activated by a crash sensor, the bag inflates automatically with harmless nitrogen gas to cushion the driver on impact. Some people imagine that the bag would pin them against the seat, but deflation occurs within a second.

Another worry has been that the bags might inflate unpredictably, or be triggered by a quick stop or low-speed accident. But there's almost no chance that this would happen. Airbag-equipped Mercedes-Benz cars, according to a company report, have logged some 5 billion miles with no inadvertent deployments. Even if an airbag inflated for no apparent reason, tests have shown that it would not cause you to lose control of your car.

For all these reasons, you should buy a car with an airbag. If you're car shopping, let the dealers know you're interested. As a paying customer, you can exert your influence for a change. But remember, airbags protect only in head-on collisions—your seat belt is still your first line of defense.

Seventy-five percent of all car crashes involving injury or death occur within twenty-five miles of home. More than half occur at speeds under forty miles per hour.

Glossary

Words in italics in the definition of a term are defined elsewhere in the glossary.

A

Abduction. Movement of limbs away from the midline of the body.

Achilles tendinitis. Inflammation of the Achilles *tendon,* which connects the calf muscles to the bones of the foot. This stress injury is most often due to tight calf muscles and is common among runners.

Acquired immune deficiency syndrome (AIDS). A fatal, incurable disease caused by a blood-borne virus (called *HIV* or human immunodeficiency virus) that attacks and eventually destroys the body's immune system. AIDS is transmitted via bodily fluids primarily through sexual relations and also by contaminated hypodermic needles and syringes, and blood transfusions if donated blood is contaminated. In addition, it can be contracted in utero or during birth.

Acute mountain sickness (AMS). A condition, characterized by shortness of breath, fatigue, headaches, nausea, and other flu-like symptoms, that occurs at high altitudes due to a lack of oxygen. Most people don't experience symptoms until they reach heights well above five thousand feet.

Adduction. Movement of limbs toward the midline of the body.

Adipose cells. Specialized cells in the body that store *fat.*

Aerobic exercise. Continuous rhythmic exercise using the large muscles of the body over an extended period of time. Aerobic exercise increases the body's demand for oxygen, thereby adding to the workload of the heart and lungs, and elevating the heart rate. Among its many benefits, it strengthens the *cardiovascular* system and allows the body to burn *fat* for energy. Aerobic activities include brisk walking, running, swimming, cycling, and cross-country skiing.

Aflatoxin. A toxin produced by several species of fungus that grow on some crops, especially peanuts, but also on wheat, corn, beans, and rice. It is known to injure the liver and may be a factor in liver *cancer* if ingested in large quantities.

Amino acids. Building blocks of *protein* molecules that are necessary for every bodily function. There are twenty different types of amino acids, which come in two forms: nonessential, which the body can produce; and essential, which the body must extract from foods.

Anaerobic exercise. Exercise in which energy is released without the use of oxygen. *Glycogen* is the primary fuel. Activities that require short bursts of energy, such as weight lifting, sprinting, and *calisthenics,* are anaerobic.

Anaphylactic shock. An overreaction of the immune system that occurs in some people in response to a substance that the person has been previously sensitized to, such as an insect sting from a bee or wasp or drugs like penicillin. This overreaction causes nausea, flushing, depressed blood pressure, irregular heartbeat, vomiting, and difficult breathing, and may lead to coma or death.

Anemia. A condition characterized by a decreased amount of *hemoglobin* circulating in the cells. The most common type is iron-deficiency anemia (usually due to a diet low in iron) in which the red blood cells are reduced in size and number, and *hemoglobin* levels are low.

Angina. Chest pain resulting from lack of blood (and therefore oxygen) to the heart muscle. The correct medical term is angina pectoris.

Antioxidants. Chemical compounds that prevent oxygen from reacting with other compounds. Some antioxidants have been shown to have *cancer*-protecting potential because they neutralize *free radicals. Beta carotene,* the *mineral* selenium, and *vitamins* C and E all act as antioxidants.

Arthritis. A term that encompasses a number of joint diseases, the most common of which is osteoarthritis, characterized by a gradual loss of *cartilage* and often an overgrowth of bone at the joints. Osteoarthritis is usually associated with aging and is divided into two forms: primary, in which there is no apparent cause, and secondary, which is the result of injury, disease, or metabolic disorder. Another more serious type is rheumatoid arthritis, which is due to chronic inflammation of joint linings, leading to the deterioration of joints.

Astigmatism. A defect of the *cornea* or lens of the eye that leads to variable blurred vision.

Atherosclerosis. A condition characterized by the accumulation of *plaque* within the arterial walls. This results in a narrowing of the arteries, which reduces blood and oxygen flow to the heart and brain as well as to other parts of the body and can lead to a heart attack, *stroke*, or loss of function or gangrene of other tissues.

ATP (adenosine triphosphate). An energy-storing compound found in the cells which releases energy when needed by the body. The body produces ATP from food.

Axons. Finger-like projections of nerve cells, or *neurons,* that serve as transmitters of information between neighboring neurons.

B

Ballistic stretching. A potentially injurious type of stretching in which one performs quick, bouncing stretches, forcing a muscle to lengthen. The muscles react by reflexively contracting or shortening, increasing the likelihood of muscle tears and soreness.

Basal cell carcinoma. The most common form of skin *cancer.* Basal cell carcinoma usually grows slowly and rarely spreads, and therefore is easily treated.

Beta carotene. A *nutrient* that the body converts to *vitamin* A. Found in orange and yellow fruits and vegetables such as cantaloupe and carrots and in green leafy vegetables such as broccoli and spinach, beta carotene may protect against some forms of *cancer.* It does not have the *toxicity* of vitamin A.

Biofeedback. A relaxation technique. An individual is provided read-outs of physiological functions that are commonly considered involuntary—*systolic blood pressure,* finger temperature or moisture, the tension of the muscles in the forehead, or any combination of these. These measurements are communicated to the individual, who is told to lower them but without any instructions on how to do this.

Blood chemistry tests. Blood tests that measure the levels of naturally occurring circulating chemicals or ingested drugs in the blood, including *glucose,* urea nitrogen, creatinine, and electrolytes such as potassium and sodium.

Blood pressure. The force of the blood against the walls of the arteries. It is measured in two ways; *systolic pressure* and *diastolic pressure.*

Botulism. A form of food poisoning caused by the bacterium Clostridium botulinum, which is commonly found in soil. Potential sources of botulism include improperly canned foods and any food contaminated by soil and subsequently mishandled. Botulism affects the nervous system, causing weakness; blurred vision; difficulty in breathing, swallowing, and speaking; and can be fatal if not diagnosed in time.

Brachialis. A muscle in the upper arm that flexes the elbow and rotates the forearm.

Brachioradialis. A muscle in the upper arm that helps to stabilize and bend the elbow.

C

Calcaneus. The heel bone.

Calisthenics. Systematic and rhythmic exercises, such as sit-ups, that are usually performed without equipment. Calisthenics are designed to tone and strengthen muscles.

Calorie. A measure of the energy released when a food is digested, more accurately called a *kilocalorie.*

Cancer. A group of diseases characterized by the uncontrolled growth of abnormal cells which can occur in any organ or tissue of the body.

Carbo-loading. An eating regimen followed by some athletes that involves consuming large quantities of *carbohydrates* several days before an endurance event or long distance competition in order to enhance performance and prevent early exhaustion. There is no evidence that carbo-loading has any benefit for anyone other than highly trained athletes.

Carbohydrates. The sugars and starches in food. Sugars are called simple carbohydrates and found in such foods as fruit and table sugar *(sucrose).* Complex carbohydrates (starches) are composed of large numbers of sugar molecules joined together, and are found in grains, legumes, and vegetables like potatoes, squash, and corn.

Carcinogen. Any substance capable of causing *cancer.*

Cardiovascular. Pertaining to the heart and blood vessels.

Cartilage. Specialized fibrous connective tissue that forms the skeleton of an embryo and much of the skeleton in an infant. As the child grows, the cartilage becomes bone. In adults, cartilage is present in and around joints and makes up the primary skeletal structure in some parts of the body, such as the ears and the tip of the nose.

Cerebellum. The part of the brain—located in the back of the head—that coordinates movement and balance.

Cerebral cortex. The outer layer of the brain containing three control areas: motor areas, which control voluntary and certain types of involuntary movement; sensory areas, which receive incoming information from the sense organs (such as the ears and eyes); and association areas, which are responsible for thought, learning, language, and personality, and may store memories.

Cerebrovascular. Pertaining to the brain and the blood vessels supplying it.

Cholesterol. A waxy, fat-like substance manufactured in the liver and found in all tissues. In foods, only animal products contain cholesterol. An excess of cholesterol in the bloodstream can contribute to the development of *atherosclerosis.*

Circuit training. A form of weight training designed for *aerobic* benefit as well as strength building. Circuit training requires the use of weight machines set up in a circuit of "stations;" the aerobic benefit comes from moving quickly from station to station between sets of exercises.

Coenzymes. Small molecules composed of nonprotein substances—often *vitamins*—that assist *enzymes* in their functions.

Collagen. The main supportive and connective tissue in the body. It forms the basic structure for *tendons, ligaments,* skin, and *cartilage.*

Complete blood count. A test that measures the composition of the blood. It includes *hemoglobin* concentration, red blood cell count, hematocrit, and white blood cell count.

Contract-relax stretching. A way of stretching muscles that allows for a reflex relaxation of the muscle. It involves contracting a muscle against resistance—usually another person—then relaxing into a static extension of the muscle while the partner pushes the muscle into a stretch that extends it farther than before.

Cornea. The transparent layer that covers the iris and pupil of the eye.

CPR (Cardiopulmonary resuscitation). A combination of chest compression and mouth-to-mouth breathing, used to help restore breathing and heartbeat until more sophisticated cardiac life support can be used.

Cross training. Regularly performing more than one *aerobic* activity to exercise different muscle groups and provide variety. Interchanging jogging with bicycling and swimming is an example of cross training.

D

Dehydration. A depletion of body fluids that can hinder the body's ability to regulate its own temperature. During exercise, one can become dehydrated if the fluids lost through perspiration are not replaced by drinking water.

Delayed-onset muscle soreness (DOMS). Discomfort believed to be a possible symptom of microscopic injury to muscle tissue. DOMS typically affects those who only exercise occasionally or perform exercise to which they are not accustomed, and usually sets in one to two days after the workout.

Dendrites. Finger-like projections of nerve cells or *neurons* that serve as receivers of information between neighboring neurons.

Dental plaque. A gummy film made up of *polysaccharides* that adheres to teeth and seals in bacteria, especially along the gum line. Other material, such as calcium and saliva, can become entrapped in it. It can lead to cavities and *periodontal disease.*

Dermatitis. A general term used to refer to eruptions or rashes on the skin. There are many causes of dermatitis—for example, contact dermatitis is skin irritation caused by contact with an irritating substance such as the *urushiol* in poison ivy.

Dextrose. A simple sugar containing one sugar unit; also another name for *glucose.*

Diabetes. A condition characterized by the body's inability to produce enough *insulin* or to use it properly. Diabetes is found in two forms. In insulin-dependent diabetes (IDDM), also known as type I or juvenile-onset, the pancreas makes little or no insulin, so the diabetic must receive insulin injections every day. More common is noninsulin-dependent diabetes (NIDDM), also known as type II or adult-onset, in which the pancreas makes insulin but either the amount is insufficiently released or the body cannot properly utilize what is available. This type of diabetes can often be controlled without insulin injections through other medications, diet, and weight management.

Diastolic blood pressure. The lowest pressure in the arteries, which occurs when the heart is relaxed between beats. It is represented by the bottom number in the fraction of a blood pressure reading.

Disaccharides. Sugars consisting of two-sugar units. For example, when *fructose* and *glucose,* two single sugars, are combined, they form the disaccharide *sucrose.*

Disc (intervertebreal disc). A ring of *cartilage* and fibrous tissue with a pulpy or gel-like center located between the vertebrae in the spine. Discs act as shock absorbers and contribute to the spine's flexibility.

Diuretic. A substance that increases fluid output through urination. Caffeine, alcohol, and a number of medications act as diuretics, and can cause the excretion of important *vitamins* and *minerals.*

Diverticulitis. A condition where diverticula (tiny pouches in the colon wall) become blocked with feces, resulting in infection and inflammation. This may cause abdominal pain, diarrhea, and fever.

Diverticulosis. A condition where tiny pouches (called diverticula) form in the wall of the colon. This condition is usually harmless and without symptoms; however, when the pouches are infected or inflamed, it can turn into *diverticulitis.*

Dysmenorrhea. The medical term for menstrual pain.

Dysplasia. A disturbance in the usual organization or appearance of cells, which may indicate a precancerous condition.

E

Edema. An abnormal accumulation of fluid in the body that can produce swelling or inflammation.

Electrocardiogram (ECG). A recording of the electroconductivity of the heart. Also referred to as an EKG. Probably the most useful test of heart function, it can detect and determine the cause of irregular heartbeats and, at times, damage to the heart muscle. It also can determine enlargement of the heart's chambers, mineral imbalances in the blood and whether someone has had or is having a heart attack. ECGs are usually performed while the individual is at rest, however, an exercising ECG (also called a stress test) can provide more information on how the heart responds under stress.

Endometrium. The lining of the uterus. Each month, if pregnancy does not occur, part of the endometrium sloughs off during *menstruation.*

Endorphins. Chemical substances produced by the central nervous system that suppress pain.

Enzymes. Proteins produced by the cells that are crucial in chemical reactions and in building up or synthesizing most compounds in the body. Each enzyme has a specific function; for example, the digestive enzyme amylase acts on *carbohydrates* in foods to break them down.

Epinephrine. A *hormone* secreted by the adrenal medulla gland in response to threatening situations. Also known as adrenaline, it causes elevated *blood pressure,* increased heart rate, and the rerouting of blood to those areas called upon in threatening situations, such as the brain, heart, and muscles.

Estrogen. One of the female sex *hormones* produced by the ovaries.

Extension. A straightening out of a joint. Kicking your knee outward from a sitting position is an example of extension.

Extensor digitorum. A slender muscle that runs along the back of the forearm and works with two smaller muscles to extend the hand and fingers.

F

Fats. The body's most concentrated source of energy, technically termed *lipids.* All fats are made up of carbon, hydrogen, and oxygen atoms arranged in combinations of glycerol and *fatty acids.* (Some fats contain other substances as their organic basis.) Fats found in foods are either in solid or liquid (oil) form. In the body, fat is part of all cell membranes, where it serves as a stored form of energy, helps cushion organs, and helps create certain *hormones.*

Fatty acids. Chemical chains of carbon, hydrogen, and oxygen atoms that are part of a *fat (lipid)* and are the major component of *triglycerides.* Depending on the number and arrangement of these atoms, fatty acids are classified as either *saturated,* polyunsaturated, or monounsaturated. (See also *unsaturated fatty acid.*)

FDA (Food and Drug Administration). The government agency that regulates and monitors food and drug safety; its many responsibilities include regulating the labeling on packaged foods, establishing safe limits of food additives, and ruling on the safety of new drugs before they are made available to the public.

Femur. The thigh bone; the largest bone in the body.

Fiber. The indigestible part of plants. Nutritionists have divided fiber into two basic types—*insoluble* and *soluble*—and have identified five major forms of fiber: cellulose, hemicellulose, lignin, pectin, and gums. Fiber is resistant to human digestive *enzymes* and therefore passes through much of the digestive tract virtually unaltered, absorbing water and helping to speed elimination. Some types of fiber are broken down by microorganisms in the large bowel into substances that can be absorbed by the body. These substances produce various physiological effects, such as inhibiting the production of *cholesterol.*

Fibula. The smaller of the two bones in the lower leg.

Flexion. The bending of a joint. Curling your fingers inward toward your palm is an example of flexion.

Free radicals. Unstable molecules, usually containing oxygen, created by normal chemical processes in the body as well as by radiation (especially X-rays) and other environmental influences. The interaction of free radicals with DNA and other macromolecules leads to impaired functioning of the cells. Free radicals are most likely an important factor in *cancer* development.

Fructose. A *monosaccharide,* sometimes known as fruit sugar. This form of sugar is sweeter than other sugars.

G

Gamma globulin. A *protein* formed in the blood that contains antibodies to all of the diseases to which an individual is immune. It can be extracted from donated blood and is used in the prevention and treatment of certain diseases, such as hepatitis A and Rh factor disorders. It is often given as an injection to individuals who may come into contact with a disease, but who are not immune to it.

Gastrocnemius. The calf muscle.

Glaucoma. A disease characterized by increased pressure in the eyeball, which can ultimately damage the optic nerve and lead to blindness. The most common form—called open-angle glaucoma—usually has no symptoms the patient can observe.

Glucose. A sugar that is the simplest form of *carbohydrate.* It is commonly referred to as blood sugar. The body breaks down carbohydrates in foods into glucose, which serves as the primary fuel for the muscles and the brain. Excess glucose is either converted by the liver to *glycogen* or turned into body fat. In foods, glucose is formed in plants via the process of photosynthesis.

Gluteus maximus. The large powerful muscle—more commonly called the buttocks—that helps to maintain the trunk's erect posture and extends, abducts, and externally rotates the hip.

Glycogen. A compound produced by the liver from *glucose* and stored in the liver and muscles. It acts as an energy source for muscles, and releases glucose from the liver to maintain blood sugar.

Gram. The metric unit of weight measurement equivalent to 1/1000 of a *kilogram.* One ounce is equal to 28.35 grams. A paper clip weighs about a gram.

GRAS (Generally recognized as safe). A list established by the *Food and Drug Administration* of food additives in long-term use and considered safe. The list is subject to revision as new facts become known.

H

Hamstrings. A group of three muscles that run along the back of the thigh.

HDL (High-density lipoprotein). A transporter of *cholesterol* from the tissues to the liver to be broken down and excreted. Often called the "good" cholesterol. There are several types of HDL.

Heme iron. The type of iron that makes up about 40 percent of the iron in meats. It is the type most easily absorbed by the body.

Hemoglobin. The oxygen-carrying *protein* of the blood found in red blood cells.

Hemorrhoid. A swollen blood vessel in the anus. Cushions of blood vessels, muscle, and connective tissue are normally present in the anus. When one of the veins becomes swollen and tender as a result of constipation, pregnancy, or *obesity,* it is called a hemorrhoid.

Hepatitis. An inflammatory disease of the liver most commonly caused by viruses, but also by alcohol, drugs, or overexposure to toxic chemicals. The viruses that cause hepatitis are spread in different ways. Hepatitis A, the most common type, is transmitted orally via food, water, or other objects that have been contaminated with feces. Hepatitis B, or serum hepatitis, is transmitted primarily through direct blood contact, as in blood transfusions or contaminated needles or syringes. Hepatitis B can also be transmitted through sexual intercourse. Hepatitis C is also transmitted through direct blood contact, primarily from intravenous drug use. It is not clear whether hepatitis C can be transmitted sexually.

High altitude pulmonary edema (HAPE). A serious, potentially life-threatening condition due to the accumulation of fluid in the lungs that may occur in individuals who ascend to heights greater than eight thousand feet.

Hippocampus. A part of the brain that screens sensory data for discard or storage.

HIV (Human immunodeficiency virus). The virus that causes *AIDS*.

Hormones. Chemical substances secreted by a variety of body organs that are carried by the bloodstream and usually influence cells some distance from the source of production. Hormones signal certain *enzymes* to perform their functions. In this way, hormones regulate such body functions as blood sugar levels, *insulin* levels, the menstrual cycle, and growth.

Humerus. The bone of the upper arm.

Hydrogenation. The process of adding hydrogen atoms to an unsaturated *fat* to make it more saturated, more solid, and more resistant to chemical change. Manufacturers often hydrogenate fats to give them a longer shelf life.

Hyperglycemia. A condition characterized by an abnormally high blood *glucose* level.

Hyperhydrosis. A condition characterized by very heavy perspiring not related to exercise. Most probably a genetic condition, it usually affects the armpits, palms, or soles of the feet.

Hypertension. High *blood pressure.* Hypertension increases the risk of heart attack, *stroke,* and kidney failure because it adds to the workload of the heart, causing it to enlarge and, over time, to weaken; in addition, it may damage the walls of the arteries.

Hypoglycemia. A condition characterized by an abnormally low blood *glucose* level. Severe hypoglycemia is rare and dangerous. It can be caused by medications such as *insulin* (diabetics are prone to hypoglycemia), severe physical exhaustion, and some illnesses. The significance of reactive hypoglycemia—a lowering of blood sugar levels after meals in some people—is uncertain, but the symptoms reported, such as lightheadedness, weakness, and rapid heart beat, usually do not correlate with blood sugar levels.

Hypothalamus. A small part of the brain that controls many unconscious functions. It regulates food intake and the release of several *hormones,* helps to main fluid balance and body temperature, and influences sexual behavior and the emotional aspects of sensory input.

Hypothermia. A condition in which body temperature drops to a dangerous level. This is most likely to occur when one remains outdoors in very cold weather for extended periods of time, particularly if one does not engage in enough physical activity to keep warm, or is wet or injured.

I

Iliotibial band. A *tendon* running along the outside of the thigh that helps to stabilize the knee joint.

Immunization. A procedure in which a dead or inactive bacteria, virus, or toxin is given orally or by injection to trigger the production of antibodies to that specific disease so that the individual is then immune to it.

Impotence. The inability to achieve and maintain an erection.

Insoluble fiber. A type of dietary *fiber* that absorbs many times its weight in water and swells up in the intestine. Found primarily in whole grains as well as in vegetables, in the peels of fruits, and on the outside of seeds and legumes, it includes cellulose, some hemicellulose, and lignin. By increasing stool bulk, insoluble fiber plays a significant role in promoting efficient waste elimination from the colon, and may help prevent colon *cancer.*

Insomnia. Difficulty in falling or staying asleep.

Insulin. A *hormone* secreted by the pancreas in response to elevated blood glucose levels. Insulin stimulates the liver, muscles, and fat cells to remove glucose from the blood for use or storage.

Interval training. A method of exercising that alternates spurts of intense exertion with lower-intensity periods in one exercise session.

Irritable bowel syndrome. A condition that occurs when the regular rhythmic contractions that normally propel waste through the intestines become irregular, resulting in constipation or diarrhea and other abdominal disorders.

Isokinetic exercise. Muscle-developing exercise performed on weight machines that provides maximal resistance through a full range of movement at a constant speed.

Isometric exercise. Strengthening exercise in which a muscle group is contracted without moving the joint to which the muscles are attached, such as pressing the hands together at the chest.

Isotonic exercise. Strength training that usually involves raising and lowering a maximal amount of weight.

K

Keratin. A *protein* found in the hair, nails, and outer layer of the skin.

Kilocalorie. The amount of heat necessary to raise the temperature of a liter of water one degree Celsius. What is usually referred to as a food *"calorie"* is more accurately a kilocalorie.

Kilogram. A metric unit of weight measurement equivalent to 2.2 pounds.

Kyphosis. Progressive rounding of the upper back.

L

Lactic acid. A byproduct of the breakdown of *glycogen* during *anaerobic* metabolism. An excess buildup of lactic acid is associated with muscle fatigue and certain forms of muscle soreness.

Lactose. The type of sugar found in milk. Lactose is a *disaccharide* composed of *glucose* and galactose.

LDL (Low density lipoprotein). A carrier of *cholesterol*, LDL delivers cholesterol to tissues and has been implicated in the accumulation of *plaque* within the arteries. Often referred to as "bad" cholesterol.

Ligaments. Bands of connective tissue that join bones together.

Lipids. The technical term for *fats,* waxes, and fatty compounds.

Lipoproteins. Molecules composed of *lipids* and *proteins* that carry *fats* and *cholesterol* through the bloodstream.

Lordosis. Exaggerated forward curvature of the lower back; sway-back.

Lumbar region. The five vertebrae in the lower spine that form the largest natural curve in the back.

Lyme disease. An infectious disease caused by bacteria spread primarily via certain species of deer ticks. Symptoms are varied, but include a rash at the site of the tick bite, chills, fever, headache, muscle and joint aches, and low fever. Several months later, more severe symptoms—such as cardiac abnormalities, neurological disorders, and recurring or chronic *arthritis*—may occur in untreated individuals.

M

Macronutrients. A category of *nutrients*—including *carbohydrates, proteins,* and *fats*—that are present in foods in large quantities.

Mammogram. A low-dose X-ray that can detect abnormalities of the breast and therefore can spot any sign of breast *cancer* at the earliest possible stage.

Maximum heart rate (MHR). The highest heart rate you can achieve during your greatest effort in exercise. MHR decreases with age, and is determined by subtracting your age from 220. MHR is used to compute your *training heart rate.*

Megadose. A quantity of a *vitamin* or *mineral* that far exceeds the *RDA,* or Recommended Dietary Allowance. In some cases, megadoses can be toxic and cause severe side effects.

Melanin. A dark pigment produced in the skin. Dark-skinned individuals produce more melanin, and melanin production increases in response to sunlight, causing the skin to become darker.

Melanoma. A malignant form of skin *cancer* that usually arises from a mole and can invade other parts of the body if not caught early.

Menopause. The state resulting in the cessation of *menstruation* that usually occurs when a woman reaches her late forties or early fifties. During menopause, *estrogen* production declines and ovulation ceases.

Menstruation. The monthly shedding of blood and the *endometrium* in a premenopausal woman who is not pregnant.

Metabolism. The sum total of the chemical reactions in the body that are necessary to sustain life. All metabolic processes are driven by energy derived from the major *nutrients* in foods.

Metatarsals. The arching bones between the ankles and the toes that form the top of your foot.

Microminerals. The *minerals* present in the body in small amounts (less than five grams). Also known as trace minerals, these include chromium, cobalt, copper, fluorine, iodine, iron, manganese, molybdenum, nickel, selenium, silicon, tin, vanadium, and zinc. The body must replenish these from foods.

Micronutrients. The *nutrients* present in foods in small amounts, such as *vitamins* and *minerals.*

Migraine. A severely painful type of headache caused by constriction of the blood vessels in head. Migraines usually affect one side of the head and may be accompanied by distorted vision, nausea, and numbness or tingling in the limbs.

Milligram. The metric unit of weight measurement that is equivalent to 1/1000 of a *gram.*

Minerals. Inorganic substances that are basic components of the earth's crust; they are also found in the human body. Humans constantly replenish their mineral supply with food and water. Minerals are crucial in a wide variety of bodily functions, including *enzyme* synthesis, regulation of the heart rhythm, bone formation, and digestion.

Monosaccharides. Sugars consisting of a single sugar molecule, such as *glucose, fructose,* and galactose.

Muscular endurance. The ability to perform repeated muscular contractions in rapid succession, such as repeatedly lifting a weight.

Muscular strength. The force a muscle produces in one effort, such as a single lift or jump.

Myoglobin. An oxygen-carrying muscle *protein* that makes oxygen available to the muscles for contraction.

N

Neurons. Active cells of the nervous system that transmit and receive messages.

Neurotransmitters. Chemicals in the brain that aid in the transmission of nerve impulses. Various neurotransmitters are responsible for different functions including controlling mood and muscle movement and inhibiting or causing the sensation of pain.

Non-REM sleep. The deepest stages of sleep characterized by general absence of body movement and slow, regular brain activity.

Nonheme iron. The type of iron that makes up all of the iron in eggs, dairy products, vegetables, fruits, grains, and enriched flours and cereals and makes up about 60 percent of the iron in animal tissue. Nonheme iron is not as well absorbed by the body as *heme iron.*

Nonoxynol-9. A spermicide used in many contraceptive foams and jellies.

Norepinephrine. A *hormone* secreted by the adrenal medulla gland in conjunction with *epinephrine* in response to threatening situations.

Nutrients. Components necessary for virtually all bodily functions that must be obtained from foods (or in some cases supplements), since the body cannot manufacture them. Nutrients include *protein, fat, carbohydrates, vitamins, minerals,* and water.

O

Obesity. A medical term that refers to the storage of excess *fat* in the body. A person is usually considered obese when his or her weight is 20 percent greater than the appropriate weight as determined by conventional height-weight tables.

Occult blood test. A test performed on a stool sample for the presence of hidden (occult) blood which can detect colon *cancer* at an early stage.

Omega-3 fatty acids. A unique group of poly-unsaturated *fatty acids* found in fish oil and some seeds (such as in linseed oil). Omega-3s in fish oil significantly reduce blood clotting. They make platelets less likely to stick together and to blood vessels, thus lessening the chance of a heart attack or *stroke.*

Opiates. Narcotic pain relievers, such as morphine.

Orthoses. Foot supports that fit in shoes to correct for abnormal foot motion and alignment. Orthoses should be designed specifically for each individual by a podiatrist or orthopedist.

Osteoporosis. A disease in which bone tissue becomes porous and brittle. The disease primarily affects postmenopausal women.

Ovulation. The monthly process in which a mature ovum (egg) is released from the ovary.

Oxalic acid. A substance that when joined with calcium in the body forms insoluble salts and hinders iron absorption from food. It is found in such vegetables as spinach, chard, and rhubarb.

P

PABA (para-aminobenzoic acid). A chemical compound that is one of the most commonly used ingredients in sunscreens. The derivatives made from it—such as Padimate O—effectively screen out the ultraviolet rays responsible for sunburn, but don't offer protection against the full spectrum of ultraviolet rays, including those that may play a role in causing skin *cancer.*

Pap smear. A diagnostic test for detecting cervical *cancer* in which a sample of cervical cells is examined for cellular changes. Among women who have regular Pap smears, the death rate from cervical cancer is almost zero.

Patella. The kneecap, which protects the front of the knee joint.

Periodontal disease. Inflammation or destruction of the supporting structures—the gums and bone—around the teeth. Periodontal disease—which is reversible in its earliest stages—is the most common cause of tooth loss in adults.

Placebo. A medication, most frequently used in medical research, that contains no active ingredients. Because people may feel better after taking medication simply because they expect to, placebos are commonly used in tests of new drugs to check whether the drug is actually having an effect.

Plantar fascia. A thick, pad-like band of tissue along the bottom of the foot. Undue stress to this area from running or jumping can cause *plantar fascitis.*

Plantar fascitis. A pain or discomfort in the heel that often travels up the sole of the foot; it is caused by a partial or full tear in the *ligament* in the arch of the foot.

Plaque (arterial). Deposits of fatty substances, such as *cholesterol,* in the inner lining of the artery walls. The buildup of these deposits can lead to *atherosclerosis.*

Polysaccharides. *Carbohydrates* that consist of many simple sugars linked together. Starch, *glycogen,* and cellulose are polysaccharides.

Premenstrual syndrome (PMS). Disruptive emotional and physical symptoms that appear to precede *menstruation* and may last two weeks or more. Though PMS has been widely publicized, physicians have yet to agree on either its cause or a reliable treatment.

Presbycusis. A common age-related degeneration of the inner ear that results in some degree of hearing loss in both ears.

Presbyopia. An eye condition due to aging in which the lens becomes less able to focus on close objects. This condition occurs to some degree in everyone over the age of forty.

Progesterone. A female sex *hormone* secreted by the ovaries. Progesterone and *estrogen* regulate changes that occur during the menstrual cycle.

Progressive muscle relaxation. A tension-reducing technique in which muscle groups from head to toe are each tensed for a few seconds and then relaxed in sequence.

Protein. Compounds composed of hydrogen, oxygen, and nitrogen present in the body and in foods that form complex combinations of *amino acids.* Protein is essential for life. Foods that supply the body with protein include animal products, grains, legumes, and vegetables.

Pruritus. The medical term for itching.

Q

Quadriceps. A group of four muscles that extend down the front of the thigh and join in a single *tendon* at the kneecap. They extend or straighten the lower leg.

R

RDA (Recommended Dietary Allowances). The estimated amount of *nutrients* needed daily to maintain good health. These estimates differ for various conditions and ages, such as women, men, children, the elderly, and pregnant and lactating women. Developed by the Food and Nutrition Board of the National Research Council, the RDAs are not minimum amounts required, but amounts recommended for optimal health.

Relaxation response. A set of changes in bodily functions that take place as a result of meditating or practicing other relaxation techniques. First described by Herbert Benson of the Harvard Medical School, the response includes a slowing of heart rate and respiration, and an increase in the brain waves associated with relaxation.

REM sleep. A phase of sleep during which the sleeper's eyes move quickly (REM stands for "rapid eye movement"), heartbeat and *metabolism* speed up, and toes and fingers twitch. Dreaming takes place during REM sleep.

Resting heart rate (RHR). The number of heartbeats per minute while the body is at rest. It is most accurately measured by taking your pulse before rising in the morning.

Retrovirus. A virus that has the ability to take over certain cells and interrupt their normal genetic function.

Rhinoviruses. One of the main groups of viruses that cause colds.

RICE. An acronym for a recommended method of acute exercise injury treatment which stands for: REST the injured body part; apply ICE; apply COMPRESSION; and ELEVATE the injured extremity above heart level.

Rotator cuff. Four small muscles that bind the shoulder's ball-and-socket joint.

Runner's knee. A condition brought on by repeated stress to the knee, which is usually signaled by dull pain at the kneecap. It most commonly affects those who run, ski, cycle, or do high-impact aerobics.

S

Salmonella. A group of bacteria that causes intestinal infection. A frequent contaminator of foods, salmonella is probably the most common cause of food poisoning.

Saturated fatty acids. *Fats* containing all the hydrogen atoms they can carry. Such fats, which are solid at room temperature, come chiefly from animal sources (such as beef, butter, whole-milk dairy products, dark meat poultry, and poultry skin) as well as tropical vegetable oils (coconut, palm, and palm kernel). Saturated fatty acids in the diet are the chief contributors to elevated blood *cholesterol* levels.

Sciatica. A severe pain along the sciatic nerve, which runs from the lower back into the leg. Strain to the lower back or a slipped disc are common causes, though often no cause can be identified.

Scoliosis. A sideways curvature of the spine.

Serotonin. A compound made from the *amino acid* tryptophan that serves as one of the brain's principal *neurotransmitters*. When a person eats a meal, the level of serotonin is raised or lowered—depending on the amounts of *proteins, carbohydrates,* and other substances consumed—and this level may affect mood.

Shin splint. A term that applies to a variety of overuse injuries that cause inflammation of muscles and *tendons* in the lower leg.

Sigmoidoscopy. A screening procedure to detect colon cancer and other abnormalities of the lower portion of the large intestine and of the rectum. The test is done by viewing the area with a long thin tube that is inserted into the rectum.

Sleep apnea. A potentially dangerous condition in which breathing stops temporarily during sleep. It is often associated with deep snoring when breathing resumes.

Solanine. A toxic substance that in large amounts is a powerful inhibitor of nerve impulses. It is found in the skin of potatoes that are damaged, old, soft, sprouted, or greenish as well as in potato sprouts.

Soleus. A flat muscle that extends along the back of the calf underneath the *gastrocnemius.*

Soluble fiber. A type of dietary *fiber* which includes pectins, some hemicellulose, and gums, found in fruits, vegetables, seeds, brown rice, oats, and oat bran. When ingested, soluble fiber can promote a softer stool and works chemically to prevent or reduce the absorption of certain substances into the bloodstream. It appears to lower blood *cholesterol* levels and may help regulate blood sugar.

Spasm. A prolonged, painful, involuntary muscular contraction.

SPF (Sun protection factor). A number on sunscreen products that indicates the relative length of time that the sunscreen will protect you against sunburn as compared to using no sunscreen. A product with an SPF of 15, for example, would allow you to stay in the sun without burning fifteen times longer, on average, than if you didn't apply sunscreen.

Sprain. An injury that damages a *ligament* or ligaments, as well as joint capsules. Ranging from small tears to serious ruptures, sprains are often the result of a sudden forceful movement.

Strain. The injury to a muscle that occurs from an excessive effort, such as lifting a heavy weight or sudden overextension of a muscle, as when you stretch to catch a baseball. When this occurs, small tears are usually present in the muscle. The thigh, groin, and shoulder are the most common sites for strains.

Stress fracture. A microscopic break in a bone caused by repeated impact. Stress fractures are common among aerobic dancers and long distance runners, and usually affect the foot, shin, or thigh.

Stress injury. An exercise-related injury—usually referring to an overuse or chronic injury—that results from the wear-and-tear of performing a repetitive activity such as cycling, running, playing tennis, or even swimming.

Stroke. A hemorrhage or a blockage in a blood vessel that supplies the brain, resulting in insufficient blood (and therefore oxygen) to a portion of the brain. The most common manifestation is some degree of paralysis, but small strokes may occur without symptoms. If recurrent, strokes can lead to mental deterioration.

Sucrose. White table sugar made from cane or beets. A combination of *fructose* and *glucose* bonded together, it also occurs naturally in many vegetables and fruits.

Swimmer's ear. A painful, itchy infection of the external ear canal that can develop after long periods of swimming or bathing. Water gets trapped in the ear canal and breaks down the skin lining, allowing bacteria or fungi to breed.

Synapses. The connections between *neurons*.

Systolic blood pressure. The maximum pressure in the arteries when the heart is contracting. It is represented by the top number in the fraction of a *blood pressure* reading.

T

Talus. The ankle bone.

Tannins. Soluble astringent substances found in some plants that may reduce iron and trace *mineral* absorption.

Tartar. Another name for dental plaque.

Temperomandibular joint syndrome (TMJ). Painful grinding, clicking, and soreness of the jawbone muscles when chewing.

Tendinitis. A condition characterized by an inflammation of the *tendons* that usually occurs from overuse, especially in those who perform one sport or movement regularly and intensely.

Tendons. The cords of connective tissue that anchor muscles to bones.

Tennis elbow. A form of *tendinitis* that is caused by forceful, repetitive movements of the arm muscle, such as in tennis, raking, and working with heavy tools. It is characterized by pain that can range from the shoulder to the wrist.

Testosterone. The principal male sex *hormone* that induces and maintains the changes that take place in males at puberty. In men, the testicles continue to produce testosterone throughout life, though there is some decline with age.

Tibia. The larger of two bones in the lower leg.

Tibialis anterior. A long muscle in front of the calf that raises the foot.

Tinnitus. Persistent or recurring ringing or other noises in the ears. When it occurs, episodes of tinnitus usually appear intermittently in middle age, then may become chronic as a person grows older.

Toxicity. The potential ability of a substance to harm a living organism. Almost any substance in food, air, and water can become toxic if taken in a high enough concentration.

Training heart rate (THR). A level of exercise intensity that enables one to gain the maximum training benefits from an *aerobic* workout. THR is computed by taking 60 percent and 80 percent of your *maximum heart rate (MHR)*. During aerobic exercise, the number of heartbeats per minute should fall between these two figures.

Trichinosis. An illness caused by eating raw or undercooked pork infested with worms called trichinae. The disease is usually characterized by muscular pain, fever, and tissue swelling.

Triglyceride. The main form of *fat* found in foods and the human body. Containing three *fatty acids* and one unit of glycerol, triglycerides are stored in *adipose cells* in the body, which, when broken down, release fatty acids into the blood.

Tubal ligation. A surgical procedure for birth control in which a woman's fallopian tubes are tied off so that fertilization of the ovum cannot take place. Tubal ligation is safe, convenient, and permanent, but it is also extremely difficult to reverse.

U

U.S. RDA. A condensed version of the *RDA* figures used by the *Food and Drug Administration* for legal regulation of food labeling. The values are based on RDAs and are used for all persons over the age of four. On food labels, they are expressed in percentages.

Unsaturated fatty acids. In foods, *fats* missing hydrogen atoms in specific places on the *fatty acid* molecule; depending on the number of missing atoms, these fats are classified as either monounsaturated or polyunsaturated. Main dietary sources are plants and fish. These fats are generally liquid at room temperature.

Urinalysis. The laboratory examination of a urine specimen. This routine examination is generally performed with a specially coated strip of paper that can reveal the presence of various substances and chemicals. Usually the sample is also inspected under a microscope for bacteria and other visible signs of urinary tract disorders.

Urushiol. The toxic material secreted by poison ivy and poison oak that causes itching, burning, and a blistery rash in those who are exposed and sensitive.

V

Vasectomy. A permanent method of birth control for men that involves cutting the vas deferens—the tube through which sperm cells pass from the testicles to the penis. The procedure is safe and effective, though irreversible to a great degree.

Vegetarian. An individual who eats a diet that omits meat. The basic categories of vegetarians include semi-vegetarians, who omit red meat; lacto-ovo vegetarians, who omit all animal foods except milk, milk products, and eggs; and vegans, who omit all animal products from their diets.

Vitamins. Organic substances (excluding the essential amino acids) that the body requires to help regulate metabolic functions. Vitamins must be ingested; the body cannot manufacture them.

W

Weight-bearing exercise. An exercise in which the legs support the body, such as in running, walking, and jumping rope.

Wisdom teeth. The last molars (in a full set of teeth) on each side of the upper and lower jaw. Because wisdom teeth may cause trouble when they grow in, which usually occurs in late adolescence, they commonly are removed.

Z

Zinc oxide ointment. A blend of zinc oxide powder and ointment that functions as a skin protector and a sunblock. Unlike chemical sunscreens—such as *PABA*—zinc oxide prevents any ultraviolet light from reaching the skin.

Index

Ultraviolet (UV) radiation, 282, 283, 284, 285
    and ozone layer, 502
    and skin cancer, 282
    and sunglasses, 311
Underwriters Laboratories (UL), 473, 475, 477
Unpasteurized milk, safety of, 166
Urea formaldehyde foam insulation (UFFI), 475
Urinalysis, 448-449
Urinary tract infection, and diaphragm use, 349
Urinometer, 449
Urologists, 431
Urushiol, 298
USDA (United States Department of
    Agriculture), 81, 89
Uterine cancer
    and oral contraceptives, 350
    and fat consumption, 96

V

Vacuum-packed foods, 344
Vaginal spermicide, 349
Vaginal sponge, 349
Valine, 105
Vanilla, 146
Vaporizers, 317, 480
Varicose veins, 279-280
Valsalva maneuver, 424
Vascular headaches, 415
Vasectomy, 350
VDT's (video display terminals),
    see Computers
Vegetables, 156-165
Vegetable oils, 195-198
    fat breakdown of, 196
Vegetarian diets, 82
    and coronary artery disease, 19
    and iron requirements, 126
Venison, 189
Ventilation:
    of gas appliances, 476-477
    of home furnaces and ranges, 482
Very-low-calorie diets (VLCs), 30, 34
Very-low-density lipoprotein (VLDL), 40
Violence on television, and stress, 406
Vitamins, 110-113
    and stress, 409
    as part of healthy diet, 70
    in vegetarian diets, 82
    Recommended dietary allowances
        (RDAs), 74-75
Vitamin A:
    and aging skin, 287
    and vitamin C in fruit juices, 151
    facts and myths concerning, 112
    function of, 110
    in fruits, 148-156
    in milk, 166
    in vegetables, 156-165
    overdose and hair loss, 302
Vitamin B-complex, 110, 112
Vitamin B_1, 112
Vitamin B_2, 112
Vitamin B_3, 112
Vitamin B_5, 112
Vitamin B_6, 110, 112
Vitamin B_{12}, 110, 112
Vitamin B_{15}, 19
Vitamin C:
    and iron absorption, 127
    and preventing cancer, 18
    and preventing colds, 317
    and vitamin A in fruit juices, 151
    and colds, 113
    food sources of, 18
    function of, 110

    in cranberries, 149
    in fruits and vegetables, 149
Vitamin D:
    and calcium absorption, 18
    deficiency and arthritis, 384
    function of, 110
    in milk, 166
Vitamin deficiency disorders, 110, 111
Vitamin E, 18, 110, 112
Vitamin K, 110, 112
Vitamin poisoning of children, 490
Vitamin supplements, 111-112
Vitamins, myths and facts concerning, 112
Vomiting, as treatment for poisoning, 491

W

Waist-to-hip ratio, calculating, 24
Walking, 252-256
    and aerobic capacity in elderly, 21
    at night, 226
    to strengthen back, 390
Walking shoes, 253
Walking speed conversion table, 253
Walnuts, 200
Warming up before exercise, 219, 220,
    370-371
Warts, 280
Water:
    bottled, 493
    consumption by Americans, 492
    sparkling, 495
    toxic substances in, 492-495
Water aerobics, 256, 257
Water beds, heated, 471
Water calisthenics, 264
Water pollution, 492-493
Water-soluble vitamins, 110
Watercress, 161
Watermelon, 156
Weight-bearing exercise:
    and bone density, 123
    to prevent arthritis, 385
    to prevent osteoporosis, 215
Weight control, 22-39
    and breakfast, 76
    and electric muscle stimulators, 27
    desirable weight, calculating, 23
    myths concerning, 26
    plans, 31-32
Weight gain, and smoking, 58-59
Weight lifting, 264-267
    and hypertension, 50, 51
    effect on back, 390
    overload principle, 265
Weight reduction:
    and longevity, 22-39
    and very-low-calorie diets, 30
    by swimming, 24
    maintaining, 35-36
    relapses, 38-39
Weights, hand and ankle, 230
Western blot assay, 360. See also AIDS.
Wet vest, for water aerobics, 257
Wheat germ vs. wheat bran, 173
White blood cell count, 442
Whole milk, 167
Whole wheat bread, 178
    vs. white bread, 177-178
Whooping cough, 450, 453
Wild game, 189
    nutritional content of, 189
Wild rice, 173
Wind-chill factor, 225, 243
Wisdom teeth, 332
Withdrawal, from smoking, 57

Women's health:
    heart disease, 24, 51
    heat tolerance, 237
    iron requirements, 125-129
    risks of alcohol consumption, 64
    risks of computer use, 469
    risks of obesity, 23
Wood-burning stoves, precautions for use of,
    472
Worcestershire sauce, 209
Workplace, accidents in, 465
World Health Organization (WHO), 469
Wrists, injuries to, 378-379

X

X-rays, 449-450
Xanthophyll, 172
Xeroderma pigmentosum, and
    light exposure, 470

Y

Yawning, 419
Yoga, 417
Yogurt, 170-171
    nutritional content of, 170

Z

Zinc, 115, 123
Zinc chloride, in toothpaste, 328
Zinc oxide, as sun protection, 285
Zirconium, 290

This book was produced by Rebus, Inc.

Publisher: Rodney M. Friedman

Editor: Thomas Dickey
Executive Editor: Patricia Calvo
Senior Editor: Jeanette Farrell
Contributing Editors: Bette Ponack Albert M.D.,
   Jeanine Barone M.S.
Managing Editor: Dale A. Ogar
Associate Publisher: Nancy Butcher
Contributors: Catherine Ritzinger,
   Jane Schechter, Karin E. Anderson
Indexer: Carney W. Mimms III

Design by: Harakawa Sisco, Inc.
Art Director: Brian Sisco
Designer: Leah Lococo
Illustrators: Susan M. Blubaugh (exercises)
   and Dana Burns-Pizer (color insert)

*The University of California,
   Berkeley Wellness Letter*

Editor and Publisher: Rodney M. Friedman
Editorial Director: Shirley Abbott Tomkievicz
Executive Editor: Michael Goldman
Managing Editor: Dale A. Ogar
Medical Editor: Bette Ponack Albert M.D.
Sports Medicine and Nutrition Editor: Jeanine Barone M.S.
Associate Medical Editor: Jane Margaretten-Ohring, R.N.
Associate Publisher: Barbara Maxwell O'Neill
Assistant Editors: Evan Hansen, Karin E. Anderson
Illustrator: Ray Skibinski